EXAM✓CRAM

CompTIA® A+
220-701 and 220-702
Fifth Edition

David L. Prowse

800 East 96th Street, Indianapolis, Indiana 46240 USA

CompTIA A+® 220-701 and 220-702 Exam Cram, Fifth Edition

Copyright © 2011 by Pearson Education, Inc.

All rights reserved. No part of this book shall be reproduced, stored in a retrieval system, or transmitted by any means, electronic, mechanical, photocopying, recording, or otherwise, without written permission from the publisher. No patent liability is assumed with respect to the use of the information contained herein. Although every precaution has been taken in the preparation of this book, the publisher and author assume no responsibility for errors or omissions. Nor is any liability assumed for damages resulting from the use of the information contained herein.

ISBN-13: 978-0-7897-4792-1
ISBN-10: 0-7897-4792-8

Library of Congress Cataloging-in-Publication Data is on file.

Printed in the United States of America

Fourth Printing: January 2012

Trademarks

All terms mentioned in this book that are known to be trademarks or service marks have been appropriately capitalized. Que Publishing cannot attest to the accuracy of this information. Use of a term in this book should not be regarded as affecting the validity of any trademark or service mark.

Warning and Disclaimer

Every effort has been made to make this book as complete and as accurate as possible, but no warranty or fitness is implied. The information provided is on an "as is" basis. The author and the publisher shall have neither liability nor responsibility to any person or entity with respect to any loss or damages arising from the information contained in this book or from the use of the CD or programs accompanying it.

Bulk Sales

Que Publishing offers excellent discounts on this book when ordered in quantity for bulk purchases or special sales. For more information, please contact

U.S. Corporate and Government Sales

1-800-382-3419

corpsales@pearsontechgroup.com

For sales outside of the U.S., please contact

International Sales

international@pearson.com

Associate Publisher
David Dusthimer

Acquisitions Editor
Betsy Brown

Development Editor
Andrew Cupp

Managing Editor
Sandra Schroeder

Project Editor
Mandie Frank

Indexer
Cheryl Lenser

Proofreader
Sally Yuska

Technical Editor
Aubrey Adams

Publishing Coordinator
Vanessa Evans

Multimedia Developer
Dan Scherf

Designer
Gary Adair

Composition
Studio Galou, LLC

Contents at a Glance

Introduction 1

CHAPTER 1 Introduction to Troubleshooting 9

CHAPTER 2 Motherboards 23

CHAPTER 3 The CPU 55

CHAPTER 4 RAM 79

CHAPTER 5 Power 103

CHAPTER 6 Storage Devices 131

CHAPTER 7 Installing and Upgrading Windows 165

CHAPTER 8 Configuring Windows 209

CHAPTER 9 Maintaining Windows 263

CHAPTER 10 Troubleshooting Windows 279

CHAPTER 11 Laptops 315

CHAPTER 12 Video, Audio, and Peripherals 351

CHAPTER 13 Printers 391

CHAPTER 14 Networking 413

CHAPTER 15 Security 459

CHAPTER 16 Safety and Professionalism 499

CHAPTER 17 Taking the Real Exams 513

Practice Exam 1: CompTIA A+ 220-701 521

Practice Exam 2: CompTIA A+ 220-702 553

Practice Exam 3: Final Prep for CompTIA A+ 220-702 587

Index 609

Table of Contents

Introduction. 1

   Target Audience 1

   About the Latest CompTIA A+ Exams. 2

   About This Book. 3

      Chapter Format and Conventions 3

      Additional Elements. 4

      The Hands-On Approach 4

      Goals for This Book. 5

   Exam Topics. 6

CHAPTER 1:
Introduction to Troubleshooting **9**

   The Six-Step A+ Troubleshooting Process. 10

      Step 1: Identify the Problem. 10

      Step 2: Establish a Theory of Probable Cause (Question the
Obvious). 11

      Step 3: Test the Theory to Determine the Cause 12

      Step 4: Establish a Plan of Action to Resolve the Problem and
Implement the Solution. 12

      Step 5: Verify Full System Functionality and if Applicable
Implement Preventative Measures 12

      Step 6: Document Findings, Actions, and Outcomes 13

      Cram Quiz 13

      Cram Quiz Answers 14

   Troubleshooting Examples and Concepts 15

      Troubleshooting Example 1: Display Issue. 15

      Troubleshooting Example 2: Power Issue 17

      Some More Troubleshooting Tidbits 18

      Cram Quiz 20

      Cram Quiz Answers 21

   Additional Reading and Resources. 22

CHAPTER 2:
Motherboards **23**

   Motherboard Components and Form Factors 24

      Motherboard Components. 24

      Form Factors. 34

Cram Quiz 37

Cram Quiz Answers 38

The BIOS 39

BIOS, CMOS, and the Lithium Battery 39

The POST 40

Accessing and Configuring the BIOS 40

Flashing the BIOS 43

Cram Quiz 44

Cram Quiz Answers 45

Installing and Troubleshooting Motherboards 46

Installing Motherboards 46

Troubleshooting Motherboards 47

Cram Quiz 51

Cram Quiz Answers 52

Additional Reading and Resources 53

CHAPTER 3:
The CPU **55**

CPU 101 56

CPU Technology 56

Brands of CPUs 62

Cooling 64

Cram Quiz 66

Cram Quiz Answers 68

Installing and Troubleshooting CPUs 69

Installing CPUs 69

Troubleshooting CPUs 74

Cram Quiz 76

Cram Quiz Answers 77

Additional Reading and Resources 78

CHAPTER 4:
RAM **79**

RAM Basics and Types of RAM 80

RAM Basics 80

Types of RAM 81

RAM Technologies 88

Cram Quiz 91

Cram Quiz Answers 93

Installing and Troubleshooting DRAM. 94
    Installing DRAM 94
    Troubleshooting DRAM 98
    Cram Quiz 100
    Cram Quiz Answers 101
  Additional Reading and Resources 102

CHAPTER 5:
Power **103**
  Understanding and Testing Power 104
    Testing an AC Outlet with a Receptacle Tester 105
    Testing an AC Outlet with a Multimeter 106
    Cram Quiz 108
    Cram Quiz Answers 109
  Power Devices. 110
    Power Strips 110
    Surge Protectors. 111
    Uninterruptible Power Supplies 112
    Cram Quiz 114
    Cram Quiz Answers 115
  Power Supplies 116
    Planning Which Power Supply to Use 116
    Installing the Power Supply 122
    Troubleshooting Power Supply Issues 123
    Heating and Cooling. 127
    Cram Quiz 128
    Cram Quiz Answers 129
  Additional Reading and Resources 130

CHAPTER 6:
Storage Devices **131**
  Magnetic Storage Media 132
    Hard Disk Drives 132
    Floppy Disk Drives. 143
    Tape Drives. 145
    Cram Quiz 146
    Cram Quiz Answers 147
  Optical Storage Media. 149
    Compact Disc (CD) 149

Digital Versatile Disc (DVD) 151

Blu-Ray 154

Cram Quiz 154

Cram Quiz Answers 155

Solid-State Storage Media 156

USB Flash Drives 156

Secure Digital Cards 159

CompactFlash Cards 161

Cram Quiz 161

Cram Quiz Answers 162

Additional Reading and Resources 163

CHAPTER 7:

Installing and Upgrading Windows **165**

Installing and Upgrading to Windows 7 166

Windows 7 Versions 166

Windows 7 Minimum Requirements and Compatibility 167

Windows 7 Installation Methods 169

Installing Windows 7 170

Upgrading to Windows 7 173

Verifying and Troubleshooting Windows 7 Installations 174

Cram Quiz 176

Cram Quiz Answers 177

Installing and Upgrading to Windows Vista 178

Windows Vista Versions 178

Windows Vista Minimum Requirements and Compatibility 179

Windows Vista Installation Methods 181

Installing Windows Vista 183

Upgrading to Windows Vista 188

Verifying and Troubleshooting Windows Vista Installations 190

Cram Quiz 193

Cram Quiz Answers 195

Installing and Upgrading to Windows XP 196

Windows XP Versions 196

Windows XP Minimum Requirements and Compatibility 197

Windows XP Installation Methods 198

Installing Windows XP 200

Upgrading to Windows XP 203

Verifying and Troubleshooting Windows XP Installations 204

Cram Quiz 205
Cram Quiz Answers 206
Additional Reading and Resources 207

CHAPTER 8:
Configuring Windows 209

Windows User Interfaces 210
Windows Components 210
Windows Applications 215
Administrative Tools and the MMC 220
Cram Quiz 222
Cram Quiz Answer 223
System Tools and Utilities 225
Managing Devices 225
Operating System Optimization. 229
User Migrations and Customizations 236
Advanced System Tools 239
Cram Quiz 245
Cram Quiz Answers 247
Files, File Systems, and Disks 248
Working with Files and File Systems 248
Managing Disks 252
Cram Quiz 260
Cram Quiz Answers 261
Additional Reading and Resources 262

CHAPTER 9:
Maintaining Windows 263

Updating Windows. 264
Service Packs 264
Windows Update 266
Cram Quiz 268
Cram Quiz Answers 269
Maintaining Hard Disks. 270
Hard Disk Utilities 270
Backups 272
Using Windows XP's NTBackup 273
Creating Restore Points 274

Cram Quiz 276
Cram Quiz Answers 276

CHAPTER 10:
Troubleshooting Windows 279

Repair Environments and Boot Errors 279
Windows Repair Tools. 279
Boot Errors 285
Cram Quiz 288
Cram Quiz Answers 289
Windows Tools and Errors. 290
Troubleshooting Within Windows 290
Stop Errors 298
Additional Windows Errors and Error Reporting 300
Restoring Windows. 301
The Six-Step Troubleshooting Process Revisited. 304
Cram Quiz 305
Cram Quiz Answers 306
Command-Line Tools 307
Windows Command Prompt 307
Recovery Command Prompt. 310
Cram Quiz 312
Cram Quiz Answers 313
Additional Reading and Resources 314

CHAPTER 11:
Laptops 315

Installing, Configuring, and Troubleshooting Visible Laptop
Components 316
Laptop 101 316
Input Devices 318
Video 324
Audio 329
Optical Discs 330
Power 330
Expansion Devices 334
Communications 336
Cram Quiz 338
Cram Quiz Answers 340

Installing, Configuring, and Troubleshooting Internal Laptop
    Components 342
        Hard Drives 342
        Memory 343
        System Board and CPU 345
        Cram Quiz 347
        Cram Exam Answers 348
    Additional Reading and Resources 349

CHAPTER 12:
Video, Audio, and Peripherals 351
    The Video Subsystem 351
        Video Cards 352
        Video Displays 361
        Video Settings and Software 363
        Cram Quiz 372
        Cram Quiz Answers 374
    The Audio Subsystem 375
        Sound cards 375
        Installing a Sound Card and Speakers 377
        Audio Quality 378
        Cram Quiz 380
        Cram Quiz Answers 381
    Input/Output, Input Devices, and Peripherals 382
        I/O Ports 382
        Input Devices and Peripherals 386
        Cram Quiz 388
        Cram Quiz Answers 389
    Additional Reading and Resources 390

CHAPTER 13:
Printers 391
    Printer Types and Technologies 392
        Types of Printers 392
        Local Versus Network Printers 397
        Cram Quiz 397
        Cram Quiz Answers 398
    Installing, Configuring, and Troubleshooting Printers 399
        Printer Installation and Drivers 399

Configuring Printers 400

Troubleshooting Printers 406

Cram Quiz 409

Cram Quiz Answers 411

Additional Reading and Resources 412

CHAPTER 14:
Networking 413

Networking Fundamentals 413

Configuring IPv4 414

IPv4 Classes 417

IPv6 420

Analyzing and Configuring the Network Adapter 422

Network Devices 424

Types of Networks 426

Common TCP/IP Protocols and Their Ports 427

Cram Quiz 430

Cram Quiz Answers 431

Network Cabling and Connectors 432

Cram Quiz 435

Exam Cram Answers 436

Troubleshooting Network Connectivity 437

Command-Line Interface Tools 437

Troubleshooting with Applications 442

Cram Quiz 444

Cram Quiz Answers 445

Installing and Configuring a SOHO Network 446

Internet and Wireless Connectivity Options 446

Setting Up a SOHO Router and Wireless Network Adapters . . . 450

Cram Quiz 455

Cram Quiz Answers 456

Additional Reading and Resources 457

CHAPTER 15:
Security 459

Basics of Data Security 460

Data Sensitivity and Security Compliance 462

Cram Quiz 463

Cram Quiz Answers 464

Authentication 465
    Usernames and Passwords 465
    Smart Cards and Biometrics 472
    Cram Quiz 473
    Cram Quiz Answers 474
Malicious Software 475
    Types of Malware 475
    Preventing and Troubleshooting Malware 477
    Cram Quiz 483
    Exam Cram Answers 484
File Security 485
    Working with Files and Folders 485
    Sharing Folders 486
    Encryption 492
    Cram Quiz 495
    Cram Quiz Answers 496
Additional Reading and Resources 497

CHAPTER 16:
Safety and Professionalism **499**

Safety and Environmental Procedures 500
    Electrical Safety 500
    ESD 502
    Physical Safety 504
    MSDS and Disposal 505
    EMI and RFI 506
    Cram Quiz 507
    Cram Quiz Answers 507
Professionalism and Communication Skills 508
    Cram Quiz 509
    Cram Quiz Answers 510
Additional Reading and Resources 511

CHAPTER 17:
Taking the Real Exams **513**

Getting Ready and the Exam Preparation Checklist 513
Tips for Taking the Real Exam 516
Beyond the CompTIA A+ Certification 519

Contents

Practice Exam 1 . . . . **521**

Practice Exam 2 . . . . **553**

Practice Exam 3 . . . . **587**

Index **609**

About the Author

David L. Prowse is a computer network specialist, author, and technical trainer. As a consultant, he installs and secures the latest in computer and networking technology. Over the past several years, he has authored several titles for Pearson Education. In addition, over the past decade he has taught CompTIA A+, Network+, and Security+ certification courses, both in the classroom and via the Internet. He runs the website www.davidlprowse.com, where he gladly answers questions from students and readers.

Dedication

To my wife Georgia, for dealing with my absurd deadlines.

Acknowledgments

First, I'd like to thank David Dusthimer who put his faith in me and turned me loose on this project.

Special thanks to Andrew Cupp, my development editor. Drew, your direction and guidance during this project, and your organization of my disoriented words and ideas really helped build what I think is a valuable text. Of course, thanks to everyone else at Pearson who was involved in this project as well!

I'd also like to acknowledge my previous and current readers, students, and visitors to my website. Thank you very much for all of your kind words, input and feedback.

We Want to Hear from You!

As the reader of this book, *you* are our most important critic and commentator. We value your opinion and want to know what we're doing right, what we could do better, what areas you'd like to see us publish in, and any other words of wisdom you're willing to pass our way.

As an associate publisher for Pearson IT Certification, I welcome your comments. You can email or write me directly to let me know what you did or didn't like about this book—as well as what we can do to make our books better.

Please note that I cannot help you with technical problems related to the topic of this book. We do have a User Services group, however, where I will forward specific technical questions related to the book.

When you write, please be sure to include this book's title and author as well as your name, email address, and phone number. I will carefully review your comments and share them with the author and editors who worked on the book.

Email: feedback@pearsonitcertification.com

Mail: David Dusthimer
          Associate Publisher
          Pearson IT Certification
          800 East 96th Street
          Indianapolis, IN 46240 USA

Reader Services

Visit our website and register this book at http://www.pearsonitcertification.com/store/product.aspx?isbn=9780789747921 for convenient access to any updates, downloads, or errata that might be available for this book.

Introduction

Welcome to the *CompTIA A+ Exam Cram*, Fifth Edition. This book prepares you for the CompTIA A+ Essentials Exam (number 220-701), and the CompTIA A+ Practical Application Exam (number 220-702) Imagine if you will, that you are at a testing center and have just been handed the passing scores for these exams. The goal of this book is to make that scenario a reality. I am very happy to have the opportunity to serve you in this endeavor. Together, we can accomplish your goal of attaining the CompTIA A+ certification.

Target Audience

The CompTIA A+ exams measure the necessary competencies for an entry-level IT professional with the equivalent knowledge of at least 500 hours of hands-on experience in the lab or field.

This book is for persons who have experience working with desktop PCs and laptops and want to cram for the A+ certification exam—*cram* being the key word. This book does not cover everything in the PC world; how could you in such a concise package? However, this guide is fairly thorough and should offer you a lot of insight...and a whole lot of test preparation.

If you do not feel that you have the required experience, have never attempted to troubleshoot a computer, or are new to the field, then I recommend the CompTIA A+ Cert Guide, which goes into much more depth than this text. On a side note, another great reference book that should be on every PC technician's shelf is the latest edition of *Upgrading and Repairing PCs* by Scott Mueller, published by Que.

There are essentially two types of people that will be reading this book: those who want a job in the IT field, and those who want to keep their job. For those of you in the first group, the new CompTIA A+ certification can have a powerful career impact, increasing the chances of securing a position in the IT world. For those in the second group, preparing for the exams serves to keep your skills sharp, and your knowledge up-to-date, making you a well-versed and well-sought after technician.

Of course I know that some of you are picking this book up solely for the practice exams, which are by the way located directly after Chapter 17, "Taking the Real Exams," and more are on the CD. But I recommend against solely studying the practice questions. This book was designed from the ground up to build your knowledge in such a way that when you get to the practice exams, they will act as the final key to passing the real exams. The knowledge in the chapters is the cornerstone, whereas the practice exam questions are the battlements. Complete the entire book and you will have built yourself an impenetrable castle of knowledge.

About the Latest CompTIA A+ Exams

The latest A+ exams (originally released in 2009) are known as the CompTIA A+ Essentials Exam (number 220-701), and the CompTIA A+ Practical Application Exam (number 220-702). There are quite a few changes and additions to the latest A+ exams including:

▶ Windows Vista has been incorporated into the new objectives.

▶ Older operating systems such as Windows 95, 98, Me, and NT have been removed.

▶ Newer multicore processor technologies such as Core 2 Duo have been added.

▶ Newer hard drive and memory technologies have been added.

▶ The A+ troubleshooting process has been updated.

▶ Increased amount of networking and security topics, with increased difficulty.

▶ As of January, 2011, CompTIA has released Version 2 of the 220-701 and 220-702 objectives and corresponding exams. This new version includes Windows 7 and IPv6. These topics have been incorporated within this (5th) edition of the book.

This book covers all these changes and more within its covers.

For more information about how the A+ certification can help your career, or to download the latest official objectives, access CompTIA's A+ webpage at http://www.comptia.org/certifications/listed/a.aspx.

> **Note**
>
> Note: Those who have been certified in the most recent version of CompTIA A+ (2006 objectives) by taking 220-601 and one of the following: 220-602, 220-603, and 220-604 exams are eligible to update their currency through taking the CompTIA A+ bridge exam (one exam, BR0-003), which covers the new 2009 objectives.

About This Book

There is a lot of new information (and changing information) on the new A+ exams, so the people at Exam Cram and I decided to start this book from scratch. Every single bit of content is all new. The book is broken down into 17 chapters, each pertaining to particular objectives on the exam. Because the official CompTIA objectives can have very long names that sometimes deal with multiple subjects, I have divided the chapters into more manageable (and memorable) topics. All the questions in this book refer to these topics. Chapter topics and the corresponding CompTIA objectives are listed in the beginning of each chapter.

For the most part, I've structured the exam topics in this book to build on one another. Because of this, I suggest that you read this entire book in order to best prepare for the CompTIA A+ exams. In the case that you want to review a particular topic, if your CD practice exam identifies a topic deficiency, for example, the topics are listed at the end of this introduction. In addition, you can use the index or the table of contents to quickly find the concept you are after.

Chapter Format and Conventions

Every Exam Cram chapter follows a standard structure and contains graphical clues about important information. The structure of each chapter includes the following:

- ▶ **Opening topics list:** This defines the topics to be covered in the chapter; it also lists the corresponding CompTIA A+ objective numbers.

- ▶ **Topical coverage:** The heart of the chapter. Explains the topics from a hands-on and a theory-based standpoint. This includes in-depth descriptions, tables, and figures geared to build your knowledge so that you can pass the exam. The chapters are broken down into between two and four topics each.

> ▶ **Cram Quiz questions:** At the end of each topic is a quiz. The quizzes, and ensuing explanations, are meant to gauge your knowledge of the subjects. If the answers to the questions don't come readily to you, consider reviewing individual topics or the entire chapter. In addition to being in the chapters, you can find a PDF of all the Cram Quiz questions compiled in one place on the CD.

> ▶ **Additional Reading and Resources:** At the end of each chapter, I list other sources of information, including books and websites, if you want to learn more about a particular topic.

> ▶ **Exam Alerts, Sidebars, and Notes:** These are interspersed throughout the book. Watch out for them!

Exam**Alert**

This is what an Exam Alert looks like. Normally, an alert stresses concepts, terms, hardware, software, or activities that are likely to relate to one or more certification test questions.

Additional Elements

Beyond the chapters, there are a few more elements that I've thrown in for you. They include:

> ▶ **Practice Exams:** There are five practice exams in total. Three of them are directly after Chapter 17 within the book. There is one for each CompTIA A+ exam and the third one—new to this fifth edition—also has questions on the new Windows 7 and IPv6 topics. This exam is also available on the CD. The other two exams are located on the CD that accompanies this book, again, one for each exam.

> ▶ **Cram Sheet:** The tear-out Cram Sheet is located right in the beginning of the book. This is designed to jam some of the most important facts you need to know for the exam into one small sheet, allowing for easy memorization.

The Hands-On Approach

For this book, I built a new desktop computer using components that I believe are a good example of what you will see in the field today, and for a while to come; and are representative of the types of technologies that will be covered in the exams. I refer to the components in this system from Chapter 2, "Motherboards," onward. I like to put things into context whenever possible. By referencing the parts in the computer during each chapter, I hope to infuse some real-world knowledge and to solidify the concepts you need to learn for the exam. I believe that this more hands-on approach can help you to visualize concepts better and recommend that every PC technician build their own PC at some point (if you haven't already). This can really help to reinforce the ideas and concepts expressed in the book. I also recommend that you work with multiple computers while going through this book: one with Windows 7, one with Windows Vista, and one with Windows XP. Or, you might attempt to create a dual-boot or three-way-boot on a single hard drive. Another option is to run one computer with one of the operating systems mentioned and virtual machines running the other operating systems. Finally, Windows 7 users might opt to include Windows XP mode, in addition to other solutions.

Within these pages I refer to various ancillary websites, most notably;

> *Microsoft's TechNet*—http://technet.microsoft.com

> *Microsoft Help and Support*—http://support.microsoft.com (previously known as the Microsoft Knowledge Base or MSKB).

As an IT technician, you will be visiting these sites often; they serve to further illustrate and explain concepts covered in this text.

Goals for This Book

I have three main goals in mind while preparing you for the CompTIA A+ exams.

My first goal is to help you understand A+ topics and concepts quickly and efficiently. To do this, I try to get right to the facts that are necessary for the exam. To drive these facts home, the book incorporates figures, tables, real-world scenarios, and simple to-the-point explanations. Also, in Chapter 17, you can find test-taking tips and a preparation checklist that gives you an orderly step-by-step approach to taking the exam. Be sure to complete every item on the checklist! For students of mine that truly complete every item, there is an extremely high pass rate for the exams.

My second goal for this book is to provide you with more than 650 *unique* questions to prepare you for the exam. Between the Cram Quizzes and the practice exams, that goal has been met, and I think it will benefit you greatly. Because CompTIA reserves the right to change test questions at any time, it is difficult to foresee exactly what you will be asked on the exam; however I think you will find that a good amount of the questions in this book are similar to the real questions. Regardless, to become a good technician, it is important to know the *concept*, not just memorize questions. To this effect each question has an explanation and maps back to the topic (and chapter) that was covered in the text. I've been using this method for more than a decade with my students (over two thousand of them) with great results.

My final goal is to provide support for this and all my titles, completing the life cycle of learning. I do this through my personal website: www.DavidLProwse.com. It has additional resources for you and is set up to take questions from you about my titles. Anyone can view the additional A+ resources, but you must register to post questions; however, all you need is a valid email address, so join my little community! I'll try my best to get to your questions ASAP. All personal information is kept strictly confidential.

Good luck to you in your certification endeavors. I hope you benefit from this book. Enjoy!

Sincerely,

David L. Prowse

Exam Topics

Table I.1 lists the exam topics covered in each chapter of the book.

TABLE I.1 **Exam Cram CompTIA A+ Exam Topics**

Exam Topic	Chapter
Troubleshooting Theory Troubleshooting Examples and Concepts	1
Motherboard Components and Form Factors The BIOS Installing and Troubleshooting Motherboards	2
CPU 101 Installing and Troubleshooting CPUs	3
RAM Basics and Types of RAM Installing and Troubleshooting DRAM	4
Understanding and Testing Power Power Devices Power Supplies	5
Magnetic Storage Media Optical Storage Media Solid State Storage Media	6

TABLE I.1 **Continued**

Exam Topic	Chapter
Installing and Upgrading to Windows 7 Installing and Upgrading to Windows Vista Installing and Upgrading to Windows XP	7
Windows User Interfaces System Tools and Utilities Files, File Systems, and Disks	8
Updating Windows Maintaining Hard Disks	9
Repair Environments and Boot Errors Windows Tools and Errors Command-Line Tools	10
Installing, Configuring, and Troubleshooting Visible Laptop Components Installing, Configuring, and Troubleshooting Internal Laptop Components	11
The Video Subsystem The Audio Subsystem Input/Output, Input Devices, and Peripherals	12
Printer Types and Technologies Installing, Configuring, and Troubleshooting Printers	13
Networking Fundamentals Network Cabling and Connectors Troubleshooting Network Connectivity Installing and Configuring a SOHO Network	14
Basics of Data Security Authentication Malicious Software File Security	15
Safety and Environmental Procedures Professionalism and Communication Skills	16
Getting Ready and the Exam Preparation Checklist Tips for Taking the Real Exam Beyond the CompTIA A+ Certification	17

CHAPTER 1

Introduction to Troubleshooting

This chapter covers the following A+ exam topics:

▶ Troubleshooting Theory

▶ Troubleshooting Examples and Concepts

You can find a master list of A+ exam topics in the Introduction.

This chapter covers CompTIA A+ 220-701 objectives 2.1 and 2.2.

Let's begin this book by talking about troubleshooting. Excellent troubleshooting ability is vital; it's probably the most important skill for a computer technician to possess. It's what we do—troubleshoot and repair problems! So it makes sense that a decent amount of questions about this subject are on the A+ exams. Every chapter of this book deals with troubleshooting to some extent; therefore, each chapter in a way is based off of this chapter. To be a good technician, and to pass the exams, you need to know how to troubleshoot hardware- *and* software-related issues. The key is to do it methodically. That's why CompTIA has incorporated a six-step troubleshooting process within the exam objectives. This chapter covers the six-step process and gives a couple basic examples of troubleshooting within this methodology. You should apply this troubleshooting theory throughout the rest of the chapters in the book.

The Six-Step A+ Troubleshooting Process

It is necessary to approach computer problems from a logical standpoint, and to best do this, we use troubleshooting theory. Several different troubleshooting methodologies are out there; in this book we focus on the CompTIA six-step troubleshooting process.

This six-step process included within the 2009 A+ objectives is designed to increase the PC technician's problem-solving ability. CompTIA expects the technician to take an organized, methodical route to a solution by memorizing and implementing these steps. This process is slightly modified from the previous version of the A+ exam, and we talk about those differences as we go through the steps. I'd like you to try to incorporate this six-step process into your line of thinking as you read through this book and whenever you troubleshoot a PC.

Step 1: Identify the problem.

Step 2: Establish a theory of probable cause. (Question the obvious.)

Step 3: Test the theory to determine the cause

Step 4: Establish a plan of action to resolve the problem and implement the solution.

Step 5: Verify full system functionality and if applicable implement preventative measures.

Step 6: Document findings, actions, and outcomes.

Let's talk about each of these six steps in a little more depth.

Step 1: Identify the Problem

In this first step we already know that there is a problem; now we have to identify exactly what it is. This means gathering information. You do this in a few ways:

> ▶ **Question the user.** Ask the person who reported the problem detailed questions about the issue. You want to find out about symptoms, unusual behavior, or anything that the user might have done of late that could have inadvertently or directly caused the problem.

▶ **Identify any changes made to the computer.** Look at the computer. See if any new hardware has been installed or plugged in. Look around for anything that might seem out of place. Listen to the computer—even smell it! For example, a hard drive might make a peculiar noise, or a power supply might smell like something is burning. Use all your senses to help identify what the problem is. Define if any new software has been installed or if any system settings have been changed. In some cases you might need to inspect the environment around the computer. Perhaps something has changed outside the computer that is related to the problem.

▶ **Review documentation.** Your company might have electronic or written documentation that logs past problems and solutions. Perhaps the issue at hand has happened before, or other related issues can aid you in your pursuit to find out what is wrong. Maybe another technician listed in the documentation can be of assistance if he has seen the problem before. Perhaps the user has documentation about a specific process or has a manual concerning the computer, individual component, software, or other device that has failed.

Keep in mind that you're not taking any direct action at this point. Instead, you are gleaning as much information as you can to help in your analysis. In this stage it is also important to back up any critical data before making any changes.

(**Exam**Alert)

Perform backups before making changes!

Step 2: Establish a Theory of Probable Cause (Question the Obvious)

In step 2 we theorize as to what the most likely cause of the problem is. Start with the most probable or obvious cause. For example, if a computer won't turn on, our theory of probable cause would be that the computer is not plugged in! This step differs from previous A+ methodologies and other troubleshooting processes in that we are not making a list of causes but instead are choosing one probable cause. In this step we also need to define whether it is a hardware- or software-related issue.

Step 3: Test the Theory to Determine the Cause

In step 3 we take our theory from step 2 and test it. Back to our example, we go ahead and plug in the computer. If the computer starts, we know that our theory is correct. At that point we move on to step 4. But what if the computer *is* plugged in? Or what if we plug in the computer and it still doesn't start? An experienced troubleshooter can often figure out the problem on the first theory but not always. If the first theory fails during testing, we go back to step 2 to establish a new theory and continue until we have a theory that tests positive. If the problem escapes us and we can't figure out what the problem is from any of our theories, it's time to escalate. Bring the problem to your supervisor so that additional theories can be established.

Step 4: Establish a Plan of Action to Resolve the Problem and Implement the Solution

Step 4 might at first seem a bit redundant, but let's delve in a little further. When a theory has been tested and works, we can establish a plan of action. In the previous scenario, it's pretty simple; plug in the computer. However, in other situations the plan of action will be more complicated; you might need to repair other issues that occurred due to the first issue. In other cases, an issue might affect multiple computers, and the plan of action would include repairing all those systems. Whatever the plan of action, after it is established, immediately implement it.

Step 5: Verify Full System Functionality and if Applicable Implement Preventative Measures

At this point we want to verify that the computer works properly. This might require a restart or two, opening applications, accessing the Internet, or actually using a hardware device, thus proving it works. Also within step 5 we want to prevent the problem from happening again if possible. Yes, of course we plug in the computer, and in this case it works, but why was the computer unplugged? The computer being unplugged (or whatever the particular issue) could be the result of a bigger problem, which we would want to prevent in the future. Whatever our preventative measures, we want to make sure that they won't affect any other systems or policies, and if they do, to get permission for the those measures first.

Step 6: Document Findings, Actions, and Outcomes

In this last step, document what happened. Depending on the company you work for, you might have been documenting the entire time, for example using a trouble ticketing system. In this step, finalize the documentation including the issue, cause, solution, preventative measures, and any other steps taken.

Documentation is extremely important; it helps us in two ways. First, it gives closure to the problem, for you and the user; it solidifies the problem and the solution, making you a better troubleshooter in the future. Second, if you or anyone on your team encounters a similar issue in the future, the history of the issue will be right at your fingertips. Most technicians don't remember specific solutions to problems that happened several months ago or more. Plus, having a written account of what transpired can help to protect all parties involved.

> **Note**
>
> Try to incorporate this methodology into your thinking when covering the chapters in this book. Apply it to any of the components, for example motherboards, adapter cards, and power supplies.

Cram Quiz

Answer these questions. The answers follow the last question. If you cannot answer these questions correctly, consider reading this section again until you can.

1. What is the second step of the A+ troubleshooting methodology?

   ○ **A.** Identify the problem.

   ○ **B.** Establish a probable cause.

   ○ **C.** Test the theory.

   ○ **D.** Document.

2. When you run out of possible theories for the cause of a problem, what should you do?

- ○ **A.** Escalate the problem.
- ○ **B.** Document your actions so far.
- ○ **C.** Establish a plan of action.
- ○ **D.** Question the user.

3. What should you do before making any changes to the computer? (Select the best answer.)

- ○ **A.** Identify the problem.
- ○ **B.** Establish a plan of action.
- ○ **C.** Perform a backup.
- ○ **D.** Escalate the problem.

4. Which of these is part of step 5?

- ○ **A.** Identify the problem.
- ○ **B.** Document findings.
- ○ **C.** Establish a new theory.
- ○ **D.** Implement preventative measures.

Cram Quiz Answers

1. B. The second step is to establish a theory of probable cause. You need to look for the obvious or most probable cause for the problem.

2. A. If you can't figure out why a problem occurred, it's time to get someone else involved. Escalate the problem to your supervisor.

3. C. Always perform a backup of critical data before making any changes to the computer.

4. D. Implement preventative measures as part of step 5 to ensure that the problem will not happen again.

Troubleshooting Examples and Concepts

The purpose of this section is to familiarize you with some introductory troubleshooting. As we progress through the book, we demonstrate more and more in depth troubleshooting of problems that might occur. Let's go ahead and give a couple basic examples of troubleshooting utilizing the methodology we just covered.

Troubleshooting Example 1: Display Issue

In this scenario you are a PC technician working for the technical services department of a mid-sized company. During the morning you get a call from a member of the graphics department. Apparently, he can't see anything on his screen. Troubleshoot!

Identify the Problem

While questioning the user you find out that the computer worked fine yesterday, but when the user came in today and started the computer, the display was blank.

While examining the computer, you can tell that it is turned on due to the power LED and can tell it is working due to the activity of the hard drive LED. The monitor has an amber LED lit next to the power button. As the user mentions, restarting the computer and turning the monitor on and off have no effect.

Establish a Theory of Probable Cause (Question the Obvious)

Once again, we look for the obvious or most probable cause. In this case you surmise that the monitor is not connected to the PC.

> **ExamAlert**
>
> Check the connections first! They are a common culprit outside and inside the computer.

You guess the monitor is not connected to the PC because the computer appears to be working normally, and the monitor seems to get power (due to the amber LED). The theory is that the video signal is not getting to the monitor from the computer.

Test the Theory to Determine the Cause

To test this theory simply go to the back of the PC and check the video connection; then check the connection on the monitor if it has screw terminals. If either is loose or disconnected, firmly connect them to see if the monitor displays anything.

If the monitor now displays video, the theory is confirmed; however, if it does not, we would need to construct a new theory. Maybe the monitor's bulb has burned out, or there is a problem with its inverter, or maybe the video card has some kind of issue. Perhaps the user neglected to tell you that he set the video resolution to a higher setting than the monitor could handle! Start with the next most likely cause and test it, moving on down the line until the cause is discovered. If you can't find the cause, escalate the problem and get others involved.

Establish a Plan of Action to Resolve the Problem and Implement the Solution

Your plan of action should include connecting the monitor to the PC securely. Maybe the plug was never screwed in, making it an easy target to get disconnected, so make sure that the plug is firmly seated and screw it in tightly. Do the same if the other end of the cable screws into the monitor. As part of your plan of action, you might want to explain what the problem was to the user and show him how to reconnect the monitor in the future.

Verify Full System Functionality and if Applicable Implement Preventative Measures

At this point we want to verify that the computer works properly. This might require a restart or two as proof, or opening applications that the user utilizes. Also within step 5 we want to prevent the problem from happening again if possible. Maybe the user inadvertently kicked the connector loose, or a member of the cleaning crew ran over the cable with a vacuum, disconnecting it from the computer. Either way, rerouting or tie-wrapping the video cable, and any other cables, might be a good idea to prevent future problems with these connections. You should also inspect the cable for any type of wear. Any possible irresponsibility of the cleaning crew should be escalated to your supervisor.

Document Findings, Actions, and Outcomes

Document according to your company's policies. This might mean using an online ticketing system or just writing things down on paper. In this scenario you should document the user and computer that had the issue, the cause of the issue, how you repaired it, and any type of preventative measures and training of the user you implemented.

Troubleshooting Example 2: Power Issue

In this scenario you are a network support specialist within an IT department that supports 500 computers. First thing in the morning, you get a call from the marketing department. From the statement it appears that several of its computers will not start. Troubleshoot!

Identify the Problem

While questioning the manager of the marketing department, you find out that the computers worked fine yesterday, but when everyone came in this morning, four of the computers grouped in one area wouldn't start.

While examining the computers, you do indeed see that none of the four computers will turn on. Not only that, but the monitors at the employees' desks are also off. So the problem is that four computers and their monitors will not turn on.

Establish a Theory of Probable Cause (Question the Obvious)

Don't forget, we are looking for the most probable cause. In this case it would appear that there is a power issue because not just one computer but all four computers and their monitors are not turning on. A possible theory is that a circuit breaker tripped causing all the electronic equipment on that circuit to fail.

Test the Theory to Determine the Cause

To test this theory we can try plugging another device into any of the outlets that are part of the supposed problem. We can also use a receptacle tester to test the affected outlets.

If the outlets test negative for power and our electrician confirms that a circuit has tripped at the main panel, we know that our theory is correct. However if the outlets test positive or have some other kind of erroneous reading, we need to troubleshoot further and most likely escalate the problem to a licensed electrician.

> **ExamAlert**
>
> If a problem is electrical, contact your building supervisor or manager so that they can contact a licensed electrician to fix the problem.

Establish a Plan of Action to Resolve the Problem and Implement the Solution

Let's say that the circuit tripped. The plan of action would simply be to reset the breaker and verify that the computers and monitors receive power.

Verify Full System Functionality and if applicable Implement Preventative Measures

At this point we want to verify that the computers and other equipment work properly. This might require a restart or two as proof and turning the monitors on and off. Also within step 5 we want to prevent the problem from happening again if possible. Chances are that the circuit was overloaded, and that's why it tripped. We need to consider taking one of the computer systems and moving it to another circuit, or possibly having the electrician add a new circuit to that area.

Document Findings, Actions, and Outcomes

Once again, document according to your company's policies. In this scenario we would document this as an issue that affected several computers. Include names of the people dealt with including any of the marketing people, electricians, and perhaps building supervisors.

Power issues are fairly common with computers. For more information on power, power supplies, and the problems you might encounter, see Chapter 5, "Power."

Some More Troubleshooting Tidbits

When working on the inside of a computer, it is imperative to protect against electrostatic discharge (ESD), which occurs when two objects of different voltages come into contact with each other. For example, if you just walked across a carpet, your body gathered a lot of static electricity, more than enough to damage a computer component. If you were to touch the component, the static electricity would discharge from you to the component, the ending result being a wasted computer component. There are several ways to protect against this including wearing an antistatic wrist strap and connecting it to the chassis of the computer, touching the chassis of the computer before handling any components, and using an antistatic mat.

Other more indirect ways to prevent this are to keep your feet stationary when working on a computer, work in a noncarpeted area, keep the humidity raised to approximately 50 percent (if possible), and use antistatic sprays. You can find more information about protecting against ESD in Chapter 16, "Safety and Professionalism."

Exam**Alert**

To prevent ESD use an antistatic wrist strap.

If a computer won't start, you should check the power cable. But what if the computer and monitor are getting power and the display is still blank? You can narrow this down to four components: video, RAM, processor, and motherboard. From a hardware standpoint, the first thing to check is whether the monitor is securely connected to the computer's video card. Next, you want to make sure that all the other components connect properly. It's not unheard of for a connector, an adapter card, or even a processor to get jarred loose. If the video card, processor, or RAM is not connected properly, they can stop the computer from booting, and nothing shows up on the screen. Also, if the motherboard has a loose main power connector, the computer will not boot. So, when troubleshooting a no-display issue, and you know that the computer and monitor are receiving power, remember the *big 4*: video, RAM, processor, and motherboard.

Another key concept that you need to remember is that a large percentage of the issues you troubleshoot are due to user error. From a customer service standpoint, this is not something you want the user to pick up from your demeanor. You don't want to accuse or blame a user; but it is something to keep in mind when questioning the user.

On a final note, when troubleshooting, try to keep a level head. Think logically about a solution to the problem. I like to tell my students to think like Mr. Spock; try not to let emotion cloud your judgment. It is understandable that at times the amount of trouble tickets might be a bit overwhelming. Just remember that you can only do what you can do. By clearing everything from your mind except for a methodical troubleshooting approach, you can obtain solutions much more efficiently, live long, and prosper.

Cram Quiz

Answer these questions. The answers follow the last question. If you cannot answer these questions correctly, consider reading this section again until you can.

1. There is a problem with the power supplied to a group of computers, and you do not know how to fix the problem. What should you do first?
   - ○ **A.** Establish a theory of why you can't figure out the problem.
   - ○ **B.** Contact the building supervisor or your manager.
   - ○ **C.** Test the theory to determine the cause.
   - ○ **D.** Document findings, actions, and outcomes.

2. You have confirmed the theory that a video card is bad and needs to be replaced. What should you do next?
   - ○ **A.** Escalate the problem.
   - ○ **B.** Document your actions so far.
   - ○ **C.** Establish a plan of action.
   - ○ **D.** Question the user.

3. A computer won't turn on when you press the power button. What should you check first?
   - ○ **A.** If an operating system is installed.
   - ○ **B.** Documentation.
   - ○ **C.** If the monitor is plugged in.
   - ○ **D.** If the computer is plugged in.

4. Which of these is part of step 1?
   - ○ **A.** Question the user.
   - ○ **B.** Document findings.
   - ○ **C.** Establish a new theory.
   - ○ **D.** Escalate the problem.

5. Which of the following are possible faulty components for having nothing on the display? (Select all that apply.)

- ○ **A.** Sound card
- ○ **B.** Video card
- ○ **C.** Processor
- ○ **D.** Network card

Cram Quiz Answers

1. B. If you can't figure out a cause to a problem and have exhausted all possible theories, escalate the problem to the appropriate persons.

2. C. After you confirm a theory, move on to step 4 to establish a plan of action, and implement the solution.

3. D. Connections are quite often the culprit outside and inside the computer. If a computer won't turn on, make sure it is plugged securely into an AC outlet.

4. A. Questioning the user is important when gathering information to identify the problem.

5. B and **C.** The big four (as I like to call them) are the video card, RAM, processor, and motherboard. If your computer is definitely getting power and there is still nothing on the display, you want to check these, most likely in order.

Additional Reading and Resources

Mueller, Scott. *Upgrading and Repairing PCs*. Que.

Soper, Mark Edward, Scott Mueller, David L. Prowse. *CompTIA A+ Certification Guide*. ISBN13: 9780789740472. Que.

Additional A+ resources: http://www.davidlprowse.com/aplus.

CHAPTER 2

Motherboards

This chapter covers the following A+ exam topics:

▶ Motherboard Components and Form Factors

▶ The BIOS

▶ Installing and Troubleshooting Motherboards

You can find a master list of A+ exam topics in the "Introduction."

This chapter covers CompTIA A+ 220-701 objective 1.2 and CompTIA A+ 220-702 objectives 1.1 and 1.2.

Without a doubt, the motherboard is the foundation of the computer. Everything connects to the motherboard, and all data is transferred through this matrix of circuitry.

In this chapter we delve into the components that make up the motherboard, the various types of motherboard form factors, the ports and interfaces you find on the face and the side of the motherboard, and the Basic Input Output System (BIOS) and show proper methods for installing and troubleshooting motherboards.

Motherboard Components and Form Factors

Over the years I have found that if a student is going to lack knowledge in one area, it's quite often going to be the motherboard. Unfortunately, this is one of the key elements in a computer system. It's the starting point for a quick and efficient computer. Because it connects to everything in the computer system, you need to know many concepts concerning it. Let's begin with the parts that make up the motherboard.

Motherboard Components

You don't need to know every single chip and circuit that resides on the motherboard. Generally, if a motherboard fails, which is uncommon, the entire board needs to be replaced. However, you do need to know the main components, interfaces, and ports of a motherboard and have some knowledge of how it transmits data. This ensures compatibility of components when you design your own system or connect replacement or additional devices to a motherboard. It also enhances your troubleshooting skills—when the time comes…muhahahah!

Main Components

I decided to build a new computer for this book (and for me I suppose) and wanted to use fairly new components. Not the latest or most expensive mind you but still current, decent parts that reflect the type of components you see in the field now and for a year or two to come. For the motherboard, I chose the Intel DP35DP. It is part of the media series of motherboards. (It wasn't because it has my initials, I swear!) Figure 2.1 shows this motherboard with callouts to the main components you need to know for the exam.

You might have noticed that this motherboard meets all the characteristics of the ATX form factor; it is indeed an ATX motherboard that we speak more of later in this chapter. And don't worry if you are confused about one or two of the components; we cover each of these as we progress through this book. Processors are covered in more depth in Chapter 3, "The CPU," RAM is covered in Chapter 4, "RAM," power is covered in more depth in Chapter 5, "Power," and SATA and IDE are covered in Chapter 6, "Storage Devices." We talk about the remainder of the listed components within this chapter.

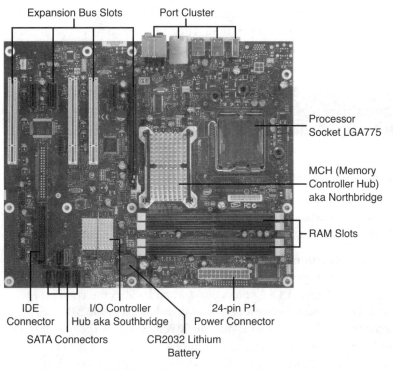

Expansion Bus Slots   Port Cluster

Processor
Socket LGA775

MCH (Memory
Controller Hub)
aka Northbridge

RAM Slots

IDE   I/O Controller   24-pin P1
Connector   Hub aka Southbridge   Power Connector
     SATA Connectors   CR2032 Lithium
                                        Battery

FIGURE 2.1   Intel DP35DP motherboard components

ExamAlert

Identify motherboard components for the exam.

Product guides usually accompany a device. But if you don't have one and want more information about the components of this or any motherboard, consider grabbing a technical document from the manufacturer's website. "Go to the source!"—that's what I always tell my students. For example, for this motherboard see the following link: http://www.intel.com/products/desktop/motherboards/DP35DP/DP35DP-overview.htm. This has all the information you can possibly want about the motherboard. If you were to click on Technical Documents, you can download a PDF of the product guide (among other documents) that includes diagrams, descriptions, installation procedures…the whole nine yards. Now I know you have seen a lot of acronyms (and there are a slew more coming), but here's a vital one for you: RTM,

"Read the Manual!" It helps when installing, configuring, and troubleshooting a device. As far as Intel goes, trust in these guys, they are some of the greatest technical documentation specialists on the planet.

ExamAlert

Go to the manufacturer's website for product documentation.

Chipsets and Busses

In a general sense, the chipset *is* the motherboard, incorporating all the controllers on the motherboard; many technicians refer to it in this way. But in the more specific sense, the chipset is composed of two main components:

▸ **Memory Controller Hub (MCH)**: On Intel motherboards this provides the connection between the processor (also known as the CPU), the RAM, and some PCI Express devices and handles the communications between them. Historically it has been known as the MCC or memory controller chip and is informally referred to as the northbridge. The MCH is used by devices that require a high speed of data transfer. It is important to note that on many AMD-based motherboards, this chip doesn't connect to the RAM; instead the RAM is accessed directly by the processor; therefore, on those AMD-based motherboards, this chip is simply referred to as the northbridge.

Note

Newer Intel Core i7 setups have a redesigned chipset that uses the Input/Output Hub (IOH) in place of the MCH. The memory controller portion is integrated to the CPU, so the IOH has connections only to the CPU and to some PCI Express devices. However, this technology is fairly new, so you will probably not see questions on the exam about it but be ready to see it in the field!

▸ **I/O Controller Hub (ICH)**: This provides the central connection point between all the secondary systems such as USB, FireWire, hard drives, and so on. It connects to the MCH through the Direct Media Interface (DMI), which is a high-speed point-to-point interconnection for the two hubs. The ICH is also known as the southbridge.

Another document available to us is the Technical Product Specification PDF. Technically this document is much more in depth, even bordering on the hypertechnical! It includes a schematic of the motherboard that shows the chipset, busses, circuitry, and chips of the motherboard and how they interconnect. From this we can see that the chipset on our motherboard is called the P35 Express chipset and contains the Intel 82P35 MCH and the Intel 82801R ICH. Figure 2.2 gives a rough idea of the connections between these hubs and the rest of the motherboard.

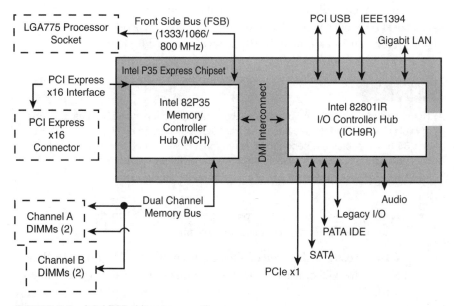

FIGURE 2.2 **Intel P35 chipset connections**

The previous figure and text gives a specific example of a chipset. However, because there are several different types of processors and manufacturers of processors, the two main chips in the chipset might be referred to as different things. In general, you can get away with using the terms northbridge, which basically connects to the CPU, and southbridge, which connects all the secondary systems.

A quick word on busses. A bus can be one wire (serial) or a group of wires working in unison (parallel) that carry data from one place to another. Parallel busses are normally designed in multiples of eight wires. That is the simple explanation and should be enough for the exam.

Three major busses (you can think of them as highways) lead to and from the MCH:

> **Front Side Bus (FSB):** This connects the MCH to the processor (CPU) socket. On our motherboard it is rated for 1,333, 1,066, or 800 MHz, which depends on what type of processor used. This bus is also referred to by Intel as the system bus in some of its documentation. When deciding on a processor, make sure that it can run at one of the FSB speeds prescribed by the motherboard. It also needs to be compatible with, and adhere to the wattage maximum, of the motherboard's socket. (Newer Core i7 systems use a different type of bus known as the QuickPath Interconnect [QPI] instead of the FSB.)

Note

The speed of the bus is rated in Hertz (Hz), a unit of frequency defined as a number of cycles per second. In this case, our front side bus can go as high as 1,333MHz or 1.33 billion cycles per second (if it is not overclocked!). For a primer on Hertz, bits, and bytes, access my website: http://www.davidlprowse.com/aplus.

> **Memory Bus:** This set of wires connects the MCH to the RAM slots. It has also been referred to as the address bus.

> **PCI Express x16 Interface:** This connects the MCH to the x16 PCIe slot used for video; usually there is only one of these slots on a motherboard.

The front side bus and memory bus are parallel; however, PCI Express works as a group of serial busses.

The ICH provides connectivity to all the secondary busses, some of which are parallel busses (IDE, Audio) and some of which are serial busses (USB, SATA, IEEE 1394, and lesser PCIe slots).

The two types of drive technologies that have ports on the face of our motherboard are IDE and SATA, which connect to the I/O Controller Hub:

> **IDE:** Integrated Drive Electronics interfaces (as shown in Figure 2.1) have 40 pins. They utilize the Parallel ATA (PATA) standard that currently specifies a maximum data transfer rate of 133MB/s. These bytes of information are transferred in parallel, for example 8 bits at a time. Hard drives, CD-ROM drives, and DVD drives can connect to IDE

ports. The IDE connector is 40 pins, but depending on the version, the cables used can have 40 or 80 conductors.

▶ **SATA:** Serial ATA is quickly eclipsing IDE. As you can see in Figure 2.1, there is only one IDE port, but there are six 7-pin SATA ports (one of which is for external connections). The reason for this is speed. Even though SATA sends data in a serial fashion, or one bit at a time, it is faster than IDE. The first generation of SATA is rated at 1.5Gbps (notice the lower case b indicating bits), equal to roughly 150MB/s. Second generation SATA, which is available on most new motherboards offers a 3.0Gbps data rate, or 300MB/s. And new generations of faster SATA are forthcoming. Once again, hard drives, CD-ROMs, and DVDs can be connected to an SATA drive.

> **Note**
>
> For more information on IDE and SATA, see Chapter 6.

A last word about chipsets: Certain applications prefer or even require specific chipsets, usually applications on the high-end side. For example, the ProTools audio platform prefers the 975 chipset with the Core 2 Duo processor (among other combinations). Graphics, engineering, and even gaming applications recommend certain chipsets as well. So before designing your computer, think about which applications you will use and whether they prefer certain chipsets.

Expansion Busses

There are six expansion busses and their corresponding adapter card slots that you need to know for the exam. They include the following:

▶ **PCI:** The Peripheral Component Interconnect bus was developed in the nineties by Intel as a faster, more compatible alternative to the deprecated ISA bus. It allows for connections to modems and to video, sound, and network adapters; however, PCI connects exclusively to the I/O Controller Hub. Because of this, other high-speed video alternatives were developed that could connect directly to the MCH. The PCI bus is used not only by devices that fit into the PCI slot, but also by devices that take the form of an integrated circuit on the motherboard. The most common PCI cards are rated at 66 MHz, and their corresponding PCI bus is 32-bits wide, allowing for a maximum data transfer rate of

266MB/s. Derivates of PCI include PCI-X, which was designed for servers, using a 64-bit bus and rated for 133 MHz/266 MHz; and Mini-PCI used by laptops. PCI slots are still found on today's motherboards (as shown in Figure 2.3) but are quickly being overtaken by PCIe technology. A comparison of PCI, AGP, and AMR is shown in Figure 2.4. A comparison of PCI and other expansion busses is shown in Table 2.1 at the end of this list of expansion busses.

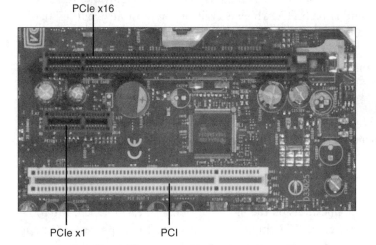

FIGURE 2.3   **PCIe x16, PCIe x1, and PCI expansion busses**

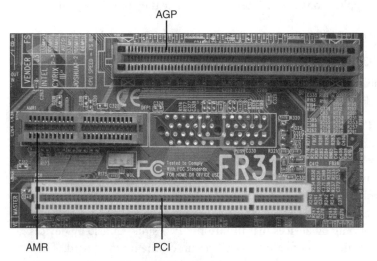

FIGURE 2.4   **AGP, AMR, and PCI expansion busses**

▶ **AGP:** Accelerated Graphics Port was developed for the use of 3D accelerated video cards and alleviated the disadvantages of PCI for video.
Originally designed as a 32-bit 66MHz bus (known as 1x), it had a maximum data transfer rate of 266MB/s. Additional versions were delivered,
for example, 2x, with a data rate of 533MB/s, effectively doubling the
fastest PCI output. (To do this the 66MHz bus was double-pumped to
an effective 133MHz.) Two more versions included 4x (quad-pumped)
offering 1GB/s, and 8x with a maximum data rate of 2GB/s. The AGP
bus connects directly to the MCH or northbridge, addressing one of the
limitations of PCI. Although there is some compatibility between cards,
it is important to note that different slots (1x, 4x, and 8x) use different
voltages. You should verify that the AGP card is compatible with the
stated voltage in the motherboard documentation. An example of an
AGP slot is shown in Figure 2.4. AGP has been overshadowed more and
more by PCIe over the past 5 years.

▶ **PCIe:** Currently the king of expansion busses, PCI Express is the high-
speed serial replacement of the older parallel PCI standard. The most
powerful PCIe slots with the highest data transfer rates connect directly to
the MCH (northbridge); the lesser PCIe slots connect to the ICH (southbridge). This expansion bus sends and receives data within *lanes*. These
lanes are considered full-duplex, meaning they can send and receive data
simultaneously. PCIe version 1 has a data rate of 250MB/s per lane, version 2 is 500MB/s, and version 3 is 1GB/s. The amount of lanes a PCIe
bus uses is indicated with an x and a number, for example, x1 (pronounced
"by one") or one lane. PCIe video cards are currently x16 (16 lanes) and
have taken the place of AGP video cards due to their improved data transfer rate. For example, a Version 2 PCIe x16 video card can transfer 8GB
of data per second (500MB × 16 = 8GB), which is far greater than AGP
could hope to accomplish. Most other PCIe adapter cards are x1, although
you might find some x4 cards as well. Of course, compatibility is key. A x1
card can go in a x1 slot or larger, but a x16 card currently only fits in a x16
slot. Figure 2.3 displays a x16 and x1 slot. Keep in mind that x4 and x16
slots are controlled by the MCH (northbridge), whereas x1 slots are controlled by the ICH, as shown in Figure 2.2. Table 2.1 shows a comparison
of PCIe and other expansion busses.

> **Note**
>
> A x32 slot is also defined in the PCIe specification. However, as of the publishing of
> this book, in general you see no more than x16 version 1 and 2 cards allowing for a
> maximum data rate of 4GB/s or 8GB/s, respectively.

> **ExamAlert**
>
> Identify the PCI, AGP, and PCIe expansion busses for the exam.

▶ **AMR and CNR:** Intel's audio/modem riser expansion slot was designed to offer a slot with a small footprint that had the capability to accept sound cards or modems. The idea behind this was to attain Federal Communications Commission (FCC) certification (which is a time-consuming and detailed endeavor) for the adapter card once, instead of having to attain FCC certifications for integrated components on motherboards over and over again with each new motherboard released. This way, the card could be transferred from system to system. The idea was flawed from the start, because adapter cards so quickly progress. This technology, and its successor CNR, are not used in today's motherboards. Figure 2.4 shows an example of AMR. Quite often, expansion busses are labeled on the motherboard just above the slot, as shown in Figure 2.4.

The Communications and Networking Riser (CNR) was Intel's adaptation of AMR and was meant for specialized networking, audio, and modem technologies. It was superior to AMR because it could be software- or hardware-controlled but had the same result as AMR and has been obsolete since about 2007.

▶ **PCMCIA:** The Personal Computer Memory Card International Association is actually an organization that develops the PC Card technology used in laptops; it is not an expansion bus itself. PC Cards (originally called PCMCIA cards) were first designed for additional storage and later for modems, network cards, combo cards, and hard drives. You have probably seen these credit card-sized devices in the past; however, they are being superseded by another technology known as ExpressCard. More information on PCMCIA, PC Card, and ExpressCard can be found in Chapter 11, "Laptops."

TABLE 2.1   **Comparison of PCI, AGP, and PCIe**

Expansion Bus	Bus Width	Frequency	Max. Data Rate
PCI	32-bit	33MHz	133MB/s
		66MHz	266MB/s
AGP	32-bit	1x = 66MHz	266MB/s
		2x = 66 MHz (double pumped to 133MHz)	533MB/s
		4x = 66MHz (quad pumped to 266MHz)	1GB/s
		8x = 66MHz (octo-pumped to 533MHz)	2GB/s
PCIe	Serial, consists of between 1 and 16 full-duplex lanes	Version 1 = 2.5GHz Version 2 = 5GHz Version 3 = 8GHz	250MB/s per lane 500MB/s per lane 1GB/s per lane

> **Note**
>
> Maximum data transfer rates are never attained, even in a lab environment. You can expect actual throughput to be substantially lower, but professionals use the maximum data rate as a point of reference and as a way of comparison.

I/O Ports and Front Panel Connectors

Without input and output ports, we really could not correspond with the computer, unless it was through telepathy, and I don't think that technology has developed yet J. These ports also take care of displaying information, printing it, and communicating with other computers. Figure 2.5 shows some typical ports as found on our motherboard.

Starting at the left and continuing counter-clockwise, we see the following in the figure:

> ▶ **IEEE 1394a:** Also known as a FireWire or i.Link, this port is used for devices that demand the low-latency transfer of data, usually concerning music or video. This port has a maximum data rate of 400Mbps.

> ▶ **USB:** Universal Serial Bus ports are used by many devices including keyboards, mice, printers, cameras, and much more. The ones shown are USB 2.0 high-speed ports and have a maximum data rate of 480Mbps.

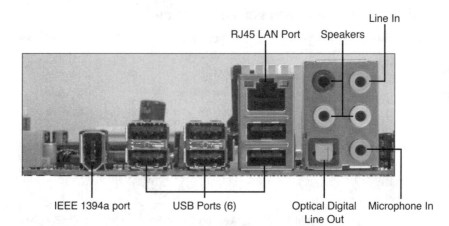

FIGURE 2.5   I/O port cluster on the back panel of the motherboard

> ▶ **Audio cluster:** There are six ports in this audio cluster including an optical digital output, microphone in, line in, and speaker outs.

> ▶ **RJ45 LAN port:** This is our wired network connection. On this particular motherboard, it is a Gigabit Ethernet LAN controller and is rated for 10/100/1000Mbps.

ExamAlert

Identify back panel connectors (I/O ports) for the exam.

Quite often, cases come with front panel ports that might be wired to the motherboard or to an adapter card. These include USB ports, audio ports, memory card readers, external SATA ports, and more.

For more information on I/O ports, see Chapter 12, "Video, Audio, and Peripherals."

Form Factors

A computer form factor specifies the physical dimensions of some of the components of a computer system. It pertains mainly to the motherboard but also specifies compatibility with the computer case and power supply. The form factor defines the size and layout of components on the motherboard. It also specifies the power outputs from the power supply to the motherboard. The most common form factors, and the ones you need to know for the exam, are ATX, microATX, BTX, and NLX. Let's discuss these a little further now.

ATX

Advanced Technology Extended (ATX) was originally designed by Intel in the mid-nineties to overcome the limitations of the now deprecated AT form factor. It has been the standard ever since. Full-size ATX motherboards measure 12 inches × 9.6 inches (305mm × 244mm). ATX motherboards have an integrated port cluster on the back and normally ship with an I/O plate that snaps into the back of the case, which fills the gaps between ports and keeps airflow to a minimum. One identifying characteristic of ATX is that the RAM slots and expansion bus slots are perpendicular to each other. Generally, ATX has seven expansion slots. For example, our DP35DP motherboard has four PCIe slots and three PCI slots. The ATX specification calls for the power supply to produce +3.3V, +5V, +12V, and −12V outputs and a 5V standby output. The original ATX specification calls for a 20-pin power connector (often referred to as P1), and the newer ATX12V 2.x specification calls for a 24-pin power connector. The additional four pins are rated at +12V, +3.3V, +5V, and ground, as shown in Table 2.2. Those pins are numbered 11, 12, 23, and 24.

TABLE 2.2 **ATX Pin Specification of the Main Power Connector**

Pin	Color	Signal	Pin	Color	Signal
1	Orange	+3.3V	13	Orange	+3.3V
				Brown	+3.3V sense
2	Orange	+3.3V	14	Blue	−12V
3	Black	Ground	15	Black	Ground
4	Red	+5V	16	Green	Power on
5	Black	Ground	17	Black	Ground
6	Red	+5V	18	Black	Ground
7	Black	Ground	19	Black	Ground
8	Grey	Power good	20	White	−5V (optional)
9	Purple	+5V standby	21	Red	+5V
10	Yellow	+12V	22	Red	+5V
11	Yellow	+12V	23	Red	+5V
12	Orange	+3.3V	24	Black	Ground

> **ExamAlert**
>
> Know the voltages supplied to an ATX motherboard by a power supply: +3.3V, +5V, +12V, –12 V outputs, and a +5V standby output.

microATX

microATX (or mATX) was introduced as a smaller version of ATX; these motherboards can be a maximum size of 9.6 inches × 9.6 inches (244 mm × 244 mm) but can be as small as 6.75 inches by 6.75 inches (171.45 mm × 171.45 mm). It is backward compatible with ATX meaning that most microATX boards can be installed within an ATX form factor case, and they use the same power connectors as ATX. Often, they have the same chipsets as ATX as well.

BTX

Balanced Technology Extended (BTX) was designed by Intel in 2004 to combat some of the issues common to ATX. More powerful processors require more power and therefore release more heat. BTX was designed with a more efficient thermal layout. There is a lower profile, and the graphics card is oriented differently than ATX, so heat is generally directed out of the case in a more efficient manner. BTX's future is uncertain because Intel and AMD processors, and most video cards' processors, are designed to use less power (and generate less heat). BTX devices are not compatible with ATX devices. One of the ways to identify a BTX motherboard is that the RAM slots and expansion busses are parallel to each other (like the old AT boards). Also, the port cluster is situated differently on a BTX board. In addition, BTX boards are slightly wider than ATX boards; they measure 12.8 inches × 10.5 inches (325mm × 267mm).

NLX

New Low Profile Extended (NLX) utilizes a riser card and a slimline case and was used for inexpensive, mass marketed PCs—the likes of which you are unlikely to see in the field anymore. Dell decided against the use of NLX that could be considered its death blow. NLX was afterward superseded by microATX and others. NLX measures from 8 inches × 10 inches to 9 inches × 13.6 inches. The CompTIA A+ exam objectives list NLX but because it is deprecated, it is doubtful that you will see any questions about this form factor.

Table 2.3 compares the ATX, microATX, BTX, and NLX form factors supplying the sizes of these motherboards and some of the characteristics that set them apart.

TABLE 2.3 **Comparison of Motherboard Form Factors**

Form Factor	Width	Depth	Identifying Characteristic
ATX	12 inches	9.6 inches	RAM slots and expansion slots are perpendicular to each other (90 degree angle).
microATX	9.6 inches	9.6 inches	Smaller than ATX but backward compatible to it.
BTX	12.8 inches	10.5 inches	RAM slots and expansion slots are parallel to each other.
NLX	9 inches	13.6 inches	Utilizes a riser card.

Exam**Alert**

Know the basics of ATX, microATX, BTX, and NLX for the exam.

Cram Quiz

Answer these questions. The answers follow the last question. If you cannot answer these questions correctly, consider reading this section again until you can.

1. What voltage does an orange pin indicate?

    ○ **A.** +12. V

    ○ **B.** +5. V

    ○ **C.** -5. V

    ○ **D.** +3.3. V

2. Which motherboard form factor measures 12 inches × 9.6 inches?

    ○ **A.** microATX

    ○ **B.** BTX

    ○ **C.** ATX

    ○ **D.** CTX

3. Which expansion bus uses lanes to transfer data?

   ○ **A.** PCI

   ○ **B.** PCI-X

   ○ **C.** PCIe

   ○ **D.** PCIa

4. Which Hub does PCIe x16 connect to?

   ○ **A.** Ethernet hub

   ○ **B.** I/O Controller Hub

   ○ **C.** UPS hub

   ○ **D.** Memory Controller Hub

5. Which of these are serial technologies? Select all that apply.

   ○ **A.** USB

   ○ **B.** IEEE 1394

   ○ **C.** PCIe

   ○ **D.** PCI

Cram Quiz Answers

1. **D.** Orange signifies +3.3 volts. Red indicates +5 volts, and yellow is +12 volts; –5 volts would be the white optional wire.

2. **C.** ATX boards measure 12 inches × 9.6 inches.

3. **C.** PCIe (PCI Express) uses serial lanes to send and receive data.

4. **D.** PCIe x16 connects to the Memory Controller Hub (MCH) directly. On AMD-based boards and newer Intel boards, this would be referred to generically as the northbridge.

5. **A, B,** and **C.** The only one listed that is not a serial technology is PCI, which is a 32-bit parallel technology.

The BIOS

BIOS, CMOS, and the Lithium Battery

The BIOS, CMOS and lithium battery have a nice, little relationship with each other. In a way, the BIOS relies on the CMOS, and the CMOS relies on the lithium battery, as shown in Figure 2.6.

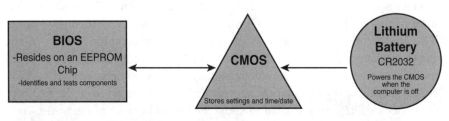

FIGURE 2.6   The BIOS, CMOS, and lithium battery

The Basic Input Output System (BIOS) is the first thing that runs when you boot the PC. The BIOS's job is to identify, test, and initialize components of the system. It then points the way to the operating system so that the OS can load up and take over. Collectively, this process is known as *bootstrapping*. Originally, the BIOS was stored on a Read-Only Memory (ROM) chip. It later progressed to a Programmable ROM (PROM) enabling the user to modify settings in the BIOS. Finally, today's system BIOS resides on an EEPROM chip on the motherboard. EEPROM stands for Electrically Erasable Programmable ROM and means that not only can we modify settings, but also fully update the BIOS by erasing it and rewriting it in a process known as *flashing*.

The complimentary metal-oxide semiconductor (CMOS) stores the contents of the BIOS's findings. For example, the type and speed of the processor, capacity of the hard drive, and current time and date. It uses little power that makes it a good choice for storing these settings. When the computer is on, the CMOS chip is powered by the power supply. However, CMOS by nature is volatile, so if it is not receiving power, it loses its stored contents.

Lithium battery to the rescue! The lithium battery powers the CMOS when the computer is shut off. The most-common battery used on today's motherboards is the CR2032, a nickel-sized battery that snaps into the motherboard and has a shelf life of anywhere from 2 years to 10 years depending on usage. The more you leave the computer on, the longer the battery will last. The lithium battery is sometimes referred to simply as the CMOS battery.

The POST

The power-on self-test (POST) is the first step in bootstrapping. The POST is essentially a piece of code that the BIOS runs to find out what type of processor is on the motherboard and verifies the amount of RAM. It also identifies busses on the motherboard, and other devices, and identifies what devices are available for booting.

The BIOS indicates any system problems that the POST finds by either on-screen display codes or beep codes. For example, a displayed 301 Error would most likely be a keyboard issue. Or one beep might indicate a memory error. This all depends on the type of BIOS used. The most common vendors of BIOS are American Megatrends (AMI) and Phoenix Technologies. Your motherboard should come with documentation about any possible BIOS error codes. If not, the documentation can usually be downloaded from the manufacturer's website; you just need to know the model number of the board. In the case of a proprietary computer (Dell, HP, and such), you need the model number of the computer to download any necessary documentation from its website.

But what happens if the display is blank? Special PCI POST adapter cards are available from companies such as JDR Microdevices that can read the system while it is booting. It usually has a two-digit hexadecimal display. If the display shows 00 or FF after the system finishes booting, everything is probably okay. However any other number would indicate a problem that can be cross-referenced in the accompanying booklet, CD, or online documentation.

Accessing and Configuring the BIOS

Accessing the BIOS must be done before the operating system boots. This can be accomplished by pressing a key on the keyboard. It can be F1, F2, F10, DEL, and so on depending on the manufacturer of and type of system. Usually, the correct key displays on the bottom-left portion of the screen when you first start the computer. If there is only a splash screen, you can press Esc to remove it, and hopefully the BIOS key displays. When you press the appropriate key, the system enters the BIOS Setup Utility, sometimes also referred to as CMOS, or just Setup, and displays a screen, as shown in Figure 2.7.

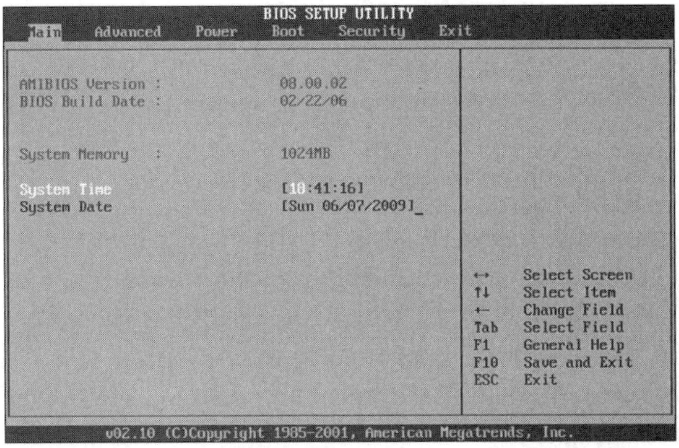

FIGURE 2.7 **The BIOS Setup Utility**

From here we can modify many things, several of which are important for the exam:

- **Time and Date:** These are normally set on the main screen. By default, operating systems retain their time and date from this, unless they synchronize to a time server.

- **Boot Device Priority:** Also known as BIOS boot order, this setting enables you to select which media will be booted: hard drive, CD-ROM, floppy, USB, and such. This feature can usually be accessed by selecting Boot on the main menu and then selecting Boot Device Priority. For a secure system, it is recommended that you set this to hard drive first, as shown in Figure 2.8.

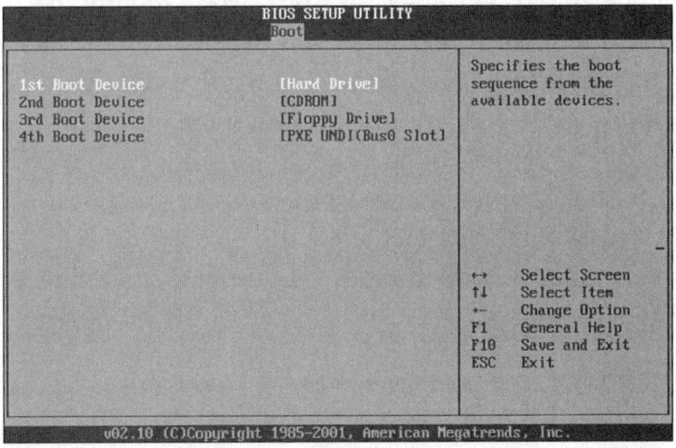

FIGURE 2.8 **BIOS boot order**

▶ **Passwords:** Two passwords are available on most BIOS: User and Supervisor. The User password (also known as a power-on password) authenticates a user before it enables the operating system to boot. The Supervisor password authenticates a user to the BIOS Setup Utility itself. For a secure system, enter a strong Supervisor password.

▶ **Power Management:** This enables you to select if power management is running and which type is used. The older Advanced Power Management (APM) enables the OS to work with the BIOS to achieve power management. This has been supplanted by the Advanced Configuration and Power Interface (ACPI) enabling the OS to take over full control of power management.

▶ **IDE Configuration:** This enables you to select and configure the hard drives and optical drives connected to the motherboard. Because most IDE and SATA drives are self-configuring, this setting is used less and less.

You can also enable or disable USB ports and legacy floppy devices and load BIOS defaults if you configure something in the BIOS that stops the system from booting.

Did you ever know someone who forgot his password? To a technician her password is like the back of her hand but maybe not to a user. And for some reason users love to set supervisory passwords in the BIOS—and then forget them. To fix this you need to turn off the computer, disconnect it, open it, and remove the lithium battery. By doing so, the CMOS forgets what it stored. The time and date probably revert to Jan. 1, 2000, or some other date in the past, and all passwords will be erased. In some cases you need to modify the BIOS Configuration Jumper Block solely, or in addition to removing the battery. This is a 3-pin jumper, usually near the lithium battery, that has three possibilities: Normal, Configuration, and Recovery. If necessary, move the jumper shunt from pins 1 and 2 (Normal) to pins 2 and 3 (Configuration); at that point you can access the BIOS without a password. Recovery mode is normally accomplished by removing the jumper altogether. A word to the wise; be ready for improperly labeled motherboards for this jumper configuration block. So you know, motherboards are usually shipped in the Normal state.

Flashing the BIOS

Flashing the BIOS is the term given to the process of erasing the BIOS firmware and rewriting it with a new version of the BIOS. It is sometimes referred to as *updating* the BIOS. It is important to check for updates to the BIOS, just like you would update an operating system. However, only flash the BIOS if your system *needs* it; for example, if your motherboard "sees" the processor but doesn't know specifically what type it is or at what speed it runs. Motherboard manufacturers release these updates quite often, and their description can tell you exactly what they fix. If you build a new computer, you should check for a BIOS update before you even install an operating system. BIOS updates close up security holes, identify new devices or identify them better, and are sometimes released simply to fix some incorrect code. There are several ways to update the BIOS, but generally you would either do it from within Windows or by using some kind of bootable media (floppy, CD-ROM, USB flash drive) to boot the system and rewrite the BIOS. Because the process varies from motherboard to motherboard, I list a few basic steps:

1. **Identify what BIOS you are running:** To do this, access the BIOS and check the main menu. There is usually some kind of code that you can check against the latest BIOS download on the manufacturer's website. If it is the same code, there is no need to update the BIOS. BIOS updates are cumulative, so you need to download and install only the newest version.

2. **Download the BIOS from the web:** This is usually downloaded in .EXE format. There is normally an instruction file you can download as well, explaining exactly how to flash the BIOS step by step.

3. **Select your method of BIOS updating:** For example, an Express BIOS Update would be done within Windows; simply download the file and double-click it to begin the process. Or a flash update could be done from a bootable floppy disk or bootable USB device. In this case there is usually a .EXE file that needs to be extracted to the bootable media and a .BAT file that will make the floppy disk bootable. You could also create your own bootable floppy if you have the wherewithal and a lot of time on your hands. With some manufacturers you can download an ISO image to be burned to a CD-ROM. After this is done, boot the computer with the CD and continue to the BIOS update. If a BIOS update were interrupted for some reason or did not complete properly, it might be necessary to recover the BIOS. To do this you need the recovery file and might need to remove the BIOS configuration jumper from the motherboard.

4. **Flash the BIOS:** Run the BIOS flash update from the appropriate media. If the media is a floppy disk or CD-ROM, restart the computer and boot to that media. Otherwise, run the BIOS update from within Windows. Some BIOS programs are nonresponsive but be careful; they are probably updating the BIOS even though it might look like nothing is happening. Let the system do it's "thing" for several minutes. *Do not* run a BIOS update during a lightning storm. Never turn off the computer during a BIOS update, and if you use a laptop, make sure that it is plugged in before starting the update.

ExamAlert

Know how to flash the BIOS for the exam!

Cram Quiz

Answer these questions. The answers follow the last question. If you cannot answer these questions correctly, consider reading this section again until you can.

1. Which component supplies power to the CMOS when the computer is off?
   - ○ **A.** Lithium battery
   - ○ **B.** POST
   - ○ **C.** Power supply
   - ○ **D.** BIOS

2. To implement a secure boot process, which device should be listed first in the Boot Device Priority screen?
   - ○ **A.** Floppy drive
   - ○ **B.** CD-ROM
   - ○ **C.** USB
   - ○ **D.** Hard drive

3. What is the term for how the BIOS readies the computer for and initiates the booting of the operating system?
   - ○ **A.** Bootlegging
   - ○ **B.** Booting
   - ○ **C.** Bootstrapping
   - ○ **D.** POST

4. How can we reset a forgotten BIOS supervisory password?

- ○ **A.** Access the BIOS by pressing F2.
- ○ **B.** Remove the battery.
- ○ **C.** Extract the .EXE contents to a floppy.
- ○ **D.** Remove the P1 connector.

Cram Quiz Answers

1. **A.** The lithium battery supplies power to the CMOS when the computer is off. This is because the CMOS is volatile and would otherwise lose the stored settings when the computer is turned off.

2. **D.** To ensure that other users cannot boot the computer from removable media, set the first device in the Boot Device Priority screen to hard drive.

3. **C.** Bootstrapping is accomplished by the BIOS. It is defined as one system readying the computer and leading to another larger system.

4. **B.** Removing the battery (and possibly moving the BIOS configuration jumper) resets the BIOS passwords.

Installing and Troubleshooting Motherboards

Installing Motherboards

You might ask, "Haven't we talked enough about motherboards?" Not quite. But installing them is easy when you know how, so this section shouldn't take too long. We'll break it down into some simple steps:

1. **Select a motherboard**: If you build a new computer, it should be designed with a compatible case and processor in mind. Also, make sure that it has the expansion ports that you need for audio, video, and so on and verify that it has the necessary I/O ports. Also, give a thought to the applications you will use and if they require or prefer a specific chipset. If you replace a motherboard, make sure that it is compatible with the system you put it in and that all the components can connect to it. If it is a proprietary computer (HP, Dell, and such), you won't have many choices on motherboards; see the computer manufacturer's website for details.

2. **Employ ESD prevention methods:** Use an antistatic strap and mat. And before touching the motherboard, place both hands on an unpainted portion of the case chassis. For more information on ESD preventative measures, see Chapter 16, "Safety and Professionalism."

3. **Ready the case:** Most cases come with brass standoffs that are already screwed directly into the case. Additional standoffs usually accompany the motherboard. Line up the motherboard's predrilled holes with the standoffs and eye it out. Add more standoffs as necessary so that the motherboard is supported properly. Some motherboards come with additional rubber standoffs that provide additional support and protection from ESD.

4. **Install the motherboard:** Carefully place the motherboard into the case so that the holes meet and line up with the brass standoffs. Secure the motherboard by screwing it in wherever there is a standoff. You might prefer to install the processor and RAM first before installing the motherboard. This has advantages and disadvantages. One advantage is that you wouldn't have to install them while the motherboard is within the case, decreasing the chances of bending the motherboard. One disadvantage is that the processor and RAM are expensive components that can be easily damaged when installing other components. Of course, in

some cases (pun intended), you will have no choice in the matter, but in general, if you worry about damaging the processor and RAM, install them last.

5. **Connect cables:** Now it's time to connect the 20-pin P1 or 24-pin P1 power cable from the power supply to the motherboard. This connector is tabbed; make sure that the tabs match up. When connected it should lock into place. Case connectors can be fitted to the motherboard as well. These wires start at the inside front of the case and have thin 2-, 3-, or 4-pin plugs on the other end. They are labeled POWER LED, POWER SW (for power switch), HDD LED, and so on. These are for the power button, reset button, and LED lights. Connect them to the corresponding ports on the edge of the motherboard closest to the front of the case. There might also be front panel ports (USB, audio), external SATA connectors, and more that need to be connected from the case to the motherboard. You can usually find documentation for these additional connections with the case.

6. **Install or re-install components:** Now it's time to install the rest of the components such as the hard drives, optical drives, and any other components. Installation of these additional components is covered in their corresponding chapters.

7. **Test the installation:** Finally, after you install anything, test it! Make sure it works. Boot the computer and access the BIOS. Tool around awhile until you are satisfied that the motherboard is functional. If there is an issue, troubleshoot the problem using the techniques discussed in the next section.

Troubleshooting Motherboards

That time has come. Remember the "big four" mentioned in Chapter 1, "Introduction to Troubleshooting." The motherboard is one of them. Here's a common issue: If you boot the computer and don't get anything on the display, and you are sure that power is not an issue and that the computer is really booting, check all connections. Chances are, it isn't the motherboard. A loose video card can cause these types of issues; make sure it is firmly pressed into its slot. Check the processor, RAM, and any connectors and other adapter cards in an attempt to rule out the motherboard as the culprit. You see, it is rare that the motherboard fails and checking these connections doesn't take long; however, removing the motherboard can be time-consuming. If you suspect a particular component has failed, for example the video card, attempt to swap out the video card with a known good device. Do the same with the RAM, even the processor. Finally, if you rule out the rest of the devices, continue troubleshooting the motherboard. Use a POST card if necessary, and if worst comes to worst, swap the motherboard with a known good one.

Let's run through a quick troubleshooting scenario using the CompTIA six-step troubleshooting methodology outlined in Chapter 1.

Motherboard Issue

In this scenario you are a PC technician working for the PC repair department of an electronics store. You are given a PC that supposedly reverts back to 12:00 AM, January 1, 2000, every time it starts. Troubleshoot!

1. **Identify the problem:** While viewing the work order, you see some of the customer comments: "PC worked fine until a few days ago. Now, every time it starts, it shows the date as Jan. 1, 2000. After changing the time and date in Windows, it reverts back to Jan 1, 2000 when restarted. Service pack 2 must have messed the computer up; I had updated to service pack 2 and that is when the problem started. Now my Outlook calendar and meetings are not synchronized to my employees' Outlook! Please fix right away!"

   A co-worker tells you the motherboard should be replaced, and your manager just wants the job done as quickly as possible.

   Remember to respect the user/customer, but don't always take his word for it. Test the computer yourself; you might find something entirely different is causing the problem, and you can save yourself a lot of time. Also, don't rush, regardless of how fast the manager wants the work done. When you rush, you risk the chance of overlooking the obvious, simple solution.

   So, while examining the computer you notice it runs Windows XP Professional and that Windows does indeed revert to Jan 1, 2000, even after you reconfigured the Date and Time Properties window. Otherwise, the computer seems to work fine, aside from Outlook synchronization issues, which is understandable. It doesn't display anything peculiar or make any strange sounds. And service pack 2 seems to have been installed correctly and is operating properly without any errors in the Event Viewer.

2. **Establish a theory of probable cause (question the obvious):** Again, we are looking for the obvious or most probable cause. Remembering your training you surmise that the lithium battery in the motherboard

has discharged causing the CMOS to lose its contents. If this happens, the BIOS has no recourse but to revert back to its earliest known time, in this case January 1, 2000. It sounds logical, so you move onto the next step.

3. **Test the theory to determine the cause:** To test this theory, you decide to restart the computer and access the BIOS. When in the BIOS, you change the time to the current time and date, and then you save the settings and shut down the computer. After turning it back on, you access the BIOS again and note that the time has once again reverted back to Jan. 1, 2000. You never accessed Windows in this procedure, so it would seem that the theory is correct. Now, if the time and date you had configured remained in the BIOS without reverting, your theory would probably be incorrect, and you would need to go back to step 2 to formulate a new theory. Although we try to establish and test theories without opening the PC, you can also test the lithium battery with a multimeter. The CR2032 lithium battery has a nominal voltage of 3.0V. If it measures below 2.0 volts, you know the battery has discharged to such a state that it cannot power the CMOS any longer.

4. **Establish a plan of action to resolve the problem and implement the solution:** Your plan of action should be to replace the CR2032 lithium battery with a new one. Implementing this requires you to shut down the PC and unplug it, open the PC, employ ESD prevention methods, and remove the CR2032 battery. This battery is easy to spot; it is shiny and is about the size of a nickel. They are usually labeled as a CR2032 as well. Removing it entails pushing on a tab and gently prying the battery out. Use something nonmetallic to do this. Then, find or requisition a new lithium battery. Next, test it with your trusty multimeter to make sure it is within proper voltage range (the closer to 3.0 volts the better). Remember that batteries slowly discharge, even when they sit on the shelf. Finally, install the battery into the motherboard.

5. **Verify full system functionality and if applicable implement preventative measures:** Now you need to make sure it works, so you boot the PC and access the BIOS. From there you update the time and date, save the settings to the BIOS, and shut down the computer. Next, boot the system again, and again access the BIOS. At this point you verify that the time and date have not reverted back to Jan. 1, 2000. If the time is correct, boot to Windows. Check the time in Windows after several "full cycles" (shutting the computer off and turning it back on) and warm boots to ensure that it works properly. As a preventative measure, you might want to recommend that the user synchronize Windows to a

time server. This can be done by opening the Date and Time Properties window, selecting the Internet Time tab, and selecting the Automatically synchronize with an Internet time server check box. This way, even if the lithium battery fails, Windows resynchronizes to the time server every time it boots. This also creates a more consistent meeting time for the user and his employees when he sets meetings in Outlook.

6. **Document findings, actions, and outcomes:** Document according to your company's policies. Complete the work order and any other paperwork necessary. Additional documentation might be required in an application such as Track-it! or another trouble-ticketing software program—and make a mental note of who the person was that said to replace the motherboard; be careful of her suggestions in the future!

Again, it is uncommon to see a motherboard fail, but if it does, it can be because of a few different things. Let's discuss several of these now.

First and probably the most common of these rarities are BIOS issues. Remember that you might need to flash the BIOS to the latest version. One example is when I built a PC for a friend who picked up an AMD 1.8GHz processor and compatible motherboard. The motherboard specifically stated that it could run 1.0GHz to 1.8GHz processors. But when I booted the system, the BIOS recognized an AMD processor but no specific speed. After running some diagnostic software, I found that the computer was rated at 100MHz processing speed. Not what my friend wanted! However, there were no BIOS updates on the manufacturer's website concerning this problem. And updating to the latest BIOS did not fix the problem. Emailing the motherboard manufacturer was the only way to fix this issue, which it was not aware of at the time because the AMD processor was so new. After a few days, a new BIOS update was released, and after flashing the system, the BIOS quickly identified the processor as 1.8GHz.

Second are ESD and other electrical issues. These might present themselves intermittently. If you find some intermittent issues, for example the computer reboots out of nowhere, or you receive random Blue Screens of Death, ESD could be the culprit. Or a surge could cause the problem. A particular wire or circuit on the motherboard could have been damaged. Document when failures occur. Swap out the motherboard with a known good one and see if the issue happens again when running through the same processes. If the issue doesn't recur, chances are the original motherboard is headed for the bit bucket. To give an example of this, let me bring you back in time, 2 years ago, to a customer of mine. In my first visit, I recommended that all computers connect to surge protectors—many were connected directly to AC outlets with no protection. During my second visit, I was presented with a computer (still not surge-protected) that crashed every time a user attempted to log on to the domain. BAM! Blue screen of death. However, he could log on locally with no problems! The Event Viewer in Windows was trying to blame the hardware, and after remembering the bad lightning storms we had the weekend before, I decided to use a POST tester on the motherboard. Sure enough, one of the circuits on the motherboard that led to the integrated network adapter had failed. However, in this case, I changed the I/O and memory address settings for the network adapter, and the problem was fixed. Other computers don't fare so well, and electrical damage can go right through the power supply to the motherboard, disabling it permanently.

Third are component failures. It is possible that a single component of the motherboard, say the SATA controller, can fail, but the rest of the motherboard works fine. This can also be verified with a POST card tester. To fix this, a separate PCI SATA card can be purchased. Then, you connect the hard drives to the new controller and disable the original SATA controller in the BIOS. Be wary though, sometimes these add-on cards can be pricey—perhaps more pricey than a new motherboard.

And last are manufacturing defects. Printed circuit boards (PCBs) are mass produced at high speed. Defects are uncommon but can occur due to mechanical problems in the machinery or due to engineering error. If you suspect a manufacturing defect, you need to replace the motherboard.

Cram Quiz

Answer these questions. The answers follow the last question. If you cannot answer these questions correctly, consider reading this section again until you can.

1. Before installing a motherboard, what should you do? (Select the best answer.)

   ○ **A.** Install the processor.

   ○ **B.** Verify that it is compatible with the case.

   ○ **C.** Employ ESD prevention methods.

   ○ **D.** Test the motherboard with a multimeter.

2. Which of the following are possible reasons for motherboard failure? (Select all that apply.)

   ○ **A.** Power surge

   ○ **B.** Manufacturer defect

   ○ **C.** CD-ROM failure

   ○ **D.** Incorrect USB device

3. How can you tell if a lithium battery has been discharged? (Select the best answer.)

- ○ **A.** Use a power supply tester.
- ○ **B.** Check within Windows.
- ○ **C.** Use a multimeter.
- ○ **D.** Plug it into another motherboard.

Cram Quiz Answers

1. **C**. Always employ ESD prevention methods before working with any components inside the computer. Although A and B are correct, they are not the best answers.

2. **A** and **B**. Power surges and manufacturing defects are possible reasons for motherboard failure. If a CD-ROM fails, it should not affect the motherboard, and any USB device can connect to a USB port (if it has the right connector). There isn't really an "incorrect" USB device.

3. **C**. Although there might be a Windows application that monitors the battery, the surefire way is to test the voltage of the lithium battery with a multimeter.

Additional Reading and Resources

Additional A+ resources: http://www.davidlprowse.com/aplus

Mueller, Scott. *Upgrading and Repairing PCs*. Que.

CHAPTER 3

The CPU

> **This chapter covers the following A+ exam topics:**
>
> ▶ CPU 101
>
> ▶ Installing and Troubleshooting CPUs
>
> You can find a master list of A+ exam topics in the "Introduction."
>
> This chapter covers CompTIA A+ 220-701 objectives 1.4 and 1.5 and CompTIA A+ 220-702 objectives 1.1 and 1.2.

The central processing unit, or CPU, is quite often referred to as the "brain" of the computer. Today's CPUs are like superbrains! A typical CPU today runs at 3GHz or higher, use two or more cores, and some can easily process 50 billion operations per second. That's a good deal more than we would have seen just 5 years ago. Some mornings I have trouble processing the thought *need coffee*! Of course we know that the human brain is much more sophisticated and functional than a CPU, but the CPU wins out when it comes to sheer calculating power.

You might hear the CPU referred to as a microprocessor, which technically it is. It's a much smaller version of the processors that were used 50 years ago. And although *microprocessor* might be a more accurate term, it has become more acceptable to refer to it as CPU, which this chapter does. However, you also see CPU manufacturers such as Intel refer to them as *processors*, so for all intents and purposes, the three terms mean the same thing. Keep in mind that a computer has other processors used by video cards and elsewhere, but know that the CPU is the main processor.

This chapter discusses some CPU technologies and cooling methods and talks about the models of CPUs offered by Intel and AMD. Afterward, the chapter demonstrates how to install and troubleshoot the CPU.

CPU 101

The CPU is often the most-expensive component in the computer; it's also one of, if not *the*, most important. The CPU's main function is to execute instructions or programs. Its speed, or *clock rate*, is measured in Hertz. For example, at 2.66GHz, a CPU operates at 2.66 billion cycles per second; we speak more to this concept in a moment. But although the speed of the CPU might be important, other factors should also play into your decision when choosing a CPU, including the chipset on the motherboard, *CPU technology*, and the *brand of CPU*. Chapter 2, "Motherboards," covers chipsets, but let's go ahead and talk about the various CPU technologies and brands of CPUs now.

CPU Technology

CPU technology is a key factor when considering a CPU. It all comes back to the motherboard; the CPU must be compatible with the motherboard in a number of ways. It is important to think about the speed (clock rate) of the CPU you want to use and whether that speed can be supported by the motherboard, and if the CPU fits in the motherboard's socket. Also, a decision has to be made as to whether to use a 32-bit or 64-bit CPU, and choose either a single-core or multi-core CPU; this will be based off the motherboard and the type of operating system you plan to install. Getting deeper into the technical side of the CPU, you might want to know the amount of cache included with the CPU, and the amount of power it requires.

Clock Rate

The *clock rate* is the frequency (or speed) of a component. It is rated in cycles per second and measured in hertz (Hz). For all practical purposes, the term clock rate is the same as the more commonly used term: *clock speed*.

Components are sold to consumers with a *maximum* clock rate, but they don't always run at that maximum number. To explain, let me use a car analogy. The CPU is often called the "engine" of the computer, like a car engine. Well, your car's speedometer might go up to 120MPH, but you'll probably never drive at that maximum—for a variety of reasons! When it comes to CPUs, the stated clock rate is the *maximum* clock rate, and the CPU usually runs at a speed less than that; in fact, it can run at any speed below the maximum.

Now, we're all familiar with speeds such as 2.4GHz, 3.0GHz, or 3.2GHz. But what is the basis of these speeds? Speed can be broken down into three categories that are interrelated:

▶ **Motherboard four clock speed:** The base clock speed of the motherboard. Also referred to as the system bus speed, this speed is generated
by a quartz oscillating crystal soldered directly to the motherboard. For
example, the base clock speed on the motherboard used in Chapter 2 is
333MHz.

▶ **External clock speed:** This is the speed of the front side bus (FSB),
which connects the CPU to the Memory Controller Hub (northbridge)
on the motherboard. This is usually variable and depends on the CPU
you install. In addition, it is determined from the base clock speed of the
motherboard. For example, our motherboard's maximum external clock
speed (or FSB) is 1333MHz. Simply put, this means that it is transferring four times the amount of data per cycle as compared to the original
base clock speed. 333 MHz × 4 = 1,333MHz.

▶ **Internal clock speed:** This is the internal speed of the CPU. For this
book I purchased the Intel Q8400 CPU that is rated at 2.66GHz. The
CPU uses an internal multiplier that is also based off the motherboard
base clock. The multiplier for this CPU is 8. The math is as follows:
base clock speed × multiplier = internal clock speed. In our example, that
would be 333MHz × 8 = 2.66GHz. Our motherboard can support faster
CPUs also, for example, the Intel Q9650 that has an internal clock
speed of 3.00GHz. This means that it has a multiplier of 9 (3.00GHz /
333MHz = 9). Some motherboards allow for overclocking (not ours),
which enables the user to increase the multiplier within the BIOS,
thereby increasing the internal clock speed of the CPU. This could possibly cause damage to the system, analogous to blowing the engine of a
car when attempting to run a 10 second ¼ mile. So approach overclocking with caution.

Note

Quite often motherboard manufacturers state only the internal and external clock
speeds (CPU and FSB); you might need to dig for more information concerning the
base clock speed. To make matters more confusing, some manufacturers refer to
the FSB as the system bus, but you can tell the difference. Just remember that the
FSB is calculated from the base clock of the motherboard. Quite often, it's multi-
plied by four. Currently, FSBs are between 800MHz and 1600MHz.

However, the external clock speed (FSB) isn't actually a factor for AMD CPUs or
newer Intel Core i7 CPUs because they have essentially done away with the FSB.
Intel just recently started using the QuickPath Interconnect (QPI) technology in
newer motherboards.

32-Bit Versus 64-Bit

The bulk of today's CPUs are 64-bit; it's a type of CPU architecture that incorporates registers that are 64 bits wide. These registers, or temporary storage areas, allow the CPU to work with and process 64-bit data types and provide support for up to one-terabyte of platform address space. 64-bit CPUs have been available for PCs since 2003. Examples of 64-bit CPUs include the AMD Phenom and Intel Duo Core CPUs.

The predecessor to the 64-bit CPU was the 32-bit CPU. Intel started developing well-known 32-bit CPUs as early as 1985 with the 386DX CPU (which ran at a whopping 33MHZ!), and AMD did likewise in 1991 with the Am386. A 32-bit CPU can't support nearly as much address space as a 64-bit CPU; 32-bit is limited to 4GB. Most editions of Windows are available in both 32-bit and 64-bit versions.

You will probably still see 32-bit technologies (such as the Pentium 4) in the field; however, due to applications' ever-increasing need for resources, these older CPUs continue to diminish, whereas 64-bit technologies (such as Core 2 Duo) will become more prevalent.

You might hear of the terms x86 and x64. x86 refers to older CPU names that ended in an 86—for example, the 80386 (shortened to just 386), 486, or 586 CPU and so on. Generally, when people use the term x86, they refer to 32-bit CPUs that enable 4GB of address space. x64 (or x86-64) refers to newer 64-bit CPUs that are a superset of the x86 architecture. This technology can run 64-bit software and 32-bit software and can address a maximum of 1TB.

Windows Vista and Windows XP come in 64-bit and 32-bit versions so that users from both generations of computers can run the software efficiently. Windows 2000 Professional was designed for 32-bit CPUs only.

Sockets

The *socket* is the electrical interface between the CPU and the motherboard. It attaches directly to the motherboard and houses the CPU. It also physically supports the CPU and heat sink and enables for easy replacement of the CPU.

The socket is either made of plastic or metal, with metal contacts for connectivity to each of the pins/lands of the CPU. A metal lever (retaining arm) locks the CPU in place. Figure 3.1 shows an example of an unlocked socket.

FIGURE 3.1   An unlocked LGA775 socket

Historically the socket has been considered a ZIF, short for zero insertion force. This means that the CPU should connect easily into the socket, with no pressure or force involved during the installation. Installing the CPU into these ZIF sockets is kind of like moving a planchette over a Ouija board until the CPU falls into place! Today's newer Land Grid Array (LGA) sockets require you to place the CPU into the socket housing, but it still doesn't require much force at all. The socket will have many pin inserts, or lands (on newer sockets), for the CPU to connect to. Pin 1 can be found in one of the corners and can be identified by one or more missing pins or pinholes depending on the type of socket. This helps you to orient the CPU, which also has the missing pin(s), or an arrow, in the corresponding corner. Here are two types of sockets you should know for the exam:

▶ **PGA:** Pin Grid Array sockets accept CPUs that have pins covering the majority of their underside. The pins on the CPU are placed in the pinholes of the socket, and the CPU is locked into place by a retaining arm. PGA has been in use since the late '80s, and is still in use on some motherboards today, but is quickly giving way to LGA.

▶ **LGA:** Land Grid Array sockets use lands that protrude out and touch the CPU's contact points. This newer type of socket (also known as Socket T) offers better power distribution and less chance to damage the CPU compared to PGA. LGA has been used since the later versions of Pentium 4 and is commonly used today.

The CPU and socket must be compatible. For example, the motherboard we use has an LGA775 CPU socket, which is common but not the only socket that Intel uses on its motherboards. The Q8400 CPU we use is designed to fit into the LGA775 socket, and several other CPUs are capable of fitting into this socket as well, but not all. For example some of Intel's Extreme CPUs are packaged differently and might need a different socket, such as the LGA771, which means a different motherboard must be used. Common sockets used by AMD are the Socket AM2 and AM2+.

> **ExamAlert**
>
> When purchasing a CPU, make sure that it is compatible with the motherboard's socket.

CPU Cache

Several types of cache are used in computers, but *CPU cache* is a special high-speed memory that reduces the time the CPU takes to access data. By using high-speed static RAM (SRAM) and because the cache is often located directly on, or even *in* the CPU, CPU cache can be faster than accessing information from dynamic RAM (DRAM) sticks. However, it will be limited in storage capacity when compared to DRAM. Cache is divided into levels:

▶ **Level 1:** L1 cache is built in to the CPU and gives fast access to *the most frequently* used data. This level cache is the first one accessed by the CPU and is usually found in small amounts. However, it is the fastest cache to be found, offering the lowest latency of any of the types of cache. One of the reasons for this is that it resides within the CPU core. Our Q8400 CPU has 4 × 32KB of L1 cache; 32KB for each core. You can find more information about multi-core technology later in this chapter.

▶ **Level 2:** L2 cache can be built on to the CPU or placed on a separate chip on the motherboard. L2 cache is accessed after L1 cache, and it serves the CPU with less frequently used data in comparison to L1 but still more frequently used than DRAM data. L2 cache feeds the L1 cache, which in turn feeds the CPU. L2 is not as fast as L1 cache but is superior to DRAM sticks. Today's CPUs have the L2 cache directly on-die, and the cache takes up the majority of the CPU's real estate. The Q8400 CPU we use for our build has a total of 4MB L2 cache.

> **Exam Alert**
>
> Know the difference between L1 and L2 cache for the exam.

▷ **Level 3:** L3 cache comes in the largest capacities of the three types of cache and has the most latency; therefore, it is the slowest. If the CPU can't find what it needs in L1, it moves to L2 and finally to L3. Or you could think of it this way: L3 cache feeds L2 cache, which feeds L1 cache, which in turn feeds the CPU with data. If the CPU can't find the data it is seeking, it moves on to the DRAM sticks. L3 cache could be on-die or on-board, but most of today's CPUs (if they use it at all) have it on-die. Newer AMD CPUs utilize a large amount of L3 cache, but most Intel CPUs do not use it, although this could obviously change in the future.

Generally, the more cache the better. The less the CPU needs to access DRAM, the faster it can calculate data.

Hyper-Threading

Intel's Hyper-Threading (HT) enables a single CPU to accept and calculate two independent sets of instructions simultaneously, simulating two CPUs. The technology was designed so that single CPUs can compete better with true multi-CPU systems but without the cost involved. In an HT environment, only one CPU is present, but the operating system sees two virtual CPUs and divides the workload, or threads, between the two.

Hyper-Threading began during the Pentium 4 days, but is not used in Intel's Core 2 CPUs. However, in 2009 it made a return with the Core i7 CPU.

> **Note**
>
> Don't confuse Hyper-Threading with HyperTransport used by AMD. HyperTransport is a high-speed, low latency, point-to-point link that increases communication speeds between various devices; AMD uses it so that CPUs can access system memory more efficiently.

Multi-Core Technologies

Whereas HT technology simulates multiple CPUs, *multi-core* CPUs physically contain two or more actual processor cores, in one CPU package. These newer CPUs can have 2, 4, or even 8 cores, each acting as a single entity, but in many cases sharing the CPU cache. This enables for more-efficient processing of data. Not only is less heat generated, but also a 1.8GHz dual-core CPU can process more data per second than a 3.6GHz single-core CPU.

Current examples of multi-core CPUs include Intel's Core 2 Duo, Core 2 Quad, and Core 2 Extreme, and AMD's X2 and Phenom CPUs. Intel's new i7 Core CPUs combine multi-core technology with Hyper-Threading enabling for as many as eight simultaneous threads in a single CPU package. It just goes on and on!

ExamAlert

Know the differences between Hyper-Threading and multi-core technologies for the exam. Hyper-Threading enables a single core CPU to calculate two instruction sets simultaneously, whereas multi-core CPUs calculate two or more instruction sets simultaneously, one instruction set per core.

Power Consumption

Power consumption of CPUs is normally rated in watts. For example, the Q8400 is rated as a 95 watt-hour CPU. This rating is known as *thermal design point (TDP)*, and it signifies the maximum power that the computer's cooling system needs to dissipate heat generated by the CPU. This doesn't mean that it always uses that much power, but it should play into your decision when planning what power supply to use and what kind of cooling system. For more information on power supplies, see Chapter 5, "Power." One hundred watts, or thereabouts, is a common amount for multi-core CPUs. They are more efficient than their predecessor single-core CPUs, such as the Pentium D that could use as much as 215 watts.

Because we are talking electricity, another important factor is voltage. CPUs are associated with a voltage range; for example, the Q8400 ranges from 0.86V—1.28V. It is important to monitor the voltage that is received by the CPU; you can do this in the BIOS. If the CPU goes beyond the specified voltage range for any extended length of time, it *will* damage the CPU. This becomes especially important for overclockers.

Brands of CPUs

For the average user, it doesn't matter too much which CPU you go with. However, for the developer, gamer, video editor, or musician, it can make or break your computer's performance. Although the CompTIA A+ objectives cover only Intel and AMD (Advanced Micro Devices), you should be aware that there are others in the market. Intel and AMD dominate the PC and laptop arena, but other companies such as VIA have made great inroads into niche markets and are moving deeper into the laptop/mobile markets as well. CPU manufacturers use the make/model system. For example, the CPU we use is the Intel (make) Core 2 Quad Q8400 Yorkfield (model).

Intel Versus AMD

Intel and AMD are both good companies that make quality products, which leads to great competition. Which is better? In all honestly, it varies and depends on how you use the CPU. You can find advocates for both (albeit subjective advocates), and the scales are constantly tipping back and forth. On any given day, a specific Intel CPU might outperform AMD, and 3 months later, a different AMD CPU will outperform an Intel. It's been that way for years now. Table 3.1 and Table 3.2 give a synopsis of currently offered CPUs by the two manufacturers, with the latest at the top and the oldest at the bottom. All these are 64-bit CPUs.

TABLE 3.1 **Comparison of Intel CPUs (as of July, 2009)**

Intel CPU	Cores	Speed	L2 Cache	Bus Speed (FSB)
Core i7 Extreme	4	3.29–3.33GHz	8MB	—
Core i7	4	2.66–3.06GHz	8MB	—
Core 2 Extreme	4	2.66–3.2GHz	4–12MB	1066–1600MHz
Core 2 Quad	4	2.4–3.0GHz	4–12MB	1066–1333MHz
Core 2 Duo	2	1.8–3.33GHz	2–6MB	800–1333MHz

> **Note**
>
> The Core i7 does away with the FSB. This is because Intel added an on-die memory controller (memory controller added directly to the CPU). Core i7 setups use a different chipset (for example the X58); within this chipset the QuickPath Interconnect (QPI) makes the connection between the CPU and the northbridge. The northbridge is referred to as the IOH (Input/Output Hub). However, you will probably not see questions concerning Core i7 on the exam because it is a fairly new technology.

TABLE 3.2 **Comparison of AMD CPUs (as of July, 2009)**

AMD CPU	Cores	Speed	L2 Cache	L3 Cache
Phenom II				
X2, X3, X4	2–4	2.4–3.1GHz	512KB	Maximum of 6144KB
Phenom X4	4	1.8–2.6GHz	512KB	2048KB
Phenom X3	3	1.9–2.5GHz	512KB	2048KB
Athlon X2 and II X2	2	1.9–3.1GHz	512KB	—

> **Note**
>
> All the AMD models listed have an on-die memory controller and use HyperTransport technology instead of a front side bus. AMD CPUs utilize L3 cache whereas Intel CPUs do not; however, AMD CPUs in general use less L2 cache than Intel.

Whatever CPU you choose, make sure that you get a compatible motherboard. A few things to watch for are compatibility with the FSB (if applicable), chipset, socket type, and voltage. However, Intel and AMD have tools on their websites that make it easy for you to find compatible motherboards.

Cooling

Now that we know a CPU can effectively use as much electricity as a light bulb, we can understand why it gets so hot. Hundreds of millions of transistors are hammering away in these powerhouses, so we need to keep it and other devices in the computer cool. This is done in a few ways as outlined in this section.

Heat Sinks

The *heat sink* is a block of metal made to sit right on top of the CPU, with metal fins stretching away from the CPU. It uses conduction to direct heat away from the CPU and out through the fins. With passive heat sinks, that's all there is to it. But with active heat sinks, a fan is attached to the top of the heat sink. The fan plugs into the motherboard for power and usually blows air into the heat sink and toward the CPU helping to dissipate heat through the heat sink fins. More powerful aftermarket CPU fans can be installed as well; just make sure that your power supply can handle the increased power requirements. In today's motherboards the chipset's northbridge and southbridge have passive heat sinks, but all new CPUs come with active heat sinks.

Traditionally heat sinks have been made of aluminum, but now you also see copper heat sinks used due to their superior conductivity.

Thermal Compound

The CPU cap and the bottom of the heat sink have slight imperfections in the metal. The best heat dissipation from CPU to heat sink would occur if the metal faces on each were completely and perfectly straight and flat, but you would find that only in a platinum-iridium alloy. So, to fill the tiny gaps and imperfections, thermal compound (aka thermal interface material or TIM) is used. One example of thermal compound is Arctic Silver, available online and at various electronics stores. Now, if this is a new installation, thermal compound is probably not needed. Most new CPUs' heat sinks have factory applied thermal compound that spreads and fills the gaps automatically after you install the heat sink and boot the computer. However, if you need to remove the heat sink for any reason, for example to clean it, thermal compound should be applied to the CPU cap before re-installing the heat sink, or installing a new heat sink. To do this, first clean any old thermal compound off of the CPU cap and the heat sink with TIM remover such as Akasa TIM-Clean. Then, clean a credit card with isopropyl alcohol or denatured alcohol. Next, apply a *small* amount of thermal compound to the center of the CPU cap. (This is the top of the installed CPU. You don't want to get any thermal compound on the actual CPU or motherboard.) With the credit card, spread the thermal compound carefully so that that you end up with a thin layer. Finally, install the heat sink. Try to do so in one shot without jostling the heat sink excessively.

> **ExamAlert**
>
> Reapply thermal compound whenever removing and re-installing a heat sink.

Fans

Case fans are also needed to get the heat out of the case. The power supply has a built-in fan that is adequate for lesser systems. However, multi-core systems should have at least one extra exhaust fan mounted to the back of the case, and many cases today come with one for this purpose. An additional fan on the front of the case can be used as an intake of cool air. If you aren't sure which way the fan blows, connect its power cable to the computer but don't mount it; then hold a piece of paper against the fan. The side that pulls the paper toward it should be the side facing the front of the computer when it is mounted. Some cases come with fans that are mounted to the top, which is also ingenious because heat rises. Another thing to consider is where the heat goes after it leaves the case. If the computer is in an enclosed area, the heat will have a hard time escaping and might end up back in the computer. Make sure there is air flow around the computer case. I have seen some people point the front of their computer toward an AC vent in the summer and even use special exhaust fans (such as bathroom fans) that butt up against the power supply or secondary exhaust fan on the case and lead hot air directly out of the house, but I digress.

Another possibility is a solution Intel developed called the Chassis Air Guide system, which is essentially a hollow tube that leads from the side of the case to the CPU, guiding cool room ambient air toward the CPU. For more information on the Intel Chassis Air Guide and Intel's Thermally Advantaged Tested Chassis list, see the following link: http://www.intel.com/go/chassis/. Of course, three or four fans can make a decent amount of noise, and they still might not be enough for the most powerful computers, especially the overclocked ones, which leads us to our next option.

Liquid Cooling Systems

Although still uncommon, liquid cooled systems are looked at as more of a viable option than they would have been 5 or 10 years ago. And newer water cooling kits can be used to not only cool the CPU, but also the chipset, hard drives, video cards, and more. A kit usually comes with a CPU water block, pump, radiator/fan, PVC tubing, and of course, coolant. The advantages are improved heat dissipation (if installed properly), higher overclocking rates, and support for the latest, hottest CPUs. The disadvantage as you can guess is the risk of a leak that can damage components. Due to the complexity of the installation, and the fact that most computers do not need this level of heat dissipation, liquid cooling is usually employed only by enthusiasts.

Cram Quiz

Answer these questions. The answers follow the last question. If you cannot answer these questions correctly, consider reading this section again until you can.

1. Which of these is the speed of the CPU?

   ○ **A.** External clock speed

   ○ **B.** FSB

   ○ **C.** Internal clock speed

   ○ **D.** System bus speed

2. Which of the following are 64-bit CPUs? (Select all that apply.)

○ **A.** Core 2 Duo

○ **B.** Phenom II

○ **C.** Pentium III

○ **D.** Celeron

3. Which is the fastest cache memory?

○ **A.** L2

○ **B.** L3

○ **C.** HTTP

○ **D.** L1

4. What does Hyper-Threading do?

○ **A.** It gives you multiple cores within the CPU.

○ **B.** It enables for four simultaneous threads to be processed by one CPU core.

○ **C.** It enables for two simultaneous threads to be processed by one CPU core.

○ **D.** It is a high-speed connection from the CPU to RAM.

5. What seals the tiny gaps between the CPU cap and the heat sink?

○ **A.** Thermal jelly

○ **B.** Peanut butter and jelly

○ **C.** 3-in-1 house oil

○ **D.** Thermal compound

6. What is the amount of power required to cool the computer?

○ **A.** FSB

○ **B.** TDP

○ **C.** MMX

○ **D.** TDK

7. Which kind of socket incorporates "lands" to ensure connectivity to a CPU?

○ **A.** PGA

○ **B.** Chipset

○ **C.** LGA

○ **D.** Copper

Cram Quiz Answers

1. **C**. The internal clock speed is the speed of the CPU, for example 2.4GHz. The external clock speed is the speed of the FSB, and the system bus speed (base clock) is what the internal clock speed is based off. An example of a base clock system bus speed would be 333MHz.

2. **A** and **B**. Intel's Core 2 Duo and AMD's Phenom II are both 64-bit CPUs. The Pentium III and Celeron are 32-bit CPUs.

3. **D**. L1 is the fastest cache memory and is located within the CPU's core.

4. **C**. Hyper-Threading allows for an operating system to send *two* simultaneous threads to be processed by a single CPU core. The OS views the CPU core as two virtual processors. Multiple cores would infer multi-core technology that means that there are two physical processing cores within the CPU package. The high-speed connection used by AMD from the CPU to RAM is Hyper-Transport.

5. **D**. Thermal compound is used to seal the small gaps between the CPU and heat sink. Did I ever tell you about the time I found grape jelly inside a customer's computer?

6. **B**. TDP (Thermal design point) is the amount of power required to cool a computer and is linked directly to the amount of heat a CPU creates.

7. **C**. LGA (Land Grid Array) is the type of socket that uses "lands" to connect the socket to the CPU. PGA sockets have pinholes that make for connectivity to the CPU's copper pins.

Installing and Troubleshooting CPUs

This section delves into the hands-on steps involved when installing or troubleshooting a CPU. Installation of CPUs has actually become easier over time, especially with the advent of LGA sockets. However, troubleshooting a CPU can be just as much of a challenge as ever. It's important to note that proper installation of a CPU can reduce the amount of CPU failures and the ensuing amount of CPU troubleshooting.

Installing CPUs

As with most computer components, installing a CPU is easy. But you must be careful, it can be easily damaged. Take it slow, and employ proper safety measures. We break it down into some simple steps:

1. **Select a CPU:** If you build a new computer, the CPU needs to be compatible with the motherboard for the type of CPU, speed, socket type, and voltage. If you upgrade a CPU, be sure that it is on the manufacturer's compatible list (which can be found on its website). This might be the motherboard manufacturer, or it could be a proprietary computer manufacturer (such as HP or Dell).

   Power down the PC, disconnect the power cable (or turn off the kill switch), open the PC, and get your boxes of components ready!

2. **Employ ESD prevention methods:** Use an antistatic strap and mat. Remove the CPU and heat sink from the package and place them on an antistatic bag. (One usually comes with the motherboard, but you should have extra ones handy.) Make sure that the CPU's lands (or pins) are facing up to avoid damage. Never touch the lands or pins of a CPU. Before touching any components, place both hands on an unpainted portion of the case chassis. For more information on ESD preventative measures, see Chapter 16, "Safety and Professionalism."

3. **Ready the motherboard:** Some technicians prefer to install the CPU into the motherboard and then install the motherboard into the case. If so, place the motherboard on the antistatic mat. (The mat should be on

a hard flat surface.) If you install the CPU directly into an already installed motherboard, clear away any cables or other equipment that might get in the way or could possibly damage the CPU, heat sink, or fan.

4. **Install the CPU:** Be careful with the CPU! It is extremely delicate! Always touch the case chassis before picking up the CPU. Hold it by the edges (the way you would properly hold a CD) and do not touch any pins, lands, or other circuitry on the CPU. If you need to put it down, put it down on an antistatic mat with the pins/lands facing up. Most of the time a CPU will be installed to either an LGA socket or a PGA socket. The following two bullets show how to install a CPU into each type of socket.

   ▶ If you install to an LGA socket, unlock the socket by releasing the retaining arm and swinging it open as far as it can go. Open the socket hatch, unhook it if necessary, and remove any plastic cover. Next, place the CPU into the socket. One corner of the CPU has an arrow that should be oriented with the socket's missing pin(s); both of these corresponding corners indicate pin 1, as shown in Figure 3.2. Carefully place the CPU into the socket. The lands on the CPU match up with the lands on the socket if it is oriented correctly. Make sure it is flush and flat within the socket. Close the cap, and secure the retaining arm underneath the tab that is connected to the socket, thus securing the CPU. Next, install the heat sink/fan assembly. On LGA sockets these usually have four plastic snap-in anchors. Carefully press each of these into and through the corresponding motherboard holes. Don't use too much force! Then turn each of them one quarter turn to lock the heat sink in place. Make sure that the heat sink is installed flush with the CPU by inspecting the assembly from the side. You want to be positive of this before turning on the computer because the thermal compound will begin to expand and fill the imperfections right away. Plug the fan into the appropriate motherboard power connector, as shown in Figure 3.3. (These are usually labeled directly on the motherboard, or see your motherboard documentation for details on where to plug in the fan.)

     Install the entire motherboard assembly into the case if that is your method of choice.

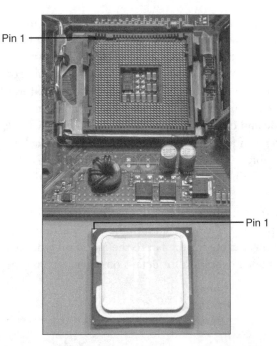

Pin 1

Pin 1

FIGURE 3.2   Orientation markings on the Q8400 CPU and LGA775 socket

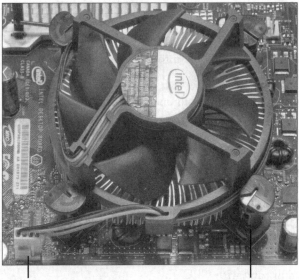

Fan Power Connector   Plastic Anchor

FIGURE 3.3   An installed multi-core CPU with connected fan

▶ If you install to a PGA socket, unlock the socket by moving the retaining arm out and upward until it is at a 90-degree angle to the motherboard. Then gently place the CPU into the ZIF socket. There will be an arrow on one corner of the CPU that should correspond to a missing pin (or arrow) on the socket. Don't use force; slide the CPU around until it slips into the socket. Look at the CPU from the side and make sure it is flush with the socket. Lock down the retaining arm to keep the CPU in place. Then attach the heat sink/fan assembly to the metal clips that are on the sides of the socket. Make sure that the heat sink is installed flush with the CPU by inspecting the assembly from the side. You want to be positive of this before turning on the computer because the thermal compound will begin to expand and fill the imperfections right away. Attach the power cable for the fan to the motherboard. (See your motherboard documentation for details on where to plug the fan in.)

> **Note**
>
> With some CPUs you might need to lock down the retaining arm *after* the heat sink/fan is installed. This depends on the CPU. Remember to RTM...read the manual!

Install the entire motherboard assembly into the case if is were your method of choice.

5. **Test the installation:** With the case still open, boot the computer to make sure that the BIOS POST recognizes the CPU as the right type and speed. Halt the POST if necessary to read the details, and when done, enter the BIOS and view the CPU information there as well. If the BIOS doesn't recognize the CPU properly, check if a BIOS upgrade is necessary for the motherboard. Also make sure that the CPU fan is functional. Then view the details of the CPU within the BIOS. Be sure that the voltage reported by the BIOS is within tolerance. Then access the operating system (after it is installed) and make sure it boots correctly. Complete several full cycles and warm boots. Finally, view the CPU(s) within Windows and with CPU-Z:

   ▶ **Within Windows:** Check in the Device Manager to make sure that the CPU is identified correctly. Navigate to Start and right-click on Computer (My Computer in XP); then select Manage from the drop-down menu. This brings up the Computer Management window. From here locate the Device Manager in the left window pane and click it. Now, from the list in the right window pane, there should be a category named Processors; click the plus sign to expand it, and the CPU you installed should be listed. In Figure 3.4 you can see a different system I am running that has a Core 2 Duo; the CPU shows up as two separate CPUs running at 2.5GHz. You can view similar information in Windows at the System Information window, which can be accessed by pressing Windows+R to open the Run prompt and typing **msinfo32** (in Vista) or **winmsd** (in XP).

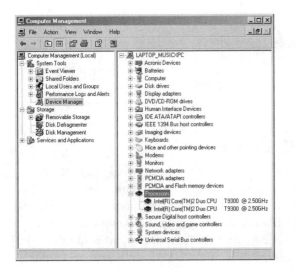

FIGURE 3.4   A Core 2 Duo CPU as shown in the Device Manager

> **With CPU-Z:** The CPU-Z program can be downloaded from http://www.cpuid.com/cpuz.php; it is freeware that gathers all the information we just saw in the Device Manager and also identifies the voltage, clock speeds, cache memory, and much more. This is *the* program to use when analyzing and monitoring your CPU, as shown in Figure 3.5. When installed (which is easy), simply run it to analyze your CPU.

Finally, if everything looks okay, close up the case, and consider monitoring the heat during the first few hours of operation. This can usually be done within the BIOS or with third-party applications within Windows. If all went well, congratulate yourself on a job well done!

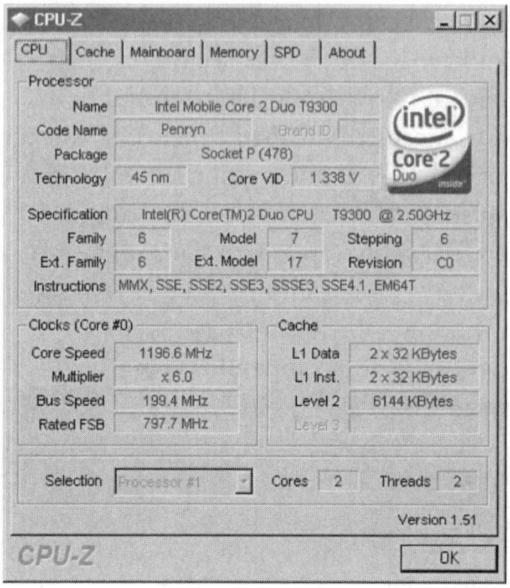

FIGURE 3.5   CPU-Z showing the same Core 2 Duo CPU

Troubleshooting CPUs

The most common issue with a CPU is when it isn't installed properly or securely. This could possibly cause a complete failure when trying to turn the system on. If this happens, always check the power first, just in case. Another possibility is that the system will turn on, and power will be supplied to the system, but nothing else will happen: no POST, no display, no hard drive activity. In either of these situations, after checking power, make sure of the following:

▸ **Check the Big Four:** Remember that the CPU is part of the big four including the video card, RAM, and motherboard. Be sure to check these other components for simple connectivity problems, which could be the real culprit and not the CPU at all. In fact, always check connections first before taking the CPU assembly apart.

▸ **Fan is connected and functional:** Some motherboards have a safeguard that disables booting if the fan is defective or not plugged in. Or you might get a message on the screen or other type warning depending on the motherboard. Be sure that the fan is plugged into the correct power connector on the motherboard (or elsewhere), and verify that it turns when the computer is on. If the fan has failed, replacement fans can be purchased; just make sure that the new fan is compatible with the heat sink and motherboard.

▶ **Heat sink is connected properly:** Make sure that the heat sink is flush with the CPU cap and that it is securely fastened to the motherboard (or socket housing).

▶ **CPU is installed properly:** Make sure it was installed flush into the socket and that it was oriented correctly. Of course, this means removing the heat sink. If you do so, you should clean off excess thermal compound and reapply thermal compound to the CPU cap before reinstalling the heat sink.

ExamAlert

When troubleshooting the CPU, be sure to first check all connections, and then make sure the fan, heat sink, and CPU are secure and installed properly.

Note

As always, turn off the computer, unplug it, and employ ESD measures before working on the inside of the computer.

Here are a few more possible symptoms of a failing CPU:

▶ Unexplained crashes during boot up or during use.

▶ The computer locks after only a short time of use.

▶ Voltage is near, at, or above the top end of the allowable range.

Sometimes, the CPU is just plain defective. It could have been received this way, or maybe it overheated. Perhaps there was a surge that damaged it, or maybe someone overclocked it too far, and it was the victim of overvoltage (and subsequent overheating). Regardless of these reasons, the CPU needs to be replaced. Now, by default CPUs come with a heat sink and fan, and if that is the case, install the CPU as you normally would. But in some cases, you can save money by purchasing the CPU only and use the existing heat sink. In this case, remember to clean excess thermal compound and then reapply thermal compound; but reapply to the CPU cap, not to the heat sink. If the CPU was installed properly, users don't usually have many problems with it (aside from the overclockers). Keep this in mind when troubleshooting the CPU, or when troubleshooting an issue that might *appear* to be a CPU issue but is actually something else altogether.

Cram Quiz

Answer these questions. The answers follow the last question. If you cannot answer these questions correctly, consider reading this section again until you can.

1. You are troubleshooting a CPU and have already cut power, disconnected the power cable, opened the case, and put on your antistatic strap. What should you do next?

   ○ **A.** Check the BIOS.

   ○ **B.** Check connections.

   ○ **C.** Remove the CPU.

   ○ **D.** Test the motherboard with a multimeter.

2. You have installed the CPU and heat sink/fan assembly. What should you do next?

   ○ **A.** Apply thermal compound.

   ○ **B.** Boot the computer.

   ○ **C.** Plug in the fan.

   ○ **D.** Replace the BIOS jumper shunt.

3. What is a possible symptom of a failing CPU?

   ○ **A.** CPU is beyond the recommended voltage range.

   ○ **B.** Computer won't boot.

   ○ **C.** BIOS reports low temperatures within the case.

   ○ **D.** Spyware is installed into the browser.

4. When deciding on a CPU for use with a specific motherboard, what does it need to be compatible with?

   ○ **A.** Case

   ○ **B.** Socket

   ○ **C.** Wattage range

   ○ **D.** PCI slots

Cram Quiz Answers

1. **B**. Check connections first; it is quick, easy, and a common culprit.

2. **C**. After installing the heat sink/fan assembly, plug in the fan to the appropriate connector on the motherboard.

3. **A**. If the CPU is running beyond the recommended voltage range for extended periods of time, it can be a sign of a failing CPU. If the computer won't boot at all, another problem might have occurred, or the CPU might have already failed. Low case temperatures are a good thing (if they aren't below freezing!) and spyware is unrelated, but we talk about it plenty in Chapter 15, "Security."

4. **B**. The CPU needs to be compatible with the socket of the motherboard. The case doesn't actually make much of a difference when it comes to the CPU. (Just make sure it's large enough!) There is no wattage range, but you should be concerned with the voltage range of the CPU, and PCI slots don't actually play into this at all because there is no direct connectivity between the two.

Additional Reading and Resources

Additional A+ resources: http://www.davidlprowse.com/aplus.

AMD official product information: http://www.amd.com/us-en/Processors/ProductInformation.

Computing tips, tricks, and solutions: http:///www.thomshardware.com.

Intel official product information: http://www.intel.com/products/processor/index.htm.

Mueller, Scott. *Upgrading and Repairing PCs*. Que.

CHAPTER 4

RAM

This chapter covers the following A+ exam topics:

▶ RAM Basics and Types of RAM

▶ Installing and Troubleshooting DRAM

You can find a master list of A+ exam topics in the "Introduction."

This chapter covers CompTIA A+ 220-701 objectives 1.2 and 1.6 and CompTIA A+ 220-702 objectives 1.1 and 1.2.

When people talk about the RAM in their computer, they are almost always referring to the "sticks" of memory that are installed into the motherboard. This is known as DRAM, or main memory, and often comes in capacities of 512MB, 1GB, or 2GB. This type of RAM has its own clock speed and must be compatible with the motherboard's RAM slots. It's not the only type of RAM, but it's the one you should be most concerned with for the exam. For all practical purposes the terms *stick, DIMM,* and *memory module* mean the same thing; they refer to the RAM installed into a motherboard's RAM slots.

The most important concept in this chapter is compatibility. There are a lot of RAM technologies to know, but the bottom line is "will it be compatible with my motherboard?" The best way to find out is to go to the RAM manufacturer's website and search for your motherboard. They usually list the matching RAM.

This chapter concentrates on SRAM and DRAM; however, there are other types, for example NVRAM that is covered in Chapter 6, "Storage Devices." In this chapter we discuss SRAM, DRAM, and DRAM types and demonstrate how to install and troubleshoot DRAM memory modules.

RAM Basics and Types of RAM

RAM Basics

Memory is the workspace for the CPU. Random-access memory (RAM) is the main memory that the CPU uses to store or retrieve data, which can be done in any order, regardless of what the CPU last accessed. The beauty of RAM is that the CPU can access any piece of memory it needs from anywhere in RAM, and any of these accesses take an equal amount of time. You often hear people associate RAM with a person's memory. But a person might take longer to recall certain memories in comparison to others. The CPU has equal access to all contents of RAM. It's fast and efficient, but the drawback is that RAM is typically cleared when the computer is shut off. To store data permanently, it would need to be written to a hard drive or other device, which is slower and less uniform in its storage and delivery of data. An example of this is when you work on a Word document; as you work, the contents of that file are stored in RAM, but when you save the file, the contents are then stored on a hard drive, or other media of your choice, which is done at a substantially slower rate.

The CPU though, is sort of closed off from memory, and the rest of the computer for that matter. It's kind of like the wizard behind the curtain. But someone does indeed pay attention to it—the memory controller chip. The memory controller is the go-between; basically, information is stored in and retrieved from RAM with the help of the memory controller. When the CPU wants to store or retrieve data to and from RAM, the memory controller is the chip that is responsible for getting the job done. It does this by moving the data along the address bus, which connects the memory controller to RAM. Figure 4.1 shows the two possible locations for the memory controller.

As you can see in the figure, the memory controller can be in one of two places:

- **Within the chipset:** In many Intel systems the memory controller is called the Memory Controller Hub (MCH). A major component within the chipset of the motherboard, it's also known as the northbridge. This design is shown on the left side of Figure 4.1.

- **Integrated to the CPU:** In other systems, the memory controller is part of the CPU (known as "on-die"), as shown on the right side of Figure 4.1. It does the same job regardless, but remember from Chapter 3, "The CPU," that AMD has been integrating the memory controller on to the CPU for some time now. And Intel's new Core i7 has an on-die memory controller as well, a major departure from the Core 2 CPU configurations. So this second design would seem to be catching on!

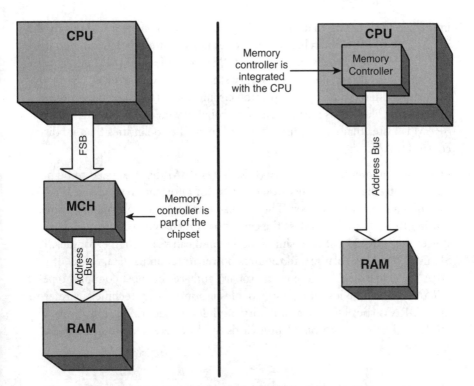

FIGURE 4.1   Comparison of the two memory controller designs

RAM discussed in this chapter is considered *volatile* (unless otherwise noted). This means that it loses any stored contents if it stops receiving power; for example, if you shut the computer off. However, not all RAM is volatile. We talk about *non-volatile* types of RAM (for example NVRAM) in Chapter 6.

Today's RAM is a set of integrated circuits (ICs) that works at high speed. These ICs could be on the motherboard, on adapter cards, within or on the processor, and of course, on those RAM sticks installed into the motherboard.

Types of RAM

Let's start by discussing the two main categories of RAM. Afterward, we move on to the types of RAM sticks you might install in a computer.

SRAM Versus DRAM

Static random-access memory (SRAM) is RAM that does not need to be periodically refreshed. Memory refreshing is common to other types of RAM and is basically the act of reading information from a specific area of memory and immediately rewriting that information back to the same area without modifying it. Due to SRAM's architecture, it does not require this refresh. You can find SRAM used as cache memory for CPUs, as buffers on the motherboard or within hard drives, and as temporary storage for LCD screens. Normally, SRAM is soldered directly to a printed circuit board (PCB) or integrated directly to a chip. This means that you probably won't be replacing SRAM. SRAM is faster than, and is usually found in smaller quantities than its distant cousin DRAM.

Dynamic random-access memory (DRAM) is RAM that *does* need to be periodically refreshed. This is because every bit of information stored in DRAM is stored in a separate capacitor. These capacitors lose their charge over time, causing the data to fade unless the capacitor is recharged or *refreshed*. It is slower than SRAM but is of simple design and can reach high capacities. Like SRAM, DRAM is volatile and requires power to retain its data. Sticks of DRAM are installed into the motherboard and are the most common type of DRAM you will be installing and troubleshooting. Many technicians refer to these DRAM sticks simply as memory modules, or just RAM. However, DRAM might also exist on adapter cards or elsewhere that we speak more about later on.

Exam Alert

Know the differences between SRAM and DRAM for the exam.

Note

Another type of memory you should know for the exam is ROM or read-only memory. Unlike the RAM types discussed in this chapter, ROM is nonvolatile, meaning that it retains its contents, even if it is not supplied with power. Historically, ROM chips could be read from but not written to. But now we have ROM chips that can do both, for example EEPROM implemented as a BIOS chip. For more information on EEPROM and the BIOS see Chapter 2, "Motherboards."

Let's talk about the different types of DRAM sticks you see in computers and how fast they can go!

SDRAM

Synchronous DRAM (SDRAM) is DRAM that is synchronized to the base clock of the motherboard (also referred to as the system bus speed). If your system bus (and corresponding memory bus) was 100MHz, you would want to install compatible 100MHz SDRAM because that SDRAM receives its clock signal from the system bus on the motherboard.

Typical SDRAM clock rates are 66MHz, 100MHz, and 133MHz; the physical RAM sticks are referred to as PC66, PC100, and PC133, respectively. Although you rarely see this type of RAM anymore, you can still purchase PC100 and PC133 versions. In stick format it is designed as a 168-pin DIMM. (You might also see SDRAM chips integrated directly to a sound or video card). DIMMs (dual in-line memory modules) have been in use for over a decade. They are the successor to the SIMM (single in-line memory module). The main difference between the two is that DIMMs have *separate* electrical contacts on each side of the module (or stick), whereas SIMMs might have contacts on both sides, but they are redundant.

Data transfer rates vary depending on the speed of the RAM, but SDRAM in general has a bus width of 64 bits (8 bytes). A 100MHz SDRAM bus can, therefore, transfer 8 bytes of data, 100 million times per second, equaling 800MB/s. Keep in mind that this data rate is a theoretical maximum, and actual data throughputs will be less.

An example of the "stick" or DIMM version of SDRAM is shown in Figure 4.2.

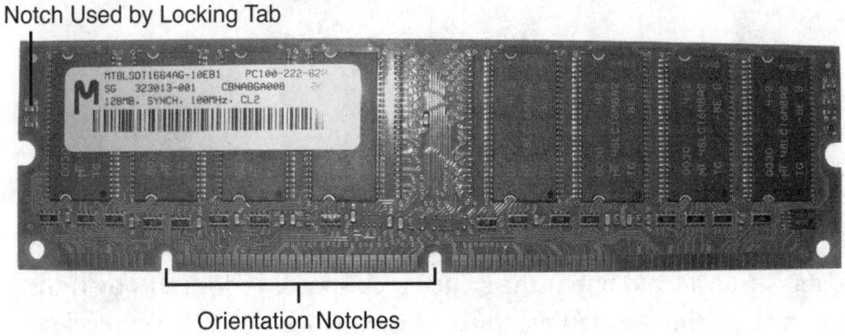

Notch Used by Locking Tab

Orientation Notches

FIGURE 4.2   A 168-Pin PC100 SDRAM 128MB stick

Notice how the stick has two notches located at the bottom, which help to orient the stick during installation. But they have another purpose; they define the functionality of SDRAM. The first notch specifies whether the SDRAM is registered, unbuffered, or reserved for future use, according to its position. Registered (or buffered) RAM has a register between the memory module and the memory controller. The register uses less electricity and requires less of a load from the memory controller, ultimately enabling for more memory modules. Historically, this was used in servers where more than four sticks of

RAM were required, but aside from some video cards, you probably won't see this on today's PCs. The second notch deals with voltage, and depending on its position, specifies whether the SDRAM stick runs at 5 volts or 3.3 volts. You might also notice that the sticker shows this RAM has a capacity of 128MB, which gives you an idea of the age of this technology; however it is still covered on the A+ exam. Finally, there is a notch on each side of the stick of RAM. These lock it into place when inserting it into the RAM slot of a motherboard. Basically, you press the stick straight down into the slot until the slot's tabs lock around the side notches.

ExamAlert

Identify SDRAM and its speeds (PC100, PC133) for the exam.

Note

A good place to go to get a "pulse" about current RAM trends is a website called www.pricewatch.com. It shows all the current types of RAM you can purchase and compares prices between vendors. Of course, this website (and others like it) compares lots of other PC equipment as well.

DDR

Let's talk about today's RAM— Double Data Rate (or DDR) is by far the most commonly used RAM on the planet. DDR is synchronized to the memory clock just like SDRAM; it's also called DDR SDRAM. The original DDR (aka DDR1) is actually SDRAM that has been double-pumped, meaning that twice the data is transferred but at the same clock speed. It does this by transferring data on the rising *and* falling edges of each clock signal (every cycle). So let's use DDR-200 as an example. Our original 100MHz system bus's transfers are doubled, so instead of 100 million transfers, it can now do 200 million transfers per second. (That's where the 200 comes from in DDR-200.) DDR also has a 64-bit wide bus allowing for 8 bytes of data per cycle. A 100MHz DDR bus can, therefore, transfer 8 bytes of data, 100 million times per second, *times 2*, equaling 1600MB/s. The equation for this data transfer rate (also known as bandwidth) is

Clock speed × bytes × 2 = Data Transfer Rate

Example: 100 MHz × 8 × 2 = 1,600MB/s

Whenever we do these types of equations, we are interested in solving for bytes because that is what these data rates measure.

> ## ExamAlert
>
> Know how to calculate the data transfer rate of DDR RAM for the exam.

You notice that people, and even manufacturers, refer to *transfers per second* as *MHz*. Although this is not completely accurate, it is common terminology. For example, DDR-200 can do 200 million transfers per second, but it is also referred to as 200MHz.

Table 4.1 gives the low-down about DDR1 memory modules including the standard names, clock speeds, how many transfers the RAM can do per second, and the total data transfer rate, also referred to as bandwidth. Finally, it shows the module name that is the name you would go by when ordering or purchasing RAM.

TABLE 4.1   **Comparison of DDR1 Types**

DDR Standard	Clock Speed	Transfers per Second	Transfer Rate	Module Name
DDR-200	100MHz	200 Million	1,600MB/s	PC1600
DDR-266	133MHz	266 Million	2,133MB/s	PC2100
DDR-333	166MHz	333 Million	2,667MB/s	PC2700
DDR-400	200MHz	400 Million	3,200MB/s	PC3200

> ## Note
>
> The DDR standards shown in this table are just that—standards as specified by JEDEC (a standardization body). However, you might see manufacturers use module names that go beyond these, for example, PC4300, which is actually based off the DDR-400 PC3200 standard. Manufacturers optimize their RAM using higher tolerance or overvolted chips, but note that motherboard manufacturers might not recommend using anything that is not standardized by JEDEC. This applies to other versions of DDR as well. Use motherboard supported and approved RAM! It can save troubleshooting time in the future.

The DDR DIMM has 184 pins and is not compatible with 168-pin SDRAM DIMMs. DDR DIMMs have one notch instead of two; this notch prevents using the wrong memory module in a RAM slot.

DDR2

DDR2 builds on the original DDR specification by increasing speed. It does this through faster signaling, which requires additional pins. Standard DDR2 DIMMs have 240 pins and cannot be used in DDR1 memory slots. As of early 2009, DDR2 was still the most common DIMM installed in new computers. Table 4.2 gives a comparison of the various types of DDR2, their speeds, and transfer rates.

TABLE 4.2   **Comparison of DDR2 Types**

DDR2 Standard	Clock Speed	Transfers per Second	Transfer Rate	Module Name
DDR2-400	200MHz	400 Million	3,200MB/s	PC2-3200
DDR2-533	266MHz	533 Million	4,266MB/s	PC2-4200
DDR2-667	333MHz	667 Million	5,333MB/s	PC2-5300
DDR2-800	400MHz	800 Million	6,400MB/s	PC2-6400
DDR2-1066	533MHz	1.066 Billion	8,533MB/s	PC2-8500

Figure 4.3 shows an example of a DDR2-800 DIMM. You might notice that the notch is in a slightly different location than with DDR DIMMs, again preventing mismatching of memory and RAM slot.

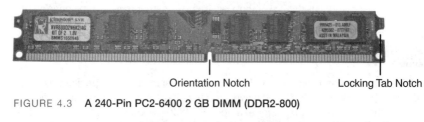

Orientation Notch   Locking Tab Notch

FIGURE 4.3   **A 240-Pin PC2-6400 2 GB DIMM (DDR2-800)**

ExamAlert

Know the amount of pins in SDRAM, DDR, and DDR2 memory modules.

It's Not the Quantity, It's the Quality!

We are all familiar with quantities of RAM like 512MB, 1GB, 2GB, and so on. For example, you might be talking to a friend or associate, or someone who just went to a computer show, who is excited that they just purchased 4GB of DDR2 RAM for her computer. Although that sounds nice, chances are the person will never use that entire amount!

What really makes the computer rock is the quality and speed of the RAM. For example, your friend might have purchased 4GB of DDR2-667 RAM, but what if you purchased 2GB of DDR2-1066 RAM? I guarantee that your RAM will outperform your friend's. Like Table 4.2 says, you can transfer 4,000MB of data per second more than your friend's computer. And whoopty-doo if your friend has 2 additional GB; some versions of Windows XP can't even access the full 4GB. *Most* Windows XP and Vista users won't ever go beyond 2GB of memory usage anyway. To prove my point, open the Windows Task Manager and view your memory usage. You can do this by right-clicking the taskbar and selecting Task Manager. Then click on the Performance tab. You should see a box that says PF Usage directly under CPU Usage (in Vista it just says Memory) check out the amount of MBs (or GBs) using. Commonly, this will be under 1GB regardless of whether you use XP or Vista. Open more applications and watch how much the number increases. Chances are it will stay below 2GB. As an example, while writing this chapter, I am running Windows XP as my OS, Windows Explorer, Microsoft Word, Excel, PowerPoint, Internet Explorer (with six tabs open), a FileZilla transfer, and a Windows Vista virtual machine, and I am using 1.47GB of memory! Now, not all the 1.47GB is stored in RAM, but the bulk of it is (more on that in Chapter 8, "Configuring Windows"). Of course, on the downside, faster RAM requires a newer and probably more expensive motherboard; as we said in Chapter 2, it always seems to lead back to the motherboard!

Currently, the pinnacle of all this RAM technology and speed is DDR3 (with DDR4 not far behind).

DDR3

When is enough enough? Never! Actually, DDR3 was designed for lower power consumption, and higher reliability, while enabling higher levels of performance. 240-pin DDR3 DIMMs are similar to DDR2 DIMMs, but are *not* backward compatible. It is probable that DDR3 will soon be the majority DIMM installed in new PCs, due to its capability to transfer twice as much data, using less voltage, basically working faster and more efficiently. Table 4.3 gives a comparison of the various types of DDR3, their speeds, and transfer rates.

TABLE 4.3 **Comparison of DDR3 Types**

DDR3 Standard	Clock Speed	Transfers per Second	Transfer Rate	Module Name
DDR3-800	400MHz	800 Million	6,400MB/s	PC3-6400
DDR3-1066	533MHz	1.066 Billion	8,533MB/s	PC3-8500
DDR3-1333	667MHz	1.333 Billion	10,667MB/s	PC3-10600
DDR3-1600	800MHz	1.600 Billion	12,800MB/s	PC3-12800
DDR3-2000	1000MHz	2.000 Billion	16,000MB/s	PC3-16000

> **Note**
>
> Laptops use smaller configurations of SDRAM, DDR, DDR2, and DDR3 with different pin configurations. These are known as SODIMMs. More information about Laptops and SODIMMs can be found in Chapter 11, "Laptops."

> **Note**
>
> The future of DDR is DDR4, which is currently used in some video cards but not available in DIMM format as of the publishing of this book.

RDRAM (Rambus)

Rambus DRAM is another type of synchronous dynamic RAM designed by the Rambus Corporation and used primarily at the turn of the millennium. Because RDRAM was proprietary and not part of the JEDEC standard, many manufacturers would not support or license it. This and other factors led to the general demise of RDRAM; when it comes to PCs, it's difficult to find it today, but a few components and gaming consoles use it. The chances of you working with it in a PC, or seeing questions on the exam about it are unlikely; however, it is briefly listed on the CompTIA A+ objectives. A few examples of RDRAM (also known as RIMMs) are PC800 (single channel, 16-bits wide, 1600MB/s bandwidth) and the more advanced RIMM 3200 (dual channel, 32-bits wide, 3200MB/s).

RAM Technologies

When you decide on the type of RAM to use, you must decide on more technical details; for example, whether to use single or dual-channel RAM that will be dictated for the most part by the motherboard. Your particular environment might need RAM that doesn't lag, so memory latency should be another consideration. There are several other lesser considerations such as whether to use single-sided or double-sided RAM, parity, or ECC RAM. For the most part, these additional factors don't play into the decision much: Your motherboard dictates whether the RAM is single-sided or double-sided, and parity and ECC RAM is more rare nowadays.

Single Channel Versus Dual Channel

Single channel is the original RAM architecture. In modern computers, there is a 64-bit bus (or data channel) between the memory and the memory controller. One or more sticks of RAM can be installed into the motherboard, but they share the same channel.

Dual channel is a newer technology that essentially doubles the data throughput. Two separate 64-bit channels are employed together resulting in a 128-bit bus. To incorporate this, the proper motherboard will have color-coded matching banks. See Figure 4.4 for an example of this.

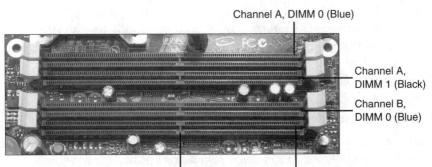

FIGURE 4.4   A motherboard's dual-channel memory slots

In the figure you can see four RAM slots. The first slot is blue and the second slot is black. Collectively they are known as Channel A. The third slot is also blue and the fourth is black, but these are known as Channel B. To use dual-channel architecture, a kit of two RAM sticks would be installed to the matching color (matching bank), for example both blue slots; one in Channel A, and one in Channel B, collectively forming the DIMM 0 bank. It is recommended that both DIMMs be identical for best performance. This means the capacity, speed, and number of chips must be the same on both DIMMs. However, if you access a website such as www.kingston.com, you can find a user-friendly memory database that tells you exactly which kits of RAM will be compatible with your motherboard. This is the easiest way to ensure a harmonious system. As a final note, it is recommended to install to banks sequentially, meaning install two memory sticks to Bank 0, and then (optionally) install two memory sticks to Bank 1.

ExamAlert

Know the difference between single and dual channel for the exam.

Memory Latency

Memory latency or CAS (Column Address Strobe) latency happens when a memory controller tries to access data from a memory module. It is a slight delay (usually measured in nanoseconds) while the memory module responds to the memory controller. It is given a rating of CAS, or more commonly CL. The higher the CL number, the longer the delay. For example, the RAM I purchased from Kingston is CL-6. The general range of DDR2 memory is between CL3 and CL6, so I'm at the slowest end of the spectrum. However, the difference between the ratings is small, so it will usually have an affect only on users that run powerful memory intensive applications, for instance graphics rendering. Video editors, graphic designers, and gamers beware! Otherwise CL6 is fine for the purpose of this computer.

Single sided Versus Double Sided

The terms single-sided and double-sided are not quite literal. Use your motherboard's documentation or a memory manufacturer's database to verify whether your motherboard accepts single-sided or double-sided memory modules, and acquire the compatible RAM from a reputable vendor. Single-sided refers to a memory module with a single "bank" of chips. The computer's memory controller can access all the chips at once. The memory module might have chips on both physical sides, or only on one side, but it is known as single-sided because the computer can address all the chips at once.

Double-sided memory modules have their chips divided into two "sides" known as banks. Only one "side" can be seen by the computer at any time. To use the second half of the storage available, the computer must switch to the second bank and can no longer read or write to the first half until it switches back again.

> **Note**
>
> Don't confuse double-sided memory and dual-channel memory when it comes to banks. An individual stick of RAM that is known as double-sided is broken down into two banks, but this has no bearing on the installation of the RAM. A bank of dual-channel RAM is two sticks of RAM that must be installed as a pair to matching color-coded slots. More often you will be concerned with dual-channel banks.

Parity Versus Nonparity

There are several types of parity in computing; RAM parity is when memory stores an extra bit (known as a parity bit) used for error *detection*. This means that the memory module can store 9 bits instead of 8 bits for every byte of data. So, parity RAM includes this extra bit, and the more common nonparity RAM does not. Parity RAM might be required when data integrity is a necessity.

ECC Versus Non-ECC

Error Correction Code (ECC) in RAM can detect *and* correct errors. Real-time applications might use ECC RAM. Like parity RAM, additional information needs to be stored, and more resources are used in general. This RAM is the slowest and most expensive of RAM types.

> **Note**
>
> Most new PCs do not support parity or ECC RAM due to the possibility of data corruption. If it is supported, but not necessary, these options can be disabled in the BIOS.

One Final Note About RAM

The main thing to "remember" when working with RAM is that it needs to be compatible with the motherboard. Check your motherboard's documentation regarding capacity per slot (or channel), maximum capacity, speed, and whether it accepts single- or dual-channel RAM. The best thing to do is to run a search on your particular motherboard at the RAM manufacturer's website to attain a complete list of a compatible RAM.

Cram Quiz

Answer these questions. The answers follow the last question. If you cannot answer these questions correctly, consider reading this section again until you can.

1. Which technology divides the RAM slots into colors?
   - ○ **A.** ECC
   - ○ **B.** Parity
   - ○ **C.** Double-sided
   - ○ **D.** Dual channel

2. Which of these is the delay it takes for a memory module to start sending data to the MCC?

  ○ **A.** DDR

  ○ **B.** Propagation

  ○ **C.** Latency

  ○ **D.** FSB

3. What is the transfer rate of DDR2-800?

  ○ **A.** 6,400MB/s

  ○ **B.** 8,533MB/s

  ○ **C.** 5,333MB/s

  ○ **D.** 800MHz

4. Which of these would you find internal to the CPU?

  ○ **A.** DRAM

  ○ **B.** DIMM

  ○ **C.** SDRAM

  ○ **D.** SRAM

5. What does SDRAM synchronize to?

  ○ **A.** FSB

  ○ **B.** CPU

  ○ **C.** System bus

  ○ **D.** PCI bus

6. Which chip designates where RAM will be stored?

  ○ **A.** ICH

  ○ **B.** MCH

  ○ **C.** CPU

  ○ **D.** FSB

7. How many pins are on a DDR2 memory module?

  ○ **A.** 168

  ○ **B.** 184

  ○ **C.** 240

  ○ **D.** 200

Cram Quiz Answers

1. **D**. Dual-channel memory configurations have two RAM slots of a particular color, each one of which is placed in a different channel; these are collectively known as DIMM 0. DIMM 1 comprises the other two slots, which are a different color, and again, each of them are placed in a separate channel.

2. **C**. Latency is the delay between the memory module and the memory controller, usually rated as CL and a number.

3. **A**. DDR2-800 can transfer 6,400MB/s; 800MHz is the doubled clock rate or speed. It has an original clock speed of 400MHz but doubles that output, so it is often referred to as 800MHz.

4. **D**. One function of SRAM is to act as CPU cache. L1 cache would be internal to the CPU or in the core. L2 would be on-die.

5. **C**. SDRAM technologies synchronize to the base clock of the motherboard (also known as the system bus speed) enabling for efficient transfer of data.

6. **B**. The Memory Controller Hub (MCH) is in charge of storing and retrieving data to and from RAM. Even though some systems use a memory controller that is part of the CPU, it is not the CPU that is in charge of this. The CPU knows what bytes it wants but not the location of those bytes.

7. **C**. DDR2 is a 240-pin architecture. 168-pin is the original SDRAM, 184-pin is the first version of DDR (DDR1), and 200-pin architectures can be found in laptops; they are known as SODIMMs.

Installing and Troubleshooting DRAM

Installing DRAM

Installing DRAM is fun and easy. Simply stated, it can be broken down into this: Orient the RAM properly, insert the RAM into the slot, and press down with both thumbs until the ears lock. Then, test. Easy! But let's take it a little further. Remember that some people refer to memory modules as DIMMs, DRAM, RAM sticks, or just plain RAM, and you could get any of these terms on the exam as well. The following describes the steps involved when installing RAM:

1. **Select the correct memory module:** The memory module must be compatible with the motherboard. Once again, this means it must be of the right size and pin configuration, the right type or standard, the correct speed, the correct size, and within voltage parameters. Don't forget to use the memory manufacturer's website. They have search engines that enable you to input the motherboard you have, by make and model, and then the search displays all the different RAM configurations that are compatible with the motherboard. If you have a proprietary computer such as an HP or Dell, the website asks for the make and model of the computer instead of the motherboard. How much simpler could it be? Be wary of websites that don't have searchable databases like these.

   For our computer I used Kingston RAM. I went to its website, plugged in the make (Intel) and the model (DP35DP) of the motherboard, and it came up with a whole slew of different DDR2 RAM stick configurations; from 256MB configs all the way up to 4GB. As you might have guessed, I chose the 4GB configuration, which is actually a kit of two 2GB sticks, running at 800MHz, which work in a dual-channel configuration, as we display in a minute. To be sure, I checked Intel's website to verify how much RAM I could use per slot and what speeds would run. The documentation shows that I could use up to 8GB maximum of DDR2 RAM, a maximum of 2GB per slot, at a top speed of 800MHz. Well, for now I don't need more than 4GB, but I can always add an identical kit later if I want; otherwise, everything sounds compatible. When the RAM is added, the BIOS should find it automatically; however, it is wise to check if any BIOS upgrades are available on the motherboard's website that deal with the latest types of RAM.

When the RAM arrives, we are ready to install. Power down the PC, disconnect the power cable (or turn off the kill switch), open the PC, and get ready!

2. **Employ ESD prevention methods:** Use an antistatic strap and mat. Before touching any components, place both hands on an unpainted portion of the case chassis. For more information on ESD preventative measures, see Chapter 16, "Safety and Professionalism." Never touch any of the pins or chips on the memory module, instead grab the module from the side edges. Remove the memory modules (could be one or more) from the package and place them on an antistatic bag.

3. **Ready the motherboard:** Some technicians prefer to install the RAM into the motherboard and then install the motherboard into the case; this can also depend on whether you are building a new computer or upgrading one. If you do choose to install the RAM to the motherboard separately, place the motherboard on the antistatic mat. (The mat should be on a hard, flat surface.) If you install the RAM directly into an already installed motherboard, clear away any cables or other equipment that might get in the way or could possibly damage the RAM during installation.

   You see a plastic tab (ear) on each side of the RAM slot in the motherboard; they are usually white. Swing them out from the slot carefully so that they end up at an angle from the slot; this enables room for the memory module to be inserted.

4. **Install the RAM:** Be careful with the RAM and the RAM slot! They are delicate! Always touch the case chassis before picking up the RAM. Hold it by the edges and do not touch any pins, or other circuitry on the memory module. If you need to put it down, put it down on an antistatic mat.

   Take a look at the slot, there should be a break in the slot somewhere near the middle (but not the exact middle); this is where the notch in the memory module will go. Gently place the memory module in the slot, pins down. If the notch does not line up with the break in the slot, you might need to turn the module around. When it appears that the RAM is oriented correctly, press down with both thumbs on the top of the memory module. Keep your thumbs as close to the edge as you can so that you can distribute even pressure to the memory module. Press down with both thumbs at the same time until the "ears" on the edge of the RAM slot close and lock on to the memory module. You might hear a click or two when it is done. You might also have to push both of the ears toward the RAM to completely lock them into place. Take a look at the memory module from the side, or compare them to other ears in unused slots; the plastic ears should be standing straight up now. You may need a bit of force to fully insert the RAM, but don't go overboard! If the motherboard is bending excessively, you are using too much force. If this is the case, make sure that the RAM is oriented correctly; the notches should match up, and the RAM should be straight within the slot. Figure 4.5 shows a bank of DDR2 memory modules installed into the blue DIMM 0 slots.

Channel A, DIMM 0 (Blue)

Locking Tabs or "Ears"

Channel B, DIMM 0 (Blue)

FIGURE 4.5   Installed Bank of DDR2 Memory Modules

Install the entire motherboard assembly into the case if that were your method of choice.

5. **Test the installation:** With the case still open, boot the computer and make sure that the BIOS POST recognizes the new RAM as the right type and speed. Halt the POST, if necessary to read the details, and when done, enter the BIOS. Next, view the details of the RAM within the BIOS. The amount is often on the main page, but you might need to look deeper for the exact configuration, depending on the motherboard. Next, access the operating system (after it is installed) and make sure it boots correctly. Complete several full cycles and warm boots. Also, at some point, you should view the RAM with CPU-Z or in Windows to verify that the operating system is seeing the correct capacity of RAM. You can do this in several places within Windows; here are a couple:

   ▶ **System Properties:** Click Start; then right-click Computer (My Computer in Windows XP) and select Properties. The total RAM should be listed within this window.

▶ **Task Manager:** We mentioned before that you can view the Task Manager by right-clicking the taskbar and selecting Task Manager. There are several other ways to open this; I like this one: Press Windows+R to bring up the Run prompt and type **taskmgr**. When it is open, go to the Performance tab and view the Physical Memory box. It should show the total physical memory. Keep in mind that 1024MB actually means 1GB. Figure 4.6 shows another computer I have running Windows Vista displaying 1GB of RAM.

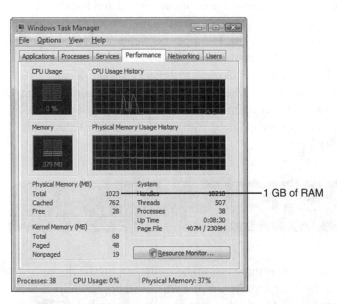

FIGURE 4.6   Windows Vista Task Manager displaying 1GB of RAM

Consider testing the RAM by seeing if you can open several applications at once without any issues or delays.

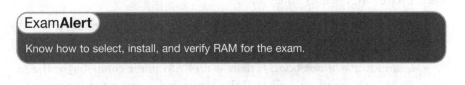

ExamAlert

Know how to select, install, and verify RAM for the exam.

Finally, if everything looks okay, close up the case, and if all went well, congratulate yourself on another job well done!

Troubleshooting DRAM

It's not common, but RAM memory modules can cause intermittent issues, or they can fail altogether. Always make sure that the RAM is fully seated within the RAM slot and that the plastic ears are locking the RAM into place. Keep in mind that an unstable system can be caused by several components including RAM. Remember to check the "big four": video card, CPU, RAM, and motherboard.

A lot of the issues you see are because a user has purchased and installed a memory stick that is not compatible, or is semicompatible, with the motherboard: wrong speed, incorrect capacity, improper configuration, and so on. Be ready for this; check the RAM compatibility against the motherboard, even if the user swears he checked it already. A good technician has her documentation available and has access to the Internet, This can help to ensure that the correct RAM has been installed originally and that it is configured properly. Some RAM manufacturers (www.kingston.com, www.crucial.com) have tools to check compatibility issues.

> **Exam**Alert
>
> Verify compatibility of RAM when troubleshooting!

Perhaps there was some kind of surge inside the computer; maybe the computer is not protected by a surge protector or UPS. Another possibility is that the RAM was damaged by ESD, and this damage manifests itself as intermittent problems. There are expensive hardware-based RAM testers that can tell you if the RAM is electrically sound and if it can process data correctly. If your company owns one, or if you can get your hands on one for a short time, you might narrow the problem down further. However, from personal experience, I have rarely needed to use these.

Here are some possible symptoms of a RAM issue and corresponding troubleshooting techniques:

- ▶ **Computer will not boot:** If there is no RAM in the computer, or the RAM is damaged, or not installed securely, it can prevent the computer from doing anything at all, aside from draining electricity from your AC outlet. For example, the power supply fan turns, but nothing else—no beeps and no displays. Add RAM if none exists. (Sounds silly but I've seen it!) If you suspect faulty RAM, or a faulty RAM slot, you can try taking the RAM out, cleaning the RAM and RAM slot if necessary (with compressed air or with Stabilant 22a or like cleaner), and putting the RAM back in, being sure to seat the memory module properly. Next, if the computer has two memory modules, try booting it with just one (if the motherboard allows it), or try moving memory modules to different slots. As mentioned in previous chapters, a POST card tester can be helpful in these situations as well. If necessary, replace the memory module with an identical one (if you have an extra one handy), or at worst, purchase a new one if you have identified the memory module as the source of the problem.

▸ **BIOS indicates a memory error:** The BIOS can indicate a memory error through a message on the screen or by beeping. If it beeps, you need to reference your motherboard documentation for the specific beep codes. Sometimes a BIOS setting can be incorrect. For example, maybe the RAM's latency setting should be configured as CL5 instead of CL6, or some other setting needs to be modified. If the computer has a saved version of the BIOS settings, you can try reverting to them, or you can try loading the BIOS defaults; I can't tell you how many times this has worked for me! Sometimes the BIOS indicates the wrong amount of RAM. If this is the case, check the RAM as explained in the first bullet. Finally, a BIOS update can be the cure; perhaps the BIOS just doesn't have the programming necessary to identify the latest type of RAM that was installed.

▸ **Memory errors occur:** Several types of memory errors are initiated by the operating system:

  ▸ **Stop error, aka BSOD or Blue Screen of Death.** This is a critical system error that causes the operating system to shut down. Most of the time, these are due to device driver errors (poor code), but they can be associated with a physical fault in memory. One example of this would be an nonmaskable interrupt (NMI). An NMI can interrupt the processor to gain its attention regarding nonrecoverable hardware errors, resulting in a BSOD. The BSOD usually dumps the contents of memory to a file (for later analysis) and restarts the computer. If you don't encounter another BSOD, it's probably not much to worry about. But if the BSOD happens repeatedly, you want to write down the information you see on the screen and cross-reference it to the Microsoft Knowledge Base (MSKB) at http://support.microsoft.com. Again, if you suspect faulty RAM, try the troubleshooting methods in the first bullet "Computer will not boot."

▶ **Page faults (hard faults), Out of memory or low on virtual memory errors.** These are usually issues with the operating system or application that was running. However, you see less and less of these with each new Windows version. If a particular application keeps failing, or if you get a particular message listing a specific memory location over and over again, it can indicate a physical problem with RAM. Be sure to document error messages and any error codes or memory locations that display on the screen.

▶ **General protection fault (GPF).** This can cause a program to fail, and in older versions of Windows, it would cause the entire OS to shut down and display a black screen. Today, these errors are uncommon and are usually related to the OS, running applications, and CPU. It is also possible that memory errors can cause a GPF, for example writing to a read-only portion of memory, or a conflict in a particular part of memory, but again, these are rare.

We troubleshoot these BSODs, page faults, and other Windows issues in Chapter 10, "Troubleshooting Windows."

Chances are you won't need them often, but a few memory testing programs are available online: GoldMemory (http://www.goldmemory.cz/), MemTest86 (http://www.memtest86.com/), PC-Diagnosys (http://www.windsortech.com/pcdiags.html), and the Windows Memory Diagnostic (http://oca.microsoft.com/en/windiag.asp) are a few examples. These can help diagnose whether a memory module needs to be replaced. But in general, trust in your senses, look at and listen to the computer to help diagnose any RAM issues that might occur.

Cram Quiz

Answer these questions. The answers follow the last question. If you cannot answer these questions correctly, consider reading this section again until you can.

1. Where can you view how much RAM you have in the computer? (Select all that apply.)

   ○ **A.** Task Manager

   ○ **B.** My Computer

   ○ **C.** System Properties

   ○ **D.** BIOS

2. How should you hold RAM when installing it?

  ○ **A.** By the edges

  ○ **B.** By the front and back

  ○ **C.** With tweezers

  ○ **D.** With an Integrated Circuit (IC) puller

3. You suspect a problem with a memory module, what should you do first?

  ○ **A.** Replace the module with a new one.

  ○ **B.** Install more RAM.

  ○ **C.** Clean the RAM slot.

  ○ **D.** Test the RAM with MemTest86.

4. If a BSOD occurs, what should you do?

  ○ **A.** Replace all the RAM.

  ○ **B.** Re-install the operating system.

  ○ **C.** Check the RAM settings in the BIOS.

  ○ **D.** Wait for it to happen again.

Cram Quiz Answers

1. A, C, and **D**. The BIOS displays what type of RAM you have and the amount. Windows has several locations in which you can discern how much RAM there is, including the Task Manager, System Properties, and System Information.

2. A. Hold RAM by the edges to avoid contact with the pins, chips, and circuitry

3. C. Clean the RAM slot and memory module. Consider using compressed air or the proper spray (like Stabilant 22a).

4. D. A singular BSOD doesn't necessarily mean that the RAM or any other components have gone bad. Often, a single BSOD occurs, but you never see it again. You want to see two or more of the same error before starting into a lengthy troubleshooting session!

Additional Reading and Resources

Additional A+ resources: http://www.davidlprowse.com/aplus

GoldMemory: http://www.goldmemory.cz/

Memory Advisor Tool: http://www.crucial.com/

MemTest86: http://www.memtest86.com/

Microsoft Help and Support : http://support.microsoft.com

Mueller, Scott. *Upgrading and Repairing PCs*. Que.

Online memory search and memory tools: http://www.kingston.com

PC-Diagnosys: http://www.windsortech.com/pcdiags.html

CHAPTER 5

Power

This chapter covers the following A+ exam topics:

▶ Understanding and Testing Power

▶ Power Devices

▶ Power Supplies

You can find a master list of A+ exam topics in the "Introduction."

This chapter covers CompTIA A+ 220-701 objectives 1.3 and 2.5 and CompTIA A+ 220-702 objectives 1.1, 1.2, and 1.4.

Everything relies on power. Clean, well-planned power is imperative in a computer system. It's so important, that I almost made this the first chapter of the book. I can't tell you how many power-related issues I have troubleshot in the past. Many of the issues that you see concerning power are due to lack of protection and improper planning, and as such you will see several questions (if not more) on the A+ exams regarding this subject.

Imagine a scenario in which you work for a technical services division of a company. You are required to install a new, more powerful power supply in a computer that contains many devices and requires a lot of electricity. You need to install the computer in a new area of the company's building. This requires you to plug the computer into an AC receptacle that has never been used or tested.

What kind of power supply should you select? How can you verify that the AC outlet is properly wired? And how can you protect the computer? This chapter answers all those questions and furnishes you with the knowledge you need to install, test, and troubleshoot power supplies and test power that comes from the wall outlet.

Understanding and Testing Power

The power for your computer is derived from electricity, which is basically the flow of electric charge. Electricity is defined and measured in several ways, most commonly:

▶ *Voltage*, a representation of potential energy; sometimes it's more simply referred to as pressure; its unit of measurement is volts (V).

▶ *Wattage* or electric power, the rate of electric energy in a circuit, measured in watts (W).

▶ *Amperage* or electric current, the movement of electric charge, measured in amperes or amps (A).

▶ *Impedance*, the amount of resistance to electricity, measured in ohms (Ω).

Each of these is covered in this chapter, but by far the most common of these that you will be testing is voltage. Here are two examples of voltages you are probably familiar with:

▶ 120 Volts AC (the voltage associated with many U.S. homes)

▶ 5 Volts DC (the voltage associated with some of the internal power connections in your PC)

The difference in these two examples (aside from the amount of volts) is that a house's outlets use alternating current (AC), in which the flow of electrons alternate, and your computer, again internally, uses direct current (DC), in which the flow of electrons is one way.

ExamAlert

In AC, electrons flow alternates.

In DC, electrons flow one way.

Back to our scenario; because you can't control who wired the AC outlet that you will be connecting the computer to, or how clean the power is that comes from your municipality, you should test the outlet prior to plugging the computer in. Two good tools to use when testing are a receptacle tester and a multimeter.

Testing an AC Outlet with a Receptacle Tester

Type B AC outlets are the most common, and might also be referred to as wall sockets, electric receptacles, or power points. It is type B that you need to be concerned with for the A+ exam. If any of the hot, neutral, or ground wires are connected improperly, the computer connected to the outlet is a sitting duck, just waiting for irreparable damage. To ensure that the AC outlet is wired properly, you can use a receptacle tester, like the one shown in Figure 5.1. These are inexpensive and are available at most home improvement stores and electrical supply shops. When you plug in the receptacle tester, it tells you if the receptacle is wired properly or indicates which wires are incorrect.

FIGURE 5.1   A common receptacle tester and labeled receptacle

In Figure 5.1 the test has passed. With this particular tester, two yellow lights tell you that the outlet is wired correctly. Any other combination of lights tells you that there is a wiring error. The different combinations are usually labeled on the tester itself; for example, an open ground error is displayed by one single, yellow light on this tester. Important: If you receive any erroneous readings or if there are no lights at all, *do not use the outlet* and contact your supervisor and/or building management so that they can bring in a licensed electrician to fix the problem.

> **ExamAlert**
>
> If you find an AC outlet is improperly wired, contact your supervisor and/or building management to resolve the problem.

Testing an AC Outlet with a Multimeter

Every PC technician should own a multimeter, and we use one throughout this chapter. A multimeter is a hand-held device that, among other things, can be used to measure amps and impedance, and to test voltage inside a computer and from AC outlets. It has two leads, a black and a red. Whenever using the multimeter, try to hold both of the multimeter leads with one hand, and hold them by the plastic handles; don't touch the metal ends. It will be like holding chopsticks but is a safer method, reducing the severity of electric shock in the uncommon chance that one occurs. To test an AC outlet with a multimeter, run through the following steps:

1. Place the multimeter's black lead in the outlet's ground. (The parts of the outlet are labeled in Figure 5.1.)

2. Place the red lead in the hot opening.

3. Turn on the multimeter to test for volts AC (sometimes labeled as VAC). Hold the leads steady and check for readings. Optimally, the reading will hover around 115 volts or 120 volts depending on where you are in the United States. Watch the readings for a minute or so. Remember the reading or range of readings that display. A common reading is shown in Figure 5.2.

4. Turn off the multimeter.

5. Remove the red lead.

6. Remove the black lead.

Red lead to hot

Black lead
to ground

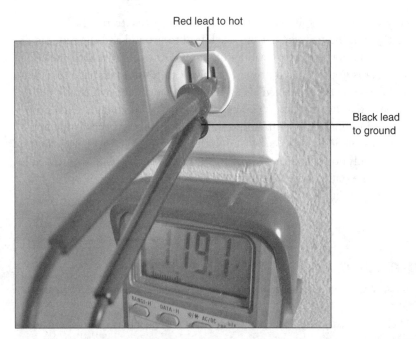

FIGURE 5.2   A receptacle tested with a multimeter

What was your reading? A steady reading closest to 120 volts is desirable. It might be less in some areas, but the key is that it's steady at one voltage; this is also known as *clean power*. If the reading fluctuates a lot, say between 113 volts and 121 volts, for example, you have one of the varieties of *dirty power*. This could be because too many devices use the same circuit or because power coming from the electrical panel or from the municipal grid fluctuates, maybe because the panel or the entire grid is under/overloaded. A quick call to your company's electrician can result in an answer and possibly a long-term fix. However, we are concerned with an immediate solution, which in this case will be to install an uninterruptible power supply (UPS) or other line-conditioning device between the computer and the AC outlet. This can regulate the output of AC to the computer.

ExamAlert

To keep an AC outlet's voltage steady, use a UPS or line conditioner.

You can also test the neutral and ground wires in this manner. You should be especially concerned with whether the ground wire is connected properly.

Previously we showed how to test this with the receptacle tester, but to test this with the multimeter, connect the black lead to ground and the red lead to neutral. This should result in a reading of 0 volts. Any other reading means that the outlet is not grounded properly, which can result in damage to a computer that connects to it. You can also use a voltage detector, which is a pen-shaped device that beeps when it comes into contact with voltage. On a properly grounded outlet, the only part that should give audible beeps is the hot. Everything else including the screw and outlet plate should not register any sounds. If sounds do register by simply touching the outlet plate with the voltage detector, the outlet is not grounded properly. If this is the case, or if you got any other reading besides 0 volts on the multimeter, contact an electrician right away.

Cram Quiz

Cram QuizAnswer these questions. The answers follow the last question. If you cannot answer these questions correctly, consider reading this section again until you can.

1. What tool would you use to test the amount of voltage that is coming from an AC outlet?

   ○ **A.** Multimeter

   ○ **B.** Voltage detector

   ○ **C.** Receptacle tester

   ○ **D.** Impedance tester

2. Which of the following is a representation of potential energy?

   ○ **A.** Wattage

   ○ **B.** Voltage

   ○ **C.** Impedance

   ○ **D.** Amperage

3. Which wire when tested should display zero volts on a multimeter?

   ○ **A.** Neutral

   ○ **B.** Hot

   ○ **C.** Ground

   ○ **D.** Red

Cram Quiz Answers

1. **A.** The multimeter is the only testing tool that can display voltage numerically.

2. **B.** Voltage is a representation of potential energy; an analogy for voltage would be water pressure in a pipe.

3. **C.** When testing the ground wire with a multimeter, it should display a reading of zero volts.

Power Devices

Utilizing proper power devices is part of a good preventative maintenance plan and helps to protect a computer. You need to protect against several things:

▶ Surges

▶ Spikes

▶ Sags

▶ Brownouts

▶ Blackouts

A *surge* in electrical power means that there is an unexpected increase in the amount of voltage provided. This can be a small increase or a larger increase known as a spike. A *spike* is a short transient in voltage that can be due to a short circuit, tripped circuit breaker, power outage, or lightning strike.

A *sag* is an unexpected decrease in the amount of voltage provided. Typically, sags are limited in time and in the decrease in voltage. However, when voltage reduces further, a brownout could ensue. During a *brownout* the voltage drops to such an extent that it typically causes the lights to dim and causes computers to shut off.

A *blackout* is when a total loss of power for a prolonged period occurs. Another problem associated with blackouts is the spike that can occur when power is restored. In the New York area, it is common to have an increased amount of tech support calls during July; this is attributed to lightning storms! Quite often this is due to improper protection.

Some devices have specific purposes, and others can protect against more than one of these electrical issues. Let's describe a few of these devices.

Power Strips

A *power strip* is a group of sockets, usually in-line, with a flexible cable that plugs into an AC outlet. It enables for multiple devices to share a single receptacle in that outlet. Due to this, a maximum wattage rating can be applied to the device, for example, 3,000 watts is a decent amount. Interesting, a computer might have a 300-watt power supply, but on the average, it might use only 100 watts of that power while running. A monitor might use between 35 watts and 100 watts depending on the type of monitor. You can check the wattage rating on the back or side of most devices. Add the total for all devices connected to the power strip, and remember not to exceed the maximum rating. This concept applies to other devices in this section including surge protectors and UPSs.

Power strips might not have surge protection functionality. If they don't have surge protection capabilities, they cannot protect from any of the electrical issues (surges and spikes) listed in the previous section.

A power strip has a master on/off switch and usually has a 15-amp circuit breaker to prevent overloading. If an overload occurs, the circuit breaker trips, cutting power, and the device can usually be reset by pressing a black button normally located somewhere near the power button. Overloads occur because the power strip tries to pull too much current (amps) from the wall outlet, or when too much current is supplied *to* the power strip. As a rule of thumb, no more than four or five computers (and monitors) should use the same power strip and, therefore, the same circuit. This calls into question whether any other AC outlets connect to the same circuit. To find this out, a qualified electrician can use a circuit testing tool and locate all the outlets on the circuit in question, or this information might be included in your building's electrical diagram. By the way, you can also calculate the amount of computers and monitors that can connect to a circuit by their amperage rating. For example, at AC (wall-outlet level) a typical computer would draw 2 to 3 amps and perhaps another 2 amps for the monitor maximum. (Keep in mind that these are estimates.) So on a standard 15-amp circuit, it would be wise to have no more than three computers and three monitors running simultaneously.

Surge Protectors

A *surge protector* or surge suppressor is a power strip that also incorporates a metal-oxide varsistor (MOV) to protect against surges and spikes. Most power strips that you find in an office supply store or home improvement store have surge protection capability. The word *varsistor* is a blend of the two terms *variable resistor*.

> **ExamAlert**
>
> To protect against surges and spikes, use a surge protector!

Surge protectors are usually rated in joules, which are a way to measure energy, and in essence, the more joules the better. For computer systems, 1,000 joules or more is recommended. This joule rating gives you a sense of how long the device can protect against surges and spikes. Surges happen more often than you might think, and every time a surge happens, part of the varsistor is burned out. The higher the joule rating, the longer the varsistor (and therefore the device) should last. Most of today's surge protectors have an indicator light that informs you if the varsistor has failed.

Because surges can occur over telephone lines, RG-6 cable lines, and network lines, it is common to see input and output ports for any or all these on a decent surge protector. Higher-quality surge protectors have multiple MOVs not only for the different connections such as AC and phone, but also have multiple MOVs for the individual wires in an AC connection.

Uninterruptible Power Supplies

An *uninterruptible power supply (UPS)* takes the functionality of a surge suppressor and combines that with a battery backup. So now, our computer is protected not only from surges and spikes, but also from sags, brownouts, and blackouts.

> **ExamAlert**
>
> Use a UPS to protect your computer from power outages!

But the battery backup can't last indefinitely! It is considered emergency power and typically keeps your computer system running for 5 to 30 minutes depending on the model you purchase. Figure 5.3 shows an example of a typical inexpensive UPS. Notice that some of the outlets on the device are marked for battery backup *and* surge protection, whereas others are for surge protection only.

Most UPS devices also act as line conditioners, protecting from over and under-voltage; they condition (or regulate) the voltage sent to the computer. The device shown, and most UPS devices today, has a USB connection so that your computer can communicate with the UPS. When there is a power outage, the UPS sends a signal to the computer telling it to shut down, suspend, or stand-by before the battery discharges completely. Most UPSs come with software that you can install that enables you to configure the computer with these options.

Battery backup and surge protection

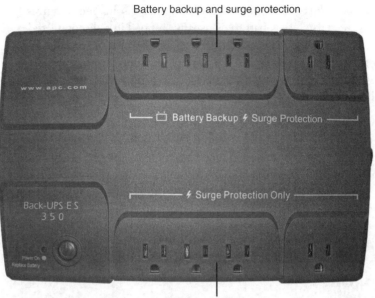

Surge protection only

FIGURE 5.3   A common UPS

UPS devices' output power capacity is rated in volt-amps (VA) and watts. Although you might have heard that volt-amps and watts are essentially the same, this is one of those times that they are somewhat different. The volt-amp rating is slightly higher due to the difference between apparent power (when in battery backup mode) and real power (when pulling regular power from the AC outlet). For example, the device in Figure 5.3 has a volt-amp rating of 350 VA but a wattage rating of 200 watts. Generally, this is enough for a computer, monitor, and a few other devices, but a second computer might be pushing it given the wattage rating. The more devices that connect to the UPS, the less time the battery can last if a power outage occurs; if too many devices are connected, there may be inconsistencies when the battery needs to take over. Thus many UPS manufacturers limit the amount of battery backup-protected receptacles. Connecting a laser printer to the UPS is *not* recommended due to the high current draw of the laser printer; and *never* connect a surge protector or power strip to one of the receptacles in the UPS, to protect the UPS from being overloaded.

ExamAlert

Do *not* connect laser printers to UPS devices.

The UPS normally has a lead-acid battery that, once discharged, requires 10 to 20 hours to recharge. This battery is usually shipped in a disconnected state. Before charging the device for use, you must first make sure that the battery leads connect to the UPS. If the battery ever needs to be replaced, a red light will usually appear accompanied by a beeping sound. Beeping can also occur if power is no longer supplied to the UPS by the AC outlet.

There are varying levels of UPS devices, which incorporate different technologies. For example, the cheaper standby UPS (known as an SPS) might have a slight delay when switching from AC to battery power, possibly causing errors in the computer operating system. Although it isn't important to know these different technologies for the exam, you should realize that some care should be taken when planning the type of UPS to be used. When data is crucial, you had better plan for a quality UPS!

Cram Quiz

Answer these questions. The answers follow the last question. If you cannot answer these questions correctly, consider reading this section again until you can.

1. Which device should you use to protect against power outages?

   ○ **A.** Multimeter

   ○ **B.** UPS

   ○ **C.** Fedex

   ○ **D.** Surge protector

2. You want a *cost-effective* solution to the common surges that can affect your computer. Which device would be the best solution?

   ○ **A.** UPS

   ○ **B.** Surge protector

   ○ **C.** Power strip

   ○ **D.** Line conditioner

3. Which of these is an unexpected increase in voltage?

   ○ **A.** Sag

   ○ **B.** Blackout

   ○ **C.** Spike

   ○ **D.** Whiteout

Cram Quiz Answers

1. **B**. The UPS is the only item listed that protects the computer from power outages like blackouts and brownouts.

2. **B**. A surge protector is the right solution at the right price. A UPS is a possible solution but costs more than a surge protector. A line conditioner also would be a viable solution but, again, is overkill. And a power strip doesn't necessarily have surge protection functionality.

3. **C**. A spike (or a surge) is an unexpected increase in voltage. A sag is a decrease in voltage, a blackout is a power outage, and a whiteout is a blizzard, which could result in a blackout!

Power Supplies

Okay, now that we've tested our AC outlet and put some protective power devices into play, let's go ahead and talk power supplies. The power supply is in charge of converting the alternating current (AC) drawn from the wall outlet into direct current (DC) to be used internally by the computer. It feeds the motherboard, hard drives, optical drives, and any other devices inside of the computer. Talk about a single point of failure! That is why many higher-end workstations and servers have redundant power supplies.

Planning Which Power Supply to Use

It is important to use a reliable brand of power supply that is UL listed (certified). There are a few other things to take into account when planning which power supply to use in your computer:

▶ Type of power supply and compatibility

▶ Wattage and capacity requirements

▶ Amount and type of connectors

Now, in our scenario we said that we need a power supply that can support many devices in our workstation; one that will output a lot of power. In this scenario the computer has two IDE hard drives, a CD-Burner, a DVD-ROM, one SATA drive, and a PCIe video card. And let's just say that we use an ATX 12V 2.0 motherboard. So we need to look for a high–capacity, compatible ATX power supply with a decent amount of connectors for our devices. Let's discuss planning now.

Types of Power Supplies and Compatibility

The most common form factor today is Advanced Technology Extended (ATX). Depending on the type of ATX, the main power connector to the motherboard will have 20 pins or 24 pins. Table 5.1 shows a few different form factors and their characteristics. The key is compatibility. In our scenario we have a previously built computer, which means that the case and motherboard are already compatible. If this computer was *proprietary*, we could go to the computer manufacturer's website to find out the exact form factor, and possibly a replacement power supply for that model computer. Some third-party power supply manufacturers also offer replacement power supplies for proprietary systems. However, if this computer was custom built, we would need to find out the form factor used by the motherboard and/or case, and should open the computer and take a look at all the necessary power connections. Then we need to find a compatible power supply according to those specifications from a third-party power supply manufacturer. Table 5.1 displays the form factors you need to know for the exam.

TABLE 5.1 **Common Power Supply Form Factors**

Form Factor	Main Power Connector	Other Characteristic
ATX	P1 20-pin connector	An older standard but you will still support it!
ATX 12V 1.0 - 1.3	P1 20-pin connector & P4 4 pin 12V connector	Supplemental 6-pin AUX connector provides additional 3.3V and 5V supplies to the motherboard.
ATX 12V 2.0	P1 24-pin connector (backward compatible)	▶ 6-pin AUX was removed. ▶ SATA power cable is required.

Figure 5.4 gives examples of a P1 20-pin (the white connector) and P1 24-pin connector (the black connector). Toward the left of the black connector you notice it has an additional four pins that can be separated from the main group of 20 pins. Both have locking tabs to keep the P1 connector fastened to the motherboard. (In the figure this is shown only on the 20-pin connector.)

FIGURE 5.4   24-pin and 20-pin power connectors

> **ExamAlert**
>
> Original ATX power supplies connect to the motherboard with a 20-pin connector. Newer ATX 12V 2.0 power supplies connect with a 24-pin connector.

There are many other types of form factors such as microATX, BTX, and NLX (covered in Chapter 2, "Motherboards") and older form factors such as AT; however, the form factors listed in Table 5.1 are the important ones to know regarding power supplies for the A+ exam. For any other form factors, just remember that the power supply, case, and motherboard all need to be compatible.

Another important piece to consider is the type of case that is used. Larger cases require longer power cables to reach the devices. You can find the measurements for the cables on the power supply manufacturer's website. There are several different types of cases that you need to be familiar with:

▸ **Desktop:** Lies horizontally, usually has one 5¼-inch drive bay.

▸ **Mini-tower:** Stands vertically, usually has two or three drive bays.

▸ **Mid-tower:** Usually has three or four bays.

▸ **Full tower:** Usually has six bays.

▸ **Slim line:** Compaq and the Playstation III and other third-party case manufacturers use this case design.

Many power supply manufacturers also make computer cases and often sell them as a package or to be purchased separately.

Wattage and Capacity Requirements

Power supplies are usually rated in watts. They are rated at a maximum amount that they can draw from the wall outlet and pass on to the computer's devices. Remember that the computer will not always use all that power the way in which a light bulb does. And the amount depends on how many devices work and how much number crunching your processor does! In addition, when computers sleep or suspend, they use less electricity. What you need to be concerned with is the maximum amount of power all the devices need collectively. Most power-supply manufacturers today offer models that range from 300 watts all the way up to 1,000 watts. Although 300 watts is a decent amount of power for many computers, it might not suffice in our scenario. Devices use a certain amount of power defined in amps and/or watts. By adding all of the devices power consumption together, we can get a clearer picture of how powerful a power supply we need. Consult the manufacturer's web page of the device for exact requirements. We said that in our scenario the computer has two IDE hard drives, a CD-Burner, a DVD-ROM, a floppy drive, and one SATA drive and a PCIe video card. It also has a quad core processor and 2GB of RAM (in two sticks).

After doing the math, it appears that the computer in our scenario needs about 400 watts or so to run smoothly. The power supply we purchase should be rated slightly higher just in case, so in this scenario we would obtain a 450-watt or 500-watt power supply. Most power supplies are rated for 15 amps, so it is important to connect the computer to a 15-amp circuit or higher.

Amount and Type of Power Connectors

It is important to know how many of each type of power connector you need when planning which power supply to use. In our scenario we need four IDE power connectors (for the two hard drives, CD-Burner, and DVD-ROM), one floppy power connector, and one SATA power connector. You need to be familiar with each of these types of power connectors for the A+ exams. Be prepared to identify them by name and by sight. Table 5.2 defines the usage and voltages for the most common power connectors: Molex, mini, SATA, and PCIe, which are displayed in Figures 5.5 through 5.8.

TABLE 5.2   **Power Connectors**

Power Connector	Usage	Pins and Voltages
Molex	IDE hard drives, optical drives, and other devices	Red (5V), black (G), black (G), yellow (12V)
Mini	Floppy drives	Red (5V), black (G), black (G), yellow (12V)
SATA	Serial ATA hard drives	15-pin, 3.3V, 5V, and 12V
PCIe	PCI Express cards	6-pin

FIGURE 5.5   Molex power connector

FIGURE 5.6   Mini power connector

FIGURE 5.7   SATA 15-pin power connector

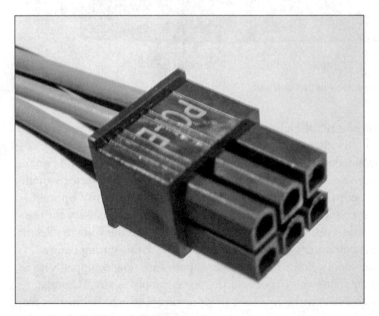

FIGURE 5.8   PCIe 6-pin power connector

Installing the Power Supply

When the power supply arrives, we can install it. But first, let's take a look at the back of the power supply to identify the components we see, as shown in Figure 5.9.

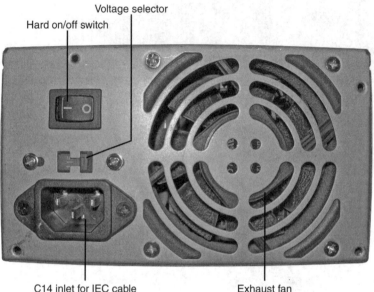

FIGURE 5.9   **Rear view of power supply**

On the top-left portion of Figure 5.9, we see a hard on/off switch sometimes referred to as a kill switch. This is a nice feature when troubleshooting PCs. Instead of disconnecting the power cable, we can shut off this switch. It works nicely in emergencies as well. Below that we see a red voltage selector switch. This should be set to 115V in the United States. It also has a 230V option to be used in other countries. (An additional adapter might be necessary for the different wall outlets you might encounter.) Never change the voltage selector switch while the computer is running. Be sure to check this setting before using the power supply. Some newer power supplies are now equipped with a universal input enabling you to connect the power supply to any AC outlet between 100V to 240V, without having to set a voltage switch. Below that we see the power cable inlet; this is known as a C14 inlet and is where we attach our power cord to the power supply. These inlets and cables that connect to them are defined by the IEC 60320 specification (previously the IEC 320 spec), and because of this many techs refer to the power cord as an IEC cable (which by the way stands for International Electrotechnical Commission).

This cord actually has a standard three-prong connector suitable for an AC outlet on one end and a C13 line socket on the other to connect to the power supply. To the right we see the power supply fan that is of great importance when troubleshooting power supplies.

If there is a power supply connected to the computer, turn off the computer and unplug the power supply. ATX motherboards are always receiving 5 volts even when they are off, if the computer is plugged in. Be sure that you are employing antistatic methods. Remove the old power supply and prepare to install the new one.

You might want to test the power supply before installing it. This can be done by connecting a power supply tester (described in the next section), plugging in the power supply to the AC outlet, and turning on the hard on/off switch. Or you can test the power supply after it is installed by simply turning the computer on.

The power supply is placed inside the case and mounted with four standard screws that are screwed in from the back of the case. In some instances, a plastic housing inside the case might need to be removed. In addition, the power supply might not fit without the removal of other devices, such as the processor, and such, but in most cases (pun intended) you should install the power supply without too much trouble. Next, connect the P1 connector to the motherboard and attach the Molex, mini, SATA, and PCIe as necessary to their corresponding devices. Note that the P1 connector (20-pin or 24-pin main connector) can be plugged in only in one way and that there is a locking tab. Also, most other connectors are molded in such a way as to make it difficult to connect them backward. If you need a lot of strength to plug in the connector, check and make sure that it is oriented correctly. Don't force the connection. Afterward, remove any antistatic protection, and finally, plug the power supply into the AC outlet, turn on the hard on/off switch (if the power supply has one), and turn on the computer. Check to see if the fan in the power supply is working and if the computer boots correctly.

Troubleshooting Power Supply Issues

Installation of the power supply was easy, and there aren't usually many issues when doing so, but power supplies don't last forever. Moreover, many issues that occur with power supplies are intermittent making the troubleshooting process a little tougher. Your best friends when troubleshooting power supplies are going to be a multimeter, power supply tester, and your eyes and ears. Of course, always make sure that the power supply connects to the AC outlet properly before troubleshooting further. Here are a couple of the issues you may encounter with power supplies:

▶ Fan failure

▶ Fuse failure

▶ Quick death

▶ Slow death

Fan failure can be due to the fact that the power supply is old, extremely clogged with dirt, or that the fan was of cheaper design (without ball bearings). However, for the A+ exam it doesn't make a difference. As far as A+ is concerned, if the fan fails, the power supply needs to be replaced, and it makes sense. Chances are, if the fan has failed, other components of the power supply are on their way out also. It is more cost-effective to a company to simply replace the power supply than to have a technician spend the time opening it and trying to repair it. More important, although it is possible to remove and replace the fan by opening the power supply, this can be a dangerous venture because the power supply holds an electric charge, so the A+ rule is to never open the power supply.

Exam Alert

Do not open a power supply! If it has failed, replace it with a working unit.

Fuse failure can occur due to an overload or due to the power supply malfunctioning. Either way, the proper course of action is to replace the power supply. Do not attempt to replace the fuse. Chances are that the power supply is faulty if the fuse is blown. If it so happens that you need to test an individual fuse that was lying around, then use your multimeter. Make sure that your red lead is connected to the ohms (Ω) input and set the meter to Ohm (Ω). Touch the probes to both ends of the fuse. A good fuse should show zero ohm or display continuity. A bad or "blown" fuse will not show any reading. This is an example of testing impedance.

If the power supply dies a quick death, it might be because of several reasons from an electrical spike to hardware malfunction. First make sure that the IEC cable is connected properly to the power supply and to the AC outlet. Sometimes, it can be difficult to tell whether the power supply has failed or if it's something else inside or outside the computer system. You should check the AC outlet with your trusty receptacle tester and make sure that a circuit hasn't tripped, and verify that any surge protectors and/or UPS devices work properly. Depending on what you sense about the problem, you might decide to just swap out the power supply with a known good one. Otherwise, move on to the following numbered steps.

If the power supply is dying a slow death and is causing intermittent errors, it could be tough to troubleshoot. If you suspect intermittent issues, first make sure that the power cord is connected securely and then try swapping out the power supply with a known good one. Boot the computer and watch it for awhile to see if the same errors occur.

Whether the power supply has apparently failed completely or is possibly causing intermittent errors, and you can't figure out the cause to this point, continue through the following steps:

1. Remove the computer case.

2. Connect a power supply tester, as shown in Figure 5.10, to the P1 connector and look at the results. (Make sure you have the correct power supply tester; this depends on whether you have a 20-pin or 24-pin power connector.) These power supply testers normally test for +12V, –12V, +5V, –5V, and 3.3V, but they might not test every individual pin. If there are error lights, no lights, or missing lights for specific voltages on the tester, replace the power supply. If all the lights are green, move on to the next step.

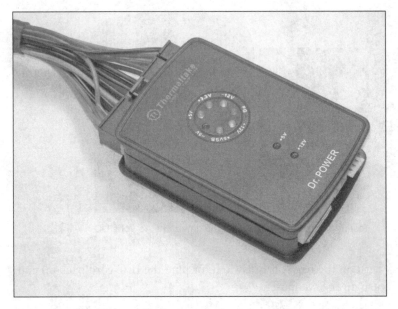

FIGURE 5.10   Testing a 24-pin P1 connector with a power supply tester

> **Note**
>
> The –5V light in the figure is not lit. This is because the –5V wire (white) is optional.
> See Chapter 2 for more information on the individual pins in an ATX connection.

> **Note**
>
> Though it's uncommon, some proprietary computer's power supplies do not light
> specific voltages, for example the 3.3V light, even though the power supply is work-
> ing properly. Check the documentation that came with the computer to see if this is
> an actual problem or a normal result.

3. Use a multimeter to test the power supply. Use the same methodology
   for testing with a multimeter as in the beginning of this chapter.

   a. Turn off the hard on/off switch. (If there is one; if not, unplug the
      IEC cord.)

   b. With the main motherboard connector (P1) inserted into the
      motherboard, connect the black lead to a ground wire (or other
      source of ground) and insert the red lead to a colored voltage wire
      in the main power connector, as shown in Figure 5.11. You need to
      dig a little bit to get the lead in there but don't press too hard.
      When the leads are stationary, move on to the next step.

FIGURE 5.11   Testing the 3.3 volt wire with a multimeter set to volts DC

   c. Turn on the hard on/off switch (or plug the IEC cord back in) and
      turn on the computer.

d. Turn on the multimeter to volts DC and view the results. In the figure you notice that we test an orange wire (which is rated for +3.3 volts). Generally, supply voltages should be within +/– 5 percent of the nominal value. Our result was +3.43 volts, which is within tolerance.

> **Note**
>
> If you have an analog multimeter, you would usually set this to 20 or higher. Just remember to move the decimal point in the reading for every increment higher than 20!

e. Shut off the multimeter and computer every time before moving to another wire. Check each of the wires for proper voltages. A chart of all the voltages for 20-pin and 24-pin connectors is available in Chapter 2.

f. If one of the wires fails or gives intermittent results, first verify you have a decent connection with the multimeter leads; then see if the wire just needs to be inserted into the main motherboard connector better, and if it continues, replace the power supply. If all the wires are fine (which is doubtful), move to the next step.

4. Swap the power supply with a known good power supply. Boot the computer and watch it for several minutes or longer to see if there are any strange and intermittent occurrences.

Remember that sometimes connections can be jarred loose inside and outside the computer. Check the IEC cord on both ends and all power connections inside the computer. This includes the main motherboard connector, Molex, mini, SATA, and PCIe connectors. Any one loose connector can have interesting results on your computer!

Heating and Cooling

Another thing to watch for is system overheating. This can happen for several reasons:

- Power supply fan failure

- Auxiliary case fan failure

- Inadequate amount of fans

► Missing or open slot covers

► Case isn't tightly closed and screwed in

Air flow is important on today's computers because processors can typically operate at 3 gflops. That creates a lot of heat. Add to that the fact that the video card and other cards have their own on-board processors, it can get hot inside the computer case. Circulation is the key word here. Air should flow in the case from the front and be exhausted out the back. Any openings in the case or missing slot covers can cause circulation to diminish. If you have a computer that has a lot of devices, or does a lot of processing, or runs hot for any other reason, your best bet is to install a case fan in the front of the case, which pulls air into the case, and a second case fan in the back of the case, which with the power supply fan helps to exhaust hot air out the back. Also, try to keep the computer in a relatively cool area and leave space for the computer to expel its hot air! Of course there are other special considerations and options, such as liquid cooling, and special processor cooling methods, such as the Intel Chassis Air Guide, but they are not covered in the A+ exam.

Cram Quiz

Answer these questions. The answers follow the last question. If you cannot answer these questions correctly, consider reading this section again until you can.

1. Which device tests multiple wires of a power supply at the same time?
   - ○ **A.** Multimeter
   - ○ **B.** Power supply tester
   - ○ **C.** Line conditioner
   - ○ **D.** Surge protector

2. Which power connector would be used to power an IDE hard drive?
   - ○ **A.** Molex
   - ○ **B.** mini
   - ○ **C.** P1
   - ○ **D.** P8/P9

3. Which of the following uses a 24-pin main motherboard power connector?
   - ○ **A.** ATX
   - ○ **B.** ATX 12V 1.3
   - ○ **C.** ATX 12V 2.0
   - ○ **D.** ATX 5V 2.0

4. The red wire in a Molex connection is rated for what voltage?

   ○ **A.** 12 volts

   ○ **B.** 5 volts

   ○ **C.** 3.3 volts

   ○ **D.** 24 volts

Cram Quiz Answers

1. **B**. The power supply tester tests 3.3V, 5V, –5V, 12V, and –12V simultaneously. A multimeter tests only one wire at a time. Line conditioners and surge protectors are preventative devices, not testing devices.

2. **A**. Molex connectors power IDE devices. Mini connectors are for floppy drives, P1 is a name used for the main motherboard connector, and P8/P9 are legacy main power connectors for AT systems.

3. **C**. ATX 12V 2.0 combined the 20-pin and 4-pin connectors used in ATX 12V 1.3 into one 24-pin connector.

4. **B**. The red wire is rated for 5 volts. The yellow wire is rated for 12 volts and 3.3 volts is associated with the main motherboard connector (to feed the processor); 24 volts is not involved in the devices we discussed in this chapter.

Additional Reading and Resources

Additional A+ resources: http://www.davidlprowse.com/aplus.

Mueller, Scott. *Upgrading and Repairing PCs*. Que. 2008.

Power Supply Calculator from Journey Systems:
http://www.journeysystems.com/?power_supply_calculator

Soper, Mark Edward; Mueller, Scott; Prowse, David L. *CompTIA A+ Certification Guide*. ISBN13: 9780789740472. Que.

CHAPTER 6

Storage Devices

This chapter covers the following A+ exam topics:

▶ Magnetic Storage Media

▶ Optical Storage Media

▶ Solid-State Storage Media

You can find a master list of A+ exam topics in the "Introduction."

This chapter covers CompTIA A+ 220-701 objectives 1.1, 1.2, and 2.5 and CompTIA A+ 220-702 objectives 1.1 and 1.2.

Everyone needs a place to store data. Whether it's business documents, audio/video files, or data backups, users must decide on the right storage medium. This can be magnetic media such as a hard drive, optical media such as a DVD, or solid-state media such as a USB flash drive. It all depends on what is stored, and how often and where it is needed. This chapter concentrates on those three categories of media and how to identify, install, and troubleshoot them.

Magnetic Storage Media

The three main types of magnetic storage are hard disk drives, floppy disk drives, and tape drives. By far the most common is the hard disk drive; this is where the operating system is normally stored. Users also store frequently accessed data on the hard drive as well, such as Word documents, music, pictures, and so on. Floppy drives are not part of the bulk of today's computers, due to their small capacity. However, in special cases they might be needed by the user, perhaps to access older data and programs. The technician, however, will use the floppy drive to boot systems with special startup and analyses disks. Tape drives are used for archival, the long-term backup of data that is not accessed often. Because floppy drives and tape drives are far less common, let's begin with hard drives.

Hard Disk Drives

Hard disk drives (HDDs) are the most common of magnetic media. They are nonvolatile, which means that any information stored on them will not be lost when the computer is turned off. They are not as fast as RAM, but are faster than most other storage mediums available; this makes them a good choice for storing permanent data that is accessed frequently.

Hard Drive 101

The hard disk drive (often shortened to hard drive or hard disk) contains one or more platters with a magnetic surface. Data is recorded to the disk by magnetizing ferromagnetic material directionally, basically, as 0s and 1s. The disk is usually made of a cobalt-based alloy. As the platters rotate at high speed, read/write heads store and read information to and from the disk. The heads are located on an actuator arm that arcs across the disk. Together, the arm and read/write heads are similar to the arm and needle combination of a record player. Figure 6.1 shows some of the components inside and outside of the drive.

The hard drive depicted in Figure 6.1 is a typical Ultra ATA 3.5-inch wide drive. This hard drive, like all internal hard drives, has a data connector and power connector. On this particular drive, the data connector attaches to the motherboard (or expansion card) by way of a ribbon cable. The power connector attaches to the power supply by way of a four-wire power cable. Regardless of the type of hard drive, always make sure that the data and power cables are firmly connected to it.

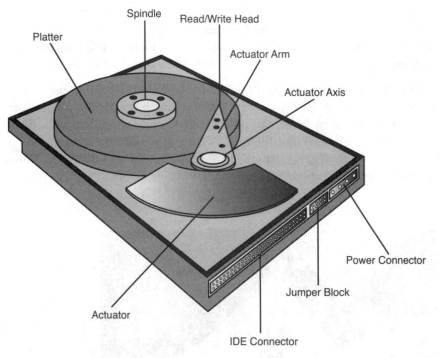

Spindle

Read/Write Head

Platter

Actuator Arm

Actuator Axis

Power Connector

Jumper Block

Actuator

IDE Connector

FIGURE 6.1   **Components of a typical hard disk drive**

PATA Versus SATA

In this corner, coming in at a maximum data throughput of 133MB/s is **PATA** (Parallel ATA). This was the standard for many years but has been all but phased out by SATA hard drives on most new computers. PATA hard drives are often referred to as Ultra ATA drives and sometimes as IDE drives. They transfer data in parallel, for example 16 bits (2 bytes) at a time. Currently, the maximum capacity Ultra ATA hard drive available for purchase is 750GB.

Internal PATA hard drives use the Integrated Drive Electronics (IDE) interface to transmit data to and from the motherboard. Every IDE port on a motherboard can have up to two drives connected to it. For a long time, motherboards would be equipped with two IDE ports, enabling for a maximum of four IDE devices. However newer motherboards often come with only one, limiting you to two IDE devices. The IDE ports on the motherboard and the hard drive manifest themselves as 40-*pin* connectors to which you can connect either a 40 or 80-*wire* ribbon cable. Newer IDE cables are all 80-wire; however, they look identical to the older 40-wire versions, except for the blue connector on one end that you find on many 80-wire cables. The cable has three connectors, one for the controller (often blue), one for the master drive (often black), and a connector in the middle of the cable for the slave drive (often gray). We talk more about master/slave configurations in a little bit. The IDE port on the hard drive is keyed for easy orientation. External PATA drives usually transfer data to the computer by way of USB or FireWire.

PATA hard drives accept a 4-pin Molex power connector from the computer's power supply. The Molex connector is keyed so that it is easier to orient when connecting to the hard drive. This power cable has four wires: Red (5V), Black (ground), Black (ground), and Yellow (12V). For more information about Molex and other power connections, see Chapter 5, "Power." Figure 6.2 shows an actual Ultra ATA hard drive's data and power connectors.

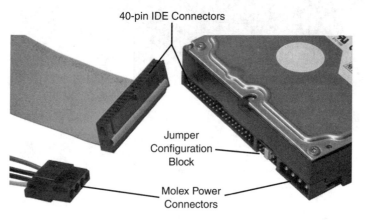

FIGURE 6.2   **PATA Ultra-ATA data and power connectors**

There is a jumper block in between the power and data connectors. This enables you to select the configuration of the hard drive. There are usually four options, which are often labeled on the drive itself:

▶ **Single:** In a single drive configuration, no jumper shunt is needed. If you want, you can connect the jumper horizontally across two pins. Although this does not configure the drive in any way, it keeps the jumper handy for future use.

▶ **Master:** Each of the motherboard's IDE connections enables for two drives. In a two-drive configuration on a single IDE cable, one must be set to drive 0 (master), and one must be set to drive 1 (slave). To set a drive to master, connect the jumper vertically to the correct pair of pins (for example, Western Digital drives use the center location; refer to Figure 6.2), and connect the black end connector of the IDE ribbon cable to the hard drive. The master hard drive is normally where the operating system would go.

▶ **Slave:** To set a drive to slave, connect the jumper vertically to the correct pair of pins (for example, Western Digital drives use the second position from the right), and connect the gray, middle connector of the IDE cable to the hard drive. The slave hard drive is where the bulk of the data would usually be stored.

▶ **Cable Select:** This drive mode automatically configures the drive as master or slave according to where you connect it to the IDE cable. This might be marked on the drive as CS.

There are currently seven versions of Parallel ATA, four of which you should know for the exam. These standards and their maximum data transfer rates are listed in Table 6.1.

TABLE 6.1 **Comparison of PATA Standards.**

Standard	Maximum Data Transfer Rate	Also Known As
ATA/ATAPI 4	33MB/s (33MHz)	ATA-4 or Ultra ATA/33
ATA/ATAPI 5	66MB/s (66MHz)	ATA-5 or Ultra ATA/66
ATA/ATAPI 6	100MB/s (100MHz)	ATA-6 or Ultra ATA/100
ATA/ATAPI 7	133MB/s (133MHz)	ATA-7 or Ultra ATA/133

> **Note**
>
> ATA-6 introduced 48-bit addressing, which allows for a maximum hard drive capacity of 144 *petabytes*. Previous versions had a maximum drive size of only 137GB.

> **Exam Alert**
>
> Know the data transfer rates for ATA-5, 6, and 7.

And in this corner, coming in at a whopping maximum data throughput of 600MB/s is SATA (Serial ATA). These drives are the most-common hard drives in use today. If you remember, the motherboard we used in Chapter 2, "Motherboards," had six SATA ports, but only one PATA IDE port, most likely for use with optical drives. So as you can surmise, hard drives, like expansion busses and several other technologies, have gone serial. A Serial ATA drive transmits serial streams of data (one bit at a time) at high-speed over two pairs of conductors and can do so in full duplex, meaning it can send and receive simultaneously. Because SATA and PATA will not interfere with each other, you can run both simultaneously; however, by default one will not mate to the other; they are not compatible without a converter board.

To transmit data the SATA drive uses a 7-pin flat (or right-angle) cable, as shown in Figure 6.3. Obviously, the motherboard should be equipped with one or more SATA connectors to use SATA hard drives. The other option would be to install an SATA PCIe or PCI expansion card. Most motherboards come with one or more SATA data cables. These cables are easily connected to the drive but to remove them, press down on the connector's metal tab at the end of the cable before pulling the cable out. Only one drive can be connected to the SATA cable.

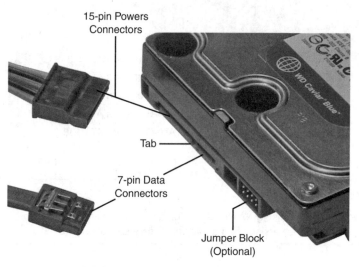

FIGURE 6.3   **SATA data and power connectors**

For power, the SATA drive utilizes a 15-pin power connector, as shown in Figure 6.3. Your power supply must be equipped with this power cable to support SATA drives. The hard drive's power connector has a vertical tab at the right side, making for easier orientation when connecting the power cable.

SATA 1.5 was the first generation of SATA devices. Currently, SATA 3.0 is the most common. Table 6.2 shows the different SATA versions you need to know for the exam.

TABLE 6.2   **Comparison of SATA Standards**

Standard	Maximum Data Transfer Rate
SATA 1.x - Known as SATA 1.5Gbit/s	150MB/s
SATA 2.x - Known as SATA 3.0Gbit/s	300MB/s
SATA 3,x - Known as SATA 6.0Gbit/s	600MB/s

> **Note**
>
> Even newer SATA 3.0 magnetic hard disks can barely transfer data at 150MB/s; however solid-state drives come close to 300MB/s (more on solid-state later in this chapter).
>
> Although SATA 6.0 has been ratified, that data rate has yet to be realized in the consumer market.

> **ExamAlert**
>
> Know the maximum data transfer rates for SATA 1.5 and 3.0.

> **ExamAlert**
>
> Know the major differences between PATA and SATA for the exam.

For this book, I decided to use the SATA 3.0 hard drive; specifically the Western Digital Caviar Blue WD5000AAKS. This model is an average hard drive when it comes to speed and other major specifications. The specifications that you should be interested in when purchasing a hard drive (PATA or SATA), and should know for the A+ exams, include the following:

▶ **Capacity:** Our example drive is marketed as a 500GB drive, but accessible capacity will vary depending on the environment the hard drive is used in. For example, after being formatted, this drive can normally hold 500,107MB. But in a RAID 1 mirrored environment, it can hold 490,402MB. Currently, the largest SATA drive capacity is 1.5TB.

▶ **Data transfer rate:** Because it is an SATA 3.0 drive, it has a theoretical maximum of 300MB/s; but we all know that the theoretical numbers are never actually achieved. This particular drive can sustain in the neighborhood of 120MB/s. This is sometimes also referred to as *data throughput*.

▶ **Rotational speed:** The platters in our example hard drive can rotate at a maximum of 7200RPM, which is common; other typical speeds for hard drives include 5400RPM and 10,000RPM.

▶ **Cache:** This drive has 16MB of cache, which is also known as a buffer. The cache on most hard drives is on-board DRAM. Compare this with CPUs that use SRAM cache that is significantly faster. Like CPUs, the hard drive's cache helps to access frequently used information faster than if it were to get the information from the magnetic disk.

▶ **Latency:** After a track has been reached by the read head, latency is the delay in time before a particular sector on the platter can be read. It is directly related to rotational speed and is usually half the time it takes for the disk to rotate once. For example, our 7200RPM drive has an average latency of 4.2ms (milliseconds), but a 10,000RPM drive has an average latency of 3.0ms.

(ExamAlert)

Understand a hard drive's specifications including capacity, data transfer rate, rotational speed, cache, and latency.

SCSI

Small Computer System Interface (SCSI) hard drives are often used in servers and power workstations that need high data throughput. You can identify a SCSI drive by the different (and usually louder) sound it makes compared to ATA drives; it's kind of like the difference between a diesel engine and a standard car engine. SCSI standards describe the devices, controllers, cables, and protocols used to send data. Part of the beauty of SCSI is that you can have up to 16 devices including the controller. They can be internal, external, or both. For the longest time SCSI was a parallel technology, but of late serial versions such as SAS (Serial Attached SCSI) have emerged. When installing SCSI devices, it is important to remember that each end of the SCSI chain must be terminated and that each device gets its own ID, between 0 and 15 (0-7 on older SCSI chains). The controller normally gets ID 7 and has its own BIOS, known as Option ROM, in which you can configure the controller, drives, and drive arrays. A driver might need to be installed to the operating system for the SCSI controller. Table 6.3 shows a few of the current SCSI technologies you might see in the field.

TABLE 6.3   **Comparison of SCSI Standards**

SCSI Standard	Maximum Data Transfer Rate	Connector Type	Transmission Type
Ultra3 SCSI	160MB/s	68-pin; 80-pin	Parallel
Ultra-320 SCSI	320MB/s	68-pin; 80-pin	Parallel
Ultra-640 SCSI	640MB/s	68-pin; 80-pin	Parallel
SAS (Serial Attached SCSI)	300MB/s	SFF 8482, 8484, 8470	Serial

ExamAlert

For the exam, know that the SCSI controller normally uses ID 7, and memorize the data transfer rates for the various SCSI Ultra versions.

Installing Hard Disk Drives

Installing hard drives is quite easy. First, make sure you employ antistatic measures and verify that the computer is off and unplugged.

Next, if it is an Ultra ATA drive (IDE), be sure to configure the jumper setting correctly. SATA drives do not need to be jumpered, unless they are coexisting with Ultra ATA drives on an IDE bus. Most internal drives are 3.5 inches, and most cases have several 3.5-inch internal bays. The drive bay might need to be removed before attaching the drive, or you might screw it directly into the chassis. Some cases have a latching screwless system. However, if you need to screw in the drive, make sure you use all four screws, and only turn the screws with a screwdriver until they are tight; don't go any further. Try to stay away from motorized screwdrivers or other tools that might have too much torque and can possibly damage the hard drive.

After the drive is screwed in or attached to the case chassis, connect the data and power connectors. For Ultra ATA drives, the data connector is keyed. There is a tab on each end of the cable (in the middle), which corresponds to a notch on the hard drive's port and on the motherboard's port. In addition, these types of cables indicate the first pin (known as Pin 1) with a colored stripe on one side of the cable. Pin 1 is normally on the upper-right corner of the hard drive's IDE port, so just match the colored stripe up to it. Or remember that the colored stripe of the IDE cable should be oriented next to the power connector. The power connector (Molex) is also keyed; it has two diagonal corners that should be oriented at the top of the connector when plugging it into the drive. Try not to force these connections; it can damage an individual pin. It should take a bit of pressure, but if it doesn't seem right, pull the connector away, and make sure it is oriented correctly. For SATA drives, attach the data connector with the exposed metal facing up, and orient the power connector according to the tab on the right side of the hard drive's port. Verify that both the data and power connectors are firmly secured to the drive and to the motherboard. A loose connector can cause a boot failure in the operating system.

Finally, test the drive and make sure it is recognized by the BIOS at the correct capacity. If for some reason, the BIOS doesn't see the full capacity, check for any possible BIOS updates. Then, either install an operating system to the drive, or verify that a current operating system (on another pre-existing disk) can see the new drive at its correct capacity. Remember that a drive might show up as slightly less than its marketed amount within the operating system, depending on the environment the drive is used in.

Preventative Maintenance and Troubleshooting Hard Drives

Hard drives will fail. It's not a matter of *if*; it's a matter of *when*, especially when it comes to mechanical drives. The moving parts are bound to fail at some point. Hard drives have an average warranty of 3 years, as is the case with the SATA drive I use in this book. It is interesting to note that most drives last around 3 years before failing. Of course, by implementing good practices, you can extend the lifespan of any hard drive, for example:

▶ **Turn the computer off when not in use:** By doing this, the hard drive is told by the operating system to spin down and enter a "parked" state. It's kind of like parking a car or placing a record player's arm on its holder. Turning the computer off when not in use increases the lifespan of just about all its devices (except for the lithium battery). You can also set the computer to hibernate, standby, or simply set your operating system's power scheme to turn off hard disks after a certain amount of inactivity, such as 5 minutes. The less the drive is in motion, the longer lifespan it will have.

▶ **Clean up the disk:** Use a hard drive cleanup program to remove temporary files, clean out the recycle bin, and so on. Microsoft includes the Disk Cleanup program in Windows. Another free program I use is called CleanUp! that you can download from the Internet after a quick

Google search. By removing the "junk" from the hard drive, there is less data that the drive has to sift through, which makes it easier on the drive when it is time to defragment.

▶ **Defragment the disk:** Defragmenting, known as *defragging* rearranges the data on a partition or volume so that it is laid out in a contiguous, orderly fashion. You should attempt to defragment the disk every month, maybe more if you are a power user. Don't worry, the operating system tells you if defragging is not necessary during the analysis stage. Over time, data is written to the drive, and subsequently erased, over and over again, leaving gaps in the drivespace. New data will sometimes be written to multiple areas of the drive, in a broken or fragmented fashion, filling in any blank areas it can find. When this happens, the hard drive has to work much harder to find the data it needs, spinning more, starting and stopping more; in general, more mechanical movement. It's kind of like changing gears excessively with the automatic transmission in your car. The more the drive has to access this fragmented data, the shorter its lifespan becomes due to mechanical wear and tear. Defragmenting the drive can be done with Microsoft's Disk Defragmenter, with the command-line **defrag **, or with other third-party programs. If using the Disk Defragmenter program, you need 15 percent free space on the volume you want to defrag. If you have less than that, you need to use the command-line option **defrag -f**. To sum it up, the more contiguous the data, the less the hard drive has to work to access that data, thus increasing the lifespan of the drive.

Exam Alert

Know the tools that are available to defragment a hard drive.

▶ **Scan the drive with antimalware:** Make sure the computer has an antimalware program installed, which includes antivirus and antispyware. Verify that the software is scheduled to scan the drive at least twice a week. (Manufacturers' default is usually every day.) The quicker the software finds and quarantines threats, the less chance of physical damage to the hard drive.

You may find several issues when troubleshooting hard drives:

▶ **BIOS does not "see" the drive:** If the BIOS doesn't see the drive you have installed, you can check a few things. First, make sure the power cable is firmly connected and oriented properly. Second, verify that the correct end of the data cable is securely connected and oriented, for example on Ultra-ATA drives, the black connector on the ribbon cable should connect to the drive. The other end of the data cable should be firmly connected to the motherboard. Next, make sure that the drive is jumpered correctly. (Or not jumpered at all, if that is the scenario.) Finally, check if there is a motherboard BIOS update to see the drive; sometimes newer drives require new BIOS code to access the drive.

▶ **Windows does not "see" a second drive:** There are several reasons why Windows might not see a second drive. Maybe a driver needs to be installed for the drive or for its controller (for example a PCI SATA card or SCSI card). Perhaps the secondary drive needs to be initialized within Disk Management. Or it can be that the drive was not partitioned or formatted. Also try the methods listed in the first bullet.

▶ **Slow reaction time:** If the system runs slow, it can be because the drive has become fragmented or has been infected with a virus or spyware. Analyze and defragment the drive. If it is heavily fragmented, the drive can take longer to access the data needed resulting in slow reaction time. You might be amazed at the difference in performance! If you think the drive might be infected, scan the disk with your antivirus/antispyware software to quarantine any possible threats. It's wise to schedule deep scans of the drive at least twice a week. More on viruses and spyware in Chapter 15, "Security." In extreme cases, you might want to move all the data from the affected drive to another drive, being sure to verify the data that was moved. Then format the affected drive, and finally move the data back. This is common in audio/video environments, and when dealing with data drives, but should not be done to a system drive, meaning a drive that contains the operating system.

▶ **Missing files at startup:** If you get a message such as NTLDR Is Missing or BOOTMGR Is Missing, these files need to be written back to the hard drive. For more on how to do this, see Chapter 10, "Troubleshooting Windows." In severe cases, this can mean that the drive is physically damaged and needs to be replaced. If this happens, the drive needs to be removed from the computer and slaved off to another drive on another system. Then the data needs to be copied from the damaged drive to a known good drive (which might require third-party programs such as SpinRite or Ontrack Data Recovery), and a new drive needs to be installed to the affected computer. Afterward, the recovered data can be copied on the new drive.

▶ **Noisy drive/lockups:** If your Ultra ATA or SATA drive starts getting noisy, it's a sure sign of impending drive failure. You might also hear a scratching or grating sound, akin to scratching a record with the record player's needle. Or the drive might intermittently just stop or lockup with one or more audible clicks. You can't wait in these situations; you need to slave off the drive in another computer immediately and copy the data to a good drive. Even then, it might be too late. However, the aforementioned programs (SpinRite or Ontrack Data Recovery, and so on) might help recover the data.

Network Attached Storage (NAS)

Another type of hard drive storage is network attached storage (NAS). This is when one or more hard drives are installed into a device known as a NAS box that connects directly to the network. The device can then be accessed as a mapped network drive from any computer on the network. A basic example of this that I use on my network is the D-Link DNS-323. It can hold two SATA drives to be used together as one large capacity or in a RAID 1 mirrored configuration for fault tolerance. RAID 1 Mirroring means that two drives are used in unison, and all data is written to both drives, giving you a mirror or extra copy of the data, in the case that one drive fails. RAID levels 0, 1, and 5 are covered in Chapter 8, "Configuring Windows." It connects to the network by way of an RJ45 port that is rated at 10/100/1000Mbps. Of course, there are much more advanced versions of NAS boxes that would be used by larger companies.

Floppy Disk Drives

As we mentioned before, floppy drives are not nearly as common as they were 10 years ago; in fact, most computers don't come with a floppy drive at all. However, some businesses might need them to access older data or programs, and technicians use them to start up a computer with special boot disks. Due to this, there is a chance you might see a question on them on the exam.

Floppy Drive Basics

The standard floppy drive is known as a 3.5-inch 1.44MB floppy drive. Historically, this has been the A: drive and possibly the B: drive in a computer. These drive letters are reserved for floppy drives and other devices; now you know why operating systems use C: by default! The floppy drive uses a "mini" floppy power connector (shown in Chapter 5), also known as Berg, and a 34-pin keyed data cable that connects to the motherboard, if your motherboard supports it.

The floppy drive is known as removable media because the floppy disks are inserted into the drive. The most common of these disks has a 1.44MB capacity. Keep in mind that you can store only 1.38MB of data to these disks due to formatting and because the boot sector takes up a small amount of space on the disk. Floppy disks are normally formatted using the FAT12 file system.

Floppy drives are installed much the same way as hard drives: They are screwed into the chassis of the case, and data and power cables connect to the floppy ports; these ports are shown in Figure 6.4. The mini power cable has a linear plastic tab that needs to face up when you connect the cable to the drive.

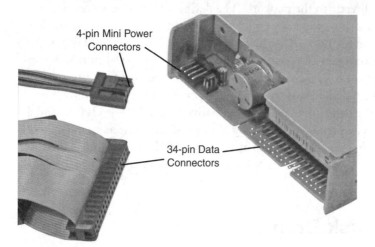

4-pin Mini Power Connectors

34-pin Data Connectors

FIGURE 6.4   Floppy data and power connectors

Floppy Drive Troubleshooting and Boot Disks

As always, make sure that the data and power cables firmly connect to the floppy drive and to the motherboard. A floppy drive fails if the data connector is connected upside down, which is possible because many floppy drive's data ports are not keyed. You will know if the data cable is upside down because the floppy drive's activity light will remain on. If a disk is placed in the drive in this state, it will be erased and/or damaged. If the floppy drive doesn't work at all, ensure that the BIOS has the floppy drive enabled. Otherwise, floppy drives are quite resilient and last a long time.

Examples of boot disks that a technician might use include Windows startup disks, to boot/repair or install a Windows computer; antivirus boot disks, to scan the boot sector of a hard drive; BIOS Flash boot disks, to update the BIOS on a computer; and specialized third-party boot disks, to repair a computer, recover data, and so on. If you plan to boot from a floppy disk, verify that the floppy drive is first in the BIOS boot order.

Tape Drives

Tape drives are devices primarily used for archival or backup of data. These devices use removable media in the form of magnetic tape cartridges, which are inserted into the tape drive. Usage of tape drives has declined greatly in recent years due to the advent of writable optical media; however, you might still see some devices in use.

The tape drive is rated in one of two ways: native capacity, for example 100GB; and compressed capacity, for example 200GB. As you can see, compressed capacity will normally be at a 2:1 ratio compared to native capacity. A common example of a tape drive is Quantum's Digital Linear Tape (DLT) and the higher capacity Super DLT.

The tape drive can be internal or external. If it is internal, it might connect to a SCSI controller card or to an IDE port. If external, you might see it connect to a SCSI port, USB, IEEE 1394, or the older parallel port.

The driver for the tape drive must be installed, and a tape drive must be used with backup software. Some drives come with their own third-party software, or you can use Windows' NTBackup. Be careful with these programs. Quite often, they backup all the data into one big compressed file, for example NTBackup backs up everything you select into one file with the .bkf extension. Be sure to use the verify option when backing up data, and consider running a test backup and restore when you first start using a tape drive to verify it works properly.

Other deprecated backup technologies related to tape drives include products from Iomega such as the ZIP or JAZ disk technology, or the SuperDisk technology. Again, these and tape drives have been all but phased out due to the popular usage of optical storage and other medias.

Cram Quiz

Answer these questions. The answers follow the last question. If you cannot answer these questions correctly, consider reading this section again until you can.

1. What is the maximum data transfer rate of SATA 1.5?

- ○ **A.** 1.5Mbps
- ○ **B.** 300MB/s
- ○ **C.** 150MB/s
- ○ **D.** 1.5GB/s

2. Which of these is the delay it takes for the hard drive to access a particular sector on the disk?

- ○ **A.** Actuator
- ○ **B.** Latency
- ○ **C.** Lag
- ○ **D.** Propagation

3. What should you do first to repair a drive that is acting sluggish?

- ○ **A.** Remove the drive and recover the data.
- ○ **B.** Run Disk Cleanup.
- ○ **C.** Run Disk Defragmenter.
- ○ **D.** Scan for viruses.

4. How much data can an Ultra ATA/100 drive transfer per second?

- ○ **A.** 133MB
- ○ **B.** 266MB
- ○ **C.** 150MB
- ○ **D.** 100MB

5. How many pins are there in a SATA drive's data and power connectors?

- ○ **A.** 40 and 4
- ○ **B.** 8 and 16
- ○ **C.** 7 and 15
- ○ **D.** 80 and 4

6. What kind of cable does a floppy drive use?

   ○ **A.** 40-pin IDE

   ○ **B.** 80-pin IDE

   ○ **C.** 34-pin IDE

   ○ **D.** 168-pin IDE

7. What is the maximum data transfer rate of an Ultra3 SCSI device?

   ○ **A.** 320MB/s

   ○ **B.** 160MB/s

   ○ **C.** 640MB/s

   ○ **D.** 300MB/s

8. In a two drive IDE configuration, drive 0 would be the _____, and drive 1 would be the _____.

   ○ **A.** Slave, master

   ○ **B.** Cable select, slave

   ○ **C.** Slave, single

   ○ **D.** Master, slave

Cram Quiz Answers

1. **C.** SATA 1.5 can transfer a maximum of 150MB/s, though most devices won't ever attain that maximum. The standard specifies the transmission of 1.5Gbps (notice the lower case 'b' for bits); 300 MB/s is the data transfer rate of SATA 3.0.

2. **B.** Latency is the delay it takes for the hard drive to access the data; it is directly related to the rotational speed (RPM) of the disk.

3. **C.** Attempt to defragment the disk. If it is not necessary, Windows lets you know. Then you can move on to other options such as scanning the drive for viruses.

4. **D**. ATA/ATAPI 6 drives can transfer 100MB/s maximum. These drives are also known as Ultra ATA/100. ATA/ATAPI 7 drives can transfer 133MB/s. SATA 1.5 drives can transmit 150MB/s, and PCI can transfer 266MB/s.

5. **C.** The SATA drive uses a 7-pin data connector and a 15-pin power connector. Ultra ATA IDE hard drives have a 40-pin data connector and 4-pin power connector. The IDE drive's cable might have 80 *conductors* or wires, but it still physically connects through 40 pins.

6. **C**. The floppy drive uses a 34-pin ribbon cable to transfer data. IDE hard drives use a 40-pin ribbon cable; 168-pin refers to the amount of pins in SDRAM.

7. **B**. Ultra3 SCSI can transfer a maximum of 160MB/s. Ultra-320 SCSI can transfer 320MB/s, Ultra-640 can transfer 640MB/s, and SAS (Serial Attached SCSI) and SATA 3.0 can transfer 300MB/s.

8. **D**. In PATA IDE two-drive configurations, drive 0 would be the master and drive 1 would be the slave. Cable select is a drive mode that autoconfigures drives as master or slave depending on their cable position. Single means a single drive configuration with no configuration necessary.

Optical Storage Media

The three main types of optical media in use today are Compact Discs (CD), Digital Versatile Discs (DVD), and Blu-Ray discs. These discs have a variety of functions, including audio, video, application, data, and so on. Some discs can be read from, and some can also be written to. Finally, some discs can be *re*written to as well. It all depends on which media you use. Now there are a lot of different versions of optical media; let's try to organize them so that they will be easier to remember. We start with the most familiar, the compact disc.

> **ExamAlert**
>
> You've probably noticed by now that most magnetic media is known as "dis*k*" and optical media is known as "dis*c*." Keep this in mind for the exam.

Compact Disc (CD)

A Compact Disc (CD) is a flat, round, optical disc used to store music, sounds, or other data. It can be read from a compact disc player. For example, audio CDs can be played on a compact disc player that is part of a stereo or a computer. However, data CDs can be read only from CD-ROM drives that are part of, or externally connected to, a computer. The A+ exam focuses on data CDs, so let's talk about some of the different data CD technologies.

Data CD Technologies

The most common acronym that comes to mind is the CD-ROM, compact disc-read-only memory. Data is written to a CD-ROM in a similar way that audio is written to a music CD; a laser shines on the reflective surface of the CD and stores data as a plethora of microscopic indentations known as lands and pits. These are the types of CDs you get when you purchase a computer program or game. They can be read from but not written to, and can be read only from a compatible CD-ROM drive. CD-ROM drives are rated in read speeds, for example 48x. The x equals 150KB/s. So to calculate a CD-ROM drive's maximum read speed, you multiply the number preceding the x by 150KB. In this example, this would be 48 x 150KB = 7.2MB/s. Most CD-ROM drives connect via IDE. Chances are the IDE connection has a maximum data transfer rate of 100MB/s, plenty for a CD-ROM running at 48x.

Over time, the technology to write to CDs was developed, enabling users to store information to CD that they would previously store on floppy disks or Zip drives. A typical CD can hold up to 700MB of data, although there are 650MB, 800MB, and other versions available. Table 6.4 describes the two most common recordable technologies.

TABLE 6.4   **Comparison of CD Recording Technologies**

CD Recording Technology	Full Name	Typical Maximum Recording Speed
CD-R	Compact Disc Recordable	48x (7.2MB/s) or 52x (7.8MB/s)
CD-RW	Compact Disc ReWritable	24x (3.6MB/s) or 32x (4.8MB/s)

Most optical drives that you can purchase for a computer today have all three compact disc functions. They can read from CD-ROMs, write to CD-Rs, and write/rewrite to CD-RWs. Usually, the read speed and CD-R speed are the same. Because CD-Rs are extremely inexpensive, this technology took off as an archival method; it was a massive nail in the coffin for technologies such as tape backup, Zip/Jaz drives, and of course floppy disks.

> **ExamAlert**
>
> Know the difference between CD-ROM, CD-R, and CD-RW.

Although there are SATA and SCSI CD-ROMs, the typical CD-ROM drive is IDE and has the same types of connectors as an Ultra ATA IDE hard drive: 40-pin data connector, 4-pin power connector (Molex), and a jumper block to set the CD-ROM drive to either master or slave. Figure 6.5 displays these connectors with the CD-ROM set to slave. It also displays the stereo audio out that connects to a sound card or to the motherboard if the sound card is integrated. This enables you to play and hear audio CDs on the CD-ROM drive.

CD-ROM discs are known as removable media; however the drive is normally fixed in the computer. It installs much like an IDE hard drive. One notable exception is that most CD-ROM drives are 5.25-inches wide. So they need to be installed to one of the larger bays in a case that has an opening on the front; this way the drive tray is accessible. Most CD-ROM drives can also play audio CDs and have a volume knob on the front. In addition, many drives have a pinhole near the volume knob. This small hole is for when a CD (or the tray) gets jammed. Use a paper clip and insert it into the hole in an attempt to free the tray and CD.

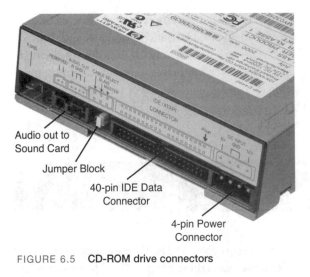

Audio out to
Sound Card

Jumper Block

40-pin IDE Data
Connector

4-pin Power
Connector

FIGURE 6.5   CD-ROM drive connectors

Digital Versatile Disc (DVD)

For data, Digital Versatile Discs, also known as Digital Video Discs, are the
successor to CDs for a variety of reasons. First, they can be used to play and
record video. Second, they have a much greater capacity than CDs. This is
because the pits etched into the surface of the DVD are smaller than CD pits
(.74 micrometers compared to 1.6 micrometers). Also, DVDs can be written
to faster than CDs. So, there are read-only DVDs and writable DVDs; however, there are a lot more variations of DVDs than there are CDs. Table 6.5
describes some of the DVD-ROM (Digital Versatile Disc-Read-Only
Memory) versions, specifications, and differences starting with the common
DVD-5 version.

TABLE 6.5   **Comparison of DVD Technologies**

DVD-ROM Technology	Sides	Total Layers	Capacity
DVD-5	1	1	4.7GB
DVD-9	1	2	8.5GB
DVD-10	2	2	9.4GB
DVD-14	2	3	13.2GB
DVD-18	2	4	17GB

The most common DVD is currently the single-sided, single-layer (SS, SL)
DVD-5 technology that can store 4.7GB of data. But some DVDs can be
written to two sides (known as dual-sided or DS); simply flip the DVD to

access the information on the other side. Layers however work differently. A DVD with two layers (known as dual layer or DL) incorporates both layers onto a single side of the disc. The second layer is actually underneath the first one; the DVD laser reads this second layer by shining through the first semi-transparent layer. By combining dual-sided and dual-layer technologies together, you end up with a DVD that can store up to 17GB of data (known as DVD-18) at 8.5GB per side.

> **ExamAlert**
>
> Know the capacity of DVD-5 for the exam.

Once again, for DVD-ROMs, and recordable DVDs, the most common by far is DVD-5. Typically a DVD drive reads these discs at 16x. However, the x in DVD speeds is different than the x in CD-ROM speeds. When it comes to DVDs, the x means approximately 1.32MB/s or about nine times the core CD speed. So, a typical 16x DVD is equal to 21MB/s. Typically, a DVD drive will read at 16x, record once at 22x or 24x, and rewrite at 6x or 8x. Table 6.6 gives a description of the different types of recordable DVDs.

TABLE 6.6   **Comparison of DVD Recordable Technologies**

DVD Recordable Technology	Capacity	Typical Write Speed*
DVD–R SL	4.707GB	22x or 24x
DVD+R SL	4.700GB	22x or 24x
DVD–R DL	8.544GB	12x
DVD+R DL	8.548GB	16x
DVD–RW SL or DL	4.707 or 8.544GB	6x
DVD+RW SL or DL	4.700 or 8.548GB	8x

*The write speeds vary from drive to drive. The stated typical speeds are the write speeds of the Samsung combo drive (DVD/CD) that I used for this book.

There is a slight difference in capacity between DVD– and DVD+ as you can see in Table 6.6. DVD– was developed by Pioneer and approved by the DVD Forum, whereas DVD+ was developed by a group of corporations headed up by Sony. Likewise, DVD–RW was developed by Pioneer and approved by the DVD Forum, and DVD+RW was developed by the same group of corporations that developed DVD+R; this group is now known as the DVD+RW Alliance. It's probably not important to know all this for the exam, because most DVD drives support all these formats. However, always check your drive to be sure before purchasing recordable DVDs.

Like most CD-ROM drives, the bulk of DVD drives connect via IDE, although this is changing slowly. IDE models have the same connections as IDE CD-ROMs and IDE hard drives: 40-pin data connector and 4-pin Molex power; they are jumpered using the same method (single, master, or slave); and are installed in the same manner, within the same 5¼ inch bay as CD-ROM drives. However, there are SATA DVD drives (the Samsung model I purchased for this book is SATA), and it connects the same way as other SATA devices. Most DVD drives are known as combo drives, meaning they can read and write to CDs and read DVDs (DVD-ROM drive), write DVDs (DVDR), and rewrite DVDs (DVDRW). The Samsung drive mentioned earlier does all these things, plus it includes the LightScribe technology that can create labels by etching text and graphics onto specially coated CDs and DVDs.

Because they are relatively cheap, DVD drives, like CD-ROM drives, are usually replaced if they fail. It could easily cost a company more money to try to repair a DVD drive, instead of simply purchasing one for between $10 to $20. However, if a problem does occur, remember to check the obvious; it takes only a few minutes. For example, if a DVD (or CD) drive tray won't open, press the eject button one time and wait. It can take a few moments for the DVD to spin down before opening. Then press it a few more times waiting a couple of moments after each time. You can also try to eject the disc from within the operating system. To do this, go to Windows Explorer, and right-click the drive in question; then select Eject. If this doesn't work, you can try to restart the computer and try the eject options again. Don't forget the pin-hole near the open button. You can slide a paperclip in there to get the tray to open. Sometimes, DVD drives have been installed with incorrect screws that are too long. This can cause damage to the drive tray. Finally, make sure that the drive is getting power! A loose Molex or SATA power connector results in the tray not opening or closing.

DVD and CD Usage

DVDs are used as much or more than CDs in computers nowadays. The only place where DVDs haven't really taken off is in the music arena. Although DVD-Audio (DVD-A) discs arguably have superior audio quality compared to audio CDs (DVD-A boasts a 24-bit rate, and up to 192kHz sampling compared to CDs 16-bit/44kHz), not many people have DVD-Audio players, so the audio CD is still by far the most common.

Blu-Ray

In 2008 the Blu-Ray Disc Association won the high-definition battle against Toshiba's HD DVD. Currently Blu-Ray is *the* standard for high-definition video. It is used by high-def movies, PlayStation 3 games, and for storing data, up to 50GB per disc, ten times the amount of a typical DVD-5 disc. The standard disc is 12cm (same size as a standard DVD or CD), is single-sided, and has a capacity of 50GB. The mini disc is 8cm, single-sided, and has a capacity of 15.6GB. Drive speeds range from 1x to 8x (with more undoubtedly on the way). 1x is equal to 36Mbps or 4.5MB/s. 8x would be eight times that core amount, which is 288Mbps or 36MB/s, which is superior to DVD write speeds. The reason you see read speeds in bits is because Blu-Ray players normally transfer data serially via SATA connections.

To play movies, games, or read the data from a Blu-Ray disc, the computer must have a compatible Blu-Ray drive. Currently, there are combo drives on the market that can read Blu-Ray discs (but not write to them, these are known as BD-ROMs), read/write DVDs, and read/write CDs.

Like CD and DVD drives, Blu-Ray drives for the PC are installed into a 5.25-inch bay in the computer case. However, Blu-Ray drives almost always have SATA connections. Keep this in mind if you upgrade a computer; the power supply needs an extra 15-pin SATA power connector, and the motherboard (or SATA card) needs to have one free SATA data port.

Cram Quiz

Answer these questions. The answers follow the last question. If you cannot answer these questions correctly, consider reading this section again until you can.

1. What does the x refer to in Compact Disc technology?

   O **A.** 150KB/s

   O **B.** 1.32MB/s

   O **C.** 133MB/s

   O **D.** 4.5MB/s

2. What type of interface does a DVD drive typically connect to?

   O **A.** PCMCIA

   O **B.** SATA

   O **C.** IDE

   O **D.** SCSI

3. What is the maximum capacity of a Blu-Ray disc?

    ○ **A.** 700MB

    ○ **B.** 4.7GB

    ○ **C.** 17GB

    ○ **D.** 50GB

4. If a user wanted to write information more than one time to a DVD, which type should you recommend? (Select all that apply.)

    ○ **A.** DVD-R

    ○ **B.** DVD–RW

    ○ **C.** DVD+RW

    ○ **D.** DVD+R

Cram Quiz Answers

1. **A.** The x in CD technology is equal to 150KB/s. A 1x drive can read or write 150KB/s, a 2x drive can read or write 300KB/s, and so on. 1.32MB/s is the 1x speed of a DVD. 133MB/s is the maximum data transfer rate of an Ultra ATA-7 connection, and 4.5MB/s is the 1x speed of a Blu-Ray disc.

2. **C.** DVD and CD drives typically connect to the motherboard by way of an IDE interface, but SATA interfaces are becoming more common.

3. **D.** Standard 12cm Blu-Ray discs have a maximum capacity of 50GB. A typical CD capacity is 700MB; 4.7GB is the capacity of the common DVD-5, and 17GB is the capacity of a DVD-18 (using both sides).

4. **B** and **C.** DVD–RW and DVD+RW are the ReWritable versions of DVDs. DVD-R and DVD+R are write-once formats.

Solid-State Storage Media

There are many types of solid-state media. Solid-state media by definition is media with no moving parts, based on the semiconductor. Most of these are implemented as large amounts of nonvolatile memory, known as flash memory and are located on a card or drive. Remember that *nonvolatile* means any data on the device is retained, even if the device is not receiving power. Examples of solid-state cards include SD cards and CompactFlash cards. Examples of solid-state drives include USB flash drives, internal SATA drives (that can take the place of a magnetic hard drive), and even PCIe drives (that are integrated into a PCIe card). In this section we focus on three types of solid-state flash media: USB flash drives, SD cards, and CompactFlash.

USB Flash Drives

The USB flash drive is probably the most familiar of all flash media. Also known as USB thumb drives, they are often retractable and can be carried on a keychain. Figure 6.6 shows an example of a USB flash drive connected to a laptop's USB port.

FIGURE 6.6 A typical USB flash drive in a laptop's USB Port

Notice that the USB flash drive is lit, indicating that it is connected to the laptop's USB port and ready to transfer data. In this scenario, the drive shows up as a volume within Windows Explorer, usually named Removable Disk. Connecting the drive is easy; just find an open USB port. But remember that you should safely remove hardware in the operating system before disconnecting the drive physically. If you don't, it can cause electrical irregularities that can damage the data on the drive. In Windows, you can either double-click the Safely Remove Hardware icon in the System Tray, or right-click it to bring up the Safely Remove Hardware window. From there click Stop to shut down power to the selected USB device. Then it can be safely removed from the physical USB port. The icon appears as a device with a green arrow above it pointing to the left and slightly down. Sometimes, if you right-click the icon and simply click Safely Remove Hardware, the device will be turned off, and the icon disappears. If your USB device has a light, make sure that light is off before physically removing the device.

ExamAlert

Remember to *safely remove* USB flash drives in the operating system before physically disconnecting them.

Tip

Sometimes, a USB or other flash-based solid-state device can't be removed with the Safely Remove Hardware option in Windows. If this happens, consider shutting down the computer before physically disconnecting the device to avoid data corruption or loss.

The advantages of a USB flash drive are obvious. For example, the drive in Figure 6.6 is an 8GB flash drive that costs in the neighborhood of $20. That is a good cost-to-MB ratio for an instantly rewritable media. It would take 2 standard DVD-RWs, or 10 standard CD-RWs, or 5,000 floppy disks to match that capacity. The best part is that no formatting is necessary, and data can simply be dragged and dropped to the drive, unlike CDs and DVDs that need to be burned. In addition, USB flash drives' read/write speed is comparable to DVD technology, averaging about 30MB/s reads and 15MB/s writes. Finally, it's *small*: it has a little footprint. What I used to carry around in a CD case is now on one flash drive on my keychain. Plus, newer flash drives are ranging all the way up to 64GB and beyond and have a much longer lifespan than just a few years ago. They can also be used to boot or install operating systems.

Let's talk about the type of memory used in this solid-state device: NAND flash memory is the core of a USB flash drive. This memory is broken up into blocks that are generally between 16KB and 512KB. Know that a USB flash drive's blocks can be written to only so many times before failures occur. With some flash drives, manufacturers estimate this at up to 1 million write/erase cycles, or 10 years of use. However, just like hard drives will never attain their maximum data transfer rate, it is doubtful that a flash drive will ever attain that maximum amount of write/erase cycles. In addition, the amount of years is subjective; it all depends on how often a user works with the flash drive. Basically, if you take the number given by the manufacturer and cut it in half, you should be in good shape, unless you are an extreme power user. Now back to NAND flash failures: Because this type of memory incurs a small amount of faults over time (as opposed to NOR flash, which should remain free of faults), a method known as Bad Block Management is implemented, which maintains a table of the faulty blocks within the USB flash device, making sure not to save data to those blocks. Blocks are broken down further into pages, which can be between 512 bytes and 4KB. Each page has error detection and correction information associated with it. All this is done to prolong the lifespan of devices using NAND memory.

Normally, USB flash drives are shipped in a formatted state, usually FAT32, possibly FAT16. This enables the drive to be accessed by just about any computer on the market and makes for easy repair of corrupted files with utilities such as ScanDisk. These drives can also be formatted as NTFS if the user wants. Sometimes NAND flash devices such as USB flash drives act up intermittently. Unless the card has failed completely, a quick reformat usually cures the flash drive of its woes. Just be sure to backup your data first! This method applies to other forms of solid-state NAND-based media.

Troubleshooting of these devices is not usually necessary, but you might see a couple of issues:

▶ Sometimes USB flash drives and other solid-state media can conflict with each other, prompting you to change the drive letter of one or more devices within Disk Management.

▶ In some cases, Windows XP SP2 will not "see" your device no matter what you do. Microsoft has released a hotfix for these types of USB controller issues. See article 892050 at http://support.microsoft.com for the download. Microsoft also has a USB Flash Drive Manager for Windows XP to aid in backing up and restoring information to and from USB flash drives.

In general, make sure that your operating system has the latest service pack and updates installed. For more information on USB, see Chapter 12, "Video, Audio, and Peripherals."

Some USB flash drives are preloaded with software that can restore data and possibly secure transferred data. The only problem with USB flash drives is that although they are small, they can't fit inside most digital cameras, cell phones, PDAs, and other hand-held devices. For that, you need something even smaller: Enter the SD card.

Secure Digital Cards

Secure Digital cards (SD cards), for the most part, are technically the same type of device as a USB flash drive. They are solid-state, use NAND memory, and have most of the same pros and cons as a USB flash drive. The difference is the form factor of the device and because of this, the usages. Instead of connecting an SD card to a USB port, it slides into a memory card reader. There are specialized memory card readers for SD cards only, and other readers that can read multiple formats of cards. Like USB flash drives, be sure to use the Safely Remove icon in Windows before physically removing the SD card. There are three sizes of SD cards: standard, miniSD, and microSD, each smaller than the last. You can still find many standard size SD cards used in cameras and some other devices but note that most cell phones and PDAs use microSD cards for additional memory. Figure 6.7 shows a full-size SD card and a microSD card. Figure 6.8 shows the standard SD card inserted into a laptop's memory card reader slot. Note that this slot can accommodate SD cards or smaller but nothing bigger than an SD card.

FIGURE 6.7   A typical microSD card (left) and a standard SD card (right)

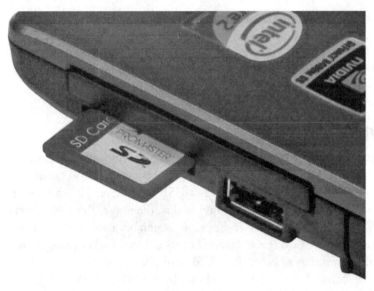

FIGURE 6.8   A standard SD card inserted in a laptop's Memory Card Reader.

Standard SD cards have capacities up to 4GB. High-capacity (SDHC) cards range up to 32GB. An upcoming specification, eXtended Capacity (SDXC), will supposedly have a maximum capacity of 2TB. When it comes to data transfer rate, SD cards are divided into three different classes: SD Class 2, 4, and 6, each with a different range of speeds. Class 6 is the fastest and ranges between 6 and 45MB/s. Some SD cards, like the one in Figure 6.7, have a write-protect tab within the notch on the left side of the card. Sliding the tab down "locks" the card so that it can be read from but not written to.

A derivative of SD is the Secure Digital Input Output (SDIO) card. This takes the capabilities of an SD card and merges them with the functionality of an I/O device. Some PDAs use this technology to integrate GPS, WLAN, Bluetooth, and many other types of radio technologies. SDIO cards do not work in standard SD card slots, but standard SD cards can be read in SDIO slots.

> **Note**
>
> Don't confuse an SDIO card with a SIM (Subscriber Identity Module) card. A SIM card identifies the user/subscriber of a phone or PDA and allows the telecommunications company to lock the phone to that SIM card. The SIM is a slightly different size than the SD and SDIO cards.

CompactFlash Cards

CompactFlash (CF) is another kind of solid-state memory that can be used in a variety of formats, the most common of which is the CompactFlash card. These are categorized as either Type I cards that are 3.3-mm thick and Type II cards that are 5-mm thick. These cards are larger than SD cards and are often used in hand-held computers, high-end cameras (Type I) and for Microdrives (Type II).

Common capacities for CF cards max out at about 32GB; however, the technology can go as high as 137GB. The cards are formatted by the manufacturer as either FAT32 or FAT, in the same manner as USB flash drives and SD cards. Like USB flash drives and SD cards, CF cards have a built-in ATA controller that makes them appear as a hard drive to the operating system; they show up as a volume within Windows Explorer. In the past CompactFlash cards used NOR memory but are typically NAND-based nowadays, like USB flash drives and SD cards. In general, CompactFlash has a lot of the same characteristics as SD cards. For example the data transfer rate ranges from 6 to 45MB/s. CF speeds have increased with each new version, starting with the original CF and moving on to CF High Speed, CF 3.0, and CF 4.0.

CompactFlash cards have taken on a new meaning as well; you can find various CF cards that have built-in Ethernet, WLAN, Bluetooth, GPS, and other technologies. The CF card is identical to a PC card from an electrical standpoint, so you see the same types of technologies in a CF card as you would in a PC card. You can use a CF card directly within a PCMCIA slot with the right adapter. For more information on PC cards and PCMCIA, see Chapter 11, "Laptops."

Cram Quiz

Answer these questions. The answers follow the last question. If you cannot answer these questions correctly, consider reading this section again until you can.

1. What should you do before physically removing a USB flash drive? (Select the best answer.)

   ○ **A.** Turn it off.

   ○ **B.** Shut down Windows.

   ○ **C.** Format the drive.

   ○ **D.** Use the Safely Remove icon.

2. How is most solid-state media formatted by the manufacturer?

   ○ **A.** As FAT32

   ○ **B.** As NTFS

   ○ **C.** As FAT16

   ○ **D.** As FAT12

3. What is the main difference between SD and SDIO?

   ○ **A.** SD cards are faster.

   ○ **B.** SDIO cards incorporate input/output functionality.

   ○ **C.** SD cards incorporate input/output functionality.

   ○ **D.** SDIO cards can identify a user's cell phone.

4. What kind of controller is built into a CF card?

   ○ **A.** SATA

   ○ **B.** IDE

   ○ **C.** ATA

   ○ **D.** SCSI

Cram Quiz Answers

1. **D**. In Windows you can either double-click the Safely Remove Hardware icon in the System Tray or right-click it to bring up the Safely Remove Hardware window. From there click Stop to shut down power to the device. Shutting off Windows is another possibility but not the best answer because it is time consuming.

2. **A**. FAT32 is the most common file system used on solid-state media such as USB flash drives, SD cards, and CF cards. FAT16 is another possibility but less common. Users have the option to reformat most of these devices as NTFS if they want.

3. **B**. SDIO cards integrate I/O functionality into a standard SD card. They are basically the same speed as SD cards. Answer D is referring to SIM cards, not SDIO cards.

4. **C**. An ATA controller is built into the CF card and many other solid-state technologies.

Additional Reading and Resources

Additional A+ resources: http://www.davidlprowse.com/aplus.

Mueller, Scott. *Upgrading and Repairing PCs*. Que.

CHAPTER 7

Installing and Upgrading Windows

This chapter covers the following A+ exam topics:

▶ Installing and Upgrading to Windows 7

▶ Installing and Upgrading to Windows Vista

▶ Installing and Upgrading to Windows XP

You can find a master list of A+ exam topics in the "Introduction."

This chapter covers CompTIA A+ 220-701 objectives 3.1 and 3.3.

Now that we have discussed the "guts" of the computer, including the motherboard, CPU, RAM, and power supplies, it's time to talk about installing operating systems. Our focus is on Windows 7 and Windows Vista, but we also discuss Windows XP and throw in little bits of Windows 2000 Professional here and there. For the 2011 updated objectives of the CompTIA 220-701 and 220-702 A+ exams, you need to know how to:

▶ Install Windows 7

▶ Install Windows Vista

▶ Install Windows XP

▶ Upgrade to Windows 7 from Windows Vista

▶ Upgrade to Windows Vista from Windows XP or Windows 2000

▶ Upgrade to Windows XP from Windows 2000

▶ Troubleshoot Windows Vista/XP installations and upgrades

> **Note**
>
> I recommend that you attempt to get your hands on a full-version copy of Windows 7 and Vista (Ultimate is preferred for both of them) and Windows XP (Professional is preferred), and a test computer to run clean installations of the operating systems, and running an upgrade from XP to Vista, as well as Vista to Win7. If you have been building a computer as you progress through this book, install to that one. This hands-on approach can help you to better visualize how operating system installs and upgrades perform.

I've broken this chapter into three main sections so that we can first focus on everything to do with Win7, then Vista, and finally XP. Installations of Windows 2000 are rare due to the fact that the OS is a decade old, so there are no step-by-step instructions on how to install it in this chapter. But have no fear, the installation of Windows XP is similar to Windows 2000; there are just a few more steps in Windows XP. The CompTIA A+ objectives mention Windows 2000, but it is doubtful that you will get many questions on the exam concerning that operating system. What I've done is to focus on Win7 first, then Vista, then XP, and where necessary I added notes about Windows 2000. Let's start by talking about how to install and upgrade Windows 7.

Installing and Upgrading to Windows 7

Before you can install Windows 7 or upgrade to it, you first need to decide which version of it you will use. Then, you should check the computer's hardware to make sure it is compatible with Windows 7. Next, you need to decide on an installation method: from DVD, as an image, or over the network. Finally, start the installation. New installations are known as "clean" installs; the other option is to upgrade. Upgrades to Windows 7 can be done directly from Windows Vista, but require more effort from Windows XP or 2000; we will cover more about upgrades to Windows 7 later in this chapter.

Windows 7 Versions

Windows 7 is an entire line of Microsoft operating systems designed for desktop PCs and laptops. Within the Windows 7 group are the versions Starter, Home Premium, Professional, and Ultimate. Starter is only available through original equipment manufacturers (OEMs), and is common among laptops. In addition, Starter is only available in a 32-bit version. However, the other versions are all available in 64-bit and 32-bit versions. In Table 7.1, the check marks indicate the components that are included in these various versions of Win7. We talk more about these components in Chapter 8, "Configuring Windows."

TABLE 7.1 **Comparison of Windows 7 Versions**

Component	Starter	Home Premium	Professional	Ultimate
Windows XP Mode	—	—	✓	✓
Domain Join	—	—	✓	✓
Backup to home or business network	—	—	✓	✓
BitLocker Encryption	—	—	—	✓

Note

There is an additional version of Win7 called Windows 7 Enterprise (not sold through retail or OEM channels), which is not covered on the exam.

Windows 7 Minimum Requirements and Compatibility

When you decide on the version of Win7 you want to use, and before installing that operating system, you should learn as much as you can about the computer you plan to install to. Components in a computer should meet Windows 7 minimum requirements and should be listed on Microsoft's website as compatible with Windows 7. Table 7.2 shows the minimum hardware requirements for Windows 7.

TABLE 7.2 **Windows 7 Minimum Requirements**

Component	Requirement
Processor	1 GHz
RAM	1 GB (32-bit) or 2 GB (64-bit)
Free disk space	16 GB (32-bit) or 20 GB (64-bit)
Video	DirectX 9 with WDDM 1.0 or higher driver
Other	DVD-ROM drive

ExamAlert

Memorize the *minimum* requirements for Windows 7.

You can use several websites and system analysis tools to check whether a system's hardware will be compatible with Windows 7. If you check a computer that already has an operating system installed, use the following tools:

▶ **Windows Compatibility Center:**
http://www.microsoft.com/windows/compatibility/

▶ **Windows Logo'd Products List:**
http://winqual.microsoft.com/HCL/Default.aspx?m=7. You can also use this site to check any hardware that you haven't installed yet that you plan on using later on.

▶**System Information:** The Windows System Information tool can be accessed by opening the Run prompt and typing `msinfo32.exe`.

▶ **Belarc Advisor:** Currently a free download, this program can be found at http://www.belarc.com/free_download.html. To run the program subsequently after installation, just access **Start > All Programs > Belarc Advisor**.

For computers without an installed operating system, consider using self-booting diagnostic programs like the following:

▶ **PC Diagnostic tools:** http://www.pc-diagnostics.com

▶ **#1-TuffTEST:** http://www.tufftest.com/

▶ **PC Check:** http://www.eurosoft-uk.com

You might also opt to make use of the Microsoft Assessment and Planning (MAP) toolkit, one of Microsoft's Solution Accelerators. This kit takes inventory of most currently deployed Microsoft operating systems and server software, analyzes the inventory, and gives in-depth reports on the assessment and analysis of those OSes and software. It is designed to simplify the planning process for IT infrastructures with multiple platform scenarios. The kit can be downloaded from the following link: http://technet.microsoft.com/en-us/library/bb977556.aspx.

Windows 7 Installation Methods

There are several types of installation methods for Windows operating systems. They include

- **Local installation from DVD-ROM:** Installation by DVD-ROM is the most common. A "local" installation is the default type. It means that you insert the DVD-ROM into the DVD-ROM drive of the computer you are sitting at, known as the local computer. When you sit at the computer and answer all the questions it asks you, it is known as an "Attended Installation;" you are attending to the computer as the install progresses. The steps for this type of installation are listed later in this chapter, in the next section titled "Installing Windows 7."

- **Network installation:** You can install Windows over the network in a variety of ways. To automate the process, Windows 7 can be installed from a server automatically, using either Windows Deployment Services, which can be installed on Windows Server 2008/2003, or the Remote Installation Services (RIS) program, which can be installed on Windows Server 2003 and Windows 2000 Server. These two server-based programs work with the Windows System Image Manager program in Win7. This program can be used to create an answer file that is used during an Unattended Installation. The answer file provides the responses needed for the installation, with no user intervention. In Windows 7, there is a single XML-based answer file called Unattend.xml.

> **Note**
>
> The Windows System Image Manager (SIM) for Win7 is part of the Windows Automated Installation Kit (AIK), which can be downloaded from www.microsoft.com, just search for "Windows Automated Installation Kit (AIK)." For detailed instructions on how to use SIM see the following link: http://technet.microsoft.com/en-us/library/dd744394(WS.10).aspx. For general information about Windows 7 deployment, see the following link: http://technet.microsoft.com/en-us/library/dd744519 (WS.10).aspx

- **Disk image:** Windows can also be installed by cloning the entire disk image of another installation. This can be done by using programs like Acronis True Image or Norton Ghost. When cloning a disk image, both computers need to be identical, or as close to identical as possible. The hard disk of the target for a cloned installation must be at least as large as the original system. To avoid Security Identifier (SID) conflicts, use the Sysprep utility. The Sysprep utility for Windows 7 is installed with the operating system and can be found by navigating to: C:\Windows\System32\Sysprep. Sysprep uses an answer file created with the System Image Manager (SIM). It creates a unique SID and makes other changes as needed to the network configuration of the system.

▶ **Installing from a recovery disc:** Computers with Windows preinstalled use a recovery disc, hidden partition, or both. This disc and/or partition contains a factory image of Windows. The purpose of this is to give users the ability to return their computer back to the state when it was first received. This means that the system partition (usually the C: drive) will be formatted, and re-imaged with Windows. This works well in a two partition system, in which the operating system is on C: and data is stored on D: or another drive letter. In this scenario, if the operating system fails and cannot be repaired, the computer can be returned to its original "factory" state, but the data won't be compromised. Whenever buying a computer from a company such as HP, Dell, and so on, make sure that they offer some kind of recovery disc, or other recovery option.

> **Note**
>
> Although it's not covered on the exam, it's also possible to install Windows 7 from a USB flash drive. This is done in essentially the same manner as installing from DVD; however, you need to partition and format the USB drive, xcopy the contents of the DVD to the flash drive, and set the BIOS to boot from USB.

> **ExamAlert**
>
> Know the difference between a local, network, disk image, and recovery disc installation.

Installing Windows 7

Now that you have decided on the version of Win7 to use and have verified compatibility of hardware, it's time to install. The Windows 7 installation is more simplified than earlier versions of Windows. This section covers the steps involved in a "clean" local installation of Win7. Keep in mind that this type of installation will remove any data currently stored on the computer's hard drive. The following steps detail an installation of Windows 7 Ultimate.

Step 1. Begin the installation from the DVD-ROM. There are two methods to perform a clean install of Windows 7 from DVD:

▶ Install Windows 7 by running the Setup program from within the current version of Windows. (This is the recommended method.) Insert the Windows 7 DVD. The disc most likely autoruns and you see a setup screen. Otherwise, just go to the DVD drive in Windows Explorer and double-click the setup.exe file to start the installation.

▶ Boot the computer from the Windows 7 DVD. This is necessary if no operating system exists on the computer. If you choose this option, do the following:

1. Make sure the DVD drive is configured as the first boot device in the system BIOS.

2. Insert the Windows 7 DVD into the system's DVD drive. (If the drive won't open while in the BIOS, insert the disc immediately after saving the BIOS during the next step.)

3. Save the BIOS and restart the system.

4. The DVD should boot automatically and start the installation, but if you are prompted to boot from the DVD, press any key. There is only a small window of time for this, approximately 5 seconds. This prompt is a protective measure; if you get the prompt, it means that there is data of some sort on the drive. Startup of the installation might take a minute or two; then you see a GUI-based window asking for information. (There is no text portion.) Setup will load Windows files for several minutes, and start the installation within the Windows GUI.

Step 2. Input the Language to install, Time and currency format, and Keyboard or input method. At this time there is also an option to learn more about the installation by clicking the What to know before installing windows link. After you input your settings for step 2, you must click Next, and then on the next screen click Install now. A few minutes or so will pass as files are copied and the installation is prepared.

Step 3. Accept the license terms.

Step 4. Select whether you are doing a custom install, which includes a clean installation or an upgrade. (Within these steps we are doing a clean installation.) If you install to a computer with no operating system, the Upgrade option will be disabled. For this exercise we are doing a clean installation so we will select Custom (advanced).

Step 5. Select where to install Windows 7. From here you can select the drive and administer partitions as you see fit. The proper disk preparation order when installing any operating system is to partition the drive, format the partition (or partitions), and start the installation (copy files). For more information on partitioning the drive during the installation process, see the section titled "Creating Partitions During a Windows Vista Installation" later in this chapter. (The steps to create partitions during the install of Windows 7 are similar to Windows Vista). If necessary, you can also load third-party drivers for the media (hard drive) to be installed to by clicking on Load Driver. These might be drivers for SATA or SCSI controllers, or other special hard disk controllers. These drivers can come from floppy disk, CD, DVD, or USB flash drive. Microsoft recommends that before you install, you check if the devices you want to use are listed at the Windows Compatibility Center: http://www.microsoft.com/windows/compatibility/ or at the Windows Logo'd Products List: http://winqual.microsoft.com/HCL. If you click on Load Driver and cannot supply a proper driver for Windows 7, or the computer cannot read the media in which the driver is stored, you need to exit the installation program. When you finish, click Next, and the system automatically copies files from the DVD, expands those files, installs features and updates, and completes the installation. The system might need to restart several times during this installation process (for example, after it installs updates and when it completes the installation), but you can let the Windows 7 installation work its magic until you get to the next step.

Step 6. Type a user name and a computer name.

Step 7. Type a password, confirm it, and type a password hint.

Step 8. Enter the Product key and decide whether to automatically activate Windows (can be delayed up to 30 days).

Step 9. Configure Windows Update to Use Recommended Settings, Install important Updates Only, or Ask Me Later. For more information on Windows Update see Chapter 9, "Maintaining Windows."

Step 10. Set the time zone, time, and date.

Step 11. Set the computer's location: home, work, or public network. (This step may not be visible if the computer is not connected to a network.)

Now it's time to start Windows. Windows 7 checks the computer's performance (which might take a while), prepares the desktop, and then logs you in. Afterwards, you can continue with initial tasks such as connecting to the Internet or transferring files and settings.

Upgrading to Windows 7

Upgrades are done in essentially the same manner as clean installs. The difference is that all the settings, applications, and user files will ultimately be kept in place *if* the upgrade is successful. It is recommended that those files and settings are backed up previous to the upgrade. However, before starting the upgrade, you should first check to see if your computer (and operating system) is compatible and if it will survive the process. Refer to Table 7.2 for the Windows 7 minimum requirements. You can also use the following utilities and websites to do this:

▶ **Windows Upgrade Advisor:** This is a website that is accessed by clicking on the Check compatibility online button when you first insert the Windows 7 DVD. Of course, the computer that you want to upgrade needs to have Internet access. You can also download the Windows 7 Upgrade Advisor from Microsoft's website.

▶ **Windows Compatibility Center:** http://www.microsoft.com/windows/compatibility/

▶ **Windows 7 Logo'd Products List:**
http://winqual.microsoft.com/HCL/Default.aspx?m=7

Only Windows Vista can be upgraded directly to Windows 7. To upgrade Windows Vista to Windows 7, make sure that service pack 1 or 2 is installed to Vista prior to the upgrade, insert the DVD, and select the Upgrade option. The steps to complete the upgrade are similar to the clean installation steps.

Windows Vista Home Basic and Home Premium versions can be upgraded to Windows 7 Home Premium. Windows Vista Business can be upgraded to Windows 7 Professional and Ultimate. Windows Vista Ultimate can only be upgraded to Windows 7 Ultimate. Any other combinations of upgrades from Vista to Win7 would require a Custom/advanced install, and would require the user to backup all data prior to the upgrade, and reinstall any applications after the upgrade is complete. To upgrade XP or 2000 to Windows 7, a user would again have to back up all files, then start the install, select Custom/advanced, and later reinstall any applications necessary and restore data files. Microsoft recommends the program Windows Easy Transfer for the backup and restoration of files. 32-bit versions of Windows cannot be directly upgraded to 64-bit versions. 32-bit and 64-bit versions of Windows 7 can be installed to a computer with a 64-bit processor. However, 32-bit processors will only accept 32-bit versions of Windows 7.

Verifying and Troubleshooting Windows 7 Installations

When you complete the clean installation or upgrade, verify that your installation has gone smoothly by testing it. For example, attempt to navigate through Windows, access administrative functions, connect to the Internet, and so on.

If you have confirmed that Windows is working normally, update the system. Install the latest service pack and additional updates as necessary. It is possible that the service pack was included on your installation media, but if not, download it and install it before going any further. Then, download any other updates that are necessary utilizing the Windows Update feature. More information about service packs and updates can be found in Chapter 9, "Maintaining Windows."

Installations usually go smoothly, but not always. If an installation fails for any reason, or if the installation completed but Windows doesn't seem to be behaving properly, consider reviewing the log files to find out more about the problem and why it occurred. Table 7.3 describes the important log files you should know and their locations.

TABLE 7.3   **Windows 7 Setup Log Files and Locations**

Log file location	Description
$windows.~bt\Sources\Panther	Log location before Setup can access the drive
$windows.~bt\Sources\Rollback	Log location when Setup rolls back in the event of a fatal error
%WINDIR%\Panther	Log location of Setup actions after disk configuration
%WINDIR%\Panther\setuperr.log	Contains information about setup errors during the installation. Start with this log file when troubleshooting. A file size of 0 bytes indicates no errors during installation.
%WINDIR%\Panther\setupact.log	Contains information about setup actions during the installation.
%WINDIR%\Inf\Setupapi*.log	Used to log Plug and Play device installations
%WINDIR%\Panther\Setup.etl	Location of Windows Setup performance events
%WINDIR%\Memory.dmp	Location of memory dump to use for bug checks

Log file location	Description
%WINDIR%\Minidump*.dmp	Location of mini memory dumps to use for bug checks
%WINDIR%\System32\Sysprep\ Panther	Location of logs generated by Sysprep

In the above table you will note the variable directory called %WINDIR%. By default, the name of this folder in Windows 7 will be "Windows." %WINDIR% is the new name of the variable previously called %systemroot%. Also, $windows.~bt is a temporary boot folder created during setup. It remains if the installation was not successful, allowing you to analyze the log files, but should be automatically deleted when the installation completes properly.

Windows 7, Vista, as well as Server 2008, include the capability to review Setup events within the Event Viewer, or by way of a script. See the following link for details: http://technet.microsoft.com/en-us/library/dd744583(WS.10).aspx.

If the system won't start, you can still view these files. However, this depends on the type of installation and how far the installation got. If it was a clean installation, you should boot to the Windows 7 DVD; select Repair your computer, then access the System Recovery Options menu, and select the Command Prompt. If it was an upgrade that didn't get far, and if Windows Vista/XP/2000 was previously installed on an NTFS drive, you can boot to the System Recovery Options in Vista, or the Recovery Console from a Windows XP or 2000 CD and view the log files from there. For more information about System Recovery Options (Win7/Vista), and the Recovery Console (XP/2000), see Chapter 10, "Troubleshooting Windows."

If you cannot start the clean installation or upgrade, check the following:

▶ **Processor speed and memory size:** Verify that your computer meets the minimum requirements for Windows 7. Refer to Table 7.2 for more information. Make sure you are installing the correct type (32-bit or 64-bit) and version of Windows 7.

▶ **Windows type and version:** Make sure you are installing the correct type (32-bit or 64-bit) and version of Windows 7 (Starter, Home Premium, and so on...).

▶ **Free disk space:** You need 16 GB/20 GB free for Windows 7 (for 32-bit and 64-bit editions respectively); the more space available, the better.

▶ **Hardware conflicts or hardware issues:** Use the Device Manager to ensure that all hardware works correctly before you start an upgrade.

▶ **Installation media:** Make sure that your DVD-ROM media is not scratched or damaged in any way. Verify that it is genuine Microsoft software and that you have the right type of media for your installation, for example, Windows 7 Full Version License or Upgrade DVD.

Cram Quiz

Answer these questions. The answers follow the last question. If you cannot answer these questions correctly, consider reading this section again until you can.

1. What is the minimum RAM requirement for Windows 7?
   - ○ **A.** 1 GB
   - ○ **B.** 256 MB
   - ○ **C.** 1536 MB
   - ○ **D.** 768 MB

2. Which log file contains information regarding Windows 7 Setup performance events?
   - ○ **A.** Setupapi*.log
   - ○ **B.** Setupact.log
   - ○ **C.** Setup.etl
   - ○ **D.** Event Viewer

3. Where can you go to find out if your current operating system can be upgraded to Windows 7?
   - ○ **A.** MSKB
   - ○ **B.** Windows Upgrade Advisor
   - ○ **C.** HAL
   - ○ **D.** Belarc Advisor

4. Which versions of Windows 7 have the capability to backup to a home or business network? (Select the best two answers.)
   - ○ **A.** Starter
   - ○ **B.** Home Premium
   - ○ **C.** Professional
   - ○ **D.** Ultimate

5. What is the minimum hard drive requirement for Windows 7?

- ○ **A.** 16 GB free space
- ○ **B.** 15 GB partition
- ○ **C.** 25 GB free space
- ○ **D.** 16 GB partition

Cram Quiz Answers

1. A. The minimum RAM requirement for Windows 7 is 1 GB for 32-bit versions, 2 GB for 64-bit versions

2. C. Setup.etl contains information regarding Windows 7 Setup performance events. Setupapi*.log is used for events about Windows 7 Plug and Play device installations. Setupact.log is a Windows Vista log file that contains information regarding *actions* during installation. The Event Viewer is an application, not a file.

3. B. The Windows Upgrade Advisor can tell you if your current operating system can be upgraded to Win7. This, and other tools like it, are located at www.microsoft.com, not at the MSKB (http://support.microsoft.com). The HAL is a file in Windows; it stands for hardware abstraction layer. Belarc Advisor is a third-party offering that analyzes your computer but does not determine whether it can be upgraded.

4. C and **D.** Windows 7 Professional and Ultimate include the capability to backup to a home or business network easily.

5. A. Windows 7 (32-bit) requires a minimum 16 GB of free space. 64-bit versions require 20 GB.

Installing and Upgrading to Windows Vista

Before you can install Windows Vista or upgrade to it, you first need to decide which version of Vista you will use. Then, you should check the computer's hardware to make sure it is compatible with Windows Vista. Next, you need to decide on an installation method: from DVD, CD, as an image, or over the network. Finally, start the installation. New installations are known as "clean" installs; the other option is to upgrade from Windows XP or 2000.

Windows Vista Versions

Windows Vista is an entire line of Microsoft operating systems designed for desktop PCs and laptops. Vista was released over a span of several months during the end of 2006 and beginning of 2007, culminating in a worldwide release on January 30, 2007. Within the Windows Vista group are the versions Home Basic, Home Premium, Business, and Ultimate, available in 64-bit and 32-bit versions. In Table 7.4, the check marks indicate the components that are included in these various versions of Vista. We talk more about these components in Chapter 8, "Configuring Windows."

TABLE 7.4 **Comparison of Windows Vista Versions**

Component	Home Basic	Home Premium	Business	Ultimate
Windows Aero	—	✓	✓	✓
Share Documents	—	✓	✓	✓
Media Center Functionality	—	✓	—	✓
Windows Complete PC Backup	—	—	✓	✓
Remote Desktop Connection	—	—	✓	✓
BitLocker Encryption	—	—	—	✓

> **Note**
>
> As you can see, Home Basic is just that: basic, with none of the bells and whistles of the other versions. The A+ exams focus on the other three versions in Table 7.4: Vista Home Premium, Business, and Ultimate.

> **Note**
>
> There are two additional versions of Vista including Vista Starter (sold in underdeveloped technology markets), and Vista Enterprise (not sold through retail or OEM channels), which are not covered on the exam.

> **ExamAlert**
>
> Know the main differences between the Vista editions Home Premium, Business, and Ultimate for the exam.

Windows Vista Minimum Requirements and Compatibility

When you decide on the version of Vista you want to use, and before installing that operating system, you should learn as much as you can about the computer you plan to install to. Components in a computer should meet Windows Vista's minimum requirements and should be listed on Microsoft's website as compatible with Vista. Table 7.5 shows the minimum hardware requirements for Windows Vista.

TABLE 7.5 **Windows Vista Minimum Requirements**

Component	Requirement
Processor	800MHz
RAM	512MB
Free disk space	15GB (20GB partition)
Other	DVD-ROM or CD-ROM drive

> **Note**
>
> The above specs are the *minimum* requirements. Microsoft *recommends* a 1GHz Processor for all versions of Vista and 1GB of RAM plus a 40GB HDD for Vista Home Premium/Business/Ultimate.

> **ExamAlert**
>
> Memorize the *minimum* requirements for Windows Vista.

You can use several websites and system analysis tools to check whether a system's hardware will be compatible with Windows Vista. If you check a computer that already has an operating system installed, use the following tools:

- **Windows Vista Compatibility Center:**
  http://www.microsoft.com/windows/compatibility/windows-vista/

- **Windows Vista Logo'd Products List:**
  http://winqual.microsoft.com/HCL/Default.aspx?m=v. You can also use this site to check any hardware that you haven't installed yet.

- **System Information:** The Windows System Information tool can be accessed by opening the Run prompt and typing `msinfo32.exe`.

- **Belarc Advisor:** Currently a free download, this program can be found at http://www.belarc.com/free_download.html. It's extremely quick and painless; all you need to do is double-click the .exe file when the download is complete. It automatically installs, looks for updates, and creates a profile of your computer that runs in a browser window. Here you can find all the hardware- (and software)-related information on one screen; it also gives you system security status. To run the program subsequently, just access Start > All Programs > Belarc Advisor.

For computers without an installed operating system, consider using self-booting diagnostic programs like the following:

- **PC Diagnostic tools:** http://www.pc-diagnostics.com

- **#1-TuffTEST:** http://www.tufftest.com/

- **PC Check:** http://www.eurosoft-uk.com

Note

The Windows Vista DVD has a Check compatibility online option, but this is meant more for upgrades, as opposed to clean installations.

Windows Vista Installation Methods

There are several types of installation methods for Windows operating systems. They include:

- ▶ **Local installation from DVD-ROM:** Installation by DVD-ROM is the most common. A "local" installation is the default type. It means that you insert the DVD-ROM into the DVD-ROM drive of the computer you are sitting at, known as the local computer. When you sit at the computer and answer all the questions it asks you, it is known as an "Attended Installation;" you are attending to the computer as the install progresses. The steps for this type of installation are listed later in this chapter, in the next section titled "Installing Windows Vista."

- ▶ **Local installation from CD-ROM:** Microsoft recommends that the DVD-ROM be used for installations of Windows Vista; however, you can order a CD-ROM version, if you can provide proof of purchase. To do so, visit this site: http://www.microsoft.com/windowsvista/1033/ordermedia/default.mspx. Keep in mind that unattended installations of Vista from CD-ROM are not possible because the Vista files span multiple CDs.

- ▶ **Network installation:** You can install Windows over the network in a variety of ways. To automate the process, Windows Vista can be installed from a server automatically, using either Windows Deployment Services, which can be installed on Windows Server 2008/2003, or the Remote Installation Services (RIS) program, which can be installed on Windows Server 2003 and Windows 2000 Server. These two server-based programs work with the Windows System Image Manager program in Vista. This program can be used to create an answer file that is used during an Unattended Installation. The answer file provides the responses needed for the installation, with no user intervention. In Windows Vista, there is a single XML-based answer file called Unattend.xml.

> **Note**
>
> The Windows System Image Manager (SIM) for Vista is part of the Windows Automated Installation Kit (AIK), which can be downloaded from www.microsoft.com, just search for "Windows Automated Installation Kit (AIK)." For a free CBT tutorial on how to use WSIM, search the Microsoft TechNet (http://technet.microsoft.com) for: "Windows Vista Virtual Lab Express: Windows System Image Manager Overview."

▶ **Disk image**: Windows can also be installed by cloning the entire disk image of another installation. This can be done by using programs like Acronis True Image or Norton Ghost. When cloning a disk image, both computers need to be identical, or as close to identical as possible. The hard disk of the target for a cloned installation must be at least as large as the original system. To avoid Security Identifier (SID) conflicts, use the Sysprep utility. The Sysprep utility for Windows Vista is installed with the operating system and can be found by navigating to: C:\Windows\System32\Sysprep. Sysprep uses an answer file created with the System Image Manager (SIM). It creates a unique SID and makes other changes as needed to the network configuration of the system.

▶ **Installing from a recovery disc:** Computers with Windows preinstalled use a recovery disc (DVD or CD), hidden partition, or both. This disc and/or partition contains a factory image of Windows. The purpose of this is to give users the ability to return their computer back to the state when it was first received. This means that the system partition (usually the C: drive) will be formatted, and re-imaged with Windows. This works well in a two partition system, in which the operating system is on C: and data is stored on D: or another drive letter. In this scenario, if the operating system fails and cannot be repaired, the computer can be returned to its original "factory" state, but the data won't be compromised. Whenever buying a computer from a company such as HP, Dell, and so on, make sure that they offer some kind of recovery disc.

Note

Although it's not covered on the exam, it's also possible to install Windows Vista from a USB flash drive. This is done in essentially the same manner as installing from DVD; however, you need to partition and format the USB drive, xcopy the contents of the DVD to the flash drive, and set the BIOS to boot from USB.

Exam Alert

Know the difference between a local, network, disk image, and recovery disc installation.

Installing Windows Vista

Now that you have decided on the version of Vista to use and have verified compatibility of hardware, it's time to install. The Windows Vista installation is more simplified than earlier versions of Windows. This section covers the steps involved in a "clean" local installation of Vista.

Step 1. Begin the installation from the DVD-ROM. There are two methods to perform a clean install of Windows Vista from DVD:

> ▶ Install Windows Vista by running the Setup program from within the current version of Windows. (This is the recommended method.) Insert the Windows Vista DVD. The disc most likely autoruns and you see the setup screen shown in Figure 7.1. Otherwise, just go to the DVD drive in Windows Explorer and double-click the setup.exe file to start the installation.

FIGURE 7.1 **Windows Vista Installation Screen**

> ▶ Boot the computer from the Windows Vista DVD. This is necessary if no operating system exists on the computer. If you choose this option, do the following:
>
> 1. Make sure the DVD drive is configured as the first boot device in the system BIOS.
>
> 2. Insert the Windows Vista DVD into the system's DVD drive. (If the drive won't open while in the BIOS, insert the disc immediately after saving the BIOS.)
>
> 3. Save the BIOS and restart the system.

    4. The DVD should boot automatically and start the installation, but if you are prompted to boot from the DVD, press any key. There is only a small window of time for this, approximately 5 seconds. This prompt is a protective measure; if you get the prompt, it means that there is data of some sort on the drive. Startup of the installation might take a minute; then you see a GUI-based window asking for information. (There is no text portion.)

Step 2. Input the Language to install, Time and currency format, and Keyboard or input method. At this time there is also an option to learn more about the installation by clicking the What to know before installing windows link. After you input your settings for step 2, you must click Next, and then on the next screen click Install now.

Step 3. Enter the Product key and decide whether to automatically activate Windows (can be delayed up to 30 days).

Step 4. Accept the license terms.

Step 5. Select whether you are doing a custom install, which includes a clean installation or an upgrade. (Within these steps we are doing a clean installation.) If you install to a computer with no operating system, the Upgrade option will be disabled.

Step 6. Select where to install Windows Vista. From here you can select the drive and administer partitions as you see fit. The proper disk preparation order when installing any operating system is to partition the drive, format the partition (or partitions), and start the installation (copy files). For more information on partitioning the drive during the installation process, see the next section titled "Creating Partitions During a Windows Vista Installation." If necessary, you can also load third-party drivers for the media (hard drive) to be installed to by clicking on Load Driver. These might be drivers for SATA or SCSI controllers, or other special hard disk controllers. These drivers can come from floppy disk, CD, DVD, or USB flash drive. Microsoft recommends that before you install, you check if the devices you want to use are listed at the Windows Vista Compatibility Center: http://www.microsoft.com/windows/compatibility/ or at the Windows Logo'd Products List: http://winqual.microsoft.com/HCL/Default.aspx?m=v. If you click on Load Driver and cannot supply a proper driver for Windows Vista, or the computer cannot read the media in which the driver is stored, you need to exit the installation program. When you finish, click Next, and the system automatically copies files from the DVD, expands those files, installs features and updates, and completes the installation. The system might need to restart several times during this installation process (for example, after it installs updates and when it completes the installation), but you can let the Vista installation work its magic until you get to the next step.

Step 7. Select a username, password, and picture.

Step 8. Select a computer name and desktop background.

Step 9. Configure Windows Update to Use Recommended Settings, Install important Updates Only, or Ask Me Later. For more information on Windows Update see Chapter 9, "Maintaining Windows."

Step 10. Set the time zone, time, and date.

Step 11. Set the computer's location: either home, work, or public location.

Now it's time to start Windows. Vista checks the computer's performance (which might take a while) and then asks you for your password (if you opted to use one) before you can access the operating system. After you have logged on with the proper password, the Welcome Center window should appear, and you can continue with initial tasks such as connecting to the Internet or transferring files and settings.

> ### ExamAlert
> Know the steps involved with installing Windows Vista.

> ### Note
> There is a short video covering the installation of Windows Vista on my website: http://www.davidlprowse.com.

Creating Partitions During a Windows Vista Installation

During the installation of Windows Vista, you can create, delete, or extend partitions as mentioned in step 6 of the previous section. There are several options; here are a few:

▶ To use all the space in the disk, either create a new partition that encompasses the entire disk or highlight the default Disk 0 Unallocated Space that Microsoft usually displays automatically, and click Next (see Figure 7.2).

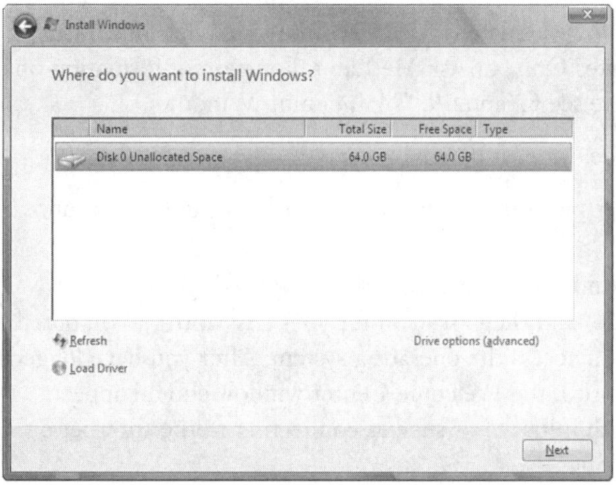

FIGURE 7.2 **Example of using an entire disk as one partition for the Windows Vista installation**

▶ To use only part of the space, click Drive options (advanced); then click New, specify the partition size, and click Apply (See Figure 7.3 and Figure 7.4).

▶ To use a preexisting partition (if this disk was used previously), highlight the partition desired and click Next. Be careful, whatever partition you select for the installation will be formatted, and all data on that partition will be erased.

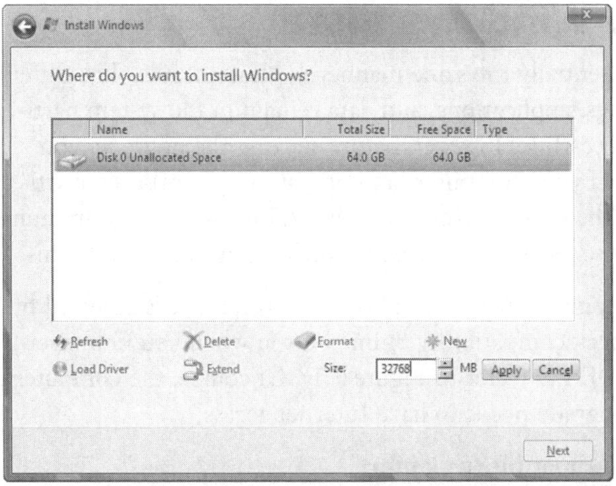

FIGURE 7.3 **Specifying a partition size**

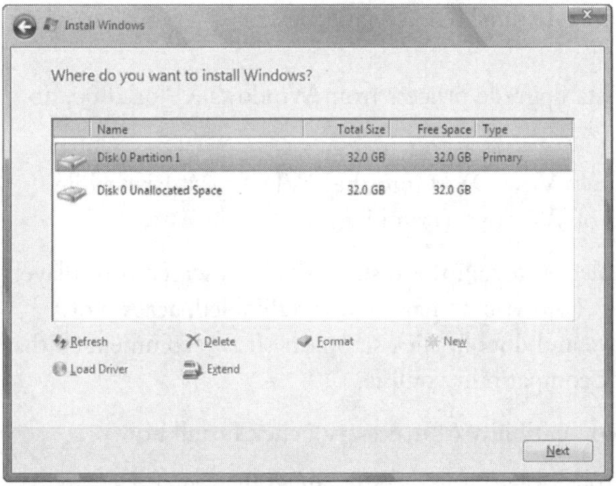

FIGURE 7.4 **Partition Table after creating a new partition, known as Partition 1**

You can also format partitions from here; they are automatically formatted as NTFS. In addition, you can extend preexisting partitions to increase the size of the partition but without losing any data.

> **Note**
>
> For more information on partitions, volumes, and formatting in Windows, see Chapter 8, "Configuring Windows."

Upgrading to Windows Vista

Upgrades are done in essentially the same manner as clean installs. The difference is that all the settings, applications, and data remain in the system partition if the upgrade is successful. However, before starting the upgrade, you should first check to see if your computer (and operating system) is compatible and if it will survive the process. Refer to Table 7.5 for the Vista minimum requirements. You can also use the following utilities and websites to do this:

▸ **Windows Vista Upgrade Advisor:** This is a website that is accessed by clicking on the Check compatibility online button when you first insert the Windows Vista DVD (refer to Figure 7.1). Of course, the computer that you want to upgrade needs to have Internet access.

▸ **Windows Vista Compatibility Center:** http://www.microsoft.com/windows/compatibility/windows-vista/

▸ **Windows Vista Logo'd Products List:** http://winqual.microsoft.com/HCL/Default.aspx?m=v

To start the Windows Vista upgrade process from Windows XP or 2000, do the following:

Step 1. Insert the Windows Vista DVD into the DVD-ROM drive while your old version of Windows is running.

Step 2. Unless you disabled Autorun, the Install Windows screen is displayed (refer to Figure 7.1). If you do have autorun disabled, access your DVD-ROM drive and double-click setup.exe. It is recommended that you select Check compatibility online.

Step 3. After checking compatibility (if necessary), click Install now.

Step 4. Next is the updates screen. It is recommended that you select the first option Go Online and Get the Latest Updates for Installation, as shown in Figure 7.5. There is also an option to send anonymous information back to Microsoft during the install. If you do not want to do this, leave the I Want to Help Make Windows Installation Better check box blank.

Step 5. Type in the product key. This should have come with your upgrade disc.

Step 6. Next, accept the terms of the license; otherwise the installation will end.

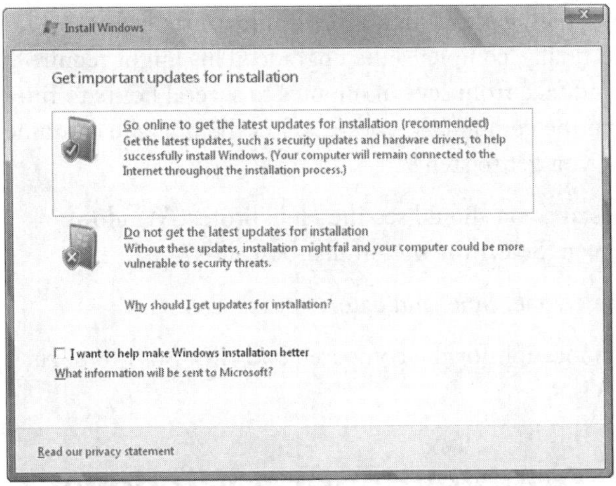

FIGURE 7.5   **Important updates window**

Step 7. In the next window, you have two options: upgrade or custom. Select the first option to upgrade the previous version of Windows to Windows Vista. If you receive any type of compatibility report window (such as the one in Figure 7.6) that say you have potential issues, consider stopping the installation for now and finding out what hardware or software needs to be replaced using the websites listed previously. Then start the upgrade again when you have fixed these issues. In some cases when you receive a compatibility report, the installation will not let you continue, and in other cases you can proceed at your own risk; but be warned, some devices or applications might not function when the upgrade completes.

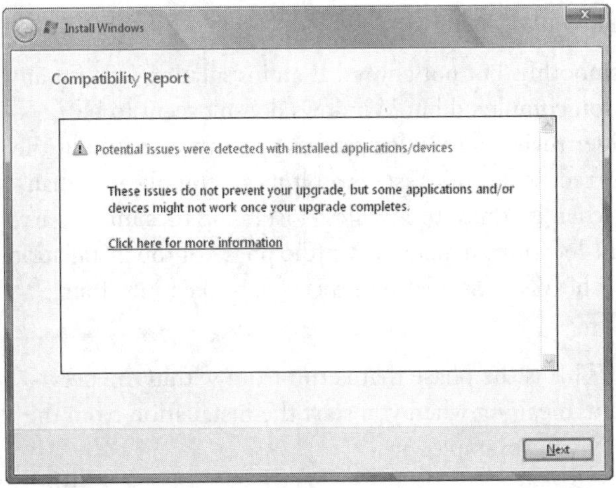

FIGURE 7.6   **Compatibility Report**

Step 8. Next, Vista copies files, gathers files, expands files, installs features and updates, and finally, completes the upgrade. This might require several restarts and take from several minutes to several hours to finish, depending on the computer's resources. Let the upgrade continue unhindered until you get to step 9.

Step 9. After the final restart, you should see the Help protect Windows automatically screen. Select the option that best suits you.

Step 10. Configure the time zone, time, and date.

Step 11. Finally, select the location for the computer, and click Start to begin using Windows Vista.

Verifying and Troubleshooting Windows Vista Installations

When you complete the clean installation or upgrade, *test it*. We previously discussed this concept a few times, but it can't be stated enough. Verify that your installation has gone smoothly by testing it. For example, attempt to navigate through Windows, access administrative functions, connect to the Internet, and so on.

If you have confirmed that Windows is working normally, update the system. As of the publishing of this book, the latest service pack (SP) for Windows Vista is SP2. It is possible that the service pack was included on your installation media, but if not, download it and install it before going any further. Then, download any other updates that are necessary utilizing the Windows Update feature. More information about service packs and updates can be found in Chapter 9, "Maintaining Windows."

Installations usually go smoothly, but not always. If an installation fails for any reason, or if the installation completed but Windows doesn't seem to be behaving properly, consider reviewing the log files to find out more about the problem and why it occurred. Windows Vista is a bit more complicated than older Windows systems when it comes to log files. Vista's log files might vary slightly and have different locations depending on the phase of the installation when they were logged. The Vista installation process is broken into four phases:

▶ **Downlevel phase:** This is the phase that is run from within the previous operating system, meaning when you start the installation from the DVD in Windows XP, for example.

▶ **Windows Preinstallation Environment phase:** Also known as Windows PE, this phase occurs after the restart at the end of the down-level phase. If installing to a new hard drive, this phase occurs when you first boot the computer to the Windows Vista DVD.

▶ **Online configuration phase:** The online configuration phase starts when a user receives the following message: Please wait a moment while Windows prepares to start for the first time. Hardware support is installed during this phase.

▶ **Windows Welcome phase:** During this phase, a computer name is selected for the computer, and the Windows System Assessment Tool (Winsat.exe) checks the performance of the computer. This is the final phase before the user first logs on.

There are log files for each phase; they are pretty much the same log files but in different locations. However, we are most concerned with the last two phases. For the most part in these two phases, the log files are in the same location. Table 7.6 covers the important log files during these two phases.

TABLE 7.6   **Windows Vista Installation Log Files**

Log file	Description	Location
setuperr.log	Contains information about setup errors during the installation. Start with this log file when trouble-shooting. A file size of 0 bytes indicates no errors during installation.	C:\Windows\Panther
setupact.log	Contains information about setup actions during the installation.	C:\Windows\Panther
miglog.xml	Contains information about the user directory structure. This information includes security identifiers (SIDs).	C:\Windows\Panther
setupapi.dev.log	Contains information about Plug-and-Play devices and driver installation.	C:\Windows\inf
setupapi.app.log	Contains information about application installation.	C:\Windows\inf
PostGatherPnPList.log	Contains information about the capture of devices that are on the system after the online configuration phase.	C:\Windows\Panther
PreGatherPnPList.log	Contains information about the initial capture of devices that are on the system during the downlevel phase.	C:\Windows\Panther
Winsat.log (Windows Welcome phase only)	Contains information about the Windows System Assessment Tool performance testing results.	C:\Windows\Performance\Winsat

ExamAlert

Know the difference between setuperr.log and setupact.log for the exam.

Note

You might notice that Vista doesn't have a setuplog.txt file like older versions of Windows does. This is because there is no text portion to the installation of Windows Vista.

Note

For a list of all log files within all phases of the Windows Vista installation, see the following link: http://support.microsoft.com/kb/927521

If the system won't start, you can still view these files. However, this depends on the type of installation and how far the installation got. If it was a clean installation, you should boot to the Windows Vista DVD; then access the System Recovery Options menu, and select the Command Prompt. If it was an upgrade that didn't get far, and if Windows XP/2000 was previously installed on an NTFS drive, you can boot to the Recovery Console from a Windows XP or 2000 CD and view the log files from there. For more information about System Recovery Options (Vista), and the Recovery Console (XP/2000), see Chapter 10, "Troubleshooting Windows."

If you cannot start the clean installation or upgrade, check the following:

▶ **Processor speed and memory size:** Verify that your computer meets the minimum requirements for Windows Vista. Refer to Table 7.5 for more information.

▶ **Free disk space:** You need 15GB free for Windows Vista; the more space available, the better.

▶ **Hardware conflicts or hardware issues:** Use the Device Manager to ensure that all hardware works correctly before you start an upgrade.

▶ **Installation media:** Make sure that your DVD-ROM (or CD-ROM) media is not scratched or damaged in any way. Verify that it is genuine Microsoft software and that you have the right type of media for your installation, for example, Vista Full Version License or Upgrade DVD.

Upgrades to Windows Vista can be especially troublesome. You might experience problems connecting to a LAN or the Internet, or some hardware might not work properly. Be sure to access the Microsoft Knowledge Base (MSKB) at http://support.microsoft.com for clues as to why these errors occur.

> **Note**
>
> For a list of specific errors concerning a Windows Vista upgrade, see the following link: http://support.microsoft.com/kb/930743

Cram Quiz

Answer these questions. The answers follow the last question. If you cannot answer these questions correctly, consider reading this section again until you can.

1. What is the minimum RAM requirement for Windows Vista?
   - ○ **A.** 2GB
   - ○ **B.** 256MB
   - ○ **C.** 512MB
   - ○ **D.** 768MB

2. Which file contains information regarding errors during a Windows Vista installation?
   - ○ **A.** Setuperr.log
   - ○ **B.** Setupact.log
   - ○ **C.** Event Viewer
   - ○ **D.** Unattend.xml

3. Where can you go to find out if your current operating system can be upgraded to Windows Vista?
   - ○ **A.** MSKB
   - ○ **B.** Windows Vista Upgrade Advisor
   - ○ **C.** HAL
   - ○ **D.** Belarc Advisor

4. Which versions of Vista have media center functionality? (Select the best two answers.)

    ◯ **A.** Home Basic

    ◯ **B.** Home Premium

    ◯ **C.** Business

    ◯ **D.** Ultimate

5. What is the hard drive requirement for Windows Vista?

    ◯ **A.** 15GB free space

    ◯ **B.** 15GB partition

    ◯ **C.** 20GB free space

    ◯ **D.** 25GB partition

6. Where can you go to find out if your computer's components are compatible with Windows Vista? (Select the best two answers.)

    ◯ **A.** Vista Compatibility Center

    ◯ **B.** MSKB

    ◯ **C.** Vista Logo'd Products List

    ◯ **D.** msinfo32.exe

7. To avoid SID conflicts when disk imaging, which program should you use in Windows Vista?

    ◯ **A.** Sysprep

    ◯ **B.** Setup Manager

    ◯ **C.** SIM

    ◯ **D.** Windows Deployment Services

8. Which of the following are possible ways to install Windows Vista? Select all that apply.

    ◯ **A.** From DVD

    ◯ **B.** From CD

    ◯ **C.** Over the network

    ◯ **D.** Using Norton Ghost

Cram Quiz Answers

1. **C.** The minimum RAM requirement for Windows Vista is 512MB. Microsoft *recommends* 1GB of RAM for Home Premium, Business, and Ultimate.

2. **A.** Setuperr.log contains information regarding errors during installation. Setupact.log contains information regarding *actions* during installation. The Event Viewer is an application, not a file, and might not contain installation details. Unattend.xml is the answer file generated by Windows SIM for unattended installations.

3. **B.** The Windows Vista Upgrade Advisor can tell you if your current operating system can be upgraded to Vista. This, and other tools like it, are located at www.microsoft.com, not at the MSKB (http://support.microsoft.com). The HAL is a file in Windows; it stands for hardware abstraction layer. Belarc Advisor is a third-party offering that analyzes your computer but does not determine whether it can be upgraded.

4. **B** and **D**. Home Premium and Ultimate include media center functionality; the others do not.

5. **A.** Vista requires 15GB of free space within a 20GB partition.

6. **A** and **C**. To find out if your computer's hardware is compatible with Vista, go to the Vista Compatibility Center or the Vista Logo'd Products List.

7. **A.** Sysprep can modify unattended installations so that every computer gets a unique SID (and other unique information). Windows SIM (System Image Manager) creates the answer files for unattended installations. Setup Manager (setupmgr.exe) is the program that Windows XP/2000 uses to create answer files. Windows Deployment Services is run on Windows Server 2008/2003 and is used to deploy operating systems across the network.

8. **A**, **B**, **C**, and **D**. Windows Vista can be installed from DVD, CD-ROM (though not recommended), over the network, and by using programs such as Norton Ghost.

Installing and Upgrading to Windows XP

Although Windows XP was released 8 years ago (as of the publishing of this book), you can still see plenty of copies of it in the field and might need to install it as well, or upgrade older Windows 2000 Professional computers to XP. The A+ exam objectives still touch on Windows 2000 Pro, which while a decade old, still exists in some dark technological corners of the universe. For the most part however, the information in this chapter refers to Windows XP. Windows 2000 works essentially the same way unless otherwise noted, for example when it comes to minimum hardware requirements.

Before you can install or upgrade to Windows XP, you first need to decide which edition of XP you'll be using. Then, you should check the computer to make sure it is compatible with Windows XP. Next, you need to decide on an installation method: from CD, floppy to CD, as an image, or over the network.

Windows XP Versions

There are several editions of Windows XP. They include:

▶ **Windows XP Home:** Designed for home users, this edition has limited networking and security capabilities.

▶ **Windows XP Professional:** This is the most common version of XP that you will see in the field. The A+ exams focus mostly on this edition. The XP Pro edition expands on the Home edition by offering the capability to connect to domains, make Remote Desktop connections, utilize the Encrypting File System (EFS), and support two physical CPUs. It is designed for power users, business people, and developers. There is a 64-bit version of this as well.

▶ **Windows XP Media Center:** This edition was developed for people concerned with audio and video. The Windows Media Center is part of the GUI that displays well on a TV and can be controlled remotely. It is also designed to playback videos and music. Normally, the Media Center edition is found preinstalled on computers that have been purchased from an OEM (original equipment manufacturer).

▶ **Windows XP Tablet PC:** This edition was designed for and can only be purchased with a tablet PC. The tablet PC is similar to a laptop but the screen can usually swivel, flip over, and be written on (hence the name tablet). These devices come with a pen-like device known as a stylus for tapping (a tablet PC's version of clicking) and writing on the screen.

ExamAlert

Know the differences between the Windows XP Home, Professional, Media Center, and Tablet PC editions.

Note

There is also Windows XP Starter, sold in technologically underdeveloped countries, and N and K editions (sold in Europe and Asia respectively), which omit Windows Media Player. These are not covered on the A+ exam.

Windows XP Minimum Requirements and Compatibility

When you have decided which version of XP you want to use, and before installing that operating system, you should learn as much as you can about the computer you plan to install to. Components in a computer should meet Windows XP's minimum requirements and should be listed on Microsoft's website as compatible with XP. Table 7.7 shows the minimum hardware requirements for Windows XP Professional and Windows 2000 Professional.

TABLE 7.7   **Windows XP and 2000 Minimum Requirements**

Component	XP Professional Requirement	2000 Professional Requirement
Processor	233MHz	133MHz
RAM	64MB	64MB
Free disk space	1.5GB (2GB partition)	650MB (2GB partition)
Other	CD-ROM or DVD-ROM	CD-ROM/Floppy drive

ExamAlert

Memorize the *minimum* requirements for Windows XP Professional and 2000.

> **Note**
>
> Windows XP Media Center edition has higher minimum requirements than XP Professional, including a 1.6GHz CPU, 256MB RAM, and a hardware-accelerated graphics card that can utilize DirectX 9.0.

> **Note**
>
> It is rare that you will install Windows 2000 Professional; however, you might still see questions about its minimum requirements on the A+ objectives.

Various websites and system analysis tools can verify that a system's hardware will be compatible with Windows XP. If you check a computer that already has an operating system installed, use the following tools:

▸ **Windows XP Logo'd Products List (formerly the HCL):** http://winqual.microsoft.com/HCL/Default.aspx?m=x

▸ **System Information:** The Windows System Information tool can be accessed by opening the Run prompt and typing **msinfo32.exe**. This takes the place of winmsd, but winmsd can still be run on Window XP and 2000 in addition to msinfo32.exe.

▸ **Belarc Advisor**: Currently a free download, this program can be found at http://www.belarc.com/free_download.html.

Windows XP Installation Methods

Following are several types of installation methods for Windows XP:

▸ **Local installation from CD-ROM:** Attended local installations by CD are the most common. Make sure that the CD-ROM drive is listed first in the BIOS boot order so that you can boot from it. Soon after starting the computer, you usually need to press a key on the keyboard to start the installation from the CD.

▸ **Booting from floppy disk and CD-ROM:** It is possible that a computer's BIOS cannot boot to CD or the CD-ROM drive is not bootable. If either of these is the case, you need to boot off the Windows Startup disks that will start the installation, install the CD-ROM drivers, and enable you to continue the installation from CD-ROM. If you install Windows XP, these disks (usually six of them) are available from http://support.microsoft.com/kb/310994. Note that there are different sets of floppy disks for Windows XP Home and XP Professional and for the specific service pack that is packaged as part of the CD. Make sure to download the correct version. If you install Windows 2000 Professional, the purchased package comes with a CD and four boot disks in the case that the computer's CD-ROM is not bootable. These disks can also be created by accessing the CD and going to the folder called bootdisk. From here, simply double-click makeboot.exe, and the program will guide you through the process of making the disks. To create disks from the CD on an older version of Windows, use makebt32.exe.

> **Note**
>
> If you can't find the boot disk that you need, you could search for it on the Internet; for example www.bootdisk.com has an image file for just about every boot disk you can imagine!

▶ **Network installation:** You can install Windows over the network in a variety of ways. To automate the process, Windows XP can be installed from a server, for example by using the Remote Installation Services (RIS) program, which can be installed on Windows Server 2003 and Windows 2000 Server. This program works along with Windows XP/2000's Setup Manager program that creates the automated answer files like unattend.txt. These files are text-based, unlike Windows Vista's unattend.xml. For more information on how this works, the differences between Vista and XP, and how to combine XP and Vista deployment technologies, see the following link: http://technet.microsoft.com/en-us/library/cc765993.aspx. Like Windows Vista, Windows XP also uses the Sysprep utility to prepare unique systems for installation over the network. It is provided on the CD-ROM at \SUPPORT\TOOLS\ in a cabinet file called DEPLOY.CAB. The most recent version of Sysprep for Windows XP can also be downloaded from the Microsoft website as part of the Windows XP Service Pack 2 Deployment Tools. See the following link for more information: http://support.microsoft.com/kb/838080

▶ **Disk image:** Windows XP (and actually any operating system) can also be installed as a disk image using programs such as Acronis True Image or Norton Ghost. When cloning a disk image, both computers need to be identical or as close to identical as possible.

> ▸ **Installing from a recovery disc:** Like Windows Vista, Windows XP
> computers that have the operating system preinstalled use a recovery
> disc (CD), hidden partition, or both. This disc and/or partition contains
> a factory image of Windows. The purpose of this is to give users the
> ability to return their computer back to the state when it was first
> received.

Installing Windows XP

After you decide on the version of XP you'd like to use, and have verified
compatibility of hardware, it's time to install. This section covers the steps
involved for a clean, local installation of Windows XP Professional off the
CD-ROM.

Step 1. Boot the computer from the CD-ROM. When doing so

1. Make sure the CD drive is configured as the first boot device in
   the system BIOS.

2. Insert the Windows XP CD-ROM into the system's CD drive. (If
   the drive won't open while in the BIOS, insert the disc immediately after saving the BIOS.)

3. Save the BIOS and restart the system.

4. The CD should boot automatically and start the installation if the
   drive is blank, but if you are prompted to boot from the CD, press
   any key. There is only a small window of time for this, approximately 5 seconds. This prompt is a protective measure; if you get
   the prompt, it means that there is data of some sort on the drive.
   When you press a key, it begins the text portion of the Windows
   XP installation.

Step 2. (Optional) Install drivers for mass storage devices. Early during the
installation process, the bottom of the screen says Press F6 if you
need to install a third party SCSI or RAID driver, as shown in Figure
7.7. This displays only for a short time. If you have such drivers, press
F6, and you will be prompted to insert the CD-ROM or floppy disk
that came with the device. Usually, installations are done to Ultra
ATA or SATA hard disks, so pressing F6 is not necessary. A similar
prompt at the bottom of the screen is shown next: Press F2 to Run
Automated System Recovery (ASR). This is not necessary during an
installation but can be used to repair an operating system that has
failed.

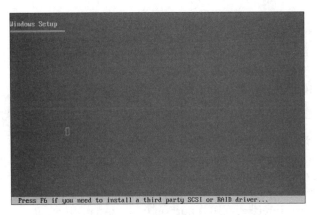

Press F6 if you need to install a third party SCSI or RAID driver...

FIGURE 7.7 **F6 prompt for optional SCSI/RAID drivers**

Step 3. Start the Install and accept the end-user license agreement (EULA). When done loading initial files, XP asks you if you want to install, repair, or quit. Press Enter to install. The next screen requires that you press F8 to agree to the EULA. You will also note that in case you make a mistake, you can press F3 at any time to quit the installation.

Step 4. Partition the drive. If you install to a new hard drive, this screen should show Unpartitioned Space. From here you can create one or more partitions (by pressing C), install to a preexisting partition, or just install to the unpartitioned space, which creates one large partition on the drive automatically, as shown in Figure 7.8. Either way, highlight the partition (or unpartitioned space) that you want to install to and press Enter.

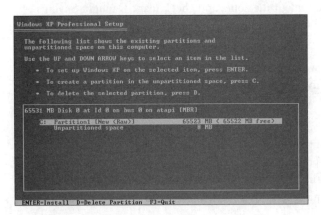

FIGURE 7.8 **Partition screen with one partition**

Step 5. Format the drive. At this point you have the option to format the partition as NTFS or FAT. NTFS is recommended and has a maximum partition size of 2TB during installation. (Hard drives are currently getting close to this number!) If you format the partition as FAT, and it is 4GB or less, it will be formatted as FAT16. If it is above 4GB, it will be formatted as FAT32, with a maximum partition size during setup of 32GB. You also have the option for a quick format; choose this option if it is a new drive or was formatted previously. If there were data files on the drive when you started the install, select the full format option. Once you press Enter, Windows automatically formats the partition, copies files to the partition, and reboots into the Graphical User Interface (GUI) portion of the installation. Sit back and relax as Windows works its magic.

Step 6. Set up regional settings. This includes the language, currency, and so on.

Step 7. Enter your name and organization. The name becomes an administrative account username.

Step 8. Enter the Product key.

Step 9. Enter a computer name and password. The computer name should be a unique name on your network and should not be the same as any other unique names (usernames, network names, domain names, and so on). Enter a secure password (more on password security in Chapter 15, "Security"), and type it again to confirm.

Step 10. Enter dialing information. This is only if the computer has a modem installed.

Step 11. Enter the date, time, time zone, and check mark Daylight Savings time if applicable. At this point, XP continues to copy files that might take a minute.

Step 12. Configure networking settings. From here you can select Typical, in which case Windows attempts to auto-configure the network adapter, or Custom, in which you can enter the settings manually.

Step 13. Select workgroup or domain. From here you can join (or create a new) workgroup, or join a domain if you possess the proper credentials and have configured TCP/IP properly in step 12. At this point, Windows continues to copy files and configures the operating system. After several minutes or more it restarts and then auto-configures the video display.

Step 14. Answer final questions. When you hear the dulcet tones of XP, you see a window that says Welcome to Windows. From here Windows checks for Internet connectivity, inquires as to how you want to connect to the Internet, asks you to register (optional), and asks you to define the users that will be accessing the computer by name. (For the primary user, you can use the same name you used in step 7). After this, the Windows desktop should appear.

Step 15. Activation of Windows. You have 30 days to activate Windows over the Internet or by telephone.

> **ExamAlert**
>
> Know the steps involved when installing Windows XP.

> **Note**
>
> There is a short video covering the installation of Windows XP on my website: http://www.davidlprowse.com

Upgrading to Windows XP

Upgrades are done in essentially the same manner as clean installs. The difference is that all the settings, applications, and data remain in the system partition if the upgrade is successful. However, before starting the upgrade, you should first check to see if your computer (and operating system) is compatible and if it will survive the process. You can use the following utilities and websites to do this:

▶ **Upgrade Advisor:** You can run the Upgrade Advisor from the Windows XP CD. Click Check System Compatibility from the Welcome to Windows XP menu; then click Check My System Automatically. (note that this upgrade advisor is no longer available for download from the Microsoft website). After the analysis is complete, the Upgrade Analyzer displays any incompatible hardware or software it finds.

▶ **Windows XP Logo'd Products List:** Formerly known as the Hardware Compatibility List or HCL, this is available at http://winqual.microsoft.com/HCL/Default.aspx?m=x.

Verifying and Troubleshooting Windows XP Installations

When you complete the clean installation or upgrade, *test it*. For example, attempt to navigate through Windows, access administrative functions, connect to the Internet, and so on. After you confirm that Windows is working normally, update the system. As of the publishing of this book, the latest service pack (SP) for Windows XP is SP3; however, some companies might still use SP2, so check your documentation, policies, and procedures to confirm. It is possible that the service pack was included on your installation media, but if not, download it and install it before going any further. Then, download any other updates that are necessary utilizing the Windows Update feature. More information about service packs and updates can be found in Chapter 9, "Maintaining Windows."

As mentioned previously, installations don't always go as planned. If an installation fails, first verify that your computer has met the minimum hardware requirements and that it doesn't have any hardware that will conflict with Windows XP. Also make sure that you have enough free disk space and that the installation media isn't damaged.

Now, let's talk about Windows XP log files. These files can be used to review what went wrong with an installation. In Windows XP, most of these files are plain text and are stored in the %systemroot% folder of the operating system. The %systemroot% folder is a variable that indicates the folder where the operating system was installed. In most cases this will be C:\Windows (C:\Winnt for Windows 2000). Table 7.8 describes the most important log files you need to know for the exam and their location within the operating system.

TABLE 7.8 **Windows XP Installation Log Files**

Log file	Description	Location
setuperr.log	Records errors (if any) during installation. This is the most important and descriptive log file for troubleshooting installation errors.	C:\Windows
setuplog.txt	Records events during the text-mode portion of installation.	C:\Windows
setupact.log	Logs all events created by the GUI-mode setup program.	C:\Windows
setupapi.log	Records events triggered by an .inf file.	C:\Windows
setup.log	The Recovery Console utilizes this to acquire information about the Windows installation during repair.	C:\Windows\repair

TABLE 7.8 **Continued**

Log file	Description	Location
comsetup.log	Installation information about Optional Component Manager and COM+ components.	C:\Windows
NetSetup.log	Information about membership to workgroups and domains.	C:\Windows\debug

Exam Alert

Know the differences between setuperr.log, setuplog.txt, and setupact.log for the exam.

If the system won't start, you can still view these files. However, this depends on the type of installation and how far the installation got. Attempt to boot to the Recovery Console from a Windows XP or 2000 CD and view the log files from there. For more information about the Recovery Console, see Chapter 10, "Troubleshooting Windows."

Cram Quiz

Answer these questions. The answers follow the last question. If you cannot answer these questions correctly, consider reading this section again until you can.

1. What is the minimum CPU requirement for Windows XP?

   ○ **A.** 133MHz

   ○ **B.** 233MHz

   ○ **C.** 800MHz

   ○ **D.** 1GHz

2. Which log file records errors during the installation of Windows XP?

   ○ **A.** setuperr.log

   ○ **B.** setuplog.txt

   ○ **C.** setup.log

   ○ **D.** setupact.log

3. Which key should be pressed if you want to install a driver for a mass storage device during the Windows XP installation?

   ○ **A.** F2

   ○ **B.** F3

   ○ **C.** F6

   ○ **D.** F8

4. What program creates answer files in Windows XP?

   ○ **A.** Windows SIM

   ○ **B.** Sysprep

   ○ **C.** RIS

   ○ **D.** Setup Manager

5. How much free disk space do you need to install Windows XP?

   ○ **A.** 2GB

   ○ **B.** 1.5GB

   ○ **C.** 650MB

   ○ **D.** 1GB

Cram Quiz Answers

1. **B.** Windows XP requires a minimum 233MHz CPU. 133MHz is the requirement for Windows 2000 Professional. For Windows Vista, 800MHz is the minimum requirement, and 1GHz is the recommended requirement for the CPU.

2. **A.** Setuperr.log records errors that occurred during installation. Setuplog.txt records events during the text portion of the installation. Setupact.log records events during the GUI portion of the installation. Setup.log is used by the Recovery Console during repair.

3. **C.** There is a short time period during the beginning of the XP installation in which you can press F6 to install mass storage drivers. F2 invokes the Automatic System Recovery (ASR), F3 quits the installation, and F8 agrees to the EULA (license).

4. **D.** Setup Manager (setupmgr.exe) is the tool that creates answer files such as unattend.txt in Windows XP. Windows SIM (System Image Manager) is used in Vista. Sysprep helps create unique installations over the network and works with the answer file. RIS or Remote Installation Services is the server component that initiates over the network installs.

5. **B.** Windows XP requires 1.5GB of free space within a 2GB partition and 650MB is the required space by Windows 2000 Professional.

Additional Reading and Resources

Additional A+ resources: http://www.davidlprowse.com/aplus

Windows Compatibility Center:
http://www.microsoft.com/windows/compatibility/

Windows 7 Logo'd Products List:
http://winqual.microsoft.com/HCL/Default.aspx?m=7

Windows Vista Logo'd Products List:
http://winqual.microsoft.com/HCL/Default.aspx?m=v

Belarc Advisor: http://www.belarc.com/free_download.html

PC Diagnostic tools: http://www.pc-diagnostics.com

#1-TuffTEST: http://www.tufftest.com/

PC Check: http://www.eurosoft-uk.com

Microsoft TechNet: Resources for IT Professionals:
http://technet.microsoft.com

Windows Upgrade Advisor: http://www.microsoft.com/windows/
windows-vista/get/upgrade-advisor.aspx

List of all log files within all phases of the Windows Vista installation:
http://support.microsoft.com/kb/927521

List of specific errors concerning a Windows Vista upgrade:
http://support.microsoft.com/kb/930743

Windows XP Logo'd Products List (formerly the HCL):
http://winqual.microsoft.com/HCL/Default.aspx?m=x

Windows XP Boot Disks: http://support.microsoft.com/kb/310994

Bootdisks and Essential Utilities: www.bootdisk.com

Comparison of Windows XP and Vista deployment technologies: http://
technet.microsoft.com/en-us/library/cc765993.aspx

Updated Sysprep tool: http://support.microsoft.com/kb/838080

CHAPTER 8

Configuring Windows

This chapter covers the following A+ exam topics:

▶ Windows User Interfaces

▶ System Tools and Utilities

▶ Files, File Systems, and Disks

You can find a master list of A+ exam topics in the "Introduction."

This chapter covers CompTIA A+ 220-701 objectives 3.2 and 3.3 and CompTIA A+ 220-702 objectives 2.2 and 2.3.

So, the computer is built, and Windows is installed; now it's time to configure the operating system! This chapter covers Windows user interfaces, system tools, utilities, and describes how to manage files and disks. Our focus is on Windows Vista, but we also discuss Windows 7, Windows XP, and to a small extent Windows 2000 Professional. However, this time, instead of breaking the sections up by the operating system, this chapter merges Windows 7, Vista, and XP together by topic. Because these operating systems are similar, you will find that many of the configurations work the same way. By default, the chapter refers to Windows Vista, but if something is different in Windows 7, XP, or 2000, it is specifically stated. You will find that navigation might be slightly different from 7 to Vista to XP, when trying to access the same feature in both operating systems. The learning curve is small though. Also, there are name changes for some of the applications in 7/Vista. For example, what used to be My Computer is now simply Computer, and what was My Network Places is just Network. This chapter refers to the Windows 7/Vista titles because they are the newer operating systems. Keep this in mind as we progress through the chapter. Also, make note that a particular setting in Windows might be arrived at from several different routes. This chapter tries to show alternative routes but doesn't cover all of them. Use the route that is the fastest and easiest for you, but try to remember as many routes as possible for the exam.

> **Note**
>
> I recommend that you run through all the configurations in this chapter on your computer(s). If you don't have computers for Windows 7, Vista, and XP available, consider running virtual machines to act as additional computers. Microsoft offers Virtual PC 2007 for free; it can be downloaded from Microsoft's website. This hands-on approach can help you to better visualize how operating systems are configured.

Windows User Interfaces

The essence of Windows is the graphical user interface (GUI), which is what Windows employs to interact with the user. Normally, a keyboard and pointing device such as a mouse are used to input information to the operating system's GUI, and whatever is inputted will be shown on the screen. Basically everything you see on the display including windows, icons, menus, and other visual indicators is part of the GUI, but remember that the GUI also governs how the user interacts with the OS.

The Windows GUI has many parts including the desktop with all its pieces, applications such as Windows Explorer and the Control Panel, and Administrative Tools such as Computer Management and the Device Manager. To master Windows, you need to learn how to navigate quickly through the GUI to the application or tool that you need. The GUI can be customized for a particular user, or it can be customized to optimize the system. Let's begin this section by talking about the various components of Windows.

Windows Components

What do you see when you start Windows? Some of the components that make up Windows include:

▶ **Desktop:** The desktop environment is basically what you see on the screen, essentially it *is* Windows, from a cosmetic standpoint. An example is shown in Figure 8.1, which displays the Start menu in the open position. The desktop is a key component of the GUI; it includes icons, wallpapers, windows, toolbars, and so on. It is meant to take the place of a person's physical desktop, at least to a certain extent, replacing calculators, calendars, and so on. The desktop is designed to be a user-friendly environment in which the user can easily save and retrieve files, make changes to the OS, and modify features. However, for more control of the OS, a user might still need advanced programs such as the command line or the Registry.

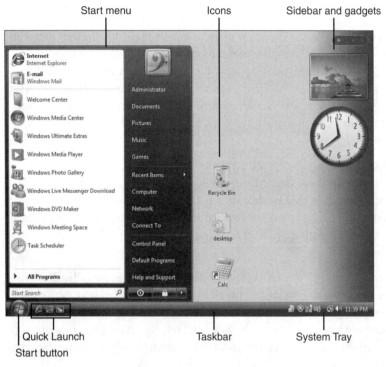

FIGURE 8.1 **Windows Vista Desktop**

> **Note**
>
> Some users refer to the desktop as just the area where the icons and shortcuts reside (the background or wallpaper) to differentiate that area from the rest of the screen.

▶ **Icons:** Icons are the little, clickable pictures you see on the desktop. They can be entire programs that run directly from the desktop, files that are stored directly on the desktop, or *shortcuts* that redirect to a program or file that is stored elsewhere in Windows. You can tell if it's a shortcut by the little arrow in the lower-left corner of the icon. Shortcuts are small, usually around 1KB to 4KB in size, which store very well on the desktop. However, storing actual files and programs on the desktop is not recommended because it can adversely affect the performance of the computer—and can quickly get really unorganized!

▶ **Taskbar:** This is the bar that spans the bottom of the desktop. It houses the Start button, Quick Launch, any open applications, and the System Tray. It can be moved to the top or either of the sides of the desktop and can be resized to fill up to 40 percent of the screen.

▶ **Start menu:** This is the main menu that is launched from the Start button. It contains a listing of all the tools within Windows and any Microsoft and third-party applications. From here you can search for files, access the Control Panel—you can get anywhere in Windows from the Start menu. It shows who is currently logged on to the system and also enables you to log off, restart, shut down, or place the computer in sleep mode.

▶ **Quick Launch:** The Quick Launch is directly to the right of the Start button. It contains shortcuts to applications or files. The beauty of the Quick Launch is that by default it is always visible, whereas shortcuts on the desktop background are covered up by open applications. Initially, the Quick Launch is enabled in Windows Vista, but it is disabled in Windows XP.

▶ **System Tray:** To the far right of the taskbar is the System Tray, otherwise known as the systray or the notification area. This houses the clock and shows the icons of applications that are running in the background. The more icons you see in the System Tray, the more resources are used, in the form of memory and CPU power, possibly making the computer less responsive.

▶ **Sidebar and gadgets:** The Windows Sidebar is a new window pane on the side of the desktop in Windows Vista. By default it is on the right side of the desktop but can be moved to the left side or closed altogether. It is primarily used to house gadgets that are mini-applications offering a variety of services, for example, connecting to the web to access weather updates and traffic, and accessing Internet radio streams. These gadgets can also interact with other applications to streamline the Windows experience. Additional gadgets can be downloaded from Microsoft. The Sidebar can be modified by simply right-clicking on it and selecting Properties; from here you can select whether the Sidebar starts when Windows does, if it is above other Windows, change its orientation, and remove gadgets. To add gadgets, click the + sign directly above the topmost gadget. Figure 8.1 displays two gadgets: a slide show and a clock.

▶ **Application windows and dialog boxes:** Application windows are the windows that are opened by programs such as Microsoft WordPad, as shown in Figure 8.2. The window consists primarily of a title bar (which says Document – WordPad), a menu bar (with the File, Edit, and other menus), a toolbar (with icons for opening, saving, and printing documents), and a work area. This program runs as an actual process known as wordpad.exe. Dialog boxes are windows that open from within another window, usually an application window. For example, Figure 8.2 shows the Computer Name/Domain Changes dialog box, which was opened from the System Properties window. System Properties (not shown) runs as a process, but the Computer Name dialog box is just part of that overall process. The dialog box prompts a user for information, in this case, for the name of the computer, and the name of the network the computer is a member of.

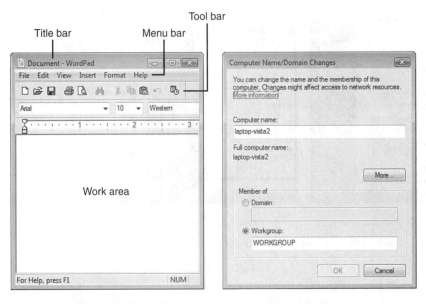

Application Window   Dialog Box

FIGURE 8.2   **An application window and a dialog box**

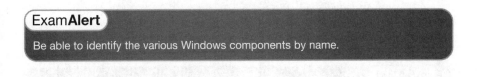

ExamAlert

Be able to identify the various Windows components by name.

Configuring the Taskbar and Start Menu

The taskbar and Start menu can be customized to just about any user's liking. To make modifications to these, right-click on the taskbar and select Properties. This brings up the Taskbar and Start Menu Properties window. The default tab is called Taskbar, from here you can unlock/lock the taskbar, auto-hide it, enable/disable the Quick Launch, and so on. The next tab is Start Menu, from here you can customize the menu by adding or removing items, selecting secondary menus, or selecting to show items as a link. You can also revert back to the Classic Start menu, which uses less computer resources and might be more accessible and memorable to people who are used to the older look of Windows. Figure 8.3 shows a default Windows Vista Start menu, a customized Start menu, and the Classic menu.

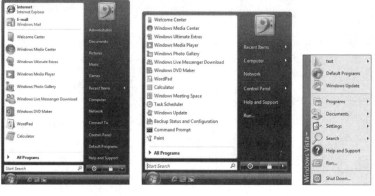

Original Start menu   Customized menu   Classic menu

FIGURE 8.3   **Standard Vista Start menu, Customized menu, and Classic menu**

As you can see, the customized menu has smaller program icons, and I added the Run command (which is *always* accessible by pressing Windows+R on the keyboard, even if you can't see it). The Classic menu is simple with only one column and shows the name of the operating system written vertically on the left side. If you select this type of menu, you can also note that several icons are automatically put on the desktop, such as Computer and Internet Explorer.

Exam Alert

Know how to switch to the Classic Start menu for the exam.

Windows Vista has two additional tabs in the Taskbar and Start Menu Properties window: Notification Area, in which you can disable items in the System Tray such as the clock or volume control, and Toolbar, in which you can add/remove toolbars to the taskbar. Windows XP and 2000 do not have these additional tabs.

Windows Aero and the Welcome Center

Windows Aero is Windows Vista's visual experience featuring translucent windows, window animations, three-dimensional viewing of windows, and a modified taskbar. You can make modifications to the look of Aero by right-clicking the desktop and selecting Personalize; then select Windows Color and Appearance, in which you can modify things such as the transparency of windows. However, Windows Aero uses a lot of resources and can be very taxing on the computer. To improve system performance (especially on older systems), you have the option to disable Aero. To do so, go back to the Personalize window and select Theme. At the Theme drop-down menu, select Windows Classic and watch the transformation in the preview window! If you want this "classic" look, click apply, and with the Theme Settings window still open, verify that this is what you want. If it is, click OK for the Theme Settings window. Note that this does not change the Start menu to classic mode; that configuration is made in the Taskbar and Start Menu Properties window.

The Welcome Center is the window that comes up automatically when you first start Windows Vista. After installing the operating system, it's a good starting point for running initial tasks such as connecting to the Internet, transferring files from another computer, adding users, and learning more about Windows Vista. The Welcome Center continues to show up every time you start Windows unless you deselect the check box at the bottom-left part of the window. To open Welcome Center later, go to Control Panel, System and Maintenance.

Windows Applications

There are lots of built-in applications within Windows. The following is a description of some of the programs you will use frequently:

- ▶ **Computer:** The Computer window can be accessed by clicking Start and selecting Computer. If you use the classic Start menu, Computer shows up as an icon on the desktop; just double-click to open it. Windows XP/2000 refers to this as My Computer. Unlike older versions of Windows, Vista's Computer window shows up as a complete two-pane window by default (known in Windows XP as Folders view). Computer is tightly integrated with Windows Explorer; Microsoft just refers to it as a folder now. From this folder you can browse through your computer to access data on the hard disk, DVD and CD-ROM, and other removable media, such as USB flash drives. By right-clicking Computer on the Start menu, you can also access things such as System Properties and Computer Management, so although it has lost some of its individuality in comparison to Windows XP/2000, it still has the same functionality within the Start menu. Figure 8.4 compares the newer Windows Vista Computer window with Windows XP's default My Computer window.

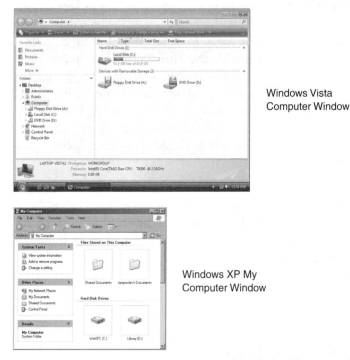

Windows Vista Computer Window

Windows XP My Computer Window

FIGURE 8.4   Vista's Computer window and XP's My Computer window

The Computer window has some additional functionality compared to Windows XP; you notice an additional toolbar in Figure 8.4 with options such as Organize and Uninstall or Change a Program.

▶ **Windows Explorer:** This works much like Computer. It can be accessed by clicking Start > All Programs > Accessories and clicking Windows Explorer. By default in Windows Vista, this brings you to the

\\%username%\\Documents folder. In Windows 7, it brings the user to the Libraries view.

Note

%username% is a variable. It refers to any real username of a particular user, for example Administrator, or DavidP. This variable enables you to refer to usernames as a collective whole. They might be different from one computer to another and from one user to the next. Whenever you see something enclosed by percentage signs (%), it is a variable name.

Actually, any folder that you access will open up within the Windows Explorer interface; the difference will be the amount of functionality given to you in the toolbar. These folders show up as different applications in the Task Manager, but they are all controlled by one process: explorer.exe. To see for yourself, open up Computer and Windows Explorer. Then open the Task Manager by right-clicking the taskbar and selecting Task Manager. From there you should see the various windows listed in the Applications tab. Next, view the process called explorer.exe within the Processes tab. You note that the Task Manager stays on top of other windows. Try an experiment: Watch explorer.exe's memory size go down as you close the Windows Explorer window and the Computer window. This should drive the point home.

Windows Vista's version of Windows Explorer incorporates the Stacks view, which groups files according to the criterion specified by the user. Stacks can be clicked on to filter the files shown in Windows Explorer. There is also the ability to save searches as virtual folders or *Search Folders*. Another new addition to Windows Explorer in Vista is the Details pane, which displays information relating to the currently selected file or folder.

Windows 7's version of Windows Explorer incorporates Libraries. *Libraries* are user-defined collections of folders that act as logical representations of the user's content. This has been incorporated into Windows to enable faster indexing and searching of important and commonly-used documents, even if they are spread out amongst the entire computer. This is done by analyzing file properties and *metadata* of files and folders; this is why Windows 7 Libraries are commonly known as *metafolders*. Metadata is information that describes a file's definition and structure, as well as how it is administered. Building on that idea, metafolders such as libraries have information that describes the definition and structure of the contents within. The Libraries portion of Windows Explorer is the default view in Windows 7. Normally, you will see the Documents, Music, Pictures, and Videos libraries when opening Windows Explorer. Double-clicking a library will show all of the folders and documents that are part of it, regardless of the location of the folder they are stored in. For example, The Documents library includes two locations by default: My Documents, and Public Documents. This can be discerned by clicking the 2 locations link. (The number of actual locations may vary from computer to computer.) You can add locations if you wish, by clicking the link, and clicking the Add button. This allows users to organize their documents and media by category, even if the files are scattered throughout the computer, and beyond to locations on the network. You can also add new libraries within the main Libraries window by right-clicking Libraries (or right-clicking the work area) and selecting New > Libraries. After a library has been created you can add folders to it by right-clicking it and selecting Properties. From there you can also specify the default folder location to save files in a library, and optimize the library. The concept of libraries has been in use for some time, especially in media players, but Windows 7 is the first Microsoft operating system to incorporate it for use with any and all files. Some third-party applications might not integrate properly with Windows libraries due to programming inadequacies. If this is the case, a user will have to store the files created in that application by navigating to the actual folder where they are to be stored, bypassing the library. Always check for updates to third-party applications that might make them library-compatible.

▶ **Control Panel:** The Control Panel (CP) is where a user would go to make system configuration changes, for example, changing the color scheme, making connections to networks, installing or modifying new hardware, and so on. The Control Panel can be opened by going to Start > Control Panel. By default, the control panel shows up in Category view. For example, in Windows Vista, System and Maintenance is a category. To see all the individual Control Panel icons, click the Classic View link on the left side. Most of the categories in Vista work basically the same in XP; however, the names are different. Within the Taskbar and Start Menu Properties window, the Control Panel option in the Start menu can be configured to show up as a sub-menu, composed of the classic view icons.

▶ **Network:** The Network window shows computers and other devices on the network. It can be opened by clicking on Start > Network. It opens in an Explorer-type window and might take a few moments to register the devices on the network. The address bar at the top of the window shows the status of the registration of devices as a bar that extends from left to right. The Network window should automatically find other computers, routers, wireless access points, and network attached devices if you are configured as a member of the network. You can add printers and wireless devices from here and open the Network and Sharing Center, in which you can add networking connections and share resources. Windows Vista's Network window takes the place of My Network Places in Windows XP.

▶ **Command Prompt:** Microsoft's Command Prompt is its command-line interface (CLI). This is the text-based interface in which you can issue commands concerning files and folders, networking, services, and so on. It can be opened in several ways including:

  ▶ Navigating to Start > All Programs > Accessories > Command Prompt.

  ▶ Press Windows+R to open the Run prompt and type **CMD** (my personal favorite). In Windows XP, Run is available directly from the Start menu. You can get to the Run prompt in Vista by clicking Start and typing **Run** in the search field. In Windows Vista, some commands need to be run as an administrator; to open the Command Prompt as an administrator, do one of the following:

    1. Click Start > All Programs > Accessories; then right-click Command Prompt and select Run as Administrator.

    2. Click Start and type **CMD** in the search field, and instead of pressing Enter, press Ctrl+Shift+Enter.

    Running the Command Prompt as an Administrator is also known as running it in *elevated mode*.

    An additional command-line called the PowerShell is integrated to Windows 7, and can be downloaded for use with other versions of Windows. The PowerShell is a combination of the Command Prompt and a scripting language (it is the successor to the Windows Script Host.) It enables administrators to perform administrative tasks that integrate scripts and executables. This can be started by navigating to Start > All Programs > Accessories > Windows PowerShell. It should be noted that if you decide to use the PowerShell in place of the Command Prompt, that you should remember to always use a space after a command, otherwise the shell will not recognize the command. For example, typing ipconfig /all would be correct, whereas ipconfig/all would not function. For administrators that run scripts often, there is also the Windows PowerShell ISE (Integrated Scripting Environment); this color codes the syntax, and is generally a more friendly environment to work in.

> **ExamAlert**
>
> Know how to open programs from the Start menu and from the Run prompt.

Administrative Tools and the MMC

Users can access the programs we mentioned in the last section, but usually aren't well versed in, or will have access to, the Administrative Tools. The administrator (that's you) of a computer or network can access these by going to Start > All Programs > Administrative Tools. There are several tools here used to configure advanced options for the computer. We cover each of them as we go through this chapter and Chapters 9, "Maintaining Windows," and 10, "Troubleshooting Windows." One example is Computer Management that you will use quite often. It has many utilities loaded into one nice, little *console* window. An example of Computer Management is shown in Figure 8.5.

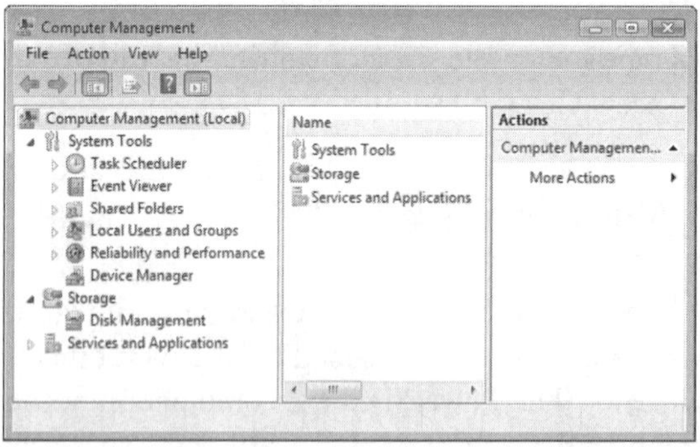

FIGURE 8.5   Windows Vista Computer Management window

Note, this is a three-pane window. The left pane has all the modules that you might work on such as the Event Viewer, Device Manager, and Disk Management. The middle pane shows the details of whatever you click on in the left pane. The right pane gives additional actions, which are also available on the menu bar. This right pane does not show up in Windows XP. There are a few other ways to open this window including:

▶ Click Start; then right-click Computer and select Manage.

▶ Access the Run prompt and type **compmgmt.msc**. The extension .msc defines the file type as a Microsoft Management Console Snap-in Control file, also known as a Microsoft Console.

> ### Note
>
> You will learn quickly that administrative functions should only be carried out by those users who have administrative privileges. Even if you have administrative privileges, a pop-up User Account Control (UAC) window displays every time you try to access tools such as Computer Management. Simply click Continue to open the program. If a user does not have administrative capabilities, they will either be blocked altogether, or when the UAC window pops up, they cannot continue. For more information on UAC, see Chapter 15, "Security."

Computer Management and other console windows can be grouped together into one master console window known as the MMC (Microsoft Management Console). The MMC acts as a shell for these other console windows. You can also use it to control remote computers in addition to the local computer (the one you sit at). And you can control what particular users see by changing the Console Mode. Finally, part of the beauty of the MMC is that it saves everything you added and remembers the last place you worked. Windows 7 and Vista uses MMC version 3.0, and Windows XP uses Version 2.0, but version 3.0 can also be downloaded for XP. To create an MMC, open the Run prompt and type **MMC**. By default, the MMC is empty. To add consoles (known as snap-ins) do the following:

1. Click File on the menu bar; then click Add/Remove Snap-in. The Add/Remove Snap-ins window should appear.

2. Select the components you want from the left by highlighting them one at a time and clicking the Add button. You notice that you need to select the local computer or a remote computer. Click OK when finished. These snap-ins should now be shown inside of the Console Root. An example MMC is shown in Figure 8.6.

3. Save the MMC. By default this window prompts you to save to the Administrative Tools folder of the user who is currently logged on.

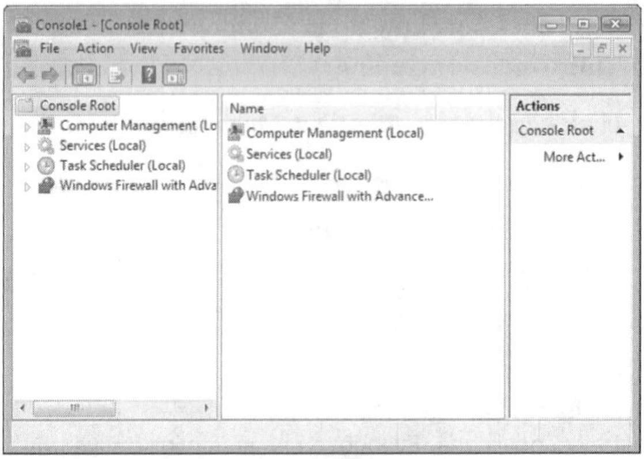

FIGURE 8.6   **Windows Vista MMC**

ExamAlert

Know how to add snap-ins to an MMC.

Cram Quiz

Answer these questions. The answers follow the last question. If you cannot answer these questions correctly, consider reading this section again until you can.

1. A small arrow at the lower-left corner of an icon identifies it as what?

    ○ **A.** A super icon

    ○ **B.** An icon headed for the Recycle Bin

    ○ **C.** A shortcut

    ○ **D.** A large file

2. The sidebar contains _____?

    ○ **A.** Gadgets

    ○ **B.** Widgets

    ○ **C.** Bracelets

    ○ **D.** Icons

3. What can a user do to cut back on the amount of resources that Windows Vista uses? (Select the two best answers.)

   ○ **A.** Increase RAM.

   ○ **B.** Use the Classic Start menu.

   ○ **C.** Turn off Windows Aero.

   ○ **D.** Use the computer less.

4. Which utility groups snap-ins into one window?

   ○ **A.** Computer Management

   ○ **B.** MSC

   ○ **C.** MCC

   ○ **D.** MMC

5. When you open Windows Explorer, what folder does it bring you to by default?

   ○ **A.** Computer

   ○ **B.** Network

   ○ **C.** Documents

   ○ **D.** Recycle Bin

6. How can the Run prompt be opened? (Select the two best answers.)

   ○ **A.** Pressing Windows+R

   ○ **B.** Pressing Windows+Run

   ○ **C.** Clicking Start and typing Run

   ○ **D.** Pressing Ctrl+Shift+Esc

Cram Quiz Answer

1. **C.** An icon with an arrow is a shortcut, redirecting to a file or program in another location in Windows. They are actually very small, from 1KB to 4 KB.

2. **A.** The sidebar contains gadgets that offer specialized information such as weather and traffic; these gadgets come from Microsoft. Widgets are the same types of small applications but they come from various vendors, can be down-loaded from the Internet, and usually work outside of the sidebar. Icons are files or programs on the desktop.

3. **B** and **C.** By using the Classic Start menu and turning off Windows Aero, the operating system will not need as much graphics computing power. Increasing RAM increases the amount of resources your computer has, but it won't decrease the amount of resources that Windows Vista uses.

4. **D.** The MMC or Microsoft Management Console can have one or more snap-ins such as Computer Management and so on. MSC is the extension that the MMC and individual console windows use. MCC stands for memory controller chip.

5. **C.** When opening Windows Explorer, the folder that is displayed is Documents, which is within the folder of the currently logged on user.

6. **A** and **C.** By pressing Windows+R on the keyboard you can open the Run prompt, or you can click Start and type **run** in the Search field. There is no Run key, so there is no Windows+Run shortcut, and pressing Ctrl+Shift+Esc would usually bring up the Task Manager. In Windows XP, the Run Prompt can be accessed directly from the Start menu.

System Tools and Utilities

Windows 7, Vista, and XP have a cornucopia of system tools and utilities. There are tools that help you to analyze and manage devices such as the Device Manager and System Information. There are also tools that can aid in optimizing the operating system and customizing the user environment. And there are advanced utilities that enable you to edit the Registry and connect remotely to other computers. Knowledge of these types of tools and utilities separates the good technician from the "okay" technician. Let's discuss how to manage devices first.

Managing Devices

A computer will probably have a dozen or more devices that all need love and attention. Taking care of a computer means managing these devices. The primary tool with which a technician does this is the Device Manager.

Device Manager

There are a few ways to open the Device Manager, for example:

▶ Open Computer Management, expand System Tools, and select Device Manager. (This and an MMC with a Computer Management snap-in are the preferred methods.)

▶ Open the System Properties window, click the Hardware tab, and select the Device Manager button. To get to the System Properties window in Vista, click Start, right-click Computer, and select Properties; then click Advanced system settings under Tasks. (Note that Device Manager is also listed under tasks.) You can also open the Run prompt and type **systempropertieshardware.exe** to directly access the Hardware tab of the System Properties window in Vista. To get to the System Properties window in Windows XP, click Start, right-click My Computer, and select Properties. The System Properties window is also accessible via the Control Panel in both Vista and XP.

▶ Open the Run prompt and type **devmgmt.msc**.

When you have the Device Manager open, you notice that there are categories for each type of device. By expanding any one of these categories, you see the specific devices that reside in your computer. Figure 8.7 shows the Device Manager with the Keyboards and Ports categories expanded.

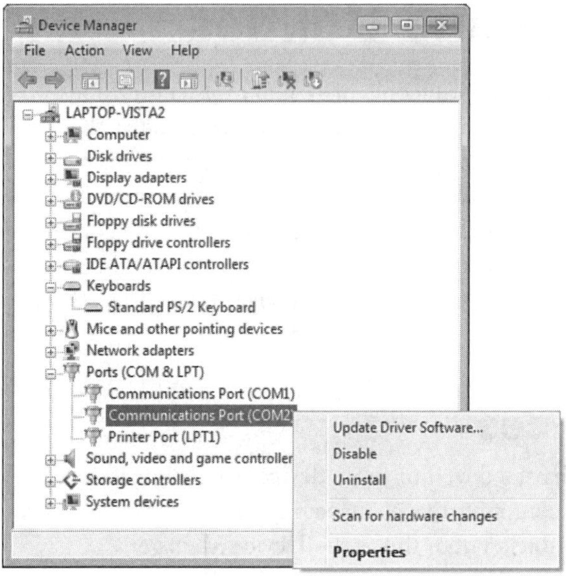

FIGURE 8.7   Device Manager in Vista

By right-clicking a specific device you can update its driver, enable or disable it, uninstall it altogether, check for any hardware changes, and access additional properties such as the driver details and resources used by the device. Figure 8.7 shows the resulting menu when right-clicking Communications Port 2. These are the standard options, but your options might be more or less depending on the device right-clicked.

ExamAlert

Know how to access the properties of a device, install drivers, and enable/disable devices in the Device Manager.

Some drivers are installed through .exe files that are downloaded from the manufacturer's website. Others are installed from within the Device Manager. The Device Manager can search for drivers automatically, or you can manually install the driver by browsing for the correct file (quite often a file with an .inf extension). Windows will attempt to install drivers automatically when it recognizes that a device has been added to the system. But usually, it is recommended that you use the driver disk that came with the device, or download the latest version of the driver from the manufacturer's website, especially when dealing with video, audio, and hard disk controller drivers.

Driver Signing

Windows device driver files are digitally signed by Microsoft to ensure quality. The digital signature ensures that the file has met a certain level of testing, and that the file has not been altered. In Windows Vista, driver signing is configured automatically, and in Windows Vista and XP, only administrators can install unsigned drivers. In Windows XP, driver signing can be configured to either ignore device drivers that are not digitally signed, display a warning when Windows detects device drivers that are not digitally signed (the default behavior), or prevent installing device drivers without digital signatures. To configure driver signing in Windows XP, open the System Properties window, click the Hardware tab, and select Driver Signing.

System Information Tool

Another tool that Windows offers for device analysis is the System Information tool. This can be accessed by navigating to Start > All Programs > Accessories > System Tools and clicking on System Information, or by opening the Run prompt and typing **msinfo32.exe**. (The .exe actually isn't necessary.) From here you can view and analyze information about hardware components, the software environment, and hardware resources used, for example Interrupt ReQuests (IRQs), as shown in Figure 8.8. An IRQ is the circuit that a device uses to "interrupt" the CPU and get its attention in an attempt to send data to it. In previous CompTIA A+ exams, a person would need to memorize each of the IRQ numbers between 0 and 15 and their corresponding device. However it is rare that IRQ conflicts occur anymore; therefore, you won't be making changes to IRQ settings often (if ever), and so the chance of a question about this on the new exams is unlikely.

DxDiag

When it comes to making sure your devices are working properly, one of the most important is the video card, and a utility you can use to analyze and diagnose the video card is DxDiag. To run the DxDiag program, open the Run prompt and type **dxdiag**. First, the utility asks if you want it to check whether the corresponding drivers are digitally signed. A digitally signed driver means it is one that has been verified by Microsoft as compatible with the operating system. After the utility opens, you can find out what version of DirectX you are running. DirectX is a group of multimedia programs that enhance video and audio, including Direct3D, DirectDraw, DirectSound, and so on. With the DxDiag tool, you can view all the DirectX files that have been loaded, check their date, and discern whether any problems were found with the files. You can also find out information about your video and sound card, what level of acceleration they are set to, and test DirectX components such as DirectDraw and Direct3D, as shown in Figure 8.9. Windows 7 ships with DirectX version 11, Windows Vista ships with DirectX version 10, whereas Windows XP currently can use up to DirectX 9.0c. However, DirectX 11 will have been released by the time this book is published. The DirectX feature is important to video gamers and other multimedia professionals.

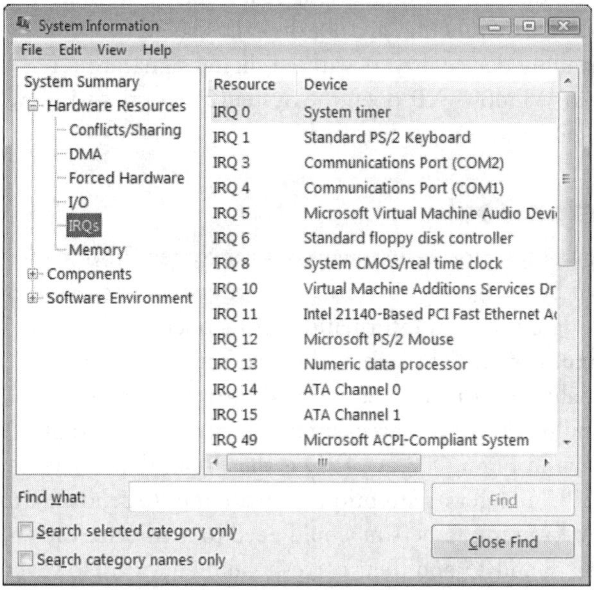

FIGURE 8.8   System Information Tool—IRQ Listing

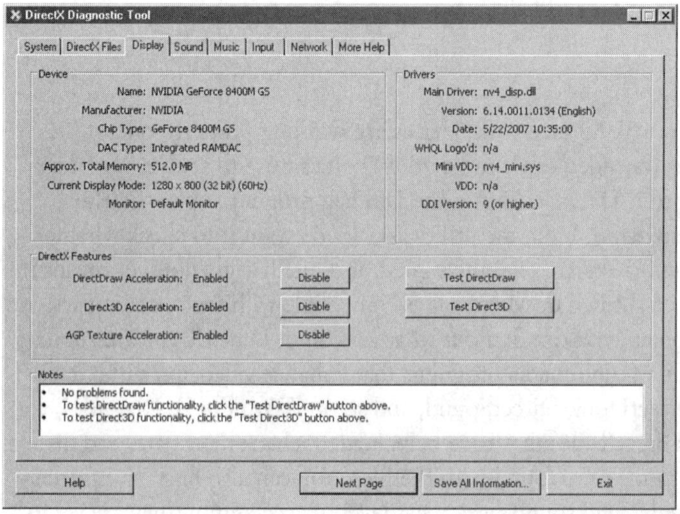

FIGURE 8.9   Windows XP DxDiag window showing the Display tab

Removing Hot Swappable Devices

When it comes to removing devices, most devices can be physically removed only if the computer has first been shut down. However, some devices can be "hot-swapped," meaning they can be removed while the power to the computer is on; no reboot is necessary. USB flash drives are an example of this; however, you should "Safely Remove" them within the operating system first. This can be done by right-clicking or double-clicking the Safely Remove icon in the System Tray and stopping the device. Other devices that can be hot swapped include printers, digital cameras, scanners, webcams, microphones, and so on.

Operating System Optimization

A fresh installation of Windows will probably not work exactly the way you want it to right from the start. It might take some tweaking and some optimization to get it just right. You will also find that systems running Windows for a while have of late suffered performance setbacks. These systems also need to be optimized. But to optimize we first need to do some system analysis of the system.

Task Manager

One simple, yet effective, tool to use when analyzing the computer is the Task Manager. There are several ways to open the Task Manager including:

▶ Right-click on the taskbar and select Task Manager.

▶ Press Ctrl+Alt+Del and select Task Manager. (If you have the Welcome Screen enabled in Windows XP, pressing Ctrl+Alt+Del alone brings up the Task Manager.)

▶ Open the Run prompt and type **taskmgr**.

▶ Press Ctrl+Shift+Esc.

The Task Manager gives you the ability to analyze your processor and memory performance in real time; this can be done from the Performance tab, as shown in Figure 8.10.

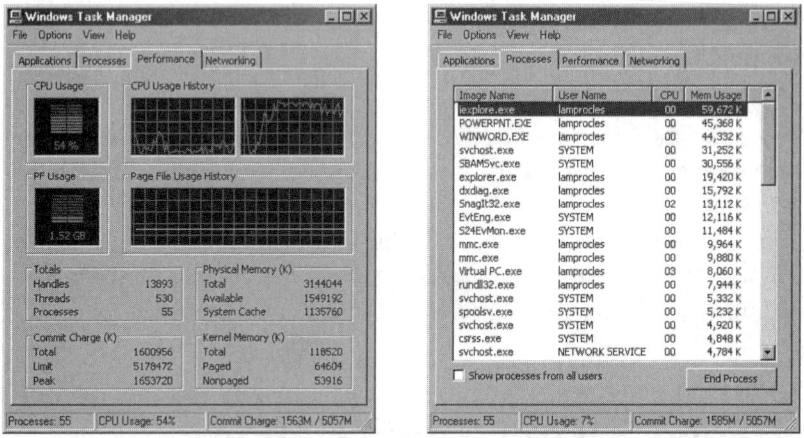

FIGURE 8.10   Windows XP Task Manager showing the Performance tab and the Processes tab

As you can see, the processor in the figure is hovering at 54 percent usage. Something is gobbling up a big portion of the processing power! You also note that nearly 1.5GB of memory is used; that's quite a bit for a Windows XP computer. What could be the reason for this? Was the processor not recognized by the BIOS properly? Is there a powerful application that is using all those resources? Maybe the computer, unbeknown to the user, is used as a zombie to send attacks out to various organizations? Or has the user turned the computer into an MP3 file server for all her friends? These are the types of things you would want to investigate. In reality, the reason for the 50 percent processor and 1.5 GB memory usage is because I am running a Windows Vista virtual machine at full power. Virtual machines can be quite a drain on the system. Now we are crossing over into the realm of troubleshooting, but then again, sometimes the lines between configuration, optimization, and troubleshooting can be blurred.

Optimizing the system can be as simple as shutting down programs. For example, in Figure 8.10, the Processes tab shows all the processes that are running and the amount of CPU and RAM resources they are using individually. A process that is hording resources can be stopped by highlighting it and clicking End Process. Programs can be turned off in the same manner from the Applications tab, but quite often the process you are looking for runs in the "background" so to speak, and although it won't show up on the Applications tab, it will show up on the Processes tab. Keep in mind that this shuts down only the process or application temporarily. If it is designated to do so, it will turn back on when the computer is rebooted. Later in this section, we discuss the programs that can be used to permanently disable programs, processes, and services. Note that the Windows XP Task Manager has four tabs in all: Applications, Processes, Performance, and Networking. Windows Vista adds to this list the Services tab, in which you can start and stop services, and the Users tab, in which you can log off or disconnect users.

> **ExamAlert**
>
> Understand how to open the Task Manager, how to read its Performance tab, and how to end processes and applications.

Optimizing the system can also mean temporarily boosting the power to a particular process. For example, if you were working within an important application that was crunching some heavy duty numbers, and you needed to increase that one process's performance, you could do so by right-clicking the process, highlighting Set Priority, and selecting an option above Normal. The higher the option on the list, the more processing power that process gets. Be wary though, changing a process's priority can have undesired effects such as system lockups or other errors. Be sure to save your work before attempting this, and consider testing it on an application before running it on something important.

> **Note**
>
> Other tools that can analyze the performance of a computer include Windows Performance Monitor, which is covered in Chapter 10, "Troubleshooting," and CPU-Z, which was covered briefly in Chapter 3, "The CPU."

Msconfig

Msconfig.exe (Microsoft System Configuration Utility) is one of the programs mentioned in the previous section that can permanently disable programs and services that are designed to run when the computer starts up, thus optimizing the system. To open this program, first open the Run prompt and then type **msconfig**. This program is built into Windows 7, Vista, and XP but is not part of Windows 2000 by default. To disable programs from starting, click on the Startup tab and uncheck mark the desired entries. Msconfig also lets you select from different boot options and can start or stop services. The

Windows XP version enables you to modify the wini.ini and boot.ini files, but the Windows Vista version does away with this because it doesn't utilize those files. We will revisit Msconfig in Chapter 10.

Virtual Memory

Virtual memory makes a program think that it has contiguous address space, when in reality, the address space can be fragmented and often spills over to a hard disk. RAM is a limited resource, whereas virtual memory is, for most practical purposes, unlimited.

There can be a large number of processes, each with its own virtual address space. When the memory in use by all the existing processes exceeds the amount of RAM available, the operating system moves pages of information to the computer's hard disk, freeing RAM for other uses. In Windows, virtual memory is known as the paging file, specifically pagefile.sys that exists in the root of C:. To view this file you need to unhide it. This can be done in Windows Explorer by clicking Tools on the menu bar and then selecting Folder Options. In the resulting Folder Options window, click the View tab and select the radio button called Show Hidden Files and Folders. Then, just below, deselect the check mark where it says Hide Protected Operating System Files. Pagefile.sys should now show up in the root of C:.

> **Note**
>
> If you cannot see the Windows Explorer menu bar in Windows Vista, press Alt+T to bring it up temporarily. Alternatively, click the Organize button, then Layout, and select Menu Bar to display it permanently.

Take a look at the size of your page file and jot down what you find. To modify the size and location of the page file, open the System Properties window, and click the Advanced tab. Next, click the Settings button within the Performance box; this will bring up the Performance Options window. Now, click the Advanced tab, and click Change in the Virtual memory box. From here you can let Windows manage the virtual memory for you, or select a custom size for the page file. The paging file has the capability to increase in size as needed. For a long time with Windows XP/2000 computers, the rule was that the page file would have an initial size of $1.5 \times RAM$, and a maximum size of $3 \times RAM$, but the page file can be increased beyond that if necessary. This rule might not be used on today's computers for a variety of reasons; however, if a user runs a lot of programs simultaneously, then increasing the page file size might be the answer for performance issues. Another option would be to move the page file to another volume on the hard drive, or to another hard drive altogether. It is also possible to create multiple paging files, or stripe a paging file across multiple disks to increase performance. Of course, nothing beats adding physical RAM to the computer, but when this is not an option, possibly because the motherboard has reached its capacity for RAM, optimizing the page file might be the solution. For more information about configuring virtual memory in Windows XP, see the following link: http://support.microsoft.com/kb/314482. Some of the techniques listed apply to Windows Vista as well.

ExamAlert

Know where to configure virtual memory, and know the location of pagefile.sys.

Working with Services

Services control particular functions in Windows such as printing, wireless networking, and so on. If a service is stopped or disabled, its corresponding program or utility will not run. You can start or stop services in the GUI or in the command line. As mentioned previously, services can be started or stopped from Msconfig or the Windows Vista Task Manager. You should also know how to do this within Computer Management and in the Command Prompt.

▶ **Start and stop services in Computer Management:** Open the Computer Management console window, click the + sign to expand Services and Applications, and then click Services. Now, in the right window pane, scroll until you find the service you want. To start a stopped service, right-click it and click Start, as shown in Figure 8.11. Alternatively, you can click the Start button on the toolbar, or double-click the service and click the Start button from the Properties window. The Properties window of the service also enables you to change the startup type, as shown in Figure 8.11. There are three startup types. At times you might need to set a service to Automatic so that the service starts automatically every time the computer boots; many services are set this way by default. Or you might want to set a service to Manual so that you have control over it. In other cases, you might want to set it to Disabled, for example, disabling the insecure Telnet service. This service is disabled by default in Windows XP (it's not even installed initially on Vista), but you never know who or what might have enabled it.

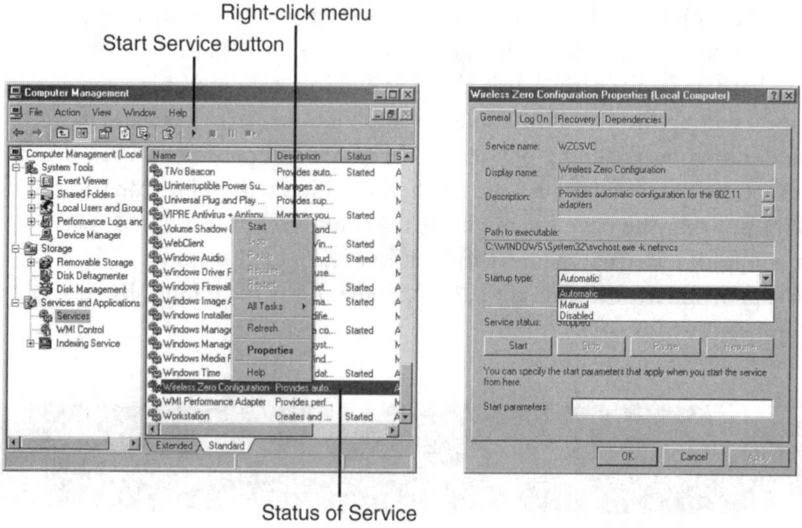

Right-click menu

Start Service button

Status of Service

FIGURE 8.11 A Common Service in the Computer Management window and its Properties window

▶ **Start and stop services in the Command Prompt:** In Windows Vista you need to run these commands as an administrator; let's review the two ways to do this.

  1. Click Start > All Programs > Accessories; then right-click Command Prompt and select Run as Administrator.

  2. Click Start and type **cmd** in the search field, and instead of pressing Enter, press Ctrl+Shift+Enter.

Windows XP does not require opening the Command Prompt as an administrator. When the Command Prompt is open, you can start a service by typing **net start** [service], for example **net start spooler** starts the Print Spooler service. **net stop spooler** stops the service.

ExamAlert

Know how to start and stop services within Computer Management and in the Command Prompt.

Power Management

Part of optimizing an operating system is to manage power wisely. You can manage power for hard disks, the display, and other devices; you can even manage power for the entire operating system.

To turn off devices in Windows Vista after a specified amount of time, navigate to Start > Control Panel. Then select Classic view in the left window pane. Next, double-click the Power Options icon. From here you can select a power plan from: Balanced, Power saver, and High performance. There are a lot of settings in this window; let's show one example. In Balanced, click Change plan settings. The Display is set to turn off in 20 minutes by default; it can be set from 1 minute to 5 hours or set to never. If you click on the Change Advanced Power Settings link, the Power Options button appears. From here you can specify how long before the hard disk turns off and set power savings for devices such as the processor, wireless, USB, PCI Express, and so on. Take a few minutes looking through these options and the options for the other power plans.

To turn off devices in Windows XP after a specified amount of time, navigate to Start > Control Panel. Then select Classic view in the left window pane. Next, double-click the Power Options icon. This opens the Power Options Properties window. From here you can tell the system when to shut off the display and the hard disks. You can also specify when the system will standby or hibernate.

Some users confuse the terms standby and hibernate; let's try to eliminate that confusion now. *Standby* means that the computer goes into a low power mode, shutting off the display and hard disks. Information that you were working on and the state of the computer is stored in RAM. The processor still functions but has been throttled down and uses less power. Taking the computer out of standby mode is a quick process; it usually requires the user to press the power button or a key on the keyboard. It takes only a few seconds for the CPU to process the standby information in RAM and return the computer to the previous working state. Hard drives and other peripherals might take a few more seconds to get up to speed. Keep in mind that if there is a loss of power, the computer will turn off and the contents of RAM will be erased, unless it is a laptop (which has a built-in battery), or if the computer is connected to a UPS; but either way, uptime will be limited. Note that some laptops still use a fair amount of power when in standby mode. *Hibernate* is different than standby in that it effectively shuts down the computer. All data that was worked on is stored to the hard drive in a file called hiberfil.sys in the root of C:. This will usually be a large file. Because RAM is volatile, and the hard drive is not, hibernate is a safer option when it comes to protecting the data and the session that you were working on, especially if you plan on leaving the computer for an extended period of time. However, because the hard drive is so much slower than RAM, coming out of hibernation will take longer than coming out of standby mode. Hibernation has also been known to fail in some cases and cause various issues in Windows.

Standby is known as "Sleep" in Windows Vista and is accessible by clicking on Start, clicking the arrow, and selecting Sleep, which is just above Shut Down. In Windows XP, Standby can be accessed by clicking Start > Shut Down and selecting Standby from the drop-down menu.

Hibernation however needs to be turned on first before it can be used. To enable hibernation in Windows Vista, open the Command Prompt as an administrator. Then type **powercfg.exe/hibernate on**; it then shows up in the shut down area of the Start menu. To turn it off, type **powercfg.exe/hibernate off**. To enable hibernation in Windows XP, go to the Power Options Properties window that we were in previously, but this time click the Hibernate tab, and check mark Enable hibernation. If you use the Welcome Screen in Windows XP, you might not see the Hibernate option. Press the Shift key and the Standby option should change to Hibernate. Otherwise, if you are not using the Welcome Screen, it should show up in the Shut Down Windows drop-down menu.

> **ExamAlert**
>
> Know the differences between Standby and Hibernate for the exam.

User Migrations and Customizations

Users often customize their own computer to a certain extent; modify colors, auto-hide the taskbar, add shortcuts, and so on. But some customizations, modifications, and migrations can be done only by the administrator.

Migrating User Data

If a user will be using a new operating system, either on the same computer or on a new computer, you might need to move his files and settings to the new system. When doing so, make sure that the destination computer has the latest service packs and updates and the same programs that are currently running on the original computer. There are a few options for migrating data:

▶ **Windows Easy Transfer:** This program enables you to copy files, photos, music, email, and settings to a Windows Vista computer; all this information is collectively referred to as *user state*. It is installed with Windows Vista and can be downloaded for Windows XP from www.microsoft.com; just search for Windows Easy Transfer for Windows XP. Either way, the program will be located in Start > All Programs > Accessories > System Tools. Files and settings can be migrated over the network or by USB cable. The data can also be stored on media like a CD, DVD, or USB flash drive until the destination Vista computer is ready. Normally you would start with the computer that has the files and settings that you want to transfer (the source computer). You can transfer the files and settings for one user account or all the accounts on the computer. All the files and settings will be saved as a single .MIG file (Migration Store). Then, you would move to the computer in which you want to transfer the files to (destination computer), and either load the .MIG file from CD, DVD, USB flash drive, or locate the file on the source computer through the use of a USB cable or network connection. For more information on how to migrate files with Windows Easy Transfer, see the following MSKB article: http://support.microsoft.com/kb/928634.

▶ **User State Migration Tool (USMT):** This is a command-line tool that can be used to migrate user files and settings for one *or more* computers. The program can be downloaded from www.microsoft.com. When installed, two different tools are used: Scanstate.exe saves all the files and settings of the user (or users) on a computer, known as the user state; and loadstate.exe transfers that data to the destination computer(s). There are many options when using the scanstate and loadstate commands, including the ability to select which users are migrated and whether the store of data is uncompressed, compressed, or compressed and encrypted. By utilizing scripting programs, the transfer of files to multiple computers can be automated over the network. For more information on how to transfer files and settings with USMT, see the following TechNet link: http://technet.microsoft.com/en-us/library/cc722032(WS.10).aspx. Windows 7 employs some additional features such as AES encryption support, and shadow copying of volumes. For more information on Windows 7 USMT improvements, see the following TechNet link: http://technet.microsoft.com/en-us/magazine/dd443646.aspx.

▶ **Files and Settings Transfer (FAST) Wizard:** This is the older version of Windows Easy Transfer and is installed by default on Windows XP. It is meant for transferring files and settings from a Windows XP, 2000, or

9x computer to a Windows XP computer but otherwise works in a similar fashion to Windows Easy Transfer. To transfer files from XP to Vista, download the Windows Easy Transfer program for XP.

> **ExamAlert**
>
> Understand the various tools that can be used to migrate user data.

Customizing the User Environment

A user might not be completely comfortable using Windows Vista, or perhaps the user's computer is not the newest or most powerful system, and Vista is making it crawl due to the resources required to run it. To create a more enjoyable user experience, and to make the best use of the resources a computer has, you might need to customize the user's environment. There are a couple ways to do this:

▶ **Revert to Classic mode:** By reverting to the original Windows look, the user might feel more comfortable, and you will free up additional resources on the computer. There are two ways to accomplish this. First, turn off Windows Aero: Right-click the desktop wallpaper and select Personalize, select Theme, and in the drop-down menu select Windows Classic; this removes the glassy translucent windows and lets the video card and processor in a lesser computer breath a sigh of relief. Second, revert to the classic Start menu: Right-click the Taskbar and select Properties, click the Start Menu tab, and select the Classic Start menu radio button. Even if you are a power user that runs intensive applications, this might be a smart solution, effectively trading style for performance. Although Windows Aero is not used in Windows XP, similar techniques can be used to revert the XP desktop and Start menu to Classic mode.

▶ **Disable visual effects:** Any special graphic effects will put a strain on the computer's performance. There are two ways to disable visual effects. First, open the Control Panel > Personalization window, select Window color and appearance; then from the Appearance Settings window, click the Effects button, and deselect all three options. Second, open the System Properties window to the Advanced tab, click the Settings button within the Performance box, and select the Adjust for Best Performance radio button. Both of these methods can be done on Windows XP as well.

A few other tools you can use to customize a user's experience are the Task Scheduler, and Regional and Language Options. The Task Scheduler (known as Scheduled Tasks in Windows XP) can run particular programs, send emails, or display messages at a scheduled time (or times) designated by the user. This program can be accessed from Start > All Programs > Accessories > System Tools (and from the Control Panel in Windows XP). Regional and Language Options is available in the Control Panel. This enables the user to modify the format of numbers, currency, and time. The user can also change how programs service the computer based on its location, and different keyboards and languages can be installed in the case that the user spends most of their time in another country.

Advanced System Tools

Several tools can affect advanced configuration changes in Windows. This section describes a few of those: the Registry Editor, Remote Desktop, and Windows Compatibility.

The Registry

The Windows Registry is a database that stores the settings for Windows Vista/XP/2000. It contains hardware and software information, and user settings. If you cannot make the modifications that you want in the Windows GUI, the Registry is the place to go. To modify settings in the Registry, use the Registry Editor; open the Run prompt and type **regedit.exe**. This displays a window like the one shown in Figure 8.12

> **Note**
>
> The Registry Editor can also be opened with the **regedt32** command. In Windows 2000 this opened a different version of the Registry Editor that is not used in Windows XP and Vista. However the **regedt32** command still works in Vista and XP; it just opens the standard Registry Editor.

The Registry is divided into several sections known as hives that begin with the letters HKEY. Table 8.1 describes the five visible hives in the Registry Editor.

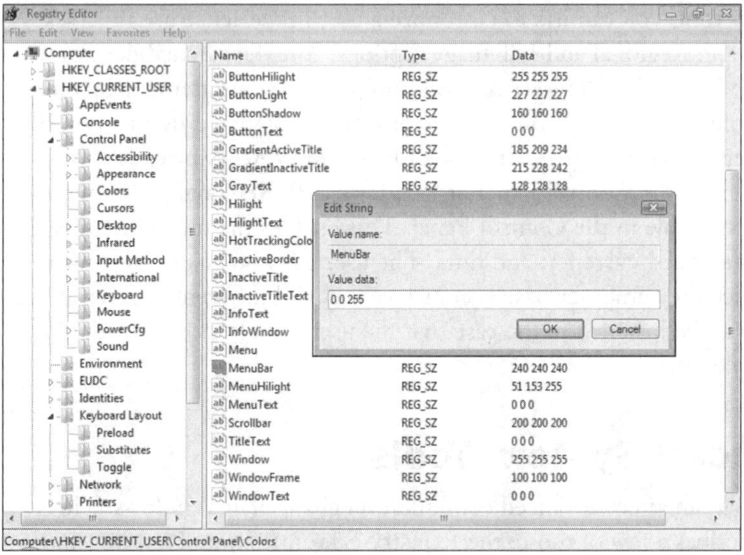

FIGURE 8.12   The Registry Editor in Windows Vista

TABLE 8.1   **Description of Registry Hives in Windows**

Registry Hive	Description
HKEY_CLASSES_ROOT	Stores information about applications' file associations and Object Linking and Embedding (OLE).
HKEY_CURRENT_USER	Stores settings that concern the currently logged on user. It is common to make changes in this hive.
HKEY_LOCAL_MACHINE	Stores hardware and software settings that are specific to the computer. This is where the bulk of a PC technician's Registry edits are made.
HKEY_USERS	Stores data corresponding to all users who have ever logged on to the computer.
HKEY_CURRENT_CONFIG	Contains information that is gathered every time the computer starts up.

Hives are also known as keys that contain other keys and subkeys. This forms the organizational system for the Registry; it is similar to folders and subfolders within Windows Explorer; however, the Registry does not store actual data files; instead it stores settings. Inside the keys and subkeys are registration entries that contain the actual settings. These can be edited, or new entries can be created. The types of entries include String values, used for decimal numbers; Binary values, used for binary entries; DWORD and QWORD entries, used for binary and hexadecimal entries; and multistring values that can have a variety of information. Registry hives are stored in \%systemroot%\ System32\Config.

Many users fear the Registry, but the technician need not. Just follow a couple simple rules: 1) Back up the Registry before making changes and 2) Don't make modifications or additions until you have a thorough understanding of the entry you are trying to modify or add. Figure 8.12 shows a Registry entry called MenuBar within HKEY_CURRENT_USER\Control Panel\Colors. By double-clicking on the MenuBar entry, an Edit String window appears as shown. Once again, the beauty of the Registry is that you can make modifications to things that normally can't be modified in the Windows GUI. MenuBar is one of these examples. In the figure the entry's string value has been changed to 0 0 255, which means the color blue. To effect this change, close the Registry Editor (no saving necessary) and log off and log back on. Some Registry changes require a reboot of the system.

As mentioned, it is important to know how to back up the Registry. It is possible to back up any individual key or the entire Registry. Let's say a user wanted to back up the Colors subkey before making changes to the MenuBar entry. The proper procedure would be to highlight the Colors subkey, click File on the Menu bar, and select Export. Then, it's as simple as selecting a location to save the Registry entry and naming it. It exports as a .reg file. A typical subkey like this is about 2KB in size. Backing up the entire Registry can be done in two ways. First, by highlighting Computer (My Computer in XP/2000), selecting Export, and saving the file. The other option is to select any Registry key; then select Export and in the Export Registry File window, select the All radio button in the Export range box. The entire Registry for Windows Vista can be upward of 200MB and 50MB for Windows XP. Later, individual keys or the entire Registry can be imported with the Import option on the File menu, in case a modification was not successful.

Lastly, you can connect to remote computers to gain partial access to their respective registries. To do this, select File, Connect Network Registry. You can then browse for computers that are members of the same network your computer is a member of, connect to them, and make modifications to those remote registries. Of course, you need to have administrative privileges on the remote computer.

ExamAlert

Know how to open the Registry Editor, modify entries, export the Registry, and connect to remote registries for the exam.

Remote Desktop

Ever want to control a computer remotely? Remote Desktop software, included with Windows Vista and Windows XP Professional, enables a user to see, and control, the GUI of a remote computer. This enables users to control other computers on the network or over the Internet without leaving their seat, and aids technicians in their attempt to repair computers, without having to go to the system that needs repair. But first, to have a remote desktop session, you need to configure the software. To do so, open the System Properties window, and select the Remote tab. From here there are two boxes of information:

▶ **Remote Assistance:** This is check marked by default. This means that connections can be made by sending Remote Assistance invitations, by email (Outlook) or via instant messaging (Windows Messenger). These invitations can be to ask for help or to offer help. This is often implemented in help desk scenarios in which a user invites a technician to take control of her computer so that it can be repaired. Invitations are made by clicking Start > Help and Support and selecting the Windows Remote Assistance link (in Vista) or Invite Someone to Help You link (in XP). If the user has access to only web-based email such as Yahoo or AOL, she can select Save invitation as a file that enables the user to attach the invitation to the web-based email message. Of course for all this to function, the Remote Assistance option must be selected in the System Properties Remote tab; plus Remote Control must be check marked, which can be enabled by clicking the Advanced button. When the proper settings are enabled, Remote Assistance calls flow right through the Windows Firewall.

▶ **Remote Desktop:** This is where you can select whether other users can connect to, and control, your computer at any time without an invitation from you. In Windows Vista, there are options to disable remote connections, enable connections with any version of remote desktop, and enable connections running Remote Desktop with Network-level Authentication for security. This is disabled by default, but if enabled, the remote users can make connections to your computer by computer name or by IP address. Finally, you can select the users that are allowed to connect to your computer. If your network is a workgroup, then the local user account(s) you select, is just that, local. For the remote user to connect, the remote computer must have an identical account (same username and password) as the one you selected on your computer, and the remote user must know the username/password. If the network is a domain, this is not an issue due to centralized administration of accounts.

> **ExamAlert**
>
> Be able to explain the difference between Remote Assistance and Remote Desktop for the exam.

To make a Remote Desktop connection to a remote computer, first make sure that the remote computer has Remote Desktop enabled. Next, click Start > All Programs > Accessories and Remote Desktop Connection. (In Windows XP the path is Start > All Programs > Accessories > Communications.) This opens the remote Desktop Connection window. Click Options for more logon settings, as shown in Figure 8.13. To make the connection, you need to supply a computer name or the IP address of the remote computer and a username and password of an account on the remote computer.

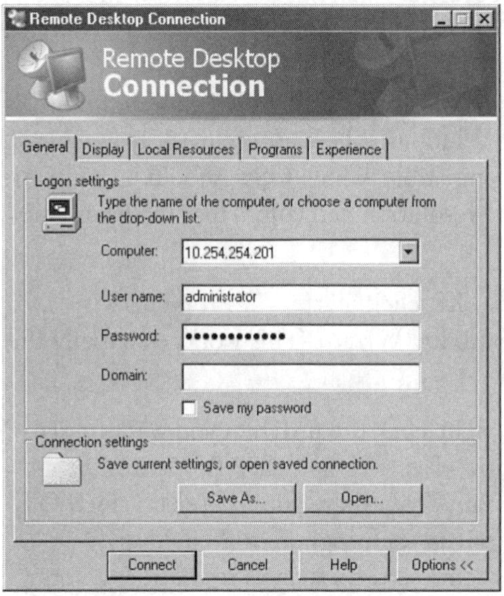

FIGURE 8.13   **Remote Desktop Connection window**

Click Connect and the screen of the other computer should show up on your local display. At this point, you can control the remote computer as if you were sitting locally at it. By default, the remote computer's screen locks and can be unlocked only with a username/password.

> **Note**
>
> Remote Desktop is based off the Remote Desktop Protocol (RDP). When Remote Desktop is enabled, this protocol is allowed through the Windows Firewall. Give strong consideration to using Network Level Authentication in Windows Vista when allowing Remote Desktop connections.

Program Compatibility Wizard

Most applications run properly on Windows Vista/XP. However, some applications that were designed for older versions of Windows might not run properly on Windows Vista/XP. To make applications written for older versions of Windows compatible with Windows Vista/XP, use the Program Compatibility Wizard, or the Compatibility tab of a file's Properties window.

► To start the wizard in Windows Vista, Click Start > Control Panel and then click the Programs icon (in category mode). Then, under Programs and Features click the link called Use an Older Program with This Version of Windows. (In Windows 7, this link is called Run programs made for previous versions of Windows.) This program asks you which programs you want to make compatible, which OS it should be compatible with, and inquires as to the resolution and colors that the program should run in.

► To start the wizard in Windows XP, click Start > All Programs > Accessories > Program Compatibility Wizard. This works essentially the same in XP as it does in Vista.

► To use the Compatibility tab, right-click the program you want to make compatible from within Windows Explorer and click Properties. From there, click the Compatibility tab. From there you can select which OS compatibility mode you want to run the program in (Windows 95/98/ME, and so forth) and define settings such as resolution, colors, and so on.

Windows XP Mode

Windows 7 can emulate the entire Windows XP OS if you so want. This is done to help with program compatibility—meaning older programs that run or perform better with Windows XP, or perhaps will *only* run with Windows XP. To do this, you must first have Windows 7 Professional or Ultimate installed. Then, additional components must be installed to emulate Windows XP. First, install Windows XP Mode, then Virtual PC, and finally the Windows XP Mode update. These additional components can be downloaded for free (as long as you have a valid copy of Windows 7) starting at the following link:

http://www.microsoft.com/windows/virtual-pc/download.aspx

Cram Quiz

Answer these questions. The answers follow the last question. If you cannot answer these questions correctly, consider reading this section again until you can.

1. What would you type to open the Device Manager in the Run prompt?

   ○ **A.** MMC

   ○ **B.** secpol.msc

   ○ **C.** CMD

   ○ **D.** devmgmt.msc

2. Where is the best place to get a driver for a video card?

   ○ **A.** CD-ROM

   ○ **B.** USB flash drive

   ○ **C.** Manufacturer's website

   ○ **D.** Microsoft's website

3. Which command opens the System Information tool?

   ○ **A.** devmgmt.msc

   ○ **B.** compmgmt.msc

   ○ **C.** winmsd.msc

   ○ **D.** msinfo32.exe

4. Which tab of the Task Manager tells you about the total usage of the CPU?

   ○ **A.** Performance

   ○ **B.** Processes

   ○ **C.** Networking

   ○ **D.** Processing

5. Where can a user go to start and stop services in Windows Vista? (Select all that apply.)

   ○ **A.** msconfig

   ○ **B.** Task Manager

   ○ **C.** Computer Management

   ○ **D.** Command Prompt

6. Which file is used by the operating system for virtual memory?

   ○ **A.** swapfile.sys

   ○ **B.** pagefile.sys

   ○ **C.** pagingfile.sys

   ○ **D.** virtualfile.sys

7. Which command should you use to stop a service in the Command Prompt?

   ○ **A.** `spooler stop`

   ○ **B.** `network stop`

   ○ **C.** `net stop`

   ○ **D.** `stop`

8. Which power management mode stores data on the hard drive?

   ○ **A.** Sleep

   ○ **B.** Hibernate

   ○ **C.** Standby

   ○ **D.** Pillow.exe

9. Which tool enables a technician to move user state data from within the command-line?

   ○ **A.** Windows Easy Transfer

   ○ **B.** Elevated mode

   ○ **C.** USMT

   ○ **D.** FAST

10. What is HKEY_LOCAL_MACHINE considered to be?

    ○ **A.** A Registry entry

    ○ **B.** A subkey

    ○ **C.** A string value

    ○ **D.** A hive

11. When users invite a technician to help repair their computer, what is this called?

    ○ **A.** Remote Desktop

    ○ **B.** Remote Assistance

    ○ **C.** RDP

    ○ **D.** Remote connectivity

Cram Quiz Answers

1. **D.** Devmgmt.msc is the Microsoft console window known as Device Manager. Typing **MMC** opens up a new blank Microsoft Management Console. **Secpol.msc** opens the Local Security Policy window. And **CMD** opens the Command Prompt.

2. **C.** The manufacturer's website is the best place to get the latest driver for your device, next on the list would be the CD-ROM that came with the device, and last, attempt to have Microsoft automatically install its version of the driver.

3. **D. Msinfo32.exe** opens the System Information tool. **Devmgmt.msc** opens the Device Manager, **compmgmt.msc** opens Computer Management, and **winmsd.msc** doesn't exist; however, **winmsd.exe** opens the System Information tool in Windows XP/2000, but **winmsd.exe** does not function in Vista.

4. **A.** The Performance tab shows the percentage of processing power used in real time. The Processes tab shows the individual processes that are running, the amount of processing power each of them is using, and the amount of memory they are utilizing. The Networking tab shows the percentage of network utilization for each network adapter. There is no Processing tab.

5. **B, C,** and **D.** All answers are correct for Windows Vista; however, keep in mind that Windows XP does not have a Services tab in the Task Manager.

6. **B.** Pagefile.sys is the virtual memory file that is located by default in the root of C:.

7. **C. Net stop** (and the service name) stops the service in the Command Prompt. For example, **net stop spooler**.

8. **B.** When a computer hibernates, all the information in RAM is written to a file called hiberfil.sys in the root of C: within the hard drive.

9. **C.** USMT (User State Migration Tool) is the command-line version that can move any or all the user states to and from multiple computers. Window Easy Transfer is the successor to FAST (Files and Settings Transfer Wizard). Elevated mode is what you need to be in when running administrative-level functions from within the Command Prompt.

10. **D.** HKEY_LOCAL_MACHINE is one of the five visible hives that can be modified from within the Registry Editor.

11. **B.** Remote Assistance calls can be made from users to invite other users to help fix a problem for them. Remote Desktop connections are the connections that a computer makes to a remote computer to control it.

Files, File Systems, and Disks

This section covers file structures, file locations, ways of manipulating files, and file systems. It also delves into how to manage disks, including how to partition and format drives, create mount points, and identify drive status. Finally, the various levels of RAID are discussed. Let's start by talking about files and file systems.

Working with Files and File Systems

Files are what makes the world go round it seems. But because there are so many of them, we need to organize them efficiently. To do so, operating systems use a directory structure. It all starts with the root of the operating system and moves on from there, as detailed in Table 8.2.

TABLE 8.2 **Directory Structure in Windows Vista**

Directory	Usage
C:\	This is the root of the C: drive, which is the drive in which the OS is usually installed. Boot files such as bootmgr and NTLDR are stored here.
C:\Windows	This folder is the %systemroot%, in which the operating system is actually installed to, folder by folder, and file by file. This is also known as %WINDIR% in Windows 7. Note: In Windows 2000, the %systemroot% is C:\Winnt.
C:\Windows\System32	Contains the core operating system files (for instance NTOSKRNL.EXE) and many applications such as cmd.exe and dxdiag.exe.
C:\Boot	This contains the Boot Configuration Data Store in Windows 7/Vista *Note: This folder might be in a different partition depending on which one is the system partition. In Windows 7, this will default to a hidden 100MB system partition.*
C:\Program Files	This is where the bulk of applications are installed to, for example Microsoft Office or Adobe Acrobat Reader.
C:\Documents and Settings	This is where all user account information is stored in Windows XP. In Windows 7/Vista, it redirects to the Users folder. (This is also known as a "junction.")
C:\Windows\Temp	This is where temporary files are stored.
C:\Windows\CSC	This is where offline files are stored. Offline files are files that you have previously selected from the network to be available to you even if the network is not available.

> **Note**
>
> If the operating system was installed to another volume, for example D:, all the paths above would be modified to reflect this. If the operating system was installed in a different folder than the %systemroot%, that would affect all subfolders of the systemroot as well.

Windows 7/Vista and XP Boot Files

After the BIOS is done bootstrapping, and the MBR and boot sector of the hard drive have been located and accessed, a loader file is accessed on the hard drive. In Windows Vista, this is the Windows Boot Manager; in Windows XP, it is NTLDR. The following files are required to start Windows 7/Vista:

▸ **Bootmgr (Windows Boot Manager):** This is the Windows loader program. It takes the place of NTLDR and determines which operating system to start.

▸ **BCD (Boot Configuration Data):** This is located in \boot\bcd; it furnishes the Windows Boot Manager with information about the operating system(s) to be booted. It is the successor to boot.ini and can be modified with MSCONFIG or with the bcdedit.exe program. BCD was developed to provide an improved mechanism for describing boot configuration data and to work better with newer firmware models such as the Extensible Firmware Interface (EFI).

The following files are required to start Windows XP:

▸ **NTLDR:** The Windows loader program determines which operating system to start (if there is more than one).

▸ **Boot.ini:** Contains the menu of operating systems that can be selected and options for booting Windows.

▸ **Ntdetect.com:** Detects the hardware installed on your system.

The following files are optional when starting Windows XP:

▸ **Ntbootdd.sys:** This device driver is used only if Windows is started from a SCSI drive whose host adapter does not have an onboard SCSI BIOS enabled.

▸ **Bootsect.dos:** This contains the boot sectors for another operating system if you multiboot.

> **Exam Alert**
>
> Memorize the required Windows Vista and XP boot files and their function.

Indexing

Because there are so many files, Windows Vista and XP offer the Indexing service to help find the files you want faster. However, indexing too much content can lead to poor operating system performance.

To adjust the indexing settings in Windows Vista, go to Start > Control Panel > System and Maintenance and click Indexing Options. From here you can modify whether folders are indexed by clicking on the Modify button and selecting or deselecting the folders you want. It is not recommended to select an entire volume (like C:) because it can cause poor performance. Use indexing for specific folders in which you store important data that you search for on a regular basis. If you don't want indexing at all, you can either deselect all folders that are check marked or disable the indexing in general. To disable indexing altogether:

1. Click Start, right-click on Computer, and select Manage. This brings up the Computer Management window.

2. From here, expand Services and Applications in the left window pane, and click Services.

3. In the right window pane, scroll down to Windows Search, right-click it, and select Stop. You can restart the service at any time by right-clicking and selecting Start. Check the startup type by right-clicking the service and selecting Properties. If the startup type is set to Automatic, you should change it to manual or disabled, otherwise the service starts back up again when you restart the computer.

You can also turn off indexing for individual drives. To do so:

1. Open Windows Explorer.

2. Right-click on the volume you want to stop indexing on; for example C:, and select Properties.

3. At the bottom of the window, deselect where it says Index This Drive for Faster Searching.

To turn off indexing in Windows XP:

1. Click Start, right-click on My Computer, and select Manage. This brings up the Computer Management window.

2. From here expand Services and Applications in the left window pane, and click Services.

3. In the right window pane, scroll down to Indexing Service, right-click it, and select Stop. You can restart the service at any time by right-clicking and selecting Start. Check the startup type by right-clicking the service and selecting Properties. If the startup type is set to Automatic, you should change it to manual or disabled; otherwise the service starts back up again when you restart the computer.

You can also turn off indexing on any volume by right-clicking the volume, selecting Properties, and deselecting Allow Indexing Service to index this disk for fast file searching.

Working with Directories in the Command Prompt

Have I mentioned yet that just about anything you can do in Windows can also be done in the Command Prompt? It's true. And sometimes the Command Prompt is faster (if you can type quickly) than the GUI. There are three commands used to work with directories in the Command Prompt, and by the way, "directory" is the original name for "folder."

▶ **CD:** Change Directory, formerly **chdir**. This command enables you to move from one directory to another. Actually, you can go from any one directory to any other using just one **CD** command.

▶ **MD:** Make Directory, formerly **mkdir**. This command creates directories.

▶ **RD:** Remove Directory, formerly **rmdir**. This command enables you to remove directories. It can also remove directories that contain files by utilizing the /S switch.

All these commands can be used in such a way in which their function affects any folder you choose within the directory structure (which used to be known as the DOS tree, but I digress). Figure 8.14 gives a sample directory structure.

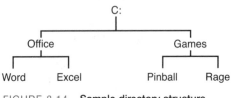

FIGURE 8.14   **Sample directory structure**

Let's say that your current position was C:\Office. From here or any other location, you can do anything to any folder in the entire directory tree. Let's give a couple examples:

▶ Change the current position to the Pinball folder. To do this, the command would be either **cd c:\games\pinball** or just **cd \games\ pinball**.

▶ Make a directory called "documents" within Word. To do this the command syntax would be **md c:\office\word\documents**.

▶ Delete the directory Excel. To do this the command would be **rd c:\office\excel**.

Note

Making directories can be quick in the command line. If you need to create several subdirectories, using the **MD** command can be quicker than clicking with the mouse in Windows Explorer. For example, to make four folders with one command, you could type: **md folder1; folder2; folder3; folder4**.

ExamAlert

Know the difference between **CD**, **MD**, and **RD** for the exam.

Managing Disks

So you have three 1TB SATA 3.0 hard disks. Now what do you do with them? You manage them. The main tool with which to do this is called Disk Management. It can be accessed by opening Computer Management, and expanding Storage.

Partitioning, Formatting, and Drive Status

The proper order for disk preparation is to partition the disk, format it, and then copy files to your heart's delight. However, sometimes you might also need to initialize new disks within Windows; this would be done before partitioning. All these things can be done within the Disk Management program. The Disk Management tool within Computer Management is the GUI-based application for analyzing and configuring hard drives. You can do a lot from here, as shown in Table 8.3. Try some of the configurations listed on a test computer. All you need is a drive with unpartitioned space.

TABLE 8.3   **Configurations in Disk Management**

Configuration	Steps involved
Initialize a new disk.	A secondary hard disk installed in a computer might not be seen by Windows Explorer immediately. To make it accessible, locate the disk (for example Disk 1), right-click where it says Disk 1, Disk 2, and such, and select Initialize Disk.
Create a primary partition.	1. Right-click on a disk's unallocated space (shown with a black header), and select New Partition, as shown in Figure 8.15. 2. Click Next for the wizard, and then select Primary Partition. 3. Select the amount of unallocated space you want for the partition and click Next. 4. Select a drive letter. 5. Choose whether you want to format at this point. 6. Review the summary screen and if it is correct, click Finish. Note: For computers with less resources, it is recommended to hold off on formatting until after the partition is created.
Create an extended partition.	1. Right-click on a disk's unallocated space (shown with a black header), and select New Partition, as shown in Figure 8.15. 2. Click Next for the wizard, and then select Extended Partition. 3. Select the amount of unallocated space you want for the partition and click Next. 4. Review the summary screen and if it is correct, click Finish.

TABLE 8.3   **Continued**

Configuration	Steps involved
Create a logical drive.	This can be done only within an extended partition that has already been created. 1. Right-click on the extended partition (shown with a green header), and select New Logical Drive, as shown in Figure 8.16. 2. Click Next for the wizard; you notice that your only option is Logical drive. Click Next. 3. Select the amount of unallocated space you want for the partition and click Next. 4. Select a drive letter. 5. Choose whether you want to format at this point. 6. Review the summary screen and if it is correct, click Finish.
Format a partition/logical drive.	1. Right-click the primary partition or logical drive and select Format. 2. In the Format *x*: window, select the file system and whether to do a quick format. If it is a new drive, quick formats are okay, but if the drive was used previously, you might want to leave this option unchecked. ALL DATA WILL BE ERASED during the format procedure.
Make a partition active.	Right-click on the primary partition and select Mark Partition as Active. You can have up to four primary partitions on a hard disk, but only one of them can be active.
Convert a basic disk to dynamic.	To change the size of a partition in Windows XP, to create simple and spanned volumes, or to implement RAID, the hard disk(s) need to be converted to dynamic. It's highly recommended that you back up your data before attempting this configuration. 1. Right-click on the hard disk in which it says Disk 0 or Disk 1 and select Convert to Dynamic Disk. 2. In the ensuing window you can select multiple disks to switch over to dynamic. This can also be done in Windows Vista; however, in Vista you now have the option to extend a partition as shown next.

TABLE 8.3 **Continued**

Configuration	Steps involved
Extend a partition (Vista only).	Windows Vista enables you to extend the size of a partition (volume) or shrink it within the Disk Management utility. It's highly recommended that you back up your data before attempting this configuration.

1. Right-click the volume to be extended.

2. Select Extend Volume. (Remember that a volume is any section of the hard drive with a drive letter.)

3. Click Next for the wizard and select how much space you'd like to add to the partition.

4. Select any other disks (with unpartitioned space) to combine with the first disk to create a spanned partition and click Next.

5. Click Finish at the summary screen.

A reboot is not required, and this process should finish quickly. This process can also be done in the Command Prompt using the **Diskpart** command.

Note: Extended partitions are not fault-tolerant; make sure you have a backup plan in place!

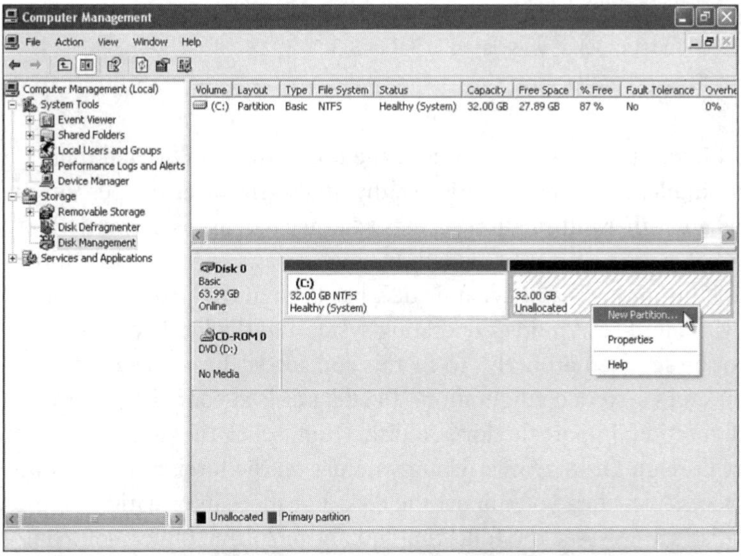

FIGURE 8.15   Creating a partition from unallocated disk space

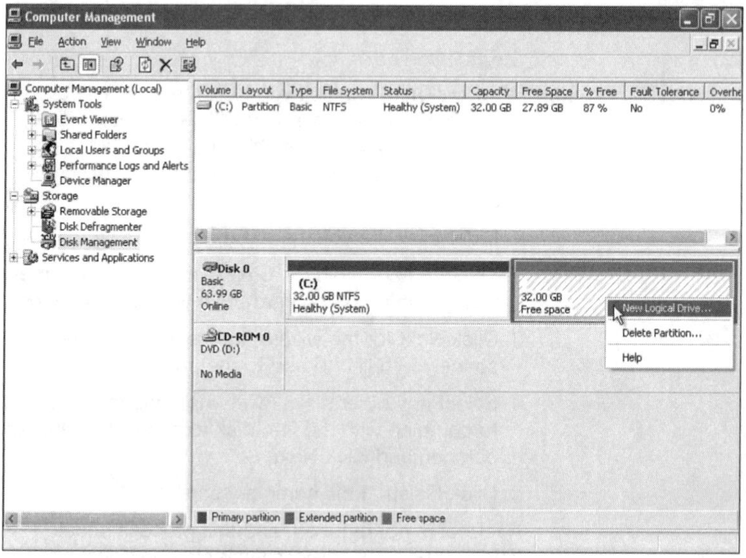

FIGURE 8.16   Creating a logical drive from within an extended partition

> **Note**
>
> The command-line version of Disk Management is called diskpart. With this tool you can accomplish most of what was listed in Table 8.3.

In Figure 8.15, we also can see the disks at the top of the window and their status. For example, the C: partition is healthy. It also shows us the percent of the disk used and other information such as whether the disk is currently formatting, if it's dynamic, or if it has failed. In some cases, you might see "foreign" status. This means that a dynamic disk has been moved from another computer (with another Windows operating system) to the local computer, and it cannot be accessed properly. To fix this and access the disk, add the disk to your computer's system configuration. To add a disk to your computer's system configuration, import the foreign disk. (Right-click the disk and then click Import Foreign Disks.) Any existing volumes on the foreign disk become visible and accessible when you import the disk. For more information on the plethora of disk statuses, see the following link: http://technet.microsoft.com/ en-us/library/cc738101(WS.10).aspx.

File System Basics

When formatting a hard drive, you have the option to format it as either the NTFS (recommended) or FAT32 file system. NTFS is a more secure and stable platform and can support larger volume sizes. It also supports encryption with the Encrypting File System (EFS). FAT32 should be used only to interact with older versions of Windows and to format devices such as USB flash drives. Depending on the cluster size used, NTFS can support up to either 16TB (4KB clusters), or 256TB (64KB cluster) partitions, but most systems will be limited to 2TB due to the limitations of partition tables on MBR-based disks. This hardware limitation applies to maximum FAT32 partition sizes of 2TB as well (aside from the installation maximum of 32GB). To go beyond this, a set of striped or spanned dynamic disks would have to be employed, creating a multidisk volume. You might have heard of FAT (specifically known as FAT16). FAT was the predecessor to FAT32. Windows XP can be installed to a FAT partition up to 4GB in size; some older flash devices also use FAT, but it is recommended to stay away from FAT16 in general because it is deprecated. One other file system of note is FAT12, which is used mostly by floppy disks. Another file system introduced by Microsoft is called the Extended File Allocation Table (exFAT) which is suited specifically for USB flash drives, but addresses the needs of many other mobile storage solutions. The successor to FAT32, it can handle very large file sizes and can format media that is larger than 32GB with a single partition. In fact, exFAT (also known as FAT64) has a recommended maximum of 512TB for partitions, with a theoretical maximum of 64 ZB (zettabytes). The file size limit when using exFAT is 16EB (exabytes). This file system can be used in Windows 7, Server 2008, Vista with SP1, XP/Server 2003 with SP2, and Windows CE 6.0. If NTFS is not a plausible solution, and the partition size needed is larger than 32GB, exFAT might be the best option. As of the writing of this book, exFAT is not used for internal IDE or SATA hard drives; instead it is used for flash memory storage and other external storage devices. exFAT is considered to be a more efficient file system than NTFS when it comes to flash memory storage; with less fragmentation, leading to more possible read/write cycles over the life of the flash memory device.

Mount Points and Mounting A Drive

You can also "mount" drives in Disk Management. A mounted drive is a drive that is mapped to an empty folder within a volume that has been formatted as NTFS. Instead of using drive letters, mounted drives use drive paths. This is a good solution for when you need more than 26 drives in your computer because you are not limited to the letters in the alphabet. Mounted drives can also provide more space for temporary files and can allow you to move folders to different drives if space runs low on the current drive. To mount a drive:

1. Right-click the partition or volume you want to mount and select Change Drive Letters and Paths.

2. In the displayed window, click Add.

3. Then browse to the *empty* folder you want to mount the volume to, and click OK for both windows.

As shown in Figure 8.17, the DVD-ROM drive has been mounted within a folder on the hard drive called Test. The figure is showing the Properties window for the folder Test. It shows that it is a mounted volume and shows the location of the folder (which is the mount point) and the target of the mount point, which is the DVD drive containing a Windows Vista DVD. To remove the mount point, just go back to Disk Management, right-click the mounted volume, and select Change Drive Letters and Paths; then select Remove. Remember that the folder you want to use as a mount point must be empty, and it must be within an NTFS volume.

FIGURE 8.17   Empty NTFS folder acting as a mount point

RAID

RAID stands for Redundant Array of Inexpensive Disks. RAID technologies are designed to either increase the speed of reading and writing data or to create one of several types of fault tolerant volumes, or both. The test requires you to know RAID levels 0, 1, and 5. Table 8.4 describes each of these.

TABLE 8.4 **RAID 0, 1, and 5 Descriptions**

RAID Level	Description	Fault Tolerant?	Minimum Number of Disks
RAID 0	Striping. Data is striped across multiple disks in an effort to increase performance.	No	2
RAID 1	Mirroring. Data is copied to two identical disks. If one disk fails, the other continues to operate. When each disk is connected to a separate controller, this is known as Disk Duplexing. See Figure 8.18 for an illustration. RAID 1 is not available in Windows XP/Vista and can be set up only in Windows Server.	Yes	2 (and 2 only)
RAID 5	Striping with Parity. Data is striped across multiple disks; fault tolerant parity data is also written to each disk. If one disk fails, the array can reconstruct the data from the parity information. See Figure 8.19 for an illustration. RAID 5 is not available in Windows XP/Vista and can be setup only in Windows Server.	Yes	3

Even though Windows Vista/XP cannot support RAID 1 and 5 from within the operating system, they *can* support hardware controllers that can create RAID 1 and 5 arrays. Some motherboards have built in RAID functionality as well. Figure 8.18 shows an illustration of RAID 1; you can see that data is written to both disks and that both disks collectively are known as the M: drive or M: *volume*. Figure 8.19 displays an illustration of RAID 5. In a RAID 5 array, blocks of data are distributed to the disks (A1 and A2 are a block, B1 and B2 are a block, and so on), and parity information is written for each block of data. This is written to each disk in an alternating fashion (AP, BP, and such) so that the parity is also distributed. If one disk fails, the parity information from the other disks will reconstruct the data. It is important to make the distinction between fault tolerance and backup. Fault tolerance means that the hard drives can continue to function (with little or no downtime) even if there is a problem with one of the drives. Backup means that we are taking the data and copying it (and possibly compressing it) to another location for archival in the event of a disaster. An example of a disaster would be if *two* drives in a RAID 5 array were to fail.

> **Note**
>
> For more information on RAID, see the Pearson title *Network+ Video Mentor*. It covers RAID and other networking topics in greater depth.

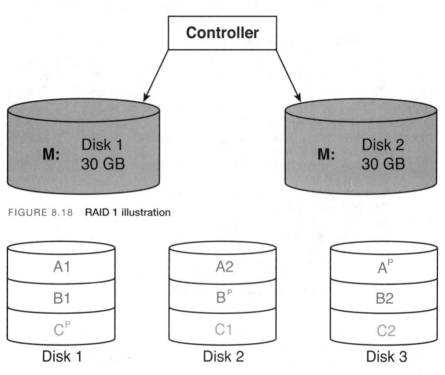

FIGURE 8.18   **RAID 1 illustration**

FIGURE 8.19   **RAID 5 illustration**

Cram Quiz

Answer these questions. The answers follow the last question. If you cannot answer these questions correctly, consider reading this section again until you can.

1. Where is NTOSKRNL.EXE located?

- ○ **A.** C:\Window
- ○ **B.** C:\Boot
- ○ **C.** C:\Windows\System
- ○ **D.** C:\Windows\System32

2. Which of these is the boot loader for Windows Vista?

- ○ **A.** BCD
- ○ **B.** Bootmgr
- ○ **C.** NTLDR
- ○ **D.** Boot.ini

3. Which command creates a directory?

- ○ **A.** CD
- ○ **B.** MD
- ○ **C.** RD
- ○ **D.** Chdir

4. Which operating system enables you to extend volumes?

- ○ **A.** Windows XP
- ○ **B.** Windows 2000
- ○ **C.** Windows Aero
- ○ **D.** Windows Vista

5. Which level of RAID uses two disks only?

- ○ **A.** RAID 0
- ○ **B.** RAID 1
- ○ **C.** RAID 5
- ○ **D.** Striping

Cram Quiz Answers

1. **D.** NTOSKRNL.EXE is located in C:\Windows\System32, otherwise referred to as \%systemroot%\System32.

2. **B.** Bootmgr (Windows Boot Manager) is the boot loader for Windows Vista. BCD is the Boot Configuration Data store, NTLDR is the boot loader for Windows XP, and Boot.ini contains the menu of OSs and boot options in Windows XP.

3. **Answer: B.** MD (Make Directory) creates directories. CD is change directory, RD is remove directory, and **chdir** is the older version of CD.

4. **D.** Windows Vista is the only (current) operating system that can extend volumes. Windows Aero is not an OS; it's the new look of the Vista GUI.

5. **B.** RAID 1 (mirroring) uses two disks only. RAID 0 (striping) can use two disks or more, and RAID 5 (striping with parity) can use three disks or more.

Additional Reading and Resources

Microsoft website: http://www.microsoft.com

Microsoft Knowledge Base (MSKB): http://support.microsoft.com

TechNet: http://technet.microsoft.com

Additional A+ resources: http://www.davidlprowse.com/aplus

David L. Prowse. *Network+ Video Mentor* First Edition. Que. 2010.

CHAPTER 9

Maintaining Windows

This chapter covers the following A+ exam topics:

▶ Updating Windows

▶ Maintaining Hard Disks

You can find a master list of A+ exam topics in the "Introduction."

This chapter covers CompTIA A+ 220-701 objective 2.5 and CompTIA A+ 220-702 objective 2.3.

Windows maintenance is important as a security precaution and as a way to prevent any strange and unforeseen issues that might occur. Bad guys are always finding ways to exploit Windows code, and as these exploits are discovered, Microsoft releases updates (also known as patches) to fix those issues.

Keeping up maintenance on the hard disk drives is one of the best things you can do for your computer. By maintaining the hard drive, you increase its lifespan and reduce the chance of corrupted files.

This chapter shows how to update Windows and how to configure the Windows Update program. It also shows how to maintain the hard disk with cleanup and defragmenting programs.

Updating Windows

Updating Windows can be done in two ways: first, by updating to the latest service pack, and second by using the Windows Update program. Let's begin by discussing service packs.

Service Packs

A service pack (SP) is a group of updates, bug fixes, updated drivers, and security fixes that are installed from one downloadable package or from one disc. Service packs are numbered, for example SP1, SP2, and so on. Installing the service pack is relatively easy and only asks a few basic questions. When those questions are answered, it takes several minutes or more to complete the update; then a restart will be required. While the service pack is installed, it rewrites many files and copies new ones to the hard drive as well.

Historically, many service packs have been cumulative, meaning that they also contain previous service packs. For example, SP2 for Windows XP includes all the updates from SP1; a Windows XP installation with no service pack installed can be updated directly to SP2, without having to install SP1 first. However, of late, you see more service packs that are incremental, for example Windows XP SP3. A Windows XP installation with no service pack *cannot* be updated directly to SP3; it needs to have SP1 or SP2 installed first before the SP3 update. Another example of an incremental service pack is Windows Vista SP2; service pack 1 must be installed first before updating to SP2 in Windows Vista.

To find out which service pack is installed to the operating system, do the following:

▶ **In Windows 7/Vista:** Click Start; then right-click Computer and select Properties. This opens the System window. In the "Windows edition" section, you should see system information including the operating system version and the service pack that is installed. If the words "service pack" do not appear, there is no service pack installed.

▶ **In Windows XP:** Click Start; then right-click My Computer and select Properties. This opens the System Properties window. Toward the top of the General tab, you should see system information including the operating system version and the service pack that is installed. If the words "service pack" do not appear, there is no service pack installed.

> **Note**
>
> You can also find out which service pack your operating system uses by opening the System Information tool (open the Run prompt and type **msinfo32.exe**). It will be listed directly in the system summary.

Service packs can be acquired through Windows Update, at www.microsoft.com on CD/DVD and through a Microsoft Developer Network (MSDN) subscription. A service pack might also have been incorporated into the original operating system distribution DVD/CD. This is known as slipstreaming. This method enables the user to install the operating system and the service pack at the same time in a seamless manner. It is also possible for system administrators to create slipstreamed images for simplified over-the-network installations of the OS and SP.

Table 9.1 defines the latest service packs as of October, 2010. You might see older operating systems in the field. (If something works, why replace it, right?) For example, Windows NT and 2000 servers might be happily churning out the data necessary to users. That's okay; just make sure that they use the latest service pack so that they can interact properly with other computers on the network. Keep in mind that this table is subject to change because new service packs can be released at any time. For example, Windows 7 SP1 is on the horizon; and when new OSes are released, it often means a new service pack for older OSes. Note also that other applications such as Microsoft Office, and server based apps like Microsoft Exchange Server, use service packs as well.

TABLE 9.1 Latest Windows Service Packs as of October 2010

Operating System	Service Pack	Type
Windows Vista	SP2	Incremental
Windows XP	SP3	Incremental
Windows 2000	SP4	Cumulative
Windows NT 4.0	SP6	Cumulative
Office 2007	SP2	Cumulative
Office 2003	SP3	Cumulative
Office 2000	SP3	Cumulative

> **ExamAlert**
>
> Memorize the latest service packs for Windows Vista, Windows XP, Windows 2000, Office 2007, and Office 2003.

Windows Update

As with any OS, Windows 7, Vista, and XP should be updated regularly. Microsoft recognizes deficiencies in the OS, and possible exploits that could occur, and releases patches to increase OS performance and protect the system. After the latest service pack has been installed, the next step is to see if any additional updates are available for download.

To install additional updates for Windows through Windows Update:

1. Click Start > All Programs > Windows Update.

2. Windows 7 and Vista open the Window Update window in which you can turn on updates or click the Install Updates button. Windows XP opens a web page in which you can select Express or Custom installation of updates. Follow the prompts to install the latest version of the Windows Update software if necessary.

3. The system (or web page) automatically scans for updates. Updates are divided into the following categories:

   ▶ **Critical Updates and Service Packs:** These include the latest service pack and other security and stability updates. Some updates must be installed individually; others can be installed as a group.

   ▶ **Windows Updates:** Recommended updates to fix noncritical problems certain users might encounter; also adds features and updates to features bundled into Windows.

   ▶ **Driver Updates:** Updated device drivers for installed hardware.

If your system is in need of updates, a shield (for the Windows Security Center) appears in the system tray. Double-clicking this brings up the Security Center window in which you can turn on automatic updates. To modify how you are alerted to updates, and how they are downloaded and installed, do the following:

▸ **Windows 7/Vista:** Click Start > Windows Update; then click the Change Settings link.

▸ **Windows XP:** Click Start > Control Panel; then select Classic view, and double-click Automatic Updates.

From here there will be four options:

▸ **Install updates automatically:** This is the recommended option by Microsoft. You can schedule when and how often the updates should be downloaded and installed.

▸ **Download updates but let me choose whether to install them:** This automatically download updates when they become available, but Windows prompts you to install them instead of installing them automatically. Each update has a check box, so you can select individual updates to install.

▸ **Check for updates but let me choose whether to download and install them:** This lets you know when updates are available, but you are in control as to when they are downloaded and installed.

▸ **Never check for updates:** This is not recommended by Microsoft because it can be a security risk but might be necessary in some environments in which updates could cause conflicts over the network. In some networks, the administrator takes care of updates from a server and sets the local computers to this option.

> **Exam Alert**
>
> Know how to install Windows updates and how to modify how they are downloaded and installed.

> **Note**
>
> Another tool that can be used online is Microsoft Update, which is similar to Windows Update, but it can update for other Microsoft applications as well. It can be found at the following link: http://windowsupdate.microsoft.com/.

Cram Quiz

Answer these questions. The answers follow the last question. If you cannot answer these questions correctly, consider reading this section again until you can.

1. Which is the latest service pack for Windows XP, and what type is it?

   ○ **A.** SP2, cumulative

   ○ **B.** SP3, incremental

   ○ **C.** SP1, incremental

   ○ **D.** SP4, cumulative

2. Which Windows Update option is not recommended?

   ○ **A.** Download Updates but Let Me Choose Whether to Install Them

   ○ **B.** Install Updates Automatically

   ○ **C.** Never Check for Updates

   ○ **D.** Check for Updates but Let Me Choose Whether to Download and Install Them

3. Where can you find out the latest service pack that is used by Windows Vista? (Select all that apply.)

   ○ **A.** System window

   ○ **B.** System Properties window

   ○ **C.** System Information

   ○ **D.** System Tools

4. In Windows Vista, where would you go to modify how you are alerted to updates?

   ○ **A.** Click Start > Windows Update; then click the Change settings link.

   ○ **B.** Click Start > Control Panel; then select Classic view, and double-click Automatic Updates.

   ○ **C.** Click Start; then right-click My Computer and select Properties.

   ○ **D.** Click Start > Windows Update; then click the Check for updates link.

Cram Quiz Answers

1. **B**. SP3 is the latest service pack for Windows XP as of October, 2010, and it is an incremental upgrade meaning that you need either SP1 or SP2 installed prior to installing SP3.

2. **C**. It is not recommended that you set Windows Update to Never Check for Updates because it is a security risk.

3. **A** and **C**. You can find out the latest SP in use by Windows Vista within the System window and the System Information tool. The SP for Windows XP can be found in the System *Properties* window.

4. **A**. To modify how you are alerted to updates and how they are downloaded and installed in Window Vista, click Start > Windows Update; then click the Change settings link.

Maintaining Hard Disks

In Chapter 6, "Storage Devices," I made a bold statement: "Hard disks *will* fail." But it's all too true; it's not a matter of *if*; it's a matter of *when*. By maintaining the hard disk with various hard disk utilities, we attempt to stave off that dark day as long as possible. To further protect data, we can back it up with programs that Windows provides to us or third-party programs. And to protect operating system files, Windows offers the System Restore utility. Let's start with some of the hard disk utilities that you will use in the field.

Hard Disk Utilities

Temporary files and older files can clog up a hard disk and cause a decrease in performance. One program used to remove these files is called Disk Cleanup. Within this program users can select which volume they want to cleanup; it then scans the volume and calculates how much space you can save. It can clean away temporary files and downloaded program files, offline web pages, Office setup files, and, older files, and empty the Recycle Bin. This program can be accessed from Start > All Programs > Accessories > System Tools > Disk Cleanup. It is recommended that all programs are closed prior to running Disk Cleanup.

> **Note**
>
> Another good disk cleanup program available freely on the web is called simply "CleanUp!"

You can also delete temporary files and Internet files manually. To remove temporary files manually, navigate to C:\Windows\Temp and remove any temp files and Internet files necessary. There are also various folders within the user profile folder (for example the Recent folder) that have temporary files. However, it is easier to remove these files with one of the programs mentioned previously. Temporary Internet files and cookies can be removed by accessing the Internet Properties window by clicking Start > Control Panel (Classic view) and double-clicking Internet Options. Within the Internet Properties window's General tab, locate the Browsing History section and click Delete. This offers you the option to remove a variety of information including temporary Internet files, cookies, history, form data, and passwords, or you can select Delete all.

> **Note**
>
> The preceding information about deleting information in Internet Explorer is based on Internet Explorer version 7.

Over time, data is written to the drive, and subsequently erased, over and over again, leaving gaps in the drivespace. New data will sometimes be written to multiple areas of the drive in a broken or fragmented fashion filling in any blank areas it can find. When this happens, the hard drive must work much harder to find the data it needs, spinning more, starting and stopping more; in general, more mechanical movement. The more the drive has to access this fragmented data, the shorter its lifespan becomes due to mechanical wear and tear. Defragmenting the drive can be done with Microsoft's Disk Defragmenter, with the command-line `defrag`, or with other third-party programs. The Disk Defragmenter is located in different places depending on whether 7/Vista or XP is used:

- ▶ **Windows 7/Vista Disk Defragmenter:** Click Start > All Programs > Accessories > System Tools > Disk Defragmenter. The program automatically analyzes volumes and lets you know if a volume needs to be defragmented.

- ▶ **Windows XP Disk Defragmenter:** Open Computer Management > Storage and click Disk Defragmenter. From here you have the option to analyze or defragment volumes.

If using the Disk Defragmenter program, you need 15 percent free space on the volume you want to defrag. If you have less than that, you need to use the command-line option `defrag -f`. Figure 9.1 shows Windows XP's Disk Defragmenter after it has completed defragmenting the D: drive.

Before clicking the Defragment button, it's recommended that the Analyze button be clicked first to find out if the drive needs to be defragmented. In Figure 9.1 there are two rows of colors. The first indicates the estimated disk usage before defragmentation, which is identified from the analysis. If a drive needs to be defragmented, this row has areas of blue and areas of red. Blue means contiguous files, which is good; red means fragmented files; the more red the more the need for defragmenting. The second row indicates estimated disk usage after defragmentation. When defragmentation is complete, the second row should show all blue or all contiguous files.

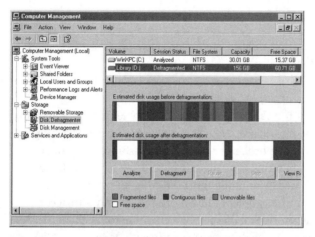

FIGURE 9.1   Windows XP Disk Defragmenter

Backups

Backing up data is critical for a company. It is not enough to rely on a fault tolerant array. Individual files or the entire system can be backed up to another set of hard disks, or to optical discs, or to tape. Windows 7, Vista, and Windows XP use three separate programs for backing up data. They are each accessed in different ways, but work in very similar ways.

Using Windows 7's Backup and Restore

Backup and Restore can back up individual files, create an image of the system, and create a system repair disc. You might have to setup the backup program prior to use, depending on your configuration. To create a backup with Windows 7's Backup and Restore:

1. Start Backup and Restore by accessing Start > Control Panel > System and Security > Backup and Restore.

2. Click the Set up backup link (if necessary) or the Back up now button if a backup device has already been set up. You will need to have an external storage device, second hard drive, or second partition to backup to. If no device or media can be found, the only other option will be to backup to the network.

3. Select the media or partition you wish to backup to and click Next.

4. Select whether Windows will automatically backup data or choose your own files to be backed up and click Next.

5. Select the folders and files you wish to backup and whether to include a system image of each drive, then click Next.

6. Review the settings, and click the Save Settings and Backup button. This will initiate the backup. Backups can be restored using this program and scheduled backups can be configured as well.

Using Windows Vista's Backup Status and Configuration

Backup Status and Configuration is the successor to Windows XP's NTBackup. It can back up individual files or an entire image of your system (using Complete PC Backup) to the removable media of your choice, for example DVD. To create a complete backup of your PC with Vista's Complete PC Backup:

1. Start the Complete PC Backup by going to Start > All Programs > Accessories > System Tools > Backup Status and Configuration.

2. Click the Complete PC Backup button.

3. Select Create a backup now and follow the directions. Have media ready that can hold an image of your operating system, for example DVD-R. Be ready; this will be a sizeable image!

Using Windows XP's NTBackup

Windows XP Professional offers the built-in program called NTBackup. This is accessible by opening the Run prompt and typing **ntbackup**. From here you can backup individual files and backup the System State, which includes everything that makes one installation of Windows XP different from another. Unfortunately, Windows XP does not include a Complete PC Backup option; however, the Automated System Recovery (ASR) option in NTBackup does enable you to back up and restore the system state (user accounts, settings, boot files, and so on).

To create an ASR backup with NTBackup:

1. Switch to Advanced Mode (if NTBackup starts in Wizard mode) and click the Automated System Recovery Wizard button. When the wizard's opening dialog appears, click Next to continue.

2. Specify where to store the backup, and click Next.

3. Click Finish to complete the wizard. You will be asked to provide a floppy disk to store configuration files.

Creating Restore Points

System Restore can fix issues caused by defective hardware or software by reverting back to an earlier time. Registry changes made by hardware or software are reversed in an attempt to force the computer to work the way it did previously. Restore points can be created manually and are also created automatically by the operating system before new applications, or hardware is installed.

To create a restore point in Windows 7/Vista:

1. Right-click Computer and select Properties. This opens the System Properties window, as shown in Figure 9.2. Alternatively, you can go to Start > All Programs > Accessories > System Tools > System Restore and click the link at the bottom of the window that says open System Protection.

2. Click the System Protection tab.

3. Click the Create button. This opens the System Protection window.

4. Enter a name for the restore point and click Create.

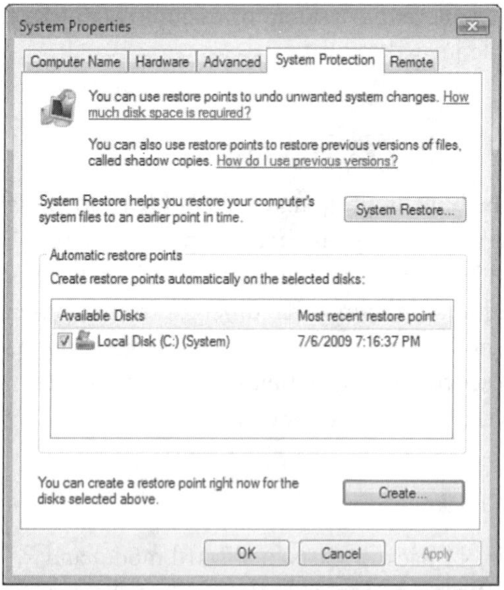

FIGURE 9.2   The System Protection Tab of the System Properties Window

To create a restore point in Windows XP:

1. Navigate to Start > All Programs > Accessories > System Tools > System Restore. This opens the System Restore window.

2. Click Create a Restore Point and then click Next.

3. Enter a name for the restore point and click Create.

If System Restore is not available, it might be turned off. Within Windows Vista you can enable or disable System Restore on any volume from the System Protection tab of the System Properties Window. Simply check or uncheck any volume that you want to enable or disable. Within Windows XP, the state of System Restore affects all drives; you can turn the utility only on and off. This is done from the System Restore tab of the System Properties Window. You can also change the amount of disk space it uses here.

Keeping a Well-Maintained Computer

In general, to keep a well-maintained computer, I tell my students to implement a six-step procedure:

1. **Use a surge protector or UPS:** Make sure the computer and other equipment connect to a surge protector, or better yet a UPS if you are concerned about power loss. For more information on surge protectors and UPSs, see Chapter 5 "Power."

2. **Update the BIOS:** Flashing the BIOS isn't always necessary; check the manufacturer's website for your motherboard to see if an update is needed. For more information on BIOS see Chapter 2, "Motherboards."

3. **Update Windows:** This includes the latest service packs and any Windows updates beyond that and setting Windows to alert if there are any new updates.

4. **Update antimalware:** This includes making sure that there is a current license for the antimalware (antivirus and antispyware) and verifying that updates are turned on and the software is regularly scanning the system. For more information on malware and antimalware, see Chapter 15, "Security."

5. **Update the firewall:** If it is the Windows Firewall, updates should happen automatically through Windows Update. However, if you have a SOHO router with a built-in firewall, or other firewall device, you need to update the device's ROM by downloading the latest image from the manufacturer's website. For more on firewalls, see Chapter 15.

6. **Maintain the disks:** This means running a disk cleanup program regularly and checking to see if the hard disk needs to be defragmented from once a week to once a month, depending on the amount of usage. It also means creating restore points, doing Complete PC Backups, or using third-party backup or drive imaging software.

Cram Quiz

Answer these questions. The answers follow the last question. If you cannot answer these questions correctly, consider reading this section again until you can.

1. Which program removes temporary files?
   - ○ **A.** Disk Backup
   - ○ **B.** Disk Cleanup
   - ○ **C.** System Restore
   - ○ **D.** Disk Defragmenter

2. If there is less than 15 percent free space within a volume, how would a user defragment it in Windows?
   - ○ **A.** With Disk Defragmenter
   - ○ **B.** With the command `defragment -f`
   - ○ **C.** With the command `defrag -f`
   - ○ **D.** With a third-party tool

3. Which program in Windows Vista creates a Complete PC Backup?
   - ○ **A.** Backup Status and Configuration
   - ○ **B.** NTBackup
   - ○ **C.** ASR
   - ○ **D.** System Restore

4. Where would you go in Windows Vista to enable System Restore? (Select the best answer.)
   - ○ **A.** System Properties window
   - ○ **B.** Advanced Protection tab of the System Properties window
   - ○ **C.** Task Manager
   - ○ **D.** System Protection tab of the System Properties window

Cram Quiz Answers

1. **B.** Disk Cleanup removes temporary files and other types of files and clears the recycle bin.
2. **C.** `defrag -f` defragments the drive even if free space is low. However, be prepared to use a lot of system resources to complete the defrag. Close any open windows before starting the process.

3. **A**. Backup Status and Configuration has an option called Complete PC Backup within Windows Vista. NTBackup is a Windows XP program that can back up individual files and the System State but not the entire PC. ASR is the Automated System Recovery option in Windows XP that backs up the System State and other data. System Restore creates restore points that deals more with settings than it does data.

4. **D**. To enable (or disable) System Restore in Windows Vista, go to the System Protection tab of the System Properties window.

CHAPTER 10

Troubleshooting Windows

This chapter covers the following A+ exam topics:

▶ Repair Environments and Boot Errors

▶ Windows Tools and Errors

▶ Command-Line Tools

You can find a master list of A+ exam topics in the "Introduction."

This chapter covers CompTIA A+ 220-701 objectives 2.1, 2.2, and 3.4 and CompTIA A+ 220-702 objectives 2.1, 2.3, and 2.4.

Now for the toughest part of working with Windows: troubleshooting. As I mentioned in Chapter 1, "Introduction to Troubleshooting," troubleshooting is the most important skill for a computer technician to possess. There are many different things that can go wrong in a computer; the majority of them are software-related. This chapter endeavors to give you the tools, utilities, and skills necessary to troubleshoot the various boot errors, stop errors, and other Windows errors that you might encounter.

Repair Environments and Boot Errors

Windows startup errors prevent you from accessing the operating system. Because of this, Windows Vista and XP have various startup tools, menus, and repair environments that you can use to troubleshoot these startup and boot errors.

Windows Repair Tools

There are many tools included with Windows Vista and XP that are designed to help you troubleshoot and repair just about any issue that might come up. Before we get into the exact issues you might face, let's discuss some of these repair tools, what they do, and where you can access them. Let's start with the Advanced Boot Options menu.

Advanced Boot Options Menu

If Windows 7/Vista/XP/2000 won't start and you don't see an error message, the culprit might be a video driver, new configuration, or other system issues. There are several startup options that can aid in fixing the problem. To access these startup options, press the F8 key immediately after the computer starts up; this brings up the Windows Advanced Boot Options menu, as shown in Figure 10.1.

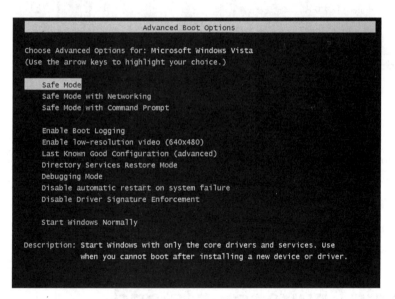

FIGURE 10.1 Windows Vista Advanced Boot Options menu

The following options are included in the Advanced Boot Options menu:

▶ **Safe Mode:** Starts system with a minimal set of drivers; used in case one of the drivers fails. Safe Mode is a good option when attempting to use System Restore.

▶ **Safe Mode with Networking:** Starts system with a minimal set of drivers and enables network support.

▶ **Safe Mode with Command Prompt:** Starts system with a minimal set of drivers but loads command prompt instead of Windows GUI.

▸ **Enable Boot Logging:** Creates a ntbtlog.txt file.

▸ **Enable low-resolution video (640x480):** Uses a standard VGA driver in place of a GPU-specific display driver, but uses all other drivers as normal. (This is called Enable VGA Mode in Windows XP/2000.)

▸ **Last Known Good Configuration:** Starts the system with the last configuration known to work; useful for solving problems caused by newly installed hardware or software.

▸ **Directory Services Restore Mode:** This is used to restore a domain controller's active directory (Windows Server). Even though it is listed, it is not used in Windows Vista/XP/2000.

▸ **Debugging Mode:** Enables the use of a debug program to examine the system kernel for troubleshooting.

▸ **Disable automatic restart on system failure (7 and Vista only):** Prevents Windows from automatically restarting, if an error causes Windows to fail. Choose this option only, if Windows is stuck in a loop in which Windows fails, attempts to restart, and fails again repeatedly.

▸ **Disable driver signature enforcement (7 and Vista only):** Enables drivers containing improper signatures to be installed.

▸ **Start Windows Normally:** This can be used to boot to regular Windows. This option is listed in case a person inadvertently pressed F8, but did not want to use any of the Advanced Boot Options.

> **ExamAlert**
>
> Know the Advanced Boot Options for the exam.

If Windows 7/Vista fails to start properly, and then restarts automatically, it normally displays the Windows Error Recovery screen and gives you the following options: Safe Mode, Safe Mode with Networking, Safe Mode with Command Prompt, Last Known Good Configuration, and Start Windows Normally. This means that Windows has acknowledged some sort of error or improper shut down and offers a truncated version of the Advanced Options Boot menu.

> **Note**
>
> There is a small window of time available to press F8; it's right between the BIOS and when the normal operating system boots. Press F8 repeatedly right after the BIOS POST begins.

> **Note**
>
> It is recommended that you attempt to repair a computer with the Advanced Boot Options *before* using Windows Vista's System Recovery Options or Windows XP/2000's Recovery Console.

Windows Recovery Environment (WinRE)

WinRE is a set of tools included in Windows 7, Windows Vista, Windows Server 2008, and other upcoming Windows operating systems. It takes the place of the Recovery Console used in Windows XP/2000. Also known as System Recovery Options, WinRE's purpose is to recover Windows from errors that prevent it from booting; it can also be instrumental in fixing issues causing a computer to "freeze" up. There are two possible ways to access WinRE:

> ▶ **Booting to the Windows Vista DVD:** This option is more common with an individual computer that had Windows Vista installed; for example, if you performed a clean installation with the standard Windows Vista DVD and made no modifications to it. To start WinRE, make sure that the DVD drive is first in the boot order of the BIOS, boot to the Windows Vista DVD (as if you were starting the installation), choose your language settings and click next, and then select Repair Your Computer, which you can find at the lower-left corner of the screen.

> **Note**
>
> Important! Do not select Install Now because that would begin the process of reinstalling Windows Vista on your hard drive.

> ▶ **Booting to a special partition on the hard drive that has WinRE installed:** This option is used by OEMs (original equipment manufacturers) so that users can access WinRE without having to search for and boot off of a Windows Vista DVD. These OEMs (computer builders and system integrators) will preinstall WinRE into a special partition on

the hard drive, separate from the operating system, so that the user can boot into it at any time. Compare this to the older Recovery Console that was installed into the same partition as the operating system. To access WinRE that has been preinstalled, press F8 to bring up the Advanced Boot Options menu, highlight Repair Your Computer, and press Enter. If you don't see Repair Your Computer in the Advanced Boot Options menu, then it wasn't installed to the hard drive, and you have to use option 1, booting from the Vista DVD. Note that you can still use option 1, even if WinRE was installed to the hard drive; for example, in a scenario where the hard drive installation of WinRE has failed.

> **Note**
>
> The process to install WinRE to the hard drive is a rather complicated one and is not covered on the A+ exam. However, if you are interested, here is a link that gives the basics of installing WinRE: http://blogs.msdn.com/winre/archive/2007/01/12/how-to-install-winre-on-the-hard-disk.aspx.

Regardless of which option you selected, at this point a window named System Recovery Options should appear, prompting you to select an operating system to repair. Most users will only have one listed. Highlight the appropriate operating system in need of repair and click Next. This displays the options at your disposal, as shown in Figure 10.2. Table 10.1 describes these options in more depth.

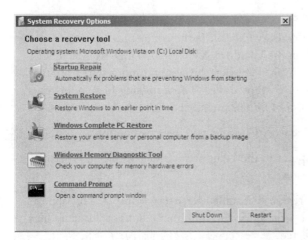

FIGURE 10.2   Windows Vista System Recovery Options window

TABLE 10.1 **Description of the Windows Vista System Recovery Options**

System Recovery Option	Description
Startup Repair	When clicked, this automatically fixes certain problems, such as missing or damaged system files that might prevent Windows from starting correctly. When you run Startup Repair, it scans your computer for the problem and then tries to fix it so your computer can start correctly.
System Restore	Restores the computer's system files to an earlier point in time. It's a way to undo system changes to your computer without affecting your personal files, such as email, documents, or photos. Note: If you use System Restore when the computer is in safe mode, you cannot undo the restore operation. However, you can run System Restore again and choose a different restore point, if one exists.
Windows Complete PC Restore	This restores the contents of a hard disk from a backup. Windows Complete PC Backup and Restore is only included with Vista Business and Vista Ultimate.
Windows Memory Diagnostic Tool	Scans the computer's memory for errors.
Command Prompt *(Replaces the Recovery Console in XP/2000)*	Advanced users can use the Command Prompt to perform recovery-related operations and also run other command-line tools for diagnosing and troubleshooting problems. Puts the user into a directory called X:\Sources. Works very much like the previous Recovery Console in Windows XP/2000, with the addition of a few new commands.

Recovery Console

The Windows XP/2000 Recovery Console is the command-line interface used for repairs. It is included on the Windows XP and 2000 CD-ROMs. The Recovery Console can be invaluable when the system cannot start from the hard drive due to missing or corrupted files. These missing files could very well block the Advanced Boot Options menu.

To start Windows XP's Recovery Console, you have two options:

Option 1: Boot the computer to the Windows XP CD-ROM and run the Recovery Console.

Option 2: Boot from a previously installed Recovery Console. This appears as part of the operating system boot menu but not if startup files have been affected.

To run the Recovery Console from CD-ROM:

1. Boot the system from the Windows XP CD.

2. When prompted, press R to start the Recovery Console. (In Windows 2000, you would press R for Repair and then C for the Recovery Console.)

3. Log into Recovery Console by selecting the installation to log into and providing the Administrator password for the operating system.

To install the Recovery Console to hard disk:

1. While in Windows, insert the Windows CD-ROM into the drive. (Close any pop-up install windows.)

2. Open the Run prompt and type **x:\i386\winnt32.exe /cmdcons**. (For this scenario, *x* is the drive letter for the CD-ROM drive, this is usually D:, but will vary from system to system.)

3. Confirm the installation by clicking Yes and restart the computer. Now, Microsoft Windows Recovery Console should appear on the boot menu. Select it to start Recovery Console.

> **ExamAlert**
>
> Memorize the different WinRE options in Vista, and know how to use the Recovery Console in XP.

Boot Errors

There are various reasons why a computer will fail to boot. If it is operating system-related, you will usually get some type of message that can help you to troubleshoot the problem. Windows 7/Vista and Windows XP have different boot files, so it stands to reason that they have different boot error messages.

Windows Vista Boot Errors

Windows Vista uses the bootmgr and BCD files during the startup process. If these files are corrupted or missing, you see corresponding error messages:

▶ **BOOTMGR is missing:** This message is displayed if the bootmgr file is missing or corrupt. This black screen will probably also say Press Ctrl+Alt+Del to Restart; however doing so will probably have the same results.

There are two methods to repair this error. The first is to boot to the System Recovery Options and select the Startup Repair option. This should automatically repair the system and require you to reboot. If this doesn't work, try the second method, which is to boot to the System Recovery Options and select the Command Prompt option. Type the command **bootrec /fixboot**, as shown in Figure 10.3.

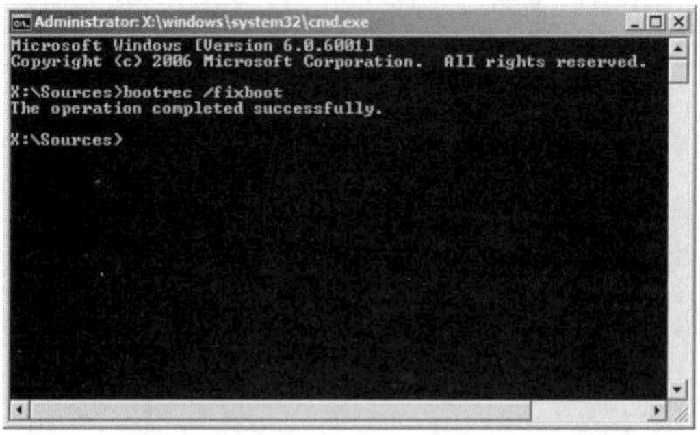

FIGURE 10.3   Repairing BOOTMGR.exe with Windows Vista's WinRE Command Prompt

> ### Note
>
> A hard drive's lifespan is not infinite. In some cases, it is not possible to repair this file, and unfortunately the hard drive will need to be replaced.

▶ **The Windows Boot Configuration Data file is missing required information:** This message means that either the Windows Boot Manager (Bootmgr) entry is not present in the Boot Configuration Data (BCD) store; or the Boot\BCD file on the active partition is damaged or missing. Additional information you might see on the screen includes File: \Boot\BCD, and Status: 0xc0000034. Unfortunately, this means that the BCD store needs to be repaired or rebuilt. Hold on to your hats; there are three methods of repair for this error:

The first method of repair is to boot to the System Recovery Options and select the Startup Repair option. This should automatically repair the system and require you to reboot. If not, move on to method 2.

The second method of repair is to boot to the System Recovery Options and select the Command Prompt option. Type **bootrec /rebuildbcd**. At this point the bootrec.exe tool either succeeds or fails. If the Bootrec.exe tool runs successfully, it displays an installation path to a Windows directory. To add this entry to the BCD store, type **Yes**. A confirmation message appears that indicates the entry was added successfully.

If the Bootrec.exe tool can't locate any missing Windows installations, you'll have to remove the BCD store and then re-create it. To do this, type the following commands:

```
Bcdedit /export C:\BCD_Backup
ren c:\boot\bcd bcd.old
Bootrec /rebuildbcd
```

Methods one and two will usually work, but if not, there is a third method which is more in depth and requires rebuilding the BCD store manually. For more information this step-by-step process can be found at the following link: http://support.microsoft.com/kb/927391.

Windows XP/2000 Boot Errors

Windows XP and 2000 use the NTLDR (boot loader), Boot.ini, NTDETECT.COM, and Ntoskrnl.exe files during startup. If any of these files are corrupted or missing, you see one of the following error messages:

▶ **NTDETECT failed:** This is displayed if the NTDETECT.COM file is missing or corrupt.

▶ **NTLDR is missing:** This is displayed if the NTLDR file is missing or corrupt.

▶ **Invalid boot.ini:** This is displayed if the boot.ini file is missing or corrupt. In some cases, the operating system will boot anyway because there is usually only one disk partition on the hard disk. If not, the file will need to be recopied to the hard disk.

To repair these issues, you can

▶ Reboot to the Windows CD and access the Recovery Console (XP/2000); then recopy the file from the Windows CD-ROM or from backup media.

▶ Reboot to the Windows CD, select Repair, and run the Emergency Repair option (Windows 2000).

▶ Repair the installation or restore of Windows. (More on restoring Windows later in this chapter).

Cram Quiz

Answer these questions. The answers follow the last question. If you cannot answer these questions correctly, consider reading this section again until you can.

1. Which option starts the system with a minimal set of drivers?

   - ○ **A.** Last Known Good Configuration
   - ○ **B.** System Restore
   - ○ **C.** Safe Mode
   - ○ **D.** Debugging Mode

2. Which tool should be used if a person wanted to do Startup Repair in Windows Vista?

   - ○ **A.** Recovery Console
   - ○ **B.** WinRE
   - ○ **C.** System Restore
   - ○ **D.** Safe Mode

3. What switch should be used to install the Recovery Console to a hard drive?

   - ○ **A.** `/recovery`
   - ○ **B.** `/winnt32`
   - ○ **C.** `/console`
   - ○ **D.** `/cmdcons`

4. What command repairs the bootmgr.exe file in Windows Vista?

   - ○ **A.** `bootrec /fixboot`
   - ○ **B.** `bootrec /fixmbr`
   - ○ **C.** `bootrec /rebuildbcd`
   - ○ **D.** `boot\bcd`

5. Which tool should be used to fix the NTLDR if it is missing or corrupt?

   - ○ **A.** Safe Mode
   - ○ **B.** `bootrec /fixmbr`
   - ○ **C.** Recovery Console
   - ○ **D.** WinRE

Cram Quiz Answers

1. **C.** Safe Mode starts the operating system with a minimal set of drivers.

2. **B.** WinRE (System Recovery Options) includes Startup Repair. The Recovery Console is used by Windows XP/2000. Safe Mode is part of the Advanced Boot Options menu, and System Restore is a different tool that is also available in WinRE and can be used in Windows XP as well.

3. **D.** **/cmdcons** is the switch (or parameter or option) that is added to the **winnt32.exe** command.

4. **A. bootrec /fixboot** is one of the methods you can try to repair bootmgr.exe in Windows Vista. **Bootrec /fixmbr** rewrites the master boot record in Vista. **Bootrec /rebuildbcd** attempts to rebuild the boot configuration store, and **boot/bcd** is where the boot configuration store is located.

5. **C.** The Recovery Console can be used to repair NTLDR if it is missing or corrupt. Safe Mode enables a user to boot into Windows with a minimal set of drivers, but this would be impossible if NTLDR is malfunctioning or nonexistent. **Bootrec /fixmbr** rewrites the master boot record in Windows Vista. WinRE is the Windows Recovery Environment in Windows Vista.

Windows Tools and Errors

Windows could fail while you are working within the operating system. Quite often, error messages will accompany these failures. There are various Windows repair tools you can use to troubleshoot these issues. The worst possible scenario is when Windows fails and cannot be repaired. In these cases, a restoration is necessary. There are several types of restoration techniques available to you in Windows as well. But before restoring the system, since it can be very time-consuming and possibly unnecessary, you should attempt to troubleshoot with Windows repair tools first.

Troubleshooting Within Windows

If there are not any boot errors, then Windows should start and operate properly. However, errors (recoverable ones) can occur while Windows is running. Devices can fail, applications can terminate for various reasons, and hardware could suffer performance issues.

Device Manager

The Device Manager can detect if a device is malfunctioning, if it has the wrong driver installed, if it has a conflicting resource (like an IRQ or I/O setting), or if it has been disabled. Figure 10.4 shows a malfunctioning PCMCIA adapter. You know it's malfunctioning because of the exclamation mark (!) within a yellow circle. The figure also shows a disabled IEEE 1394 adapter, the proof is indicated by the red X. These devices won't work properly until they are fixed.

Of course, we can't just leave these devices this way! A clean Device Manager is a good sign of a healthy computer. When a user opens this program, they should see nothing but collapsed categories; none of them should be open. Conflicting resources like IRQs and I/O settings are really a thing of the past and are controlled automatically. But it is certainly possible for a device driver issue. Perhaps the driver failed, or the wrong one was installed initially, or a device was updated with the wrong type of driver. Either way, we would need to repair it by opening the Device Manager, right-clicking on the device with the exclamation point, and selecting Properties. Take a look at Figure 10.5. Notice the title at the top of the screen: It says Texas Instruments PCIxx12 Cardbus Controller. Then underneath where it says Manufacturer, you see the name Vadem. Well, that's a different manufacturer altogether, so something went wrong along the way. (Really, I broke it for demonstration purposes!)

FIGURE 10.4   **Device Manager window in Windows XP showing a disabled device and a malfunctioning device**

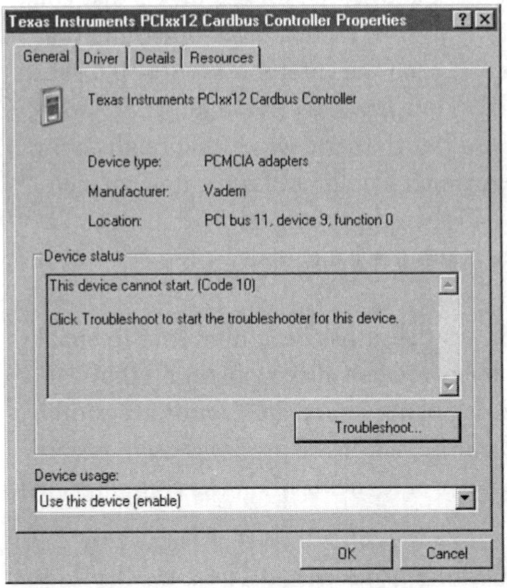

FIGURE 10.5   **PCMCIA Device Properties window**

To repair this, install the correct Texas Instruments driver. This might be on the hard drive already, or maybe the user has a disc that came with the computer containing this driver. Perhaps it needs to be downloaded from the

Internet. Internet installs are usually quite easy; download the .exe (or .zip) file and double-click it to install. But if the driver is already on the computer, it might be a bit more detailed. For example, you might need to find a specific .inf file, or you might need to search for the driver within Windows' driver database (a manual install), which is what we will do in the following steps:

1. In the Properties window of the device, click the Driver tab.

2. Click Update Driver. The wizard appears.

3. Click the Install from a List or Specific Location radio button and click next.

4. The next screen tries to find the driver automatically; you can try this, but chances are it will just reinstall the same driver that was already there. Instead, click the Don't Search. I Will Choose the Driver to Install radio button and click Next.

5. On the next screen, you see compatible hardware. If the list of compatible hardware does not match with the name of your device, deselect the Show Compatible Hardware check box. Then, you get a list of manufacturers and models. If the manufacturer/model that you want is not on the list, you need to click Have Disk and search for the driver that could be elsewhere on the system, on removable media, or is something that you downloaded, or will download from the Internet. Figure 10.6 shows the correct driver being selected. This driver is served up by Windows, so it is a Microsoft driver. However, for other devices, you might want to use the manufacturer's driver, which would have to be downloaded from their website. Click next and then finish to complete the installation. Sometimes a restart of the computer is necessary.

As mentioned, a red X on a device means that it has been disabled. To enable it, simply right-click it and select Enable. You can also enable it on the General tab of its Properties sheet. It is possible to create a hardware profile that disables certain devices. To find out if a hardware profile is used, restart the computer and watch for a hardware profile menu when the computer first boots.

Codes can be helpful when troubleshooting issues with devices. If a device is malfunctioning or is configured incorrectly, it should show a code number within its Properties sheet on the General tab. Table 10.2 gives a few examples of these codes.

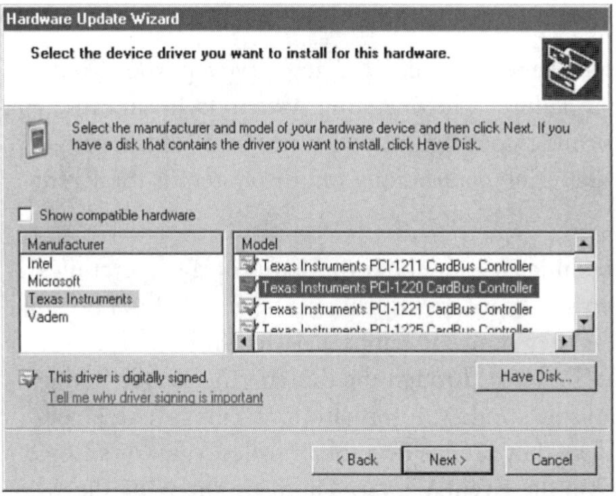

FIGURE 10.6 Driver selection by manufacturer and model

TABLE 10.2 **Description of Codes in the Device Manager**

Device Manager Code Number	Problem	Recommended Solutions
Code 1	This device is not configured correctly.	Update the driver.
Code 3	The driver for this device might be corrupted, or your system might be running low on memory or other resources.	Close some open applications. Uninstall and reinstall the driver. Install additional RAM.
Code 10	Device cannot start.	Update the driver. View MSKB article 943104 for more information.
Code 12	This device cannot find enough free resources that it can use. If you want to use this device, you need to disable one of the other devices on this system.	You can use the Troubleshooting Wizard in Device Manager to determine where the conflict is, and then disable the conflicting device. Disable the device.

Note

These are just a few examples of the codes you might see in the Device Manager. For a complete list, see the following link: http://support.microsoft.com/kb/310123.

Event Viewer

Applications are a boon and a bane to mankind. They serve a purpose, but sometimes they are prone to failure. The operating system itself can cause you grief as well by underperforming, locking up, or causing other intermittent issues. One good tool for analyzing applications and the system is the Event Viewer.

The Event Viewer tells a technician a lot about the status of the operating system and programs. It informs as to informational events, warns about possible issues, and displays errors as they occur. It can be accessed from Start > All Programs > Administrative Tools, or through the System Tools node in the Computer Management console window. Information, warnings, and errors are stored in log files. In Vista they are inside a folder called Windows Logs; in XP they are directly within the Event Viewer. There are three log files located inside the Event Viewer that you should know for the exam:

▶ **System:** The System log contains information, warnings, and errors about hardware, device drivers, system files, and so on. This log deals primarily with the operating system.

▶ **Application:** The Application log contains events about programs that are built into Windows, such as the Command Prompt or Windows Explorer, and might contain information about applications that have been loaded after the operating system was installed.

▶ **Security:** The Security log holds information that was gathered for auditing and security purposes; for example, it might log who logged on to the computer, or who tried to gain access to a particular file.

An event can be viewed by double-clicking on it, as shown in Figure 10.7.

In Figure 10.7, you can see an Event with a simple description: The Windows Security Center Service Has Started. It's self-explanatory and is a typical example of an informational event. The fact that this service started is standard procedure. However, if you are getting any warnings (indicated by an exclamation point), they should be investigated when time is available. And if errors are received (indicated by an X), they should be investigated right away; an example of an error is shown in Figure 10.8.

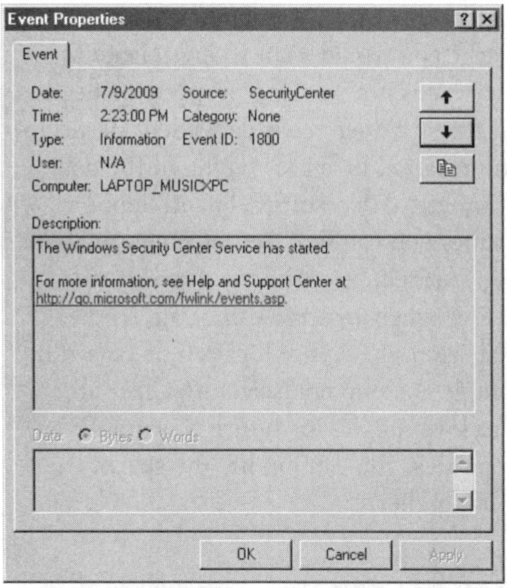

FIGURE 10.7 **Event Properties window**

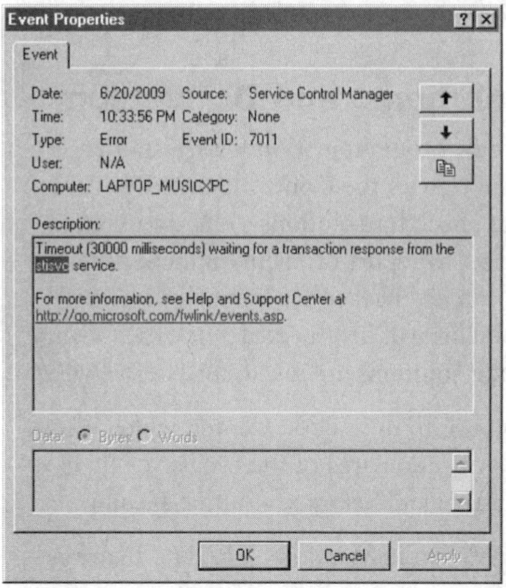

FIGURE 10.8 **Event Properties window showing an error**

The error in Figure 10.8 is showing that the operating system was expecting a transaction from the stisvc service but never received it due to a timeout. This service is installed by Windows to help interact with digital cameras and graphical input devices. If something like this happens only once, it isn't usually a big deal, but if you see it regularly, you would want to investigate further. Perhaps a device that uses the service is not working properly or needs a new driver, or maybe the service that the stisvc service is dependent on needs to be restarted. You can find more information by either typing in the code number for the event or the description into Microsoft Help and Support: http://support.microsoft.com. Sometimes you can find out information about these types of services just by running a search, but it is best to go to the source that is Microsoft. You never know when an error can occur, so the Event Viewer logs should be reviewed regularly. Entire logs can be erased by right-clicking on the log file (for example System) and selecting Clear all events. The system asks if you want to save the log for future viewing. By right-clicking a log and selecting Properties, you can modify the size of the log, and in Vista can disable logging altogether.

> **ExamAlert**
>
> Be able to describe the System, Application, and Security log files for the exam.

Problem Reports and Solutions, and Dr. Watson

Problem Reports and Solutions is a new program in Windows Vista that can be accessed directly within the Classic view of the Control Panel. Problem Reports and Solutions enables you to check for solutions to hardware and software problems. Windows can be set to report problems and check for solutions automatically, or solutions can be checked for manually when a problem occurs. To modify how problems will be reported, click the Change settings link. Problem descriptions and solutions are saved, for later viewing.

In Windows 7 this functionality is built into the Action Center, which can be accessed by clicking its icon in the notification area of the taskbar or by navigating to Start > Control Panel > System and Security > Action Center.

This program took the place of Dr. Watson in Windows XP/2000 that was used as a system and application failure analysis tool. Dr. Watson can be accessed in XP/2000 by opening the Run prompt and typing **drwtsn32**. Application failures that are listed in Dr. Watson are rare and are often listed in the Application log of the Event Viewer as well.

Performance

Another tool that you can use to analyze and troubleshoot applications is called Performance in Windows XP and is known specifically as the Reliability and Performance Monitor in Windows Vista. This program tracks how much your devices are utilized; for example, what percentage of the processor is used, or how much RAM.

This tool can be accessed within Administrative Tools. When you open the Reliability and Performance Monitor in Windows Vista, it opens to a window that graphs the usage of the CPU, disks, network, and memory, as shown in Figure 10.9; these are ActiveX graphs like the ones used in the Performance tab of the Task Manager.

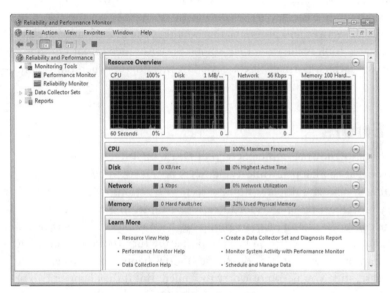

FIGURE 10.9   Resource overview within the Reliability and Performance Monitor of Windows Vista

By clicking on Performance Monitor, you can track the usage of any device in the computer (known as objects), in a variety of measurements (known as counters). By default this screen tracks only the CPU. This screen is similar to the default screen that comes up in Windows XP's Performance window. In XP, this screen automatically tracks the Processor, RAM, and hard disk. By clicking the + sign toward the top of the window, you can add devices to track, and in a myriad of ways. Information can be viewed in different formats like line charts and histograms and can also be viewed in Report view. They can be exported as well. However, any objects that are added in this program are not saved when you close the window. But it is possible to configure the program so that it saves your additions; enter the MMC. (You remember the MMC from Chapter 9, "Maintaining Windows.") From an MMC a user can add the ActiveX Control called System Monitor that *is* the Performance Monitor. You can also add Performance Logs and Alerts to log your findings and alert you to any changes or tripped thresholds. The MMC saves its contents and remembers the last place you were working in, which works great if you are going to be analyzing the same things day in and day out.

Msconfig

Msconfig can help troubleshoot various things, from operating system startup issues to application and service problems. From Msconfig (open the Run prompt and type **msconfig**), one can select different modes of startup, for example loading only basic devices, or diagnostic startup. A user can also shut down individual services and programs that would normally be loaded at start-up, an invaluable tool. Aside from that, some of the Advanced Boot Options can be accessed, which normally are accessed by pressing F8 when the system starts up.

Stop Errors

A stop error (also known as a Blue Screen of Death or BSOD) is the worst type of error that can happen while Windows is operating. It completely halts the operating system and displays a blue screen with various text and code. Anything you were working on is for the most part lost. In some cases, it reboots the computer after a memory dump has been initiated. (This is also known as auto-restart.) If not, you need to physically turn the computer off at the power button and turn it back on. Some BSODs happen only once, and if that is the case, then you need not worry too much. But if they happen two or three times or more, you should investigate why. Quite often they are due to a corrupt driver file. If you see two columns of information with a list of drivers and other files, that is probably the case. Look at the bottom of the second (or last) column and identify the driver that has failed, for example cdrom.sys. These drivers can become corrupt for a variety of reasons and would need to be replaced when you boot into Windows, or if you can't boot into Windows, replaced from within WinRE's Command Prompt (Vista) or the Recovery Console (XP/2000). Less commonly a BSOD might be caused by a memory error that will have additional code that you can research on Microsoft's websites (MSKB and TechNet).

By default, two things happen when a Stop error occurs:

▶ An event will usually be written to the System Log within the Event Viewer, if that option has been selected in the Startup and Recovery window, as shown in Figure 10.10. When a STOP error is written to the System Log, it is listed as an Information entry, not as an Error entry. The STOP error will be listed as "The System Has Rebooted from a Bugcheck. The Bugcheck was (Error Number)." Use the error number to look up the problem, and hopefully find a solution, on the MSKB and/or TechNet.

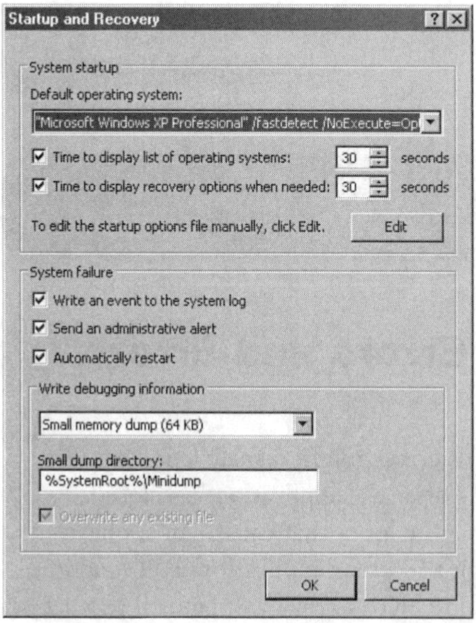

FIGURE 10.10 **Startup and Recovery window**

The settings shown in Figure 10.10 can be accessed in the following ways:

▶ **In Windows Vista:** Click Start, right-click Computer, select Properties, click the link for Advanced system settings, select the Advanced tab, and click the Settings button in the Startup and Recovery box.

▶ **In Windows XP:** Click Start, right-click My Computer, select Properties, select the Advanced tab, and click the Settings button in the Startup and Recovery box.

▶ Windows will write debugging information to the hard drive for later analyses with programs such as Dumpchk.exe; this debugging information is essentially the contents of RAM. The default setting in Windows

XP is to only write a portion of the contents of RAM, known as a Small Memory Dump; this is written to %systemroot%\Minidump, as shown in Figure 10.10. Or you could configure Windows to do a Kernel memory dump, which is the default in Windows Vista. The Kernel memory dump is saved as the file %systemroot\MEMORY.DMP that is larger than the minidump file. Both operating systems support the option for a Complete Memory Dump, which dumps the entire contents of RAM to a file once again named MEMORY.DMP. This must be where the phrase "My computer just took a dump..." comes from! For more information on how to analyze the debugging information resulting from these stop errors, see the following link: http://support.microsoft.com/kb/315263.

> **ExamAlert**
>
> Know how to make configuration changes in the Startup and Recovery window.

Additional Windows Errors and Error Reporting

Windows errors less serious than STOP errors might display a pop-up window like the one shown in Figure 10.11 after the application has closed. Figure 10.12 shows a critical error (runaway loop) that caused an application to close. However, the operating system and other applications still function. Figure 10.13 displays a critical application error known as a general protection fault (GPF) that also caused the application to fail, but again, without crashing the operating system.

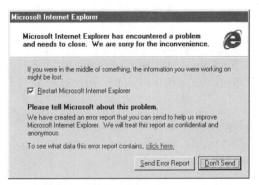

FIGURE 10.11   An Internet Explorer error

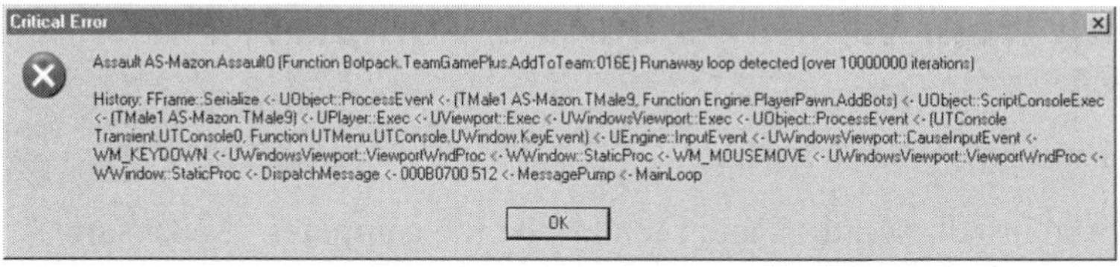

FIGURE 10.12   A critical error

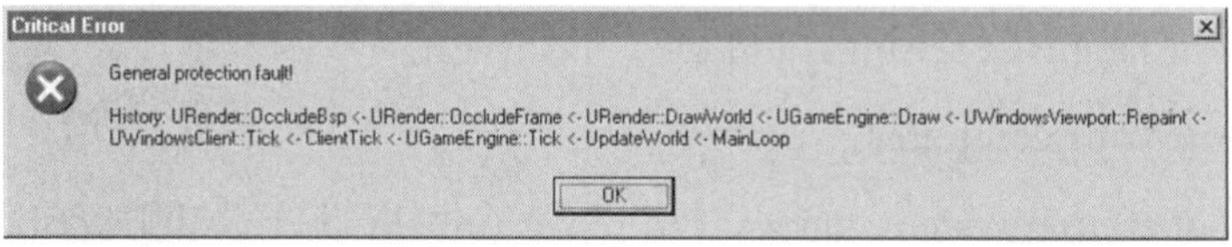

FIGURE 10.13   A General Protection Fault (GPF)

As you can see, Windows Vista/XP/2000 can recover from these types of errors and continue to function. More information can be found about the error in the Event Viewer, and in the case of Figure 10.11, the error report information can be viewed just by clicking on the link Click Here within the error window. You also have the option of sending an error report to Microsoft, in the hopes of acquiring a solution or fix.

To enable/disable error reporting in Windows Vista, navigate to Control Panel > System and Maintenance > Problem Reports and Solutions > Change settings > Advanced settings. To find out if any new solutions are available, click the Check for New Solutions link within Problem Reports and Solutions.

To enable/disable error reporting in Windows XP, navigate to the System Properties window, Advanced tab, and click the Error Reporting button.

Restoring Windows

Beyond even stop errors, a complete system failure is when a system cannot be repaired. When this happens, the only options are to reinstall or to restore Windows. There are several methods for restoring Windows. Chapter 9 showed how to back up the system and create System Restore points. Now let's show how to restore entire system backups, restore data, and restore the computer to an earlier point in time.

Restoring from Windows Vista's Complete PC Backup

To restore a system from the backup:

1. Insert the installation disc, and then restart the computer. (Make sure that the DVD drive is listed first in the BIOS boot order.)

2. Press any key when prompted to do so to boot off of the DVD.

3. Choose your language settings, and then click Next.

4. Click Repair your computer.

5. Select the operating system you want to repair (usually there will be only one), and then click Next.

> **Note**
>
> If you are restoring a 64-bit system using a 32-bit Complete PC backup or a 32-bit system using a 64-bit Complete PC backup and have more than one operating system installed, do not select an operating system. If an operating system is selected by default, clear the selection by clicking a blank area of the window, and then click Next.

6. On the System Recovery Options menu, click Windows Complete PC Restore, and then follow the instructions. Insert the last DVD of the backup set when prompted to do so.

Restoring from Windows XP's ASR Backup

To restore a system with ASR, you need the Windows XP Professional CD, the ASR backup media, the ASR floppy disk, and the computer must have a floppy drive. Follow these steps to restore the system:

1. Boot to the Windows XP CD.

2. Press F2 to start Automated System Recovery.

3. Insert the ASR floppy disk.

4. Provide the backup media when asked for it.

When ASR is finished, applications need to be reinstalled and any data backups need to be restored.

Restoring to an Earlier Condition in Windows Vista and XP

To restore your system to an earlier condition in Windows Vista

1. Access the System Protection tab again, and this time click the System Restore button. This opens the System Restore window.

2. Select either Recommended restore, or Choose a different restore point.

3. The Recommended restore point asks you to confirm. If you choose a different restore point, you will need to select the appropriate one and confirm.

4. The system initiates the restore and automatically restarts.

Windows Vista also enables you to undo a system restore, if it did not repair the problem.

To restore your system to an earlier condition in Windows XP

1. Close any open programs and save your work before you start the process.

2. Navigate to Start > All Programs > Accessories > System Tools > System Restore. This opens the System Restore window.

3. Click Restore My Computer to an Earlier Time and click Next.

4. Select a date from the calendar. (Dates that have restore points are in bold text.)

5. Select a restore point and click Next. The system will shut down, restart, and start the restore.

Using System Restore with Advanced Boot Options

If you cannot boot into Windows XP, try starting your computer using the Safe Mode option; then start System Restore . Click Restore My Computer to an earlier time, and click next. This returns your system to a previous state.

You can also start a System Restore with Safe Mode with Command Prompt option. If you are prompted to select an operating system, use the arrow keys to select the appropriate operating system for your computer, and then press enter. Log on as an administrator or with an account that has administrator credentials. At the command prompt, type **%systemroot%\system32\ restore\rstrui.exe**, and then press Enter. Follow the instructions that appear on the screen to restore your computer to a functional state.

If System Restore is not available, it might be turned off. Within Windows Vista you can enable or disable System Restore on any volume from the System Properties window > System Protection tab. Simply check or uncheck any volume that you want to enable or disable. Within Windows XP, the state of System Restore affects all drives; you can only turn the utility on and off. This is done from the System Properties window > System Restore tab. You can also change the amount of disk space it uses here.

Be aware that System Restore is not necessarily the first thing you should try when troubleshooting a computer. Simply restarting the computer has been known to "fix" all kinds of issues. It's also a good idea to try the Last Known Good Configuration. This can be accessed within the Windows Advanced Boot Options menu by pressing F8 when the computer first boots.

Note

Third-party programs such as Ghost and Acronis True Image can be used to restore a system from an image file, but the end result all depends on how long ago you imaged the machine in the first place. Factory recovery discs can also be used, but these usually return the operating system back to its original state. Any data would have to be restored afterward from some sort of backup.

ExamAlert

Know the various ways a system can be restored.

The Six-Step Troubleshooting Process Revisited

Remember to try to use the CompTIA six-step troubleshooting process when troubleshooting software issues. They are

Step 1: Identify the problem.

Step 2: Establish a theory of probable cause. (Question the obvious.)

Step 3: Test the theory to determine the cause.

Step 4: Establish a plan of action to resolve the problem and implement the solution.

Step 5: Verify full system functionality and if applicable implement preventative measures.

Step 6: Document findings, actions, and outcomes.

By using a methodical troubleshooting process like this one, you are organizing your thoughts and actions, and probably, saving time and effort in the long run.

ExamAlert

Memorize the six-step CompTIA troubleshooting process for the exam.

Cram Quiz

Answer these questions. The answers follow the last question. If you cannot answer these questions correctly, consider reading this section again until you can.

1. What could a yellow exclamation point in the Device Manager indicate?

   ○ **A.** Disabled device

   ○ **B.** Event Viewer error

   ○ **C.** Incorrect driver

   ○ **D.** Device is not installed

2. Which log file in the Event Viewer contains information concerning auditing?

   ○ **A.** System

   ○ **B.** Application

   ○ **C.** Internet Explorer

   ○ **D.** Security

3. A Stop error could manifest itself as what?

    ○ **A.** A BSOD

    ○ **B.** An Event Viewer error

    ○ **C.** A Dr. Watson error

    ○ **D.** Internet Explorer error

4. Which tools can be used to restore a computer? (Select all that apply.)

    ○ **A.** Complete PC Backup

    ○ **B.** ASR

    ○ **C.** Dr. Watson

    ○ **D.** System Restore

Cram Quiz Answers

1. C. A yellow exclamation point could indicate an incorrect device driver or other malfunction of a device. A disabled device would be indicated by a red x. If the device is not installed, it will either not show up on the list at all, or it will show up in a category named Unknown devices.

2. D. The Security log contains information about auditing and other security events.

3. A. A BSOD (Blue Screen of Death) is what results from a Stop error in Windows.

4. A, B, and **D.** Complete PC Backup is the Windows Vista solution for backing up the entire hard drive. Automatic System Recovery (ASR) restores the system state of the computer. System Restore brings the computer back to an earlier point in time.

Command-Line Tools

Let's face it; the command-line interface, or CLI, is where the extreme techs live. Some things are just easier to do in the command line, or the functionality needed might be accessible only in the command line. In this section we cover two groups of commands: First, ones that run from within Windows, and second, ones that should be run within the Recovery Console (XP) or the Command Prompt option in WinRE's System Recovery Options (Vista). Commands use what are known as switches. For example, if you typed **DIR /?**, the switch would be **/?**. Switches are also referred to as parameters or options.

Windows Command Prompt

Microsoft's name for the command line is the Command Prompt. The Command Prompt can be found in Start > All Programs > Accessories. However, if you troubleshoot Windows Vista, you probably need to run the Command Prompt in elevated mode (as an administrator), which can be done in one of two ways:

1. Click Start > All Programs > Accessories; then right-click Command Prompt and select Run as Administrator.

2. Click Start and type **cmd** in the search field, and instead of pressing Enter, press Ctrl+Shift+Enter.

Chkdsk

By running the command **chkdsk**, this tool checks a disk, fixes basic issues like lost files, and displays a status report; it can also fix some errors on the disk by using the **/F** switch. Here's an example of the three stages of results when running the chkdsk command:

```
The type of the file system is NTFS.
Volume label is WinXPC.
WARNING!  F parameter not specified.
Running CHKDSK in read-only mode.
CHKDSK is verifying files (stage 1 of 3)...
File verification completed.
CHKDSK is verifying indexes (stage 2 of 3)...
Index verification completed.
CHKDSK is recovering lost files.
Recovering orphaned file ~WRL3090.tmp (59880) into directory file
28570.
```

```
Recovering orphaned file ~DFA188.tmp (59881) into directory file
28138.
CHKDSK is verifying security descriptors (stage 3 of 3)...
Security descriptor verification completed.
Correcting errors in the master file table's (MFT) BITMAP attribute.
Correcting errors in the Volume Bitmap.
Windows found problems with the file system.
Run CHKDSK with the /F (fix) option to correct these.
 31471300 KB total disk space.
 13053492 KB in 56091 files.
    16340 KB in 4576 indexes.
        0 KB in bad sectors.
   133116 KB in use by the system.
    65536 KB occupied by the log file.
 18268352 KB available on disk.
     4096 bytes in each allocation unit.
  7867825 total allocation units on disk.
  4567088 allocation units available on disk.
```

Notice that the utility warned us that the /F switch was not specified, and because of this it ran in read-only mode. Also notice that the orphaned files were recovered, although they are just .tmp files, and most likely not necessary for the functionality of Windows. Finally, the program found issues with the file system; if we wanted to repair these, we would have to use the /F option. Be sure that you really need to run chkdsk with the /F parameter before doing so. For example, if the system seems to function properly, but the standard chkdsk command gave an error, it might not be absolutely necessary to run chkdsk with the /F parameter.

SFC

System File Checker (SFC) is a Windows Vista/XP/2000 utility that checks protected system files. It replaces incorrect versions or missing files with the correct files. SFC can be used to fix problems with Internet Explorer or other Windows applications. To run SFC, open the command prompt and type **SFC** with the appropriate switch. A typical option is **SFC /scannow**, which scans all protected files immediately. Another is **SFC /scanonce**, which scans all protected files at the next boot. If SFC finds that some files are missing, you are prompted to reinsert the original operating system disc, so the files can be copied to the DLL cache.

Convert

The convert command enables you to convert a volume that was previously formatted as FAT32 over to NTFS, without losing any data. An example of the convert command would be **convert d: /FS:NTFS**, which would convert the hard disk volume D: to NTFS. Sometimes you might encounter older computers' hard drives (or flash media) that require being formatted as NTFS for compatibility with other devices and networked computers.

Format

Format is a command used to format magnetic media such as hard drives and solid-state media such as USB flash drives to the FAT, FAT32 or NTFS file systems. An example of formatting a USB flash drive in the command line would be **format F:**. The type of file system that the media will be formatted to can be specified with the switch **/FS:filesystem**, where file system will equal either FAT, FAT32, or NTFS. For more information on the various switches available with format, type **format /?**.

Diskpart

The Diskpart utility is the command-line counterpart of Windows' Disk Management program. This program needs to be run by typing **diskpart** before any of the diskpart actions can be implemented. This brings the user into the DISKPART> prompt. From here you can create, delete, and extend volumes, assign drive letters, make a partition active, and so on. Essentially, everything that was covered in the Disk Management portion of Chapter 9 can be done with Diskpart. When you finish using Diskpart, type **exit** to return back to the standard command prompt.

Defrag

This is the command-line version of the Disk Defragmenter. To analyze a disk, type the command **defrag –a**. If a volume needs to be defragmented, but has less than 15 percent free space, use the **–f** parameter.

Xcopy

The Xcopy command is meant to copy large amounts of data from one location to another; entire directory trees even. One example of its usage would be to copy the contents of a Windows Vista DVD-ROM over to a USB flash drive so that you can use the USB flash drive as installation media. The command for this would be **xcopy d:*.* /E/F e:**. This is assuming that D: is the DVD-ROM drive, and E: is the USB flash drive. ***.*** means all files with all extensions within the D: drive. **/E** indicates that all folders and subfolders will be copied including empty ones. **/F** displays full source and destination files while copying. For more information about Xcopy type **xcopy /?**.

> **Exam Alert**
>
> Memorize as many of the commands mentioned in this section as you can!

Recovery Command Prompt

Windows Vista's System Recovery Options Command Prompt and Windows XP's Recovery Console are used to repair issues with the operating system. For example, a system file causing the system to fail at startup can be copied from installation media. This environment can also be used to edit files and run commands that can fix the boot sector and master boot record. In this section I refer to both Windows Vista's System Recovery Options Command Prompt and Windows XP's Recovery Console collectively as "recovery Command Prompts" for easier reading.

Edit

The **edit** command can be used to create and modify text files within Windows or within a recovery Command Prompt. For example, maybe the boot.ini file in Windows XP needs to be modified. Within the root of C: the command to modify this would be simply **edit boot.ini**. Here is an example of a default Windows XP boot.ini file that has some incorrect information:

```
[boot loader]
timeout=30
default=multi(0)disk(0)rdisk(0)partition(1)\WINNT
[operating systems]
multi(0)disk(0)rdisk(0)partition(1)\WINDOWS="Microsoft Windows XP
Professional" /fastdetect /NoExecute=OptIn
```

Did you notice the error? The default %systemroot% folder name in Windows XP is **\Windows**, not **\Winnt**, as is incorrectly shown in line 3. Line 3 contains what is called an Advanced RISC Computing (ARC) path. It tells us the type of disk being used, which disk and partition the operating system is installed to, and finally the installation folder. Errors within an ARC path can be easily fixed with the **edit** command, or you could simply delete the file, and Windows XP would re-create a default boot.ini automatically upon restart. However, the file that XP re-creates automatically would be a default file, assuming one hard drive with the operating system installed to the C: drive. Any other configurations would require the boot.ini be modified. For example, if Windows was installed to D: instead of C:, the "partition" section of the ARC path would have to be modified to partition(2). If using SATA or IDE hard drives, the default setting for rdisk is 0, which means the first hard drive; the default setting for partition is 1, which means the first partition on the drive. Note that the partition setting does *not* start with 0. For more information on ARC paths, an older but still valid article can be found at: http://support.microsoft.com/kb/102873.

Copy

The **copy** command obviously copies files from one location to another. An example of its usage in a recovery-based Command Prompt would be to replace a missing NTLDR file in Windows XP. To do this, the file would have to be copied from the CD-ROM to the hard disk. Assuming that all drive letters are standard (hard disk is C: and CD-ROM drive is D:), the syntax for this would be **copy d:\i386\ntldr c:**. This copies the NTLDR file from the I386 folder on the CD-ROM to the root of C: on the hard drive.

Expand

Sometimes you can't just copy files from a DVD/CD to the hard drive. Many of these files are compressed. If a file ends with an underscore, for example ntoskrnl.ex_ then it is a compressed file and has to be expanded. Let's just say that it was a dark day and that ntoskrnl.exe had failed. You can't do much without that core operating system file. To fix the problem in the recovery Command Prompt, you would expand the file from DVD/CD to the hard drive. In a standard environment where the hard drive is C: and the DVD/CD drive is D:, the syntax would be **expand D:\i386\ntoskrnl.ex_ C:\Windows\System32\ntoskrnl.exe**. This decompresses the file and places a copy of the decompressed version on the hard drive. Be sure to type the entire name of the file in the destination; otherwise, you will need to rename the file.

> **Note**
>
> The **edit**, **copy**, and **expand** commands can also be used within Windows in the Command Prompt.

Other Recovery Environment Commands

If Windows Vista has startup issues, you can use several commands:

- ► **bootrec /fixboot**—Replaces the bootmgr file and writes a new Windows Vista compatible boot sector to the system partition.

- ▶ **bootrec /fixmbr**—Rewrites the Windows Vista compatible master boot record to the system partition.

- ▶ **bootrec /rebuildbcd**—Repairs the BCD store.

- ▶ **bootrec /ScanOs**—This scans all disks for installations compatible with Windows Vista. This option also displays the entries that are currently not included in the BCD store. Use this command if there are Windows Vista installations that the Boot Manager menu does not list.

If Windows XP has startup issues, there are a couple of commands that you can use:

- ▶ **FIXMBR**—Use this command to repair the MBR of the system partition. Use this command if a virus has damaged the MBR and Windows cannot start.

- ▶ **FIXBOOT**—Use this command to write new Windows boot sector code to the system partition.

> **Note**
>
> For an advanced description of the Recovery Console and all its commands, see the following link: http://support.microsoft.com/kb/314058.

Cram Quiz

Answer these questions. The answers follow the last question. If you cannot answer these questions correctly, consider reading this section again until you can.

1. Which command can fix lost files?

- ○ **A. Defrag**
- ○ **B. Diskpart**
- ○ **C. Chkdsk**
- ○ **D. FIXMBR**

2. Which Recovery Console command will decompress a file as it copies it to the hard drive?

- ○ **A. Extract**
- ○ **B. Expand**
- ○ **C. Compress**
- ○ **D. Encrypt**

3. Which command can copy multiple files and entire directory trees?

- ○ **A. Copy**
- ○ **B. Cut**
- ○ **C. Paste**
- ○ **D. Xcopy**

4. Which command will write a new boot sector and replace the bootmgr file in Windows Vista?

- ○ **A. bootrec /fixboot**
- ○ **B. bootrec /fixmbr**
- ○ **C. bootrec /rebuildbcd**
- ○ **D. bootrec /ScanOs**

Cram Quiz Answers

1. **C.** **Chkdsk** verifies the integrity of a disk and can fix lost (or orphaned) files.

2. **B.** The expand command decompresses files that are compressed on the CD, such as ntoskrnl.ex_.

3. **D.** **Xcopy** can copy an entire disc of information with just one command (with parameters).

4. **A.** **Bootrec /fixboot** replaces the bootmgr file and writes a new Windows Vista compatible boot sector to the system partition.

Additional Reading and Resources

Microsoft Help and Support, formerly known as the Microsoft Knowledge Base (MSKB): http://support.microsoft.com

TechNet: http://technet.microsoft.com

Additional A+ resources: http://www.davidlprowse.com/aplus

CHAPTER 11

Laptops

This chapter covers the following A+ exam topics:

▶ Installing, Configuring, and Troubleshooting Visible Laptop Components

▶ Installing, Configuring, and Troubleshooting Internal Laptop Components

You can find a master list of A+ exam topics in the "Introduction."

This chapter covers CompTIA A+ 220-701 objectives 1.10 and 2.4 and CompTIA A+ 220-702 objective 1.3.

Ah, the laptop. The beauty of laptops is that they are portable, and all the connections are right at your fingertips. However, quite often there is a trade-off in performance and in price. This chapter assumes a basic knowledge of laptops, and jumps straight into how to install, configure, and troubleshoot laptop devices.

Laptops were originally designed for niche markets, but today are used in businesses almost as much as desktop PCs are. Laptops (also known as notebooks or portable computers) have integrated displays, keyboards, and pointing devices making them easy to transport and easy to use in confined spaces. There are plenty of other portable devices on the market today including PDAs, Ultra-Mobile PCs, and more, but the bulk of the portable devices that you will troubleshoot are laptops; it is laptops that are covered on the CompTIA A+ exams. For the exams, it is important to identify the components of a laptop and the ports that surround the machine, how to install and configure hardware, and how to take care of and troubleshoot the laptop. In many respects, laptops work the same way as desktop computers. This chapter focuses on the differences that make a laptop stand out from the desktop PC.

Installing, Configuring, and Troubleshooting Visible Laptop Components

In this section, we discuss the visible components of the laptop such as the keyboard and the display. These two devices are probably the most prone to failure, so we discuss some methods and step by steps on how to repair them. In addition, we talk about a laptop's audio, power, expansion busses, and optical disc drives.

Laptop 101

For the exam, it is important to identify the main components of a laptop and its ports. Figure 11.1 shows some of the main components of the laptop.

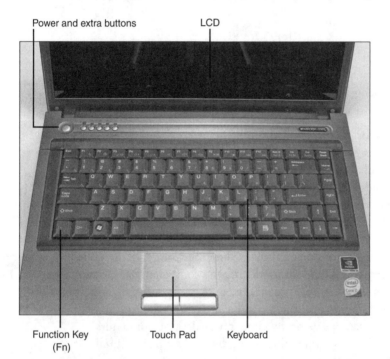

FIGURE 11.1 **A typical laptop's main components**

The main components of the laptop include the liquid crystal display (LCD), keyboard (with special Fn key), touch pad, the power button, and extra buttons. The extra buttons offer additional functionality, for example; enabling and disabling wireless, turning the sound on or off, and opening applications such as Internet Explorer and Outlook.

A laptop manufacturer needs to squeeze in ports wherever they can find space, so quite often you find ports on three of the sides of the laptop. Figures 11.2 through 11.4 identify the various ports around the sides of the laptop.

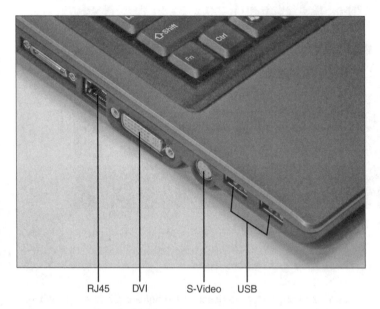

RJ45   DVI   S-Video   USB

FIGURE 11.2   **A typical laptop's ports part A**

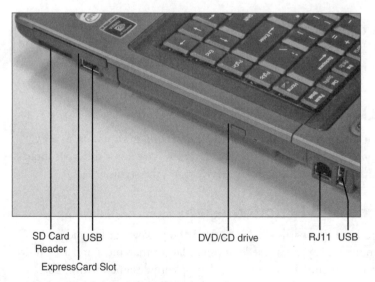

SD Card   USB   DVD/CD drive   RJ11 USB
Reader

ExpressCard Slot

FIGURE 11.3   **A typical laptop's ports part B**

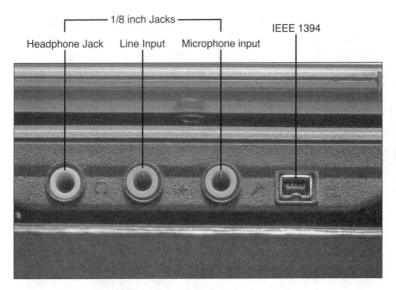

FIGURE 11.4 A typical laptop's ports part C

Note

The ports in Figures 11.2 through 11.4 are described in detail in Chapter 12, "Video, Audio, and Peripherals."

ExamAlert

Be able to identify the main components and ports of a laptop for the exam.

Input Devices

Inputting information to a laptop is just like inputting information to a PC, except all of the devices are miniaturized. Laptops have a few different input devices including keyboards, pointing devices, and the stylus.

Keyboards and Function Keys

Some laptops have keyboards similar to the 101-key keyboard found on a PC including a numeric keypad; these laptops are larger than most and are known as desktop replacements. However, most laptops are designed with a small form factor in mind, and this means a smaller keyboard. For example, the keyboard in Figure 11.5 has 86 keys. But as you note in the figure, a user has the option of using the Fn key. The Fn key (Function key) is a modifier key used on most laptops. This is designed to activate secondary functions of other keys (usually marked in blue). For example, in Figure 11.5 the F8 key has the secondary function "volume up," but only if you are pressing the Fn key at the same time.

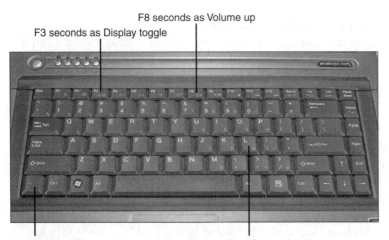

FIGURE 11.5 **A typical laptop keyboard**

Using this method, much more functionality can be incorporated into the keyboard without the need for additional keys. This idea has since grown to include all kinds of controls; for instance, using media player controls, putting the computer to sleep, and a variety of other functions including enabling an external monitor (as shown in Figure 11.5); on this laptop the F3 key seconds as a display toggle between the built-in LCD and an external monitor. In addition, the entire numeric keypad is added to the keyboard as secondary keys. For example, in Figure 11.5 the L key seconds as the number 3, but this will work only if the Number Lock (Num Lk) key has been enabled. (The Fn key is not necessary for the numeric keypad to work.) Quite often, users forget about the Num Lk key, and when they try to type, strange garbled code comes out! Simply press the Num Lk key once to fix the problem. This is also common if the user works with an external keyboard at the office and disconnects it when they leave the office.

> **ExamAlert**
>
> Press the Num Lk key to enable/disable the numeric keypad on a laptop.

Personally, I have had a dozen people I know approach me telling me that their laptop's keyboard wasn't working properly. Over time I've noticed several culprits: overuse, loose ribbon cables, spilled coffee, or users simply pounding the tar out of the keyboard! Here are a couple of problems you might encounter:

> **Stuck keys:** Stuck keys could occur because of overuse, damage to the individual key's switch, or if liquid was spilled on the keyboard. (And if a stuck key is the worst that happens due to a liquid spill, consider yourself lucky!) Stuck keys can be identified by the fact that the key fails to work in Windows, or if the BIOS reports a 3xx error. (It might say something similar to "Keyboard stuck key failure.") If there is a BIOS error, look for a two-digit hexadecimal code just before the 3xx error. This code identifies which key(s) is stuck. Of course, you have to access your BIOS documentation to find out which key a particular hexadecimal code refers to. (In some cases this will be based off of the standard ASCII printable character code.) By removing the keycap and cleaning the keyswitch underneath, you can usually fix the problem. If not, the entire keyboard will probably have to be replaced. See Table 11.1 for more information.

> **Loose connection:** If the laptop is moved around and jostled a lot, as many laptops are, it could possibly cause loose connections. One of these is the ribbon cable that connects the keyboard to the motherboard. To fix this, the keyboard will have to be lifted away from the laptop and the ribbon cable attached securely. Follow the steps listed in Table 11.1 to accomplish this.

> **Damaged keyboard:** Users who inadvertently drop heavy items onto the keyboard or operate the keyboard with a heavy hand might cause a warped or bent keyboard. Some brands of laptops suffer from this more than others. This is usually impossible to repair, and the keyboard will need to be replaced, as shown in Table 11.1.

TABLE 11.1   **Steps Involved in Replacing a Laptop Keyboard**

Step	Procedure
1. Prepare the laptop for surgery!	Shut down the laptop, unplug it, and disconnect the battery. Then employ ESD prevention measures. Because there is nowhere on a laptop to connect an antistatic wrist strap or mat, you need to connect these to the chassis of a nearby unplugged desktop computer, or a proper earth bonding point of some sort.

TABLE 11.1   **Continued**

Step	Procedure
2. Remove the trim.	Usually the keyboard is held in place by a piece of trim or an entire plastic housing (also known as a bezel). The trim might be in-between the keyboard and the monitor, or it might surround the keyboard. The plastic housing might have to be pried out with a thin flat tool, which can be a little tricky. You can use wooden trim sticks, which are thin, cylindrical pieces of wood that have an angled edge to get underneath plastic housings (available at drug stores, and some hardware stores), or use a very fine flathead screwdriver. In addition, some laptops come with a special tool to remove trim, bezels, and hinge covers. Go slow and be gentle with these plastic parts that snap in and out of the laptop case.
3. Remove the screws.	When the trim is removed, you should see two screws. You might need a small Phillips head screwdriver or a small Torx screwdriver. (Most laptops require smaller Torx screwdrivers than PCs do, as low as T8 or even T6.)
4. Disconnect the keyboard.	When the keyboard can be lifted up, you can see it is connected to the system board by a ribbon cable, also known as a flex cable. Figure 11.6 shows the keyboard lifted up and back displaying the flex cable connector. Be gentle with this cable and its connection. The connector usually has two locking tabs, one on each end of the flex cable connector. Unlocking this is a delicate procedure; the locks need to be pulled out only a little bit to unlock the flex cable. Some technicians use an extremely small screwdriver or a toothpick to move these tabs into the unlocked position. On many systems, this also enables you access to the hinges that can remove the display.
5. Replace the keyboard.	A new keyboard can sometimes be purchased from the manufacturer, but you might not find out the part # you need from the manufacturer by giving them the model # of the laptop. If you can't find the part #, or the manufacturer will not supply the component you need, look for the part number on the bottom of the keyboard and search for that part on the Internet. After you acquire the correct part (always check the part # of the new keyboard against the old one), connect the flex ribbon cable, lock it on both sides with those tiny locking tabs, screw in the keyboard, and replace the plastic trim.
6. Test the keyboard.	Verify that the new keyboard works by testing every key within a word processor like WordPad, and test Fn enabled keys as well.

FIGURE 11.6   **Keyboard Flex Cable Connector**

> **Note**
>
> Step 1 should be employed whenever you replace parts in the laptop.

> **ExamAlert**
>
> Understand the steps involved when replacing keyboards for the exam.

If a user needs access to a laptop right away before it can be repaired, a temporary solution would be to connect a USB or PS/2 external keyboard. This
should be recognized automatically by Windows. There are USB to PS/2
adapters available if the laptop has only USB ports, and the only keyboard
accessible is PS/2. Examples of sites where these types of adapters can be
acquired include www.cablestogo.com, and www.cyberguys.com.

> **Note**
>
> When repairing a laptop, try to document the process as you go. Write down what
> you see and how and where cables and screws were attached. Also make note of
> how devices were oriented before they were removed. Label any parts that you
> remove for easier identification later on. If available, refer to the manufacturer's doc-
> umentation that came with the laptop.

Pointing Devices

Whereas a PC uses a mouse, the laptop uses a pointing device. The bulk of laptops come with a pointing device known as a touch pad. By gliding a finger across the touch pad surface, a user can move the cursor on the screen. Touch pads also comes with two buttons that take the place of a mouse's buttons. In portable computing lingo, the word "click" is replaced with the word "tap." In addition to using the buttons, most touch pad surfaces can also be tapped or double-tapped upon, just by tapping with the finger. The buttons are oriented in such a way as to be used with the thumb. Touch pads can be replaced though it is uncommon to do so; they are connected by two cables similar to the flex cable that connects the keyboard. However, you might have to remove other devices first to get at the touch pad. You might also have to work from the bottom and from the top of the laptop; this will depend on the brand of laptop. Some touch pad buttons can be replaced the way keys on the keypads are. Touch pads are sometimes referred to as track pads as well.

Pointing devices can often be turned off within Windows, usually through the laptop manufacturer's software. Watch out for situations in which the entire device was disabled or perhaps just the pad portion of the touch pad was disabled. It's also possible to disable tapping ability of the touch pad, while still allowing movement of the cursor.

Another common type of pointing device is the pointing stick, known within IBM/Lenovo laptops as the TrackPoint. This device manifests itself as a smaller rubber cap (that looks like an eraser head) just above the B key, and two buttons that work essentially the same as a touch pad's buttons. External keyboards are also sold with integrated TrackPoint devices.

Of course external mice can be connected to the laptop or its docking station as well. These would be connected to USB or PS/2 ports or could be wireless devices that connect via Bluetooth.

Stylus/Digitizer

A stylus is a writing tool, usually a thin plastic "pen" looking device used to take the place of a mouse by tapping and "writing" on a touch screen (also known as a digitizer screen). This method is widely used in tablet PCs, PDAs, and handheld computers. Whenever you sign for a package from a package company, you sign with a stylus on a touch screen. This takes the place of pencil and paper.

Video

A laptop's video subsystem is composed of a liquid crystal display (LCD) and a graphics processor unit (GPU):

- ▶ **LCD:** A flat panel display that consists of two sheets of polarizing material surrounding a layer of liquid crystal solution. It connects to the motherboard by way of a flex ribbon cable and gets its power from an inverter board.

- ▶ **GPU:** The GPU is the processor for video. On a laptop it is usually integrated with the motherboard. In some cases it is part of the chipset and utilizes RAM as shared video memory. In others scenarios, namely more powerful laptops, it is a separate processor that has its own memory and possibly is situated upon its own circuit board.

Most of today's LCD screens are thin-film transistor (TFT) active-matrix displays, meaning they have three transistors for each pixel, which are contained within a flexible material. These are located directly behind the liquid crystal material. In general, LCDs use low amounts of power, generate a small amount of heat, and cause very little in the way of interference and emissions.

Display Controls

Brightness can be adjusted from the keyboard on most laptops. On the laptop keyboard shown previously in Figure 11.5, pressing the Fn and F4 key will decrease brightness, and pressing the Fn and F5 key will increase brightness. There usually aren't contrast controls on a laptop's LCD.

Resolution is the amount of pixels, measured horizontal by vertical, on the display, and is user selectable. The higher the resolution, the more that can be fit on the screen, which is beneficial to a certain point, especially if the laptop's screen isn't very big. Table 11.2 shows some of the common resolutions that laptops use currently.

TABLE 11.2 **Common Laptop Resolutions**

Resolution Standard	Full Name	Pixels (HxV)	Aspect Ratio
WXGA	Widescreen Extended Graphics Array	1280x800	16:10 (1.6:1)
HD	High-Definition display similar to WXGA	1366x768	16:9 (1.78:1)
WSXGA+	Widescreen Super Extended Graphics Array Plus	1680x1050	16:10 (1.6:1)
HD	High-Definition display similar to WSXGA+	1680x945	16:9 (1.78:1)

> **Note**
>
> For more about resolution and the different resolution modes available, see Chapter 12, "Video, Audio, and Peripherals."

Laptops' active-matrix screens are usually set to run at one specific resolution. The laptop used during the writing of this book uses a default resolution of 1280x800 pixels. If the resolution is changed to something else, the laptop usually scales the resolution, making the picture unclear and perhaps not even fit on the screen correctly. Because of this you're really stuck with the default resolution. Sometimes this default resolution can be a bit tough on the eyes, for example if the laptop's display runs at WXGA 1280x800 but the screen size is only 13.3 inches. If a user plans on using the laptop for long periods of time, they should consider a laptop with a larger display or an external display.

That brings us to the capability to send video signal to an external monitor. Some people refer to this technology as *screen switching*. Most laptops come with an external connection (either VGA or DVI or both) for a second monitor. When this monitor is plugged in, it can be enabled by pressing the display toggle key, otherwise known as the secondary monitor button. On the laptop used in this chapter, this can be done by pressing the Fn key and the F3 key simultaneously; however, it can be a different key than F3 on other brands of laptops. The icon on the key usually looks like an open laptop viewed from the side with a monitor to its right. Normally, you have the option to display the desktop to the laptop, to the external display, or a copy of the desktop to both. Many laptops offer a greater resolution to external displays than they can provide internally, but only when the external display is being used exclusively. For example, the laptop used in this chapter can run a resolution of 1280x800 on the integrated display but can run at 1920x1200 on the external monitor (again, exclusively). If the external monitor won't display anything, make sure that the cable is firmly connected to the external port, verify that the external monitor is plugged in and on, and then try cycling through the various video options by pressing the button several times, waiting a few seconds each time. Make sure you are holding down the Fn key while doing so. Finally, restart the computer if necessary. This can get a little trickier if using a projector as the second display. Sometimes, the projector might need time to warm up or might need to be configured via its on-screen display (OSD). Locate the projector's documentation for more details.

Well, displaying the same desktop on two monitors is great, but what if you want to take it to the next level and *stretch out* the Windows desktop across two monitors? That would be known as DualView.

> **Note**
>
> For more about video settings, see Chapter 12 "Video, Audio, and Peripherals."

DualView

DualView is a Windows feature that extends the desktop across to a second display; it enables you to spread applications over two monitors that effectively work together as one. This works well for applications that are very wide; for instance, a wide spreadsheet that requires some heavy left-to-right scrolling, an audio/video application with many tracks of information, or in the case that more than one window needs to be open and visible at the same time. The secondary screen used in DualView does not have a taskbar; it just has the wallpaper that you normally use. When DualView is used on a laptop, the laptop is always the primary monitor, and the other monitor cannot be selected as primary, meaning it cannot have the taskbar, Start button, and so on. To enable DualView, follow these steps:

1. Connect a secondary monitor to the DVI or VGA port on the laptop. Newer laptops have a DVI port. But you can still connect older SVGA monitors, just use a DVI to VGA adapter. (These come with many of today's video cards.)

2. Turn on the secondary monitor.

3. Open the Display Settings window in Vista, or the Display Properties window in XP.

   ▶ **In Vista:** Right-click the desktop and select Personalize. Then select Display Settings. This opens the Display Settings window.

   ▶ **In XP:** Right-click the desktop and select Properties. This opens the Display Properties window. Select the Settings tab.

4. Click on the Display drop-down menu. Multiple Monitors should be listed. If it is not listed, the laptop might not support DualView.

5. Select the monitor with the number 2, either in the display, or in the drop-down menu and check mark Extend My Windows Desktop on to this Monitor, as shown in Figure 11.7. By using the Identify button, and dragging the monitors around in the display window, you can arrange your monitors so that they match their physical position.

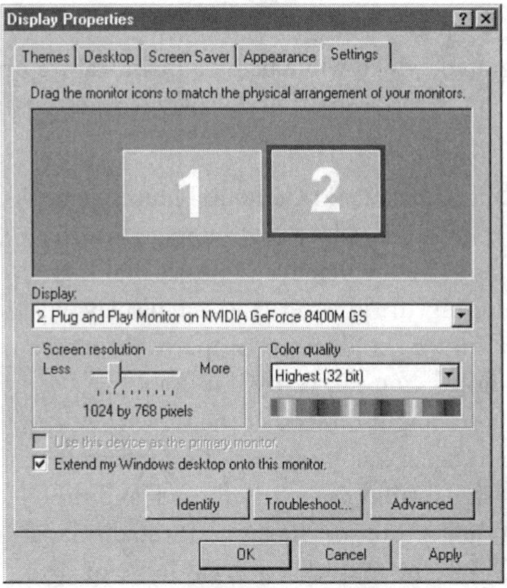

FIGURE 11.7   Windows XP DualView configuration

6. Click Apply. The mouse should extend all the way across both monitors now. Verify that the secondary monitor is functional by dragging a window to that display. If all is good, click OK to close the Display Settings/Display Properties window.

When DualView is implemented, screen switching will not function; to use screen switching, DualView first has to be disabled. Some laptops' video adapters do not support DualView, or they might need a software upgrade to support it.

Note

Windows' Multiple Monitor technology builds off DualView but cannot currently be used on laptops. It works with desktop PCs and can drive up to ten monitors, any one of which can be the primary monitor. In Windows XP, different video adapters with different drivers can be used, but in Windows Vista, the same driver must be used for all adapters. Many video adapters today come with two DVI outputs standard for just this sort of scenario. Other video adapters don't support Multiple Monitor or need a software upgrade to do so.

Troubleshooting Video Issues

The video display in laptops is integrated, which while being a main feature of the portability of laptops can be a point of failure as well. Display failures can be broken down into a few categories:

▶ **Damaged inverter:** The LCD is lit by a Cold Cathode Fluorescent Lamp (basically a bulb). The lamp is driven by a high-voltage inverter circuit. Because the inverter runs at high voltage, and possibly at high temperatures, it is prone to failure. If the inverter fails, the display will go dark; however, an external monitor should work properly. Another possibility is that the lamp has failed. You can verify if it is an inverter/lamp issue by shining a flashlight directly at the screen. When you do this you should be able to make out Windows! This means that the display is getting the video signal from the motherboard, and the problem, most likely, is indeed the inverter or the lamp. If the display's flex cable that connects the LCD to the motherboard was loose or disconnected, nothing would show up on the screen at all. The inverter circuit is usually situated on its own circuit board. To replace this circuit board follow the steps in Table 11.3.

▶ **Damaged LCD screen:** An LCD could be damaged in a variety of ways. For example you might see a crack in the screen, or a portion of the screen doesn't display properly. If this is the case, the LCD will have to be replaced, follow steps 1–3 in Table 11.3 to open the display assembly.

▶ **Worn out lamp:** A laptop's lamp will usually last a long time. However, at some point the lamp will start to wear out. You might notice a dimmer screen than before, or a reddish/pinkish hue to the screen, or maybe a loss of color. All these things indicate the possibility of a worn out lamp. To replace the lamp, follow the steps in Table 11.3 but during steps 4 and 5, instead of replacing the inverter, replace the lamp.

TABLE 11.3   **Steps to Replace a Damaged Inverter Board**

Step	Procedure
1. Prepare the laptop for surgery!	Shut down the laptop, unplug it, and disconnect the battery. Then employ ESD prevention measures.
2. Remove the display.	To remove the display, the keyboard will have to be removed first. (Depending on the brand of laptop, there might be a few other items to unscrew and remove.) Then, remove the screws holding the hinges down to the base of the laptop. Finally, disconnect the flex cable and any other connectors from the display to the system board.

TABLE 11.3 **Continued**

Step	Procedure
3. Open the display.	There are several screws that hold the display together located on the plastic bezel that surrounds the LCD. These screws are covered with either tape or plastic domes. Remove the tape/domes and then remove the screws. Pry the plastic bezel open (carefully!) and remove the LCD.
4. Remove the inverter.	The inverter often has two connectors: one for the high-voltage connection that leads to the power source and a flex cable that connects to the LCD. Disconnect these, and remove the inverter. As always, hold circuit boards by the edges and try not to touch any actual circuits or chips. Note: At this stage, the bulb could be replaced (if it failed) on some laptops. It is usually located on the back of the LCD at the very bottom. However, some LCDs have nonremovable bulbs. If this is the case, the entire LCD will have to be replaced.
5. Install the new inverter.	LCD inverters can be purchased from a variety of places online including the manufacturer of the laptop, or of the display. Verify that you are getting the correct part#. Connect the flex cable and the other connector to the inverter board.
6. Rebuild the display.	Now the tough part. The LCD must be put back into the bezel. Then the bezel needs to be snapped together and screwed in. Replace the tape or domes that covered the screws. Then reconnect the display assembly to the rest of the laptop; the hinges normally connect with a few screws. Next, reconnect the flex cable and any other connectors from the display to the system board. Finally, reconnect and screw in other components like the keyboard.

Exam Alert

Warning! The inverter should not be handled if the laptop is on! Be sure to turn off and unplug the laptop and remove the battery before removing an inverter.

Audio

Almost all laptops have an integrated sound card (often a Mini-PCI card) and speakers. These work in the same manner as a PC's sound card and speakers, just on a smaller scale. Quite often, a laptop comes equipped with a speaker out/headphone out connector, line in connector, microphone connector, and perhaps an IEEE 1394 (FireWire) connector. For more information on audio, see the section titled "The Audio Subsystem" in Chapter 12.

A laptop's volume can be adjusted in one of two ways:

▶ **Volume knob/button:** Older laptops have a knob, which can sometimes be a little hard to find. This can be the culprit when a user informs you that they cannot hear anything from their speakers. Newer laptops use a button, usually one that is activated with the Fn key (refer to Figure 11.5). Most new laptops have an on-screen display that shows the volume level as you adjust it.

▶ **Software adjustment:** Volume can be adjusted within Windows Vista by navigating to Start > Control Panel > Sound and then accessing the Speakers Properties window and adjusting the volume slider. Volume can be adjusted in Windows XP by navigating to Start > Control Panel > Sounds and Audio Devices, and then adjusting the volume slider. From here you can also place a volume icon on the taskbar (within the System Tray) for easy access to the volume control and to the Sounds and Audio Devices window. Vista places an icon within the System Tray automatically. Most sound cards come with their own software as well in which a user can adjust volume, the equalizer, and more. This software might place an icon within the System Tray as well.

Optical Discs

Due to the amount of abuse a typical laptop receives, it is not uncommon to see a DVD or CD drive fail. However, optical disc drives are usually easy to replace on a laptop, easier than on a desktop PC in fact. Most of the time there will be two screws on the bottom of the laptop that hold the DVD or CD drive in place. When removed, the drive can be slid out of the side of the laptop. Drives that can be installed simply by sliding them into a slot are becoming more and more commonplace; most laptops incorporate them. Check your laptop's documentation for a compatible replacement (or upgrade), or check the bottom of the drive itself for part numbers that you can use to find a replacement drive online.

Power

Laptops are designed to run on battery power, but laptops can run only between 2 and 5 hours on these batteries. So, the laptop comes with an AC power adapter to plug into an AC outlet; these adapters should always be carried with the laptop. How many times have I heard from a user that they forgot their power brick! Recommend to users that they always put the AC adapter back in the laptop case.

The worst is when a laptop won't turn on! Without power a user can't do anything. When troubleshooting power problems, envision the entire chain of power in your mind (or write it on paper), from the AC outlet, to the AC adapter, all the way to the power button on the laptop. There are a few things you can check if it appears that the laptop is not getting any power.

▶ **Check the power LED:** Most laptops have a power LED just above the keyboard. If this lights up, then maybe it isn't a power problem at all. For example, the user might start the laptop, see nothing on the display, and determine that the laptop has no power, when in reality, it is a display issue. Many laptops also have hard drive and wireless LEDs, which can tell you more about the status of the laptop, without being able to see anything on the screen.

▶ **Check connections:** Verify that the laptop is firmly connected to the AC adapter and that the AC Adapter is firmly connected to the AC outlet.

▶ **Make sure the user uses the right power adapter:** Swapping power adapters between two different laptops is not recommended, but users try to do it all the time. Two different laptop models made by the same manufacturer might use what appear to be similar power adapters, with only one or two volts separating them; however, the laptop usually won't power on with that "slightly" different power adapter. Laptop AC adapters are known as fixed input power supplies, meaning they work at a specific voltage. The adapter is not meant to be used on another model laptop. Unfortunately, a user might have plugged in the incorrect power adapter, and the laptop worked fine for 4 or 5 hours, because it was actually running on battery power, but the user might not have noticed, even though the system should have notified the user when the battery was low (and critical). If you do suspect that an AC power adapter is faulty, consider testing your theory by swapping it out with an *identical* power adapter. Chances are a company will have extra power adapters or will have several laptops of the same make and model. Another power adapter-related issue could be that the user is trying to work in another country. To do this, the user needs an auto-switching AC adapter, meaning that it can switch from 120 to 240 VAC automatically. Some laptops do not come with auto-switching AC adapters, but after-market versions can be purchased for many models of laptops. Remember that an additional adapter might be necessary to make the actual connection to the AC outlet in foreign countries.

▶ **Check the battery and voltage:** It might sound silly, but check if the battery hasn't been removed for some odd reason. Also, check if the battery is fully inserted into the battery compartment. There is usually a locking mechanism that should hold the battery in place. Finally, test the battery's voltage. Batteries last a finite amount of time. They can be recharged (known as cycles) by the laptop just so many times before failure. After a few to several years, the battery won't hold a charge any longer or will lose charge quickly. In some cases you can try discharging and recharging the battery a few times to "stimulate" it, but in most scenarios the battery will have to be replaced. In general, lithium-ion batteries last longer if the laptop is operated and stored at the right temperature ranges. Acceptable operating range for laptops is from 50–95°F (10–35°C), and acceptable storage ranges are from –4–140°F (–20–60°C).

> **Note**
>
> For more information on how to prolong lithium-ion batteries (the most common laptop battery), see the following link: http://batteryuniversity.com/parttwo-34.htm.

▶ **Check if standby or hibernate mode has failed:** If the user regularly puts the laptop into standby or hibernate mode, they could encounter issues once in a while. In some cases, the power button needs to be held down for several seconds to reboot the machine out of a failed power down state. This might have to be done with the battery removed. If either of these modes failed, check the Event Viewer for any relative information, and possibly turn off hibernation and or standby mode until the situation has been rectified.

▶ **Reconnect the power button:** In rare cases the power button might have been disconnected from the system board. To fix this the laptop will have to be opened up; usually removing the keyboard and laptop housing gives access to the buttons.

▶ **Check the AC outlet:** Make sure the AC outlet that the user has plugged the laptop into is supplying power. A simple test would be to plug a lamp, clock, or other device into the outlet, but a more discerning and safe test would be to use a receptacle tester. For more information on testing AC outlets see Chapter 5, "Power."

There are a few different types of batteries that a laptop might use including Lithium-ion (Li-ion), Nickel-metal hydride (NiMH), and Nickel-cadmium (NiCd), but Li-ion is by far the most common. They have the best energy to weight ratio and don't suffer from "memory effect" like NiCd batteries. They also discharge slowly when they are not used.

However, you can't run on batteries forever! So Windows includes alarms that can be set to notify the user when the battery is getting low, and *real* low, known as critical. These alarms are set in Power Options.

To modify battery alarms in Windows XP, click Start > Control Panel, and in Classic mode double-click the Power Options icon. Select the Alarms tab; from here the low battery and critical battery alarm thresholds can be modified. Additional settings like the power scheme used, what to do when the lid of the laptop is closed, and enabling hibernation can also be modified in the Power Options Properties dialog box. To conserve battery power, consider setting the display and hard disk to turn off after the computer has been idle for 5 minutes; this can be done from the Power Schemes tab.

Power options on portable systems running Windows Vista can be modified by going to the Control Panel, selecting Classic view, and double-clicking the Power Options applet. By default in Vista, there are three Preferred plans: Balanced, Power saver, and High performance; however, users can create their own power plans as well. Each of these plans can be modified by clicking on the Change plan settings link. There are a lot of settings in this window; let's show one example. In Balanced, click Change plan settings. The Display is set to turn off in 20 minutes by default; it can be set from 1 minute to 5 hours, or set to never. If you click on the Change advanced power settings link, the Power Options button appears. From here you can specify how long before the hard disk turns off, and set power savings for devices such as the processor, wireless, USB, and PCI Express. To configure alarms in Vista, go to the Battery area and Low battery notification. Take a few minutes looking through these options, and the options for the other power plans. Almost all of today's laptops use the Advanced Configuration and Power Interface (ACPI), which enables Windows to control the device power management instead of the BIOS.

ExamAlert

Know where to modify battery alarms in Windows XP and Vista.

Expansion Devices

There are several ways to expand upon your laptop, including external and internal expansion slots and docking stations. Let's talk about each of these briefly.

▶ **External expansion busses:** The most common types of external expansion busses are called PC Card (also known as PCMCIA), CardBus, and ExpressCard; I'm talking about those 2-inch-wide slots on the side of the laptop. These expansion busses accept credit card-size devices that can be added to a laptop to increase memory, or add functionality in the form of networking, hard disks, and more. They are hot swappable, meaning they support hot plugging into the expansion slot while the computer is powered on.

PC Cards must be supported by the computer on two levels: the card level (Card Services) and the socket level (Socket Services). Card Services deal with the installation of compatible drivers to the operating system and enable the allocation of system resources automatically. Socket Services is the BIOS level software interface that provides access to the sockets (slots) in the computer.

PC Cards have a 16-bit bus width and can be used in PC Card slots and CardBus slots. However, CardBus cards have a 32-bit bus width (essentially they are PCI); they look similar to PC Cards but cannot be used in a PC Card slot. ExpressCard (also known as PCI ExpressCard) is a separate technology altogether and not compatible with either of the other two (without an adapter). It looks similar to the others, but you can identify it by a cutout in one corner of the card. Also, PC Cards and CardBus cards have a 68-pin connector, whereas ExpressCard has a 26-pin connector. PC Card and CardBus were the most-used expansion cards in laptops for many years, but since 2006 have been losing ground to ExpressCard, especially in higher-end laptops. This is yet another example of a technology that is moving from parallel to serial data transfer. A manufacturer of ExpressCard devices can select to design them using the PCI Express technology or USB 2.0 technology depending on what type of card they make. For example, an ExpressCard soundcard wouldn't need the speed of PCI Express, so it would probably be designed from a USB 2.0 standpoint. Table 11.4 breaks down the characteristics of PC Card, CardBus, and ExpressCard expansion busses.

TABLE 11.4 **PC Card, CardBus, and ExpressCard Details**

Technology	Type	Data transfer Rate	Typical Usage
PC Card	Type I (3.3mm thick)	20MB/s	RAM, Flash memory
PC Card/ CardBus	Type II (5mm thick)	PC Card = 20MB/s CardBus = 133MB/s	Network adapters, modems
PC Card/ CardBus	Type III (10.5mm thick)	PC Card = 20MB/s CardBus = 133MB/s	Hard drives
ExpressCard	PCI Express mode USB mode	2.5 Gbps (250MB/s) 480 Mbps (60MB/s)	External SATA drives, soundcards, Ethernet devices, and so on

ExamAlert

Memorize the differences between the PC Card, CardBus, and ExpressCard expansion busses for the exam.

Note

Many owners of high-end laptops complain about the quality of the integrated soundcards and look for alternatives. To meet this need, some manufacturers such as Creative Labs make high-quality ExpressCard soundcards that rival the latest soundcard technology in desktop computers.

▶ **Internal expansion busses:** As far as internal expansion busses go, laptops use Mini-PCI and Mini-PCI Express. These are about a quarter the size of their desktop computer counterparts and work essentially the same, although there might be less performance in the laptop versions. For example Mini-PCI has a maximum data transfer rate of 133MB/s, which is one-half of some PCI cards in desktops. They might be used as video cards or as wireless cards. Replacing them can be a bit of a chore on some laptops. You'll need to remove the keyboard first, then disconnect a cable or two from the Mini-PCI card, and remove two screws that hold the card in place. (The card is often flat against the system board.) By the way, when replacing components like this, be sure to put the keyboard upside down on an antistatic bag, and put Mini-PCI cards in an antistatic bag as well until you are ready for them.

▶ **Docking Stations:** The docking station expands the laptop so that it can behave more like a desktop computer. By connecting the laptop to the docking station, and adding a full-size keyboard, mouse, and monitor, the user doesn't actually touch the laptop anymore except per-haps to turn it on. Most laptops can *hot dock*, meaning they can connect to the docking station while powered on. The docking station recharges the laptop's battery, and possibly a second battery, and has connections for video, audio, networking, and expansion cards. Docking stations might even have an optical disk drive or additional hard disk; it all depends on the brand and model. If all these extras aren't necessary, a user might require only a *port replicator*, which is a similar device but it has only ports; for example, video, sound, network, and so on.

> **Note**
>
> Of course, you can also expand your laptop by using integrated USB and IEEE 1394 ports and built-in memory card readers. For more information on USB and IEEE 1394, see Chapter 12, "Video, Audio, and Peripherals." For more information on memory cards, see Chapter 6, "Storage Devices."

Communications

Communicating quickly and efficiently is key in business environments. To do so, laptops use a variety of different devices including the following:

▶ **Ethernet:** Most laptops today come equipped with wired and wireless Ethernet adapters to connect to a local area network (LAN) or a wireless local area network (WLAN). The wired connection presents itself as an RJ45 port and can typically transfer data at 1000, 100, and 10Mbps, auto-negotiating its speed to the network it is connected to. Wireless connections are made with an internal Mini-PCI card that can connect to 802.11n, g, and b networks (a maximum of 300, 54, and 11Mbps, respectively). It is also possible to connect wired or wireless network adapters to USB ports or to ExpressCard or PC Card slots. Otherwise, these technologies work the same on a laptop as they do on a desktop computer. For more information on wired and wireless LAN technolo-gies, see Chapter 14 ,"Networking." There is usually a WLAN button (located near the power button) that can enable/disable the wireless adapter. Keep this in mind when troubleshooting. If this is disabled, the laptop cannot connect wirelessly, even if the device is enabled in the Device Manager. Many laptops use proprietary software for the configu-ration of wireless network connections, instead of using the built-in Windows Wireless Zero Configuration program. In some cases, it might be easier to disable the proprietary application and use Wireless Zero Configuration instead.

▶ **Bluetooth:** Bluetooth adapters enable a laptop to connect to other Bluetooth devices over short distances, thus joining or creating a personal area network (PAN). A Bluetooth adapter might be included inside the laptop as an individual Mini-PCI card or as a combo Bluetooth/WLAN Mini-PCI card. External USB and ExpressCard Bluetooth adapters and remote controls are also available. For more information on Bluetooth, see Chapter 14, "Networking." Many laptops come with WLAN and Bluetooth capabilities; however, the two technologies compete over frequencies. It is recommended that a user make use of only one at a time if possible. Buttons are usually available on the laptop (near the power button) for enabling/disabling WLAN and Bluetooth.

▶ **Infrared:** Infrared or IrDA wireless ports can be used to transfer data between the laptop and another computer, PDA, or other mobile device over short distance. Unlike Bluetooth, IrDA connections must be line-of-sight. Built-in IrDA ports are not seen as often on laptops as Bluetooth but can be purchased in USB format if necessary.

▶ **Cellular WAN:** Connecting to the Internet through 3G cellular WAN cards has become more popular over the past few years. Telecommunications providers like Verizon, Sprint, and AT&T offer cellular WAN ExpressCards (also known as wireless WAN cards) and USB-based travel routers. Some laptops are designed with built-in Mini-PCI cellular devices (sometimes called modems).

▶ **Modem:** The standard dial-up modem can still be found on many laptops. This circuitry is often built into the motherboard but can also be a Mini-PCI card or a separate card altogether. If the modem fails and it is integrated into the motherboard, the entire motherboard would have to be replaced (which would be costly) or a PC Card, ExpressCard, or USB version could be purchased.

ExamAlert

Know the various ways that a laptop could communicate with other computers for the exam including wired and wireless Ethernet, Bluetooth, IrDA, Cellular WAN, and dial-up modems.

Cram Quiz

Answer these questions. The answers follow the last question. If you cannot answer these questions correctly, consider reading this section again until you can.

1. Which kinds of ports can typically be found on a laptop? (Select all that apply.)

   ○ **A.** RJ45

   ○ **B.** USB

   ○ **C.** IEEE 1284

   ○ **D.** DVI

2. When a user types, a laptop's screen displays letters and numbers instead of only letters. What should you check first?

   ○ **A.** Fn key

   ○ **B.** LCD cutoff switch

   ○ **C.** Num Lk key

   ○ **D.** Scroll Lock key

3. Which of the following are possible reasons that a laptop's keyboard might fail completely? (Select the best two answers.)

   ○ **A.** A stuck key.

   ○ **B.** A disconnected ribbon cable.

   ○ **C.** The user spilled coffee on the laptop.

   ○ **D.** The keyboard was disabled in the Device Manager.

4. What kind of video technology do most laptops incorporate currently?

   ○ **A.** TFT Active Matrix

   ○ **B.** Passive Matrix

   ○ **C.** CRT

   ○ **D.** TFT Passive Matrix

5. What is a common resolution on today's laptops?

   ○ **A.** 640x480

   ○ **B.** 800x600

   ○ **C.** 1280x800

   ○ **D.** 2048x1536

6. If a user wanted to stretch their desktop across two monitors, what Windows technology would they look for?

○ **A.** Multiple monitor

○ **B.** Video replication

○ **C.** SideCar

○ **D.** DualView

7. What are two possible reasons why a laptop's display suddenly went blank?

○ **A.** Damaged inverter

○ **B.** Damaged LCD

○ **C.** Burned out lamp

○ **D.** Incorrect resolution setting

8. What is the most common battery used by today's laptops?

○ **A.** Double AA batteries

○ **B.** Lithium-ion (Li-ion)

○ **C.** Nickel-metal hydride (NiMH)

○ **D.** Nickel-cadmium (NiCd)

9. Where would a user go to modify the battery alarms in Windows?

○ **A.** Display Properties window

○ **B.** Power Properties window

○ **C.** BIOS

○ **D.** Power Options window

10. A user doesn't see anything on his laptop's screen. He tries to use AC power and thinks that the laptop is not receiving any. What are two possible reasons for this?

○ **A.** Incorrect AC adapter.

○ **B.** The AC adapter is not connected to the laptop.

○ **C.** Windows won't boot.

○ **D.** The battery is dead.

11. Which of the following has the fastest data transfer rate?

○ **A.** CardBus

○ **B.** ExpressCard PCIe

○ **C.** PC Card

○ **D.** ExpressCard USB

12. Which of the following are ways that a laptop can communicate with other computers? (Select all that apply)

   ○ **A.** Bluetooth

   ○ **B.** WLAN

   ○ **C.** Ultraviolet

   ○ **D.** Cellular WAN

Cram Quiz Answers

1. **A, B,** and **D.** RJ45, USB, and DVI ports are all common on a laptop. However, IEEE 1284 printer ports are not common.

2. **C.** The number lock key (Num Lk) can enable or disable the numeric keypad. This might be necessary if the user inadvertently turned it on or disconnected an external keyboard from the laptop. Pressing the Function (Fn) key is not necessary when pressing the Num Lk key. The LCD cutoff switch is used to turn off the bulb that lights the LCD. The scroll lock key is used very little but is meant to lock any scrolling done with the arrow keys.

3. **B** and **C.** A laptop's keyboard could fail due to a disconnected or loose keyboard ribbon cable. It could also fail if a user spilled coffee on the laptop, or through general abuse, or by being dropped on the ground, and so on. One stuck key will not cause the entire keyboard to fail, and on most laptops, the keyboard cannot be disabled in the Device Manager.

4. **A.** TFT active matrix LCDs are the most common in laptops today. Passive matrix screens have been discontinued, although you might see an older laptop that utilizes this technology. There is no TFT passive matrix, and cathode ray tubes (CRTs) were used only on the first laptops many years ago. Due to a CRT's weight and heavy power usage, it is not a good solution for laptops.

5. **C.** 1280x800 (WXGA) is a common resolution used by today's laptops. 640x480 and 800x600 are older VGA modes that can't fit much on the screen. 2048x1536 (QXGA) is a higher resolution than most laptops' video adapters can display. For more information on resolutions see Chapter 12, "Video, Audio, and Peripherals."

6. **D.** DualView enables a laptop running Windows XP or Vista to stretch the desktop across two monitors. It is a basic version of Multiple Monitor that is only available on desktop PCs. SideCar is a third-party hardware/software solution that enables a desktop PC or laptop to stretch the desktop over multiple monitors but is not included in Windows.

7. **A** and **C.** A damaged inverter or burned out bulb could cause a laptop's display to go blank. You can verify if the LCD is still getting a signal by shining a flashlight at the screen. A damaged LCD usually works to a certain extent and will either be cracked, have areas of Windows missing, or show other signs of damage. An incorrect resolution settings usually makes Windows look garbled on the screen.

8. **B.** There are a few different types of batteries that a laptop might use including Lithium-ion (Li-ion), Nickel-metal hydride (NiMH), and Nickel-cadmium (NiCd), but Lithium-ion is by far the most common. Believe it or not, some laptops (namely children's) can run on 4 AA batteries, but it is not common or feasible in today's business environments.

9. **D.** To change the thresholds for battery alarms, a user would access the Power Options window.

10. **A** and **B.** An incorrect adapter will usually not power a laptop. The laptop used must be exact. And of course, if the laptop is not plugged in properly to the adapter, it won't get power. Windows doesn't play into this scenario. And if the battery was dead, it could cause the laptop to not power up, but only if the AC adapter was also disconnected; the scenario states that the user is trying to use AC power.

11. **B.** ExpressCard in PCI Express mode (PCIe) has the highest data transfer rate at 250MB/s. The next fastest would be CardBus, followed by ExpressCard in USB mode, with PC Card bringing up the rear.

12. **A**, **B**, and **D.** Laptops can communicate with other computers through Bluetooth, WLAN, IrDA, and Cellular WAN wireless connections, plus wired connections like Ethernet (RJ45) and dial-up (RJ11).

Installing, Configuring, and Troubleshooting Internal Laptop Components

Now that you know how to troubleshoot the visible components of a laptop, let's discuss the internal components a little bit. Because they are not exposed, these devices won't fail as often as components such as the keyboard and the display, but sometimes failures still occur. At times you might need to replace a hard drive (and possibly recover the drive's data), add or swap out memory, and possibly switch out a CPU, motherboard, or both. Dealing with hard drive trouble and working with RAM is more common, so let's begin with those.

Hard Drives

So far, we mentioned a few times that hard drives will fail; it's just a matter of when. And laptop hard drives are more susceptible to failure than desktop computers due to their mobility and the bumps and bruises that laptops regularly sustain. Laptops are available with PATA (IDE) or SATA hard disks, though more and more are coming standard with SATA. The bulk of the hard drives in laptops are 2.5-inches wide, as opposed to a desktop computer's 3.5-inch hard drive. Obviously, the smaller form factor is necessary in today's laptops. Ultra-small laptops and other small portable devices might use a hard disk as small as 1.8 inches.

2.5-inch SATA hard drives use the same connectors as their 3.5-inch counterparts, another benefit of using SATA. Because of this, no adapters are needed when transferring information from a laptop drive to a desktop drive (which is common when attempting to recover data). However, 2.5-inch PATA drives use a different connector than their 3.5-inch counterparts. Remember from Chapter 6 that a 3.5-inch PATA desktop hard drive has a 40-pin IDE connector for data and a 4-pin Molex connector for power. The problem is that a 2.5-inch PATA hard drive just doesn't have the space for these types of connectors. So a different 44-pin IDE connector was developed, which is much smaller and contains both the data *and* the power pins in one 44-pin package. However, this means that an adapter is necessary if you want to transfer data from the 2.5-inch PATA drive to a 3.5-inch PATA drive. An example of this adapter is shown in Figure 11.8.

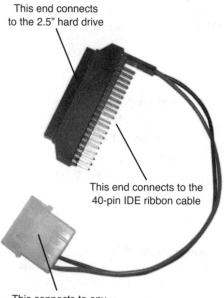

This end connects
to the 2.5" hard drive

This end connects to the
40-pin IDE ribbon cable

This connects to any
available Molex connector

FIGURE 11.8   44-pin to 40-pin IDE adapter

44-pin 2.5-inch PATA hard drives have four additional pins to the right of the
IDE connector; these are used for master/slave configurations, which might
be necessary to configure when rescuing data from a laptop drive. Of course,
to rescue data from a hard drive, you first have to remove it. Laptop hard
drives can be accessed from one of three places. The first, and maybe the most
common, is from an access panel on the bottom of the laptop. The second is
from underneath the keyboard. And the third would be from the side of the
laptop. In this last scenario, the hard drive is inside of a caddy that has a handle for easy removal; it should slide right out of the side of the laptop. In the
third scenario, the hard drive would have to be removed from the caddy, and
in any scenario there will usually be some kind of bracket that has to be
unscrewed from the drive when replacing it. Hold on to this bracket for the
new hard drive.

Memory

Most of today's laptops use DDR SDRAM like desktop computers do. But
once again, we are dealing with a much smaller device, so the memory is also
smaller; it is known as a SO-DIMM or small outline dual in-line memory
module. Table 11.5 shows the four types of SO-DIMMs and their pin formats.

As with desktop RAM, different versions of memory in laptops are not compatible; for example, you can't put a DDR2 SO-DIMM into a DDR SO-DIMM slot.

TABLE 11.5 **SO-DIMM Versions**

Memory Type	Module Format	Version
SDRAM	144-pin	PC66—PC133
DDR	200-pin	DDR-200—DDR-400
DDR2	200-pin	DDR2-400—DDR2-1066
DDR3	204-pin	DDR3-800—DDR3-2000

> **Note**
>
> For more information on RAM types, see Chapter 4, "RAM."

RAM has a center notch that helps to orient the RAM during installation. This notch will usually be in a different location for DDR, DDR2, and DDR3.

Installing RAM to a laptop is usually quite simple. Often it is located on the bottom of the laptop underneath an access cover. In other laptops it might be underneath the keyboard, or there could be one stick of RAM under the keyboard and a second (usually for add-ons) under an access cover underneath the laptop. Consult your laptop's documentation for the exact location of the RAM compartment. Sometimes the compartment has a small icon identifying it as the location for memory. Table 11.6 shows the steps involved in adding RAM to a laptop. Keep in mind that SO-DIMMs, and their corresponding memory board, are much more delicate than their counterparts in a desktop computer.

TABLE 11.6 **Installing a SO-DIMM to a Laptop**

Step	Procedure
1. Prepare the laptop for surgery!	Shut down the laptop, unplug it, and disconnect the battery. Then employ ESD prevention measures.
2. Review your documentation.	Review your documentation to find out where RAM is located. For this step we assume that the RAM can be added to a compartment underneath the laptop.

TABLE 11.6 **Continued**

Step	Procedure
3. Open the memory compartment.	Usually there will be two screws that you need to remove to open the memory compartment door. Often, these are captive screws and will stay in the door. But if they are not, store them in a safe place and label them.
4. Insert the RAM.	There could be one or two slots for RAM. One of them might already be in use. Some laptops support dual-channel memory. If this is the case and you install a second memory module, make sure it is identical to the first.
	Insert the memory module at a 45-degree angle into the memory slot, aligning the notch with the keyed area of the memory slot. Press the module into the slot; then press the module down toward the circuit board until it snaps into place (GENTLY!). Two clips, one on either side, lock into the notches in the side of the memory module. Press down once again to make sure it is in place. See Figure 11.9 for an example of an installed SO-DIMM. There are actually two SODIMMs on top of each other, the one on top is farther to the left. Note the locking clips holding the memory module into place.
5. Close the compartment and test.	Screw the compartment door back on to the laptop. Then boot the computer into the BIOS and make sure it sees the new memory module. Finally, boot into Windows and make sure that the operating system sees the new total amount of RAM, and verify that applications work properly.

System Board and CPU

I mentioned before that the worst thing that could happen to a laptop is if it doesn't start. Let me rephrase; that would be the worst thing that could happen to a *user*. The worst thing for a tech would be if the system board failed. This is because it would require almost a complete disassembly of the unit to repair, which is very time-consuming and requires heavy documentation to get all the parts back together properly when done. However, CPU replacement (and upgrading) is not quite as difficult but still requires removing at least the keyboard, and more than likely, a few other components that will be in the way; documentation is still very important when replacing a CPU.

Memory slot   Locking clip

Notch   Locking clip

FIGURE 11.9   **Installed SO-DIMM**

Sometimes a system board's lithium battery needs replacement. This is done in the same manner as it is within a desktop computer; however, you need to remove the keyboard, and perhaps other devices and connections, to get access to the battery. Most laptops come with the same CR2032 battery that desktop models use; however, a few laptops (and other handheld devices) come with a rechargeable system board lithium battery that has a shelf life of up to 10 years, but this is a fairly new technology.

Before you do decide to take this type of plunge into a laptop, one thing to keep in mind is that a lot of companies will purchase 1- to 3-year warranties for the laptops they use. Even though there is a cost involved in doing this, it is usually the wise choice. If the laptop did fail, the alternative would be to have a technician spend several hours (at least) disassembling, testing, replacing, and reassembling the laptop; all of which could cost the company more money in man hours than it would have to just get the warranty. Warranties are a type of insurance, and this type is usually acceptable to a company. So check your company's policies and procedures first before doing these types of repairs.

Before removing a CPU or other internal components, employ ESD prevention measures. If the CPU is surface-mounted, you cannot remove it; if it has failed the entire system board would have to be removed. But if it is socketed (which is more likely on newer laptops), with either a pin grid array (PGA) or ball grid array (BGA), it can be removed. Usually there is some kind of locking arm mechanism that must be unlocked to remove the CPU from the socket. Common sockets for mobile Intel CPUs include the Socket M (for several CPUs including the Core 2 Duo) and Socket P (for Core 2). Keep in mind that upgrade ranges for laptop CPUs are usually quite narrow. If a CPU fails, it is usually best to install an identical CPU. If you do plan to upgrade a CPU, check the documentation carefully to make sure that the exact model laptop (and it's motherboard) can support the faster CPU. After removing the CPU, be sure to place it on top of an antistatic bag with the pins facing up. When installing CPUs, employ the same delicate procedure as you would with a desktop PC. These CPUs require no force to insert them into the socket.

> **Note**
>
> For more information on installing motherboards and CPUs into desktops, see Chapter 2, "Motherboards," and Chapter 3, "The CPU."

> **Note**
>
> The Internet has plenty of sites that can offer some free repair tips, for example: http://repair4laptop.org and http://www.laptoprepair101.com. Another good resource for laptop repair is the book *Upgrading and Repairing Laptops* by Scott Mueller.

Cram Quiz

Answer these questions. The answers follow the last question. If you cannot answer these questions correctly, consider reading this section again until you can.

1. What is the pinout for a stick of SO-DIMM DDR RAM?

   ○ **A.** 200

   ○ **B.** 168

   ○ **C.** 144

   ○ **D.** 204

2. How many pins are in a laptop's PATA hard drive?

○ **A.** 40

○ **B.** 200

○ **C.** 68

○ **D.** 44

3. How are SODIMMs installed to a laptop?

○ **A.** By pressing straight down

○ **B.** Into a ZIF socket

○ **C.** On a 45-degree angle

○ **D.** On a 90-degree angle

4. What should you do when upgrading a CPU in a laptop? (Select all that apply.)

○ **A.** Check documentation to see if the CPU is supported.

○ **B.** Install more RAM.

○ **C.** Employ antistatic measures.

○ **D.** Remove the system board.

Cram Exam Answers

1. A. DDR SODIMM modules have 200 pins. Desktop SDRAM has 168 pins. SODIMM SDRAM has 144 pins, and DDR3 SODIMMs have 204 pins.

2. D. A laptop's PATA hard drive has a 44-pin IDE connection that includes the four power pins.

3. C. SODIMMs are installed to a laptop at a 45-degree angle unlike a desktop's DDR memory that is installed by pressing straight down. ZIF sockets refer to CPUs.

4. A and **C.** When upgrading a CPU in a laptop, check for laptop documentation to see if the faster CPU is supported; then employ ESD prevention measures. More RAM is not necessary when upgrading a CPU, but it could help the laptop get the best out of the CPU if an open memory slot is available. Usually the system board does not have to be removed to replace or upgrade a CPU.

Additional Reading and Resources

Battery University. http://batteryuniversity.com.

Mueller, Scott. *Upgrading and Repairing Laptops*. Que.

CHAPTER 12

Video, Audio, and Peripherals

This chapter covers the following A+ exam topics:

▶ The Video Subsystem

▶ The Audio Subsystem

▶ Input/Output, Input Devices, and Peripherals

You can find a master list of A+ exam topics in the "Introduction."

This chapter covers CompTIA A+ 220-701 objectives 1.7, 1.8, and 1.9 and CompTIA A+ 220-702 objectives 1.1, and 1.2.

Video makes a computer sparkle, audio makes it rock, and input devices and peripherals make it extremely accessible. This chapter describes the technologies and devices that transform the computer from a boring block of metal to a multimedia juggernaut. We could talk about video and audio for days, but lucky for you this chapter has a page limit! So we'll stick to what you need to know for the exam.

This chapter is broken down into three sections. First, the video subsystem, which includes the video card and display. Second, the audio subsystem, which includes the sound card and speakers. And closing it out are input/output ports, devices, and peripherals. However, the bulk of the information in this chapter pertains to video, so let's begin with that first.

The Video Subsystem

The computer can be broken down into several subsystems, the video subsystem being one of the most important. The video subsystem includes the video card (or integrated video), the card's expansion bus, internal connections, external connections between the video card and the display, the display itself, and the video driver. This section details those portions of the video subsystem. Of course, it's also vital to know how to install and configure video cards and how to troubleshoot any issues that might occur.

Video Cards

Today's video cards are like little self-contained computers! They have a processor, known as a graphics processing unit (GPU), and a substantial amount of RAM. When deciding on a video card to use, there are several things to take into account including the expansion bus that the card will connect to, the card's GPU speed and amount of memory, the connectors it offers, if there is an expansion slot available for it on the motherboard, whether the video card will fit in the case, and whether the case has adequate power and cooling capabilities for the card.

Expansion Busses: PCI, PCIe, AGP

Before purchasing and installing a video card, make sure that the motherboard in the computer has a corresponding open expansion slot for the card. There are three expansion busses that can be used by video cards: Peripheral Component Interconnect (PCI), Accelerated Graphics Port (AGP), and PCI Express (PCIe), with PCIe being the most common expansion bus slot in today's motherboards. Because PCIe and AGP have high data transfer rates, those expansion slots connect directly to the northbridge of a motherboard's chipset. PCI however, has a lesser data transfer rate; therefore, PCI slots connect to the southbridge. Table 12.1 reviews the three expansion busses' characteristics and differences. The color listed for each expansion bus is typical but not definite because some motherboard manufacturers select their own proprietary colors. Figure 12.1 shows a comparison of these expansion bus slots.

TABLE 12.1 **Video Card Expansion Busses**

Expansion Bus	Typical Color	Distance from edge of Motherboard	Data Transfer Rate
PCI	White	Closest to the edge	133MB/s or 266MB/s
AGP	Brown	Farthest from the edge	266MB/s—2GB/s
PCIe	Black	Slightly farther from the edge than PCI	250MB/s—1GB/s per lane

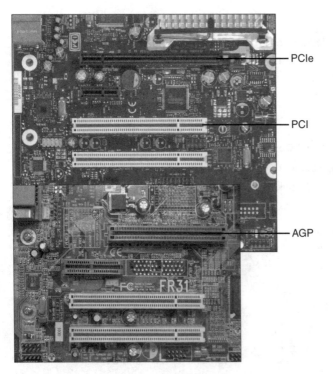

PCIe

PCI

AGP

FIGURE 12.1   **PCIe, PCI, and AGP expansion bus slots**

Exam Alert

Know the differences between PCI, AGP, and PCIe for the exam.

PCI Express won the battle against AGP as soon as the PCIe x16 card was released, which could initially transfer 4GB of data per second, double that of AGP. Since then, PCI Express has only gotten faster. PCI video cards are less common; although, an old PCI card works great in a pinch, and many motherboards still come with PCI slots. PCI also works well in some Multiple Monitor scenarios.

Installing a video card to a PCI or to an AGP slot is easy; just press the card straight down into the slot, and screw it into the chassis. However, PCI Express cards require a little bit more work, which is discussed later in this chapter. For more information on expansion busses, see Chapter 2, "Motherboards."

Connector Types

After a video card is decided on, that will probably dictate the connector used. Most of today's PCIe video cards come with one or two DVI outputs, but there are several other connectors that you see in the field. Table 12.2 details these. Figure 12.2 shows a video card's two DVI ports and the other ports described in Table 12.2.

TABLE 12.2   **Video Card Connectors**

Connector Type	Full Name	Description
VGA (also known as SVGA)	Video Graphics Array	15-pin D-sub, usually blue, known as DE15F. Used for older monitors that display VGA, SVGA, and XGA resolutions.
DVI	Digital Visual Interface	High-quality connections used with LCD displays. Carries uncompressed digital video, is partially compatible with HDMI. Types include ▶ **DVI-D:** Digital-only connections ▶ **DVI-A:** Analog-only connections ▶ **DVI-I:** Digital and analog ▶ **DVI-DL:** Dual link (There are dual-link versions for DVI-I and DVI-D.) ▶ **M1-DA:** Digital, analog, and USB
HDMI	High-Definition (HD) Multimedia Interface	Used mainly for high-definition television. Can carry video and audio signals. Most video cards do not offer HDMI, but instead offer DVI: ▶ **Type A:** Supports all HD modes, compatible with DVI-D connectors ▶ **Type B:** Double-video bandwidth, supports higher resolutions ▶ **Type C:** Used in portable devices ▶ **Type D:** Smallest connector, also used in portable devices
S-Video	Separate Video	Used for standard-definition video, no audio signal. Uses a mini-DIN 4-pin or 7-pin connector.
Component/RGB	Component Video	Used to send analog or digital signal over three wires: red, green, and blue, each wire ending with an RCA plug. Can send high-definition signals digitally.

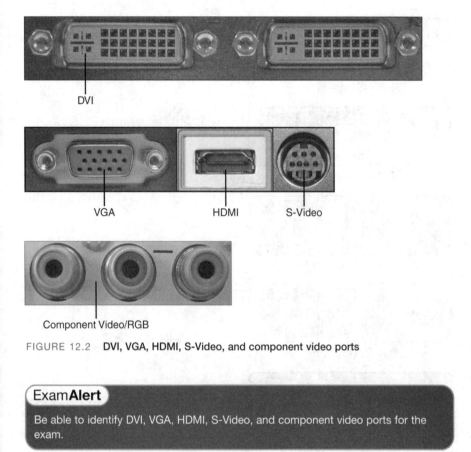

FIGURE 12.2 **DVI, VGA, HDMI, S-Video, and component video ports**

ExamAlert

Be able to identify DVI, VGA, HDMI, S-Video, and component video ports for the exam.

Many DVI connectors on a video card look the same; however, it is the monitor's cable and plug that define which type of DVI it can support. Figure 12.3 shows an illustration of the various DVI plugs, and their associated pins, that you might see on the end of a monitor cable.

A computer's DVI connector is usually compatible with HDMI and VGA. Adapters and adapter cables are available if a user wants to connect a VGA monitor or HDMI television to the DVI port of a computer.

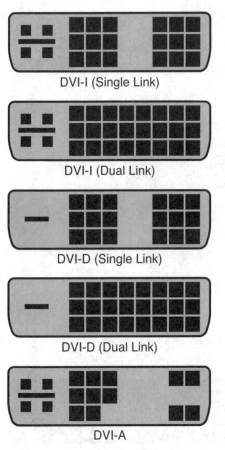

DVI-I (Single Link)

DVI-I (Dual Link)

DVI-D (Single Link)

DVI-D (Dual Link)

DVI-A

FIGURE 12.3 **Various DVI plug connector pins**

Video Card Chipset, GPU, and Memory

The video card I selected for this book is the Gigabyte GeForce GTX 260. It was mentioned before that today's video cards are like computers unto themselves. To a certain extent this is true. These cards have a chipset, similar to a motherboard's chipset, but more simplified; it takes care of the connection between the graphics processing unit (GPU) and the RAM on the card. A video card name, such as GTX 260, is also the chipset name of the card. The GPU of a video card is measured quite like a CPU. For example, the GPU in the GTX 260 runs at 630MHz; this is known as its core clock. Likewise, a video card's RAM is measured like a motherboard's RAM. Many video cards already in the field use DDR and DDR2. Newer cards use DDR3, and some video cards are being developed during the writing of this book that use DDR4. Video card RAM is known as GDDR or Graphics Double Data Rate.

The GTX 260 has 896MB of DDR3 RAM, which runs at a whopping speed of 2,000MHz, and the memory bus is 448-bits wide. These numbers are usually ahead of motherboard RAM, especially in the bus width category. For example, motherboards are just now supporting DDR3 RAM (the motherboard used in this book supports only DDR2), and even with Dual Channel architecture, a motherboard's maximum memory bus width is only 128-bit. Most new video cards (as of the writing of this book) are PCI Express x16, meaning they have a bus speed of 16 and can connect only to a PCIe x16 slot. Because today's video cards have powerful GPUs, the GPU will have its own heat sink and fan, or the entire card will be enclosed and will have its own exhaust fan, thus cooling the GPU, chipset, and RAM.

Installing and Troubleshooting Video Cards

Video cards, like other adapter cards, are inserted into an expansion bus slot and then screwed into the chassis of the case to keep them in place. However, PCI Express cards require the installer to do a few more things. And keep in mind that newer PCIe cards are *big*. When deciding on a video card like this one, make sure it fits in the computer case first! The following steps describe how to install a PCIe video card:

Step 1. **Check if the card is compatible:** Verify that there is an open, compatible slot on the motherboard. Also, make sure that the card is compatible with the operating system. For more information on OS compatibility, see Chapter 7, "Installing and Upgrading Windows."

Step 2. **Ready the computer:** Make sure that the computer is turned off and unplugged. Then implement ESD prevention measures (antistatic mat, antistatic wrist strap, and so on).

Step 3. **Ready the video card:** Remove the card from the package and place it on an antistatic bag until it is ready to be inserted. (Make sure the card is sealed when first opening it. In rare cases, used cards are repackaged and resold as new.)

Step 4. **Document:** If the computer had a video card already, document how and where it was connected. Otherwise, review documentation that came with the motherboard and video card, so a plan can be put into place as to where to install the card, and what cables need to be connected to the card (and how they should be routed through the case).

Step 5. **Prepare the slot:** Use a Phillips head screwdriver to remove the slot cover (or covers) where the card will be installed. Newer PCIe cards inhabit the space used by two slot covers. On most PCIe slots there will be a thumb lever. Open this gently. When the card is inserted, the lever locks the card into place. In some cases, this lever isn't necessary.

Step 6. **Install the card to the slot:** Insert the card, using both thumbs, with equal pressure, straight down into the slot. Try not to wiggle the card in any direction. Press down until the card snaps into place and you can't see any of the gold edge connectors. If it doesn't seem to be going in, don't force it. There might be something in the way; for example, one of the slot covers hasn't been removed, or the thumb lever isn't in the correct position.

Step 7. **Connect cables:** PCIe cards need their own power connection (or two). These are 6-pin PCIe power connectors. Many cases come with PCIe power connectors, but if not, most PCIe video cards have a 6-pin PCIe to Molex adapter (or two). Next, make any SLI connections necessary, if you have two or three video cards (less common). Then, connect optional cables, for example, an S/PDIF header cable to the motherboard, and any other ancillary cables. When complete, it should look something like Figure 12.4.

FIGURE 12.4   An installed PCIe GTX 260 video card

Step 8. **Test:** Testing is simple; plug the monitor into the video card's port, and boot the computer. If you don't get anything on the display, it's time to troubleshoot. Make sure that the monitor is connected securely to the correct port. Then (after shutting down the PC) make sure that the card is seated properly and that the power connections and any other connections are connected firmly. Listen for any beep codes that might be issued by the BIOS POST. Check if the computer is booting without video; this can be done by watching the LED lights on the front of the case and listening for the power supply fan and hard drive activity.

Step 9. **Install the driver:** When the system boots properly, install the driver from the manufacturer's CD. If for some reason there weren't a CD supplied with the device, or it is missing, go to the manufacturer's website and download the latest version of the driver for the *exact* model of the video card.

Step 10. **Test again:** Now that the driver is installed, test again. Verify that the card is seen as the correct make and model in the Device Manager. Then make sure the display can output the desired resolution. Keep in mind that some video cards can output a higher resolution than a monitor can support. If the computer is used for graphics or gaming, open the appropriate application and verify that it works as expected. For example, check for fluidity, quick response, frame rate, and so on.

ExamAlert

Know how to install and test a video card for the exam.

When troubleshooting video issues, there are a number of things to check including

- ► **Connections:** If nothing is showing up on the display, first make sure that the monitor is plugged into the video card properly (and to the correct video port); then verify that the monitor is connected to the AC outlet and is powered on. If the image on the display is scrambled, check that it is connected to the correct port on the video card because some cards come with DVI and VGA ports.

- ► **Resolution setting:** In the case that the resolution was set too high, or to a resolution not supported by the monitor, boot into low resolution VGA mode or Safe Mode. This starts the computer with a resolution of 640x480. Then modify the resolution setting in the Display Properties window. More on resolution later in this chapter.

- ► **Check the driver:** Maybe the driver failed, or perhaps the wrong driver was installed during installation, or maybe an update is necessary. If there is nothing on the display, or if the image is distorted, or if the monitor only displays a lower resolution, boot into low res mode or Safe Mode, and update the driver from within the Device Manager.

- ► **Check the version of DirectX:** DirectX is a Windows technology that includes video, animation, and sound components. It helps a computer get more performance out of multimedia, games, and movies. The DirectX Diagnostic Tool (DxDiag) helps to troubleshoot DirectX-related issues. This tool gives information about the installed version of DirectX and whether it is operating correctly, among other things. The DirectX Diagnostic Tool can be started by opening the Run prompt and typing **dxdiag**.

▶ **Check inside the computer:** I usually leave this for last because it is time-consuming to open the system, unless I have a sneaky suspicion that one of the connections inside the computer is loose. Check if the card is seated properly. In areas where the temperature and humidity change quickly, the card could be unseated due to thermal expansion and contraction. (Some refer to this as chip creep or card creep!) Also, if the computer were moved recently, it could cause the card to come out of the slot slightly. Verify that the power connections and other cables are not loose. Check all other connections inside the PC in the case that it isn't a video problem.

Once again, verify that it is actually a video problem. Don't forget about the "big four." When you can't see anything on the display and you know the computer is receiving power, you can narrow it down to video, RAM, processor, and the motherboard. If the system appears to boot; if you can hear the hard drive accessing data, and can see hard drive activity from the LED light on the front of the case, it is most likely a video problem.

SLI and TV Tuner/Capture Cards

Gamers are always looking to push the envelope when it comes to video performance. It's possible to take video to the next level by incorporating a technology known as Scan Line Interleave (SLI). This is when a computer has two (or more) identical video cards that work together for greater performance and higher resolution. The SLI compatible cards are bridged together to essentially work as one unit. The GTX 260 video card mentioned previously supports SLI, as shown in Figure 12.4. It is important to have a compatible motherboard and ample cooling when attempting this type of configuration. Currently this is done with two or more PCI Express video cards and is most commonly found in gaming rigs.

Home entertainment enthusiasts often have a computer hooked up to their home theater. If this is the case, they probably install a TV tuner card. These cards can accept the signal from a cable or satellite provider and then send it back out to the TV or other devices in the home theater. Most TV tuners also act as capture cards, meaning that they can capture the signal and record TV programs. The purpose of all this is to record shows onto the computer and basically use the computer as a digital video recorder (DVR), among other things. By using Window Media Center, which is built-in to Windows Vista and comes as a separate edition for Windows XP, users can control their TV experience. TV tuner cards are available with PCI Express, PCI, ExpressCard (for laptops), and USB interfaces.

Video Displays

Regardless of what type of video card (or cards) is in a computer, it all means nothing if the computer doesn't have an output device. The most common video output device in a computer system is the liquid crystal display (LCD).

LCD

A liquid crystal display (LCD) is a flat panel display that consists of two sheets of polarizing material surrounding a layer of liquid crystal solution. Most of today's LCD screens are thin-film transistor (TFT) active-matrix displays, meaning they have three transistors for each pixel, which are contained within a flexible material. The transistors store the electrical state of each pixel, while all the other pixels are updated. These transistors are located directly behind the liquid crystal material. In general, LCDs use low amounts of power, generate a small amount of heat, and cause little in the way of interference and emissions. Common LCD resolutions include WXGA, SXGA+, UXGA, WSXGA+, and WUXGA. Generally, an LCD will be designed for one resolution, known as the *native resolution*; it's the resolution that the LCD works best at. If this is the case, any other resolution selected will be scaled and will usually appear stretched or compressed. If a user complains of these symptoms, check the LCDs documentation to find its native resolution, and switch to that resolution in the Display Properties window. More on video resolution later in this chapter.

Another measure of an LCD is contrast ratio. Contrast ratio is a comparison of the brightest and darkest colors (white and black) that can be generated on a display. It can be measured statically, or dynamically (known as DC). Generally, the higher the contrast ratio, the better. Dynamic will always be a higher number than static. For example, the monitor used for this book (Samsung 2343BWX) has a static contrast ratio of 1000:1 and a dynamic contrast ratio of 20000:1.

When it comes to cleaning displays, be careful; liquid can possibly get between the bezel and the screen; when it infiltrates the display assembly, bad things can happen! To avoid this, conservatively spray the cleaner on to a soft, clean, lint-free cloth first; then carefully clean the display with the cloth. Many manufacturers of displays recommend using isopropyl alcohol diluted with water; basically no more than 50 percent of the solution should be alcohol; the rest should be water. Isopropyl alcohol can be found in most supermarkets and drug stores; the higher the purity level the better, for example 90 percent purity is acceptable; it will say this directly on the bottle. Again, use the solution conservatively, apply it to the cloth first, and try not to get any on the plastic bezel, apply to the screen only. It usually isn't necessary to clean the screen very often; once every 3 to 6 months is fine unless you work in a very dirty environment. Instead of cleaning the screen, you can also try removing the dust (which can affect visibility) with a soft lint-free cloth or a canister of compressed air. This might help as an added step before cleaning the screen to avoid streaking. There are also various spray cleaners available at electronics stores and online; some of them are simply expensive isopropyl alcohol/water solutions! But personally, for over a decade I have simply mixed my own isopropyl/water solution for use on LCDs, CRTs, laptop LCDs, handheld computers, PDAs, and cell phones, and have never had a problem.

CRT

A cathode ray tube (CRT) is an older type monitor that uses a vacuum tube display and utilizes three electron guns to display the colors red, green, and blue to a fluorescent screen. (Red, green, and blue are the three primary colors of the computer display world.) These colors are grouped into triads and are emitted by phosphors within the screen so that a user can see the image on the display. A triad consists of three "dots," red, green, and blue. One way that CRTs are measured is in dot pitch, which is the distance between two like colors of adjacent triads. The lower the dot pitch, the better the CRT's image quality because the triads are closer together. CRTs are higher in emissions and interference than LCDs.

Projectors

Video projectors can be plugged into a computer's external video port to project the computer's video display to a projection screen. An extremely bright bulb is necessary to project this image to the screen. The light output is measured in *lumens*. More lumens are necessary for locations with a higher amount of ambient light (existing light in the room). Projectors are used for presentations and for teaching and are common in conference rooms and training centers; however, some schools and companies opt to go for large flat-screen TVs instead of using projectors, even though projectors can usually project a larger image. Projectors are available in CRT, LCD, and DLP versions. The CRT and LCD technologies work in a similar fashion to the monitor technologies of the same name, whereas DLP uses light valves with rotating color wheels. Common display resolutions for projectors include SVGA (800x600), XGA (1024x768), and high-definition resolutions such as 720p and 1080p; the price of the projector increasing with each type of resolution mentioned, and with other characteristics such as the brightness, contrast, and noise. A video projector can be used with a laptop, by utilizing the display toggle button, or can be used with a computer that has a video card with dual outputs.

Video Settings and Software

So, you've selected and installed a video card, and the monitor is connected to the computer. What next? Now it's time to install drivers (if not done already during the installation process) and configure settings in Windows such as the color depth, resolution, refresh rate, plus features such as Multiple Monitor, and on-screen settings.

Drivers

Device drivers (otherwise known as software drivers) are programs that enable the operating system to communicate with the actual device. For example, a video driver enables the operating system to interact with the video card. The driver simplifies the amount of work that an application needs to do by acting as a go-between for the application and the device.

Video drivers (or the lack thereof) have been known to cause plenty a headache for technicians. However, if a couple of simple rules are adhered to, many of the plaguing video driver issues can be avoided:

▶ Use the *manufacturer's* driver. When you install a video card, Windows attempts to use a Microsoft version of the driver. This is usually not the best option, especially for newer cards. Instead, use the driver that came on disc with the device, or better yet, access the manufacturer's website to download the latest driver for the device. You can check the date of the driver on the website against the date listed in the Device Manager to see if you currently have the latest.

▶ Watch out for new operating systems. Newer operating systems don't always have all the kinks worked out. Sometimes new hardware will not operate properly with a new operating system until updates have been released, or the first service pack has been issued for the operating system. Before installing a new operating system, verify that the device is listed as compatible. For example, when installing Windows Vista, visit the Windows Vista Compatibility Center. (For more information on compatibility, see Chapter 7.) Make sure to update the operating system after the installation is complete.

To work with video drivers in Windows, open the Device Manager and then expand the Display Adapters category. This shows the video card. Right-click the device and select Properties; then select the Driver tab. This shows a lot of information including the manufacturer of the driver. If it says Microsoft, consider downloading the latest driver from the manufacturer's website. If it says NVIDIA, ATI, or something else, then you already have a manufacturer's version of the driver, though it might not be the latest. From this window you can also see the date of the driver, update the driver to the latest version, roll back the driver if a new installation has failed, or uninstall the driver completely.

Sometimes, if a driver fails, the system will not display anything on the screen. If this happens, try pressing F8 during startup and boot into either Enable Low-Resolution Video (in Vista), Enable VGA Mode (in XP), or if those don't work, attempt to boot into Safe Mode. These start the computer without the normal video driver and instead will use a basic VGA driver at 640x480 resolution. In some cases, the computer automatically asks you if you want to start in Safe Mode, recognizing that there is a video issue. Note that Enable Low-Resolution Video and Enable VGA Mode use a basic VGA driver, but all other drivers work normally. However, Safe Mode starts the system with a minimal set of drivers. If a driver does fail, Internet access might be required to download the latest driver. This is not available in Safe Mode, but it is available in either of the low resolution modes named previously.

Color Depth

Color depth (also known as bit depth or color quality) is a term used to describe the amount of bits that represent color. For example, 1-bit color is known as monochrome, those old screens with a black background and one color for the text, like in old *Six Million Dollar Man* episodes, or like Neo's computer in *The Matrix!* But what is 1-bit? 1-bit in the binary numbering system means a binary number with one digit; this can be a zero or a one, for a total of two values: usually black and white. This is defined in scientific notation as 2^1, (2 to the 1st power equals 2). Another example would be 4-bit color, used by the ancient but awesome Commodore 64 computer. In a 4-bit color system you can have 16 colors total. In this case $2^4 = 16$. Of course 16 colors aren't nearly enough for today's applications; 16-bit, 24-bit, and 32-bit are the most common color depths used by Windows.

Now that you know the basics, take a look at Table 12.3 that shows the different color depths used in Windows.

TABLE 12.3 **List of Color Depths used in Windows**

Color Depth	Amount of Colors	Calculation
8-bit	256	2^8
16-bit	65,536	2^{16}
24-bit	16,777,216	2^{24}
32-bit	4,294,967,296	2^{32}

8-bit color is used in VGA mode, which is uncommon for normal use, but you might see it if you boot into Safe Mode, or other advanced modes that disable the normal video driver. 16-bit is usually enough for the average user who works with basic applications; however, many computers are configured by default to 24-bit or 32-bit (also known as 3 bytes and 4 bytes respectively). Most users will not have a need for 32-bit color depth; in fact, it uses up resources that might be better put to work elsewhere. If the user works only on basic applications, consider scaling them down to 24-bit or 16-bit to increase system performance. However, gamers, graphics artists, and other designers probably want 32-bit color depth. Some applications and games have the capability to work outside of Windows when it comes to color depth, and a user can select a different color depth for the application than what they use for Windows.

To modify color depth do the following:

▶ **In Windows Vista:** Right-click the desktop and select Personalize. Then click the Display Settings link. A drop-down menu for color depth is located near the bottom-right part of this window, as shown in Figure 12.5.

▶ **In Windows XP:** Right-click the desktop and select Properties. Then click the Setting tab within the Display Properties window. A drop-down menu for color depth is located near the bottom right of this window, as shown in Figure 12.5.

Resolution

Display resolution is described as the amount of pixels (picture elements) on a screen. It is measured horizontally by vertically (HxV). The more pixels that can be used on the screen, the bigger the desktop becomes, and a user can fit more windows on the display. The word *resolution* is somewhat of a misnomer and will also be referred to as *pixel dimensions*. Table 12.4 shows some of the typical resolutions used in Windows.

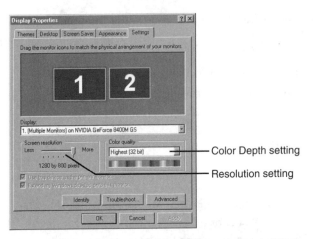

FIGURE 12.5 Color depth and resolution settings in Windows XP

TABLE 12.4 **List of Resolutions Used in Windows**

Resolution Type	Full Name	Pixel Dimension	Aspect Ratio
VGA*	Video Graphics Array	640x480	4:3 (1.333:1)
SVGA*	Super Video Graphics Array	800x600	4:3 (1.333:1)
XGA	eXtended Graphics Array	1024x768	4:3 (1.333:1)
WXGA min. (720p)	Widescreen eXtended Graphics Array minimum	1280x720	16:9 (1.78:1)
WXGA	Widescreen eXtended Graphics Array	1280x800	16:10 (1.6:1)
WXGA (HD)	Widescreen eXtended Graphics Array (High Definition)	1366x768	16:9 (1.78:1)
SXGA	Super eXtended Graphics Array	1280x1024	5:4 (1.25:1)
SXGA+	Super eXtended Graphics Array Plus	1400x1050	4:3 (1.333:1)
UXGA	Ultra eXtended Graphics Array	1600x1200	4:3 (1.333:1)
WSXGA+	Widescreen Super Extended Graphics Array Plus	1680x1050	16:10 (1.6:1)
WSXGA+ (HD)	Widescreen Super Extended Graphics Array Plus (High-Definition)	1680x945	16:9 (1.78:1)
WUXGA	Widescreen Ultra eXtended Graphics Array	1920x1200	8:5 (1.6:1)
HD 1080P and 1080i	Full High Definition	1920x1080	16:9 (1.78:1)

* VGA and SVGA modes are usually seen only if you attempt to boot the system into Safe Mode or other advanced boot mode, or if the video driver has failed.

Aspect ratio can be defined as an image's width divided by its height; for example, XGA's resolution is 1024x768. If we divide the width (1024) by the height (768), our result would be 1.333. You also hear this referred to as a four-to-three ratio (4:3). This means that for ever 4 pixels running horizontally, there are 3 pixels running vertically. Wider resolutions have a higher first number, for example 16:9. Most current laptops and desktop LCD screens use a widescreen format by default, either 16:9 or 16:10, though you can still purchase LCD monitors that are based off the 4:3 ratio.

A common resolution for older desktop LCDs is XGA; however, even though they are older, you still see them in the field for a while. In fact, I have one running in DualView mode off my laptop right now. Today's common resolutions for desktop LCDs and laptops are WXGA, SXGA+, UXGA, and WSXGA+. Display resolutions continue to get larger; there are a dozen or so higher standards that aren't listed in Table 12.4. For example, the monitor used during the writing of this book has a maximum resolution of 2048x1152, which is known as QWXGA (Quad Wide eXtended Graphics Array). Keep in mind however, that the maximum resolution of a monitor can be achieved only if the video card can support it. Video cards' maximum resolution is rated in two ways: maximum digital resolution and maximum VGA resolution. The VGA number is usually less than the digital number.

ExamAlert

Memorize the basic differences between XGA, WXGA, SXGA+, UXGA, WSXGA+, and WUXGA for the exam.

To modify screen resolution in Windows do the following:

▸ **In Windows Vista:** Right-click the desktop and select Personalize. Then click the Display Settings link. Toward the bottom-left part of the window is a box called Resolution, which has a slider that enables you to configure the pixel dimensions. Drag the slider to the appropriate resolution. This slider is indicated in Figure 12.5.

▸ **In Windows XP:** Right-click the desktop and select Properties. Then click the Setting tab within the Display Properties window. Toward the bottom-left part of the window is a box called Screen resolution, which has a slider that enables you to configure the pixel dimensions. Drag the slider to the appropriate resolution. This slider is indicated in Figure 12.5.

Sometimes a user might set the resolution too high, resulting in a scrambled or distorted display. This can happen when video cards support higher resolution modes than the monitor does. If this happens, reboot the computer into either Enable Low Resolution Video (Enable VGA Mode in XP) or Safe Mode and adjust the resolution setting to a level that the monitor can support.

A video card's amount of memory dictates the highest resolution and color depth settings. You can multiply the resolution by the color depth to find out how much memory will be needed. For example, if a user wanted to run a 1920x1080 resolution at 32-bit color (4 bytes of color), the equation would be $1920 \times 1080 \times 4$, which would equal approximately 8MB, easily covered by most video cards. But keep in mind that this is the bare minimum needed to display Windows and that more will be necessary for advanced GUIs such as Windows Aero. Much more video memory is necessary to run games and graphics programs. Some desktop computers and laptops have integrated video, which use shared video memory. This means that instead of the video device having its own memory, it shares the motherboard's RAM. Motherboard RAM will usually be slower than a video card's memory, and there will probably be less available. Due to this, a PCI Express video card is recommended over integrated video for computers that run resource-intensive applications and games.

Refresh Rate

Refresh rate is generally known as the amount of times a display is "painted" per second. It is more specifically known as *vertical refresh rate*. Refresh rate works differently in LCDs and CRTs.

On a CRT, the display is painted in horizontal lines one at a time from top to bottom, at high speed. This is done by an electron beam. When the entire display has been painted, it is considered one refresh. By default on many systems, this is set to occur 60 times per second, or 60 Hz. However, to reduce eye strain when working with CRTs, it is possible to increase this number to a higher amount, for example 72Hz or 85Hz, which reduces *flicker*. The faster the screen is painted, the less a user's eyes have to work to register what they see. Keep in mind that the video card must support a higher refresh rate to match the monitor.

On an LCD, refresh rate works differently because LCDs use a completely different technology to paint the screen. Instead of painting the screen at x times per second, the liquid crystal material is illuminated. However, you can still modify the Windows refresh rate, which effectively configures how many times per second a new image is received from the video card. This is usually set to 60Hz and is not configurable on most LCDs. Flicker is not as much of an issue on LCDs because the backlight (lamp) is set to it's own rate, usually at 200Hz. Because refresh rate is not configurable on most LCDs, you might not see this measurement in an LCDs specifications (aside from the newer 120Hz models).

To modify the Windows refresh rate for CRTs or LCDs:

► **In Windows Vista:** Right-click the desktop and select Personalize. Then click the Display Settings link. Click the Advanced Settings button and click the Monitor tab. Select the Screen refresh rate from the drop-down menu.

► **In Windows XP:** Right-click the desktop and select Properties. Then click the Setting tab within the Display Properties window. Click the Advanced button and then click the Monitor tab. Select the Screen refresh rate from the drop-down menu.

Don't confuse the refresh rate with frames per second (frames/s or fps). Although the two are directly related, they are not the same thing. For example, if playing a video game that is set to run at 90 frames/s, the game attempts to send those frames of video data from the video card to the monitor. However, the monitor might be limited to a 60Hz refresh rate. If this is the case, the video card attempts to display the additional frames within the given refresh rate, causing a sort of blur, which might or might not be acceptable to the user. To many users in the gaming community, the higher the frames/s, the better. But to actually attain a higher frame rate, a higher refresh rate will also be necessary. With a CRT monitor this was historically 85Hz or higher; with an LCD monitor, this higher refresh rate wasn't available until recently with newer 120Hz technologies. The LCD used for the writing of this book runs at a native refresh rate of 60Hz. An example of an LCD that runs at 120Hz is the Samsung 2233RZ.

OSD and Degaussing

The on-screen display (OSD) can help configure picture quality. It can aid in fixing problems of all types including distortion, picture size, centering, and contrast and brightness. The OSD is superimposed on top of the monitor's display and can usually be accessed by pressing a Menu button or other like button on the monitor either below the display or on one of the sides of the monitor. From there, arrow buttons enable the user to make modifications to the settings. Typical settings for LCDs and CRTs include picture size, picture centering, contrast, and brightness. Keep in mind that laptop displays usually have only a brightness setting.

CRT displays also offer the ability to *degauss* the screen. Degaussing is the process of decreasing an unwanted magnetic field in the CRT. The CRT has a metal plate near the front of the monitor that picks up magnetic fields, which over time produce discoloration or other undesired effects on the screen. To degauss the screen (and remove the unwanted effects), there is usually a degauss option within the OSD menu, or there will be a degauss button directly on the monitor. If pressed, the whole screen distorts and shakes for a moment, and then should return to normal, without the discoloration or other undesired effects. Be careful with the degauss feature, it is not meant to be used often.

Multiple Monitor

Multiple Monitor (also referred to as DualView) is a Windows feature that extends the desktop across to multiple displays; it enables you to spread applications over two or more monitors that effectively work together as one. This works well for applications that are very wide, or if a user needs to see multiple windows at the same time. The additional screens used in Multiple Monitor do not have a taskbar; they just have the wallpaper or background that was selected. It is possible to select any of the monitors connected to the computer as the primary monitor, meaning the one with the Start button, taskbar, and so on. To enable Multiple Monitor, follow these steps:

Step 1. Connect an additional monitor to one of the extra video ports on the computer. Newer video cards have a DVI port. But you can still connect older SVGA monitors; just use a DVI to VGA adapter. (These are included with many of today's video cards.)

Step 2. Turn on the secondary monitor.

Step 3. Open the Display Settings window in Vista or the Display Properties window in XP.

> ▶ **In Windows Vista:** Right-click the desktop and select Personalize. Then select Display Settings. This opens the Display Settings window.

> ▶ **In Windows XP:** Right-click the desktop and select Properties. This opens the Display Properties window. Select the Settings tab.

Step 4. Click on the Display drop-down menu. Multiple Monitors should be listed. If it is not listed, the video card (or cards) might not support Multiple Monitor, or a driver upgrade might be necessary. Check your video card documentation to find out if it supports Multiple Monitor.

Step 5. Select the monitor with the number 2, either in the display or in the drop-down menu, and check mark Extend My Windows Desktop on to This Monitor. By using the Identify button and dragging the monitors around in the display window, you can arrange your monitors so that they match their physical position.

Step 6. Click Apply. The mouse should extend all the way across both monitors now. Verify that the secondary monitor is functional by dragging a window to that display. If all is good, click OK to close the Display Settings/Display Properties window.

Step 7. Repeat steps 1–6 for additional monitors beyond the second. Up to ten can be used with the Multiple Monitor feature.

It is possible to use multiple video cards, but keep in mind that the Windows Vista version of Multiple Monitor works only with identical video cards and drivers. Windows XP might work with different cards/drivers, but it is not recommended. Some applications (for example video players) might not work perfectly on a secondary screen. This depends on the type of video played, the application, and the type of monitor used.

Exam Alert

Know how to set up Multiple Monitor in Windows Vista/XP.

Note

For laptops, the Multiple Monitor feature is known as DualView and can have only a maximum of two monitors. Also, the laptop display is always the primary monitor in DualView setups. For more information on DualView and laptops, see Chapter 11, "Laptops."

For more information on Multiple Monitor/DualView, see the following link: http://www.microsoft.com/windowsxp/using/setup/hwandprograms/monitors.mspx.

Cram Quiz

Answer these questions. The answers follow the last question. If you cannot answer these questions correctly, consider reading this section again until you can.

1. Which expansion bus slot is typically white in color?
   - ○ **A.** PCIe
   - ○ **B.** AGP
   - ○ **C.** PCI
   - ○ **D.** LCD

2. Which of the following supports digital only connections?
   - ○ **A.** DVI-A
   - ○ **B.** DVI-D
   - ○ **C.** DVI-I
   - ○ **D.** VGA

3. When installing a video card, what should you do before inserting the card into the slot?
   - ○ **A.** Connect cables
   - ○ **B.** Install drivers
   - ○ **C.** Test
   - ○ **D.** Prepare the slot

4. A user set the resolution in Windows too high resulting in a scrambled distorted display. What should you do?
   - ○ **A.** Upgrade the video driver.
   - ○ **B.** Boot into low resolution mode.
   - ○ **C.** Boot into the recovery console.
   - ○ **D.** Check the video connections.

5. Which of the following uses a TFT active-matrix display? (Select all that apply.)
   - ○ **A.** LCD
   - ○ **B.** CRT
   - ○ **C.** Projector
   - ○ **D.** Laptop

6. Where is the best place to get the latest driver for a video card?

- ○ **A.** Microsoft
- ○ **B.** CD-ROM
- ○ **C.** A friend
- ○ **D.** Manufacturer's website

7. How many colors are there if the color depth in Windows is set to 24-bit?

- ○ **A.** 16
- ○ **B.** 65,536
- ○ **C.** 16,777,216
- ○ **D.** 24

8. A computer is set to 1280x1024 resolution. Which standard is it using?

- ○ **A.** XGA
- ○ **B.** SXGA
- ○ **C.** UXGA
- ○ **D.** WXGA

9. What resolution does Windows use when started in Safe Mode?

- ○ **A.** 800x600
- ○ **B.** 1024x768
- ○ **C.** 640x480
- ○ **D.** 1280x800

10. What is a common refresh rate for an LCD?

- ○ **A.** 30Hz
- ○ **B.** 60Hz
- ○ **C.** 200Hz
- ○ **D.** 60MHz

11. What is the maximum amount of monitors a user can have in a Multiple Monitor environment?

- ○ **A.** 10
- ○ **B.** 2
- ○ **C.** 4
- ○ **D.** 1

Cram Quiz Answers

1. **C.** Peripheral Component Interconnect (PCI) slots are usually white in color. PCIe are often black or blue, AGP slots are often brown, and LCD is a type of monitor.

2. **B.** DVI-D supports digital-only connections, which are common on newer LCDs. DVI-A supports analog-only. DVI-I supports both digital and analog, and VGA is an analog connection.

3. **D.** Before inserting the card into the slot, prepare the slot by manipulating any locking mechanism and removing the appropriate slot cover(s).

4. **B.** Boot into a low-resolution mode. In Windows Vista this is called Enable Low Resolution Mode, and in XP it is called Enable VGA Mode. Safe Mode is another valid option, but keep in mind that Safe Mode loads Windows with a minimal set of drivers, and you can't access the Internet if necessary.

5. **A** and **D**. Liquid Crystal Displays normally use the TFT active-matrix technology. Laptops have LCDs so they use the same technology.

6. **D.** The manufacturer's website is the best place to get the latest driver. The CD-ROM supplied with the card is usually satisfactory, but it will not be the latest driver.

7. **C.** 24-bit color is equal to 16,777,216 colors in total, otherwise known as 2^{24} power. Sixteen colors would be 4-bit, 65,536 colors would be 16-bit, and there is no setting that allows for 24 colors.

8. **B.** Super eXtended Graphics Array (SXGA) resolution is 1280x1024.

9. **C.** Safe Mode boots the computer with a minimal set of drivers including the video driver. Due to this, the resolution is set to 640x480 VGA mode.

10. **B.** A typical refresh rate for LCDs is 60Hz.

11. **A.** The Multiple Monitor feature in Windows Vista/XP supports up to 10 monitors. A laptop supports a lesser version of Multiple Monitor known as DualView, which supports a maximum of 2 monitors.

The Audio Subsystem

In some environments, sound is not required; but more often than not, it is either desired or is mandatory. So although troubleshooting sound is not as common as troubleshooting video (in most environments), it is still something that a technician will do fairly commonly in the field.

The audio subsystem consists of the sound card, the expansion bus used, audio ports, connectivity in the form of internal and external audio cables, speakers, sound card drivers, and any additional third-party audio software. The sound card is the basis for audio, so let's begin by discussing that device now.

Sound cards

The sound card is responsible for generating sound from the data sent to it by either the CD-ROM drive or the operating system. Sound cards can be integrated into the motherboard, installed to PCI and PCIe slots, and can be connected to USB and IEEE 1394 ports. However, the typical soundcard is installed to a slot on the motherboard.

In the computer built for this book, I decided to go with the Creative Labs Sound Blaster X-Fi Titanium. It's a PCIe x1 card, which means that it can fit within a x1, x4, or x16 slot. It has most of the ports a user would need for outputting and inputting sound. Figure 12.6 shows the ports on the back of this card and the integrated audio ports on the back of the motherboard used in Chapter 2.

Most sound cards are color-coded. This color scheme is defined by the PC System Design Guide, version PC 99 (which was finalized as version PC 2001). It specifies the following colors for the TRS 1/8 inch mini-jacks like the ones shown in Figure 12.6:

▶ **Light blue:** Line input. Sometimes this seconds as a microphone input.

▶ **Pink:** Microphone input.

▶ **Lime green:** Main output for stereo speakers or headphones. Can also act as a line out.

▶ **Black:** Output for surround sound speakers (rear speakers).

▶ **Gray/Brown:** Output for additional two speakers in a 7.1 system (middle surround speakers).

▶ **Orange:** Output for center speaker and subwoofer.

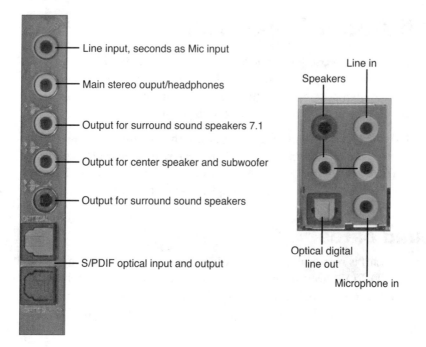

FIGURE 12.6 A typical sound card's ports and integrated audio ports on a motherboard

ExamAlert

Know the PC 99 audio port color codes for the exam.

On the sound card in Figure 12.6, note an optical input and output. This is known as an Sony/Phillips Digital Interconnect Format (S/PDIF) port. This particular version of S/PDIF is called TOSLINK. It delivers high-quality digital sound over fiber optic cable. It is also known as a *digital optical port*. It is considered by some to be sonically superior to the analog 1/8-inch mini-jacks described previously. The S/PDIF output can be used to connect to a home theater system or other receiver; this enables the user to play CDs, MP3s, and so on, on the system of their choice. The input can connect recording equipment, game consoles and so on, enabling a user to bring high-quality audio into the computer to be manipulated as the user sees fit. Cables connecting TOSLINK ports can be a maximum of 10 meters, but are normally found in 5 meter lengths.

Installing a Sound Card and Speakers

Installing a sound card is much like installing any other card. First be sure that the card is compatible with the installed operating system. Then employ ESD prevention measures. The card should be inserted into a PCI or PCIe slot by pressing straight down with both thumbs, making sure not to wiggle the card in any direction; this way the contacts will not get damaged. Make sure it is fully inserted; you shouldn't see any of the gold-colored edge contacts. Then screw the card in where the slot cover used to be within the case.

However, we aren't finished. Now we need to connect any front panel case connections that the card might support, hook up the CD-ROM drive if necessary, connect the speakers, and finally install the driver for the card:

- **Make front panel connections:** One common type of front panel connection is known as Intel High Definition Audio. This uses a 10-pin cable that goes from a compatible sound card (or motherboard if sound is integrated) to the front of an AC'97 compatible case. It is keyed at pin 8 so that the cable cannot be connected upside down. This port enables a user to connect headphones and a microphone to the front of the case instead of having to connect them to the sound card on the back of the computer. Creative Labs and other manufacturers also offer advanced devices that can be installed to a 5.25-inch bay so that the user can have greater access to connections, volume, and so on.

- **Connect the CD-ROM drive:** Newer computers running Windows XP or Vista do not need a CD audio cable. Music CDs are played directly through the data connection, be it IDE or SATA. However, to play audio CDs on an older computer with an older operating system, you need to connect a CD audio cable from the sound card to the CD-ROM drive. The two options are to connect a 4-pin analog cable or a 2-pin digital cable if your CD-ROM drive supports it. These two ports are usually located on the edge of the sound card and can be found on the back of the CD-ROM drive. Without this cable, audio CDs cannot be heard from the computer's speakers on older systems. Many newer sound cards do not even offer a CD audio cable port, and newer SATA CD-ROM drives and DVD/CD combo drives will not have the CD audio cable port.

- **Connect the speakers:** Back in the day a pair of speakers would be connected to the sound card, and you were done. But now, you might be using a 5.1 or 7.1 system, and if so, you need to color coordinate! 5.1 surround sound means that the system is using five regular speakers (left, right, center, back left, and back right) and one speaker for low frequencies, which is usually a subwoofer. 7.1 builds upon this by adding two additional surround speakers. Normally, the lime green output is for the first two speakers (or headphones), which gives standard stereo 2.1 output (two speakers + sub). The black output is for two rear speakers, and the orange output is for the center channel and the subwoofer; an AC outlet will be necessary to power the subwoofer. A grey, brown, or other dark port is used for two additional speakers (middle surround) in a 7.1 system. Another option is to use the digital fiber optical output or digital coaxial output. There are a lot of options, so read the manual on the sound card and the speakers when trying to hook everything together, and pay attention to the little icons that are engraved into the back of the sound card next to the ports.

▶ **Install the driver and software:** Installing a sound card driver is usually done from the Installation CD that accompanies the sound card. It's also wise to check the manufacturer's website for any critical updates to the driver files. The CD usually comes with additional software to take control of the sound card. Keep in mind that this software might conflict with other audio software, or media player software that was already installed on a PC. Consider using one or the other for things such as volume, equalization, and sound effects. Disable or uninstall any unused audio applications or media players to avoid conflicts.

ExamAlert

Know how to install sound cards, connect speakers, and connect other internal audio connections for the exam.

Audio Quality

Audio quality is measured in several ways, but it all starts with the sampling rate and the amount of bits per sample (known as bit depth). Standard audio CDs have a sampling rate of 44kHz, sampling 16 bits at a time (known as 16-bit) per channel, using two channels (known as stereo or 2.1). This is referred to collectively as 16-bit/44kHz and is considered CD-quality. For stereo output of music this has been the standard ever since CDs were first developed in the 1980s. Songs are recorded to the CD in an uncompressed format known as a .WAV file. Another measurement you might see or hear of is the total data rate (or bit rate). This is the amount of bits that the CD plays per second and is calculated as sampling rate × bits × channels, or $44,100 \times 16 \times 2 =$ 1,411,200 bits, or 1411kbps. A standard audio CD is designed to play a maximum of 74 minutes of music at 1411kbps. To find the total capacity of an audio CD, we would multiply 1,411,200 bits × 74 (minutes) × 60 (seconds). This would come to a total of 783 million bytes, essentially a 750MB CD.

There are technologies that use higher data rates, and technologies that use lower data rates. For example, DVD-Audio (DVD-A) can be recorded at a maximum of 24-bit/192kHz in stereo. Given this fact, many sound cards (including the one installed during this chapter) can output at 24-bit/192kHz. And DVD-Audio might go beyond just two speakers; it might be designed for 5.1 surround sound; however, it would be at a lesser sampling rate. On the other end of the spectrum, MP3s, which are compressed versions of audio files, generally range between 128kbps and 320kbps. Compare this to CD quality that is 1411kbps. However, MP3s and other compressed audio files are done in a smart way to retain CD-quality sound. Table 12.5 compares CDs, DVDs, and a couple types of compressed music files.

TABLE 12.5 **Comparison of Audio Types**

Audio Type	Sampling Rate	Bit Depth	Data Rate
Audio CD	44kHz	16-bit	1411kbps
DVD-Audio	192kHz maximum	24-bit maximum	9.6Mbps
MP3 (MPEG Layer-3)	n/a	n/a	128—320kbps (typically)
WMA (Windows Media Audio)	n/a	n/a	48—192kbps (typically)

ExamAlert

Know the basic differences between Audio CDs, DVD-Audio, and compressed music files for the exam.

Media players like Windows Media Player (which is built in to Windows) and Winamp can play audio CDs, DVD-Audio, and compressed files such as .mp3 and .wma. Certain versions of these programs can also "rip" CDs, taking the song from the CD, and creating a compressed .wma or .mp3 from it (if the CD is not encrypted). These compressed files can be anywhere from one-tenth to one-fourth the size of the original .WAV file on CD. They can then be transferred to just about any type of device including portable music players, USB flash drives, SD cards, and so on.

Cram Quiz

Answer these questions. The answers follow the last question. If you cannot answer these questions correctly, consider reading this section again until you can.

1. What types of cables are used to connect speakers to a sound card? (Select all that apply.)

   ○ **A.** 1/8-inch mini-jacks
   ○ **B.** DVI
   ○ **C.** S/PDIF
   ○ **D.** RCA

2. Which of the following are commonly used expansion busses for sound cards? (Select all that apply.)

   ○ **A.** AGP
   ○ **B.** PCI
   ○ **C.** PCIe
   ○ **D.** AMR

3. What standard is followed by most sound card manufacturers for the colors of the 1/8 mini-jacks?

   ○ **A.** PCI
   ○ **B.** PC 99
   ○ **C.** PC 100
   ○ **D.** PCIe

4. What is the total data rate of an audio CD?

   ○ **A.** 320kbps
   ○ **B.** 160kbps
   ○ **C.** 1411kbps
   ○ **D.** 9.6Mbps

Cram Quiz Answers

1. **A** and **C**. The colored connectors on the back of the sound card are known as TRS 1/8-inch mini-jacks. S/PDIF is the optical output (and possibly input) found on the back of the sound card. DVI is a video port, and RCA is another port that can be used for video and audio but won't be found on the back of a sound card; however, RCA might be found on I/O drives that are loaded into the front of a computer in a 5.25-inch bay, enabling for greater connectivity on the computer's front panel.

2. **B** and **C**. PCI Express (x1) and PCI are common expansion busses for sound cards. AGP is for video-only, and AMR, although it used to be utilized for combination sound/modem cards, it is rarely seen today.

3. **B**. PC 99 specifies the color scheme used by all kinds of equipment including a sound card's 1/8 mini-jacks.

4. **C**. 1411kbps is the total data rate (or bit rate) of an audio CD. 320 kbps is the maximum data rate for MP3, 160kbps is a common data rate for WMA files, and 9.6Mbps is the total data rate of DVD-Audio.

Input/Output, Input Devices, and Peripherals

To take advantage of a computer, the appropriate input/output devices and peripherals must be connected to the proper input/output (I/O) ports. Keyboards, mice, and multimedia devices can be connected to a variety of ports, most commonly, USB. This section briefly describes those devices and the ports they connect to.

I/O Ports

I/O ports enable a user to input information by way of keyboard, mouse, and microphone; plus they enable the output of information to printers, monitors, USB devices, and so on. The CompTIA A+ exams require a person to describe USB, IEEE 1394 (FireWire), serial, and parallel ports. The most common of these by far is USB.

USB

Universal Serial Bus (USB) ports are used by many devices including keyboards, mice, printers, cameras, and much more. The USB port enables data transfer between the device and the computer and usually powers the device as well. The speed of a USB device's data transfer depends on the version of the USB port, as shown in Table 12.6.

TABLE 12.6　**Comparison of USB Versions**

USB Version	Name	Data Transfer Rate
USB 1.0	Low-speed	1.5Mbps
USB 1.1	Full-speed	12Mbps
USB 2.0	High-speed	480Mbps
USB 3.0	Super-speed	5.0Gbps

The most common of these is USB 2.0, although USB 1.1 ports are also common in older computers. USB 1.0 is deprecated, and although the USB 3.0 specification was completed in 2008, only a handful of compliant devices were developed in 2010. However, many more are expected in 2011.

ExamAlert

Memorize the specifications for USB versions 1.1 and 2.0 for the exam.

A computer can have a maximum of 127 USB devices. However, most computers have only four or six USB ports. To add devices beyond this, a USB hub can be used, but no more than five hubs can be in a series of USB devices. All cables connecting USB devices must comply with their standard's maximum length. USB version 1.1 cables are limited to 3 meters in length (a little less than 10 feet), and USB version 2.0 cables can be a maximum length of 5 meters (a little more than 16 feet). The standard USB cable has four pins: a +5 V pin for power, positive and negative data pins, and a ground pin. Most USB connections are half-duplex, meaning that the device can send or receive data, but not both simultaneously.

There are various plugs used for the different types of USB connections. The most common are Type A and Type B, which are 4-pin connectors, but there are also mini- and micro-connectors, which are 5-pin. Type A connectors are the type you see on the back of a computer or on the side of a laptop. Figure 12.7 displays an illustration of these connectors.

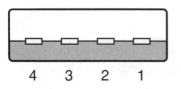

Type A

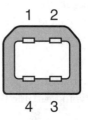

Type B

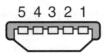

Mini-A

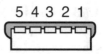

Mini-B

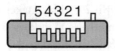

Micro-AB

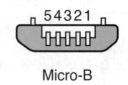

Micro-B

FIGURE 12.7 **USB connectors**

Type A and Type B connectors are commonly used for printers and other larger devices. Mini- and micro-connectors are often used for handheld computers, PDAs, digital cameras, portable music players, and cell phones. However, some companies create proprietary cables and connectors for their devices based off of the USB specifications. These devices will not connect properly to Type A, Type B, mini- or micro-connectors.

By default, a USB device is designed to be a host *or* a slave. The host is in charge of initiating data transfers. However, USB version 2.0 introduced On-The-Go (OTG), which enables a device to act as both host *and* slave. This is more common in handheld computers, PDAs, and cell phones, devices that connect with either mini- or micro-plugs.

USB devices connect to what is known as a root hub, regardless of whether they are USB version 1.1 or 2.0 devices. The USB devices, root hub, and host controllers can be viewed from within Windows in a couple of ways:

▶ **Device Manager:** Within Device Manager, click Universal Serial Bus Controllers to expand it. The root hub and controllers are listed within. Individual devices will be listed under such categories as Human Interface Devices.

▶ **System Information:** Open System Information by opening the Run prompt and typing **msinfo32**. Expand Components, and select USB.

▶ **Third-party tools:** Third-party tools such as UVCView can analyze your USB devices, ports, root hub, and controllers.

When troubleshooting USB devices, keep a few thing in mind:

▶ **Verify that USB is enabled in the BIOS:** It is possible to enable/disable USB within the BIOS. Keep this in mind when troubleshooting USB devices that are not functioning whatsoever. The user might have inadvertently set this to disabled, or perhaps the computer was shipped in that state.

▶ **Make sure the computer is running USB 2.0:** If the computer is USB 2.0-compliant from a hardware standpoint, make sure it is running USB 2.0 on the software side. Some versions of Windows support only USB 1.1 by default, but with an update can support USB 2.0. This makes a huge difference in the speed of data transfer. Sometimes Windows informs the user that an update to USB 2.0 is available and that the USB devices work faster if this update is completed.

▶ **Verify connectivity:** Make sure the device is plugged in and that it is using the correct cable. Some incompatible USB plugs might look similar to the correct plug and might even connect to a device.

One of the problems with USB is how it suffers from latency. Due to this fact, users who work with audio and video prefer a zero-latency connection such as IEEE 1394.

IEEE 1394

The Institute of Electrical and Electronics Engineers (IEEE) is a nonprofit organization that creates standards regarding cables and connectors and other technology related to electricity. One common standard is IEEE 1394, also known by the brand name versions FireWire, i.Link, and Lynx. It is a port used for devices that demand the low-latency transfer of data in real time, usually music or video. Up to 63 devices can be powered by a computer, with no more than 16 devices per chain. Table 12.7 describes some of the IEEE 1394/FireWire versions.

TABLE 12.7 **Comparison of IEEE 1394/FireWire Versions**

IEEE 1394 Version	Data Transfer Rate	Connector Type	Cable Length Between Devices
IEEE 1394a	400Mbps	4-circuit and 6-circuit	4.5 meters (15 feet)
IEEE 1394b	800Mbps[1]	9-circuit[2]	10 meters (100 meters with Category 5e cable)
FireWire 400	400Mbps	4-circuit and 6-circuit	4.5 meters
FireWire 800	800Mbps	9-circuit[2]	10 meters
FireWire S1600	1.6Gbps	9-circuit	10 meters
FireWire S3200	3.2Gbps	9-circuit	10 meters

[1]The full IEEE 1394b specification describes data rates of 1,600Mbps and 3,200Mbps in addition to 800 Mbps.

[2]IEEE 1394b and FireWire 800 devices are backward compatible to 4-circuit and 6-circuit connectors on a computer but at a reduced data rate of 400Mbps.

Exam Alert

Memorize the specifications for IEEE 1394a and b, and FireWire 400 and 800 for the exam.

Serial Versus Parallel

USB and FireWire are both serial busses that were designed to be faster than the original serial bus, which for the most part utilizes the RS-232 standard for the transmission of data. The original 9-pin serial ports are known as DE-9 connectors. (Some people incorrectly refer to them as DB-9 connectors.) These are used with external modems and to communicate directly with networking equipment such as routers. It is rare to see these integrated into today's motherboards anymore, but in networking environments, you might see them on older computers/laptops or perhaps added on as a PCI card so that a network engineer can communicate with various networking equipment. These ports send data serially, meaning one bit at a time. Generally Windows limits these ports to 115.2Kbps (115,200bps). Dial-up connections through an external modem are limited to 56Kbps.

Parallel connections can deliver more than one bit simultaneously, usually in multiples of eight. This way, one, two, or more bytes of information can be sent at one time. An example of a parallel port is the deprecated 25-pin DB-25 port, also known as a printer port, although other devices like scanners and older SCSI devices could connect to that port. Later, additional types of parallel connectors were developed for the SCSI standard. See Chapter 6, "Storage Devices," for more information on SCSI.

PS/2

The PS/2 connector is used for connecting keyboards and mice to a desktop computer or laptop. The PS/2 port was originally introduced in the late '80s as part of IBM's Personal System/2 computer. Keyboards and mice connect via a 6-pin Mini-DIN connector. In the PC 99 color scheme, PS/2 keyboard ports are purple, and PS/2 mouse ports are green. Most manufacturers comply with this standard, although you may see a few (such as Compaq) that have historically used their own color schemes.

Though PS/2 had almost a 20-year run, these connectors are extremely rare on new computers; they were the standard until USB became popular. PS/2 keyboards are automatically configured as Interrupt ReQuest (IRQ) 1, and PS/2 mice are configured as IRQ 12 on a Windows system.

Input Devices and Peripherals

Let's briefly discuss the types of devices used to input information and the various peripherals a technician might see in the field.

The usual suspects include the keyboard, for typing information in Windows, and the mouse, for manipulating the GUI. These two are known as human interface devices (HID). Some other devices that you might not have seen yet include KVM switches, touch screens, digital cameras, web cameras, microphones, biometric devices, bar code readers, and MIDI devices. Table 12.8 describes these devices.

TABLE 12.8 **Description of Various Input Devices and Peripherals**

Device	Description	Types and Connections
Keyboard	Used to type text and numbers into a word processor or other application.	101-key keyboard is standard USB, PS/2, and wireless connections
Mouse	Used to control the GUI, works in two dimensions. Might have two or more buttons and a scroll wheel to manipulate Windows.	Ball mouse, optical mouse USB, PS/2, and wireless connections
KVM Switch	Enables a user to control two or more computers from one **K**eyboard, **V**ideo display, and **M**ouse (KVM).	Passive: works off computer's USB power Active: plugs into an AC outlet
Touch screen	A video display that detects the presence of either a finger, stylus, or light pen that enables interaction with Windows.	Used in tablet PCs, PDAs, iPhones
Digital Cameras (digicam)	Takes still photographs and/or video using an electronic image sensor. Images are displayed on screen and can be saved to solid-state media such as SD cards and CompactFlash.	Can be a single device or integrated into PDAs and mobile phones Can connect to the PC via USB
Web cameras (webcam)	Enables a user to monitor other areas of a home or building, communicate via video telephony, and take still images.	Can connect to a PC via USB, to a LAN via RJ-45, or a WLAN via 802.11n, g, or b
Microphones	Enables the user to record his or her voice, or other sounds to the computer. Common usages are webcasts, podcasts, for voice-overs while screen capturing, and for gaming.	Can connect to a PC via 1/8-inch mini-jack (sound card) or via USB
Biometric devices	Analyze what a person is. Used for authentication purposes, for example a fingerprint reader.	May be integrated to the PC or can be connected via USB, or connected to the network
Bar code readers	Reads bar codes, for example linear barcodes, 2D barcodes, Post Office barcodes, and such.	Connects to the PC via USB, PS/2 ,or might be integrated into handheld computers and PDAs
MIDI devices	Musical Instrument Digital Interface. Enables computers, music keyboards, synthesizers, digital recorders, samplers, and so on to control each other and exchange data.	Uses a 5-pin DIN connector

Troubleshooting any of the devices in Table 12.8 is usually quite easy. Make sure that the device is connected properly to the computer (or has a working wireless connection), and verify within the Device Manager that the latest drivers are installed for the device. Then, find out if any additional software is necessary for the device to function. Portions of the software might have to be installed to the device and to Windows.

Cram Quiz

Answer these questions. The answers follow the last question. If you cannot answer these questions correctly, consider reading this section again until you can.

1. What is the data transfer rate (speed) of USB 2.0?
   - A. 12Mbps
   - B. 400Mbps
   - C. 480Mbps
   - D. 5Gbps

2. What is the maximum amount of USB devices a computer can support?
   - A. 4
   - B. 63
   - C. 127
   - D. 255

3. Which type of USB connector is normally found on a desktop PC or laptop?
   - A. Type A
   - B. Type B
   - C. Type C
   - D. Type D

4. A user calls you with a complaint that *none* of his USB devices are working. What is the most probably cause?
   - A. The USB 2.0 controller has failed.
   - B. The root hub is not configured.
   - C. USB is disabled in the BIOS.
   - D. USB is disabled in Windows.

5. What is the maximum data transfer rate of IEEE 1394a?

○ **A.** 400Mbps

○ **B.** 800Mbps

○ **C.** 1,600Mbps

○ **D.** 3,200Mbps

Cram Quiz Answers

1. **C.** USB 2.0 has a maximum data transfer rate of 480Mbps. 12Mbps is the data rate for USB version 1.1; 400Mbps is the data rate of IEEE 1394a (FireWire 400). And 5 Gbps is the data rate for the new USB 3.0.

2. **C.** USB can support up to 127 devices on one computer. However USB hubs will be necessary to go beyond the amount of USB ports (usually 4 or 6) commonly found on a system. FireWire supports up to 63 devices.

3. **A.** Type A connectors are almost always included on desktop PCs and laptops.

4. **C.** If none of the USB devices are working, chances are that USB has been disabled in the BIOS. This might be company policy so that users can't access USB drives or boot the computer to one. If the USB 2.0 controller fails, the USB 1.1 controller should kick in (at a slower data transfer rate, of course). The USB root hub requires no configuring; it is auto-configured by Windows. Although it might be possible to disable one USB device at a time in Windows, it will be uncommon; disabling all the devices in Windows is rare.

5. **A.** IEEE 1394a specifies a maximum data transfer rate of 400Mbps. IEEE 1394b specifies 800Mbps, 1,600Mbps, and 3,200Mbps.

Additional Reading and Resources

Video card information:

- **NVIDIA:** http://www.nvidia.com/page/home.html
- **Gigabyte:** http://www.gigabyte.com.tw/Products/VGH/Default.aspx

Creative Labs sound card information: http://www.creativelabs.com

Additional A+ resources: http://www.davidlprowse.com/aplus

CHAPTER 13

Printers

This chapter covers the following A+ exam topics:

▶ Printer Types and Technologies

▶ Installing, Configuring, and Troubleshooting Printers

You can find a master list of A+ exam topics in the "Introduction."

This chapter covers CompTIA A+ 220-701 objectives 1.11 and 2.3 and CompTIA A+ 220-702 objective 1.5.

Printers are the number two output device right behind video displays. Their main purpose is to output hard copy versions of what you see on the computer screen. Most printers connect via USB, although you also encounter printers that connect directly to the network—and on the rare occasion, printers that connect to parallel ports. Some printers also act as fax machines, copiers, and scanners; these are known as multifunction devices or multifunction printers (MFPs).

Generally, Windows Vista behaves the same as Windows XP when it comes to printing. So whenever one operating system is mentioned in this chapter, the same applies to the other operating system, unless otherwise stated.

This chapter is broken into two sections. First are printer types and technologies, and second is installing, configuring, and troubleshooting printers.

Printer Types and Technologies

Businesses utilize several types of printers. The most common business-oriented printer is the laser printer. However inkjet printers are more prevalent in the home due to their lower cost and their capability to print in color with excellent resolution. A technician might also encounter thermal and impact printers. Some printers connect directly to a computer; others connect to the network or to a print server. This section describes the four main types of printers and how they function; it also discusses the differences between local and network printers.

Types of Printers

Each type of printer has its own characteristics that affect how a technician installs, configures, and troubleshoots them. The most common type of printer that a business would use is the laser printer; this type of printer also happens to be the most complicated and difficult to troubleshoot.

Laser Printers

Laser printers can produce high-quality text and graphics on cut sheets of paper; printers that print to individual pieces of paper are known as *page printers*. The bulk of laser printers print in black, but there are also color laser printers, which of course are more expensive. They are called laser printers because inside the printer is a laser beam that projects an image of the item to be printed onto an electrically charged drum; this image is later transferred to the paper. Text and images that are shown on paper are created from electrically charged toner, which is a type of powder stored in a replaceable toner cartridge. The type of toner used can vary from one brand to the next, but they all work essentially the same way.

Known also as a photoelectric or photosensitive drum, the laser printer drum is at the center of the whole laser printing process, but there are a couple of other important components including the primary corona wire, transfer corona wire, fusing assembly, and of course, the laser itself. These components are shown in Figure 13.1.

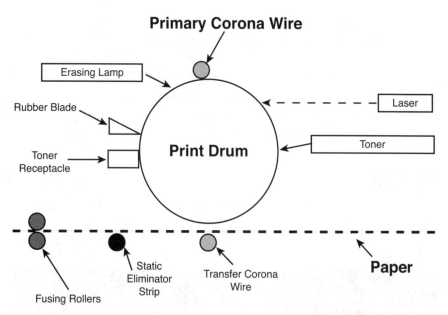

FIGURE 13.1   Components involved in the six-step laser printing process

The following list describes the six-step laser printing process:

1. **Cleaning:** A rubber blade removes excess toner from the drum as it spins. An erasing lamp removes any leftover charge on the drum bringing it to zero volts.

2. **Conditioning:** Also known as charging. A negative charge is applied to the drum by the primary corona wire, which is powered by a high-voltage power supply within the printer.

3. **Writing:** Also known as exposing. The laser is activated and "writes" to the drum as it spins. Where the laser hits the drum, it dissipates the negative charge toward the center of the drum that is grounded. The "written" areas of the drum now have a lesser negative charge.

4. **Developing:** The surface of the drum that was previously exposed to the laser is now applied with negatively charged toner. This toner has a higher charge than the areas of the drum that were written to.

5. **Transferring:** The toner, and therefore the text or image, is transferred to paper as the drum rolls over it. On many laser printers, the paper slides between the drum and a positively charged corona wire (known as the transfer corona wire). The transfer corona wire applies the positive charge to the paper. Because the paper now has a positive charge, and

the toner particles on the drum have a negative charge, the toner is attracted to the paper. (When it comes to voltages, opposites attract.) In many printers the paper passes by a static elimination device (often a strip), which removes excess charge from the paper.

6. **Fusing:** The toner is fused to the paper. The paper passes through the fusing assembly that includes pressurized rollers and a heating element that can reach approximately 400 degrees F (or about 200 degrees C).

> **Note**
>
> On some laser printers, the cleaning stage occurs at the end of the fusing stage, cleaning off the photosensitive drum and reducing its voltage to zero.

> **Exam Alert**
>
> Know the six-step laser printing process (also known as the electrophotographic printing process) for the exam.

In some laser printers the drum, laser, and primary corona wire are contained within the toner cartridge. Issues that are caused by these components can usually be fixed just by replacing the toner cartridge.

> **Note**
>
> Toner cartridges are replaceable; they are known as *consumables*. Whatever material it is that actually prints on to paper is usually considered a consumable, regardless of the type of printer.

Laser printers have some advantages over other printers:

▶ **Speed:** A laser printer can print anywhere from 10 to 100 pages per minute depending on the model and whether it is a color or black-and-white laser printer.

▶ **Print quality:** The laser printer commonly prints at 600DPI (dots per inch), which is considered *letter quality*, but 1,200DPI and higher resolution printers are also available.

Inkjet Printers

Inkjet printers are common in small offices, in home offices, and for personal use. They can print documents but more commonly print photographs and graphical information in color; most of the time they connect to the computer by way of USB.

The inkjet printer works by propelling ink onto various sizes of paper. Many inkjets store ink in multiple ink cartridges that are consumable; they have to be replaced when empty. Some inkjet printers stop operating if just one of the ink cartridges is empty. Two common types of inkjet printers are the thermal inkjet and the piezoelectric inkjet:

▸ **Thermal inkjets:** These account for the bulk of consumer inkjets and are the more recognizable type. To move the ink to the paper, heat is sent through the ink cartridge, forming a bubble (known as the thermal bubble) that pushes the ink onto the paper; immediately afterward another charge of ink is readied. The reservoir of ink is within the ink cartridge; this is where the heat transfer occurs. HP and Canon develop many models of thermal inkjet printers. Don't confuse thermal inkjets with thermal printers.

▸ **Piezoelectric inkjets:** These account for the bulk of commercial inkjets. The printing processes within a piezoelectric inkjet and a thermal inkjet are similar; however, the piezo inkjet applies current to the ink material, causing it to change shape and size, forcing the ink onto the paper. The reservoir of ink is in another area outside of where the current is applied. This process enables longer print head life as compared to thermal inkjets. Epson develops many models of piezoelectric inkjet printers. Piezoelectric inkjets can also be found in manufacturing assembly lines.

The inkjet print process is fairly simple:

1. The paper or other media is pulled or moved into position by a roller mechanism, or moved into position by an assembly line's conveyor belt as with some piezoelectric inkjets.

2. The print head, located on a mechanical arm, moves across the paper, placing black and colored ink as directed by the print driver.

3. At the end of the line, the paper or media is advanced, and the print head either reverses direction and continues to print (often referred to as Hi-Speed mode) or returns to the left margin before printing continues.

4. After the page is completed, the paper or other media is ejected.

Thermal Printers

Thermal printers produce text and images by heating specially coated thermal paper. It is typical to see thermal printers used in point-of-sale systems, gas station pumps, and so on. Thermal printers consist of the following parts:

- ▶ **Thermal head:** This generates the heat and takes care of printing to the paper.

- ▶ **Platen:** This is the rubber roller that feeds the paper past the print head.

- ▶ **Spring:** Applies pressure to the print head, which brings the print head into contact with the paper.

- ▶ **Circuit board:** Controls the mechanism that moves the print head.

To print, thermal paper is inserted between the thermal head and the platen. The printer sends current to the thermal head, which in turn generates heat. The heat activates the thermo-sensitive coloring layer of the thermal paper, which becomes the image.

Impact Printers

Impact printers use force to transfer ink to paper, for example, a print head striking a ribbon with paper directly behind it, similar to a typewriter. This type of printer is somewhat deprecated although certain environments might still use it: auto repair centers, warehouses, accounting departments, and so on.

One type of impact printer, the daisy-wheel, utilizes a wheel with many petals, each of which has a letter form (an actual letter) at the tip of the petal. These strike against the ribbon that impresses ink upon the paper that is situated behind the ribbon. But by far the most common type of impact printer is the dot-matrix.

Dot-matrix printers are also known as line printers because they print text one line at a time and can keep printing over a long roll of paper, as opposed to page printers that print to cut sheets of paper. Dot-matrix printers use a matrix of pins that work together to create characters, instead of a form letter. The print head that contains these pins strikes the ribbon that in turn places the ink on the paper. Print heads either come with 9 pins or 24 pins, with the 24-pin version offering better quality, known as *near letter quality* (NLQ). Dot-matrix printers are loud and slow but are cheap to maintain.

Local Versus Network Printers

A local printer is one that connects directly to a computer, normally by USB, or parallel connection. When a user works at a computer, that computer is considered to be the local computer. So, if a printer is connected to that computer, it is known as the local printer.

A network printer is one that connects directly to the network or to a print server device. Network printers are shared by more than one user on the computer network. Usually, network printers are given an IP address and become yet another *host* on the network. If the printer connects directly to the network, it is usually by way of a built-in RJ45 port on the printer, just like how a computer's network card connects to the network. A print server could be a computer or smaller black box device. Many SOHO routers from Linksys and D-link offer print server capabilities. In this case the printer connects via USB to the print server/router, and a special piece of software is installed on any client computers that want to print to that printer.

Regardless of whether a printer is local or on the network, it can be controlled by Windows, described in the following section.

Cram Quiz

Answer these questions. The answers follow the last question. If you cannot answer these questions correctly, consider reading this section again until you can.

1. Which type of printer uses a photoelectric drum?
    - ○ **A.** Impact
    - ○ **B.** Dot-Matrix
    - ○ **C.** Laser
    - ○ **D.** Inkjet

2. During which step of the six-step laser printing process is the transfer corona wire involved?
    - ○ **A.** Developing
    - ○ **B.** Transferring
    - ○ **C.** Fusing
    - ○ **D.** Cleaning

3. Which stage of the six-step laser printing process involves extreme heat?

    ○ **A.** Fusing

    ○ **B.** Transferring

    ○ **C.** Exposing

    ○ **D.** Writing

4. What is the most common type of consumer-based printer?

    ○ **A.** Thermal printer

    ○ **B.** Laser printer

    ○ **C.** Thermal inkjet

    ○ **D.** Impact printer

5. What is the rubber roller that feeds the paper past the print head known as?

    ○ **A.** HVPS

    ○ **B.** Cartridge

    ○ **C.** Spring

    ○ **D.** Platen

6. What is a common amount of pins in a dot-matrix printer's print head?

    ○ **A.** 40

    ○ **B.** 24

    ○ **C.** 8

    ○ **D.** 184

Cram Quiz Answers

1. C. The laser printer is the only type of printer that uses a photoelectric drum.

2. B. The transfer corona wire gets involved in the six-step laser printing process during the transferring step.

3. A. The fusing step uses heat (up to 200 degrees Celsius) and pressure to fuse the toner permanently to the paper.

4. C. The thermal inkjet is the most common type of printer used in the consumer market today.

5. D. The platen is the rubber roller that feeds the paper past the print head.

6. B. Dot-matrix printer print heads usually have 24 pins or 9 pins.

Installing, Configuring, and Troubleshooting Printers

Physically installing printers and installing device drivers is usually straightforward, but the configuration of printers in Windows is more complex because so many configurable options exist. Troubleshooting as always should be approached from a logical standpoint. This section covers the installation, configuration, and troubleshooting of printers.

Printer Installation and Drivers

When installing printers focus on several things:

▸ **Compatibility:** Make sure that the printer is compatible with the version of Windows that runs on the computer that controls the printer. Check the Windows Vista/XP Logo'd Products List to verify this. If the printer is to connect to the network, make sure that it has the right type of compatible network adapter to do so.

▸ **Installing printer drivers:** Generally, the proper procedure is to install the printer driver to Windows before physically connecting the printer. However, if the driver already exists on the computer, the printer can simply be connected. Usually, the best bet is to use the driver that came on disc with the printer, or download the latest driver from the manufacturer's website. Verify that the driver to be installed is the correct one and that it is for the correct operating system, and version of the operating system, for example 32-bit or 64-bit versions of Windows. Printer drivers are installed in a similar fashion to other drivers described in this book, but Windows includes a wizard specifically for printers called the Add Printer Wizard. This can be accessed by navigating to Start and opening the Control Panel in Classic mode; then select Printers (in Vista) or Printers and Faxes (XP). Any current printers should be listed in the right window pane. From there, right-click anywhere in the work area and select Add Printer.

▸ **Connecting the device:** In general, devices connecting via USB or IEEE 1394 can be connected without turning the computer off. (That is, they are hot-swappable.) However, devices that connect to a parallel, SCSI, or serial port require that the computer be shut down first. (Parallel ports are less common today, but if a user wants to connect a printer to one, they need to use a compatible IEEE 1284 cable that has a 25-pin parallel connector on one end and a centronics connector on the other.) Plug the USB or other connector cable into the computer first, and then connect the printer to an AC outlet. (It's recommended to use a surge protector for printers but is generally *not* recommended to use a UPS for a laser printer.) Verify that the device turns on.

▶ **Calibrating the printer:** Color laser printers, inkjet printers, and multi-function printers might need to be calibrated before use. This involves aligning the printing mechanism to the paper and verifying color output. Usually the software that accompanies the printer guides a user through this process. In some cases, these calibration tests can be done via the small display on the printer.

▶ **Testing the printer:** First test the printer by printing a test page in Windows. This can be done by locating the printer in the Printers window (Printers and Faxes in XP), right-clicking it, and selecting Properties; then click the Print Test Page button on the General tab. The resulting page should show the operating system the local computer runs and various other configuration and driver information. If the page can be read properly and the Windows logo is using the correct colors, the test passed. Some printers offer a test page option on the small display of the printer as well. After a test page has been printed, it might be wise to try printing within the most used applications as well, just to make sure they work properly. Some applications might behave differently, and some configurations of printers in Windows could cause a particular application to have print failures.

Configuring Printers

Configuration of printers can be done in one of two places. The first is the small display that might be included on a printer; these are more common on laser printers. These menu driven displays are usually user-friendly and intuitive. But the second, and the one that I'd like to focus on in this section, is within Windows, specifically by double-clicking the printer icon within the Printers window and by accessing the Properties page of the printer. Both of these can be done by accessing the Printers page (Printers and Faxes page in XP). To open this window navigate to Start, open the Control Panel in classic mode, and select Printers (Printers and Faxes in XP). Another option would be for a user to open Windows Explorer and navigate to Control Panel; then select Printers. To open a printer simply double-click it. To manage it's properties right-click the printer in question and select Properties. If you work with printers often, consider placing a shortcut to the printer or printers on the desktop or within the Quick Launch. Several items can be configured by double-clicking the printer and within the Printer Properties window including Managing print jobs, setting the priority of the printer, configuring the print spooler, and managing permissions.

Managing Printers and Print Jobs

To manage a printer or an individual print job, just double-click the printer in which the job was sent to. A window similar to Figure 13.2 should display on the monitor.

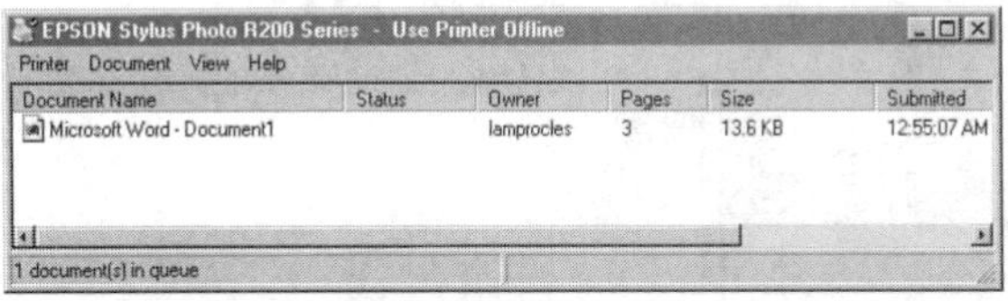

FIGURE 13.2 **A typical printer window with one print job**

In Figure 13.2 you can notice that one print job called Document1 is listed. If the job went to the printer properly, it would say Printing under the Status column. Any other message would mean that the job was either spooled, queued, stopped, or has failed. These jobs can be paused, restarted, or stopped completely if they are not printing properly. This can be done by right-clicking in the job or by selecting the Document menu. Keep in mind that larger documents take longer to spool before they start printing. In addition to this, all documents can be paused or canceled, or the entire printer can be taken offline from the Printer menu. Use these tools to troubleshoot any printing misqueues.

Printer Priority

Printer priority can be configured within the Advanced tab of a printer's Properties page, as shown in Figure 13.3.

The priority of a printer can be configured from 1 to 99; 99 being the highest. This is useful in two situations:

▶ **Scenario 1:** Let's say that several users and their manager share a printer. Chances are that you would want to give the manager the highest priority when it comes to print jobs. It is possible to install two software printers in Windows that point to the same physical printer. The first software printer could be given a higher priority (say 99) and a share name such as "manager," with permissions that allow access only by the manager. The second software printer would be given a lower priority (say 50) and use a share name such as "users." After the client computers are configured properly to access the correct printers, the manger should always get precedence over other print jobs on the shared physical printer.

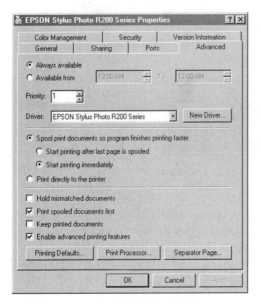

FIGURE 13.3   **Printer priority and spooling**

▶ **Scenario 2:** Imagine that there are two or more physical printers that have been combined to create a printer pool. Each printer in the pool can be given a different priority. One printer in the pool is often set aside for managers and executives with a higher priority than the others.

Print Spooling

Whenever a job goes to print there are three possible options:

▶ **Print directly to the printer:** This means that the print job goes right to the printer without any delays. This relies solely on the amount of memory in the printer (which can be increased BTW just like in computers). Of course, if the print job is larger than the amount of RAM in the printer, the job will probably fail. Usually a better solution is to spool the document.

▶ **Start printing immediately:** This is the first of two spooling options. When this setting is selected, one page at a time of the document will be *spooled* to the hard disk drive. When an entire page has been spooled, it is sent to the printer for printing. This repeats until all the pages of the document have been spooled and ultimately printed. This is the default setting in Windows and is usually the best option, as shown in Figure 13.3.

▶ **Start printing after last page is spooled:** This means that the entire document will be spooled to the hard drive, and then pages are sent to the printer for printing. This is usually slower than "Start printing immediately" but might have fewer issues such as stalls or other printing failures.

The spooler is controlled by the Print Spooler service. Not only can you have issues in which print jobs or printers stop working, but the Print Spooler service can fail also. This service can be started, stopped, and restarted from the GUI and from the Command Prompt:

▶ **Adjusting the Print Spooler service in Computer Management:** Open the Computer Management console window; then click the + sign to expand Services and Applications and click Services. Now, in the right window pane, scroll until you find the Print Spooler service. To start a stopped service, right-click it and click Start. Alternatively, you can click the Start or other buttons on the toolbar.

▶ **Adjusting the Print Spooler service in the Command Prompt:** In Windows Vista you need to run these commands as an administrator; let's review the two ways to do this.

   1. Click Start > All Programs > Accessories; then right-click Command Prompt and select Run as Administrator.

   2. Click Start and type **cmd** in the search field, and instead of pressing Enter, press Ctrl+Shift+Enter.

Windows XP does not require opening the Command Prompt as an administrator. When the Command Prompt is open, you can start the Print Spooler service by typing **net start spooler**. Typing **Net stop spooler** stops the service.

ExamAlert

Know how to configure spooling and how to start and stop the Print Spooler service within Computer Management and in the Command Prompt.

New XPS Feature in Windows Vista

Windows Vista incorporates the XML Paper Specification (XPS) print path. The XPS spooler is meant to replace the standard Enhanced Metafile print spooler that Windows has used for years. With XPS (part of the Windows Presentation Foundation) Vista provides improved color and graphics support, and support for the CMYK colorspace, and reduces the need for colorspace conversion.

This is implemented as the Microsoft XPS Document Writer that can be found in Start > Control Panel > Printers. A document created within any application in Windows can be saved as an .XPS file to be later viewed on any computer that supports XPS. It can also be printed from any computer that supports XPS, but will print only with proper fidelity if the computer has an XPS-compliant printer.

Printer Pooling

Printer pooling takes multiple separate printers and combines them to form a team of printers that work together to complete print jobs as quickly as possible. This can be accomplished from the Ports tab of the printer's Properties window. Normally a printer will be shown next to the port it connects to. To add a second installed printer to the pool, click Enable printer pooling; then check mark the other printer listed, as shown in Figure 13.4

As you can see in Figure 13.4, the Printer Pooling option has been selected, and a second printer (HP LaserJet 5) has been check marked that adds it to the pool along with the Epson Stylus printer. At this point, any jobs sent to the first printer that can't be processed right away will be transferred to the second printer. This is a one-way printer pool; two-way printer pools are also possible but aren't done as much. Quite often, printer pools consist of all identical printers.

Note

Remote printers can be connected to and controlled from the Ports tab. This can be done by adding a port and then entering the IP address of the printer to be controlled, or the computer name of the computer that the remote printer connects to.

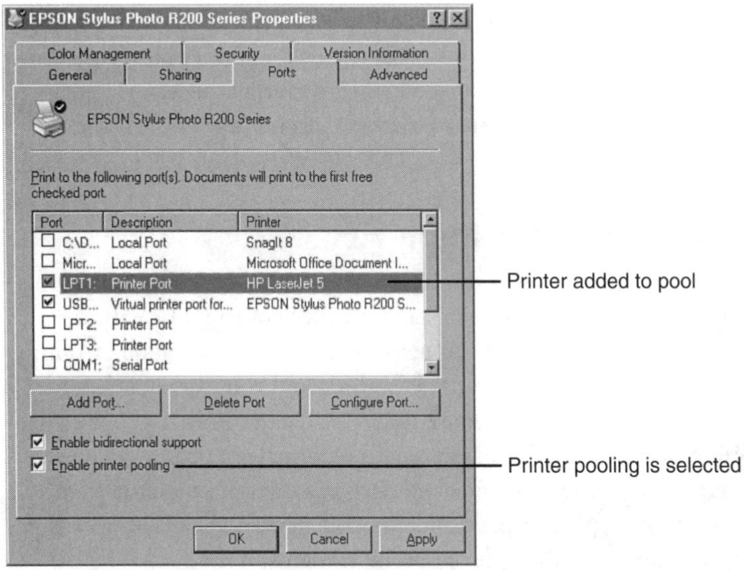

FIGURE 13.4   Enabled printer pooling option

Sharing Printers and Managing Permissions

A printer must first be shared before other users can send print jobs to it. There are two steps involved in sharing printers in Windows. First, printer sharing in general must be enabled:

▶ To enable Printer Sharing in Windows Vista, go to Start > Control Panel > Network and Sharing Center; click the down arrow for Printer Sharing and select the radio button labeled Turn on Printer Sharing.

▶ To enable Printer Sharing in Windows XP, go to Start > Control Panel > Network Connections. Then right-click any network adapter and select Properties. Check mark File and Printer Sharing for Microsoft Networks. This is normally enabled by default.

Next, the individual printer needs to be shared. This can be done in the Sharing tab of the printer's Properties window. Click the Share This Printer radio button and give the printer a share name. Note that the share name does not need to be the same as the printer name. Click OK, and the printer should show up as shared within the Printers window.

Permissions can be set for a printer in the Security tab of the printer's Properties window. Users and groups can be added in this window, and the appropriate permission can be assigned including Print, Manage Printers, and

Manage Documents. Regular users normally are assigned the Print permission, whereas administrators get all permissions, enabling them to pause the printer or cancel all documents (Manage Printers), and pause, cancel, and restart individual documents. For more information on permissions, see Chapter 15 "Security."

Selecting a Separator Page

Separator pages help users to find the start and end points of their print job. The separator page might be printed as a blank piece of paper or with the username and title of the document to be printed. This can be added from the Advanced tab by clicking the Separator Page button. From there click the browse button that shows the System32 folder by default. Initially four separator pages are in this folder, the most common of which are pcl.sep and pscript.sep. However, some companies opt to use a custom separator page. Click the appropriate separator page and click open; then click OK. The separator page will be added to the appropriate documents.

> **Note**
>
> There are a lot of other settings in the printer Properties window. Spend some time looking through the various tabs and configurations to better prepare yourself for the exam.

Troubleshooting Printers

Sometimes companies have paid consultants that take care of all printers and copying machines, and sometimes taking care of these devices is the job of the in-house IT guy. Either way, it is a good idea to know some of the basic issues that can occur with printers and how to troubleshoot them. Table 13.1 describes some of these issues and possible solutions. Some of these issues, for example paper jams and resulting error codes, might be displayed on a printer's LCD.

TABLE 13.1 **Printer Problems and Solutions**

Printer Issue	Possible Solution
Paper jams	1. Attempt to turn the printer on and off in the hopes that the printer will clear the jam itself. This is known as power cycling the printer.

TABLE 13.1 **Continued**

Printer Issue	Possible Solution
	2. Remove paper trays and inspect them for crumpled papers that can be removed by grabbing both ends of the paper firmly and pulling or rotating the rollers to remove it. In general, clear the paper path.
	3. Verify that the right paper type is in the printer. If the paper is too thin or thick, it might cause a paper jam. Also, watch for paper that has been exposed to humidity.
	4. Check for dirty or cracked rollers. A temporary fix for dirty rubber rollers is to use isopropyl alcohol. A permanent fix would be to replace the roller.
	5. Check if the fusing assembly has overheated. Sometimes the printer just needs time to cool, or perhaps the printer is not in a well enough ventilated area. In uncommon cases the fuser might have to be replaced. Be sure to unplug the printer and let the printer sit for an hour or so before doing so due to the high temperatures of the fuser. The fusing assembly can usually be removed with a few screws.
Blank paper	1. Empty toner cartridge. Install a new one.
	2. Toner cartridge was installed without the sealing tape removed.
	3. Transfer corona wire has failed. If the transfer corona wire fails, there will be no positive (opposite) voltage to pull the toner to the paper. Replace the wire.
Error codes	If a specific error is shown on the printer's LCD, read it. It might tell you exactly what the error is and how to fix it, or at least what the error is. On some printers it displays an error number. Check your printer's documentation to find out what the error means.
Out of memory error	If this happens, check if the user's computer is spooling documents. The setting with the least chance of this error is the Start Printing Immediately spool setting. You might also need to restart the Print Spooling service. If a user tries to print a large image, he might need to change settings in the application in which the image was made. In some cases, the printer's RAM might need to be upgraded. Whenever installing RAM to a printer, take all the same precautions you would when working on a PC.
Lines and smearing	Black lines can be caused by a scratch in the laser printer drum or a dirty primary corona wire. Usually, the toner cartridge needs to be replaced. White lines could be caused by a dirty transfer corona wire; this can be cleaned or replaced. Wide white vertical lines can occur when something is stuck to the drum. Smearing can occur if the fusing assembly has failed; in this case you might also notice toner coming off of the paper easily.
	If it is an inkjet, one or more ink cartridges might need to be replaced, or the printer might need to be calibrated.

TABLE 13.1 **Continued**

Printer Issue	Possible Solution
Garbage printout	This can occur due to an incorrect driver. Some technicians like to try "close" drivers. This is not a good idea. Use the exact driver for the exact model of the printer that corresponds to the appropriate version of the operating system. A bad formatter board or printer interface can also be the cause of a garbage printout. These can usually be replaced easily by removing two screws and a cover.
Ghosted image	Ghosted images or blurry marks can be a sign that the drum has some kind of imperfection or is dirty. Especially if the image reappears at equal intervals. Replace the drum (or toner cartridge). Another possibility is that the fuser assembly has been damaged and needs to be replaced.
No connectivity	If there is no connectivity, check the following: ▸ Printer is plugged into an AC outlet and it is "online." ▸ Printer is securely connected to the local computer or to the network. ▸ The computer has the correct print driver installed. ▸ The printer is shared to the network. ▸ The printer has a properly configured IP address. (This can be checked on the LCD display of most networkable laser printers.) ▸ Remote computers have a proper connection over the network to the printer.

In general, when working with printers, try to keep them clean and use printer maintenance kits. Like changing the oil in a car, printers need maintenance also. HP and other manufacturers offer maintenance kits that include items such as fusers, rollers, separation pads, and instructions on how to replace all these items. Manufacturers recommend that this maintenance be done every once in a while, for example every 200,000 pages printed. When you finish installing a maintenance kit, be sure to reset the maintenance count.

When troubleshooting printers, don't forget to RTM! Read The Manual! Most printers come with one, and they often have a troubleshooting section toward the back. In some cases, the manual will be in PDF format on the disc that accompanied the printer. Regardless of whether a manual accompanied the printer or if it can't be found, the manufacturer will usually have the manual on its website in addition to a support system for its customers. Use it! And keep in mind that many products come with a warranty, or the customer might have purchased an extended warranty. I remember one time I was troubleshooting two-color laser printers. They were only two weeks old when they failed. When the manufacturer knew the error code that was flashing on the printer's display, it didn't want to hear anything else; it simply sent out a tech the next day because the device was under warranty. To sum up, let the manufacturer help you. If it doesn't cost the company anything, it can save you a lot of time and aggravation.

Cram Quiz

Answer these questions. The answers follow the last question. If you cannot answer these questions correctly, consider reading this section again until you can.

1. When connecting a laser printer's power cable, what type of device is not recommended?

   ○ **A.** Surge protector

   ○ **B.** Line conditioner

   ○ **C.** UPS

   ○ **D.** AC outlet

2. When finished installing a new printer and print drivers, what should you do? (Select all that apply.)

   ○ **A.** Calibrate the printer.

   ○ **B.** Install the print drivers.

   ○ **C.** Check for compatibility.

   ○ **D.** Print a test page.

3. Which is the faster option when it comes to spooling documents?

   ○ **A.** Print directly to the printer.

   ○ **B.** Start printing immediately.

   ○ **C.** Start printing after the last page is spooled.

   ○ **D.** Start printing after the separator page.

4. What command turns off the print spooler?

   ○ **A.** `net disable print spooler`

   ○ **B.** `net stop print spooler`

   ○ **C.** `net restart spooler`

   ○ **D.** `net stop spooler`

5. What is it known as when two printers are joined together so that they can work as a team?

   ○ **A.** Printer pooling

   ○ **B.** Printer spooling

   ○ **C.** pscript.sep

   ○ **D.** Printer joining

6. What window in Windows Vista enables printer sharing?

   ○ **A.** Network Connections

   ○ **B.** Network and Sharing Center

   ○ **C.** Network

   ○ **D.** My Network Places

7. How can a paper jam be resolved? (Select all that apply.)

   ○ **A.** Clear the paper path.

   ○ **B.** Use the right type of paper.

   ○ **C.** Check for damaged rollers.

   ○ **D.** Check for a damaged primary corona wire.

8. What is a possible reason for having blank pages come out of a laser printer?

   ○ **A.** Failed transfer corona wire

   ○ **B.** Failed primary corona wire

   ○ **C.** Failed fusing assembly

   ○ **D.** Damaged roller

9. What is a possible reason for having black lines show up on printouts?

   ○ **A.** Scratch on the laser printer drum

   ○ **B.** Damaged roller

   ○ **C.** Damaged transfer corona wire

   ○ **D.** Scratch on the fusing assembly

Cram Quiz Answers

1. **C**. An uninterruptible power supply (UPS) is not recommended for laser printers due to the high draw of the laser printer.

2. **A** and **D**. After the printer is installed, meaning it has been connected, and the drivers have been installed, you should calibrate the printer (if necessary) and print a test page. Before starting the installation, you should check for compatibility with operating systems, applications, and so on.

3. **B**. Start Printing Immediately is the faster print option when spooling documents. Print Directly to the Printer doesn't use the spooling feature, and there is no Start Printing After the Separator Page.

4. **D**. The command **net stop spooler** stops or turns off the print spooler service.

5. **A**. Printer pooling is when two or more printers are combined to get print jobs out faster.

6. **B**. The Network and Sharing Center in Windows Vista is where printer sharing is enabled.

7. **A, B**, and **C**. There are several possible reasons why a paper jam might occur. The paper could be stuck somewhere in the paper path, the paper could be too thick, or the rollers could be damaged.

8. **A**. If the transfer corona wire has failed, there is no way for the toner to be "attracted" to the paper, resulting in blank sheets coming out of the printer.

9. **A**. A scratch on the laser printer drum can account for black lines showing up on printouts. Another culprit can be a dirty primary corona wire.

Additional Reading and Resources

Additional A+ resources: http://www.davidlprowse.com/aplus

Soper, Mark Edward; Mueller, Scott; Prowse, David L.. *CompTIA A+ Certification Guide*. ISBN13: 9780789740472. Que.

CHAPTER 14

Networking

This chapter covers the following A+ exam topics:

▶ Networking Fundamentals

▶ Network Cabling and Connectors

▶ Troubleshooting Network Connectivity

▶ Installing and Configuring a SOHO Network

You can find a master list of A+ exam topics in the "Introduction."

This chapter covers CompTIA A+ 220-701 objectives 4.1, 4.2, and 4.3 and CompTIA A+ 220-702 objectives 3.1, and 3.2.

Virtually every business has one or more computer networks, and it seems that nowadays just about every home has a network as well. But what is a computer network? The simple answer: A computer network is two or more computers that communicate. For the more in-depth answer, read on!

We use networks so that computers can share files, access databases, collaborate on projects, connect to the Internet, and send email. Important considerations in networking include the technologies used, devices, protocols, cabling; plus the installation, configuration, and troubleshooting of networks. Other things to think about are how the network is organized, what types of communications are necessary, in what way devices share information, how the network is secured, and what is the effect of the network on the budget. As you can see, so much is dependent on a well-designed, quick and efficient, and cost-effective network, making this an important chapter for the exam. Let's begin by discussing the building blocks of networks: networking fundamentals.

Networking Fundamentals

To network your computer, you first need a network adapter. Networking expansion cards for desktop computers include PCI, and PCIe, whereas laptops use PC Cards, ExpressCards, and Mini-PCI.

USB network adapters are also available that enable a computer to connect to the network via a USB port. It is sometimes referred to as a network interface card (NIC). Adapters integrated into the motherboard of the PC or laptop are common. This adapter is either equipped with an RJ45 jack that enables for a wired connection to the network or has a wireless antenna built-in for connectivity to wireless networks. Some computers have both types of adapters. When the adapter is physically installed, drivers for the network adapter are installed much like any other drivers. This enables the operating system to communicate with the network adapter and transmit data over the network.

After a driver is installed, a communications protocol is needed. In most cases the protocol is installed automatically. The most commonly used protocol is Transmission Control Protocol/Internet Protocol (TCP/IP). TCP/IP is actually a suite that includes many protocols, some of which you have probably heard of, for example, HTTP, or FTP. The version of TCP/IP that the exams focus on is TCP/IPv4, more simply known as IPv4. Unless stated otherwise in this chapter, when I use the term IP or TCP/IP, I refer to IPv4. Let's show how to configure IP settings now.

Configuring IPv4

Configuring IP works the same way in most versions of Windows. First we navigate to the Internet Protocol (TCP/IP) Properties window, which we refer to as the IP Properties window.

> **In Windows XP:** Navigate to Start > Control Panel > Network and Internet Connections. Select the Control Panel icon Network Connections. Then right-click the Local Area Connection icon and select Properties. Finally, highlight Internet Protocol and click the Properties button.

> **In Windows Vista:** Navigate to Start > Control Panel > Network and Internet > Network and Sharing Center. Select the Manage My Network Connections link (change adapter settings link in Windows 7). Then right-click the Local Area Connection icon and select Properties. Finally, highlight Internet Protocol Version 4 and click the Properties button.

ExamAlert

Memorize how to navigate to the IP Properties window for the exam!

Note

These are the default paths. You can shorten these considerably. For example, in Windows XP if you added the My Network Places option in the Start Menu, just right-click that and select properties. In Windows Vista, if you have the Network option in the Start menu, right-click that and select properties. There are other ways to save time, for example using a shortcut or utilizing a network connection link in your System Tray. Use the fastest method available!

The first item to be configured is the IP address. The IP address is the unique assigned number of your computer on the network. IP addresses consist of four octets. Each octet's value can be between 0 and 255. Each number is separated by a dot. For example: 192.168.0.100. The binary equivalent of 0–255 would be 00000000 through 11111111. For example, 192 is equal to 11000000 in binary. Because each octet contains 8 bits, and there are four octets, the IP address collectively is a 32-bit number but is normally expressed in dotted-decimal notation.

There are two main types of addresses: dynamic and static. Dynamically assigned addresses are more common for a client computer; this is when the computer seeks out a DHCP server so that it can get its IP information automatically. In Figure 14.1, you note a radio button that says Obtain an IP Address Automatically. If you select this, the rest of the information becomes grayed out, and the computer attempts to get that IP information from a host such as a D-Link router or DHCP server. This is common; in fact it's the default configuration for Windows. Static addresses are when we configure the IP information manually. Figure 14.1 shows an example of statically configured IP settings in the Local Area Connection properties window. In the figure we configured the computer to use the address 192.168.0.100, but the IP address differs from machine to machine depending on several factors. Remember that the address should be unique for each computer on the network.

ExamAlert

Know the difference between static and dynamic IP addresses.

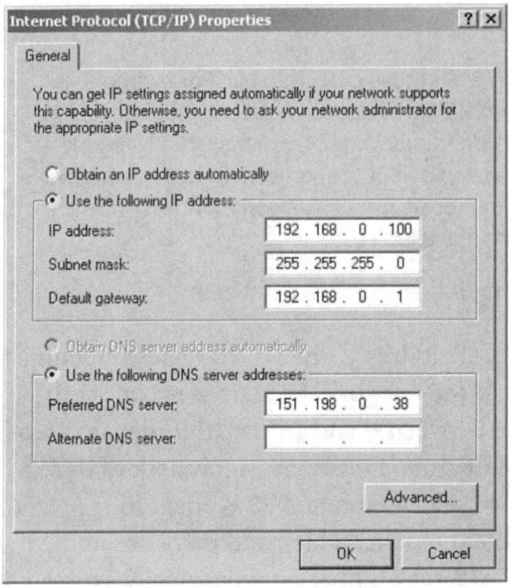

FIGURE 14.1 IP Properties window with an example IP configuration

There is another possibility when it comes to IP addresses, and that is when the computer self-assigns an address. This is known as *automatic private IP addressing (APIPA)* and happens when a computer cannot contact a DHCP server to obtain an IP address. If APIPA self-assigns an address, it will be on the 169.254.0.0 network.

IP addresses are divided into two sections: the network portion, which is the number of the network the computer is on, and the host portion, which is the individual number of the computer. The subnet mask defines which portion of the IP address is the network number and which portion is the individual host number. In this case the subnet mask is 255.255.255.0. The 255s indicate the network portion of the IP address. So, 192.168.0 is the network this computer is a member of. The zeros (in this case there is only one of them) indicate the host number, so 100 is the individual number of this computer. Quite often the subnet mask will be configured automatically by Windows after you type in the IP address.

The gateway address is the IP address of the host that enables access to the Internet or to other networks. The IP address of the gateway should always be on the same network as the computer(s) connecting to it. In Figure 14.1 we know it is because the first three octets are 192.168.0. If a computer is not configured with a gateway address, it cannot connect to the Internet.

ExamAlert

To use the gateway, computers must be on the same network number as the gateway device.

The DNS server address is the IP address of the host that takes care of domain name translation to IP.

When you use your browser to connect to a website, you might type something like www.davidlprowse.com. What you need to remember, however, is that computers actually communicate by IP address, not by name. So the DNS server takes care of translating the name davidlprowse.com to its corresponding IP address and forwarding that information back to your computer. When your computer knows the IP address of the website, it can go ahead and start a session with the website and transmit and receive files. Notice in Figure 14.1 that the DNS server address is on a completely different network than our computer. This is typical, in this case the DNS server is run by the Internet service provider (ISP) who provides me with my cable Internet connection. However, DNS servers can also be run internally by a company; this happens more often with larger companies. That brings us to how the different network numbers are categorized.

IPv4 Classes

When working with classful IP addresses, the first number in the IP address dictates what class the address is part of. For example, suppose you use 192.168.0.100. In that case, the first number is 192, which means that the IP address is part of a Class C network.

Table 14.1 shows the various classes and their associated IP address ranges. Table 14.2 shows the IP classes and their associated default subnet masks, which as we mentioned, identify which portion of the IP address is the network portion and which is the host portion.

Take a look at Table 14.1 and try to get a feel for the different IP Classes available. You realize that this classification system was created to appease different organizations of different sizes. If you have a small network at home, it is simplest and most common to use Class C.

TABLE 14.1 **IP Classifications**

IP Class	Range	Number of Networks	Number of Hosts Per Network	Total Hosts Worldwide	Who Uses It?
A	1–126	126	16,777,214	2,113,928,964	Large Corps, ISPs
B	128–191	16384	65534	1,073,709,056	Corps, Universities, ISPs
C	192–223	2,097,152	254	532,676,608	Small companies and organizations
D	224–239	—	—	—	Multi-Cast testing
E	240–255	—	—	—	Future Use

You probably noticed that the number 127 was skipped. That is because this network number is reserved for loopback testing. Technically, it is part of the Class A range, but it cannot be configured as an IP address within the IP Properties window.

You might have also noticed that there are only 254 possible hosts per network in Class C instead of 256. This is because you can never use the first or the last address in the range; the first is actually the network number and the last is the broadcast address!

The total hosts, for all classes combined, is 3,720,314,628. That's just under four billion—and we are getting close to that number of used IP addresses today. Some analysts guess that we will run out of IPv4 addresses by 2012, and this is one of the reasons for IPv6.

> **ExamAlert**
>
> You need to memorize the IP ranges of IPv4 for the Network+ exam. Most important are the Class A, B, and C ranges.

TABLE 14.2 **IP Class Ranges and Their Equivalent Binary Values and Default Subnet Masks**

IP Class	Binary Equivalent	Default Subnet Masks
A: 1-126	00000001-01111110	255.0.0.0 Net.node.node.node
B: 128-191	10000000-10111111	255.255.0.0 Net.net.node.node
C: 192-223	11000000-11011111	255.255.255.0 Net.net.net.node

TABLE 14.2 **Continued**

IP Class	Binary Equivalent	Default Subnet Masks
D: 224-239	11100000-11101111	255.255.255.255 Net.net.net.net
E: 240-255	11110000-11111111	—

Notice in Table 14.2 how the number 255 in a subnet mask coincides with the name *net*. Also, notice the 0 coincides with the name *node*. Net is the network portion of the IP address, whereas node is the host or computer portion of the address.

ExamAlert

Memorize the default subnet masks for Class A, B, and C.

It is also important to know the difference between private and public addresses. A private address is one that is not displayed directly to the Internet and is normally behind a firewall. Typically, these are addresses that a SOHO router would assign automatically to clients. A list of reserved private IP ranges is shown in Table 14.3. Public addresses are addresses that are displayed directly to the Internet; they are addresses that anyone could possibly connect to around the world. Most addresses, besides the private ones listed in Table 14.3, are considered public addresses.

TABLE 14.3 **Private IP Ranges (As Assigned By the IANA)**

IP Class	Assigned Range
Class A	10.0.0.0–10.255.255.255
Class B	172.16.0.0–172.31.255.255
Class C	192.168.0.0–192.168.255.255

ExamAlert

Memorize the private IP ranges for Class A, B, and C.

IPv6

IPv6 is the next generation of IP addressing. Used on the Internet and on some LANs and WANs, it is designed to meet the inadequacies of IPv4. IPv6 is slowly gaining popularity in today's networks, but is still the underdog compared to IPv4. One of the main reasons for the development of IPv6 was the rapidly approaching global shortage of IPv4 addresses. Where IPv4 (a 32-bit system) can have approximately 4 billion total theoretical addresses, IPv6 (128-bit) can have a total of 340 undecillion theoretical addresses; a far greater total. Various limitations of the system will drastically reduce that number, but the remaining result is still orders of magnitude above and beyond the IPv4 system. However, IPv6 is also known for security. IPsec is a fundamental piece of the IPv6 puzzle, and if used properly can offer much more secure communications than IPv4. IPv6 also supports larger packet sizes known as jumbograms. Table 14.4 summarizes some of the differences between IPv4 and IPv6.

TABLE 14.4   **IPv4 Versus IPv6**

IPv4	IPv6
32-bit	128-bit
4 billion addresses	340 undecillion addresses
Less secure	More secure, IPsec is embedded
65,536 byte packet size max	4 billion bytes max

IPv6 addresses are 128-bit hexadecimal numbers that are divided into eight groups of four numbers each. The most commonly used type is the unicast address which defines a single IP address on a single interface (such as a network adapter). Windows auto-configures a unicast address when IPv6 is installed. The address will either start with FE80, FE90, FEA0, or FEB0 (collectively, this range is shown as FE80::/10). Every Windows computer with IPv6 installed also receives a loopback address that is ::1. The IPv6 address ::1 is the equivalent to IPv4's loopback address of 127.0.0.1.

There are three types of IPv6 addresses as shown in Table 14.5

TABLE 14.5 **IPv6 Address Types**

IPv6 Type	Address Range	Description
Unicast	Global Unicast, begins at 2000	Address assigned to one interface Link-Local, begins at FE80::/10 Loopback is ::1
Anycast	Uses the Unicast structure	Address assigned to a group of interfaces. Packets are delivered to the first interface only.
Multicast	FF00::/8	Address assigned to a group of interfaces. Packets are delivered to all interfaces.

Here's an example of an IPv6 address:

```
2001:7120:0000:8001:0000:0000:0000:1F10
```

IPv6 addresses are broken down into three sections: the global routing prefix, in this case 2001:7120:0000, a subnet which is 8001 and the individual interface ID, shown as 0000:0000:0000:1F10.

This is the full address, but you will more commonly see truncated addresses. There are two ways to truncate, or shorten, an IPv6 address. First is to remove leading zeroes. Any group of 4 zeroes can be truncated down to a single zero; basically zero is always zero, so the additional zeroes are not necessary. Also, one consecutive group of zeroes can be truncated as a double colon ::. In the example we have 12 consecutive zeroes that can be truncated all the way down to a double colon. The end result of both of these abbreviations would be:

```
2001:7120:0:8001::1F10
```

IPv6 addresses can be assigned statically as well; this can be done within the Internet Protocol Version 6 Properties window, which can be accessed from Local Area Connection Properties; it is listed right next to IPv4.

The CompTIA A+ objectives only cover the basics about IPv6 address lengths and conventions, and how they compare to IPv4. However, IPv6 is definitely the way of the future, and as such I would recommend that you take some time to investigate it further. My CompTIA Network+ Video Mentor and the CompTIA Network+ Cert Guide go into more depth about IPv6. Those titles are listed at the end of the chapter.

Analyzing and Configuring the Network Adapter

When analyzing the network adapter, we can use several status indicators, some are hardware-based and some are software-oriented.

The first type of indicators are physical; they show up as LED lights on the network adapter itself. Different network adapters have different LED lights, but typically you have a connectivity LED and an activity LED. The connectivity LED tells you if you have a good connection to a router or switch by displaying a solid color. Usually, solid yellow means connectivity at 10Mbps; solid green means connectivity at 100Mbps. (Green is sometimes used for 1000Mbps as well.) However, if the connectivity LED is blinking, then you know there is an intermittent connection that should be troubleshot. The activity LED blinks when data is passing through the network adapter; the color of this LED doesn't make a difference unless it is the only LED available on the network adapter.

The second type of indicators are logical and show up in the operating system. These normally manifest themselves in the System Tray and can be put there by Windows or by the manufacturer of the network adapter, depending on whether you let Windows install the card or if you used the additional software that came with the network adapter. Figure 14.2 displays a Local Area Connection Status icon used by Windows; it appears as two monitors diagonally, one on top of the other.

Local Area
Connection
status icon

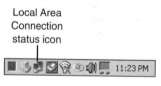

FIGURE 14.2   **Local Area Connection Status icon**

If you were to right-click the status icon and select Status, you would see the status of the adapter, as shown in Figure 14.3

From the default General tab, we can see what our "speed" is, how long we have been connected, and how many bytes have been sent and received. Also, if we click on the Properties button, it brings us to the Local Area Connection properties window—a nice shortcut! If we click on the Support tab, we see our IP configuration and can have Windows attempt to repair the adapter if there were an issue.

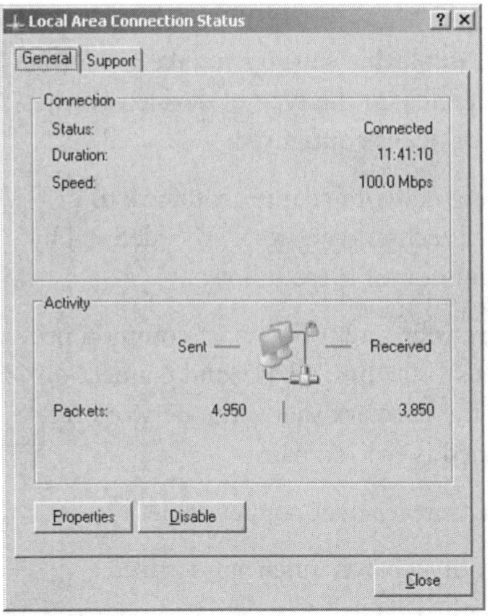
Local Area Connection Status
General
Support
Connection
Status:
Connected
Duration:
11:41:10
Speed:
100.0 Mbps
Activity
Sent
Received
Packets:
4,950
3,850
Properties
Disable
Close

FIGURE 14.3 **Local Area Connection Status window**

How well your network adapter operates depends on a few different factors including bandwidth, latency, and what duplex setting it is configured for.

In computer networking, bandwidth refers to the maximum data throughput of the connection and is measured in bits per second (bps). In Figure 14.3 we saw that our speed was 100Mbps; this would also be known as bandwidth. To get this speed, every link in the networking chain must operate at 100Mbps including the network adapter, cables, and central connecting devices such as SOHO router, switch, or hub. If any one of those links runs at less than 100Mbps, the entire connection would be brought down to 10Mbps.

Latency is the time it takes for sent data packets to be received by a remote computer. An easy way to show this would be to *ping* another computer, for example open the CLI and type **`ping davidlprowse.com`**, the ensuing replies should show a time= amount, probably around 100ms. This tells us that the ping packet took a round-trip time of 100 milliseconds to get from your computer to the destination and back.

There are two duplex settings that a network adapter can be set for: half-duplex and full-duplex. Half-duplex means that your network adapter can send or receive data but not at the same time; full-duplex means that the adapter can do both simultaneously thus doubling the maximum data throughput. This can be configured by navigating to the Device Manager and then going to the properties of the network adapter. Finally, access the Advanced tab and the Speed & Duplex setting (or like name). This is normally set to auto-negotiation, but you can modify the speed or duplexing settings to take full advantage of your network. Of course, this depends on the type of device your network adapter connects to and how that device is configured.

The most common type of network that a network adapter connects to is Ethernet. Ethernet is a family of network technologies for LANs defined by the IEEE 802.3 standards. The most common of these follow:

▶ **802.3u:** Specifies 100Mbps data transfer rates. The most common protocol is 100BASE-TX that indicates 100Mbps, a baseband connection (meaning that every computer on the network shares the network frequency used), and that the cable used is twisted pair.

▶ **802.3ab:** Specifies 1000Mbps data transfer over copper cable.

▶ **802.3z:** Specifies 1000Mbps data transfer over fiber optic cable.

Network Devices

There are several types of network devices that you will run into in the field. Some are designed to offer connectivity to other computers; others are designed to offer connectivity to other networks. Let's discuss a few of these now:

▶ **Hub:** A hub is a central connecting device that enables computers to physically connect to each other. It regenerates and passes on the electrical signals initiated by computers. It is used in Ethernet networks only. Other network technologies have a different name for this device. A hub is actually a simple device; it connects multiple computers together and amplifies and passes on the electrical signal. Internally, the hub actually has only one trunk circuit that all the ports connect to. All bandwidth, for example 10Mbps or 100Mbps within the hub, is shared among all computers connected to the hub. Hubs are also known as multiport repeaters.

▶ **Repeater:** Repeaters enable a network administrator to extend the electrical signal beyond the standard 100 meters if a cable run needs to go farther than that. Generally, they have two ports, one for an incoming cable and one for an outgoing cable. When an electrical signal has traveled 100 meters on a standard network cable (twisted pair), it attenuates or loses power to the point at which it cannot be understood at the receiving end.

▶ **Switch:** Ethernet Switching was developed in 1996 and quickly took hold as the preferred method of networking. A switch, like a hub, is a central connecting device that all computers connect to, and like a hub it regenerates the signal, but that's where the similarity ends. A switch takes the signal and sends it to the correct computer instead of broadcasting it out to every port. This can effectively make every port an individual entity, and it increases data throughput exponentially. Switches employ a matrix of copper wiring instead of the standard trunk circuit and intelligence to pass information to the correct port. This means that each computer has its own bandwidth, for example 10Mbps or 100Mbps.

▶ **Router:** A router is used to connect two or more networks together to form an internetwork. They are used in LANs and WANs and on the Internet. This device routes data from one location to another, usually by way of IP address and IP network numbers. Routers are intelligent and even have their own text-based OS known as an IOS (Internetwork Operating System).

▶ **Wireless Access Point (WAP):** A WAP enables data communications over the air if your computer is equipped with a wireless networking adapter. They transmit their data over radio waves either on the 2.4GHz or 5GHz frequencies. This brings mobility to a new level. Some WAPs also have a router built in, such as the D-Link Router we use in this chapter. This enables wireless computers to not only communicate with each other but to access the Internet as well! Many of these devices also come equipped with a firewall. At this point they are referred to as multifunction network devices, SOHO routers, or simply routers.

▶ **Proxies:** A proxy server is a computer or device that is between the network client computers and the Internet. Proxies cache information for the clients to increase performance and to conserve Internet connection bandwidth. The most common type is the HTTP proxy. This stores website information requested by a client so that subsequent clients can get that same information much quicker without having to connect to the actual website. A proxy server will usually be on the same network as the client computer. The client computer can be configured to utilize the proxy server by opening Internet Explorer, clicking Tools, Internet Options, selecting the Connections tab, and clicking the LAN settings button. From here the user needs to type in the IP address of the proxy server.

Types of Networks

There are several network types that you need to be cognizant of for the exam including:

▶ Local area network (LAN)

▶ Wide area network (WAN)

▶ Workgroup

▶ Domain

▶ Virtual private network (VPN)

A local area network (or LAN) is a group of computers in a small geographic area, for example in one room, a house, or in one building. If you have more than one computer in your home that share an Internet connection, they would be considered a LAN.

A wide area network (or WAN) is usually two or more LANs connected together. This covers a larger geographic area and requires the services of a telecommunications provider or ISP.

Workgroups and domains are more logical groupings of computers. A workgroup (sometimes also referred to as peer-to-peer) is usually a small group of computers, often ten or less, which share the same network name. No one computer controls the network, and all systems are considered equal. A domain builds on this by having one or more computers that are in control of the network, enabling for more computers, and centralized administration. Domains also get a name and are sometimes also referred to as client/server networks. Figure 14.4 shows the Computer Name Changes window accessible from the System Properties window, in which we can change the name of the workgroup that we are a member of, join new workgroups, or join domains.

Virtual private networks (VPNs) were developed so that telecommuters, salespeople, and others could connect to the office from a remote location. If set up properly, the remote logon connection is seamless and appears as if you are actually at the LAN in the office. You log on just as you would if you were at your desk at headquarters. VPNs give the user access to all the resources that they get when logging on locally. VPNs are superior to older dial-up connections because they take advantage of the more powerful infrastructure of the Internet and faster connections such as cable, DSL, and so on. A VPN connection can be identified by an additional network connection in the System Tray, as an additional network connection when using the ipconfig command, or as a pop-up window that comes up during the logon process, for example the kind used by Cisco VPN software.

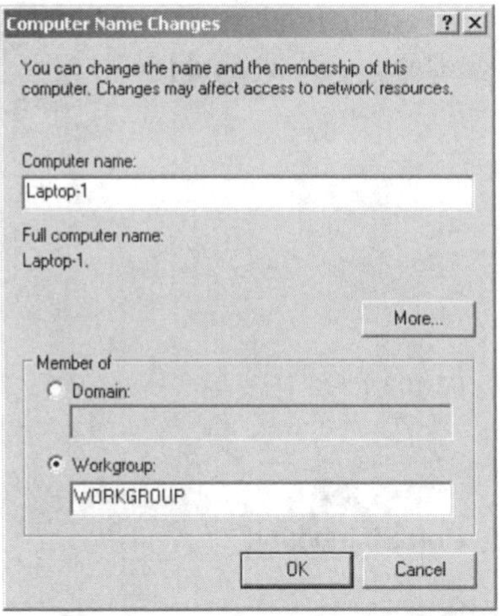

FIGURE 14.4   Windows XP Computer Name Changes window

Common TCP/IP Protocols and Their Ports

For two computers to communicate, they must both use the same protocol.

For an application to send or receive data, it must use a particular protocol designed for that application and open up a port on the network adapter to make a connection to another computer. For example, let's say you want to visit www.google.com. You would open up a browser and type in `http://www.google.com`. The protocol used is HTTP, short for Hypertext Transfer Protocol. That is the protocol that makes the connection to the web server: google.com. The HTTP protocol selects an unused port on your computer (known as an outbound port) to send and receive data to and from google.com. On the other end, google.com's web server has a specific port open at all times ready to accept sessions. In most cases the web server's port is 80, which corresponds to the HTTP protocol. This is known as an inbound port. Figure 14.5 shows this.

The local computer on the bottom-left part of Figure 14.5 has been given the IP address 172.30.250.3, a Class B private address. It uses port 3266 to go out to the Internet and start a session with google.com. For security purposes this is a dynamically assigned port and will be different every time you connect to another web server, but it will normally be somewhere in the thousands. The session is accepted by google.com's web server, using the public IP address 66.102.1.100, inbound port 80. Conversely, if you want to run your own web server at home and sell widgets and such, that web server would need to have port 80 open to the public at all times. If it were ever closed, you would lose sales! People's computers that connected to your web server would use dynamically assigned ports.

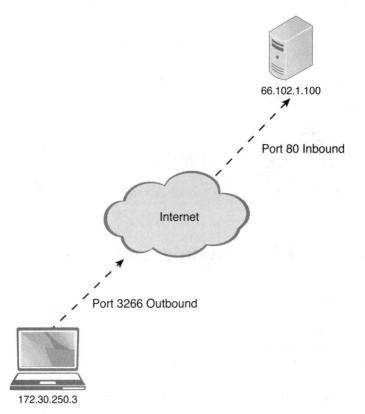

FIGURE 14.5 **HTTP in action**

There are 65536 ports in total, numbered between 0 and 65535, and almost as many protocols! Don't worry; you need to know only a few for the exam, which are listed in Table 14.6.

TABLE 14.6 **Common Protocols and Their Ports**

Protocol	Port Used
FTP	21
SSH	22
TELNET	23
SMTP	25
HTTP	80

TABLE 14.6   **Continued**

Protocol	Port Used
POP3	110
HTTPS	443

(Exam**Alert**)

Know these seven common protocols and their corresponding ports for the exam!

The ports mentioned in Table 14.6 are the inbound ports used by the computer that runs the service:

▶ **FTP:** the File Transfer Protocol allows computers to transfer files back and forth. When you connect to a FTP server, that FTP server will have port 21 open. Some type of FTP client software is necessary to connect to the FTP server, this could be done in the command-line within the FTP shell, or by using a GUI-based application like FileZilla.

▶ **SSH:** Secure Shell enables data to be exchanged between computers on a secured channel. This protocol offers a more secure replacement to FTP and TELNET. The Secure Shell server housing the data you want to access would have port 22 open.

▶ **TELNET:** Short for **Tel**ecommunication **net**work provides remote access to other hosts within the CLI. It uses port 23 but is an insecure and somewhat deprecated protocol. However, because some companies still use it to access routers and other hosts, you might see a question about it on the exam.

▶ **SMTP:** Simple Mail Transfer Protocol sends email. When you send email from home, it goes to an SMTP server (which has inbound port 25 open) at your ISP and is then sent off to its destination. A good way to remember this is by using the mnemonic device *Send Mail To People.*

▶ **HTTP:** Hypertext Transfer Protocol transfers web pages and other web-based material from a web server to your web browser. It is normally done in a compressed format but not in a secured format. Web servers have port 80 open by default.

▶ **POP3:** Post Office Protocol Version 3 is used by email clients to retrieve incoming email from a mail server. The POP3 mail server uses port 110.

▶ **HTTPS:** Hypertext Transfer Protocol Secure sends and receives information like HTTP but includes the Transport Layer Security protocol (successor of the Secure Sockers Layer [SSL] protocol) to encrypt the information, most commonly when making purchases/payments online or when logging in to a confidential website. The HTTPS server has port 443 open.

Cram Quiz

Answer these questions. The answers follow the last question. If you cannot answer these questions correctly, consider reading this section again until you can.

1. Which protocol uses port 22?

   ○ **A.** FTP

   ○ **B.** TELNET

   ○ **C.** SSH

   ○ **D.** HTTP

2. Which of these addresses needs to be configured to enable a computer access to the Internet or to other networks?

   ○ **A.** Subnet mask

   ○ **B.** Gateway address

   ○ **C.** DNS address

   ○ **D.** MAC address

3. Which LED blinks when data is passed through the network adapter?

   ○ **A.** Activity

   ○ **B.** Connectivity

   ○ **C.** Full-duplex

   ○ **D.** Amber

4. The Computer Name Changes window enables you to add your computer to these two types of networks. (Select two.)

   ○ **A.** Domains

   ○ **B.** VPNs

   ○ **C.** LANs

   ○ **D.** Workgroups

5. The IP address 128.0.0.1 would be part of what IPv4 class?

   ○ **A.** Class A

   ○ **B.** Class B

   ○ **C.** Class C

   ○ **D.** Class D

Cram Quiz Answers

1. **C.** SSH uses port 22, FTP uses port 21, TELNET uses port 23, and HTTP uses port 80.

2. **B.** The gateway address must be configured to enable a computer access to the Internet through the gateway device. By default, the subnet mask defines the IP address's network and host portions. The DNS server takes care of name resolution, and the MAC address is the address that is burned into the network adapter; it is configured at the manufacturer.

3. **A.** The activity LED blinks when data is passed through the network adapter. The connectivity LED should remain solid.

4. **A and D.** This window enables you to set whether the computer connects to a workgroup or domain.

5. **B.** The IP address 128.0.0.1 is part of the Class B range that encompasses 128-191.

Network Cabling and Connectors

The most common type of cable used in today's networks is twisted pair. It is referred to as twisted pair because the copper wires inside of the cable are twisted together into pairs throughout the entire length of the cable. Regularly, admins use UTP cable, short for unshielded twisted pair. Today, the most frequently used twisted pair types are Category 5, 5e, and 6. Table 14.7 shows the various categories of twisted pair and the data transfer rates they can support.

TABLE 14.7 **UTP Categories and Speeds**

Category UTP	Maximum Data Transfer Rate
Category 3	10 Mbps
Category 5	100 Mbps
Category 5e	Rated for 100 Mbps and gigabit networks
Category 6	Rated for 100 Mbps and gigabit networks

> Note
>
> Depending on the manufacturer of Category 5e and Category 6, and the type of Category 6, maximum data throughput amounts vary.

Network data transfer rates (also known as speed or bandwidth) are normally measured in bits because networks normally transfer data serially, or one bit at a time. 100Mbps is 100 megabits per second. 1Gbps is equal to 1 gigabit per second (known as a gigabit network).

Most wiring standards are based on the original BOGB standard, which specifies that wire pair colors go in this order: blue, orange, green, brown. The 568A and B standards are based on this. Generally speaking, the most common standard you see is the 568B standard. Any physical cabling equipment used in the network must comply with this standard. This includes cables, patch panels, jacks, and even connectors! The connector used with twisted pair networks is known colloquially as the RJ45 (more specifically the 8P8C connector). RJ45 plugs connect to each end of the cable, and these connect to RJ45 sockets within network adapters and on hubs/switches.

As you can see in Figure 14.6, RJ45 plugs look a lot like the plugs that connect your telephone (known as RJ11). However, the RJ45 plug is larger and contains eight wires whereas the RJ11 plug can hold only a maximum of six.

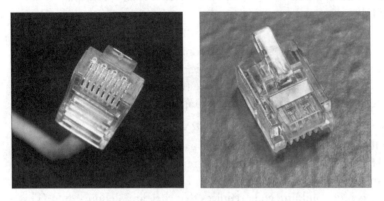

RJ45   RJ11

FIGURE 14.6   **RJ45 and RJ11 plugs**

You can use several tools to test the various categories of twisted pair cable. They include:

- **Patch testers:** These are designed to test patch cables. Both RJ45 ends are connected to the patch tester to test each individual wire (pin). Pressing a button illuminates eight LED lights that correspond to the eight pins in the cable. In a standard straight-through patch cable, both ends should be wired in the same order. Straight-through patch cables connect computers directly to hubs or switches and are the more common type of patch cable. Another type of cable, the crossover cable connects computers directly to each other; these require a different wiring scheme on one end of the cable, essentially 568B on one end, and 568A on the other. The problem with a patch tester is that you need both ends of the cable in one location, so it cannot test longer cable runs.

- **Continuity testers:** These test those longer cable runs. They check for continuity on each pin to make sure that each end is wired properly. These testers usually consist of a handheld device that connects to one end of a network connection that indicates test results, and terminators that connect to the other end of the cable, which send the signal back to the tester. Some continuity testers can also act as testing devices for phone lines and more.

▶ **Time-domain reflectometers (TDR):** These measuring instruments can locate faults in a cable or discontinuities in a connector. They transmit a short pulse across the cable. If the cable is installed properly, no signal will be reflected back to the TDR, but if there are any impedance discontinuities, an error signal will be reflected back and displayed on the TDR.

UTP has a few disadvantages; it can be run only 100 meters before signal attenuation, it's outer jacket is made of plastic, and it has no shielding, making it susceptible to electromagnetic interference (EMI) and susceptible to unauthorized network access in the form of wire tapping.

Because the UTP cable jacket is made of PVCs (plastics) and can be harmful to humans if they catch on fire, most municipalities require that plenum-rated cable be installed in any area that cannot be reached by a sprinkler system. A plenum is an enclosed space used for airflow. For example, if cables are run above a drop ceiling, building code requires that they are plenum-rated: This means that the cable has a special Teflon coating or is a special low-smoke variant of twisted pair, reducing the amount of PVCs that are released into the air in the case of fire.

ExamAlert

To meet fire code, use plenum-rated cable above drop ceilings and anywhere else necessary!

Because UTP is susceptible to EMI, a variant was developed known as STP or shielded twisted pair. This includes metal shielding over each pair of wires, reducing external EMI and the possibility of unauthorized network access. A couple of disadvantages of STP include higher cost of product and installation, and the fact that the shielding needs to be grounded to work effectively.

When dealing with EMI, a better option is to use fiber optic cable. Because fiber optic cables transmit data by way of light instead of electricity, they can send signals much further than copper wires, and EMI doesn't even play into the equation. Due to this, fiber optic cable is the most secure type of cable.

You might encounter single mode and multimode fiber; for the most part single-mode fiber is used over longer distances, but both types are capable of supporting 1000Mbps and 10Gbps networks, and can be run farther than twisted pair cable. A couple types of connectors used with fiber include ST and SC, as shown in Figure 14.7. Some of the newer types of connectors include LC and MTP.

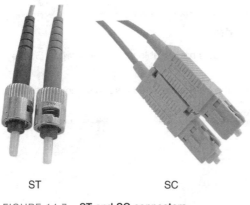

ST   SC

FIGURE 14.7   **ST and SC connectors**

Coaxial cable is another way to transfer data over a network. This cable has a single conductor surrounded by insulating material, which is then surrounded by a copper screen, and finally an outer plastic sheath. Some networking technologies still use coaxial cable; for example, cable Internet connections use coaxial cable (known as quad shield coaxial cable) with RG-6 connectors (previously RG-59). But older coaxial cabled LANs that used RG-58 connectors are a thing of the past, and it is extremely unlikely that you will see a LAN using coaxial cable.

Cram Quiz

Answer these questions. The answers follow the last question. If you cannot answer these questions correctly, consider reading this section again until you can.

1. Which of the following would be suitable for 100Mbps networks? (Select all that apply.)

   ○ **A.** Category 3

   ○ **B.** Category 5

   ○ **C.** Category 5e

   ○ **D.** Category 6

2. Which type of cable would you use if you were concerned about EMI?

   ○ **A.** Plenum-rated

   ○ **B.** UTP

   ○ **C.** STP

   ○ **D.** Coaxial

Exam Cram Answers

1. **B, C,** and **D.** The only cable listed that is not suitable would be category 3; it is only suitable for 10Mbps networks.

2. **C.** STP or shielded twisted pair is the only cable listed here that can reduce electromagnetic interference.

Troubleshooting Network Connectivity

Okay, now that we've shown some of the basics of networking, let's get into a little bit of network troubleshooting. To troubleshoot client connectivity properly, we need to know a little bit more about command-line interface (CLI) tools and some of the applications available to us. Let's begin with CLI tools.

Command-Line Interface Tools

There are many command-line tools that we can use in Windows to help us troubleshoot situations; in this section we delve into six of them. To open the command-line interface (known as the Command Prompt in Windows), do one of the following:

▶ Click Start > All Programs > Accessories > Command Prompt.

▶ Open the Run prompt (by pressing Windows +R) and type **cmd**.

▶ (Vista only) Click Start and type `Command Prompt` within the search field; then double-click the Command Prompt shortcut from the list that appears.

Ipconfig

Internet protocol configuration or ipconfig displays current TCP/IP network configuration values. This is one of the first tools you should use when troubleshooting network connectivity. If you type **ipconfig** you get results similar to the following:

```
Windows IP Configuration
Ethernet adapter Local Area Connection:
        Connection-specific DNS Suffix  . :
        IP Address. . . . . . . . . . . : 192.168.0.100
        Subnet Mask . . . . . . . . . . : 255.255.255.0
        Default Gateway . . . . . . . . : 192.168.0.1
```

Ipconfig combined with the /all switch shows more information including the DNS server address and MAC address, which is the hexadecimal address that is burned into the ROM of the network adapter.

ExamAlert

To view additional IP configuration information such as DNS servers and MAC addresses, use the `ipconfig/all` command.

This command can offer a lot of information about a problem. For example, if a person cannot connect to any Internet resources, it could be because the gateway address is improperly configured. Remember that the gateway address must be on the same network number as the IP address of the client computer. If a user can't connect to any websites, but they can download email, it could be that the DNS server address is incorrectly configured. Ipconfig also tells you whether the client computer's IP address is obtained from a DHCP server, or assigned via APIPA, and whether it is a private or public address.

Note

Linux operating systems use a similar command called `ifconfig`. However, in Linux computers you can also modify the IP address with this command.

Ping

Ping tests whether another host is available over the network. It's the easy way to see if another host is "alive." Let's say your gateway's IP address was 192.168.0.1. To ping that computer you would type **ping 192.168.0.1**, as an example and hopefully get the following output:

```
Pinging 192.168.0.1: with 32 bytes of data:
Reply from 192.168.0.1: bytes=32 time<1ms TTL=64
Reply from 192.168.0.1: bytes=32 time<1ms TTL=64
Reply from 192.168.0.1: bytes=32 time<1ms TTL=64
Reply from 192.168.0.1: bytes=32 time<1ms TTL=64
Ping statistics for 192.168.0.1:
    Packets: Sent = 4, Received = 4, Lost = 0 (0% loss),
Approximate round trip times in milli-seconds:
    Minimum = 0ms, Maximum = 0ms, Average = 0ms
```

Notice the replies indicate that the host is alive.

Any other message would indicate a problem, for example the Request Timed Out or Destination Host Unreachable messages would require further troubleshooting. Keep in mind that if it's the local computer that is configured incorrectly, you might not be able to ping anything! Also watch for the amount of time the ping took to reply back. A longer latency time could indicate network congestion.

You can also use ping to test whether a computer has TCP/IP installed properly, even if it isn't wired to the network! To do this use the **ping 127.0.0.1** command. This IP address is known as the loopback address, is used for testing, and is available on every host. It differs from the IP addresses we talked about previously (for example 192.168.0.100) in that it works internally. This command essentially enables you to ping yourself, meaning you can test the local computer's network connection without a valid IP configuration and without a physical connection to the network. Replies are simulated within local computer; they prove if the network adapter and TCP/IP have been installed properly. However, it does not prove if TCP/IP has been *configured* properly.

Tracert

Tracert, short for traceroute, builds on ping in that it send packets to destinations beyond the local computer's network. It pings each router along the way between you and the final destination. An example of tracert output follows:

```
Tracing route to davidlprowse.com [216.97.236.245]
over a maximum of 30 hops:
  1     6 ms     5 ms     5 ms  bdl1.eas-ubr16.atw-
eas.pa.cable.rcn.net [10.21.80.1]
  2    10 ms     9 ms     9 ms  vl4.aggr1.phdl.pa.rcn.net
[208.59.252.1]
  3    10 ms     9 ms    18 ms  ge3-0.core2.phdl.pa.rcn.net
[207.172.15.35]
  4    11 ms    13 ms    12 ms  pos6-0.core3.nyw.ny.rcn.net
[207.172.19.11]
  5   133 ms   203 ms   133 ms  ge6-1.core4.nyw.ny.rcn.net
[207.172.19.114]
  6    13 ms    11 ms    12 ms  tge2-1.border1.nyw.ny.rcn.net
[207.172.19.109]
  7    11 ms    11 ms    11 ms  207.172.9.74
  8    12 ms    11 ms    14 ms  te2-4.ccr01.jfk02.atlas.cogentco.com
[154.54.6.49]
  9    12 ms    11 ms    11 ms  te9-1.ccr04.jfk02.atlas.cogentco.com
[154.54.25.137]
 10    17 ms    18 ms    25 ms  te3-1.ccr02.dca01.atlas.cogentco.com
[66.28.4.82]
 11    59 ms    60 ms    60 ms  te7-3.ccr02.iah01.atlas.cogentco.com
[66.28.4.90]
 12    55 ms    53 ms    54 ms  te3-1.ccr01.sat01.atlas.cogentco.com
[154.54.27.114]
 13    80 ms    80 ms    81 ms  te4-1.ccr01.elp01.atlas.cogentco.com
[154.54.27.141]
```

```
14   211 ms    225 ms    208 ms  te4-1.ccr01.phx02.atlas.cogentco.com
[154.54.27.78]
15   155 ms    237 ms    243 ms  te3-1.ccr01.san01.atlas.cogentco.com
[154.54.27.109]
16    82 ms     82 ms     82 ms  vl3806.na21.b006590-
1.san01.atlas.cogentco.com [66.28.67.74]
17    82 ms     82 ms     82 ms  38.112.242.138
18    86 ms     86 ms     86 ms  unused-240-180-214.ixpres.com
[216.240.180.214]
19    98 ms     96 ms     97 ms  lwdc.dbo2.gi9-4.host1.23680.
americanis.net [38.96.20.2]
20    97 ms     96 ms     96 ms  zosma.lunarpages.com [216.97.236.245]
Trace complete.
```

Note that there are three pings per line item measured in milliseconds (ms). Also note that every line item contains a router name and IP address. It starts by sailing through the various routers in our ISP, RCN.net. It ends at a server named zosma.lunarpages.com that hosts www.davidlprowse.com (as of the writing of this book). If you saw any asterisks in the place of the millisecond amounts, you might question whether the router is functioning properly. If the tracert stops altogether before saying Trace Complete, you would want to check your network documentation to find out which router it stopped at, and/or make sure that the router is troubleshot by the appropriate personnel.

Netstat

Moving on to another concept, netstat shows the network statistics for the local computer. The default command displays sessions to remote computers. In the following example, I connected to www.google.com and ran the netstat command. Output follows:

```
Active Connections
   Proto  Local Address        Foreign Address        State
   TCP    laptop-musicxpc:1395 8.15.228.165:http      ESTABLISHED
   TCP    laptop-musicxpc:1396 he-in-f101.google.com:http
ESTABLISHED
```

This output shows that there are two established TCP sessions (they're actually both to the same website) to google.com. In the local address column we see our computer called laptop-musicxpc and the outbound ports it uses to access the website, 1395 and 1396. In the foreign address column, we see an IP address and the protocol used (http) and in the second session, a hostname followed by the protocol (again http). The protocol used by google.com corresponds to port 80. This command can tell us a lot about our sessions. For example, if a session times out, or if it closes completely; this shows up in the State column. To see this information numerically, try using the –n switch after the netstat command. Netstat has a lot of other options; to view these type **netstat /?**.

Nslookup

Nslookup queries DNS servers to discover DNS details including the IP address of hosts. For example, if I want to find the IP address of davidlprowse.com, I would type **nslookup davidlprowse.com**. The resulting output should look something like this:

```
Non-authoritative answer:
Name:    davidlprowse.com
Address:  216.97.236.245
```

So from the output, we now know the IP address that corresponds to the domain name davidlprowse.com. Nslookup means name server lookup and can aid in finding DNS servers and DNS records in a domain as well. If the command nslookup is typed by itself, it brings the user into the nslookup shell. From here several commands can be utilized; to find out more about these type **?**. To exit the nslookup shell type **exit**, press Ctrl+C, or press Ctrl+Break.

Net

The **net** command is actually a collection of commands. In Chapter 13, "Printers," we used the **net stop** command to stop the print spooler. In networking you might use the **net view** command to see what computers are currently available on the network or the **net send** command to send messages to other users via the command line. For the exam you should know the types of **net** commands that enable you to view or create mapped network drives. To view any currently mapped network drives, simply type **net use**. To create a mapped network drive, use the following syntax:

```
net use x: \\computername\sharename
```

X: is the drive letter, in this case X is a variable; you can use whatever drive letter you want if it's available. Computername is the name of the remote host you want to connect to, and sharename is the share that was created on that remote host.

There is a network share on another computer on my network called C$. The following syntax shows the command to connect to it and the resulting output:

```
net use f: \\laptop-musicxpc\c$
The command completed successfully.
```

In this example, we used F: as our drive letter; the computer we connected to is called laptop-musicxpc and the share is C$ (the default hidden share). For more information on the net command, type **net /?**. For more information on the **net use** command type **net use /?**.

Troubleshooting with Applications

We can use applications to help us troubleshoot client connectivity as well. In this section, we focus on a mail application and the Windows Firewall.

Sometimes users complain that they can connect to the Internet but they can't access their email. This can be because they connect to POP3 and SMTP mail servers and their email configuration is incorrect. Figure 14.8 shows the E-mail Accounts window of Outlook.

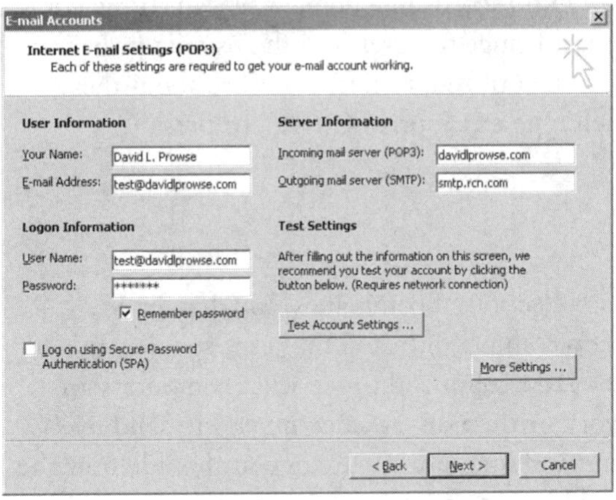

FIGURE 14.8   Outlook E-mail Accounts window

This can be accessed in Outlook by going to Tools > E-mail Accounts, selecting View or change existing email accounts, and selecting the appropriate one to modify. Outlook Express works in much the same way, but the navigation might be slightly different. Notice the incoming mail server (POP3) and the Outgoing mail server (SMTP). If these server names are not exact, the client cannot access her mail. Or let's say that the SMTP server is configured properly but the POP3 server is not. Then the user could send messages but not receive them. The same goes for IMAP4 servers (Internet Message Access Protocol 4); be sure that the server name is configured correctly. IMAP4 is another protocol used for incoming mail, less common than POP3, but it enables a user to store mail folders on the email server and access those folders from other computers. Of course the username and password need to be exact as well, but improperly configured mail servers are a common reason why email fails!

The Windows Firewall is meant to protect client computers from malicious attacks and intrusions, but sometimes it can be the culprit when it comes to certain applications failing. When you turn on the firewall, the default setting is to shield all inbound ports (effectively closing them). This means that certain applications that need to communicate with a remote host might not work properly. Or if the client computer wanted to host some services such as FTP or a web server, the firewall would block them. That's where exceptions come in. You can still use the firewall, but you can specify applications that are exceptions to the rule. You can also do this by port number, so for example, if I want to run an FTP server, I can add port 21 as an exception. Figure 14.9 shows an example of exceptions.

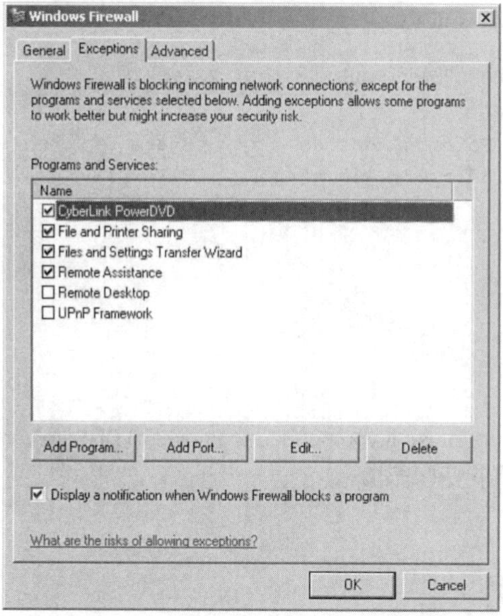

FIGURE 14.9   Windows Firewall exceptions

In this example, we have four applications that are not blocked from incoming connections. This way, these applications can communicate with the Internet and the Internet can communicate with them, but we aren't sacrificing the entire security of the system. All other incoming connections will be blocked. You can find more information on firewalls in Chapter 15, "Security."

Cram Quiz

Answer these questions. The answers follow the last question. If you cannot answer these questions correctly, consider reading this section again until you can.

1. Which command tests whether another computer is alive on the local area network?

   ○ A. AGP
   ○ B. Nslookup
   ○ C. Netstat
   ○ D. Ping

2. Which would be the best command to test for a router that is in another state?

   ○ A. Ipconfig
   ○ B. Tracert
   ○ C. Nbtstat
   ○ D. SSH

3. Which command would display the following output?

```
Active Connections
  Proto   Local Address          Foreign Address         State
  TCP     laptop-musicxpc:1395   8.15.228.165:http       ESTABLISHED
```

   ○ A. Ping
   ○ B. Ipconfig
   ○ C. Nbtstat
   ○ D. Netstat

4. Which would be the best command to use if you needed to know the DNS server address that was configured on a computer?

   ○ A. Ipconfig
   ○ B. Ping
   ○ C. Ipconfig/all
   ○ D. Netstat -n

5. A user can receive mail, but they can't send it. Which of the following servers is most likely configured incorrectly?

   ○ A. SMTP
   ○ B. POP3
   ○ C. FTP
   ○ D. HTTP

Cram Quiz Answers

1. **D.** Ping tests whether another host on the network is available.

2. **B.** Tracert can attempt to connect to hosts that are outside of the local area network such as a router in another state. The **tracert** command will test each router along the way between the local computer and the destination computer.

3. **D.** **Netstat** shows sessions like the ones displayed here.

4. **C.** **Ipconfig /all** shows DNS server addresses; remember that the default ipconfig will not; it will show only the configured IP address, subnet mask, and gateway address.

5. **A.** The client computer uses the SMTP server to send mail; if they can't send, check the SMTP settings. The POP3 server retrieves mail. FTP servers transfer files, and HTTP servers are used for World Wide Web pages.

Installing and Configuring a SOHO Network

Small office home office (SOHO) networks are extremely common. As such, you should know how to install and configure them for the A+ exams. In this chapter, we cover wireless technologies and multifunction network devices. But first, we need to decide which type of Internet connection to use. This depends on what is available to us, but they include dial-up and broadband options such as Digital Subscriber Line (DSL), cable, satellite, and Integrated Services Digital Network (ISDN) and cellular.

Internet and Wireless Connectivity Options

There are a lot of different options for connecting to the Internet including the venerable dial-up, DSL, cable Internet, and more. The type of Internet connection dictates download speeds to the clients on a SOHO network. Next, a decision should be made about whether to connect client computers to the network in a wired fashion or as wireless. Another factor in the decision-making process will be whether any Bluetooth-enabled devices need to access the network.

Dial-Up

Strange as it might seem, dial-up Internet is still used by millions, and in some areas of the United States, it is the only Internet connectivity available. Dial-up connections are inexpensive but at the cost of slow data throughput and dropped connections. To connect to a dial-up service, a user needs four things: a working phone line, an account with an ISP, a modem to dial-up to the ISP's networks, and some type of software to control the dial-up connection, for example dial-up networking. The modem serves to modulate and demodulate signals that travel between the computer and the phone line. It sends and receives data in a serial fashion, meaning one bit at a time. It is now possible to purchase devices that enable multiple computers to share the dial-up modem. The modem can be an internal adapter card or an external device that connects to a serial port. The difference is that the internal card incorporates a universal asynchronous receiver transmitter (UART) that converts the serial information coming in from the phone line into parallel data to be sent to the processor. The external modem relies on the UART that is built into the serial port of the computer. Dial-up utilizes the plain old telephone service/public switched telephone network (POTS/PSTN).

DSL

Digital subscriber line (DSL) builds on dial-up by providing full digital data transmissions over phone lines but at high speeds. DSL modems connect to the phone line and to the PC's network adapter or to a SOHO router enabling sharing among multiple computers. One of the benefits of DSL is that you can talk on the phone line and transmit data at the same time. There are several derivatives of DSL, but for the exam you need only know of two:

▸ **ADSL (Asymmetrical Digital Subscriber Line):** ADSL can run on your home telephone line so that you can talk on the phone and access the Internet at the same time. Users are generally limited to approximately 500Kbps upload and 1Mbps download speed, although there can be lags and spikes in these numbers. Upload speed is always slower than download speed. It is usually not as fast as cable Internet.

▸ **SDSL (Symmetrical Digital Subscriber Line):** SDSL is installed (usually to companies) as a separate line and is more expensive. SDSL data transfer rates can be purchased at 384K, 768K, 1.1M, and 1.5M. The upload and download speed are the same, or symmetrical unlike ADSL.

Cable Internet

Broadband cable, used for cable Internet and cable TV, offers higher speeds than DSL and can usually get up to an average of 5Mbps to 7Mbps, although the serial connection has the theoretical capability to go to 18Mbps. One website, DSLreports.com, commonly shows people connecting with cable at 10Mbps. Like most Internet connectivity options, cable Internet is shared by the customer base. The more users that are on the Internet, the slower it becomes for everyone.

Satellite

Satellite connectivity uses a parabolic antenna (satellite dish) to connect via line of sight to a satellite; it is used in places in which standard landline Internet access is not available. The satellite is in geosynchronous orbit, at 22,000 miles (35,406 Km) above the Earth. The "dish" connects to coax cable that runs to a switching/channeling device for your computers. Today's satellite connections offer speeds close to traditional broadband access. One of the issues with satellite is electrical and natural interference. Another problem is latency. Due to the distance (44,000 miles total) of the data transfer, there can be a delay of .5 seconds to 5 seconds.

ISDN

Integrated Services Digital Network (ISDN) is a digital technology developed to combat the limitations of PSTN. Users can send data, talk on the phone, fax, all from one line. It is broken down into two types of services:

- ▶ **BRI: Basic Rate ISDN:** 128Kbps. Two equal B channels at 64Kbps each for data and one 16Kbps D channel for timing.

- ▶ **PRI: Primary Rate ISDN:** 1.536Mbps, runs on a T-1 circuit; 23 equal 64Kbps B channels for data and one 64Kbps D channel for timing.

Many companies still use ISDN for video conferencing or as a fault-tolerant secondary Internet access connection. Data commuters use this if DSL or cable is not available.

Cellular

Cellular has become more popular of late as a means to access the Internet from mobile devices. The term *cellular* has grown to encompass several different technologies such as GSM, CDMA, GPRS, EDGE, and more. Although it's not necessary to know these technologies for the exam, you might want to know 3G and 4G because they are all the rage right now.

3G (short for third-generation telecommunications) has been in use for several years. Many new phones and PDAs are equipped to connect to 3G networks. The main purpose is to enable these mobile devices to send data at higher speeds. However, these speeds vary depending on the vendor, the country you are in, and whether you move while you send data. For stationary transmissions, possible data rates range from 2Mbps to 14Mbps; for moving transmissions, data rates fall below 1Mbps. Of course, network congestion also has a hand in 3G data rates. Manufacturers suggest that a user can expect 384Kbps while stationary or walking and less than that in a moving car. There are millions of 3G users; 3G devices are available for laptops in the form of PC Cards and embedded within PDAs. 3G is made out to be the best thing since sliced bread by ISPs and telecommunications companies, but it is questionable whether it has really lived up to expectations.

4G (short for fourth generation), currently in development, is expected to completely replace current networks and create a much faster, more secure IP solution. This is where the real increases in data rates are expected; from 100Mbps in a moving vehicle to 1Gbps when stationary. One of the goals is to have a data rate of 100Mbps between any two points in the world at any time. 4G devices will be available for laptops, PDAs, and cell phones the same way that 3G devices are currently available.

802.11 Wireless

Up until now, we have been talking about Internet connectivity. Now I'd like to move over to wireless options for the LAN. The 802.11x series of protocols defines the various speeds, frequencies, and protocols used to transmit data over radiowaves in small geographic areas using unlicensed spectrums.

There are four different 802.11 derivatives you need to know for the exam: 802.11a, 802.11b, 802.11g, and 802.11n. Table 14.8 shows these technologies and the characteristics that differentiate them.

TABLE 14.8   **802.11x Standards**

802.11 Version	Maximum Data Rate	Frequency	Modulation Protocol Used
802.11a	54Mbps	5 GHz	OFDM
802.11b	11Mbps	2.4GHz	DSSS
802.11g	54Mbps	2.4GHz	OFDM
802.11n	600Mbps 300Mbps is typical	5 and/or 2.4GHz	OFDM

ExamAlert

Know the data rates and frequency used for each of the 802.11 versions!

Note

OFDM is orthogonal frequency-division multiplexing, a common modulation method. DSSS is direct-sequence spread spectrum, a less-used modulation technique.

The key with wireless is to make sure that your access point (AP) and wireless network adapters are compatible.

Bluetooth

This is a short-range radio technology aimed at simplifying communications and synchronization among network devices. Bluetooth is divided into three classes. Class I has a maximum transmission range of 100 meters, Class II (the most common) has a range of 10 meters, and Class III is short range and hardly used at 1 meter. An example of Bluetooth technologies would be the common Motorola Bluetooth wireless headsets. These and other Bluetooth devices need to be *paired* either with your cellular phone or your PC to transmit data. Bluetooth data transfer rates are broken down into two versions, as shown in Table 14.9.

TABLE 14.9 **Bluetooth Versions**

Version	Maximum Data Rate
Version 1	721Kbps
Version 2	2.1Mbps

> **Note**
>
> Version 3 was just adopted in early 2009, offering higher data rates, low energy, and more security but is not covered in the 2009 A+ exams.

Setting Up a SOHO Router and Wireless Network Adapters

Okay! Now that we have Internet connectivity and wireless out of the way, let's talk about the setup and configuration of our SOHO router. These devices have been called a plethora of different names, from the nice-router, switch, firewall, access point, and multifunction network device to the not-so-nice, which we can't mention here! Let's put it this way, you will troubleshoot SOHO routers, but much of the troubleshooting will be due to user error. Each manufacturer has their own interface, and some manufacturers are not the best with technical support or in the writing of their manual. In this section, I refer to a D-Link DIR655 that has served me well and is one of the easier devices to understand.

Most SOHO routers are set up to be plug-and-play, meaning that computers can be plugged in and they can communicate with each other and access the Internet. But a word of caution, you don't want to use the default settings that the manufacturer gives you; they are quite insecure. So the first thing we want to do is to log in to the router so that we can make some changes. To do this, open a browser window and type the IP address of the router. For our D-Link DIR655, the default address is 192.168.0.1, the login is admin, and no password. A web-based emulator of this router is available at http://support.dlink.com/Emulators/dir655/index.html. If for some reason this link does not work, or is changed, simply go to www.dlink.com, search for DIR-655, and when at the product page click Support, select your country, and click Emulator.

The first thing we want to do is to update the firmware so that we have the latest options and security available. This can be done in the Tools\Firmware section. Always make sure the router's firmware is updated before proceeding to configure it.

Next we access the Manual Internet Connection Setup button toward the bottom of the default screen. From here we see that the router is set up by default to obtain its WAN IP address automatically from the ISP, but in some cases you need to use a static IP address, or perhaps configure a secure connection to the Internet with Point to Point Tunneling Protocol (PPTP) or Layer 2 Tunneling Protocol (L2TP). Figure 14.10 shows these options.

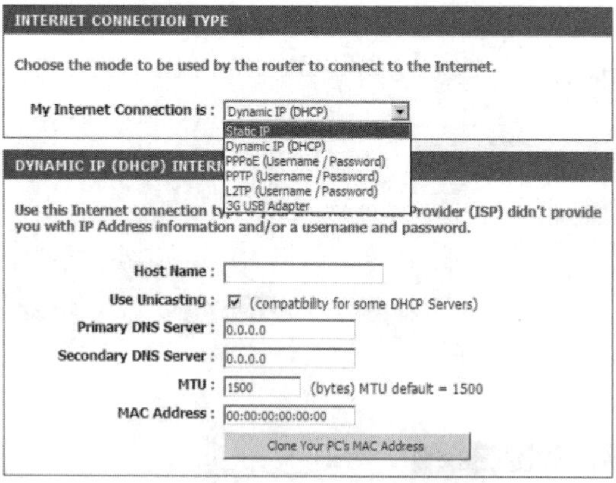

FIGURE 14.10   D-Link Internet connection options

If we selected any of the other options, we would have to input the correct information including IP address, username, and so forth. This information should be provided to you by the ISP you connect to.

Next we take a look at the network settings by clicking on the link called Network Settings on the left side. As shown in Figure 14.11, this is where we can change the LAN IP address and subnet mask of the router and enable or disable the DHCP server.

Now we take a look at the wireless settings; to do this, click on the Wireless Settings link on the left and then select the Manual Wireless Network setup at the bottom of the screen. That displays a window like the one shown in Figure 14.12.

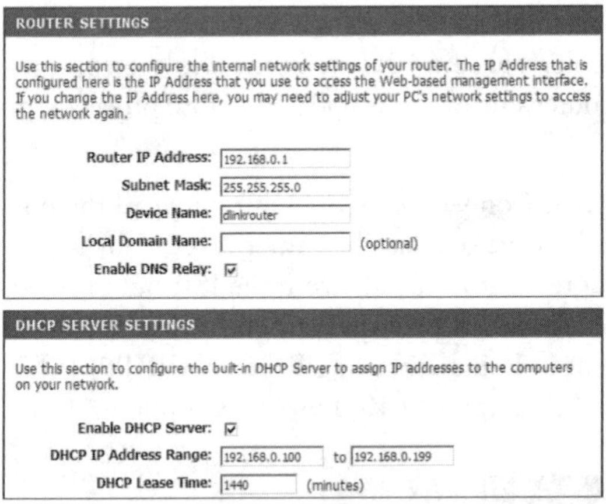

FIGURE 14.11   D-Link network settings

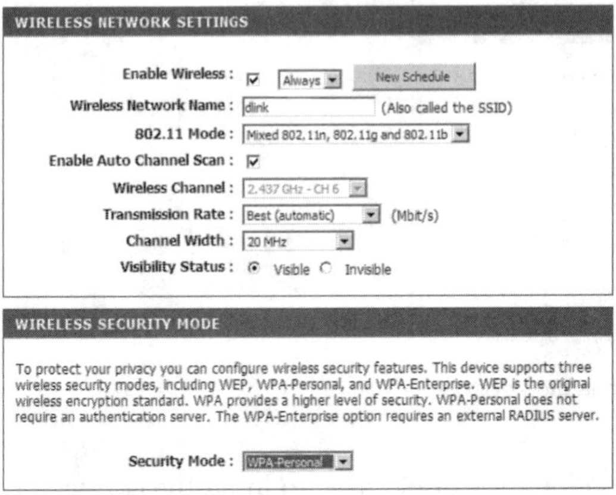

FIGURE 14.12   D-Link wireless network settings

From here, we can enable or disable the wireless radio and select the 802.11 technology of our choice. We can also modify the SSID (or Service Set Identifier) that is listed in the figure as Wireless Network Name and enable or disable SSID broadcasts, which is listed in the figure as Visibility Status. It's a good idea to modify the SSID. Think about it; thousands of people are using D-Link routers that all default to the same SSID! And finally, we can modify our encryptions settings for wireless. WPA2 utilizing AES is the most secure encryption that this router offers. Table 14.10 shows the characteristics of the various encryption methods.

TABLE 14.10 **Wireless Encryption Methods**

Wireless Encryption Protocol (Key Size)	Description	Encryption Level
WEP	Wired Equivalent Privacy	64-bit
WPA2	Wi-Fi Protected Access	256-bit
TKIP	Temporal Key Integrity Protocol	128-bit
AES	Advanced Encryption Standard	128-bit, 192-bit, and 256-bit

Note

WEP also has 128-bit and 256-bit versions, but these versions are not commonly found in wireless network hardware.

More SOHO Router Security

To offer a secure device, D-Link incorporated two types of firewalls into its DIR-655 device and most of its other products. The first is a network address translation (NAT) firewall that hides an entire network of IP addresses (the internal IP addresses), for example 192.168.0.100, behind a single publicly-displayed IP address. The second is a stateful packet inspection (SPI) firewall, which monitors packets according to each session that they belong to. Many devices offer these technologies today to protect the consumer's computers on the LAN.

Beyond this, SOHO routers offer MAC filtering technology. We mentioned that the MAC address is the unique address that is applied to the network adapter by the manufacturer. You can create a list of the MAC addresses on your network and insert that into the SOHO router. This way, only computers that have MAC addresses on the list can send any data through the router. On the D-Link DIR655, this applies to wireless *and* wired connections, but on some devices it is only wireless connections. An example of a MAC address would be **00–1e–68–55–ba–01**; be prepared to see the numbers separated by colons instead of hyphens as well.

It is also recommended to change the administrator username (if possible) and password. Remember that a strong password is one that is at least 8 alphanumeric characters, with at least one capital and one special character. The best passwords incorporate all these ideas but are 14 characters or more. Finally, back up the settings to your computer in the case that you need to reset the device in the future.

Some More SOHO Tidbits

Most people are wireless crazy nowadays, but don't forget that these SOHO routers normally come with four wired LAN ports. Some people love wired connections, and this D-Link device is considered 10/100/1000BASE-T. That means that it can auto-negotiate connections at 10bps, 100Mbps, and 1000Mbps (1Gbps). The BASE applies to any speed, and it is short for base-band, meaning every computer on the network shares the same channel or frequency. The T is short for twisted pair. By default, unshielded twisted pair cables can send data 100 meters before the electronic signal attenuates to such a point where it is useless.

> **ExamAlert**
>
> UTP cables can send data 100 meters maximum (328 feet).

These devices can usually do another two things concerning ports:

▶ **Port forwarding:** This forwards an external network port to an internal IP address and port. This enables you to have a web server, FTP server, and other servers, but you need to have only one port open on the WAN side of the router. It can be any port you like; of course, you would need to tell people which port they need to connect to if it is not a standard one.

   The D-Link device we have been using takes this to a new level by enabling what it calls Virtual Servers, making the process a lot more user-friendly. So, for example, you might have an FTP server running internally on your LAN; its IP address and port might be 192.168.0.100:21 (notice how the colon separates the IP address from the port), but you would have users on the Internet connect to your router's WAN address, for example 65.43.18.1 and any port you want. The router takes care of the rest, and the forwarding won't be noticed by the typical user.

▶ **Port triggering:** This enables you to specify outgoing ports that your computer uses for special applications, and their corresponding inbound ports will be opened automatically when the sessions are established. This is helpful for things like bit torrents.

Finally, we need to place our SOHO router. It is important to keep the device away from any electrical sources such as outlets, UPS, microwaves, and so on and any large amounts of metal to avoid interference.

The basement is probably not the best place for a router due to the thick walls, copper pipes, and most likely your main electrical panel. The antennas should be either at a 90-degree angle from each other or pointing toward where the computers are. The more centralized the router is, the better the wireless access your computers will get.

Wireless Network Adapters

Wireless network adapters require additional configuration compared to wired network adapters. This includes scanning for wireless networks, possibly typing the SSID of the wireless access point, specifying a channel, selecting the type of wireless encryption protocol to correspond with what is used by the wireless access point, and entering the security passphrase for that wireless encryption type that has been configured on the router.

Cram Quiz

Answer these questions. The answers follow the last question. If you cannot answer these questions correctly, consider reading this section again until you can.

1. Which of the following is the fastest wireless protocol?
   - ○ **A.** 802.11b
   - ○ **B.** 802.11g
   - ○ **C.** 802.11n
   - ○ **D.** 802.11x

2. What is the maximum data rate of Bluetooth Version 2?
   - ○ **A.** 721Kbps
   - ○ **B.** 100Mbps
   - ○ **C.** 2.1Gbps
   - ○ **D.** 2.1Mbps

3. Which of these is a valid MAC address?
   - ○ **A.** 00:3e:2b:1d:11:ff
   - ○ **B.** 192.168.0.100
   - ○ **C.** 00:3g:2b:1d:11:fe
   - ○ **D.** 2001:0000:0000:01

4. Which of these hides an entire network of IP addresses?

   ○ **A.** SPI

   ○ **B.** NAT

   ○ **C.** SSH

   ○ **D.** FTP

5. Which of the following use the 2.4-GHz frequency range? (Select all that apply.)

   ○ **A.** 802.11b

   ○ **B.** 802.11a

   ○ **C.** 802.11g

   ○ **D.** 802.11n

Cram Quiz Answers

1. C. 802.11n has a theoretical maximum data rate of 600Mbps; however, 300Mbps is the norm.

2. D. Version 2 has a maximum data rate of 2.1Mbps, Version 1 maxes out at 721Kbps.

3. A. Answer A is the valid MAC address. B is an IP address, C is not valid because the letter G is not part of the hexadecimal numbering system, and D appears to be a truncated IPv6 address.

4. B. Network Address Translation hides an entire network of IP Addresses. SPI or Stateful Packet Inspection is the other type of firewall that today's SOHO routers incorporate.

5. A, C, and **D.** The only protocol that does not use the 2.4GHz frequency is 802.11a.

Additional Reading and Resources

Prowse, David L. *CompTIA Network+ Video Mentor*, First Edition. Que. 2009.

Harwood, Mike. *CompTIA Network+ N10-004 Cert Guide*, First Edition. Que. 2010.

Additional A+ resources: http://www.davidlprowse.com/aplus

Additional Network+ resources: http://www.davidlprowse.com/netplus

CHAPTER 15

Security

This chapter covers the following A+ exam topics:

► Basics of Data Security

► Authentication

► Malicious Software

► File Security

You can find a master list of A+ exam topics in the "Introduction."

This chapter covers CompTIA A+ Objectives 220-701: 5.1 and 5.2 and 220-702: 4.1 and 4.2.

The 2009 A+ exams and the updated 2011 version of the A+ exams have an increased amount of security objectives. This is understandable because everyone should have some basic knowledge on security. Computers and computer networks are constantly at risk, and new risks are always rearing their ugly head.

This chapter concentrates on demonstrating how to secure an individual computer system. But you must ask yourself some questions: What kind of computer am I trying to secure? What operating system is it using, and what applications are loaded? How will the files be protected? What type of hardware is employed, and what BIOS is in place? And, what are the security policies of my company? We'll answer all these questions in the hope that you end up with a secure computer.

> **Note**
>
> The CompTIA A+ objectives focus primarily on individual computer security but make a few references to network and wireless security; these few additional points are covered in Chapter 14, "Networking," in the section titled "Installing & Configuring a SOHO Network."

Basics of Data Security

Data security is the act of protecting data from threats and possible corruption. You need to be aware of several types of threats:

▶ **Malicious software:** Known as malware, this includes computer viruses, worms, trojan horses, spyware, rootkits, adware, and other types of unwanted software. Everyone has heard of a scenario in which a user's computer was compromised to some extent due to malicious software.

▶ **Unauthorized access:** This is access to computer resources and data without consent of the owner. It might include approaching the system, trespassing, communicating, storing and retrieving data, intercepting data, or any other methods that would interfere with a computer's normal work. Access to data must be controlled to ensure privacy. Improper administrative access would fall into this category as well.

▶ **System failure:** This refers to computer crashes, or individual application failure. This could happen due to three reasons: user error, malicious activity, or hardware failure.

▶ **Social engineering:** The act of manipulating users into revealing confidential information or performing other actions detrimental to the user. Almost everyone gets emails nowadays from unknown entities making false claims or asking for personal information (or money!); this is one example of social engineering.

> **ExamAlert**
>
> Know the possible threats to a computer system for the exam!

Many data security technologies can protect against, or help recover from, the above threats. Several common ones are listed here:

▶ **Authentication:** This is the verification of a person's identity, and it helps protect against unauthorized access. It is a preventative measure that can be broken down into three categories:

  ▶ Something the user knows, for example a password or PIN

  ▶ Something the user has, for example a smart card or other security token

  ▶ Something the user is, for example the biometric reading of a fingerprint or retina scan

▶ **Anti-malware software:** This is software that protects a computer from the various forms of malware, and if necessary, detects and removes them. Types include antivirus and antispyware software. Well-known examples include Norton AntiVirus, McAfee VirusScan, Windows Defender, and Spyware Doctor. Nowadays, a lot of the software named "antivirus" can protect against spyware as well.

▶ **Data backups:** This must be the fifth time we've mentioned backing up data in this book, but it's worth the reminder! Backups won't stop damage to data, but they can enable you to recover data after an attack or other compromise, or system failure. From programs such as NTbackup and Bacula to enterprise-level programs such as Tivoli and Veritas, data backup is an important part of security. Note that fault-tolerant methods such as RAID 1 and 5 are good preventative measures against hardware failure but might not offer protection from data corruption or erasure. For more information on RAID, see Chapter 6, "Storage Devices."

▶ **Encryption:** This is the act of changing information using an algorithm known as a cipher to make it unreadable to anyone except users who possess the proper "key" to the data. Examples of this include HTTPS, Kerberos, and PGP. We talk more about encryption later in this chapter.

▶ **Data removal:** Proper data removal goes far beyond file deletion or the formatting of digital media. The problem with file deletion/formatting is data remanence, or the residue, that is left behind, from which re-creation of files can be accomplished by some less-than-reputable people with smart tools. Companies typically employ one of three options when met with the prospect of data removal:

   ▶ **Clearing:** This is the removal of data with a certain amount of assurance that it cannot be reconstructed. The data is actually recoverable with special techniques. In this case, the media is recycled and used within the company again. The data wiping technique (also known as shredding) is used to clear data from media by overwriting new data to that media. Several software programs are available to accomplish this.

   ▶ **Purging:** Also known as sanitizing, this is once again the removal of data, but this time, it's done in such a way so that it cannot be reconstructed by any known technique; in this case the media is released outside the company. Special software (or other means) are employed to completely destroy all data on the media.

▶ **Destruction:** This is when the storage media is physically destroyed through pulverizing, incineration, and so on. At this point, the media can be disposed of in accordance with municipal guidelines.

▶ **User awareness:** The wiser the user, the less chance of security breaches. Employee training and education, easily accessible and understandable policies, security-awareness emails, and online security resources all help to provide user awareness. These methods can help to protect from all the threats mentioned previously.

> **ExamAlert**
>
> Educating the user is an excellent method when attempting to protect against security attacks.

Data Sensitivity and Security Compliance

Sensitive data is information that can result in a loss of security, or loss of advantage to a company, if accessed by unauthorized persons. Quite often, information is broken down into two groups: classified (which requires some level of security clearance) and nonclassified. ISO/IEC 17799:2005 (now known as ISO/IEC 27002:2005) is a security standard that among other things, can aid companies in classifying their data. Although you don't need to know the contents of that document for the exam, you should have a basic idea of how to classify information. For example, classification of data can be broken down as shown in Table 15.1.

TABLE 15.1 **Example of Data Sensitivity Classifications**

Class	Description
Public information	Information available to anyone.
Internal information	Used internally by a company but if it becomes public, no critical consequences results.
Confidential information	This information can cause financial and operational loss to the company.
Secret information	This data should never become public and is critical to the company.
Top secret information	The highest sensitivity of data, very few should have access; security clearance may be necessary.

In this example, loss of public and internal information probably won't affect the company very much. However, unauthorized access, misuse, modification, or loss of confidential, secret, or top secret data can affect users' privacy, trade secrets, financials, and the general security of the company. By classifying data and enforcing policies that govern who has access to what information, a company can limit its exposure to security threats.

Many companies need to be in compliance with specific laws when it comes to the disclosure of information. In the United States there are two acts you should know about, as shown in Table 15.2. In addition, there are several bills in process that will probably be passed in the near future regarding data-breach notification.

TABLE 15.2   **Acts Passed Concerning the Disclosure of Data**

Act	Acronym	Description
Sarbanes-Oxley	SOX	Governs the disclosure of financial and accounting information. Enacted in 2002.
Health Insurance Portability and Accountability Act	HIPAA	Governs the disclosure and protection of health information. Enacted in 1996.

Many computer technicians have to deal with SOX and HIPAA at some point in their careers, and although the acts create a lot of paperwork and protocol, the expected result is that they will help companies protect their data.

Cram Quiz

Answer these questions. The answers follow the last question. If you cannot answer these questions correctly, consider reading this section again until you can.

1. Which method would you use if you were disposing hard drives as part of a company computer sale?

   ○ **A.** Destruction

   ○ **B.** Purging

   ○ **C.** Clearing

   ○ **D.** Formatting

2. Which of these governs the disclosure of financial data?

   ○ **A.** SOX

   ○ **B.** HIPAA

   ○ **C.** GLB

   ○ **D.** Top secret

3. Which of the following is the verification of a person's identity?

   ○ **A.** Authorization

   ○ **B.** Accountability

   ○ **C.** Authentication

   ○ **D.** Password

4. Which of the following is not an example of malicious software?

   ○ **A.** Rootkits

   ○ **B.** Spyware

   ○ **C.** Viruses

   ○ **D.** Browser

Cram Quiz Answers

1. **B.** Purging (or sanitizing) removes all the data from a hard drive so that it cannot be reconstructed by any known technique.

2. **A.** SOX, or Sarbanes-Oxley, governs the disclosure of financial and accounting data.

3. **C.** Authentication is the verification of a person's identity. Authorization to specific resources cannot be accomplished without previous authentication of the user.

4. **D.** A web browser (for example, Internet Explorer) is the only one listed that is not an example of malicious software. Although a browser can be compromised in a variety of ways by malicious software, the application itself is not the malware.

Authentication

As previously mentioned, authentication is the verification of a person's identity. Its purpose is to help protect against unauthorized access. This preventative measure can be something the user knows, for example a password, something the user has such as a smart card, or something the user is, for example, a user's fingerprint read by a biometric device. Let's discuss each of these now.

Usernames and Passwords

The username/password combination is the most common type of authentication when it comes to gaining access to computers. The username is known to all parties involved and can be seen as plain text when typed. In some cases, the user has no control over what the username will be, or it will be the name or email address of the user. However, the password is either set by the user or created automatically for the user. It is common knowledge that a strong password is important for protecting a user account, whether the account is with a bank, at work, or elsewhere. But what is a strong password? Many organizations define a *strong* password as a password with at least 8 characters, including at least one uppercase letter, one number, and one special character. The *best* passwords have the same requirements but are 14 characters or more. Many password checker programs are on the web, for example Microsoft's password checker at http://www.microsoft.com/protect/yourself/password/checker.mspx. Table 15.3 shows a strong password and a "best" password as checked by this program.

TABLE 15.3   **Strong and Stronger Passwords**

Password	Strength of Password
locrian7	Strong
This1sV#ryS3cure	Very strong or "best"

Notice the first password is using the | pipe symbol instead of the letter L. This is a special character that shares the \ backslash key on the keyboard. In the second password we have 16 characters, 3 capital letters, 2 numbers, and a partridge in a pear tree, um, I mean one special character ☺. Just checking if you are still with me! Of course a partridge wouldn't help your password security, but the other methods make for an extremely strong password that would take a super-computer many years to crack.

Changing your password at regular intervals is important as well. The general rule of thumb is to change your password as often as you change your toothbrush. However, because this is a subjective concept (to put it nicely!), many organizations have policies concerning your password. It might need to meet certain requirements, or be changed at regular intervals, and so forth. Figure 15.1 shows an example of the default password policy on a Windows XP Professional computer. This can be accessed by navigating to Start > All Programs > Administrative Tools > Local Security Policy. When in the Local Security Settings window, continue to Security Settings > Account Policies > Password Policy.

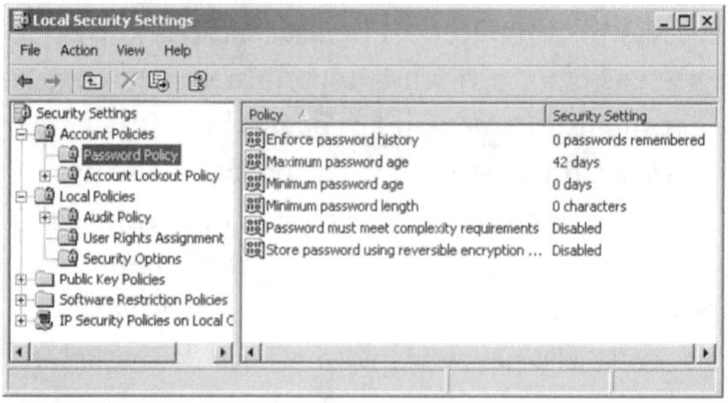

FIGURE 15.1 Default password policy in Windows XP

As you can see in the figure, there are several items that we can configure or could be configured by the network administrator centrally if the computer is part of a domain. The four important ones for the exam include:

▸ **Enforce password history:** When this is defined, users cannot use any of the passwords that are remembered in the history. If you set the history to 3, then the last three passwords cannot be used again when it is time to change the password.

▸ **Maximum and minimum password age:** This defines exactly how long a password can be used. The maximum is initially set to 42 days but does not affect the default Administrator account. To enforce effective password history, the minimum must be higher than zero.

> **Note**
>
> To avoid any chance of overriding the maximum password age policy, create Windows XP user accounts in the Local Users and Groups section of the Computer Management console instead of within the User Accounts applet of the Control Panel.

▶ **Minimum password length:** This requires that the password must be at least the specified amount of characters. For a strong password policy, set this to eight or more.

▶ **Passwords must meet complexity requirements:** This means that passwords must meet three of these four criteria: uppercase characters, lowercase characters, digits between 0 and 9, and nonalphabetic characters (special characters).

> **Note**
>
> For more information on password best practices, see the following link:
> http://technet.microsoft.com/en-us/library/cc784090.aspx

Now that we have a secure password, and a password policy in place, let's talk about securing the logon process and user accounts for Windows XP and Vista. There are several things we can do to secure these:

1. **Disable the Welcome screen and Fast User Switching:** Although these are convenient features, they can be security risks. To disable both of these in Windows XP, navigate to Start > Control Panel > User Accounts (and User Accounts again if you are in Category view); then select Change the way users log on or off. Deselect both check boxes.

> **Note**
>
> To remove these in Windows Vista, you need to access the Local Group Policy Editor. Although you shouldn't see this on the exam, you can find out how to do it at my website: http://www.davidlprowse.com/aplus.

This also enables you to open the Windows Security dialog box by pressing Ctrl+Alt+Del, which previously would have brought up the Task Manager. From the Windows Security dialog box, you can see who is logged on to the computer and the name of the computer. You can also lock the computer. The advantage of locking the computer is that you can leave your applications open while you take a break, go to lunch, and such. If you log off the system, all applications are closed. Of course, from the Windows Security dialog box you can also change your password, run the Task Manager, log off, or shut down the computer.

2. **Enable Ctrl+Alt+Del login functionality:** Setting up the computer so a user must press Ctrl+Alt+Del before logging on secures the computer in more ways than one. To do this, open the Local Security Settings window previously mentioned.

> **Note**
>
> A quick way to get to the Local Security Settings window is by bringing up the Run prompt and typing `secpol.msc`.

This time navigate to Security Settings > Local Policies > Security Options and then locate the item listed as Interactive Logon: Do Not Require CTRL+ALT+DEL. Double-click it and select the Disabled radio button (this is a double negative); then log off and log back on. The Ctrl+Alt+Del window should appear.

3. **Rename and password protect the Administrator account:** It's nice that Windows XP and Vista have incorporated a separate administrator account: the problem is that by default the account has no password. To configure this account, navigate to Computer Management > System Tools > Local Users and Groups > Users and locate the Administrator account. By right-clicking the account, you see a drop-down menu in which you can rename it and/or give it a password. (Just remember the new username and password!) Now it's great to have this additional administrator account on the shelf just in case the primary account fails; however Vista disables this account by default. To enable it, right-click the account and select Properties. In the General tab, deselect the Account is disabled check box. Alternatively, open the command line and type **net user administrator /active:yes**.

> **Note**
>
> Alternatively, you can use the User Accounts applet in the Control Panel to accomplish these tasks for any account in Vista, and for any account except Administrator in XP, but using Computer Management is recommended due to the fact that it is more consistent and thorough.

4. **Verify that the Guest account (and other unnecessary accounts) are disabled:** This can be done by navigating to Computer Management > System Tools > Local Users and Groups > Users, and right-clicking the account in question, selecting properties and then selecting the check box named Account Is Disabled. It is also possible to delete accounts (aside from built-in accounts such as the Guest account); however, companies usually opt to have them disabled instead, so that the company can retain information linking to the account.

5. **Set the Account lockout threshold:** If a user attempts to log on to a system and is unsuccessful, the user will be locked out of the system (after a specified number of attempts). The settings and thresholds for this can be configured in the Local Security Settings window. Navigate to Security Settings > Account Policies > Account Lockout Policy. From here you can set the threshold to a certain amount of invalid logons, set how long the user will be locked out, and how long until the lockout counter is reset. If an account is locked out and you need to unlock it immediately, follow one of the options at the end of step 3.

ExamAlert

Know how to enable/disable accounts, reset passwords, and modify password policy for the exam!

It's important to note that when logging on to a Microsoft network, the logon process is secured by the Kerberos protocol, which is run by the Domain Controller. This adds a layer of protection for the username and password as they are being authenticated across the network. When a user is going to take a break or go to lunch, they should lock the computer. This can be done by pressing Windows+L. When doing so, the operating system goes into a locked state, and the only way to unlock the computer is to enter the username and password of the person who locked the computer. The difference between this and logging out is that a locked computer keeps all the session's applications and files open, whereas logging out closes all applications and open files.

User Account Control (UAC)

User Account Control (UAC) is a security component of Windows Vista that keeps every user (besides the actual Administrator account) in standard user mode instead of as an administrator with full administrative rights—even if they are a member of the administrators group. It is meant to prevent unauthorized access and avoid user error in the form of accidental changes. With UAC enabled users perform common tasks as non-administrators, and when necessary, as administrators, without having to switch users, log off, or use Run As.

Basically, UAC was created with two goals in mind. First, to eliminate unnecessary requests for excessive administrative-level access to Windows resources. And second, to reduce the risk of malicious software using the administrator's access control to infect operating system files. When a standard end user requires administrator privileges to perform certain tasks such as installing an application, a small pop-up UAC window appears notifying the user that an administrator credential is necessary. If the user has administrative rights and clicks Continue, the task will be carried out, but if they do not have sufficient rights, the attempt fails. Note that these pop-up UAC windows do not appear if the person is logged on with the actual Administrator account.

In Windows Vista, you can turn off UAC by going to Start > Control Panel > User Accounts and Family Safety. Then select User Accounts and Turn User Account Control On or Off. From there UAC can be turned on and off by checking or unchecking the box. If a change is made to UAC, the system needs to be restarted. Note that if you use the Classic View in the Control Panel, User Accounts and Family Safety is bypassed. Windows 7 adds some functionality to UAC. To access the UAC settings in Windows 7, the path is Start > Control Panel > User Accounts and Family Safety. Then select User Accounts, and click the Change User Account Control settings link. Unlike Vista, where you can only turn UAC on or off, Windows 7 displays a slider that enables you to select from four different settings:

▶ **Always notify:** This will configure the OS to notify the user whenever software installations are started, or when any changes to Windows settings are attempted by the user.

▶ **Default: Notify me only when programs try to make changes to my computer:** This configures the OS to notify the user if a program attempts to make a change, but not when the user attempts to make a change to settings.

▶ **Notify me only when programs try to make changes to my computer (do not dim my desktop):** This is essentially the same as the last item, but the desktop is not dimmed when the notifications appear.

▶ **Never notify:** This effectively turns UAC off, and UAC will not notify the user regardless of the program or user change.

So, UAC, by default, notifies a user before changes are made to a computer that requires administrator-level permission. In Windows Vista this can be turned off altogether only, whereas in Windows 7 it can be controlled with a little bit more definition. Of course, a user will need administrative rights in order to make changes to UAC settings.

> **ExamAlert**
>
> Be sure to know how to turn UAC on and off for the exam!

BIOS Security

The BIOS can be the victim of malicious attacks as well; for mischievous persons it can also act as the gateway to the rest of the system. Protect it! Or your computer just might not boot. Here are a few ways to do so:

▶ **Use a BIOS password:** The password that blocks unwanted persons from gaining access to the BIOS is also known as the supervisor password. Don't confuse it with the user password (or power-on password) that is employed so that the BIOS can verify a user's identity before accessing the operating system. Both of these are shown in Figure 15.2.

On a semi-related note, many laptops come equipped with *drive lock* technology; this might simply be referred to as an HDD password. If enabled, it prompts the user to enter a password for the hard drive when the computer is first booted. If the user of the computer doesn't know the password for the hard drive, the drive will lock and the OS will not boot. An eight digit or like hard drive ID usually associates the laptop with the hard drive that is installed, as shown in Figure 15.2. On most systems this password is clear by default, but if the password is set and forgotten, it can usually be reset within the BIOS. Some laptops come with documentation clearly stating the BIOS and drive lock passwords.

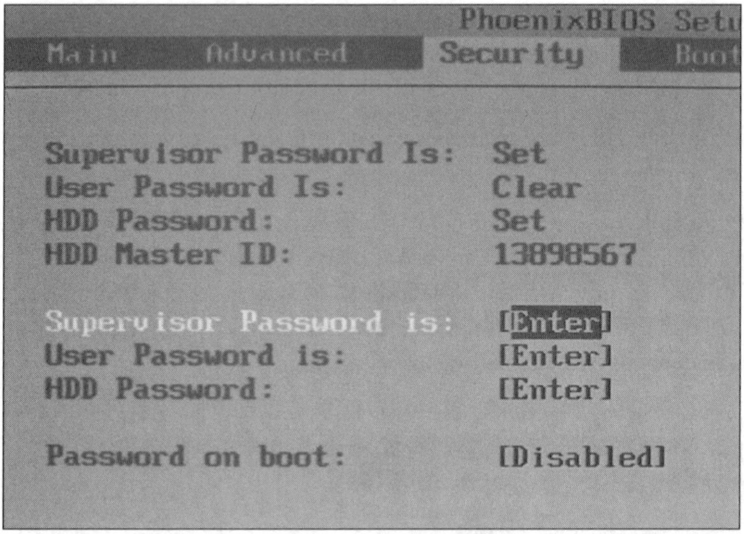

```
                                    PhoenixBIOS Setu
     Main         Advanced          Security          Boot

    Supervisor Password Is:     Set
    User Password Is:           Clear
    HDD Password:               Set
    HDD Master ID:              13898567

    Supervisor Password is:     [Enter]
    User Password is:           [Enter]
    HDD Password:               [Enter]

    Password on boot:           [Disabled]
```

FIGURE 15.2   **BIOS and drive lock passwords**

▶ **Flash the BIOS:** *Flashing* is the term used to describe the updating of the BIOS. By updating the BIOS to the latest version, you can avoid possible exploits and BIOS errors that might occur. All new motherboards issue at least one new BIOS version within the first 6 months of the motherboard's release. For more information on BIOS updating, see Chapter 2, "Motherboards."

▶ **Configure the BIOS:** Setup the BIOS to reduce the risk of infiltration. For example, change the BIOS boot order (boot device priority) so that it looks for a hard disk first and not any type of removable media. Also, if company policy requires it, disable removable media including the floppy drive and USB ports.

Smart Cards and Biometrics

The smart card falls into the category of "something a person has." It's the size of a credit card and has an embedded chip that stores and transacts data for use in secure applications such as hotel guest room access, prepaid phone services, and more. Smart cards have multiple applications, one of which is to authenticate users by swiping the device against a scanner, thus securing a computer or a computer room. It might also be used as part of a multifactor authentication scheme in which there is a combination of username/password (or PIN) and a smart card. Advanced smart cards have specialized cryptographic hardware that utilizes algorithms such as RSA and 3DES (more on these encryption types later in this chapter). A smart card might incorporate a processor or an RFID chip as well. A smart card security system will usually be composed of the smart card itself, smart card readers, and a back-office database that stores all the smart card access control lists and history.

Biometrics fall into the category of "something a person is." Examples of bodily characteristics that are measured include fingerprints, retinal patterns, iris patterns, and even bone structure. Biometric readers, for example fingerprint scanners, are becoming more common on laptops or as USB devices; biometric information can also be incorporated into smart card technology. One example of biometrics hardware is the Microsoft Fingerprint Scanner, which is USB-based.

> **Note**
>
> There is a fourth type of authentication based on something a person does. Examples of this include signature and voice recognition; however, this is not covered in the CompTIA A+ objectives.

Cram Quiz

Answer these questions. The answers follow the last question. If you cannot answer these questions correctly, consider reading this section again until you can.

1. Which of the following is the strongest password?

   ○ **A.** locrian#

   ○ **B.** Marqu1sD3S0d

   ○ **C.** This1sV#ryS3cure

   ○ **D.** Thisisverysecure

2. Which of the following would fall into the category of "something a person is?"

   ○ **A.** Passwords

   ○ **B.** Passphrases

   ○ **C.** Fingerprints

   ○ **D.** Smart Cards

3. Which of these is a security component of Windows Vista?

   ○ **A.** UAC

   ○ **B.** UPS

   ○ **C.** Gadgets

   ○ **D.** Control Panel

4. What key combination helps to secure the logon process?

   ○ **A.** Windows+R

   ○ **B.** Ctrl+Shift+Esc

   ○ **C.** Ctrl+Alt+Del

   ○ **D.** Alt+F4

Cram Quiz Answers

1. **C.** Answer C incorporates case-sensitive letters, numbers, and special characters and is 16-characters long.

2. **C.** Fingerprints are an example of something a person is. The process of measuring that characteristic is known as biometrics.

3. **A.** User Account Control (UAC) adds a layer of security to Windows Vista to protect against malware and user error, and conserve resources.

4. **C.** Ctrl+Alt+Del is the key combination that is used to help secure the logon process. It can be added by configuring the Local Security policy.

Malicious Software

Malicious software, or *malware*, is software that is designed to infiltrate a computer system and possibly damage it without the user's knowledge or consent. Malware is a broad term used by computer guys to include viruses, worms, trojan horses, spyware, rootkits, adware, and other types of unwanted software.

Of course, we don't want malware to infect our computer system, but to defend against it we first need to define it and categorize it. Then we can put preventative measures into place. It's also important to locate and remove or quarantine malware from a computer system.

Types of Malware

There are several types of malware that you need to know for the exam. For the past several years there has been an emphasis shift from viruses to spyware. Most people know about viruses and have some kind of antivirus software running. However, many people are still confused about exactly what spyware is, how it occurs, and how to protect against it. Because of this, computer professionals spend a lot of time fixing spyware issues and training users on how to protect against them in the future. However, viruses are still a valid foe; let's start by discussing them.

Viruses

A *virus* is code that runs on a computer without the user's knowledge; it infects the computer when the code is accessed and executed. It also has reproductive capability and can spread copies of itself throughout the computer. By infecting files that are accessed by other computers, the virus can spread to those other systems as well.

One well-known example of a virus is the "Love Bug." Originating in 2000, this virus would arrive by an email titled "I love you" with an attachment named love-letter-for-you.txt.vbs, or one of several other permutations of this fictitious love. Some users would be tricked into thinking this was a text file, but the extension was actually .vbs, short for Visual Basic script. This virus deleted files, sent usernames and passwords to its creator, infected 15 million computers, and supposedly caused $5 billion in damage. Educate your users on how to screen their email!

There are several different types of viruses that you might encounter:

▶ **Boot Sector:** Initially loads into the first sector of the hard drive; when the computer boots, the virus then loads into memory.

▶ **Macro:** Usually placed in office documents and emailed to users in the hopes that the user will open the document, thus executing the virus.

▶ **Program:** This type of virus infects executable files.

▶ **Polymorphic:** Can change every time is it executed, in an attempt to avoid antivirus detection.

▶ **Stealth:** Uses various techniques to go unnoticed by antivirus programs.

▶ **Multipartite:** This is a hybrid of boot and program viruses. It attacks the boot sector or system files first and then attacks the other.

> **Exam Alert**
>
> For viruses to do their dirty work, they first need to be executed by the user in some way.

Worms

Worms are much like viruses except that they self-replicate whereas a virus does not.

> **Exam Alert**
>
> The difference between viruses and worms is that worms self-replicate!

Worms take advantage of backdoors and security holes in operating systems and applications. They look for other systems on the network or through the Internet that are running the same applications and replicate to those other systems. When it comes to worms, there is no need for the user to access and execute the malware. A well-known example of a worm is Nimda (admin backward) which propagated automatically through the Internet in 22 minutes back in 2001, causing widespread damage. It propagated through network shares, mass emailing, and operating system vulnerabilities.

Trojan Horses

Trojan Horses, or simply trojans, appear to perform desired functions but are actually performing malicious functions behind the scenes. These are not technically viruses and can easily be downloaded without noticing them. Remote access trojans (RATs) are the most common type of Trojan, for example Back Orifice or NetBus; their capability to allow an attacker higher administration privileges than the owner of the system makes them dangerous as well.

Spyware

Spyware is a type of malicious software that is either downloaded unwittingly from a website or is installed along with some other third-party software. Usually, this malware collects information about the user without the user's consent. It could be as simple as a piece of code that logs what websites you access, to a program that records your keystrokes. Spyware is also associated with advertising (those pop-ups that just won't go away!) and could possibly change the computer configuration without any user interaction, for example redirecting a browser to access websites other than those desired. *Adware* usually falls into the realm of spyware because it pops up advertisements based on what it has learned from spying on the user. *Grayware* is another general term used to describe applications that are behaving improperly, but without serious consequences. It is associated with spyware, adware, and joke programs. Very funny...not.

> **Note**
>
> Malware can be distributed throughout the Internet by way of a *botnet*—a collection of compromised computers (known as zombies) running software installed by worms or other malware. It's a vicious circle!

There are other types of malware such as rootkits and logic bombs, but for the most part the previously mentioned malware are the ones you'll see on the exam.

Preventing and Troubleshooting Malware

Now that we know the types of malware, let's talk about how to stop them before they happen, and how to troubleshoot them if they do happen. Unfortunately, given the amount of computers you will work on, they *will* happen.

If a system is affected by malware, it might be sluggish in its response time, display unwanted pop-ups and incorrect home pages, or applications (and maybe even the whole system) could lock up or shut down unexpectedly. Quite often malware uses CPU and memory resources directly or behind the scenes, causing the system to run slower than usual. In general, a technician should look for erratic behavior from the computer, as if it had a mind of its own! Let's go over viruses and spyware and show how to prevent them and troubleshoot them if they do occur.

Preventing and Troubleshooting Viruses

There are several things that we can do to protect a computer system from viruses. First, every computer should have antivirus software running on it. McAfee, Norton, and Vipre are examples of manufacturers of AV software, but there are many others. Second, the AV software should be updated, which means that the software will require a current license; this is renewed yearly with most providers. When updating, be sure to update the AV engine *and* the definitions if you are doing it manually. Otherwise, set the AV software to automatically update at periodic intervals, for example every week. It's a good idea to schedule regular scans of the system within the AV software.

> **Exam Alert**
>
> Be sure to update antivirus software regularly!

Next, we want to make sure that the computer has the latest service packs and updates available. This goes for the operating system and applications such as Office. Backdoors into operating systems and other applications are not uncommon, and the OS manufacturers often release fixes for these breaches of security. In Windows XP, Automatic Updates can be configured by going to Start > Control Panel > Automatic Updates. From here you have several options:

- ▸ Automatic—This automatically downloads and installs updates at specific intervals entered by the user.

- ▸ Download updates for me, but let me choose when to install them.

- ▸ Notify me but don't automatically download or install them.

- ▸ Turn off Automatic Updates.

Configure Automatic Updates according to your company's policy. You can also check if your computer is up to date by going to Start > All Programs > Windows Update. It directs you to a website that prompts you to install a Windows Update component and then checks if the computer has the latest security (and other) patches. In Windows Vista, you can check for updates directly within the Automatic Updates program. To access the preceding options, one additional step is required: clicking on the Change settings link.

It's also important to make sure that a firewall is available, enabled, and updated. A firewall will close all the inbound ports to your computer (or network) in an attempt to block intruders. The Windows Firewall is a built-in feature of Windows XP/Vista, and you might also have a SOHO router with a built-in firewall. By using both, you will have two layers of protection from viruses and other attacks. You can access the Windows Firewall by navigating to Start > Control Panel > Windows Firewall. Keep in mind that you might need to set exceptions for programs that need to access the Internet. This can be done by the program, or the port used by the protocol, and can be configured in the Exceptions tab, enabling specific applications to communicate through the firewall while keeping the rest of the ports closed.

Finally, educate users as to how viruses can infect a system. Instruct them on how to screen their emails and tell them not to open unknown attachments. Show them how to scan removable media before copying files to their computer.

By utilizing these methods, virus infection can be severely reduced. However, if a computer is infected by a virus, you want to know what to look for so that you can "cure" the computer.

Here are some typical symptoms of viruses:

- ▶ Computer runs slower than usual.
- ▶ Computer locks up frequently or stops responding altogether.
- ▶ Computer restarts on its own or crashes frequently.
- ▶ Disk drives and/or applications are not accessible or don't work properly.
- ▶ Strange sounds occur.
- ▶ You receive unusual error messages.
- ▶ Display or print distortion.
- ▶ New icons appear or old icons (and applications) disappear.

▶ There is a double extension on a file attached to an email that was opened, for example: .txt.vbs or .txt.exe.

▶ Antivirus programs will not run or can't be installed.

▶ Files have been corrupted or folders are created automatically.

Before making any changes to the computer, make sure that you back up critical data and verify that the latest updates have been installed to the OS and the AV software. Then, perform a thorough scan of the system using the AV software's scan utility; if allowed by the software, run the scan in Safe Mode.

ExamAlert

If at all possible, scan in Safe Mode!

Hopefully, the AV software will find and quarantine the virus(es) on the system. In the case that the AV software's scan does not find the issue, or if the AV software has been infected and won't run, you can try using an online scanner such as Trend Micro's HouseCall: http://housecall.trendmicro.com/ or download Microsoft's Malicious Software Removal Tool: http://www.microsoft.com/security/malwareremove/default.mspx.

In rare cases, you might need to delete individual files and remove Registry entries. This might be the only solution when a new virus has infected a system and there is no antivirus definition released. Instructions on how to remove viruses in this manner can be found on AV software manufacturers' websites.

When it comes to boot sector viruses, your AV software is still the best bet. The AV software might utilize a boot disk to accomplish this, or it might have boot shielding built in. Some BIOS programs have the capability to scan the boot sector of the hard drive at startup; this might need to be enabled in the BIOS setup first. It is also possible to use the DOS **SYS** command to restore the first sector or the **FDISK/MBR** command to repair the master boot record within the boot sector, but a DOS-based boot disk will be necessary to do this; it will need to be created on a DOS-based computer or downloaded from the Internet. Windows 2000 and XP offer the **FIXMBR** command available from the Recovery Console. Windows Vista offers the bootrec /fixmbr command from within the System Recovery Options Command Prompt. Keep in mind that the DOS, Recovery Console, and System Recovery Options Command Prompt methods might not fix the problem; in fact, they might render the hard drive inoperable depending on the type of virus. It is best to use the AV software's various utilities that you have purchased for the system.

Worms and Trojans can be prevented and troubleshot in the same manner as viruses. There are scanners for trojans as well, for example: http://www.windowsecurity.com/trojanscan/. In some cases, AV software will scan for worms and trojans in addition to viruses.

Preventing and Troubleshooting Spyware

Preventing spyware is much like preventing viruses as far as updating the operating system and using a firewall. Also, because spyware has become much more common, antivirus companies have begun adding antispyware components to their software. Here are a few more things you can do to protect the computer in the hopes of preventing spyware:

▶ **Download and install antispyware protection software.** For example, Windows Defender, available at http://www.microsoft.com/windows/products/winfamily/defender/default.mspx. Other options include Spyware Doctor with Antivirus, SpyBot S&D (free), or one of the antivirus programs previously mentioned if it includes spyware protection. Be sure to keep the antispyware software updated.

▶ **Adjust Internet Explorer security settings.** This can be done by clicking Tools on the menu bar, selecting Internet Options, and accessing the Security tab. From there the security level can be increased, and trusted and restricted sites can be established. (It's a good thing.) Internet Explorer 7 and higher also have a phishing filter that can be turned on by going to Tools, Phishing Filter and clicking Turn on Automatic Website Checking. This attempts to filter out fraudulent online requests for usernames, passwords, and credit card information, which is also known as web-page spoofing. Higher security settings can also help to fend off session hijacking; that is the act of taking control of a user session after obtaining or generating an authentication ID.

▶ **Uninstall unnecessary applications and turn off superfluous services** (for example, Telnet and FTP if they are not being used).

▶ **Educate users on how to surf the web safely.** User education is actually the number one method of preventing malware! Only access sites believed to be safe, and only download programs from reputable websites. Don't click OK or Agree to close a window; instead press Alt+F4 on the keyboard to close that window. Be wary of file-sharing websites and the content stored on those sites. Be careful of emails with links to downloadable software that could be malicious.

▶ **Consider technologies that discourage spyware.** For example, use a browser that is less susceptible to spyware. Consider running a browser within a virtual machine, or take it to the next level and use a thin-client computer!

Here are some common symptoms of spyware:

▶ The web browser's default home page has been modified.

▶ A particular website comes up every time you perform a search.

▶ Excessive pop-up windows appear.

▶ The network adapter's activity LED blinks frequently when the computer shouldn't be transmitting data.

▶ The firewall and/or antivirus programs turn off automatically.

▶ New programs, icons, and favorites appear.

▶ Odd problems occur within windows (slow system, applications behaving strangely, and such).

▶ The Java console appears randomly.

To troubleshoot and repair systems infected with spyware, first disconnect the system from the Internet. Then, try uninstalling the program from Add/Remove Programs in Windows XP, or Programs and Features in Windows Vista. Some of the less malicious spyware programs can be fully uninstalled without any residual damage. Be sure to reboot the computer afterward and verify that the spyware was actually uninstalled! Next, scan your system with the AV software to remove any viruses that might have infested the system, which might get in the way of a successful spyware removal. Once again, do this in Safe Mode if the AV software offers that option.

> **Note**
>
> In some cases, Safe Mode is not enough, and you need to boot off a CD (Knoppix or BartPE, for example) and then rerun the scans.

Next, scan the computer with the antispyware software of your choice in an attempt to quarantine and remove the spyware. Other programs such as HijackThis can be used in an attempt to remove malware, but be careful with these programs as you will probably need to modify the Registry. Only remove that which is part of the infection.

Finally, you need to make sure that the malware will not re-emerge on your system. To do this, check your home page setting in your browser, verify that your hosts file hasn't been hijacked (located in C:\WINDOWS\system32\drivers\etc), and make sure that unwanted websites haven't been added to the Trusted Sites within the browser.

On a final and sad note, sometimes computers become so infected with malware that they cannot be saved. In this case, the data should be backed up (if necessary by removing the hard drive and slaving it to another system), and the operating system and applications reinstalled.

Cram Quiz

Answer these questions. The answers follow the last question. If you cannot answer these questions correctly, consider reading this section again until you can.

1. Which of the following is the best mode to use when scanning for viruses?

   ○ **A.** Safe Mode

   ○ **B.** Last Known Good Configuration

   ○ **C.** Command Prompt only

   ○ **D.** Boot into Windows normally

2. Which of the following is a common symptom of spyware?

   ○ **A.** Infected files

   ○ **B.** Computer shuts down

   ○ **C.** Applications freeze

   ○ **D.** Pop-up windows

3. Which of the following is one way to prevent spyware?

   ○ **A.** Use firewall exceptions.

   ○ **B.** Adjust Internet Explorer security settings.

   ○ **C.** Adjust the Internet Explorer home page.

   ○ **D.** Remove the spyware from Add/Remove Programs.

CramQuiz Malicious Software

4. What key combination should be used to close a pop-up window?
   - ○ **A.** Windows+R
   - ○ **B.** Ctrl+Shift+Esc
   - ○ **C.** Ctrl+Alt+Del
   - ○ **D.** Alt+F4

Exam Cram Answers

1. **A.** Safe Mode should be used (if your AV software supports it) when scanning for viruses.

2. **D.** Pop-up windows are common to spyware. The rest of the answers are more common symptoms of viruses.

3. **B.** Adjust the Internet Explorer security settings so that security is at a higher level, and add trusted and restricted websites.

4. **D.** Alt+F4 is the key combination that is used to close an active window. Sometimes it is okay to click the X, but malware creators are getting smarter all the time and the X could be a ruse.

File Security

File security is a feature of most operating systems that controls what files and folders a user has access to. To allow access to a folder, that folder must first be shared. Then permissions can be granted or denied to specific users or groups of users. Because files are securable in Windows, access to them is regulated by an Access Control Model. But before we get into sharing and permissions, let's talk a little more about files and folders.

Working with Files and Folders

Previously we covered the basics of files and folders and how to access and work with them in the GUI and in the command line. To further understand how to secure files, let's review the available file attributes. They start with the group of attributes known as RASH:

- *Read-only:* Write-protects the file so that it cannot be modified.

- *Archive:* Its purpose is to quickly determine if a file requires backing up; it is set when a file is overwritten or modified by the operating system.

- *System:* Indicates that the file is integral and important to the operating system; it protects the file.

- *Hidden:* Makes a file invisible when applications attempt to display a list of files.

There are two more attributes: *compression*, which decreases the size of a file so that it uses less space on a volume, and *encryption*, which converts the file (using a cipher) so that it cannot be read by others. We'll talk more about encryption later in this chapter.

It is important to note that the *system* attribute protects a file. Viruses and other malicious attacks could possibly remove the system attribute (and read-only attribute) in an attempt to make modifications to the file or delete the file. For example, if a virus, worm, or RAT gained access to a system with the correct administrative privileges, removing the file would be as simple as using the following syntax:

```
attrib -r -a -s -h filename
del filename
```

When checking if viruses exist or have done damage to a system, use the **attrib** command in the root directory to verify that the proper attributes are set on system files. Here are some of the important root directory system files to watch out for:

- boot.ini

- NTDETECT.COM

- ntldr

- pagefile.sys

By default, all of the preceding files should be set to ASHR except for page-file.sys that should be set to ASH. If there have been any modifications to them, use the **attrib** command to reset them—you might also want to verify that they weren't corrupted, and if you suspect foul play, recover the original files from the installation CD (or service pack CD).

System files and folders are quite often hidden from view to protect the system. In some cases you can simply click on the link Show the Contents of This Folder, but to permanently configure the system to show hidden files and folders navigate to Windows Explorer, Tools menu, and click Folder Options. Then select the View tab and under Hidden Files and Folders select the Show Hidden Files and Folders radio button, as shown in Figure 15.3. Note that in Windows Vista, the menu bar can also be hidden; to view it press Alt+T on the keyboard. To configure the system to show protected system files, deselect the Hide Protected Operating System Files check box, located two lines below Show Hidden Files and Folders. This enables you to view files such as ntldr and boot.ini.

> **ExamAlert**
>
> To view files such as ntldr and boot.ini, deselect the Hide Protected Operating System Files check box.

Sharing Folders

Folders and files need to be shared so that other users on the local computer and on the network can gain access to them. Windows operating systems use an Access Control Model for securable objects like folders. This model takes care of rights and permissions, usually through discretionary access control lists (DACL) that contain individual access control entries (ACEs). All the shared folders can be found by navigating to Computer Management > Shared Folders > Shares, as shown in Figure 15.4.

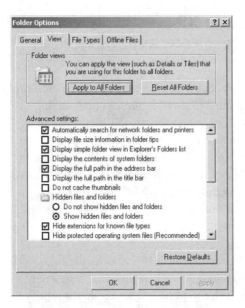

FIGURE 15.3   **The View tab of the Folder Options window**

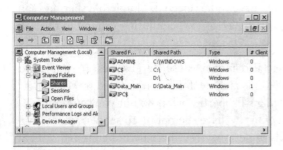

FIGURE 15.4   **Windows XP Shares**

Here we also see the hidden *administrative shares* that can be identified by the $ on the end of the share name. These shares cannot be seen by standard users when browsing to the computer over the network; they are meant for administrative use. Note that every volume (C: or D:, for example) has an administrative share. Although it is possible to remove these by editing the Registry, it is not recommended because it might cause other networking issues. You should be aware that only administrators should have access to these shares.

Sharing folders differs slightly in Windows XP and Windows Vista, so let's briefly discuss each one now.

Sharing Folders in Windows XP

There are two different ways to share folders in Windows XP: By utilizing simple file sharing or by using standard network shares.

Simple file sharing is enabled by default, but if you need to turn it on, you can do so by navigating to the Tools menu in Windows Explorer and selecting Folder Options. From the Folder Options window, click the View tab and scroll to the end of the list. The last option is Use Simple File Sharing; if it is check marked, then it is enabled. To share a file or folder for other *local* users on the computer, simply drag it to the Shared Documents folder, usually listed directly after Control Panel in the left window pane of Windows Explorer; this is known as a *local share*. To share a folder for access by remote users on the network, right-click the folder to be shared, and select Sharing & Security. Next, check mark the Share This Folder on the Network check box. At that point, you can give it a share name that by default is the same as the folder name. Now remote users can either browse to your computer or map a network drive to view the folder's contents. Keep in mind that by sharing the folder in this manner, any user can access the folder, but by default the files will be read-only. For users to modify the files, the option Allow Network Users to Change My Files would have to be selected. Simple file sharing is an example of *share-level security*, which has slowly been losing ground to the more secure *user-level security*.

To use standard network shares (also known as user-level security), simple file sharing must be disabled. When this is done, folders are shared by accessing the same Sharing tab of the folder's Properties window, but you can notice that the window has changed. Now, we have the option to set permissions for the folder. There are two levels of permissions: Share permissions and NTFS permissions.

► Share permissions can be accessed from the Sharing tab by clicking the Permissions button. From here you note that the Everyone group has read-only access by default. The other two permissions available to us are Change and Full Control.

► NTFS permissions are accessed from the Security tab. Here we have six default levels of permissions from Read and Write to Full Control, as shown in Figure 15.5.

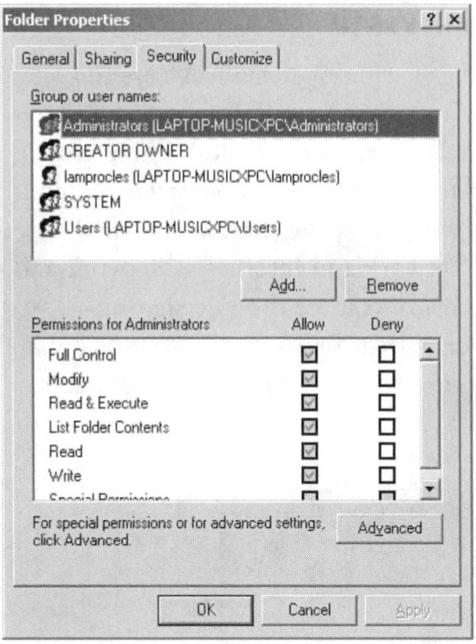

FIGURE 15.5   Security tab of a folder's Properties window

ExamAlert

NTFS permissions are modified in the Security tab of the folder's Properties window.

The weakest of these permissions is Read, and the strongest, of course, is Full Control. You also note that we have the option to Allow access or Deny access and that this can be done by the users or by their user group, thus the term user-level security. Generally, if you want users to have access to the folder, you would add them to the list and select Allow for the appropriate permission. If you don't want to allow them access, normally you simply wouldn't add them. But in some cases, an explicit Deny is necessary. This could be because the user is part of a larger group that already has access to a parent folder, but you don't want the specific user to have access to this particular subfolder.

Of course, permissions can get very in-depth; for more information on simple file sharing and the associated permissions see the following link: http://support.microsoft.com/kb/304040/. For more information on NTFS permissions see: http://technet.microsoft.com/en-us/library/bb727008.aspx.

Sharing Folders in Windows Vista

Windows Vista does not enable simple file sharing by default. Access to shared folders in Vista normally requires a username and password. (So share-level security has, for the most part, gone the way of the dodo.) There are once again two different ways of sharing folders; by using a wizard or doing it manually. First however, we need to make sure that file sharing is turned on! To do this, navigate to Control Panel > Network and Internet > Network and Sharing Center. Under Sharing and Discovery you see the File sharing option; make sure it is turned on. Also verify that Network discovery is on so that other computers can "see" the computer that will be hosting the shares, as shown in Figure 15.6.

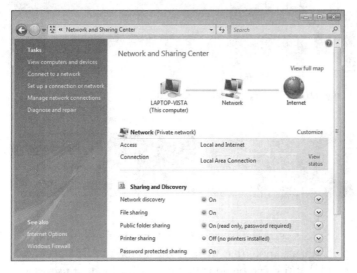

FIGURE 15.6   **Network and Sharing Center**

You will note a few other settings. First is Public Folder Sharing. Although you can share any folder you want, the Public folder was created as a default share that any user on the local computer or other computers can access. It takes the place of the Shared Documents folder in Windows XP. The Public folder can be found by navigating to Start > Documents and then selecting Public under Favorite Links. This setting can be configured so that network users can open files in the Public folder, or open *and* modify them, or the setting can be turned off so that only local users can see the files. Second is Password Protected Sharing. If this is on, a remote user needs to type a username and password to gain access to a share, but if it is off, any user can connect automatically, which is not recommended as it is not secure.

Now, you can enable/disable the wizard previously mentioned by navigating to Windows Explorer, Tools menu, and click Folder Options. Then select the View tab, scroll to the bottom, and either select or deselect the Use Sharing Wizard check box. If you use the wizard and attempt to share a folder by right-clicking it and selecting Share, a window pops up prompting you to select the users that will have access to the folder. The appropriate users are then added to the list and configured as a Reader, Contributor, or Co-author. If you choose not to use the wizard, and want to share a folder, right-click the folder and select Share; then click the Advanced Sharing button. In the Advanced Sharing window, check mark the option for Share This Folder. From there, Share permissions can be added the same way as in Windows XP simply by clicking the Permissions button. To add NTFS security permissions, cancel out of the Advanced Sharing window and select the Security tab; NTFS permissions work the same way as in Windows XP. For more information on File sharing in Windows Vista see the following link: http://technet.microsoft.com/en-us/library/bb727037.aspx.

Permission Inheritance and Propagation

If you create a folder, the default action it takes is to inherit permissions from the parent folder. So any permissions that you set in the parent will be inherited by the subfolder. To view an example of this, locate any folder within an NTFS volume (besides the root folder), right-click it and select Properties, access the Security tab, and click the Advanced button. Here you see an enabled check box named Inherit from Parent the Permission Entries (and so on) toward the bottom of the window, as shown in Figure 15.7. This means that any permissions added or removed in the parent folder will also be added or removed in the current folder. In addition, those permissions that are inherited cannot be modified in the current folder. To make modifications in this case, deselect the Inherit from Parent the Permission Entries (and so on) check box. When you do so, you have the option to copy the permissions from the parent to the current folder or remove them entirely. So by default, the parent is automatically propagating permissions to the subfolder, and the subfolder is inheriting its permissions from the parent. You can also propagate permission changes to subfolders that are not inheriting from the current folder. To do so, select the Replace Permission Entries on All Child Objects (and so on) check box. This might all seem a bit confusing, and you will probably not be asked many questions on the subject. Just remember that folders automatically inherit from the parent unless you turn inheriting off—and you can propagate permission entries to subfolders at any time by selecting the Replace option.

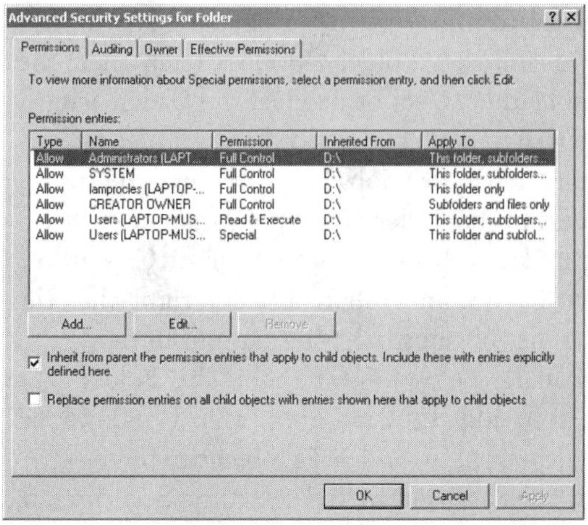

FIGURE 15.7 Advanced Security Settings window

Moving and Copying Folders and Files

This subject (and the previous one) is actually an MCSE type concept, so we'll try to keep this simple. Moving and copying folders have different results when it comes to permissions. Basically, it breaks down like this:

▶ If you *copy* a folder on the same or to a different volume, the folder inherits the permissions of the parent folder it was copied to (target directory).

▶ If you *move* a folder to a different location on the same volume, the folder retains its original permissions.

> **Note**
>
> Keep in mind that when you move data, the data isn't actually relocated; instead the pointer to the file or folder is modified.

Encryption

Encryption is the process of converting information, with the use of a cipher (algorithm), making it unreadable by other users unless they have the correct "key" to the information. Cryptography is the practice of hiding information. In a cryptosystem, information is protected by disguising it.

Types of Encryption

There are two main types of encryption algorithms:

▶ **Symmetric key:** This encryption system uses a common shared key between the sender and the receiver. It is quick and easier to implement than an asymmetric system. One logistical issue with symmetric keys is that the shared key must be communicated between the users securely before file transfer can commence. Examples of symmetric key technology include Encrypting File System (EFS), BitLocker, WEP, WPA, Kerberos, AES, 3DES, and Rivest's cipher.

▶ **Asymmetric key:** This system uses two keys; one is public, the other private. Users encrypt data with the public key of the target computer. Upon receipt of the data, the target uses a private key to decrypt the data. One issue with asymmetric is ensuring that the public key is authentic; to be certain, organizations will use a PKI or public key infra-structure. Examples of asymmetric key technology include RSA and ECC.

Exam Alert

Know the difference between symmetric key and asymmetric key technologies.

Another type of encryption is used for verifying the integrity of files that are downloaded; this is known as *hashing*. A hash is a mathematically generated number that ensures message integrity. Examples of hash algorithms include Secure Hash Algorithm (SHA) and Message-Digest algorithm 5 (MD5).

Encryption in Windows

There are a few different encryption technologies used in Windows. For example, whenever you log on to a Windows network, that authentication is secured with the Kerberos protocol. Another example is when you want to encrypt one or more files or folders. In this case Windows uses the Encrypting File System (EFS), a component of NTFS. Follow the steps below to encrypt a file in Windows:

1. Locate the file, right-click it, and select Properties. This brings up the General tab within the file's Properties window.

2. At the bottom of the General tab, click the Advanced button. This brings up the Advanced Attributes window.

3. Check the box labeled Encrypt Contents to Secure Data.

4. Click OK for both windows. (When you do so, the system should ask whether you want to encrypt the parent folder and the file or just the file. It's recommended that the file's parent folder be encrypted as well.)

The file should now appear green within Windows Explorer. To unencrypt the file and return it to normal, simply deselect the check box.

> **Note**
>
> Windows XP Home edition doesn't include EFS.

EFS is considered a symmetric key technology but actually uses symmetric and asymmetric keys. Any individual or program that does not have the correct key cannot read the encrypted file. If a file needs to be decrypted and the original user (owner of the key) isn't available, an EFS recovery agent will need to be used. In many cases, the default recovery agent is the built-in Administrator account. It is important to note a few more items: One is that EFS isn't designed to protect data while it is transferred from one computer to another; the other is that it is not designed to encrypt an entire disk.

To encrypt an entire disk, you need some kind of full disk encryption software. There are several currently available on the market; one developed by Microsoft is called BitLocker—available only on Vista Ultimate and Vista Enterprise. This software can encrypt the entire disk which, after complete, is transparent to the user. However, there are some requirements for this including:

▶ A Trusted Platform Module (TPM): A chip residing on the motherboard that actually stores the encrypted keys.

or

▶ An external USB key to store the encrypted keys.

and

▶ A hard drive with two volumes, preferably created during the installation of Windows. One volume is for the operating system (most likely C:) that will be encrypted; the other is the active volume that remains unencrypted so that the computer can boot. If a second volume needs to be created, the BitLocker Drive Preparation Tool can be of assistance and can be downloaded from Windows Update.

BitLocker software is based on the Advanced Encryption Standard (AES) and uses a 128-bit key. Keep in mind that a drive encrypted with BitLocker usually suffers in performance compared to a nonencrypted drive and could have a lesser shelf life as well.

> **Note**
>
> Windows sessions over the Internet can be encrypted by utilizing Microsoft Challenge-Handshake Authentication Protocol (MS-CHAP) and MS-CHAP Version 2. These authenticate a user or a networked computer to an authenticating entity such as an Internet access provider. This is sometimes used with virtual private network (VPN) connections and can be enabled within the Advanced Security Settings window within the VPN adapter's Properties page.

Cram Quiz

Answer these questions. The answers follow the last question. If you cannot answer these questions correctly, consider reading this section again until you can.

1. Which operating system offers simple file sharing?
   - **A.** Windows XP
   - **B.** Windows Vista
   - **C.** Windows 2000
   - **D.** DOS

2. Where would you turn on file sharing in Windows Vista?
   - **A.** Control Panel
   - **B.** Local Area Connection
   - **C.** Network and Sharing Center
   - **D.** Firewall properties

3. Which option will enable you to view ntldr?
   - **A.** Enable Hide protected operating system files
   - **B.** Disable Show hidden files and folders
   - **C.** Disable Hide protected operating system files
   - **D.** Remove the –R attribute

4. Which type of encryption technology is used with the BitLocker application?

- ○ **A.** Symmetric
- ○ **B.** Asymmetric
- ○ **C.** Hashing
- ○ **D.** WPA2

Cram Quiz Answers

1. **A.** Windows XP uses simple file sharing by default. However, most network admins opt to use standard sharing; also, there is no simple file sharing when computers are members of a domain. The approximate equivalent of this in Windows Vista would be known as Disable Password Protected Sharing.

2. **C.** The Network and Sharing Center is where you would enable file sharing in Windows Vista.

3. **C.** To view ntldr, you need to disable the Hide protected operating system files check box. Keep in mind that you should have already enabled the Show hidden files and folders radio button.

4. **A.** BitLocker uses symmetric encryption technology based off AES.

Additional Reading and Resources

Barrett, Diane, et al. *CompTIA Security+ Exam Cram*, Second Edition. Que, 2009.

Additional A+ resources: http://www.davidlprowse.com/aplus

CHAPTER 16

Safety and Professionalism

This chapter covers the following A+ exam topics:

▶ Safety and Environmental Procedures

▶ Professionalism and Communication Skills

You can find a master list of A+ exam topics in the "Introduction."

This chapter covers CompTIA A+ 220-701 objectives 6.1 and 6.2 and CompTIA A+ 220-702 objective 1.4.

In this chapter you learn how to safely work inside a computer and how to properly operate the computer. By using *electrostatic discharge (ESD)* prevention methods, you protect your computer's components. Utilizing proper ergonomics helps to protect your body from the possible long–term, damaging effects of operating the computer. Other safety issues covered include electrical safety, physical safety, *material safety data sheets (MSDSs)* and disposal of equipment, and *electromagnetic interference (EMI)* and *radio frequency interference (RFI)*, all of which you might get questions about on the A+ exams.

This chapter also covers the correct way to approach customers. By being professional and utilizing good communication skills, you increase the chances to receive a good customer reaction. Also, these skills help you to get to the heart of the issue and can help to make you more efficient, saving time as you repair computer problems. Throughout the rest of the book, you learned how to repair the computer. Now put those abilities together with a professional demeanor and good communication skills, and there should be no lack of new customers in the future.

Safety and Environmental Procedures

Safety first! Remember to put safety on the top of your priority list when dealing with computers, power, networking, and anything else in IT. Let's talk about some of the things to watch out for when working on computers, how to keep yourself and the computer safe, and how to be environmentally conscious.

Electrical Safety

Electricity is a great energy that should be treated as such. Before working on any computer component, turn off the power and disconnect the device from the AC outlet. If a device such as a power supply or video monitor has a label that says, "No serviceable components inside," take the manufacturer's word for it and send the component to the proper repair facility, or simply replace the component. The message on the device is intended to keep a person out, usually because the internal components might hold an electrical charge.

Be sure to use your multimeter and power supply tester properly. If you do not know how to use these, refer to Chapter 5, "Power," or escalate the issue to another person in your company. If you find issues with AC outlets, or other AC equipment, refer this to your manager or building supervisor. Do not try to fix these issues yourself. If you find an issue like this in a customer's home, tell them about the problem and recommend that they have the AC outlet repaired before going any further.

Do not open power supplies. As far as the A+ exam is concerned, if a power supply goes bad, replace it, even if you think it is just the fan and would be an easy repair. It is known as a *field replaceable unit (FRU)* for a reason. Although it is possible to repair power supplies, it should be done only by trained technicians. Remember that the power supply holds a charge; this alone should be enough to keep you away from the internals of the power supply. But in addition to that, the amount of time it would take a person to repair a power supply would cost more to a company than just buying a new one and installing it.

It is recommended that you do not open CRT monitors; these also carry a lethal charge. Instead, refer these monitors to a company that is specialized in monitor repair. If you work outside, but near the CRT monitor, disconnect any antistatic wrist strap being worn. If for some reason you decide to disregard this warning and do work on a CRT monitor, be sure to discharge the anode. To do this follow these instructions:

1. Turn off the monitor and unplug it.

2. Carefully remove the outer housing of the monitor.

3. Using a wire with alligator clips on both ends, attach one end to part of the metal frame of the monitor; attach the other end to the metal portion of an insulated, long, flat-blade screwdriver.

4. Holding the insulated handle, carefully slide the flat end of the screwdriver underneath the insulation that covers the anode until the screwdriver comes into contact with the anode. There will be a pop or crackling noise as the anode is discharged. Hold the screwdriver there for several seconds before carefully removing it.

LCD monitors aren't as simple as CRTs; I can't really tell you *not* to work on them, especially because laptops integrate them. Regardless, it is again recommended that the failed monitor (or laptop) be sent to the proper repair organization, or to the manufacturer if the device is within warranty. However, if a technician does decide to work on the LCD, one thing to be careful of are capacitors; these are normally near the LCD power supply and hold a charge. Also, make sure that the device is turned off and unplugged, and if it is a laptop, that the battery has been removed. One of the items that can fail on an LCD monitor is the backlight inverter. The inverter is usually mounted on a circuit board, and if it fails, either a fuse needs to be replaced or the entire inverter board. The inverter is a high-voltage device; try not to touch it, and be especially sure not to touch it if the LCD device is on. A lot of this is common sense, but it is worthwhile to always be sure—like measuring twice before you cut. For more information on repairing laptop LCDs, see Scott Mueller's *Upgrading and Repairing Laptops* and accompanying videos published by Que.

ExamAlert

Do not touch an LCD's inverter, if the device is on!

Another device that you need to make sure you turn off and unplug is the laser printer. Extremely dangerous high voltages are inside a laser printer. On a related note, watch out for the fuser if the printer were recently used; the fuser runs hot!

Finally, it is important to match the power requirement of your computer equipment with the surge protector, or uninterruptible power supply (UPS), that it connects to. Verify that the amount of watts your computer's power supply requires is not greater than the amount of power your surge protector can provide; the same goes for the watts (or volt-amps) that the UPS can provide. In addition, be sure that you do not overload the circuit that you connect to. For more information regarding electricity used by your computer, see Chapter 5. For additional information about electrical safety, see the electrical safety and health topics at OSHA's website: http://www.osha.gov/SLTC/electrical/index.html.

ESD

Electrostatic discharge (ESD) occurs when two objects of different voltages come into contact with each other. The human body is always gathering static electricity, more than enough to damage a computer component, for example, that $500 video card you just purchased! ESD is a silent killer. If you were to touch a component without proper protection, the static electricity could discharge from you to the component, most likely damaging it, but with no discernable signs of damage. Worse yet, it is possible to discharge a small amount of voltage to the device and damage it to the point at which it works intermittently, making it tough to troubleshoot. It takes only 30 volts or so to damage a component. On a dry winter day, you could gather as much as 20,000 volts when walking across a carpeted area! You can equalize the electrical potentials in several ways, allowing you to protect components from ESD, including the following:

▶ **Use an antistatic wrist strap:** The more common kind is inexpensive and takes only a moment to put on and connect to the chassis of the computer. (The chassis is an unpainted portion of the frame inside the case.) By doing so you constantly discharge to the case's metal frame instead of to the components that you handle. Of course, the chassis of the computer can absorb only so much ESD, so consider another earth-bonding point to connect to or try to implement as many other antistatic methods as possible. Most wrist straps come equipped with a resistor (often 1 megaohm) that protects the user from shock hazards when working with low-voltage components.

More advanced types of wrist straps are meant to connect to an actual *ground*; a ground strip or the ground plug of a special dedicated AC outlet. These are used in more-sophisticated repair labs. Do not attempt to connect the alligator clip of a basic wrist strap (purchased at an office store) to the ground plug of an outlet in your home.

▶ **Touch the chassis of the computer:** Do this before handling any components to further discharge yourself. This is also a good habit to get into if an antistatic strap is not available.

▶ **Use an antistatic mat:** Place the computer on top of the antistatic mat and connect the alligator clip of the mat to the computer's chassis in the same manner that you did with the wrist strap. (Some people stand on the mat and connect its alligator clip to the computer, which is also an option.)

▶ **Use antistatic bags:** Adapter cards, motherboards, and the like are normally shipped in antistatic bags; hold on to them! When installing or removing components, keep them either inside or on top of the bag until you are ready to work with them.

▶ **Don't touch any of the chips or circuits:** When handling circuit boards, handle them from the edge. When handling adapter cards, hold them by the bracket at the edge of the card.

▶ **Use antistatic wipes:** Use products, such as Endust, to clean the outside of monitors, computer cases, and keyboards; they apply a certain amount of ESD protection.

▶ **Use antistatic sprays:** These can be sprayed on clothing or on the floor or table in which a technician works.

A few less direct ways to reduce ESD follow:

▶ **Keep your feet stationary:** When working on the computer and touching components, keep your feet stationary to reduce friction.

▶ **Work in a noncarpeted area:** Carpeting creates additional friction that leads to ESD. Some computer labs have special tiling with antistatic properties, but if you work for a company that doesn't have a proper lab or repair room, consider using an uncarpeted warehouse space or uncarpeted cafeteria. If you work at home, consider uncarpeted areas such as the kitchen, basement, or garage.

▶ **Raise the humidity:** By increasing the humidity to 50 percent (if possible), you decrease the chance of friction and ultimately decrease the chance of ESD. Did you ever notice that electrostatic discharges happen more readily during the winter? This is because of the lower humidity during that season.

▶ **Don't use a vacuum cleaner:** Vacuum cleaners can be a deadly source of ESD. When cleaning those dust-bunnies out of the computer, do it outside, and consider using compressed air or other specialized cleaning kits. Use Stabilant-22a or a similar cleaner to enhance the contacts connectivity when you finish.

Remember ESD needs to happen only once, and that $500 video card you try to install is toast!

Physical Safety

Physical safety considerations include the following:

▸ Securing cables

▸ Using caution with heavy items

▸ Not touching hot components

▸ Considering workplace ergonomics

Cables can be a trip hazard. Employ proper cable management by routing cables away from high-traffic areas and keep computer cables stowed away and tie-wrapped. Network cables should have been installed permanently within the walls and ceiling, but sometimes you might find a rogue cable. If you discover a cable lying on the floor, or hanging from the ceiling, alert your network administrator or your manager. Do not attempt to reroute the network cable yourself. You don't know what data is transferred on the cable. Because network cabling is monitored by municipalities the same way other electrical work is done, only qualified, trained technicians should take care of the network wiring.

Be careful with heavy items, such as a rack-mounted UPS, which could weigh up to 100 pounds. If it needs to be moved, ask for assistance, use proper moving equipment, or have the appropriate building personnel move the item for you. When moving items, bend at the knees, and lift with your legs, not with your back.

Watch for hot components. Processors and hard drives can run extremely hot in some computers. Allow them to cool before handling them to avoid minor burns. This goes for components within a laser printer such as the fuser assembly. Sometimes power supplies burn out. This could be accompanied by a significant amount of heat and possibly smoke. Be patient and handle these carefully.

You probably won't get any questions on the exam about this, but ergonomics are important when operating the computer. Ergonomics can affect the long-term health of the computer operator. It is important to keep the wrists and hands in-line with the forearms and to use proper typing technique. Keep the elbows close to the body and supported if possible. The lower back should be supported as well, and your head and neck should be straight and in-line with the back; the shoulders should be relaxed. Keep the top of the monitor at or just below eye level. Take breaks at least every 2 hours to avoid muscle cramps and eyestrain. To further reduce eyestrain, increase the refresh rate of the monitor if possible. For more information on ergonomics, see OSHA's information on computer workstations at http://www.osha.gov/SLTC/etools/computerworkstations/index.html.

MSDS and Disposal

Products that use chemicals require material safety data sheets (MSDSs). These are documents that give information about particular substances, for example the ink in inkjet cartridges. Information in the MSDS includes

▶ Proper treatment if the substance is ingested or comes into contact with the skin.

▶ How to deal with spills and other hazards.

▶ How to dispose of the substance.

▶ How to store the substance.

It's easy to find MSDSs; most companies have them online. You can search for them at the manufacturer's website or with a search engine. For example, the following link has all the Hewlett Packard MSDSs: http://www.hp.com/hpinfo/globalcitizenship/environment/products/msds-specs.html. Click on any category and then a specific product to see its MSDS. An MSDS identifies the chemical substance, possible hazards, fire-fighting measures, handling and storage, and so on. Make sure you have Adobe Acrobat Reader installed because most MSDSs are in PDF format.

Recycling and proper disposal are also important. Batteries should not be thrown away with normal trash because they contain chemicals. First, you should check your local municipal or EPA guidelines for proper disposal of batteries, and in some cases, you will find that there are drop-off areas for these, either at the town municipal center, or sometimes at office and computer supply stores. This applies to alkaline, lithium (for example CR2032), lithium-ion, and NiCd batteries.

> **ExamAlert**
>
> Check your local municipal and EPA guidelines for disposal of batteries and other equipment.

Ink and toner cartridges can usually be sent back to the manufacturer, or quite often office supply stores and printer repair outfits will take them for later recycling. Some municipalities have a method for recycling electrical devices in general.

EMI and RFI

Electromagnetic interference (EMI) is an unwanted disturbance that affects electrical circuits. Network interference could be caused by EMI. For example, if an unshielded network cable was inadvertently draped over a fluorescent light above the drop ceiling. The light's EMI could cause data loss on that cable. Keep network cables away from lights, junction boxes, and any other AC electrical sources. Anything with magnets (speakers, CRTs, UPSs) should be kept away from the computer, and cables should be routed away from these devices. It's possible that lightning can cause EMI line noise to occur within the power cable. A good surge protector or line-conditioning device should deflect this.

Radio frequency interference (RFI) is closely related to EMI. For the A+ exam, some things to consider include cordless phone and microwave usage. Because these devices can also inhabit the 2.4 GHz frequency range used by 802.11b, g, and n networks, they can interfere with the network signal. Be sure that all devices are on different channels (1, 6, and 11 are the nonoverlapping ones) and that the microwave is not physically near any wireless devices.

Cables can act as antennas for radiated energy and should be shielded if possible.

Cram Quiz

Answer these questions. The answers follow the last question. If you cannot answer these questions correctly, consider reading this section again until you can.

1. If a power supply fails, what should you do?

   ○ **A.** Replace it.

   ○ **B.** Repair it.

   ○ **C.** Use a different computer.

   ○ **D.** Switch it to a different voltage setting.

2. Which of the following are ways to avoid ESD? (Select three.)

   ○ **A.** Use an antistatic wrist strap.

   ○ **B.** Use a vacuum cleaner.

   ○ **C.** Use an antistatic mat.

   ○ **D.** Touch the chassis of the computer.

3. What document can aid you in the event of a chemical spill?

   ○ **A.** MSKB

   ○ **B.** MSDS

   ○ **C.** MCSE

   ○ **D.** DSS

Cram Quiz Answers

1. **A.** Replace the power supply. It can be dangerous to try to repair it and is not cost-effective to the company.

2. **A, C, D.** Antistatic wrist straps, mats, and touching the chassis of the computer are all ways to stop ESD.

3. **B.** The material safety data sheet (MSDS) defines exactly what a chemical is, what the potential hazards are, and how to deal with them.

Professionalism and Communication Skills

For the A+ exams, professionalism and communication consists of seven categories:

▶ **Punctuality:** Be on time! If a customer has to wait, he might become difficult before you even begin. If you are running late, contact the customer, apologize, and let him know that you will be late.

▶ **Listen to the customer:** Don't interrupt the customer, even if you think you know what the problem is before she has fully explained the situation. Be respectful and allow her to complete her explanation. Her tale just might give you clues as to what the *real* problem is. Listen carefully but be assertive when eliciting answers.

▶ **Be positive:** Try to maintain a positive attitude, even if the customer thinks the situation is hopeless, or if the customer is frustrated. Sometimes problems that appear to be the worst have the easiest solutions! And there is *always* a solution. It's just a matter of finding it.

▶ **Speak clearly:** Use proper language, and speak slowly and clearly so the customer can fully understand what you tell them. Avoid computer jargon and acronyms (for example WPA or TCP/IP). By using computer jargon, the customer might think that you are insecure and cannot clearly explain things. Stay away from the techno-babble. The customer expects you to know these things technically but to explain them in a simple manner.

▶ **Set and meet expectations:** When you have a clear idea of what the customer's trouble is, set a timeline; offer a reasonable assessment of how long it will take to fix the issue and what will be involved. Stay in contact with the customer giving him updates at certain intervals—every half hour for smaller jobs and perhaps two or three times a day for larger jobs. If applicable, offer different repair or replacement options as the job progresses. At first you might inform a customer that it appears a power supply needs to be changed. Later you might find that an optical drive also needs to be replaced. Keep the customer up to date and offer options. Whatever the service, be clear as to the policies of your company and provide the proper documentation about the services you will be performing. After you finish the job, follow up with the customer to verify that the computer runs smoothly and that he is satisfied.

▶ **Avoid distractions:** Cell phone calls should be screened and left to go to voicemail unless it is an emergency. The same goes for emails that arrive on your PDA and text messages on the phone. If other customers call, explain to them that you are with a customer and will call them back shortly, or have your manager or co-worker take care of them if they are available. Avoid talking to co-workers when dealing with customers. The customer wants to feel valued and wants to get her problem fixed in a timely manner. Try to avoid personal interruptions in general.

▶ **Deal with customers professionally:** Understand that customers can come from all walks of life. By being patient, understanding, and respectful, you show customers that you are a professional and serious about fixing their computer problems. Never argue with customers or take a defensive or offensive stance. This is another one of those times in which I like to think of Mr. Spock. Approach customers' computer problems and complaints from a scientific point of view. Try not to make light of a customer's computer issues, no matter how simple they might seem, and avoid being judgmental of any possible user error. Never ask things such as "What did you do?" or "Who was working on this?" because these questions can come across as accusations. Ask computer-oriented open-ended questions when eliciting answers from the customers, for example "What is wrong with the computer?" or "What can you tell me about this computer?" Stick with the senses; questions such as "What type of strange behavior did you *see* from the computer?" keeps customers more relaxed and can help you to narrow down the cause of the problem. If customers don't come across clearly, restate what you believe to be the issue, or repeat your question to them so that you can verify understanding and so both of you will be on the same page.

Cram Quiz

Answer these questions. The answers follow the last question. If you cannot answer these questions correctly, consider reading this section again until you can.

1. How will speaking with a lot of jargon make a technician sound?

    ○   **A.** Competent

    ○   **B.** Insecure

    ○   **C.** Smart

    ○   **D.** Powerful

2. A customer experiences a server crash. When you arrive, the manager is upset about this problem. What do you need to remember in this scenario?

    ○ **A.** Stay calm and do the job as efficiently as possible.

    ○ **B.** Imagine the customer in his underwear.

    ○ **C.** Avoid the customer and get the job done quickly.

    ○ **D.** Refer the customer to your supervisor.

3. Which of the following are good ideas when dealing with customers? (Select two.)

    ○ **A.** Speak clearly.

    ○ **B.** Ignore them.

    ○ **C.** Avoid distractions.

    ○ **D.** Explain to them what they did wrong.

Cram Quiz Answers

1. B. Too much computer jargon can make an end user think that you do not have the qualifications needed and are masking it with techno-babble.

2. A. There isn't much you can do when a customer is upset except fix the problem!

3. A and C are correct. Speak clearly so that customers understand you and avoid distractions so that the customers know they have your complete attention.

Additional Reading and Resources

Mueller, Scott. *Upgrading and Repairing Laptops*. Que.

CHAPTER 17

Taking the Real Exams

This chapter provides the following tools and information to help you be successful when preparing for and taking the CompTIA A+ 220-701 and 220-702 exams:

▶ Getting Ready and the Exam Preparation Checklist

▶ Tips for Taking the Real Exam

▶ Beyond the CompTIA A+ Certification

Getting Ready and the Exam Preparation Checklist

The CompTIA A+ certification exams can be taken by anyone; there are no prerequisites although CompTIA recommends prior experience working with computers. For more information on CompTIA and the A+ exam, go to http://www.comptia.org/certifications/listed/a.aspx. To acquire your A+ certification, you need to pass two exams: 220-701, and 220-702, each of which is 100 questions. Although it is possible, I don't recommend taking both exams on the same day, but instead spacing them a week or so apart. These exams are administered by two testing agencies: Sylvan Prometric (www.2test.com) and Pearson Vue (www.vue.com). You need to register with one of those test agencies to take the exams.

It is important to be fully prepared for the exam, so I created a checklist that you can use to make sure you have covered all the bases. The checklist is shown in Table 17.1. Go through the checklist twice, once for each exam. For each exam place a check in the status column as each item is completed. Do this first with the 220-701 exam and then again with the 220-702 exam. I highly recommend completing each step in order and taking the 220-701 exam first. Historically, my readers and students have benefited greatly from this type of checklist.

TABLE 17.1 **Exam Preparation Checklist**

Step	Item	Details	220-701 Status	220-702 Status
1.	Complete the Practice Exam in the book.	Directly after this chapter are three practice exams. On the first run-through of this checklist, take the first exam, which is geared toward the 220-701 exam. On the second run-through of this checklist, take the second and third, which are geared toward the 220-702 exam. Your goal should be to get at least 80% correct on each exam. Keep taking them until you have reached 80%. (100% would be preferable!)		
2.	Complete the Practice Exam on the CD.	The CD contains three practice exams. On the first run-through of this checklist, take the first exam, which is geared toward the 220-701 exam. On the second run-through of this checklist, take the second and third, which are geared toward the 220-702 exam. Your goal should be to get at least 80% correct on each exam. Keep taking them until you have reached 80%. (Again, 100% would be preferable!)		
3.	*(Optional)* Complete any other testing engine software you acquired.	Pearson Education (and other companies) offer additional test software. Although some readers use this book solely, others have additional testing resources; complete these in this step.		
4.	Create your own cheat sheet.	Although there is a Cram Sheet in the beginning of this book, you should also create your own. See Table 17.2 for an example. The act of writing down important details helps to commit them to memory. Keep in mind that you will not be allowed to take this or the Cram Sheet into the actual testing room.		
5.	Register for the exam.	Do not register until you have completed the previous steps; you shouldn't register until you are fully prepared. When you are ready, schedule the exam to commence within a day or two so that you won't forget what you learned!		

TABLE 17.1 **Continued**

Step	Item	Details	220-701 Status	220-702 Status
		Registration can be done over the phone or online, although online is much easier. Register at one of the two websites:		
		▶ Sylvan Prometric: www.2test.com		
		▶ Pearson Vue: www.vue.com		
		You need to input your personal information into a secure website. Afterward, you will be assigned an ID#, which you can refer to for all your exams. They accept payment by major credit card for the exam fee.		
		To save some money, consider purchasing discounted exam vouchers from places such as http://www.getcertified4less.com/. If you choose to do this, you pay the company that provides you with the voucher (which is sent to you by email). Then, when you register for the exam with Sylvan or Vue, you input the voucher number, instead of paying by credit card.		
6.	Study the Cram Sheet and cheat sheet.	The Cram Sheet is a fold out in the beginning of this book. Study from this and your cheat sheet during the day or two between when you registered and the day of the exam.		
		(If your exam gets delayed for any reason, go back to steps 1 and 2 and retake the practice exams until once again the test day is a day or two off.)		
7.	Take the exam!	Check mark each exam to the right as you pass them. Good luck!		

Table 17.2 gives a partial example of a cheat sheet that you can create to aid in your studies. Fill in the appropriate information in the right column. For example, the first step of the six-step troubleshooting process is "Identify the problem."

TABLE 17.2 **Example Cheat Sheet**

Concept	Fill in the Appropriate Information Here
The six-step troubleshooting process	1.
	2.
	3.
	4.
	5.
	6.
The four form factors you should know	
The three types of DDR and their data transfer rates	
The EP printing process	
Six types of expansion busses and their maximum data transfer rates	
Windows Vista startup files	
Windows XP startup files	
Etc.*	

*Continue Table 17.2 in this fashion on paper. The key is to write down various technologies, processes, step-by-steps, and so on to commit them to memory.

Tips for Taking the Real Exam

Some of you readers will be new to exams. This section is for you. For other readers who have taken exams before, feel free to skip this section or use it as a review.

The exam is conducted on a computer and is multiple choice. You have the option to skip questions. If you do so, be sure to "mark" them before moving on. There is be a small check box that you can select to mark them. Feel free to mark any other questions that you have answered but are not completely sure about. When you get to the end of the exam, there will be an item review section, which shows you any questions that you did not answer and any that you marked.

The following list includes tips and tricks that I have learned over the years. I've taken at least 20 certification exams in the past decade, and the following points have served me well:

▶ **Pick a good time for the exam:** It would appear that the least amount of people are at test centers on Monday and Friday mornings. Consider scheduling during these times. Otherwise, schedule a time that works well for you, when you don't have to worry about anything else. Keep in mind that Saturdays can be busy.

▶ **Don't over-study the day before the exam:** Some people like to study hard the day before; some don't. My recommendations are to study off the Cram Sheet and your own cheat sheets, but in general, don't overdo it. It's not a good idea to go into overload the day before the exam.

▶ **Get a good night's rest:** A good night's sleep (7 to 9 hours) before the day of the exam is probably the best way to get your mind ready for an exam.

▶ **Eat a decent breakfast:** Eating is good! Breakfast is number two when it comes to getting your mind ready for an exam, especially if it is a morning exam.

▶ **Show up early:** Both testing agencies recommend that you show up 30 minutes prior to your scheduled exam time. This is important; give yourself plenty of time, and make sure you know where you are going. You don't want to have to worry about getting lost or being late. Stress and fear are the mind killers. Work on reducing any types of stress the day of and the day before the exam. By the way, you really do need extra time because when you get to the testing center, you need to show ID, sign forms, get your personal belongings situated, and be escorted to your seat. Have two forms of ID (signed) ready for the administrator of the test center. Turn your cell phone or smartphone off when you get to the test center; they'll check that, too.

▶ **Bring ear plugs:** You never know when you will get a loud testing center, or worse yet, a loud test taker next to you. Ear plugs help to block out any unwanted noise that might show up. Just be ready to show your ear plugs to the test administrator.

▶ **Brainstorm before starting the exam:** Write down as much as you can remember from the Cram and cheat sheets before starting the exam. The testing center is obligated to give you *something* to write on; make use of it! By getting all the memorization out of your head and on "paper" first, it clears the brain somewhat so that it can tackle the questions. I put paper in quotation marks because it might not be paper; it could be a mini dry erase board or something similar.

▶ **Take small breaks while taking the exam:** Exams can be brutal. You have to answer one hundred questions while staring at a screen for an hour. Sometimes these screens are old and have seen better days; these older flickering monitors can cause a strain on your eyes. I recommend small breaks and breathing techniques. For example, after going through every 25 questions or so, close your eyes, and slowly take five deep breaths, holding each one for 5 seconds, and releasing each one slowly. Think about nothing while doing so. Remove the test from your mind during these breaks. It takes only ½ a minute, but can really help to get your brain refocused.

▶ **Use the process of elimination:** If you are not sure about an answer, first eliminate any answers that are definitely *incorrect*. You might be surprised how often this works. This is one of the reasons why it is recommended that you not only know the correct answers to the practice exams' questions, but also know *why* the wrong answers are wrong. The testing center should give you something to write on; use it by writing down the letters of the answers that are incorrect to keep track.

▶ **Use your gut instinct:** Sometimes a person taking a test just doesn't know the answer; it happens to everyone. If you have read through the question and all the answers and used the process of elimination, sometimes this is all you have left. In some scenarios, you might read a question and instinctively know the answer, even if you can't explain why. Tap into this ability. Some test takers write down their gut instinct answer before delving into the question and then compare their thoughtful answer with their gut instinct answer.

▶ **Don't let one question beat you!** Don't let yourself get stuck on one question. Skip it and return to it later. When you spend too much time on one question, the brain gets sluggish. The thing is with these exams you either know it or you don't. And don't worry too much about it; chances are you are not going to get a perfect score. Remember that the goal is only to pass the exams; how many answers you get right after that is irrelevant. If you have gone through this book thoroughly, you should be well prepared, and you should have plenty of time to go through all the exam questions with time to spare to return to the ones you skipped and marked.

▶ **If all else fails, guess:** Remember that the exams might not be perfect. A question might seem confusing or appear not to make sense. Leave questions like this until the end, and when you have gone through all the other techniques mentioned, make an educated, logical guess. Try to imagine what the test is after, and why they would be bringing up this topic, vague or strange as it might appear.

▶ **Review all of your answers:** Use the time allotted to you to review the answers. Chances are you will have time left over at the end, so use it wisely!

Beyond the CompTIA A+ Certification

After you pass the exams, consider thinking about your technical future. Not only is it important to keep up with new technology and keep your technical skills sharp, but technical growth is important as well.

Usually, companies wait at least 6 months before implementing new operating systems and other applications on any large scale, but you will have to deal with it sooner or later, most likely sooner. Microsoft is always releasing new products. Consider getting access to the latest Microsoft software and operating systems, and practice installing, upgrading, configuring, and troubleshooting them. And Microsoft isn't the only player in town, although the A+ exams focus on it almost exclusively. Apple regularly releases new operating systems for its computers, and several types of Linux operating systems are slowly gaining acceptance and PC market share. Consider becoming proficient in these other operating systems.

To keep on top of the various PC technologies, think about subscribing to periodicals and accessing technology websites on a regular basis. After all, a technician's skills need to be constantly honed and kept up-to-date. My website has lists of websites, periodicals, and other sources that I utilize.

Information Technology (IT) people need to keep learning to foster good growth in the field. Consider taking other certification exams after you complete the A+. The CompTIA A+ certification acts as a springboard to other certifications. For example, the CompTIA Network+ is designed to identify a technician's knowledge of network operating systems, equipment, and networking technologies. The CompTIA Security+ takes this to another level, evaluating the technician's knowledge of how to secure networks and PCs, and their applications. Another nonvendor-specific certification is the CWNA. This one proves a technician's knowledge of wireless networks and wireless devices. And of course, there are vendor-specific certifications from Microsoft, Cisco, Check Point, and many others. Now that you know exactly how to go about passing a certification exam, consider more certifications to bolster your resume. The best advice I can give is to do what you love. From an IT perspective, I usually break it down by technology, as opposed to by the vendor. For example, you might want to learn more about email systems, or securing internetworks, or you might prefer to work on databases. Whatever the field, learn as much as you can about that field and all its vendors to stay ahead.

I wish you the best of luck in your IT career endeavors. And remember that I am available to answer any of your questions about this book via my website: http://www.davidlprowse.com.

Practice Exam 1

CompTIA A+ 220-701

The 100 multiple-choice questions provided here help you to determine how prepared you are for the actual exam and which topics you need to review further. Write down your answers on a separate sheet of paper so that you can take this exam again if necessary. Compare your answers against the answer key that follows this exam.

1. Which of the following are the most common expansion busses on today's motherboards? (Select all that apply.)
   - ○ **A.** PCI
   - ○ **B.** PCIe
   - ○ **C.** AMR
   - ○ **D.** AGP

2. Which adapter card slot has a 32-bit wide data path or "bus"?
   - ○ **A.** USB
   - ○ **B.** PCI
   - ○ **C.** PCIe
   - ○ **D.** ISA

3. While you are working at a customer site, a friend calls you on your cell phone. What should you do?
   - ○ **A.** Ignore the call for now.
   - ○ **B.** Go outside and take the call.
   - ○ **C.** Answer the phone as quietly as possible.
   - ○ **D.** Text your friend.

4. You spill an unknown chemical on your hands. What should you do?
   - ○ **A.** Call 911.
   - ○ **B.** Call the building supervisor.
   - ○ **C.** Consult the MSDS for the chemical.
   - ○ **D.** Ignore it.

5. You would normally plug speakers into what type of port?

    ○ **A.** Parallel

    ○ **B.** VGA

    ○ **C.** 1/8-inch TRS

    ○ **D.** 1/4-inch TRS

6. At the beginning of the workday, Susan informs you that her computer is not working. When you examine the computer, you notice that nothing is on the display. What should you check first?

    ○ **A.** Check whether the monitor is connected to the computer.

    ○ **B.** Check whether the monitor is on.

    ○ **C.** Check whether the computer is plugged in.

    ○ **D.** Reinstall the video driver.

7. A user complains that his NIC (network interface card) is not functioning and has no link lights. The weather has been changing drastically over the past few days, and humidity and temperature have been rising and falling every day. What could be the direct cause of this problem? Select the best answer.

    ○ **A.** Thermal expansion and contraction

    ○ **B.** Thermal sublimation

    ○ **C.** Chip creep

    ○ **D.** POST errors

8. Beep codes are generated by what?

    ○ **A.** CMOS

    ○ **B.** RTC

    ○ **C.** POST

    ○ **D.** Windows

9. How should you apply spray cleaner to a monitor?

    ○ **A.** Spray the cleaner directly on the monitor screen.

    ○ **B.** Spray the cleaner on the top of the monitor and wipe down.

    ○ **C.** Spray evenly on the monitor.

    ○ **D.** Spray the cleaner on a clean, lint-free cloth first.

10. What is the second step of the A+ troubleshooting methodology?

- ○ **A.** Identify the problem.
- ○ **B.** Establish a probable cause.
- ○ **C.** Test the theory.
- ○ **D.** Document.

11. This is the most common type of RAM architecture used by laptops.

- ○ **A.** DIMM
- ○ **B.** RIMM
- ○ **C.** SODIMM
- ○ **D.** SDRAM

12. Where are the Registry hives stored?

- ○ **A.** \%systemroot%\Windows
- ○ **B.** \%systemroot%\Windows\System32\Config
- ○ **C.** \%systemroot%\System32
- ○ **D.** \%systemroot%\System32\Config

13. Where is the system tray located in Windows XP?

- ○ **A.** In System Tools
- ○ **B.** In the System32 folder
- ○ **C.** On the taskbar
- ○ **D.** Within the Start menu

14. What is the proper order for installing Windows XP?

- ○ **A.** Start installation, partition, format drive
- ○ **B.** Start installation, format, partition drive
- ○ **C.** Start installation, initialize, format, partition drive

15. Bob is having an issue with his display. He guesses that a problem exists with the video driver. How should he boot his Windows XP system to bypass the video driver?

- ○ **A.** Press F8, and then select Safe Mode.
- ○ **B.** Press F6.
- ○ **C.** Press Ctrl, and then select Safe Mode.
- ○ **D.** Press F1.

16. Windows service packs are _____.

    ○ **A.** A new version of the operating system

    ○ **B.** Resource Kit utilities

    ○ **C.** Compilations of software updates and patches

    ○ **D.** Driver updates

17. In Windows Vista, an MMC is blank by default. What would you add to the MMC?

    ○ **A.** Applets

    ○ **B.** Files

    ○ **C.** Directories

    ○ **D.** Snap-ins

18. What is the minimum amount of RAM needed to install Windows Vista?

    ○ **A.** 128MB

    ○ **B.** 256MB

    ○ **C.** 512MB

    ○ **D.** 1GB

19. This type of printer uses a toner cartridge.

    ○ **A.** Ink jet

    ○ **B.** Laser

    ○ **C.** Dot matrix

    ○ **D.** Daisy wheel

20. Which of the following indicate a network-ready printer?

    ○ **A.** An RJ-11 jack

    ○ **B.** A USB connector

    ○ **C.** An RJ-45 jack

    ○ **D.** A SCSI connector

21. Which device stores data even when the computer is off?

    ○ **A.** RAM

    ○ **B.** Processor

    ○ **C.** Hard drive

    ○ **D.** Power supply

22. If you were to connect an ATX power supply to a compatible ATX mother-board, what type of connector would you use?

   ○ **A.** P8/P9

   ○ **B.** P1

   ○ **C.** Molex

   ○ **D.** Berg

23. Which of the following connectors can you use to connect a keyboard? Select all that apply.

   ○ **A.** PS2

   ○ **B.** USB

   ○ **C.** PCI

   ○ **D.** Parallel

24. What type of RAM stick is PC3200?

   ○ **A.** SDRAM

   ○ **B.** RIMM

   ○ **C.** DDR

   ○ **D.** EEPROM

25. To which type of expansion slot would you install a x16 card?

   ○ **A.** PCI

   ○ **B.** PCIe

   ○ **C.** AGP

   ○ **D.** PCI-X

26. Where is the memory controller located in a Core 2 Duo system?

   ○ **A.** On the CPU

   ○ **B.** On memory

   ○ **C.** Within the chipset

   ○ **D.** Within the PCIe controller

27. Russ's computer has a 60GB IDE hard drive that contains his operating system. He wants to add a second IDE hard drive to his computer. How should he configure the two drives?

   ○ **A.** Russ should configure the new drive as master and set the old drive as slave.

   ○ **B.** Russ should configure both drives as slaves.

   ○ **C.** Russ should configure both drives as master.

   ○ **D.** Russ should configure the new drive as slave and the old drive as master.

28. What is the most common output on today's new video cards?

   ○ **A.** VGA

   ○ **B.** DVI

   ○ **C.** HDMI

   ○ **D.** Component Video

29. Which would be the fastest connection for your external hard drive?

   ○ **A.** USB

   ○ **B.** Parallel

   ○ **C.** PS2

   ○ **D.** IDE

30. Stuart wants to format his IDE hard drive in such a way so that it can accept a 300GB partition for the installation of Windows XP. What's the best type of file system for him to choose?

   ○ **A.** FAT

   ○ **B.** FAT16

   ○ **C.** FAT32

   ○ **D.** NTFS

31. A user hands you her laptop in the hopes that you can repair it. What should you do first before making any changes?

   ○ **A.** Back up the important data.

   ○ **B.** Reinstall the operating system.

   ○ **C.** Open the laptop and analyze the components inside.

   ○ **D.** Modify the Registry.

32. You successfully modified the Registry on a customer's PC. Now the customer's system gets onto the Internet normally. What should you do next?

○ **A.** Bill the customer.

○ **B.** Move on to the next computer.

○ **C.** Document your solution.

○ **D.** Run Disk Defrag.

33. What part of the computer checks all your components during boot?

○ **A.** CMOS

○ **B.** POST

○ **C.** BIOS

○ **D.** EEPROM

34. You just built a PC, and when it first boots you hear some beep codes. If you don't have the codes memorized, what are the best devices to examine first? (Select all that apply.)

○ **A.** RAM

○ **B.** CD-ROM

○ **C.** Video card

○ **D.** CPU

35. Although not used as often as a Phillips screwdriver, this tool is sometimes used to remove screws from the outside of a computer case or from within a laptop.

○ **A.** Monkey wrench

○ **B.** Torx wrench

○ **C.** Channel lock

○ **D.** Pliers

36. To move your CPU's speed beyond its normal operating range is called

_____.

○ **A.** Overclocking

○ **B.** Overdriving

○ **C.** Overpowering

○ **D.** Overspeeding

37. Tim installs a new CPU in a computer. After a few hours, the processor starts to overheat. Which of the following might be the cause?

    ○ **A.** The CPU is not locked down.

    ○ **B.** The CPU is not properly seated.

    ○ **C.** Thermal compound was not applied.

    ○ **D.** The CPU is not compatible with the motherboard.

38. What tool should always be used when working on the inside of the computer?

    ○ **A.** Cordless drill

    ○ **B.** Antistatic strap

    ○ **C.** Multimeter

    ○ **D.** Screwdriver

39. Which password is used in the BIOS (CMOS) to prevent end users from accessing the BIOS contents?

    ○ **A.** Supervisor

    ○ **B.** User

    ○ **C.** Administrator

    ○ **D.** Local

40. On a laptop, which of these would least likely be a pointing device?

    ○ **A.** Serial mouse

    ○ **B.** PS/2 mouse

    ○ **C.** USB mouse

    ○ **D.** Touchpad

41. Ben's laptop has two Type II expansion slots. Which of the following would not work with his laptop?

    ○ **A.** One Type III PC Card and one Type I PC Card

    ○ **B.** One Type II PC Card

    ○ **C.** Two Type I PC Cards

    ○ **D.** One Type III PC Card

42. Most laptops use what kind of hard drive interface?

    ○ **A.** SCSI

    ○ **B.** ATA

    ○ **C.** ATAPI

    ○ **D.** PCIe

43. Which key on a laptop aids in switching to an external monitor?

    ○ **A.** Fn

    ○ **B.** Ctrl

    ○ **C.** Alt

    ○ **D.** Shift

44. Which file is the boot loader in Windows XP?

    ○ **A.** NTDETECT.COM

    ○ **B.** Boot.ini

    ○ **C.** ntldr

    ○ **D.** NTOSKRNL.EXE

45. What tool enables you to create a partition in Windows Vista/XP?

    ○ **A.** Disk Administrator

    ○ **B.** Disk Management

    ○ **C.** Computer Management

    ○ **D.** Disk Cleanup

46. Which type of partition should an operating system be installed to?

    ○ **A.** Primary

    ○ **B.** Extended

    ○ **C.** Volume

    ○ **D.** Logical drive

47. What is the minimum requirement of RAM for Windows XP?

    ○ **A.** 64MB

    ○ **B.** 128MB

    ○ **C.** 256MB

    ○ **D.** 32MB

48. What should you do first before performing an upgrade to an operating system?

    ○ **A.** FDISK the drive.

    ○ **B.** Back up critical data.

    ○ **C.** Back up the old OS.

    ○ **D.** Format the drive.

49. Where can you find and manage system resources allocated to devices?

- ○ **A.** In System Settings
- ○ **B.** In the Performance Console
- ○ **C.** In the Device Manager
- ○ **D.** In the Command Prompt

50. What is the default initial size of virtual memory in Windows XP?

- ○ **A.** 1.5 times RAM
- ○ **B.** 3 times RAM
- ○ **C.** 6 times RAM
- ○ **D.** The same as the amount of RAM on the system

51. What is the boot loader file in Windows Vista called?

- ○ **A.** ntldr
- ○ **B.** BOOTMGR
- ○ **C.** Boot.ini
- ○ **D.** BCD

52. What tool enables you to find out how much memory a particular application is using?

- ○ **A.** MSCONFIG
- ○ **B.** Task Manager
- ○ **C.** CHKDSK
- ○ **D.** System Information

53. Which utility verifies the files on a disk?

- ○ **A.** CHKDSK
- ○ **B.** DEFRAG
- ○ **C.** Disk Cleanup
- ○ **D.** ATTRIB

54. How can you restart the Print Spooler service. Select all that apply.

- ○ **A.** Enter **net stop spooler** and then **net start spooler** in the command line.
- ○ **B.** Enter **net stop print spooler** and then **net start print spooler** in the command line.
- ○ **C.** Go to Computer Management > Services and restart the Print Spooler service.
- ○ **D.** Go to Computer Management > Services and Applications > Services and restart the Print Spooler service.

55. Where is the Windows Update feature located in Windows XP?

- ○ **A.** Start > All Programs > Accessories
- ○ **B.** Start > All Programs
- ○ **C.** Start > All Programs > Control Panel
- ○ **D.** Start > All Programs > Administrative Tools

56. What tool would you be using if you were setting the computer to boot with the Selective Startup feature?

- ○ **A.** Task Manager
- ○ **B.** Recovery Console
- ○ **C.** Safe mode
- ○ **D.** MSCONFIG

57. Which of the following should not be connected to a UPS?

- ○ **A.** PC
- ○ **B.** Monitor
- ○ **C.** Laser printer
- ○ **D.** Speakers

58. Which of these is not a connector you might find on a printer?

- ○ **A.** RJ-45
- ○ **B.** USB
- ○ **C.** PCIe
- ○ **D.** Centronics

59. Dan finishes installing a printer for a customer. What should he do next?

  ○ **A.** Verify that the printer prints in Microsoft Word.

  ○ **B.** Print a test page.

  ○ **C.** Restart the spooler.

  ○ **D.** Set up a separator page.

60. A client brings in a printer that is giving a paper-feed error. What is the most likely cause?

  ○ **A.** The compression rollers

  ○ **B.** The developing rollers

  ○ **C.** The paper tray

  ○ **D.** The pickup rollers

61. The IP address 192.168.1.1 uses what addressing scheme?

  ○ **A.** 64-bit

  ○ **B.** 32-bit

  ○ **C.** 128-bit

  ○ **D.** 40-bit

62. This is the most commonly used protocol suite on local area networks.

  ○ **A.** DLC

  ○ **B.** IPX/SPX

  ○ **C.** NETBEUI

  ○ **D.** TCP/IP

63. When running cable through drop ceilings, what type of cable do you need?

  ○ **A.** PVC

  ○ **B.** Category 5

  ○ **C.** Strong cable

  ○ **D.** Plenum

64. What is the maximum distance at which a Class 2 Bluetooth device can receive signals from a Bluetooth access point?

  ○ **A.** 300 feet (approx. 100 meters)

  ○ **B.** 30 feet (approx. 10 meters)

  ○ **C.** 3 feet (approx. 1 meter)

  ○ **D.** 15 feet (approx. 5 meters)

65. The wireless protocol 802.11g has a maximum data transfer rate of what?

- ○ **A.** 11Mbps
- ○ **B.** 600Mbps
- ○ **C.** 480Mbps
- ○ **D.** 54Mbps

66. This type of virus propagates itself by tunneling through the Internet and networks.

- ○ **A.** Macro
- ○ **B.** Phish
- ○ **C.** Trojan
- ○ **D.** Worm

67. What user account permissions are needed to install device drivers on Windows Vista?

- ○ **A.** User
- ○ **B.** Guest
- ○ **C.** Administrator
- ○ **D.** Power user

68. Which component of Windows Vista enables users to perform common tasks as nonadministrators, and when necessary, as administrators, without having to switch users, log off, or use Run As?

- ○ **A.** USMT
- ○ **B.** UAC
- ○ **C.** USB
- ○ **D.** VNC

69. What can you do to secure your WAP/router? (Select all that apply.)

- ○ **A.** Change the default SSID name.
- ○ **B.** Turn off SSID broadcasting.
- ○ **C.** Enable DHCP.
- ○ **D.** Disable DHCP.

70. You have been given the task of installing a new hard drive on a server for a customer. The customer will be supervising your work. What should you ask the customer first?

   ○ **A.** What is the administrator password?

   ○ **B.** Are there any current backups?

   ○ **C.** Do you want me to shut down the server?

   ○ **D.** Which version of Windows Server is this?

71. Clinton needs a more secure partition on his hard drive. Currently, the only partition on the drive (C:) is formatted as FAT32. He cannot lose the data on the drive but must have a higher level of security, so he is asking you to change the drive to NTFS. What is the proper syntax for this procedure?

   ○ **A.** `Change C: /FS:NTFS`

   ○ **B.** `Change C: NTFS /FS`

   ○ **C.** `Convert C: /FS:NTFS`

   ○ **D.** `Convert C: NTFS /FS`

72. You work in an Internet cafe. The computers there need to be accessible by anyone. What type of password should you set in the BIOS?

   ○ **A.** User

   ○ **B.** Administrator

   ○ **C.** Supervisor

   ○ **D.** Guest

73. When you connect to a website to make a purchase by credit card, you want to make sure the website is secure. You are using Internet Explorer. What are two ways you can tell whether a site is secure?

   ○ **A.** Look for the padlock (in the locked position) toward the top or bottom of the screen.

   ○ **B.** Look for the padlock (in the unlocked position) toward the top or bottom of the screen.

   ○ **C.** Look for the protocol HTTP in the address or URL bar.

   ○ **D.** Look for the protocol HTTPS in the address or URL bar.

74. Which type of software helps protect against viruses that are attached to email?

   ○ **A.** Firewall software

   ○ **B.** Antivirus software

   ○ **C.** Windows Defender

   ○ **D.** Hardware firewall

75. When is the one time you should *not* use an antistatic strap?

    ○   **A.**   When replacing a hard drive

    ○   **B.**   When upgrading a processor

    ○   **C.**   When working on a CRT

    ○   **D.**   When opening a power supply

76. You are running some cable from an office to a warehouse space. As you are working in the warehouse, a 55-gallon drum falls from a pallet and spills what smells like ammonia. What should you do first?

    ○   **A.**   Call 911.

    ○   **B.**   Call the building supervisor.

    ○   **C.**   Get out of the area.

    ○   **D.**   Save the computer.

77. You are working just outside a server room that is being built and you hear a loud popping sound from inside. As you enter the server room, you notice an electrician lying on the floor with an electrical cord in his hand. What should you do first?

    ○   **A.**   Call 911.

    ○   **B.**   Call the building supervisor.

    ○   **C.**   Pull the electrician away from the cord.

    ○   **D.**   Turn off the electrical power at the source.

78. While you are upgrading a customer's server hard drives, you notice looped network cables lying all over the server room floor. What should you do?

    ○   **A.**   Ignore the problem.

    ○   **B.**   Call the building supervisor.

    ○   **C.**   Tell the customer about safer alternatives.

    ○   **D.**   Notify the administrator.

79. You and a co-worker are running network cables above the drop ceiling. The co-worker accidentally touches a live AC power line and is thrown off the ladder and onto the ground. He is dazed and can't stand. He is no longer near the AC power line. What should you do first?

    ○   **A.**   Cut the power at the breaker.

    ○   **B.**   Move the co-worker farther down the hall.

    ○   **C.**   Apply CPR.

    ○   **D.**   Call 911.

80. What should be done with a lithium-ion battery that won't hold a charge any longer?

    ○ **A.** Throw it in the trash.

    ○ **B.** Return it to the battery manufacturer.

    ○ **C.** Contact the local municipality and inquire as to their disposal methods.

    ○ **D.** Open the battery and remove the deposits.

81. Which of the following is not assertive communication?

    ○ **A.** I know how bad it is when data is lost!

    ○ **B.** Could you explain again exactly what you would like done?

    ○ **C.** Do your employees always cause issues on computers like these?

    ○ **D.** What can I do to help you?

82. After removing malware/spyware from a customer's PC for the third time, what should you do?

    ○ **A.** Tell him you can't fix the system again.

    ○ **B.** Do nothing; the customer pays every time.

    ○ **C.** Show him how to avoid the problem.

    ○ **D.** Change his user permissions.

83. Active communication includes which of the following?

    ○ **A.** Filtering out unnecessary information

    ○ **B.** Declaring that the customer doesn't know what he or she is doing

    ○ **C.** Clarifying the customer's statements

    ○ **D.** Mouthing off

84. A customer has a malfunctioning PC, and as you are about to begin repairing it, the customer proceeds to tell you about the problems with the server. What should you say to the customer?

    ○ **A.** Wait until I finish with the PC.

    ○ **B.** I'm sorry, but I don't know how to fix servers!

    ○ **C.** Is the server problem related to the PC problem?

    ○ **D.** I have to call my supervisor.

85. This device can store a maximum of 1.44MB on a removable disk.

   ○ **A.** Floppy drive

   ○ **B.** CD-ROM

   ○ **C.** ROM

   ○ **D.** Compact Flash

86. If you have a flat-panel monitor, what type of technology is most likely being used? Select the best answer.

   ○ **A.** LCD

   ○ **B.** CRT

   ○ **C.** RGB

   ○ **D.** DVI

87. What is the PC equivalent of FireWire?

   ○ **A.** IEEE 1284

   ○ **B.** USB

   ○ **C.** IEEE 1394

   ○ **D.** ISA

88. A user calls and complains that he cannot get onto the Internet, although he could just minutes before. What should you say to the user?

   ○ **A.** What is your IP address?

   ○ **B.** Wait 10 minutes, and then try it again.

   ○ **C.** Do you remember the last thing that you did?

   ○ **D.** Let me get my supervisor.

89. Which of the following could cause the POST to fail?

   ○ **A.** CPU

   ○ **B.** Power supply

   ○ **C.** CD-ROM

   ○ **D.** Memory

   ○ **E.** Hard drive

90. Which of these is part of step five of the CompTIA A+ troubleshooting process?

   ○ **A.** Identify the problem.

   ○ **B.** Document findings.

   ○ **C.** Establish a new theory.

   ○ **D.** Implement preventative measures.

91. Which expansion bus uses lanes to transfer data?

   ○ **A.** PCI

   ○ **B.** PCI-X

   ○ **C.** PCIe

   ○ **D.** PCIa

92. Which of the following are 64-bit CPUs? (Select all that apply.)

   ○ **A.** Core 2 Duo

   ○ **B.** Phenom II

   ○ **C.** Pentium III

   ○ **D.** Celeron

93. Which kind of socket incorporates "lands" to ensure connectivity to a CPU?

   ○ **A.** PGA

   ○ **B.** Chipset

   ○ **C.** LGA

   ○ **D.** Copper

94. What is a possible symptom of a failing CPU?

   ○ **A.** CPU is beyond the recommended voltage range.

   ○ **B.** Computer won't boot.

   ○ **C.** BIOS reports low temperatures within the case.

   ○ **D.** Spyware is installed into the browser.

95. What is the transfer rate of DDR2-800?

   ○ **A.** 6,400MB/s

   ○ **B.** 8,533MB/s

   ○ **C.** 5,333MB/s

   ○ **D.** 800MHz

96. How should you hold RAM when installing it?

- ○ **A.** By the edges
- ○ **B.** By the front and back
- ○ **C.** With tweezers
- ○ **D.** With an IC puller

97. Which device should you use to protect against power outages?

- ○ **A.** Multimeter
- ○ **B.** UPS
- ○ **C.** Fedex
- ○ **D.** Surge protector

98. Which of the following uses a 24-pin main motherboard power connector?

- ○ **A.** ATX
- ○ **B.** ATX 12V 1.3
- ○ **C.** ATX 12V 2.0
- ○ **D.** ATX 5V 2.0

99. What is the maximum data transfer rate of SATA Version 1.x?

- ○ **A.** 1.5Mbps
- ○ **B.** 300MB/s
- ○ **C.** 150MB/s
- ○ **D.** 1.5GB/s

100. What does the X refer to in Compact Disc technology?

- ○ **A.** 150KB/s
- ○ **B.** 1.32MB/s
- ○ **C.** 133MB/s
- ○ **D.** 4.5MB/s

Answers at a Glance

1. A and B	**35.** B	**69.** A, B, and D
2. B	**36.** A	**70.** B
3. A	**37.** C	**71.** C
4. C	**38.** B	**72.** C
5. C	**39.** A	**73.** A and D
6. B	**40.** A	**74.** B
7. A	**41.** A	**75.** C
8. C	**42.** B	**76.** C
9. D	**43.** A	**77.** D
10. B	**44.** C	**78.** C
11. C	**45.** B	**79.** D
12. D	**46.** A	**80.** C
13. C	**47.** A	**81.** C
14. A	**48.** B	**82.** C
15. A	**49.** C	**83.** C
16. C	**50.** A	**84.** C
17. D	**51.** B	**85.** A
18. C	**52.** B	**86.** A
19. B	**53.** A	**87.** C
20. C	**54.** A and D	**88.** C
21. C	**55.** B	**89.** A and D
22. B	**56.** D	**90.** D
23. A and B	**57.** C	**91.** C
24. C	**58.** C	**92.** A and B
25. B	**59.** B	**93.** C
26. C	**60.** D	**94.** A
27. D	**61.** B	**95.** A
28. B	**62.** D	**96.** A
29. A	**63.** D	**97.** B
30. D	**64.** B	**98.** C
31. A	**65.** D	**99.** C
32. C	**66.** D	**100.** A
33. B	**67.** C	
34. A and C	**68.** B	

Answers with Explanations

1. **A** and **B**. Peripheral Component Interconnect (PCI) and PCI Express (PCIe) are the most common expansion busses on today's motherboards. Audio Modem Riser (AMR) was phased out years ago, and Accelerated Graphics Port (AGP) has been succeeded by PCIe x16 expansion bus slots, although you will still see some AGP devices in the field. See the section titled "Motherboard Components and Form Factors" in Chapter 2, "Motherboards," for more information.

2. **B**. Standard PCI has a 32-bit data path, allowing it to send 32 bits of data simultaneously across the bus. USB sends only 1 bit at a time (serially) and does not work with adapter cards. PCIe is much faster than PCI and behaves in a serial fashion. ISA is an older legacy bus architecture that sends data at 16 bits max. See the section titled "Motherboard Components and Form Factors" in Chapter 2, "Motherboards," for more information.

3. **A**. While on the job site, limit phone calls to emergencies or if your employer calls you about another customer. See the section titled "Professionalism and Communication Skills" in Chapter 16, "Safety and Professionalism," for more information.

4. **C**. If it is not life threatening, consult the MSDS to determine the proper first aid (if any). See the section titled "Safety and Environmental Procedures" in Chapter 16, "Safety and Professionalism," for more information.

5. **C**. 1/8" TRS jacks (also known as mini-jacks) are the most common for speaker connections. Parallel ports are normally used for printers or scanners. VGA is a type of video port. The larger ¼-inch TRS connections are for instrument cables or full-size stereo connections. See the section titled "The Audio Subsystem" in Chapter 12, "Video, Audio, and Peripherals," for more information.

6. **B**. When troubleshooting a computer system, always look for the most likely and simplest solutions first. The fact that Susan might not have turned her monitor on when she first came in is a likely scenario. Afterward, you could check whether the computer is on, if the computer and monitor are plugged into the AC outlet, and whether the monitor is plugged into the computer. Reinstalling the video driver is much further down the list. See the section titled "The Video Subsystem" in Chapter 12, "Video, Audio, and Peripherals," for more information.

7. **A**. Thermal expansion and contraction happens when humidity changes quickly. This can lead to what some technicians refer to as "chip creep" or "card creep." Although there might have been chip creep, the direct cause of the problem was most likely thermal expansion/contraction. POST errors would not be the cause of the error but in some cases could give you diagnostic information leading to the cause. Thermal sublimation deals with a specific type of printing process and is not involved in the problem. While in the computer, you might want to check other adapter cards in the case that they were affected by this phenomenon as well. See the section titled "Networking Fundamentals" within Chapter 14, "Networking," for more information.

8. **C**. As the POST checks all the components of the computer, it may present its findings on the screen or in the form of beep codes. See the section titled "The BIOS" within Chapter 2, "Motherboards," for more information.

9. **D**. Never spray any cleaner directly on a display. Spray on a lint free cloth first, and then wipe the display gently. Try not to get any liquid in the cracks at the edge of the screen. See the section titled "The Video Subsystem" in Chapter 12, "Video, Audio, and Peripherals," for more information.

10. **B**. The second step is to establish a theory of probable cause. You are looking for the obvious or most probable cause for the problem. See the section titled "Troubleshooting Theory" within Chapter 1, "Introduction to Troubleshooting," for more information.

11. **C**. SODIMM (small outline dual in-line memory module) is the most commonly used RAM by laptops. Regular DIMMs are normally used in desktop computers, some of those types include SDRAM, DDR, and RIMMs or RDRAM. See the section titled "Installing, Configuring, and Troubleshooting Internal Laptop Components" in Chapter 11, "Laptops," for more information.

12. **D**. Remember that %systemroot% is a variable. It takes the place of whatever folder contains the operating system. This will usually be Windows (for Windows Vista/XP) and Winnt (for Windows 2000). For example, if you were to run a default installation of Windows XP, the path to the Registry hives would be C:\Windows\System32\Config. See the section titled "System Tools and Utilities" in Chapter 8, "Configuring Windows," for more information.

13. **C**. The system tray is the area toward the bottom-right of your screen. It contains the time, and any applications (shown as icons) currently running in memory. See the section titled "Windows User Interfaces" in Chapter 8, "Configuring Windows," for more information.

14. **A**. To properly install Windows XP (and virtually any operating system), you must start the installation from your media (CD, USB, or network image) and then partition the drive so that there is, at minimum, a primary partition of at least 2GB (2048MB). Then, you format the partition and copy files. See the section titled "Installing and Upgrading Windows XP" within Chapter 7, "Installing and Upgrading Windows," for more information.

15. **A**. When Windows XP is first starting, pressing F8 brings up the Windows Advanced Boot Options menu, which includes several options for Safe mode (among other options). Ctrl brings up a special menu that contains only the Safe mode options (not available in Windows Vista). When you enter Safe mode, the video driver is bypassed and only a simple VGA driver is loaded, allowing Bob to troubleshoot his video driver. (F5 also brings up the Windows Advanced Boot Options menu on some systems.) See the section titled "Repair Environments and Boot Errors" in Chapter 10, "Troubleshooting Windows," for more information.

16. **C**. Microsoft releases many patches for its operating system and normally bundles these bug fixes together as service packs. See the section titled "Updating Windows" in Chapter 9, "Maintaining Windows," for more information.

17. **D**. The MMC (Microsoft Management Console) is a blank shell until you add snap-ins (such as Computer Management) for functionality. See the section titled "Windows User Interfaces" in Chapter 9, "Maintaining Windows," for more information.

18. **C**. Windows Vista requires a minimum of 512MB of RAM for installation. Microsoft *recommends* 1GB of RAM. See the section titled "Installing and Upgrading Windows Vista" in Chapter 7, "Installing and Upgrading Windows," for more information.

19. **B**. Laser printers use toner cartridges. Inkjet printers use ink cartridges. Dot matrix printers and Daisy Wheel printers use a ribbon. See the section titled "Printer Types and Technologies" in Chapter 13, "Printers," for more information.

20. **C**. The RJ-45 jack enables a connection to a twisted-pair (most likely Ethernet) network. See the section titled "Printer Types and Technologies" in Chapter 13, "Printers," for more information.

21. **C**. The hard disk drive (HDD) stores data permanently on a magnetic disk even when the computer is off. When the computer is turned off, the RAM and processor are both cleared of data. The power supply has no data storage capabilities. See the section titled "Magnetic Storage Media" in Chapter 6, "Storage Devices," for more information.

22. **B**. P1 is the connector used to connect an ATX power supply to an ATX motherboard. The P1 connector might be 20-pin or 24-pin depending on the version of ATX. P8/P9 is an older standard used primarily with AT boards. Molex is a four-pin standard used to power such devices as hard drives. And Berg (also called mini) is commonly known as a floppy drive connector. See the section titled "Power Supplies" in Chapter 5, "Power," for more information.

23. **A** and **B**. Keyboards can connect to PS2 or USB ports. Peripheral Component Interconnect (PCI) slots are used by adapter cards such as video cards. Parallel connections are legacy connections used by devices such as printers. See the section titled "Input/Output, Input Devices, and Peripherals" in Chapter 12, "Video, Audio, and Peripherals," for more information.

24. **C**. PC3200 is an example of Double Data Rate (DDR) RAM. SDRAM is an older, slower type of RAM (for example PC100 or PC133). RIMM is another name for RDRAM by the Rambus Corporation, which is uncommon. EEPROM is the chip that stores the BIOS on your motherboard. See the section titled "RAM Basics and Types of RAM" in Chapter 4, "RAM," for more information.

25. **B**. PCI Express (PCIe) slots accept x1, x4, and x16 cards (pronounced "by sixteen"). PCI is an older expansion bus that can accept video cards but they have no particular designation like PCIe. AGP works with video cards but the cards are normally numbered as 1x, 2x, 4x, and 8x (pronounced eight x). PCI-X is used mostly in servers, for example with network adapters. See the section titled "The Video Subsystem" in Chapter 12, "Video, Audio, and Peripherals," and the section titled "Motherboard Components and Form Factors" in Chapter 2, "Motherboards," for more information.

26. **C**. On Core 2 Duo, Quad, and Extreme systems, the memory controller is located within the chipset and is known as the Memory Controller Hub (MCH). On AMD systems and newer Intel systems, the memory controller is located "on-die" meaning on the CPU. See the section titled "Motherboard Components and Form Factors" in Chapter 2, "Motherboards," for more information.

27. **D**. The operating system should be contained within the master drive. By setting the jumper to master on the old drive and setting the jumper to slave on the new drive, Russ will accomplish that. Selecting any other setting listed above might result in problems booting to the operating system. Another option is to use the cable select jumper setting that will attempt to automatically configure the new drive as a slave. Note that this can only be done if the drive is equipped with that jumper setting. See the section titled "Magnetic Storage Media" in Chapter 6, "Storage Devices," for more information.

28. **B**. During the writing of this book DVI (Digital Visual Interface) is the most common type of video connector on new video cards. VGA was the most common for many years previous to DVI. HDMI is more common on televisions, and Component Video is the least common. See the section titled "The Video Subsystem" in Chapter 12, "Video, Audio, and Peripherals," for more information.

29. **A**. USB would be the fastest connection for the external drive. Parallel external hard drives transmit data at a 10th of the speed. IDE is an internal technology (whereas *EIDE* would be external). To date, there are no PS2 hard drives. See the section titled "Input/Output, Input Devices, and Peripherals" in Chapter 12, "Video, Audio, and Peripherals," for more information.

30. **D**. NTFS offers partition sizes of up to 2TB (with a theoretical maximum of 256TB). FAT32 is limited in the partition sizes it can accept; this amount is 32GB during installation, and 137GB otherwise. FAT and FAT16 are essentially the same thing and are limited to 2GB and 4GB partitions. See the section titled "Files, File Systems, and Disks" in Chapter 9, "Configuring Windows," for more information.

31. **A**. Back up data before making any changes to the computer. This way, if your changes affect the functionality of the system, you can always restore the data later. You should do this before making any changes to the software or OS and before opening the computer. See the section titled "Maintaining Hard Disks" in Chapter 8, "Maintaining Windows," for more information.

32. **C**. Documentation is the final step in the troubleshooting process. This helps you to better understand and articulate exactly what the problem (and solution) was. If you see this problem in the future, you can consult your documentation for the solution. Plus, others on your team can do the same. In addition, it is common company policy to document all findings as part of a trouble ticket. See the sections titled "Troubleshooting Theory" and "Troubleshooting Examples" in Chapter 1, "Introduction to Troubleshooting," for more information.

33. **B**. The POST (Power-On Self-Test) is part of the Basic Input Output System (BIOS). It runs a self-check of the computer system during boot and stores many of the parameters of the components within the CMOS. EEPROM is a type of ROM chip on which the BIOS might reside. BIOS is known as firmware. See the section titled "The BIOS" within Chapter 2, "Motherboards," for more information.

34. **A** and **C**. It is common to have an unseated RAM stick or video card. These are the most common culprits of beep codes during the POST. If the CPU is not installed properly, you might not even get any beep codes at all. And the CD-ROM's functionality has little bearing on the POST. See the section titled "Troubleshooting Examples" within Chapter 1, "Introduction to Troubleshooting," for more information.

35. **B**. The Torx wrench is a special tool used to remove screws from the outside of a case; often, proprietary companies such as Compaq use these screws. It can also be used to remove screws (albeit smaller ones) from a laptop. The standard is the size T-10 Torx wrench. See the section titled "Installing, Configuring, and Troubleshooting Internal Laptop Components" in Chapter 11, "Laptops," for more information.

36. **A**. Overclocking is the act of increasing your CPU's operating speed beyond its normal rated speed. See the section titled "CPU 101" in Chapter 3, "The CPU," for more information.

37. **C**. Without the thermal compound applied, the processor might overheat after a few hours. If the CPU is not locked down, or is not properly seated, the PC will simply fail to boot. If the CPU is not compatible with the motherboard, either it will not fit the socket or the PC will not boot. See the section titled "Installing and Troubleshooting CPUs" in Chapter 3, "The CPU," for more information.

38. **B**. Always use an antistatic strap to avoid ESD (electrostatic discharge). Power tools and battery-operated tools such as cordless drills should be avoided. Although multimeters and screwdrivers are tools you *might* use, they might not always be necessary, whereas the antistatic strap should always be worn. See the section titled "Safety and Environmental Procedures" in Chapter 16, "Safety and Professionalism," for more information.

39. **A**. The supervisor (or system) password is used so that only the technician can get into the BIOS (CMOS). The user password is used to password pro-tect whatever operating system is running on the computer, but it does it from the firmware level. An "administrator" password is something used in Windows, and a local password is something used in software. See the sec-tion titled "The BIOS" in Chapter 2, "Motherboards," and the section titled "Authentication" in Chapter 15, "Security," for more information.

40. **A**. Serial devices (and the port in general) are found less and less often on lap-tops. (They are extinct on new laptops.) As these are the slowest (and bulki-est) devices, they have given way to external USB mice and the touchpad. Even PS/2 mice are becoming increasingly rare. See the section titled "Installing, Configuring, and Troubleshooting Visible Laptop Components" in Chapter 11, "Laptops," for more information.

41. A. There is not enough room for a Type III PC Card and a Type I PC Card. However, a single Type III PC Card will work in a laptop with two Type II PC Card slots. See the section titled "Installing, Configuring, and Troubleshooting Visible Laptop Components" in Chapter 11, "Laptops," for more information.

42. B. Most laptops either use PATA or SATA hard drive interfaces, which are collectively known as ATA devices. See the section titled "Installing, Configuring, and Troubleshooting Internal Laptop Components" in Chapter 11, "Laptops," for more information.

43. A. The Fn (Function) key is used for a variety of things, including toggling between the built-in LCD screen and an external monitor/TV. The Fn key is usually blue and offers a sort of "second" usage for keys on the laptop. See the section titled "Installing, Configuring, and Troubleshooting Visible Laptop Components" in Chapter 11, "Laptops," for more information.

44. C. ntldr is the first file to be loaded from the hard drive when the computer is started, it is known as the boot loader. See the section titled "Files, File Systems, and Disks" in Chapter 8, "Configuring Windows," for more information.

45. B. Disk Management is a tool found in Computer Management and allows for the creation, deletion, and formatting of partitions and logical drives. To view this application, right-click My Computer and select Manage. Then click the Disk Management icon. See the section titled "Files, File Systems, and Disks" in Chapter 8, "Configuring Windows," for more information.

46. A. Primary partitions are the first partitions created on a disk. An OS should always be installed to a primary partition, but before installing the OS, the primary partition should be set to active. See the section titled "Files, File Systems, and Disks" in Chapter 8, "Configuring Windows," for more information.

47. A. Windows XP needs only 64MB to be installed. Microsoft recommends more, but 64 is the bare minimum needed to run the system. See the section titled "Installing and Upgrading Windows XP" in Chapter 7, "Installing and Upgrading Windows," for more information.

48. B. Upgrades can cause issues, worst of which is a loss of data. To protect against this, be sure to back up the *important* files before proceeding with the OS upgrade. See the section titled "Installing and Upgrading Windows Vista" in Chapter 7, "Installing and Upgrading Windows," for more information.

49. C. System resources such as IRQ settings and input/output address ranges are located in the Device Manager. See the section titled "System Tools and Utilities" in Chapter 8, "Configuring Windows," for more information.

50. A. By default, Windows XP (when first installed) analyzes the amount of RAM in the computer and sets the hard drive's initial virtual memory size to 1.5 times that amount. Maximum size is set to 3 times RAM. So, for example, if a user has 1GB of RAM (1024MB), the initial virtual memory file (PAGEFILE.SYS) is 1.5GB (1536MB), and the maximum file size is 3GB (3072MB). See the section titled "System Tools and Utilities" in Chapter 8, "Configuring Windows," for more information.

51. B. the BOOTMGR file (Boot Manager) is the boot loader file for Windows Vista. NTLDR is the boot loader for Windows XP. Boot.ini contains the menu of operating systems for Windows XP. BCD is the Windows Vista Boot Configuration Data store, which takes the place of boot.ini. See the section titled "Files, File Systems, and Disks" in Chapter 8, "Configuring Windows," for more information.

52. B. The Task Manager enables you, via a click of the Processes tab, to view all current processes that are running and how much memory each of them uses. See the section titled "Files, File Systems, and Disks" in Chapter 8, "Configuring Windows," for more information.

53. A. CHKDSK is the only utility that *verifies* files on the hard drive. DEFRAG defragments files, Disk Cleanup removes old and temporary files, and ATTRIB changes the attributes of a file. See the section titled "Command-Line Tools" in Chapter 10, "Troubleshooting Windows," for more information.

54. A and **D**. In the command line, this service is simply known as *Spooler*. Type **net stop spooler** and **net start spooler** to restart the service. In Computer Management, the Print Spooler service is found inside the Services applet, which is inside of Services and Applications in Computer Management. See the section titled "Installing, Configuring, and Troubleshooting Printers" in Chapter 13, "Printers," for more information.

55. B. Windows Update is simply located in Start > All Programs; it is at the top of the list before the first divider. See the section titled "Updating Windows" in Chapter 9, "Maintaining Windows," for more information.

56. D. MSCONFIG enables you to modify the startup selection. See the section titled "System Tools and Utilities" in Chapter 8, "Configuring Windows," for more information.

57. C. Laser printers use large amounts of electricity, which in turn could quickly drain the battery of the UPS. See the section titled "Installing, Configuring, and Troubleshooting Printers" in Chapter 13, "Printers," for more information.

58. C. Printers might connect via RJ-45, USB, or Centronics. However, PCIe is an internal expansion bus that printers do not use. See the section titled "Installing, Configuring, and Troubleshooting Printers" in Chapter 13, "Printers," for more information.

59. B. If the test page prints properly, it should be unnecessary to print a page in Word. Restarting the spooler is not needed if the printer has just been installed. The spooler should be running. See the section titled "Installing, Configuring, and Troubleshooting Printers" in Chapter 13, "Printers," for more information.

60. D. Paper-feed errors are often caused by the pickup rollers, which are in charge of feeding the paper into the printer. See the section titled "Installing, Configuring, and Troubleshooting Printers" in Chapter 13, "Printers," for more information.

61. B. There are 32 bits in a standard IPv4 address. In this case, the binary equivalent of the IP numbers would be 192 = 11000000, 168 = 10101000, 1 = 00000001, and 1 = 00000001. If you count all the binary bits up, you end up with 32 in total. Therefore, the address is a 32-bit dotted-decimal address. See the section titled "Networking Fundamentals" in Chapter 14, "Networking," for more information.

62. D. TCP/IP (Transmission Control Protocol/Internet Protocol) is the most commonly used protocol suite on local area networks (LANs). See the section titled "Networking Fundamentals" in Chapter 14, "Networking," for more information.

63. D. Plenum-rated cable needs to be installed wherever a sprinkler system cannot get to. This includes ceilings, walls, and plenums. The reason for this is that the PVCs in regular cable give off toxic fumes in the case of a fire. Plenum rated cable has a protective covering which burns slower and gives off less toxic fumes. See the section titled "Network Cabling and Connectors" in Chapter 14, "Networking," for more information.

64. B. Class 2 Bluetooth devices have a maximum range of 30 feet (approximately 10 meters). Class 2 devices are the most common (for example, Bluetooth headsets). Class 1 is 30 feet (approx. 100 meters), and Class 3 is 3 feet (approx. 1 meter). The maximum length of a standard USB cable is 15 feet (approx. 5 meters). See the section titled "Installing and Configuring a SOHO Network" in Chapter 14, "Networking," for more information.

65. D. 802.11g has a maximum DTR of 54Mbps. 802.11b runs at a maximum of 11Mbps. 802.11n draft runs at a maximum of 600Mbps (300 Mbps typical). USB 2.0 Hi-Speed runs at a maximum of 480Mbps. See the section titled "Installing and Configuring a SOHO Network" in Chapter 14, "Networking," for more information.

66. D. Worms travel through the Internet and through LANs. Macros are viruses that attach to programs like Microsoft Word. Trojans are viruses that look like programs and phishing is an attempt to fraudulently acquire information. See the section titled "Malicious Software" in Chapter 15, "Security," for more information.

67. C. The administrator is the only account level that can install device drivers. See the section titled "Authentication" in Chapter 15, "Security," for more information.

68. B. With UAC (User Account Control) enabled, users perform common tasks as nonadministrators, and when necessary, as administrators, without having to switch users, log off, or use Run As. See the section titled "Authentication" in Chapter 15, "Security," for more information.

69. A, B, and **D.** WAP/router devices come with a standard, default SSID name (that everyone knows). It is a good idea to change it. After PCs and laptops have been associated with the wireless network, turn off SSID broadcasting so that no one else can find your WAP. Disabling DHCP and instead using static IP addresses remove one of the types of packets that are broadcast from the WAP. See the section titled "Installing and Configuring a SOHO Network" in Chapter 14, "Networking," for more information.

70. **B**. Always check whether there are backups and physically inspect and verify the backup before changing out any drives. See the section titled "File Security" in Chapter 15, "Security," for more information.

71. **C**. The convert command turns a FAT32 drive into a NTFS drive without data loss, allowing for a higher level of data security. The proper syntax is **convert** *volume* **/FS:NTFS**. See the section titled "Command-Line Tools" in Chapter 10, "Troubleshooting Windows," for more information.

72. **C**. The BIOS has several password types including: user and supervisor. The supervisor password is the password needed to actually access the BIOS. The user password is what acts as a safeguard from anyone getting into the operating system. Because these computers can be used by anyone, the user password is not necessary. However, the supervisor password is important to thwart end users from accessing the BIOS (and possibly changing important settings). Administrator is an account type in the operating system, as is guest. See the section titled "Authentication" in Chapter 15, "Security," for more information.

73. **A** and **D**. The padlock in the locked position tells you that the website is using a secure certificate to protect your session. HTTPS (Hypertext Transfer Protocol Secure) also defines this in the Secure Sockets Layer (SSL) protocol. See the section titled "Networking Fundamentals" in Chapter 14, "Networking," for more information.

74. **B**. Antivirus software (such as McAfee or Norton) updates automatically so as to protect you against the latest viruses. Firewalls protect against intrusion but not viruses. Windows Defender protects against spyware/malware. See the section titled "Malicious Software" in Chapter 15, "Security," for more information.

75. **C**. When opening a CRT, there is a special procedure for discharging and working on the unit. When replacing items such as CPUs, RAM, and hard drives, always use an antistatic strap. However, you should never open a power supply (and so a trick answer). See the section titled "Safety and Environmental Procedures" in Chapter 16, "Safety and Professionalism," for more information.

76. **C**. If there is something that is immediately hazardous to you, you must leave the area. See the section titled "Safety and Environmental Procedures" in Chapter 16, "Safety and Professionalism," for more information.

77. **D**. If the electrician is being electrocuted, you do not want to touch him. Because it appears that the power is still on, turn it off at the source (if it is not near the sparking wire). This will usually be the circuit breaker, cut the power from there. Then call 911. Do not move the cord or the electrician; you could be next. See the section titled "Safety and Environmental Procedures" in Chapter 16, "Safety and Professionalism," for more information.

78. **C**. You need to explain to the customer that there is a safer way. See the section titled "Safety and Environmental Procedures" in Chapter 16, "Safety and Professionalism," for more information.

79. **D**. Because the immediate danger is gone, call 911 right away. The next call would be to the building supervisor to shut the power off. See the section titled "Safety and Environmental Procedures" in Chapter 16, "Safety and Professionalism," for more information.

80. **C**. Every municipality has their own way of recycling batteries. See the section titled "Safety and Environmental Procedures" in Chapter 16, "Safety and Professionalism," for more information.

81. **C**. Asking a customer something like this is just plain rude; this type of communication should be avoided. See the section titled "Professionalism and Communications Skills" in Chapter 16, "Safety and Professionalism," for more information.

82. **C**. Teach the user how to avoid this problem. The customer will then be more likely to come back to you with other computer problems. See the section titled "Professionlism and Communications Skills" in Chapter 16, "Safety and Professionalism," for more information.

83. **C**. For instance, if you are unsure exactly what the customer wants, always clarify the information or repeat it back to the customer so that everyone is on the same page. See the section titled "Professionlism and Communications Skills" in Chapter 16, "Safety and Professionalism," for more information.

84. **C**. Try to understand the customer before making any judgments about the problems. Make sure it isn't a bigger problem than you realize, before making repairs that could be futile. See the section titled "Professionlism and Communications Skills" in Chapter 16, "Safety and Professionalism," for more information.

85. **A**. The floppy disk drive (FDD) stores a maximum of 1.44MB on a removable disk (1.38MB of which is actual data). CD-ROM drives use removable discs; however, the maximum they can store is much greater. The acronym ROM usually refers to a chip on a circuit board that is not removable. Compact Flash comes in varying sizes (all greater than 1.44MB) and is considered a card, not a disk. See the section titled "Magnetic Storage Media" in Chapter 6, "Storage Devices" for more information.

86. **A**. Liquid Crystal Display (LCD) is most commonly the type of technology that a flat panel monitor uses. Cathode Ray Tube (CRT) is an older type of tube technology resulting in a much bulkier monitor. RGB simply stands for red, green, blue (the three primary colors of a CRT monitor). And DVI is short for Digital Video Input, a port you would find on a video card. See the section titled "The Video Subsystem" in Chapter 12, "Video, Audio, and Peripherals," for more information.

87. **C**. IEEE 1394 is the PC equivalent of FireWire. FireWire was originally developed by Apple, and although the two names are often used interchangeably, the PC standard is IEEE 1394. USB is the Universal Serial Bus, a similar standard but with a different architecture and data transfer rate. IEEE 1284 is a PC standard for printer cables. ISA is the Industry Standard Architecture, a legacy 16-bit adapter card slot. See the section titled "Input/Output, Input Devices, and Peripherals" in Chapter 12, "Video, Audio, and Peripherals," for more information.

88. **C**. Questioning the user can often lead to what caused the issue. Of course, you do not want to accuse the user of anything; instead, just ask what the user did for his or her last steps taken on the computer. See the section titled "Professionlism and Communications Skills" in Chapter 16, "Safety and Professionalism," for more information.

89. **A** and **D**. The CPU and memory need to be installed properly for the POST to run (and to pass). The hard drive and CD-ROM might or might not be installed properly, but they are not necessary for the POST to complete. If the power supply is defective, the system will simply not boot and will not even get to the POST. See the section titled "The BIOS" in Chapter 2, "Motherboards," for more information.

90. **D**. Implement preventative measures as part of step 5 to ensure that the problem will not happen again. See the section titled "Troubleshooting Theory" in Chapter 1, "Introduction to Troubleshooting," for more information.

91. **C**. PCIe (PCI Express) uses serial lanes to send and receive data. PCI and PCI-X are parallel technologies, and PCIa is not a known technology. See the section titled "Motherboard Components and Form Factors" in Chapter 2, "Motherboards," for more information.

92. **A** and **B**. Intel's Core 2 Duo and AMD's Phenom II are both 64-bit CPUs. The Pentium III and Celeron are 32-bit CPUs. See the section titled "CPU 101" in Chapter 3, "The CPU," for more information.

93. **C**. LGA (Land Grid Array) is the type of socket that uses "lands" to connect the socket to the CPU. PGA sockets have pinholes that make for connectivity to the CPU's copper pins. See the section titled "CPU 101" in Chapter 3, "The CPU," for more information.

94. **A**. If the CPU is running beyond the recommended voltage range for extended periods of time, it can be a sign of a failing CPU. If the computer won't boot at all, another problem might have occurred, or the CPU might have already failed. Low case temperatures are a good thing (if they aren't below freezing!) and spyware is unrelated. See the section titled "Installing and Troubleshooting CPUs" in Chapter 3, "The CPU," for more information.

95. **A**. DDR2-800 can transfer 6,400MB/s. 800MHz is the doubled clock rate or speed. It has an original clock speed of 400MHz, but doubles that output, so it is often referred to as 800MHz. See the section titled "RAM Basics and Types of RAM" in Chapter 4, "RAM," for more information.

96. **A**. Hold RAM by the edges to avoid contact with the pins, chips, and circuitry. See the section titled "Installing and Troubleshooting RAM" in Chapter 4, "RAM," for more information.

97. **B**. The UPS is the only item listed that protects the computer from power outages like blackouts and brownouts. See the section titled "Power Devices" in Chapter 5, "Power," for more information.

98. **C**. ATX 12V 2.0 combined the 20-pin and 4-pin connectors used in ATX 12V 1.3 into one 24-pin connector. See the section titled "Power Supplies" in Chapter 5, "Power," for more information.

99. **C**. SATA Version 1.x can transfer a maximum of 150MB/s, though most devices won't ever attain that maximum. The standard specifies the transmission of 1.5Gbps. (Notice the lowercase "b" for bits.) 300 MB/s is the data transfer rate of SATA Version 2.x. See the section titled "Magnetic Storage Media" in Chapter 6, "Storage Devices," for more information.

100. **A**. The X in CD technology is equal to 150 KB/s. A 1X drive can read or write 150KB/s, a 2X drive can read or write 300KB/s, and so on. 1.32 MB/s is the 1X speed of a DVD. 133MB/s is the maximum data transfer rate of an Ultra ATA-7 connection, and 4.5MB/s is the 1X speed of a Blu-Ray disc. See the section titled "Optical Storage Media" in Chapter 6, "Storage Devices," for more information.

Practice Exam 2

CompTIA A+ 220-702

The 100 multiple-choice questions provided here help you to determine how prepared you are for the actual exam, and which topics you need to review further. Write down your answers on a separate sheet of paper so that you can take this exam again if necessary. Compare your answers against the answer key that follows this exam.

1. What is the delay in the RAM's response to a request from the memory controller called?

    ○ **A.** Latency

    ○ **B.** Standard deviation

    ○ **C.** Fetch interval

    ○ **D.** Lag

2. In a standard ATX-based computer, how many IDE devices can be installed?

    ○ **A.** 1

    ○ **B.** 2

    ○ **C.** 4

    ○ **D.** 8

3. What is the minimum number of hard drives necessary to implement RAID 5?

    ○ **A.** 2

    ○ **B.** 5

    ○ **C.** 3

    ○ **D.** 4

4. Which of the following precautions should be taken so that ESD does not cause damage to a computer that is being repaired? Select all that apply.

- ○ **A.** Use an antistatic strap.
- ○ **B.** Wear shoes with rubber soles.
- ○ **C.** Spray antistatic spray on the components.
- ○ **D.** Put the computer on an antistatic mat.

5. You start a new computer and nothing seems to happen. Upon closer inspection, you can hear the hard drive spinning; however, nothing is coming up on the monitor. Which of the following would *not* be a reason for this?

- ○ **A.** The monitor is not on.
- ○ **B.** The video card is not properly seated.
- ○ **C.** The monitor is not connected to the PC.
- ○ **D.** The PC is not connected to the AC outlet.

6. What is the easiest way to monitor the battery health of a UPS?

- ○ **A.** Use the UPS monitoring software.
- ○ **B.** Use a voltmeter.
- ○ **C.** Replace the battery every year.
- ○ **D.** Use Event Viewer.

7. A computer you are working on has a lot of dust inside. How should you clean this?

- ○ **A.** Disassemble the power supply and remove the dust.
- ○ **B.** Use a vacuum to clean up the dust.
- ○ **C.** Use a surface dust cleaning solution.
- ○ **D.** Use compressed air to remove the dust.

8. What function is performed by the external power supply of a laptop?

- ○ **A.** Increases voltage
- ○ **B.** Stores power
- ○ **C.** Converts DC power to AC power
- ○ **D.** Converts AC power to DC power

9. Which one of the following keys is found only on a laptop?

   ○ **A.** Ctrl key

   ○ **B.** Fn key

   ○ **C.** Shift key

   ○ **D.** Numlock key

10. Which of the following commands creates a new directory in the Windows Command Prompt?

   ○ **A.** CD

   ○ **B.** MD

   ○ **C.** RD

   ○ **D.** SD

11. To learn more about the **PING** command, what would you enter at the command line?

   ○ **A.** PING HELP

   ○ **B.** HELP PING

   ○ **C.** PING /?

   ○ **D.** PING ?

12. Which syntax will enable you to see your computer's MAC address?

   ○ **A.** IPCONFIG /?

   ○ **B.** IPCONFIG /everything

   ○ **C.** PING /everything

   ○ **D.** IPCONFIG /all

13. A customer's computer is using FAT16. What file system can you upgrade it to when using the **convert** command?

   ○ **A.** NTFS

   ○ **B.** HPFS

   ○ **C.** FAT32

   ○ **D.** NFS

14. How do you change the virtual memory in Windows XP?

○ **A.** Click Start > Settings > Control Panel > Virtual Memory.

○ **B.** It is not possible.

○ **C.** Go to the System Properties window, click the Advanced tab, select Performance Options. Click Change and enter the new virtual memory.

○ **D.** Go to the System Properties window and select Performance Options. Click Change and enter the new virtual memory.

15. How can you configure Windows XP's virtual memory to optimal settings?

○ **A.** Set the virtual memory to No Paging File.

○ **B.** Set Windows to Automatically Manage Size.

○ **C.** Manually set the virtual memory settings to 1MB.

○ **D.** Set the virtual memory manually to one-third of RAM.

16. Jake's Windows Vista computer has several programs running in the system tray that take up a lot of memory and processing power. He would like you to turn them off permanently. What tool should you use to do this?

○ **A.** MSCONFIG.EXE

○ **B.** SYSEDIT.EXE

○ **C.** `IPCONFIG /RELEASE`

○ **D.** Task Manager

17. What is a common risk when installing Windows drivers that are unsigned?

○ **A.** System stability may be compromised.

○ **B.** Files might be cross-linked.

○ **C.** The drive might become fragmented.

○ **D.** Physical damage to devices might occur.

18. Which of the following answers can be used to keep disk drives free of errors and Windows XP running efficiently? Select all that apply.

○ **A.** Disk Management

○ **B.** Disk Defragmenter

○ **C.** Check Disk

○ **D.** System Restore

○ **E.** Scheduled Tasks

19. Tom has a 30GB hard disk partition (known as C:). He has 1.5GB free space on the partition. How can he defrag the partition?

   ◯ **A.** He can run the Disk Defragmenter in Computer Management.

   ◯ **B.** He can run **DEFRAG.EXE** **−f** in the command line.

   ◯ **C.** He can run **DEFRAG.EXE** **−v** in the command line.

   ◯ **D.** He can run the Disk Defragmenter in Computer Management with the Vigor option.

20. Buzz gets an error that says "Error log full." Where should you go to clear his Error log?

   ◯ **A.** Device Manager

   ◯ **B.** System Information

   ◯ **C.** Recovery Console

   ◯ **D.** Event Viewer

21. What is Windows Vista's recovery environment known as? (Select all that apply.)

   ◯ **A.** WinRE

   ◯ **B.** Recovery Console

   ◯ **C.** Advanced Boot Options

   ◯ **D.** System Recovery Options

22. A user's time and date keeps resetting to January 1st, 2000. What is the most likely cause?

   ◯ **A.** The BIOS needs to be updated.

   ◯ **B.** Windows needs to be updated.

   ◯ **C.** The Windows Date and Time Properties window needs to be modified.

   ◯ **D.** The lithium battery needs to be replaced.

23. What would you need to access to boot the computer into Safe Mode?

   ◯ **A.** WinRE

   ◯ **B.** Recovery Console

   ◯ **C.** Advanced Boot Options

   ◯ **D.** System Restore

24. What command repairs the bootmgr.exe file in Windows Vista?

- ○ **A.** `bootrec /fixboot`
- ○ **B.** `bootrec /fixmbr`
- ○ **C.** `bootrec /rebuildbcd`
- ○ **D.** `boot/bcd`

25. If you get a Code 1 message about a particular device in the Device Manager, what should you do?

- ○ **A.** Close applications and install RAM.
- ○ **B.** Disable the device.
- ○ **C.** Update the driver.
- ○ **D.** Reinstall the driver.

26. Which tool checks protected system files?

- ○ **A.** Chkdsk
- ○ **B.** Xcopy
- ○ **C.** Scandisk
- ○ **D.** SFC

27. What are the six steps of the laser-printing process in order?

- ○ **A.** Cleaning, charging, writing, developing, transferring, fusing
- ○ **B.** Charging, cleaning, writing, developing, transferring, fusing
- ○ **C.** Cleaning, charging, writing, transferring, developing, fusing
- ○ **D.** Charging, cleaning, writing, transferring, developing, fusing

28. How many pins would you see in a high-quality printhead on a dot matrix printer?

- ○ **A.** 24
- ○ **B.** 15
- ○ **C.** 8
- ○ **D.** 35

29. Which of the following would indicate a secured HTTP server?

- ○ **A.** HTTPSSL://www.davidlprowse.com
- ○ **B.** HTTPS://www.davidlprowse.com
- ○ **C.** HTTP://www.davidlprowse.com
- ○ **D.** HTTP://www.davidlprowse.com/secure

30. The IP address 192.168.1.1 should have what default subnet mask?

- ○ **A.** 255.255.0.0
- ○ **B.** 255.255.255.0
- ○ **C.** 255.0.0.0
- ○ **D.** 255.255.255.255

31. Joey's computer was working fine for weeks, and suddenly it cannot connect to the Internet. Joey runs the command `ipconfig` and sees that the IP address his computer is using is 169.254.50.68. What can he conclude from this?

- ○ **A.** The computer cannot access the DHCP server.
- ○ **B.** The computer cannot access the POP3 server.
- ○ **C.** The computer cannot access the DNS server.
- ○ **D.** The computer cannot access the WINS server.

32. Which of the following commands ping the loopback address?

- ○ **A.** `PING 127.0.0.1`
- ○ **B.** `PING 10.0.0.1`
- ○ **C.** `PING 1.0.0.127`
- ○ **D.** `PING \\localhost`

33. Which of these is an example of social engineering?

- ○ **A.** Asking for a username and password over the phone
- ○ **B.** Using someone else's unsecured wireless network
- ○ **C.** Hacking into a router
- ○ **D.** A virus

34. Which of the following settings must be established if you want to make a secure wireless connection? Select all that apply.

- ○ **A.** The brand of access point
- ○ **B.** The wireless standard used
- ○ **C.** The encryption standard used
- ○ **D.** The SSID of the access point

35. A co-worker is traveling to Europe and is bringing her computer. She asks you what safety concerns there might be. What should you tell her?

- ○ **A.** That computer is not usable in other countries.
- ○ **B.** Check for a compatible power adapter for that country.
- ○ **C.** Use a line conditioner for the correct voltage.
- ○ **D.** Check the voltage selector on the power supply.

36. A customer wants you to replace the fan in her power supply. What should you do?

- ○ **A.** Order the correct replacement fan and replace it.
- ○ **B.** Clean the inside of the power supply first.
- ○ **C.** Unplug the power supply first.
- ○ **D.** Refuse the customer.

37. Which of these tools can protect you in the case of a surge?

- ○ **A.** Torx wrench
- ○ **B.** Antistatic strap
- ○ **C.** Voltmeter
- ○ **D.** Antistatic mat

38. You are at a customer's office you have visited before. You can guess what the problem is, and when the customer mentions getting an IP address of 169.254..., you immediately know how to fix the problem. However, as you ponder the solution, you notice that the customer is now talking about his server. What should you do?

- ○ **A.** Fix the IP problem while the customer talks.
- ○ **B.** Hold up your hand and tell him that you understand the problem.
- ○ **C.** Let the customer finish what he is saying.
- ○ **D.** Leave the job site.

39. While you are working on a customer's computer at her home, she informs you that she needs to leave for about 10 minutes and that her 8-year-old son can help you with anything if you need it. What should you do?

- ○ **A.** Tell the customer to get back home as soon as possible.
- ○ **B.** Tell her that you are not responsible for the child.
- ○ **C.** Tell her that an adult must be home while you work.
- ○ **D.** Tell her that the child must be removed.

40. After installing a new hard drive on a Windows XP computer, Len tries to format the drive. Windows XP does not show the format option in Disk Management. What did Len forget to do first?

    ○ **A.** Run CHKDSK

    ○ **B.** Partition the drive

    ○ **C.** Defragment the drive

    ○ **D.** Copy system files

41. What is the thickness of a Type II PC Card?

    ○ **A.** 0.3 inches (7.5mm)

    ○ **B.** 0.129 inches (3.3mm)

    ○ **C.** 0.2 inches (5.0mm)

    ○ **D.** 0.41 inches (10.5mm)

42. What type of adapter card is normally plugged into an AGP adapter card slot?

    ○ **A.** Modem

    ○ **B.** Video

    ○ **C.** NIC

    ○ **D.** Sound

43. Which of the following recovery options uses a floppy disk?

    ○ **A.** WinRE

    ○ **B.** ASR

    ○ **C.** NTBackup

    ○ **D.** Recovery Console

44. To prevent damage to a computer and its peripherals, the computer should be connected to what?

    ○ **A.** A power strip

    ○ **B.** A power inverter

    ○ **C.** An AC to DC converter

    ○ **D.** A UPS

45. A computer has 512MB of RAM. It also has 64MB of shared video memory. How much RAM is available to the operating system?

   ◯ **A.** 512MB

   ◯ **B.** 256MB

   ◯ **C.** 448MB

   ◯ **D.** 576MB

46. Jennifer just installed a DVD-ROM drive and a CD-RW drive in a PC. When she boots the system, she sees only the DVD-ROM drive. What is the most likely cause of this problem?

   ◯ **A.** The drives are jumpered incorrectly.

   ◯ **B.** The Molex connector is not connected to the CD-RW drive.

   ◯ **C.** The IDE cable to the CD-RW drive is upside down.

   ◯ **D.** The CD-RW drive has not been initialized.

47. Which of the following components could cause the POST to beep several times and fail during boot?

   ◯ **A.** Sound card

   ◯ **B.** Power supply

   ◯ **C.** Hard drive

   ◯ **D.** RAM

48. Which of the following is the proper boot sequence of a PC?

   ◯ **A.** CPU, POST, boot loader, operating system

   ◯ **B.** Boot loader, operating system, CPU, RAM

   ◯ **C.** POST, CPU, boot loader, operating system

   ◯ **D.** CPU, RAM, boot loader, operating system

49. Which of the following has the fastest data throughput?

   ◯ **A.** CD-ROM

   ◯ **B.** Hard drive

   ◯ **C.** RAM

   ◯ **D.** USB

50. Roger informs you that none of the three SCSI drives can be seen on his SCSI chain. What should you check?

- ○ **A.** Whether the host adapter is terminated and that the disks have consecutive IDs of 1, 2, and 3
- ○ **B.** Whether the SCSI adapter has an ID of 7 or 15, and whether all the disks are terminated and have consecutive IDs of 0, 1, and 2
- ○ **C.** Whether the host adapter has an ID of 0, and whether the disks are terminated with the same ID
- ○ **D.** Whether the SCSI adapter has an ID of 7, and whether both ends of the chain are terminated, and that each disk has a unique ID

51. What type of power connector is used for a x16 video card?

- ○ **A.** Molex 4-pin
- ○ **B.** Mini 4-pin
- ○ **C.** PCIe 6-pin
- ○ **D.** P1 24-pin

52. Louis attempts to boot his computer. A message on the screen says "Hard disk not found." The computer has a single PATA IDE hard disk. What is the most likely cause of the problem?

- ○ **A.** IDE cable is not connected.
- ○ **B.** IDE cable is installed upside down.
- ○ **C.** IDE drive is not jumpered correctly.
- ○ **D.** Wrong type of IDE cable.

53. How can a paper jam be resolved? (Select all that apply.)

- ○ **A.** Clear the paper path.
- ○ **B.** Use the right type of paper.
- ○ **C.** Check for damaged rollers.
- ○ **D.** Check for a damaged primary corona wire.

54. What could cause a ghosted image on the paper outputted by a laser printer?

- ○ **A.** Transfer corona wire
- ○ **B.** Primary corona wire
- ○ **C.** Pickup rollers
- ○ **D.** Photosensitive drum

55. Which log file contains information about Windows Vista setup errors?

   ○ **A.** setupact.log

   ○ **B.** setuperr.log

   ○ **C.** unattend.xml

   ○ **D.** setuplog.txt

56. Mary installed a new sound card and speakers; however, she cannot get any sound from the speakers. What could the problem be? Select all that apply.

   ○ **A.** Speaker power is not plugged in.

   ○ **B.** Sound card driver is not installed.

   ○ **C.** Sound card is plugged into the wrong slot.

   ○ **D.** Speaker connector is in the wrong jack.

57. You just upgraded the CPU. Which of the following can make your computer shut down automatically after a few minutes?

   ○ **A.** Wrong CPU driver

   ○ **B.** Wrong voltage to the CPU

   ○ **C.** Incorrect CPU has been installed

   ○ **D.** The CPU has overheated

58. When you reboot a computer, you get a message stating "No OS present, press any key to reboot." What is the most likely problem?

   ○ **A.** The hard drive is not jumpered properly.

   ○ **B.** The hard drive is not getting power.

   ○ **C.** There is no active partition.

   ○ **D.** The hard drive driver is not installed.

59. Which kind of current does a typical desktop PC draw from a wall outlet?

   ○ **A.** Direct current

   ○ **B.** Neutral current

   ○ **C.** Alternating current

   ○ **D.** Draw current

60. You are installing an IDE CD-ROM. Currently, there is an IDE hard drive configured on the primary controller as master. There are no other drives. What is the correct setting for the CD-ROM?

    ○ **A.** Primary controller, slave

    ○ **B.** Secondary controller, slave

    ○ **C.** Secondary controller, master

    ○ **D.** Primary controller, cable select

61. Normally, when your PC boots, it sounds one beep. Today, there is a series of beeps, and the PC does not boot. What should you check? Select all that apply.

    ○ **A.** Unseated RAM

    ○ **B.** Unseated NIC

    ○ **C.** Unseated modem

    ○ **D.** Unseated video

62. If a lot of data is flowing through a network card, what should the link light look like?

    ○ **A.** Unlit

    ○ **B.** Rapid, erratic flashing

    ○ **C.** Solid green

    ○ **D.** Solid yellow

63. Russ wants to run his video-editing software at a resolution of 1280 x 1024 with True Color (24 bits). His PC has an older 2MB video card. Can he run these video settings?

    ○ **A.** Yes

    ○ **B.** No

64. Which of the following hides the file APLUS.DOC?

    ○ **A.** `attrib +H aplus.doc`

    ○ **B.** `attrib ?H aplus.doc`

    ○ **C.** `attrib +R aplus.doc`

    ○ **D.** `attrib aplus.doc /H`

65. What is the proper way to format a floppy disk as a bootable disk?

- ○ **A.** `format /s`
- ○ **B.** `format a: /s`
- ○ **C.** `format a: /system`
- ○ **D.** `format a: /boot`

66. Paul's Device Manager shows a red *X* over one of the devices. What does this tell you?

- ○ **A.** The device's driver has not been installed.
- ○ **B.** The device is not recognized.
- ○ **C.** The device is disabled.
- ○ **D.** The device is in queue to be deleted.

67. Which of the following is not an advantage of NTFS over FAT32?

- ○ **A.** NTFS supports file encryption.
- ○ **B.** NTFS supports larger file sizes.
- ○ **C.** NTFS supports larger volumes.
- ○ **D.** NTFS supports more file formats.

68. In Windows XP, which of the following paths enables a program to start for every person who logs on to Windows?

- ○ **A.** Documents & Settings > Programs > Start menu > Startup
- ○ **B.** Documents & Settings > All Users > Start menu > Programs > Startup
- ○ **C.** Documents & Settings > Start menu > Programs Startup
- ○ **D.** Documents & Settings > Default User > Startup

69. Which of the following parameters (switches) copy all files, folders, and subfolders, including empty subfolders in the TEST folder?

- ○ **A.** `xcopy *.* c:\test /T /S`
- ○ **B.** `xcopy *.* c:\test /S`
- ○ **C.** `xcopy *.* c:\test /E`
- ○ **D.** `xcopy *.* c:\test /S /T`

70. Which Windows utility is used to prepare a disk image for duplication across the network?

   ○ **A.** XCOPY

   ○ **B.** SYSPREP

   ○ **C.** Ghost

   ○ **D.** Image Clone

71. You need to configure a service to start when Windows XP boots. Which tool enables you to accomplish this?

   ○ **A.** MMC

   ○ **B.** Local Security Policy snap-in

   ○ **C.** Services snap-in

   ○ **D.** Disk Management snap-in

72. Steve just installed a second hard disk in his Windows Vista computer. However, he does not see the disk in Windows Explorer. What did he forget to do? Select all that apply.

   ○ **A.** Format the drive

   ○ **B.** Partition the drive

   ○ **C.** Run FDISK

   ○ **D.** Initialize the drive

   ○ **E.** Set up the drive in the BIOS

73. To install a SCSI hard disk during a Windows XP/2000 installation, which key must be pressed?

   ○ **A.** F2

   ○ **B.** F3

   ○ **C.** F6

   ○ **D.** F8

74. You just upgraded the president's computer's video driver. Now, the Windows XP system will not boot. Which of the following should you try first?

   ○ **A.** Access the Recovery Console.

   ○ **B.** Boot into Safe mode and roll back the driver.

   ○ **C.** Reinstall the operating system.

   ○ **D.** Boot into Directory Services Restore mode.

75. After you install Windows, the computer you are working on displays a blue screen of death (BSOD) when rebooting. Which of the following are possible causes? Select all that apply.

- ○ **A.** BIOS needs to be flashed to the latest version
- ○ **B.** IRQ conflict
- ○ **C.** Virus in the MBR
- ○ **D.** Incompatible hardware device

76. Which of the following does not allow you to add drivers in Windows?

- ○ **A.** Add New Hardware Wizard
- ○ **B.** Manufacturer's driver disk
- ○ **C.** Device Manager
- ○ **D.** Drivers applet in Control Panel

77. You recently installed a program on Jason's Windows XP computer while logged on as Jason. Where would the location of the installation's cache files most likely be?

- ○ **A.** C:\Documents and Settings\Jason\Local Settings\Temp
- ○ **B.** C:\Documents and Settings\Jason\TEMP
- ○ **C.** C:\Documents and Settings\Local Settings\Application Data
- ○ **D.** C:\Documents and Settings\Local Settings\Temp

78. Mary's computer is running Windows XP. In the Device Manager, you notice that the NIC has a black exclamation point. What does this tell you?

- ○ **A.** The device is disabled.
- ○ **B.** The wrong driver is installed.
- ○ **C.** The device is malfunctioning.
- ○ **D.** The incorrect driver is installed.

79. In Windows Vista, when will a computer dump the physical memory?

- ○ **A.** When the wrong processor is installed
- ○ **B.** When a device is missing drivers
- ○ **C.** When the computer was shut down improperly
- ○ **D.** When the computer detects a condition from which it cannot recover

80. To create a restore point, what must you do?

   ○ **A.** Run Disk Defragmenter from the MMC.

   ○ **B.** Run NTBackup from the Control Panel.

   ○ **C.** Run the System Restore program from the System Tools menu.

   ○ **D.** Run the Disk Cleanup program from the System Tools menu.

81. What is printing in duplex?

   ○ **A.** Printing on both sides of the paper

   ○ **B.** Printer collation

   ○ **C.** Two-way printer communication

   ○ **D.** Printing to file

82. Special paper is needed to print on what kind of printer?

   ○ **A.** Dot matrix

   ○ **B.** Thermal

   ○ **C.** Laser

   ○ **D.** Inkjet

83. Which environmental issue affects a thermal printer the most?

   ○ **A.** Moisture

   ○ **B.** ESD

   ○ **C.** Dirt

   ○ **D.** Heat

84. Which of the following can you not do from the Printer Properties screen?

   ○ **A.** Modify spool settings

   ○ **B.** Add ports

   ○ **C.** Pause printing

   ○ **D.** Enable sharing

85. Where are software firewalls usually located?

   ○ **A.** On routers

   ○ **B.** On servers

   ○ **C.** On clients

   ○ **D.** On every computer

86. For multiple computers to make a physical, electrical connection on a network, what device must be in play?

   ○ **A.** Router

   ○ **B.** Hub

   ○ **C.** Bridge

   ○ **D.** Gateway

87. What is the minimum category cable needed for a 100BASE-T network?

   ○ **A.** Category 2

   ○ **B.** Category 3

   ○ **C.** Category 4

   ○ **D.** Category 5

88. You are not using simple file sharing. In Windows XP, how would you share your CD-ROM drive to the rest of the network?

   ○ **A.** Drag the CD-ROM to the Shared Network folder.

   ○ **B.** In My Computer, right-click the CD-ROM icon, and then click Sharing.

   ○ **C.** In My Computer, click the CD-ROM icon, and then click Sharing.

   ○ **D.** Select Start > Settings > Control Panel, and then click Network > File and Print Sharing.

89. Which of these IP addresses can be routed across the Internet?

   ○ **A.** 127.0.0.1

   ○ **B.** 192.168.1.1

   ○ **C.** 129.52.50.13

   ○ **D.** 10.52.50.13

90. The IP address of Davidprowse.com is 10.255.200.1. You can ping the IP address 10.255.200.1 but cannot ping Davidprowse.com. What is the most likely cause?

   ○ **A.** Davidprowse.com is down.

   ○ **B.** The DHCP server is down.

   ○ **C.** The DNS server is down.

   ○ **D.** THE ADDS server is down.

91. If a person takes control of a session between a server and a client, it is known as what type of attack?

- ○ **A.** DDoS
- ○ **B.** Smurf
- ○ **C.** Session hijacking
- ○ **D.** Malicious software

92. Making data appear as if it is coming from somewhere other than its original source is known as what?

- ○ **A.** Hacking
- ○ **B.** Phishing
- ○ **C.** Cracking
- ○ **D.** Spoofing

93. You are setting up auditing on a Windows XP Professional computer. If set up properly, which log should have entries?

- ○ **A.** Application log
- ○ **B.** System log
- ○ **C.** Security log
- ○ **D.** Maintenance log

94. You are called upon to replace some hard drives on a server. As you enter the server room, you see water dripping from the ceiling. What should you do?

- ○ **A.** Place a bucket under the water leak and continue replacing the hard drives.
- ○ **B.** Place a bucket under the water leak and log the incident.
- ○ **C.** Notify building services and the system administrator.
- ○ **D.** Send an email to the system administrator.

95. You are working on a very old printer and it starts to smoke. What should you do?

- ○ **A.** Turn off the printer.
- ○ **B.** Call 911.
- ○ **C.** Unplug the printer.
- ○ **D.** Tell the printer it is bad to smoke.

96. Which Windows Vista System Recovery Option attempts to automatically fix problems?

   ○ **A.** System Restore

   ○ **B.** Startup repair

   ○ **C.** Complete PC Restore

   ○ **D.** Recovery Console

97. The message The Windows Boot Configuration Data File Is Missing Required Information appears on the screen. What command would you type to repair this issue?

   ○ **A.** `bootrec /fixboot`

   ○ **B.** `bootrec /fixmbr`

   ○ **C.** `bootrec /rebuildbcd`

   ○ **D.** `boot\bcd`

98. What is the fourth step of the CompTIA 6-step troubleshooting process?

   ○ **A.** Identify the problem.

   ○ **B.** Establish a theory of probable cause.

   ○ **C.** Establish a plan of action.

   ○ **D.** Document findings.

99. You are asked to fix a problem with a customer's domain controller that is outside the scope of your knowledge. What action should you take?

   ○ **A.** Learn on the job by trying to fix the problem.

   ○ **B.** Tell the customer that the problem should be reported to another technician.

   ○ **C.** Assure the customer that the problem will be fixed very soon.

   ○ **D.** Help the customer find the appropriate channels to fix the problem.

100. How should you remain in the face of adversity?

   ○ **A.** Wavering

   ○ **B.** Decisive

   ○ **C.** Positive

   ○ **D.** Certain

Answers at a Glance

1. A	35. D	69. C
2. C	36. D	70. B
3. C	37. B	71. C
4. A and D	38. C	72. A, B, and D
5. D	39. C	73. C
6. A	40. B	74. B
7. D	41. C	75. A and C
8. D	42. B	76. D
9. B	43. B	77. A
10. B	44. D	78. C
11. C	45. C	79. D
12. D	46. B	80. C
13. A	47. D	81. A
14. C	48. A	82. B
15. B	49. C	83. D
16. A	50. D	84. C
17. A	51. C	85. C
18. B and C	52. A	86. B
19. B	53. A, B, and C	87. D
20. D	54. D	88. B
21. A and D	55. B	89. C
22. D	56. A, B, and D	90. C
23. C	57. D	91. C
24. A	58. C	92. D
25. C	59. C	93. C
26. D	60. C	94. C
27. A	61. A and D	95. C
28. A	62. B	96. B
29. B	63. B	97. C
30. B	64. A	98. C
31. A	65. B	99. D
32. A	66. C	100. C
33. A	67. D	
34. C and D	68. B	

Answers with Explanations

1. **A**. Memory latency or CAS (Column Address Strobe) latency happens when a memory controller tries to access data from a memory module. It is a slight delay (usually measured in nanoseconds) while the memory module responds to the memory controller.The memory controller (also known as the northbridge or MCH) has a specific speed at which it operates. If the CPU asks the chip for too much information at once, this might increase latency time while the memory controller works. See the section titled "RAM Basics and Types of RAM" in Chapter 4, "RAM," for more information.

2. **C**. In a standard ATX-based computer, the motherboard has two IDE interfaces (primary and secondary), each of which can support two devices, a master and a slave. See the section titled "Magnetic Storage Media" in Chapter 6, "Storage Devices," for more information.

3. **C**. Because RAID 5 uses striping *with parity,* a third disk is needed. You can have more than three disks as well. Two disks are enough for plain RAID 0 striping and is the exact number you need for RAID 1 mirroring. See the section titled "Files, File Systems, and Disks" in Chapter 8, "Configuring Windows," for more information.

4. **A** and **D**. The antistatic strap and mat are the best ways to avoid ESD. As another precaution, you can touch the chassis of the computer (unpainted surface) to discharge yourself. See the section titled "Safety and Environmental Procedure" in Chapter 16, "Safety and Professionalism," for more information.

5. **D**. If the PC is not connected to the AC outlet, the hard drive will *not* spin, so it isn't a possible reason for why nothing is coming up on the monitor, given the question's scenario. All other answers are possible reasons for why nothing is showing up on the display. Also, the monitor might not be plugged in. See the section titled "The Video Subsystem" in Chapter 12, "Video, Audio, and Peripherals," for more information.

6. **A**. Most UPS devices come with software that you can use to monitor the battery health. However, to do this you need to connect the UPS to the PC by way of a USB cable. See the section titled "Power Devices" in Chapter 5, "Power," for more information.

7. **D**. Compressed air is safe. However, you might want to do this outside. See the section titled "Safety and Environmental Procedure" in Chapter 16, "Safety and Professionalism," for more information.

8. **D**. The external power supply of the laptop converts AC to DC for the system to use and for charging the battery. See the section titled "Power Supplies" in Chapter 5, "Power," for more information about power supplies.

9. **B**. The function (Fn) key is a secondary key that is not normally seen on a PC, but is almost always on a laptop. The purpose of this key is to access additional features of the laptop. See the section titled "Installing, Configuring, and Troubleshooting Visible Laptop Components" in Chapter 11, "Laptops," for more information.

10. **B**. **MD** (or `mkdir`) is short for make directory. **CD** is change directory. **RD** is remove directory, and SD deals with memory cards and is not a valid command in the Command Prompt. See the section titled "Command-Line Tools" in Chapter 10, "Troubleshooting Windows," for more information.

11. **C**. To learn more about any command, type the command and then **/?**. Entering anything else in this case would make the command **PING** try to connect to and test that name. **HELP** by itself will give you a list of commands. You can get specific information about any of the commands in that list by entering **HELP** [*command*]. For example: the syntax **HELP RD** gives you the specific help file for the **RD** command. But there are several commands that this does not work with (mainly networking commands such as **PING** and **IPCON-FIG**). See the section titled "Troubleshooting Networking Connectivity" in Chapter 14, "Networking," for more information.

12. **D**. The **/all** switch shows everything you need to know about your network connection, including the MAC address. See the section titled "Troubleshooting Networking Connectivity" in Chapter 14, "Networking," for more information.

13. **A**. `Convert` is used to upgrade FAT and FAT32 volumes to NTFS without loss of data. HPFS is the High Performance File System developed by IBM and not used by Windows. NFS is the Network File System, something you would see in a storage area network. See the section titled "Command-Line Tools" in Chapter 10, "Troubleshooting Windows," for more information.

14. **C**. Changing virtual memory in Windows XP is done in the Performance Options screen. Answer D is missing the step of selecting the Advanced tab. There is no Virtual Memory applet in the Control Panel. See the section titled "System Tools and Utilities" in Chapter 8, "Configuring Windows," for more information.

15. **B**. Of the potential answers listed, the best or optimal settings are implemented by allowing Windows to manage the size. However, note that the default setting for virtual memory is 1.5 times RAM, with a maximum of 3 times RAM. See the section titled "System Tools and Utilities" in Chapter 8, "Configuring Windows," for more information.

16. **A**. MSCONFIG can turn programs on and off in the Startup tab. By modifying this, you effectively create a selective startup. Task Manager can turn off programs, but only temporarily; when the system restarts, those programs will run again. It is important to note that Windows 2000 does not have MSCON-FIG.EXE built in, but it can be added as a download from the Internet. See the section titled "System Tools and Utilities" in Chapter 8, "Configuring Windows," for more information.

17. **A**. By installing a driver that is not signed by Microsoft, you are risking instability of the operating system. See the section titled "System Tools and Utilities" in Chapter 8, "Configuring Windows," for more information.

18. **B** and **C**. Disk Defragmenter keeps Windows XP running more efficiently by making the files contiguous, lowering the amount of physical work the hard drive has to do. Check Disk checks the hard drive for errors. See the sections titled "Windows Tools and Errors" and "Command-Line Tools" in Chapter 10, "Troubleshooting Windows," for more information.

19. **B**. You need to have 15 percent free space on your partition to defrag it in the Disk Defragmenter GUI-based utility. However, you can force a defrag on a partition even if you don't have enough free space by using the **–f** switch in the command line. The **–v** switch gives you verbose (or wordy) output. There is no Vigor option. See the section titled "Maintaining Hard Disks" in Chapter 9, "Maintaining Windows," for more information.

20. **D**. The Event Viewer contains the error logs; they are finite in size. You could either clear the log or increase the size of the log. The other three do not contain error logs. See the section titled "Windows Tools and Errors" in Chapter 10, "Troubleshooting Windows," for more information.

21. **A** and **D**. The Windows Vista recovery environment (WinRE) is also known as System Recovery Options. The Recovery Console is only available in Windows XP/2000. Advanced Boot Options is the menu that can be accessed by pressing F8, which is available in Vista/XP/2000. See the section titled "Repair Environments and Boot Errors" in Chapter 10, "Troubleshooting Windows," for more information.

22. **D**. If the time and date keep resetting to a time like January 1, 2000, chances are that the lithium battery needs to be replaced. Any of the other options will not fix the problem. See the sections titled "The BIOS" and "Installing and Troubleshooting Motherboards" in Chapter 2, "Motherboards," for more information.

23. **C**. The Advanced Boot Options menu has many options including Safe Mode. This menu can be accessed by pressing F8 when the computer first boots up. See the section titled "Repair Environments and Boot Errors" in Chapter 10, "Troubleshooting Windows," for more information.

24. **A**. `bootrec /fixboot` is one of the methods you can try to repair bootmgr.exe in Windows Vista. `Bootrec /fixmbr` rewrites the master boot record in Vista. `Bootrec /rebuildbcd` attempts to rebuild the boot configuration store, and boot\bcd is where the boot configuration store is located. See the section titled "Repair Environments and Boot Errors" in Chapter 10, "Troubleshooting Windows," for more information.

25. **C**. A Code 1 message means that a device is not configured correctly. Usually this means that the driver should be updated. See the section titled "Windows Tools and Errors" in Chapter 10, "Troubleshooting Windows," for more information.

26. **D**. SFC (System File Checker) checks protected system files and replaces incorrect versions. None of the other options check *system* files. See the section titled "Command-Line Tools" in Chapter 10, "Troubleshooting Windows," for more information.

27. **A**. First, the drum is cleaned; then the primary corona wire applies a negative charge to the drum. Third, the "laser" writes to the drum, increasing the voltage of those areas written to. Next, the image is developed, meaning that toner is attracted to the written areas of the drum. At this point, the paper has entered under the toner cartridge and his applied a positive charge by the transfer corona wire. While this is happening, the negatively charged toner is transferred to the paper. Finally, the loose toner is fused to the paper by heat (350° to 400° F) and pressure rollers. See the section titled "Printer Types and Technologies" in Chapter 13, "Printers," for more information.

28. **A**. High-quality dot matrix printheads can come in 9, 18, or 24 pins, with 24 being the highest quality. See the section titled "Printer Types and Technologies" in Chapter 13, "Printers," for more information.

29. **B**. When you connect to a secure web server, you should see the protocol HTTPS and a secure padlock in the locked position or something of the sort. See the section titled "Networking Fundamentals" in Chapter 14, "Networking," for more information.

30. **B**. 192.168.1.1 is a private Class C address and therefore should have the subnet mask 255.255.255.0, the standard default subnet mask for Class C. (See the following table) See the section titled "Networking Fundamentals" in Chapter 14, "Networking," for more information.

Table 1: Subnet Masks

Class	Subnet Mask	Example IP Address
A	255.0.0.0	10.0.0.1
B	255.255.0.0	128.0.0.1
C	255.255.255.0	192.168.1.1

31. **A**. If you get any address that starts with 169.254, it means the computer has self-assigned that address. It is known as an APIPA address (Automatic Private IP Addressing). Normally, DHCP servers will not use this network number. A simple `ipconfig/release` and `ipconfig/renew` might fix the problem, given that a DHCP server is actually available. The POP3 server is for incoming mail, the DNS server is for resolving domain names to IP addresses, and the WINS server is for resolving NETBIOS names to IP addresses. See the section titled "Networking Fundamentals" in Chapter 14, "Networking," for more information.

32. **A**. 127.0.0.1 is the built-in loopback IP address for every computer with TCP/IP installed. Alternatively, you could ping any number on the 127 network or ping localhost without the double backslash. See the section titled "Troubleshooting Network Connectivity" in Chapter 14, "Networking," for more information.

33. **A**. Social engineering is the practice of obtaining confidential information by manipulating people. Using someone else's network is just theft. Hacking into a router is just that, hacking. And a virus is a self-spreading program that might or might not cause damage to files and applications. See the section titled "Basics of Data Security" in Chapter 15, "Security," for more information.

34. **C** and **D**. To make a secure connection, you first need to know the SSID (service set identifier) of the AP and then the encryption being used (for example, WEP or WPA). Knowing the wireless standard being used can help you verify whether your computer is compatible (802.11b or g), and the brand of access point isn't really helpful. See the section titled "Installing and Configuring a SOHO Network" in Chapter 14, "Networking," for more information.

35. **D**. Most power supplies have selectors for the United States and Europe (115 and 230 volts). However, your co-worker will probably need an adapter, too; otherwise, the plug may not fit. See the section titled "Power Supplies" in Chapter 5, "Power," for more information.

36. **D**. Do not open the power supply. It might hold a *lethal* charge. Also, although it is possible that you *could* fix the power supply, it is more cost-effective and a more efficient use of time to just order a new one. Plus, if the fan is bad on the power supply, chances are that something else will fail in there, too. Of course, you need to refuse *nicely*. See the sections titled "Power Supplies" in Chapter 5, "Power," and "Professionalism and Communication Skills" in Chapter 16, "Safety and Professionalism," for more information.

37. **B**. Most antistatic straps come with a 1 mega ohm resistor, which can protect against surges. See the section titled "Safety and Environmental Procedures" in Chapter 16, "Safety and Professionalism," for more information.

38. **C**. Always pay attention and allow the customer to finish. Customers might give you valuable clues about a more sinister problem. See the section titled "Professionalism and Communication Skills" in Chapter 16, "Safety and Professionalism," for more information.

39. **C**. Whenever working in someone's home, make sure that there is an adult available. See the section titled "Professionalism and Communication Skills" in Chapter 16, "Safety and Professionalism," for more information.

40. **B**. You must partition the drive before formatting. Copying files can be done only after formatting is complete. CHKDSK has little value on an unformatted drive. Something else not mentioned here is that a second drive would have to be *initialized* in Windows XP before use. See the section titled "Files, File Systems, and Disks" in Chapter 8, "Configuring Windows," for more information.

41. **C**. PC Cards come in the following sizes. (See Table 2.) See the section titled "Installing, Configuring, and Troubleshooting Visible Laptop Components" in Chapter 11, "Laptops," for more information.

Table 2: PC Card Sizes

PC Card	Size (metric)	Size (U.S.)
Type I	3.3mm	0.129 inches
Type II	5.0mm	0.2 inches
Type III	10.5mm	0.41 inches

42. **B**. The AGP (Accelerated Graphics Port) expansion slot is used primarily for video. See the section titled "Motherboard Components and Form Factors" in Chapter 2, "Motherboards," for more information.

43. B. ASR (Automated System Recovery) is a recovery option used by Windows XP. When an ASR backup is created Windows XP requests a blank floppy disk for additional ASR information. WinRE is the Windows Vista Recovery Environment which includes several System Recovery Options. NTBackup allows a user to backup files but isn't really considered a recovery option unless using ASR. The Recovery Console is run from the Windows XP/2000 CD.

44. D. A UPS (uninterruptible power supply) protects computer equipment against surges, spikes, sags, brownouts, and blackouts. Power strips, unlike surge protectors do not protect against surges. See the section titled "Power Devices" in Chapter 5, "Power," for more information.

45. C. The amount of shared video memory is subtracted from the total RAM. The remainder is what the operating system has left to work with. See the section titled "Installing, Configuring, and Troubleshooting Internal Laptop Components" in Chapter 11, "Laptops," for more information.

46. B. Molex power is most likely the culprit. The Molex connector might not be connected at all or might be loose. Improper jumper settings might be an issue, but not the most likely. It is very hard to install the IDE cable to a CD-RW drive upside down because they are keyed. CD-RW drives do not need to be initialized in Windows XP, only secondary hard drives. See the section titled "Optical Storage Media" in Chapter 6, "Storage Devices," for more information.

47. D. RAM is one of the big four (RAM, CPU, motherboard, and video) that can cause the POST to fail. Different RAM errors can cause the POST to make a different series of beeps. Consult your motherboard documentation for more information about the different beep codes. See the section titled "Installing and Troubleshooting RAM" in Chapter 4, "RAM," for more information.

48. A. The CPU must be installed correctly for the POST to begin. After the POST is successful, the boot loader then runs (for example, NTLDR), and then the operating system comes up. You might also see "power good" as a possible step directly after CPU and before POST. This means that the power to the CPU has been verified. See the section titled "The BIOS" in Chapter 2, "Motherboards," for more information.

49. C. RAM is much faster than the rest of the options listed. For instance, if you have PC3200 DDR RAM (aka DDR-400), your peak transfer rate is 3200MBs. The rest of the following devices are listed in descending order: hard drive (typically 133, 150, or 300MBs), USB (typically 60MBs), and CD-ROM (typically 7.5MBs). See the section titled "RAM Basics and Types of RAM" in Chapter 4, "RAM," for more information.

50. D. The adapter should use the ID 7. Both ends of the SCSI chain need to be terminated. Each disk needs a unique ID. The particular ID you give the disks doesn't matter. See the section titled "Magnetic Storage Media" in Chapter 6, "Storage Devices," for more information.

51. C. A x16 card is a PCI Express card. They require one or two PCIe 6-pin power connectors. See the section titled "Power Supplies" in Chapter 5, "Power," for more information.

52. A. The most likely cause would be that the IDE ribbon cable is not connected. It is nearly impossible to install an IDE cable upside down because it is keyed. In a computer with only one drive, the jumper setting will probably not affect whether it can boot; it can be jumpered as master or as single (no jumper) and still function. 40-wire or 80-wire cables can be used with PATA IDE drives. They both have 40 *pins.* Generally, a drive will work with either cable, but perhaps not at the maximum speed. See the section titled "Magnetic Storage Media" in Chapter 6, "Storage Devices," for more information.

53. A, B, and **C.** There are several possible reasons why a paper jam might occur. The paper could be stuck somewhere in the paper path, the paper could be too thick, or the rollers could be damaged. See the section titled "Installing, Configuring, and Troubleshooting Printers." in Chapter 13, "Printers," for more information.

54. D. Ghosted images or blurry marks could be a sign that the drum has some kind of imperfection or is dirty. Especially if the image reappears at equal intervals. Replace the drum (or toner cartridge). Another possibility is that the fuser assembly has been damaged and needs to be replaced. See the section titled "Installing, Configuring, and Troubleshooting Printers" in Chapter 13, "Printers," for more information.

55. B. Setuperr.log contains information about setup errors during the installation of Windows Vista. Start with this log file when troubleshooting. A file size of 0 bytes indicates no errors during installation. Setupact.log contains the events that occurred during the installation. Unattend.xml is the answer file used by Windows Vista during unattended installations. Setuplog.txt records events that occurred during the text portion installation of Windows XP. Windows Vista does not have a text portion during installation. See the section titled "Installing and Upgrading to Windows Vista" in Chapter 7, "Installing and Upgrading Windows," for more information.

56. A, B, and **D.** Always make sure that the speaker power (if any) is plugged into an AC outlet, and that the speakers are on (if they have a power button). When a sound card is first installed, Windows should recognize it and either install a driver through plug-and-play or ask for a driver CD. For best results, use the manufacturer's driver, the latest of which can be found on their website. Make sure that you plug the speakers into the correct 1/8-inch RCA jack. The speaker out is the one with concentric circles and an arrow pointing out. Or you might have 5.1 surround sound; in which case, you would use the standard front speaker jack, which is often a green jack. Finally, it's quite hard to plug a sound card into a wrong slot. For example, if you have a PCI 32-bit sound card (a common standard), you can then plug that sound card into any of the available PCI slots on your motherboard, and it will be recognized. (Word to the wise, if you ever remove the sound card when upgrading, make sure you put it back in the same slot.) PCI cards will not fit in ISA, AGP, or PCIe slots. See the section titled "The Audio Subsystem" in Chapter 12, "Video, Audio, and Peripherals," for more information.

57. D. The CPU could overheat if thermal compound has not been applied correctly (common) or if it is not seated properly (rare). As part of the boot process, power needs to verify the CPU. If the wrong voltage is running to the CPU, the system won't even boot. If an incorrect CPU has been installed, the system will probably not boot, especially if the BIOS doesn't recognize it. Finally, the CPU doesn't use a driver, instead the BIOS recognizes it (or doesn't, if it needs a BIOS update) and passes that information to the operating system. See the section titled "Installing and Troubleshooting CPUs" in Chapter 3, "The CPU," for more information.

58. C. The primary partition must be set to active to boot to the operating system. If there is only one drive, the jumper setting probably won't matter, and if it is wrong, the drive simply won't be seen by the BIOS. The same holds true for power; if the drive does not get power, the BIOS will not recognize it. Finally, hard drives do not need drivers to simply be recognized. See the section titled "Files, File Systems, and Disks" in Chapter 8, "Configuring Windows," for more information.

59. C. Alternating current is the standard in the U.S.; your computer should be connected to a 120V AC outlet. Other countries might use 230V AC connections. Direct current works inside the computer. The power supply converts between the two! See the section titled "Power Supplies" in Chapter 5, "Power," for more information.

60. C. The default is to install the CD-ROM to the secondary controller and set the jumper as master. It is common to have magnetic disks on the primary IDE channel and optical discs on the secondary IDE channel. See the section titled "Magnetic Storage Media" in Chapter 6, "Storage Devices," for more information.

61. A and **D**. If any one of the big four (RAM, video, CPU, and motherboard) is not installed properly, the system will not boot. However, the system can start even if the modem and NIC are not seated properly. See the section titled "Troubleshooting Examples" in Chapter 1, "Introduction to Troubleshooting," for more information.

62. B. When data is flowing through the activity light, it should blink or flash rapidly but not in an erratic fashion. You see solid green (100Mbps) or yellow (10Mbps) on the *link* light. If it is unlit, the cable is not connected properly or the device is malfunctioning. See the section titled "Troubleshooting Network Connectivity" in Chapter 14, "Networking," for more information.

63. B. To find out how much RAM you need on your video card, you just multiply the two resolution numbers together and then multiply by the amount of bytes of color. For example, 1280 x 1024 x 3 = 3.9MB. A system running in 24-bit color (16,777,216 colors) equates to 3 bytes of color. His card has only 2MB of RAM. See the section titled "The Video Subsystem" in Chapter 12, "Video, Audio, and Peripherals," for more information.

64. A. The syntax for this would be `attrib` `+H` [*filename*]. `–H` removes the attribute, making the file visible. `+R` makes the file read-only. `/H` is an invalid switch. See the section titled "File Security" in Chapter 15, "Security," for more information.

65. **B**. To format the floppy, you have to include its drive letter, which most likely would be A. You also need the switch, which is `/s`. So the syntax would be `format a: /s.` Many companies will do something similar when prepping hard drives of computers that they are selling. In that case, the syntax would be `format c: /s`. For more information about `format`, you can enter `format /?.` See the section titled "Magnetic Storage Media" in Chapter 6, "Storage Devices," for more information.

66. **C**. The red *X* tells you that the device is disabled. In many cases, it can easily be enabled by right-clicking it and selecting Enable. If the driver had not been installed, the device would most likely be sitting in a category called Unknown Devices. If the device is not even recognized by Windows, it will not show up on the list or will show up under Unknown Devices. There is no queue to be deleted. See the section titled "Windows Tools and Errors" in Chapter 10, "Troubleshooting Windows," for more information.

67. **D**. NTFS and FAT32 support the same number of file formats. See the section titled "Files, File Systems, and Disks" in Chapter 8, "Configuring Windows," for more information.

68. **B**. The All Users profile is meant to serve any user who logs on to Windows. See the section titled "Files, File Systems, and Disks" in Chapter 8, "Configuring Windows," for more information.

69. **C**. `/E` is needed to copy the files, directories, subdirectories, *including* empty subdirectories. `/S` will copy files, directories, and subdirectories, but *not* empty subdirectories. If you add `/T` on to the end, you get just the empty directories copied. See the section titled "Command-Line Tools" in Chapter 10, "Troubleshooting Windows," for more information.

70. **B**. SYSPREP is one of the utilities built in to Windows for image deployment over the network. Ghost and Image Clone are third-party offerings. XCOPY copies entire directories (in the same physical order, too) but not from one system to another. SYSPREP preps the system to be moved as an image file. See the section titled "Installing and Upgrading Windows Vista" in Chapter 7, "Installing and Upgrading Windows," for more information.

71. **C**. The Services snap-in lists all the services that you can start, stop, restart, and modify. Snap-ins are added to a Microsoft Management Console (MMC), but the Services snap-in is available by default in Computer Management. See the section titled "Windows User Interfaces" in Chapter 8, "Configuring Windows," for more information.

72. **A, B**, and **D**. For secondary drives, you must go to Disk Management and initialize, partition, and format them. FDISK is an older DOS command. Today's computers' BIOS should see the drive automatically with no configuration needed. In special cases a hard disk might require special drivers. See the section titled "Files, File Systems, and Disks" in Chapter 8, "Configuring Windows," for more information.

73. **C**. Right at the beginning of the text portion of the installation of Windows XP/2000, F6 must be pressed (you would see it on the bottom) to install other third-party drivers (for example, an Adaptec SCSI card). F2 is commonly used to get into the BIOS. F3 is the key to quit the Windows installation. F8 is used to get into the Advanced Boot Options (including Safe mode). See the section titled "Installing and Upgrading Windows XP" in Chapter 7, "Installing and Upgrading Windows," for more information.

74. **B**. By rolling back the driver (which is done in the Device Manager) while in Safe mode, you can go back in time to the old working video driver. The Recovery Console will not help you with drivers. Reinstalling the OS would wipe the partition of the president's data (and probably wipe you of your job). Directory Services Restore mode (although listed in the Advanced Startup Options) is only for Windows Server domain controllers. Note that Last Known Good configuration would probably be able to help you, but not in all cases. See the section titled "Repair Environments and Boot Errors" in Chapter 10, "Troubleshooting Windows," for more information.

75. **A** and **C**. Older PCs might need the BIOS to be upgraded before an installa-tion. Always flash the latest BIOS before performing an upgrade or fresh install. Always check the hardware on the HCL before performing an install or upgrade. IRQ conflicts will not cause BSODs, but they will render the affected devices inoperable. Viruses in the MBR could cause the computer to simply not boot. See the section titled "Windows Tools and Errors" in Chapter 10, "Troubleshooting Windows," for more information.

76. **D**. There is no Drivers applet in the Control Panel, but all the other answers are valid. See the section titled "System Tools and Utilities" in Chapter 8, "Configuring Windows," for more information.

77. **A**. C:\Documents and Settings\Jason\Local Settings\Temp is the correct path. Unless you installed the program so that all users can access it, this should be the location. Temp is shown as Temp, not TEMP, in the operating system. There will always be a profile name inside of this sort of path (for example, Jason). Answers C and D do not show this. See the section titled "Files, File Systems, and Disks" in Chapter 8, "Configuring Windows," for more information.

78. **C**. The exclamation point tells you that the device is malfunctioning. You might have to update the driver. See the section titled "Windows Tools and Errors" in Chapter 10, "Troubleshooting Windows," for more information.

79. **D**. If the computer fails and cannot recover, you usually see some type of criti-cal or stop error. At this point, you must restart the computer to get back into the operating system. The reason for the physical dump of memory is for later debugging. The physical dump writes the contents of memory (when the com-puter failed) to a file on the hard disk. Missing drivers will not cause this error, but a failed driver might. If the wrong processor is installed, you can probably not get the system to boot at all. Shutting down the computer improperly just means that the computer recognizes this upon the next reboot and asks whether you want to go into Safe mode. See the section titled "Windows Tools and Errors" in Chapter 10, "Troubleshooting Windows," for more information.

80. **C**. System Restore is the tool used to create restore points. See the section titled "Maintaining Hard Disks" in Chapter 9, "Maintaining Windows," for more information.

81. **A**. When printing "duplex," it means that you are printing on both sides of the paper, if the printer has that capability. See the section titled "Printer Types and Technologies" in Chapter 13, "Printers," for more information.

82. **B**. Regular paper can be used on all the listed printers except for the thermal printer. Thermal printers use specially coated paper that is heated to create the image. See the section titled "Printer Types and Technologies" in Chapter 13, "Printers," for more information.

83. **D**. Heat is the number one enemy to a thermal printer. See the section titled "Printer Types and Technologies" in Chapter 13, "Printers," for more information.

84. **C**. Pausing printing in general and pausing individual documents is done by double-clicking on the printer in question and making the modifications from the ensuing window. All the others can be modified from the Printer Properties screen. See the section titled "Installing, Configuring, and Troubleshooting Printers" in Chapter 13, "Printers," for more information.

85. **C**. Software-based firewalls, such as the Windows Firewall, are normally running on the client computers. See the section titled "Malicious Software" in Chapter 15, "Security," for more information.

86. **B**. You need a central connecting device such as a hub or switch to make the physical connection between computers on a network. Also, the computers need NICs to connect physically to the hub or switch. Many SOHO "routers" have a four-port hub/switch built in. See the section titled "Networking Fundamentals" in Chapter 14, "Networking," for more information.

87. **D**. Of the answers listed, only Category 5 can transmit data fast enough for the 100BASE-T standard. See the section titled "Network Cabling and Connectors" in Chapter 14, "Networking," for more information.

88. **B**. Just right-click the device you want to share (if you are not using simple file sharing). See the section titled "File Security" in Chapter 15, "Security," for more information.

89. **C**. The only public address (needed to get onto the Internet) is 129.52.50.13. All the others are private IPs, meant to be behind a firewall. The following table lists the standard private IP networks ranges. See the section titled "Networking Fundamentals" in Chapter 14, "Networking," for more information.

Table 3: Private IP Networks

Class	IP Networks
A	10.0.0.0
B	172.16.0.0–172.31.0.0
C	192.168.1.0–192.168.255.0

90. C. The purpose of a DNS server is to resolve (convert) hostnames and domain names to the IP address. Computers normally communicate via IP address, but it is easier for humans to type in names. If Davidprowse.com is down, you cannot ping the corresponding IP address at all. If the DHCP server is down, your workstation will probably not have an IP on the network and again will not ping the corresponding IP address. ADDS is Active Directory Directory Services, meaning a domain controller, which doesn't have much to do with this, except that in many smaller companies, the domain controller and DNS server are one and the same. See the section titled "Networking Fundamentals" in Chapter 14, "Networking," for more information.

91. C. Session hijacking is when an unwanted mediator takes control of the session between a client and a server (for example, an FTP or HTTP session). See the section titled "Malicious Software" in Chapter 15, "Security," for more information.

92. D. Spoofing is when a malicious user makes data or email appear to be coming from somewhere else. See the section titled "Basics of Data Security" in Chapter 15, "Security," for more information.

93. C. After Auditing is turned on and specific resources are configured for auditing, you need to check the Event Viewer's Security log for the entries. These could be successful logons or misfired attempts at deleting files; there are literally hundreds of options. The Application log contains errors, warnings, and informational entries about applications. The System log deals with drivers and system files and so on. A System Maintenance log can be used to record routine maintenance procedures. See the section titled "Windows Tools and Errors" in Chapter 10, "Troubleshooting Windows," for more information.

94. C. If you ever see anything like this in a server room, you need to contact the network or system administrator and the building superintendent right away. See the section titled "Safety and Environmental Procedures" in Chapter 16, "Safety and Professionalism," for more information.

95. C. Turning the printer off might not be enough. It might be seriously malfunctioning, so pull the plug. See the section titled "Safety and Environmental Procedures" in Chapter 16, "Safety and Professionalism," for more information.

96. B. Startup repair attempts to fix issues automatically. This is available in Windows Vista's WinRE System Recovery Options. See the section titled "Repair Environments and Boot Errors" in Chapter 10, "Troubleshooting Windows," for more information.

97. C. `Bootrec /rebuildbcd` attempts to rebuild the boot configuration store. `Bootrec /fixboot` is one of the methods you can try to repair bootmgr.exe in Windows Vista. `Bootrec /fixmbr` rewrites the master boot record in Vista. Boot\bcd is where the boot configuration store is located. See the section titled "Repair Environments and Boot Errors" in Chapter 10, "Troubleshooting Windows," for more information.

98. **C.** The fourth step of the CompTIA 6-step troubleshooting process is Establish a plan of action to resolve the problem and implement the solution. Identify the problem is step 1. Establish a theory of probable cause is step 2. Document findings is step 6. See the section titled "Troubleshooting Theory" in Chapter 1, "Introduction to Troubleshooting," for more information.

99. **D.** Make sure that the customer has a path toward a solution before dismissing the issue. Do *not* try to fix the problem if the scope of work is outside your knowledge. See the section titled "Professionalism and Communication Skills" in Chapter 16, "Safety and Professionalism," for more information.

100. **C.** Always have a positive outlook. The customer will have fewer concerns, and you will be more relaxed. See the section titled "Professionalism and Communication Skills" in Chapter 16, "Safety and Professionalism," for more information.

Practice Exam 3

Final Prep for CompTIA A+ 220-702

The 50 multiple-choice questions provided here are meant to act as a final practice test in preparation for the 220-702 exam. It is a bit more difficult than Practice Exam 2, and the first 220-702 practice exam located on the disc that accompanies this book, and as such it should be taken last. This exam is also available on the CD. This practice exam helps you to determine how prepared you are for the actual exam, and which topics you need to review further. Write down your answers on a separate sheet of paper so that you can take this exam again if necessary. Compare your answers against the answer key that follows this exam.

1. What is the bit length of an IPv6 address?
   - ○ **A.** 32-bit
   - ○ **B.** 64-bit
   - ○ **C.** 128-bit
   - ○ **D.** 256-bit

2. What is the minimum CPU requirement for Windows 7?
   - ○ **A.** 233 MHz
   - ○ **B.** 500 MHz
   - ○ **C.** 800 MHz
   - ○ **D.** 1 GHz

3. A user cannot connect to a printer with the following UNC path: \\10.10.1.5\printer1. Which of the following paths would be the best solution?
   - ○ **A.** ipp://10.10.1.5/printer1
   - ○ **B.** https://10.1.1.5/printer1
   - ○ **C.** //10.10.1.5/printer1
   - ○ **D.** http:\\10.10.1.5\printer1

4. Which of the following descriptions classifies the protocol IMAP?

○ **A.** A protocol that allows real-time messaging

○ **B.** An e-mail protocol that allows users to selectively download messages

○ **C.** An e-mail protocol that allows users to send but not to receive messages

○ **D.** A protocol that authenticates users who are sending e-mail

5. Your boss calls you and tells you he is trying to install an external hard drive on his laptop. All of the USB ports are already in use. He explains that there is another port on the side of the laptop that looks similar to a USB port, but it has a bevel on one side. What is he attempting to describe to you?

○ **A.** USB 2.0 port

○ **B.** IEEE 1394

○ **C.** PCMCIA

○ **D.** Centronics

6. Which of the following are user-defined collections of folders that act as logical representations of the user's content?

○ **A.** Metadata

○ **B.** My Documents

○ **C.** Libraries

○ **D.** Public Documents

7. A user asks you to explain a message that comes up on the computer display before the operating system boots. The message states that the BIOS logged a chassis intrusion. What would be your explanation to the user?

○ **A.** The CD drive tray is open

○ **B.** The CPU is loose

○ **C.** A malicious individual has hacked the system

○ **D.** The computer case has been opened

8. You are experiencing intermittent connectivity to the website www.davidlprowse.com and want to check the status of the connectivity to that Web server over a span of half an hour. Which of the following commands should you use?

○ **A.** Ping –t

○ **B.** Ipconfig/all

○ **C.** Nslookup

○ **D.** Ping –l

9. Which command-line tool in Windows XP will find all of the unsigned drivers in the computer?

   ○ **A.** sigverif

   ○ **B.** dxdiag

   ○ **C.** ping

   ○ **D.** msconfig

10. James is a LAN Administrator in charge of printers. Which of the following should he check first if a Windows XP user is trying to print a document and gets the error message "Print sub-system not available"?

   ○ **A.** Correct printer driver is installed.

   ○ **B.** Printer has been added.

   ○ **C.** Spooler service is running.

   ○ **D.** Printer has power from the jack.

11. One of your customers wishes to have broadband Internet access set up in their home office. They are on a tight budget and don't want to pay for additional equipment. Which of the following technologies would be the best solution?

   ○ **A.** Cable modem

   ○ **B.** T-3

   ○ **C.** ISDN

   ○ **D.** T-1

12. Your manager's Windows computer locks up after the graphical user interface starts to load up. However, the computer will boot in Safe Mode. When you access the Event Viewer, you see an entry that states that a driver failed. Which of the following would help you further diagnose the problem?

   ○ **A.** Run sigverif

   ○ **B.** Enable Boot Logging. Then, in Safe Mode analyze the ntbtlog.txt file

   ○ **C.** Disable Driver Signature Enforcement

   ○ **D.** Access Debugging Mode

13. A user who is part of a workgroup reports that they cannot print to a new printer. Everyone else in the workgroup can print to the new printer and the user can still automatically send print jobs to the old printer. Which of the following can fix the problem for the user? (Select the two best answers.)

    ○ **A.** Add the new printer to the user's computer.

    ○ **B.** Clear the print queue on the new printer.

    ○ **C.** Change the user's password and permissions.

    ○ **D.** Set the new printer as the default printer.

14. Which of the following commands would be used to fix errors on the system disk?

    ○ **A.** Xcopy

    ○ **B.** Tracert /w

    ○ **C.** Diskpart

    ○ **D.** Chkdsk /F

15. Which of the following versions of Windows 7 can run in Windows XP mode, join domains, and utilize BitLocker encryption?

    ○ **A.** Starter

    ○ **B.** Home Premium

    ○ **C.** Ultimate

    ○ **D.** Professional

16. A customer's computer is running Windows Vista Ultimate 32-bit. The customer would like to upgrade to Windows 7. Which of the following operating systems can the person's computer be upgraded directly to?

    ○ **A.** Windows 7 Professional 32-bit

    ○ **B.** Windows 7 Professional 64-bit

    ○ **C.** Windows 7 Ultimate 32-bit

    ○ **D.** Windows 7 Ultimate 64-bit

17. You replaced two 1 GB DIMMS with two 2 GB DIMMS on a Windows Vista 32-bit computer. When you reboot the computer the BIOS recognizes 4 GB of RAM, but the operating system only shows approximately 3 GB. Which of the following is the most likely reason for this?

    ○ **A.** The new RAM is not the correct speed

    ○ **B.** Vista only sees 3 GB of RAM

    ○ **C.** The new RAM is not the correct type

    ○ **D.** There is a memory hole in the BIOS

18. In Windows 7, which of the following folders might be stored in a hidden partition by default?

   ◯ **A.** \Boot

   ◯ **B.** \Windows

   ◯ **C.** \Documents and Settings

   ◯ **D.** \Bootmgr

19. What is the IPv6 loopback address?

   ◯ **A.** 127.0.0.1

   ◯ **B.** FE80::/10

   ◯ **C.** ::1

   ◯ **D.** localhost

20. One of your customers has a wireless network that is secured with WEP. The customer wants to improve data encryption so that the transmission of data has less of a chance of being compromised. Which of the following should you do?

   ◯ **A.** Reconfigure the network to use WPA

   ◯ **B.** Use MAC address filtering

   ◯ **C.** Modify the WEP key every week

   ◯ **D.** Disable the SSID broadcast

21. One of your coworkers just installed a newer, more powerful video card in a customer's computer. The computer powers down before it completes the boot process. Before the installation, the computer worked normally. Which of the following is the most likely cause of a problem?

   ◯ **A.** The video card is not compatible with the CPU

   ◯ **B.** The monitor cannot display the higher resolution of the new video card

   ◯ **C.** The computer's RAM needs to be upgraded

   ◯ **D.** The power supply is not providing enough wattage for the new video card

22. You need to find out which ports are open in the Windows Firewall. Which of the following will allow you to show the configuration?

   ◯ **A.** arp –a

   ◯ **B.** netsh firewall show logging

   ◯ **C.** netsh firewall show state

   ◯ **D.** ipconfig /all

23. You get a complaint from a customer that her computer started receiving pop-up ads after they installed an application within Windows. What is most likely the problem?

   ○ **A.** The installed application contains a logic bomb

   ○ **B.** The installed application is a worm

   ○ **C.** The installed application is a Trojan horse

   ○ **D.** The installed application included adware

24. Which of the following commands is used to display hidden files?

   ○ **A.** dir /o

   ○ **B.** dir /a

   ○ **C.** dir /d

   ○ **D.** dir /?

25. Your organization has an Active Directory domain. One of the users, Bill, should not have read access to a folder named Accounting. The Accounting folder is shared on a network server, on a partition formatted as NTFS. How can you stop Bill from having read access to the folder without impacting any other users on the network?

   ○ **A.** Remove Bill from all domain groups that have access to the Accounting folder

   ○ **B.** Deny read access to the Accounting folder for Bill through local access security

   ○ **C.** Deny read access to the Accounting folder for any group that Bill is a member of

   ○ **D.** Deny read access to the Accounting folder for Bill through shared access security

26. A customer brings in a laptop with a non-functioning LCD screen that always remains black; however, when you connect the laptop to an external monitor the laptop boots to Windows normally. Which of the following actions should you take first?

   ○ **A.** Replace the inverter

   ○ **B.** Replace the LCD panel with a compatible model

   ○ **C.** Check the functionality of the LCD cutoff switch

   ○ **D.** Install a different video card

27. In Windows Vista, which of the following commands should be used to verify that a previous system shutdown was completed successfully?

- ○ **A.** ipconfig
- ○ **B.** chkntfs
- ○ **C.** chkdsk
- ○ **D.** sfc

28. Logging on to a network with a user name and password is an example of what?

- ○ **A.** Authorization
- ○ **B.** Identification
- ○ **C.** Identity proofing
- ○ **D.** Authentication

29. Which of the following versions of Windows uses the Sync Center for synchronization of off-line files?

- ○ **A.** Windows Vista
- ○ **B.** Windows XP Home
- ○ **C.** Windows 2000 Professional
- ○ **D.** Windows XP Professional

30. An administrator cannot connect to a network volume. Which of the following is the best path for the administrator to use?

- ○ **A.** \\computername\C$
- ○ **B.** \\ipaddress\sharename
- ○ **C.** //computername/C$
- ○ **D.** http://computername/C
- ○ **E.** \\computername\sharename

31. Your boss asks you to install a new wireless network. Which of the following should you implement on the wireless network to help prevent unauthorized access? (Select the two best answers.)

- ○ **A.** Install additional wireless access points
- ○ **B.** Use WPA2
- ○ **C.** Broadcast the SSID
- ○ **D.** Use a MAC filtering
- ○ **E.** install a signal booster

32. In Windows 7, which of the following enable administrators to perform administrative tasks that integrate scripts over a network?

- ○ **A.** PowerShell
- ○ **B.** Command Prompt
- ○ **C.** Command-line
- ○ **D.** Windows Script Host

33. Which of the following tools should you use in Windows 7 to migrate user files and settings for multiple computers?

- ○ **A.** Files and Settings Transfer Wizard
- ○ **B.** Windows Easy Transfer
- ○ **C.** User State Migration Tool
- ○ **D.** Profile Transfer Tool

34. Which of the following file systems is suited specifically for USB flash drives?

- ○ **A.** FAT32
- ○ **B.** FAT64
- ○ **C.** NTFS
- ○ **D.** FAT16

35. Which of the following programs in Windows 7 saves problem descriptions and solutions?

- ○ **A.** Dr. Watson
- ○ **B.** Problem Reports and Solutions
- ○ **C.** Action Center
- ○ **D.** Performance Monitor

36. Windows XP uses which of the following protocols to configure and monitor printer device status?

- ○ **A.** SMTP
- ○ **B.** SNMP
- ○ **C.** IPX/SPX
- ○ **D.** IPP
- ○ **E.** DNS

37. A program has been detected collecting information such as the computer name and IP address and sending that information to a specific IP address on the Internet. What kind of threat is this an example of?

- ○ **A.** Spyware
- ○ **B.** Virus
- ○ **C.** Rootkit
- ○ **D.** Spam

38. A customer of yours has a home office. Which of the following technologies would benefit from the use of QoS?

- ○ **A.** SSID
- ○ **B.** Instant messaging
- ○ **C.** E-mail
- ○ **D.** VoIP

39. Which of the following are descriptions or examples of unicast IPv6 addresses? (Select the two best answers.)

- ○ **A.** An address assigned to a group of interfaces where the packets are delivered to all interfaces
- ○ **B.** An address assigned to one interface
- ○ **C.** An address assigned to a group of interfaces where the packets are delivered to the first interface only
- ○ **D.** A loopback address of ::1

40. Which of the following is the best solution for repairing a hard drive when a computer displays an "NTLDR is missing error" upon booting?

- ○ **A.** Recovery Console with the fixmbr command.
- ○ **B.** Recovery Console with the fixboot command.
- ○ **C.** Recovery Console with the chkdsk command.
- ○ **D.** Recovery Console with the bootcfg /rebuild command.

41. Where can a user's Desktop folder be found in Windows Vista by default?

- ○ **A.** C:\Users\%username%\desktop
- ○ **B.** C:\Documents and Settings\%username%\desktop
- ○ **C.** C:\System Volume Information\%username%\desktop
- ○ **D.** C:\Users\System32\%username%\desktop

42. A technician gets a call from a customer with a Windows XP computer. The customer has just installed a new program. When the customer opens a file, it opens in a program that the customer does not want to use. Which of the following is the correct navigational path to change the file extension?

○ **A.** Control Panel > Tools > Folder Options > Offline Files > Advanced

○ **B.** Control Panel > Tools > Folder Options > View > Restore Defaults

○ **C.** Control Panel > Tools > Folder Options > View > Reset All Folders

○ **D.** Control Panel > Tools > Folder Options > File Types

43. You want to prevent Windows 7 from loading particular applications. What tool would you use to accomplish this?

○ **A.** Dir

○ **B.** Msconfig

○ **C.** Regedit

○ **D.** MD

44. You are building a new PC for a customer. Which of the following is the most valid reason why you would select SATA 2.0 over the original SATA 1.0?

○ **A.** You are installing an external SATA drive

○ **B.** You are attempting to implement hot-swapping functionality

○ **C.** You are trying to optimize the system for audio and video

○ **D.** You do not want to use jumpers

45. You are building a new PC and want to select a motherboard that will support the Scalable Link Interface (SLI) technology so that you can install two SLI video cards connected by a bridge. Which of the following expansion slots should the motherboard have for your two video cards?

○ **A.** Two AGP slots

○ **B.** Two PCIe slots

○ **C.** A PCI and PCIe slot

○ **D.** An AGP and PCIe slot

46. Which of the following **chkdsk** switches can repair data from bad sectors? (Select the two best answers.)

○ **A.** /?

○ **B.** /R

○ **C.** /X

○ **D.** /F

○ **E.** /V

47. How can an IDE hard disk be set up as a slave drive? (Select the two best answers.)

○ **A.** Set the hard disk's jumper to the slave position

○ **B.** Configure the disk as a slave in the BIOS

○ **C.** Connect the hard disk to the secondary IDE port of the mother-board

○ **D.** Connect the hard disk to the slave connector of a cable select cable.

48. One of your customers uses IMAP to download their e-mail. One day, the customer complains that their e-mail client is not downloading e-mail. Which port should you check is opened?

○ **A.** 110

○ **B.** 143

○ **C.** 25

○ **D.** 23

49. Which type of motherboard enables the use of a riser card?

○ **A.** New Low-Profile Extended (NLX)

○ **B.** Advanced Technology Extended (ATX)

○ **C.** Balanced Technology Extended (BTX)

○ **D.** Micro Advanced Technology Extended (Micro ATX)

50. In Windows 7, which of the following command-line utilities is used to verify the integrity of protected system files?

○ **A.** Expand

○ **B.** SFC

○ **C.** Chkdsk

○ **D.** Chkntfs

Answers at a Glance

1.	C	26.	C
2.	D	27.	B
3.	A	28.	D
4.	B	29.	A
5.	B	30.	A
6.	C	31.	B and D
7.	D	32.	A
8.	A	33.	C.
9.	A	34.	B
10.	C	35.	C.
11.	A	36.	B
12.	B	37.	A.
13.	A and D	38.	D
14.	D	39.	B and D
15.	C	40.	B
16.	C	41.	A
17.	B	42.	D
18.	A	43.	B
19.	C	44.	C
20.	A	45.	B
21.	D	46.	B and D
22.	C	47.	A and D
23.	D	48.	B
24.	B	49.	A
25.	D	50.	B

Answers with Explanations

1. **C**. IPv6 addresses are 128-bit. They are displayed as hexadecimal numbers separated by colons. An example of an IPv6 address would be 2001:7120:0000:8001:0000:0000:0000:1F10. IPv4 addresses are 32-bit; an example of an IPv4 address would be 192.168.1.1. See the section titled "Networking Fundamentals" in Chapter 14, "Networking," for more information.

2. **D**. 1 GHz is the minimum CPU requirement for Windows 7. 233 MHz is the minimum requirement for Windows XP. 800 MHz is the minimum requirement for Windows Vista. See the section titled "Installing and Upgrading to Windows 7," in Chapter 7, "Installing and Upgrading Windows" for more information.

3. **A**. IPP stands for the Internet Printing Protocol. It is a common standard used for remote printing. IPP paths are similar to HTTP paths, but instead they begin with the letters ipp. IPP supports access control, authentication and encryption enabling secure printing. Some organizations prefer to use IPP instead of UNC paths. Although answer B could be a possibility, it would be more likely to use IPP instead of HTTPS. However, the IP address in answer B is also incorrect; the second octet is a 1 instead of a 10. Answer C isn't correct syntax; two slashes should be preceded by some kind of protocol such as IPP or HTTP. Or if this was meant to be a UNC, the slashes should be backslashes; however, a UNC was the original path that failed, so it is incorrect either way. Answer D is showing backslashes in the path instead of the proper slashes. See the section titled "Installing, Configuring, and Troubleshooting Printers" in Chapter 13, "Printers," for more information about printer configurations.

4. **B**. IMAP is the Internet Message Access Protocol which allows an e-mail client to access e-mail on a remote mail server. Generally the e-mail client software will leave the messages on the server until the user specifically deletes them. So, the user can selectively download messages. This allows multiple users to manage the same mailbox. Real-time messaging can be accomplished by using instant messaging and chat programs. IMAP, like POP3, allows users to download, or receive messages, but it does not send messages; a protocol such as SMTP would be used to send mail. IMAP, like POP3, authenticates the user, but again not for sending e-mail, but when receiving e-mail.

5. **B**. The IEEE 1394 6-pin connector looks similar to a USB port, but one ends will be beveled or curved. So answer B is the best answer. However, don't confuse the 6-pin connector with the 4-pin IEEE 1394 connector, which is smaller than a USB connector. PCMCIA or PC Card slots are approximately the size of a credit card. Centronics connectors are large ports on printers and other similar devices. See the section titled "Input/Output, Input Devices, and Peripherals" in Chapter 12, "Video, Audio, and Peripherals," for more information.

6. **C**. Libraries are commonly known as metafolders; they are logical representations of a user's content. For example, one library in Windows 7 is called Documents. The Documents library includes two default locations: My Documents and Public Documents. See the section titled "Windows User Interfaces" in Chapter 8, "Configuring Windows," for more information.

7. **D**. A chassis intrusion means that the computer case has been opened. Some BIOS programs have the capability to detect this. This is a security feature that informs the user of a possible breach. As a PC technician, you should check the computer inside and out for any possible tampering. The BIOS program will not detect if the CD-ROM drive is open. If the CPU was loose, the computer would not boot, and there would be nothing to display. It is possible that a malicious individual has hacked, or attempted to hack, the system, but this is not necessarily the case, although you should check just to make sure. See the section titled "The BIOS" in Chapter 2, "Motherboards," for more information.

8. **A**. Ping –t is a continuous ping. It will ping the Web server with ICMP echo packets until you manually stop the operation. You can stop the operation by pressing Ctrl+C on the keyboard. When you do so, an average of the ping results will be displayed, as well as the total packets that were sent, received, and lost. Ipconfig/all displays the configuration of your network adapter. Nslookup enables you to find out a domains corresponding IP address, as well as carry out other name's server configurations. Ping –l is a four packet ping, but the –l parameter enables you to modify the size of the packet being sent. See the section titled "Troubleshooting Network Connectivity" in Chapter 14, "Networking," for more information.

9. **A**. The sigverif.exe tool can be used to check for unsigned drivers within your operating system. Unsigned drivers are drivers that have not been verified by Microsoft. If you receive error messages and are troubleshooting, run this command from the Run prompt. When the check is finished, unsigned drivers will be displayed. This list is also stored in a file called sigverif.txt within the %systemroot%. Dxdiag is short for DirectX diagnostics. It is used to test the functionality of audio and video devices. Ping is used to test whether or not another host is on the network. Msconfig (the Microsoft System Configuration Utility) is a tool used to troubleshoot the startup process of Windows. See the section titled "Windows Tools and Errors" in Chapter 10, "Troubleshooting Windows," for more information.

10. **C**. If a "print sub-system not available" message or similar message appears, it most likely means the spooler has stalled. This can be turned back on within the Services section of Computer Management, or by issuing the command net start spooler in the Command Prompt. If the wrong printer driver was installed, the user would either get a message stating that the printer is not available, or the document would print but the information would be garbled. If the printer has not been added, the user would not be able to print any documents to any printers, and therefore should not get an error message. If the printer is not getting power, the user would most likely get a message stating that the printer is not available. See the section titled "Installing, Configuring, and Troubleshooting Printers" in Chapter 13, "Printers," for more information.

11. A. Installing cable Internet would be the best solution given the parameters of this scenario. It is the cheapest of the four technologies listed and it is a broadband Internet solution. ISDN is generally known as a narrowband technology. Although there is a type of Broadband ISDN, that is designed to handle high-bandwidth applications and is quite expensive. T-1 and T-3 lines are dedicated high-speed connections that will not fit the customer's tight budget. See the section titled "Installing and Configuring a SOHO Network" in Chapter 14, "Networking," for more information.

12. B. Boot Logging can be enabled from Windows Advanced Boot Options Menu (ABOM); it is generally the fourth option. Once this is enabled, the system will automatically create a file called ntbtlog.txt. Afterwards, you can access the system by booting into Safe Mode, once again from the ABOM. Sigverif is a program that can be run in Windows that verifies whether drivers have been signed by Microsoft. Disabling Driver Signature Enforcement is another ABOM option; you might use this to help fix the issue, but not to diagnose the problem. Debugging Mode is another ABOM option, but in this scenario you don't necessarily need to debug the system, but rather repair the individual driver that failed to load up. See the section titled "Repair Environments and Boot Errors" in Chapter 10, "Troubleshooting Windows," for more information.

13. A and D. If a user cannot print to a brand-new printer, yet everyone else can print to it, you should check if the printer is installed on that user's computer, and if it is set as the default printer. If the printer has not yet been installed, there will be no print queue to clear. However, if the printer has been installed, then the next thing to check would be if the print queue has failed. You could also check the print spooler. If the user was able to print to an older printer that was also shared by other users in the workgroup, then you should not have to change the user's password or permissions. See the section titled "Installing, Configuring, and Troubleshooting Printers" in Chapter 13, "Printers," for more information.

14. D. Chkdsk /F allows you to fix errors on a disk. It does not fix all errors, but checks for disk integrity, bad sectors, and similar issues. Xcopy copies files and directory trees; Microsoft recommends using Robocopy on newer Windows operating systems. Tracert /w analyzes the path to another computer with a specific timeout per reply. Diskpart is the command-line tool that enables you to make changes to the operating system's partition table. See the section titled "Command-Line Tools" in Chapter 10, "Troubleshooting Windows," for more information.

15. C. Windows 7 Ultimate can run in Windows XP mode, join domains, and utilize BitLocker encryption. Starter and Home Premium can do none of these. Windows 7 Professional cannot utilize BitLocker encryption. On a side note, Windows 7 Enterprise can also run BitLocker, although it was not one of the listed answers. See the section titled "Installing and Upgrading to Windows 7" in Chapter 7, "Installing and Upgrading Windows," for more information.

16. **C**. Windows Vista Ultimate can only be upgraded to Windows 7 Ultimate. 32-bit versions of Windows cannot be directly upgraded to 64-bit versions of Windows. See the section titled "Installing and Upgrading to Windows 7" in Chapter 7, "Installing and Upgrading Windows," for more information.

17. **B**. Although Windows Vista can address 4 GB of RAM, Windows Vista 32-bit (and Windows XP 32-bit) systems and applications can use only 3.12 GB of RAM. This is because these operating systems reserve the remainder for devices in what is known as MMIO or memory-mapped I/O. See the section titled "Installing and Upgrading to Windows Vista" in Chapter 7, "Installing and Upgrading Windows," for more information.

18. **A**. The \Boot folder will be located in a hidden partition, by default, which is separate from the C drive. The Windows folder is where the operating system is installed to; it is also known by the variables: %systemroot% or %WINDIR%, and is located in the C: drive by default. \Documents and Settings is also located in C: by default. Bootmgr is the Windows Boot Manager, which is the Windows loader program; it is a file, not a folder. See the section titled "Files, File Systems, and Disks" in Chapter 8, "Configuring Windows," for more information.

19. **C**. ::1 is the IPv6 loopback address. If you were to type any one of the following three commands: ping ::1, ping localhost, or ping loopback, on an IPv6-enabled Windows computer, the computer would ping the internal loopback address ::1. 127.0.0.1 is the IPv4 loopback address. FE80::/10 is the address range used by Windows when auto-configuring a unicast IPv6 address. Localhost is another name for a local computer; the name corresponds with the ::1 address. See the section titled "Networking Fundamentals" in Chapter 14, "Networking," for more information.

20. **A**. The best solution is to upgrade the wireless network from WEP to WPA. WEP is a deprecated wireless encryption protocol and should be updated to a newer and more powerful protocol if at all possible. If this is not possible, it would be wise to use a strong WEP key, and modify it often. MAC address filtering will not increase the level of data encryption, but it will filter out unwanted computers when they attempt to connect to the wireless access point. Disabling the SSID broadcast will deter any new computers for making initial connections to the wireless access point. See the section titled "Installing and Configuring a SOHO Network" in Chapter 14, "Networking," for more information.

21. **D**. Today's video cards can be very powerful, and might require a more powerful power supply than is in the computer currently. Video cards need to be compatible with the motherboard, not necessarily with the CPU. If the monitor could not display the higher resolution, the operating system would still boot but you would probably see garbled information on the screen. Because a video card comes with its own RAM, the computer's RAM usually does not need to be upgraded. See the section titled "The Video Subsystem" in Chapter 12 "Video, Audio, and Referrals", and "Power Supplies" in Chapter 5, "Power," for more information.

22. **C**. Netsh firewall show state is a command that can be run in the Command Prompt that will display any currently open ports. Other commands can also show open ports such as netstat –a. However, arp-a will show a table of hosts that the local computer has connected to in recent history; it displays the IP address and MAC address of those remote computers. Netsh firewall show logging will display the location of the firewall log, its maximum file size, and whether any packets were dropped. Ipconfig /all displays the configuration of your network adapters. See the section titled "Troubleshooting Network Connectivity" in Chapter 14, "Networking," for more information.

23. **D**. If a computer starts receiving pop-up advertisements after an application has been installed, the application probably included adware. While pop-up ads are not necessarily harmful to a computer, the rest of the answers including Trojan horse, worms, and logic bombs will usually be more serious. See the section titled "Malicious Software" in Chapter 15, "Security," for more information.

24. **B. Dir /a** can be used to display hidden files. Specifically, dir /ah can be used to show hidden files only. Dir /o deals with various sort orders of files, for example alphabetical. Dir /d sorts files by column in wide format. Dir /? displays the help file for the dir command. For more information about utilities in the Command Prompt, see the section titled "Command-line Tools" in Chapter 10, "Troubleshooting Windows," for more information.

25. **D**. The best option in this scenario would be to deny read access to the Accounting folder for Bill through shared access security. You would not use local access security because the folder is shared from a network server within your Active Directory domain. Also, if you remove Bill from all domain groups that have access to the accounting folder, Bill will probably lose access to other folders as well. If you deny read access to the accounting folder for any group that Bill is a member of, you will probably impact other users on the network negatively. See the section titled "File Security" in Chapter 15, "Security," for more information.

26. **C**. Check the functionality of the LCD cutoff switch first before opening the laptop and replacing parts. The LCD cutoff switch turns off the monitor when the laptop is closed; these are prone to failure. Although the LCD panel and inverter could possibly fail, it is less common and because they require a lot of time and effort to replace, they should be checked afterwards. Generally, a laptop's video card is the least common component to fail, although it can be replaced on some laptops. See the section titled "Installing, Configuring, and Troubleshooting Internal Laptop Components" in Chapter 11, "Laptops," for more information.

27. **B**. Chkntfs can check to see if a previous system shutdown completed successfully. Generally, you would check this on the system drive, for example C:. If the drive is okay and the system did complete the shut down successfully, you'll get a message such as "C: is not dirty." Otherwise, you will get a message telling of the error. Chkdsk checks the integrity of the disk. Ipconfig displays the configuration of your network adapters. SFC scans the integrity of all protected system files and can replace them with the correct versions if necessary. See the section titled "Command-Line Tools" in Chapter 10, "Troubleshooting Windows," for more information.

28. **D**. Authentication is when a person's identity is confirmed or verified through the use of a specific system. Authorization to specific resources cannot be accomplished without previous authentication. Identification is when a person is in a state of being identified. Identity proofing is an initial validation of an identity. See the section titled "Authentication" in Chapter 15, "Security," for more information.

29. **A**. Windows Vista is the only operating system listed that uses the Sync Center. It is also available in Windows Vista Business and Ultimate. However, it is not available in Windows Vista Starter, Home Basic, or Home Premium. See the section titled "Installing and Upgrading to Windows Vista" in Chapter 7, "Installing and Upgrading Windows," for more information on Windows versions.

30. **A**. The UNC \\computername\C$ or \\ipaddress\C$ would be the best option. This allows the administrator to connect to the hidden share for the root of C if the administrator has issues connecting to a network volume with a particular share name, they should use the hidden share. This can be done by computer name or by IP address. It would not be necessary to connect utilizing HTTP. Also, it is not wise to share the C: drive with a share name called "C." See the section titled "File Security" in Chapter 15, "Security," for more information.

31. **B and D.** By using WPA2 (the strongest type of encryption on most wireless access points) you ensure a high level of encryption, helping to reduce unauthorized access. Using MAC filtering will filter out unwanted computers by checking their MAC address when the computers first try to connect. Additional wireless access points and signal boosters would increase the chances of unauthorized access. Broadcasting the SSID also increases the chance of unauthorized access, because any wireless device will see the name of your network. When all wireless devices have made their initial connection to the wireless access point, consider disabling the SSID broadcast. See the section titled "Installing and Configuring a SOHO Network" in Chapter 14, "Networking," for more information.

32. **A**. The Windows 7 PowerShell enables administrators to perform administrative tasks that integrates scripts and executables, and can be run over a network. It is a combination of the Command Prompt and a scripting language. The PowerShell is the successor to the Windows Script Host. The Command Prompt is Windows version of a command-line. It is not as functional as the PowerShell. See the section titled "Windows User Interfaces" in Chapter 8, "Configuring Windows," for more information.

33. C. The User State Migration Tool (USMT) is a command-line tool that can be used to migrate user files and settings for one or more computers in Windows 7 as well as Windows Vista. Windows 7 employs additional features such as AES encryption support and shadow copying of volumes of information. The Files and Settings Transfer Wizard is an older version of Windows Easy Transfer that is used with Windows XP, 2000, and other older operating systems. Windows Easy Transfer enables you to copy files, photos, music, and settings, but not for multiple computers. See the section titled "System Tools and Utilities" in Chapter 8, "Configuring Windows," for more information.

34. B. FAT64 (also known as exFAT) is suited specifically for USB flash drives, and many other mobile storage solutions. It is the successor to FAT32, and can format media that is larger than 32 GB with a single partition. Older file systems such as FAT32 and FAT16 are very limited as to the partition size. NTFS can be a good solution for USB flash drives, but FAT64 was developed specifically for USB flash drives and is the better solution if you have an operating system that will support it such as: Windows 7, Windows Server 2008, Windows Vista with service pack one, and so on. See the section titled "Files, File Systems, and Disks" in Chapter 8, "Configuring Windows," for more information.

35. C. The Action Center in Windows 7 can save problem descriptions and solutions; this is done in the archived messages section. The Action Center could be considered the successor to the Problem Reports and Solutions of Windows Vista, as well as the successor to the older Dr. Watson in Windows XP. Performance Monitor is a program that tracks how much of your device's resources are being utilized, for example what percentage of the processor is used. See the section titled "Windows Tools and Errors" in Chapter 10, "Troubleshooting Windows," for more information.

36. B. The Simple Network Management Protocol (SNMP) can be used to monitor remote computers and printers. This requires the installation of SNMP on the appropriate hosts. SMTP is the Simple Mail Transfer Protocol which deals with the sending of e-mail. IPX/SPX is a Novell-based communications protocol that has been all but phased out by TCP/IP. IPP is the Internet Printing Protocol which allows hosts to print documents to a remote printer without the need for UNC paths. DNS is the Domain Name System which resolves domain names to their corresponding IP addresses. For more information on networking protocols see the section titled "Networking Fundamentals" in Chapter 14, "Networking," for more information.

37. A. Spyware is a type of malicious software that is usually downloaded unwittingly by a user or is installed by third-party software. It collects information about the user and the user's computer without the user's consent. A virus is code that runs on the computer without the user's knowledge; it infects a computer when the code is accessed and executed. A rootkit is software designed to gain administrator-level control over a computer system without being detected. Spam is the abuse of electronic messaging systems such as e-mail. See the section titled "Malicious Software" in Chapter 15, "Security," for more information.

38. **D**. Voice over IP (VoIP) is a streaming telephony application. Streaming applications such as VoIP and online games can benefit from QoS. QoS stands for Quality of Service, which is the capability to provide different priorities to different applications. It guarantees network bandwidth for real-time streaming of the media applications such as VoIP. The SSID is the name or identifier of a wireless network. Instant messaging and e-mail are not streaming applications, therefore they would not benefit from the use of QoS. See the section titled "Installing and Configuring a SOHO Network" in Chapter 14, "Networking," for more information.

39. **B and D.** Unicast IPv6 addresses are addresses assigned to one interface on a host. Examples of unicast IPv6 addresses include Global unicast addresses that begin at 2000, link-local addresses that begin at FE80::/10, and the loopback address ::1. Addresses assigned to a group of interfaces where the packets are delivered to all interfaces are known as multicast addresses. Addresses assigned to a group of interfaces where the packets are delivered to the first interface only are known as anycast addresses. See the section titled "Networking Fundamentals" in Chapter 14, "Networking," for more information.

40. **B**. The Recovery Console is a system recovery tool used in Windows XP and 2000. There are a lot of different commands that can be issued in this mode. If the NTLDR file has been damaged or is missing, it can be re-written to the hard disk by issuing the fixboot command while in the Recovery Console. NTLDR can also be manually copied from the CD-ROM disc if necessary. The fixmbr command will rewrite the master boot record of the hard drive. The chkdsk command will check the integrity of the disk. Bootcfg /rebuild can be used to scan for the operating system installations and rebuild that information into the boot.ini file. See the section titled "Repair Environments and Boot Errors" in Chapter 10, "Troubleshooting Windows," for more information.

41. **A**. Every user profile gets a Desktop folder by default. This folder will be located within the user profile folder, which is shown in the answer as a variable %username%. In a standard Windows Vista configuration, the Documents and Settings and System Volume Information folders will be hidden and access will be denied. The System32 folder is inside the Windows folder, not the Users folder. See the section titled "Files, File Systems, and Disks" in Chapter 8, "Configuring Windows," for more information.

42. **D**. The File Types section of the Folder Options dialog box is where program associations can be set. The user has the ability to decide what programs will open any known file extensions. The other locations each serve a different purpose. Offline files can only be modified if fast user switching is turned off; however, this is not associated with file types. Restore Defaults and Reset All Folders deals with the file and folder settings but is not associated with file types. See the section titled "Files, File Systems, and Disks" in Chapter 8, "Configuring Windows," for more information.

43. **B**. The System Configuration tool (MSconfig) can be used to modify how the system boots, what services will be loaded, and what applications will be loaded at startup. Dir will show the contents of a directory in the command-line. The Registry Editor (Regedit) is used to access and modify the registry database. MD is short for make directory; it is used to create directories or folders from within the command-line. See the section titled "System Tools and Utilities" in Chapter 8, "Configuring Windows," for more information.

44. **C**. SATA 2.0 (maximum transfer rate of 300 MB/s) can send and receive twice as much data as SATA 1.0 (maximum transfer rate of 150 MB/s). This makes it the better choice for audio and video applications and would be the most valid reason why you would select it for a new computer. When building a new computer, you would most likely start with an internal drive. You might add an external drive later, but regardless, just having an external drive is not a reason to use SATA 2.0 over SATA 1.0. SATA drives are not hot-swappable by default, whether they are internal or external. Special drive enclosures can be purchased to make an SATA drive hot-swappable, however. Neither SATA 1.0 nor SATA 2.0 use jumpers. IDE drives are the most well-known for their use of jumpers. See the section titled "Magnetic Storage Media" in Chapter 6, "Storage Devices," for more information.

45. **B**. For SLI to work properly, you will need two identical PCIe (PCI Express) slots. Although older SLI cards were available for PCI, the technology cannot span different expansion slots. See the section titled "The Video Subsystem" in Chapter 12, "Video, Audio, and Peripherals," for more information.

46. **B and D.** /F is used to fix errors on the disk, which includes bad sectors. /R locates bad sectors only and recovers readable information; which implies a portion of /F. /? Is the help switch for the chkdsk command. /X forces the volume to dismount. /V displays the path and name of each file. See the section titled "Command-Line Tools" in Chapter 10, "Troubleshooting Windows," for more information.

47. **A and D.** The hard disk can be jumpered to the slave position and connected to the motherboard, or it can be jumpered to CS (cable select) and connected to the appropriate connector of the cable select cable. This needs to be done manually and physically; it is not set up in the BIOS. Both the primary and secondary IDE ports of a motherboard can have master *and* slave drives. See the section titled "Magnetic Storage Media" in Chapter 6, "Storage Devices," for more information.

48. **B**. Port 143 needs to be open to download e-mail via IMAP. Port 110 corresponds to POP3. Port 25 is SMTP. Port 23 is Telnet. See the section titled "Networking Fundamentals" in Chapter 14, "Networking," for more information.

49. **A**. NLX motherboards allow for the use of riser cards. They are common to computer manufacturers who wish to have a computer case with a small footprint, yet with the capability to have a lot of internal devices by building vertically and horizontally, making the most use of the space available in the case. The motherboard and case must be compatible. ATX, BTX, and Micro ATX don't allow for riser cards. See the section titled "Motherboard Components and Form Factors" in Chapter 2, "Motherboards," for more information.

50. **B**. SFC (system file checker) is a command-line utility used to check the integrity of protected system files. It can replace incorrect versions and missing files. Expand is a command used to inflate compressed files such as those found on an installation CD (for example, ntoskrnl.ex_ can be expanded to ntoskrnl.exe). Chkdsk allows you to check for errors on a disk. Chkntfs can check to see if a previous system shutdown completed successfully. A typical option for SFC is /scannow, which scans all protected system files immediately. See the section titled "Command-Line Tools" in Chapter 10, "Troubleshooting Windows," for more information.

Index

Symbols

% (percentage signs), 217

%username% variable, 217

#1-TuffTEST, 168, 180

3G, 448

4G, 448

32-bit CPU (central processing units), 58

64-bit CPU (central processing units), 58

220-701 CompTIA A+ practice exam

    exam answers, 540-552

    exam questions, 521-539

220-702 CompTIA A+ practice exams

    exam answers, 573-586, 598-608

    exam questions, 553-572, 587-597

802.3ab standard, 424

802.3u standard, 424

802.3z standard, 424

802.11 wireless, 449

A

AC (alternating current), 104

AC outlets

    electrical safety, 500

    regulating output, 107

    testing

        via multimeters, 106, 108

        via receptacle testers, 105

Accelerated Graphics Port (AGP), 352

Acronis True Image, 304

actions, documenting (six-step troubleshooting process), 13

    display issue example, 17

    power issue example, 18

Add/Remove Snap-ins window, 221

address types, IPv6, 421

addresses

IP addresses, 415

private addresses, 419

public addresses, 419

administrative privileges, 221

administrative shares, 487

administrative tools, 220-221

ADSL (Asymmetrical Digital Subscriber Line), 447

Advanced Boot Options menu, 280-281

adware, 477

AGP (Accelerated Graphics Port), 352, 31, 33

AMD CPU (central processing units), 63-64

amperage (A), 104

AMR (audio/modem riser) buses, 32

analyzing network adapters, 422-424

answers to practice exams

practice exam 1, 540-552

practice exam 2, 573-586

practice exam 3, 598-608

anti-malware software, 461

HDD (hard disk drives) maintenance, 141

updates, 275

antistatic devices, ESD (electrostatic discharges), 503

antistatic wrist straps, 19, 502

antivirus software, 478, 480-481

anycast addresses, 421

APIPA (automatic private IP addressing), 416

application windows, 212

applications

troubleshooting network connectivity with, 442-443

Windows applications

Command Prompt, 219

Computer, 215-216

Control Panel, 218

Network, 218

PowerShell, 219

Windows Explorer, 216-218

Archive file attribute, 485

aspect ratio, 367

asymmetric key encryption, 493

Asymmetrical Digital Subscriber Line (ADSL), 447

attrib command, 486

ATX (Advanced Technology Extended)

motherboards, 24, 35-37

power supplies, 116-117

audio

laptop audio subsystem, 329-330

overview, 375

quality, 378-379

sound cards

installing, 377-378

overview, 375-376

speakers, installing, 377

audio clusters, 34

authentication

biometrics, 473

BIOS security, 471-472

definition of, 460

logon process, 467-469

passwords

changing, 466

password policy, 466-467

strong passwords, 465

smart cards, 472

UAC (User Account Control), 470-471

usernames, 465

automatic private IP addressing (APIPA), 416

Automatic Updates, 478

AV (antivirus) software, 478, 480-481

B

Backup and Restore (Windows 7), 272-273

Backup Status and Configuration (Windows Vista), 273

backups, 461. *See also* restore points
Windows 7, 272-273
Windows Vista, 273
Windows XP, 273

bar code readers, 387

Basic Rate ISDN (BRI), 448

batteries
disposal of, 505
laptop batteries, 333
lithium batteries
BIOS password resets, 42
CMOS, 39

Belarc Advisor, 168, 180, 198

biometric devices, 387

biometrics, 473

BIOS (Basic Input Output System), 39, 44-45
accessing, 40
configuring, 40-41
downloading, 43
flashing, 43-44
identifying version of, 43
passwords, resetting, 42
POST (power-on self-tests), 40
security, 471-472
Setup utility, 40-41
troubleshooting
memory errors, 99
motherboard-related issues, 50
updating, 43
HDD (hard disk drive) maintenance, 275

blackouts, 110

blank paper (printers), troubleshooting, 407

Blu-Ray data storage, 154

Blue Screen of Death (BSOD), 298-300

Bluetooth, 337, 449-450

Boot Device Priority (BIOS boot order), 41

boot disks, 145

boot errors
Windows Vista Boot Errors, 285-287
Windows XP/2000 Boot Errors, 287

boot files, 249

boot sector viruses, 476

BOOTMGR is missing (error message), 285

bootrec command, 311

bootstrapping
BIOS (Basic Input Output System), 39-40
POST (power-on self-tests), 40

botnets, 477

BRI (Basic Rate ISDN), 448

brownouts, 110

BSOD (Blue Screen of Death), 298-300
troubleshooting, 99

BTX (Balanced Technology Extended)
motherboards, 36-37
power supplies, 118

buses. *See also* expansion buses
AGP (Accelerated Graphics Port) buses, 31, 33
AMR (audio/modem riser) buses, 32
CNR (Communications and Networking Riser) buses, 32
FSB (Front Side Buses), 28
external clock speeds, 57
IDE (Integrated Drive Electronics) buses, 28-29
BIOS configuration, 42
memory buses, 28
PCI (Peripheral Component Interconnect) buses, 29, 32
PCI Express x16 Interface, 28
PCIe (Peripheral Component Interconnect Express) buses, 31, 33
SATA (Serial ATA) buses, 29
speed ratings, 28

C

cable Internet, 447

cable select drive configurations (PATA), 135

cables, 432-435

EMI (electromagnetic interference), 506

physical safety, 504

RFI radio frequency interference), 506

caches

CPU, 60-61

HDD (hard disk drives), 138

cameras, 387

CAS (Column Address Strobe) latency (RAM), 90

case fans, 65-66

cathode ray tube (CRT), 362

causes (problem identification process)

establishing theory of probable cause, 11

display issue example, 15-16

power issue example, 17

testing theory of probable cause, 12

display issue example, 16

power issue example, 17

CD (Compact Discs)

CD-R, 150

CD-ROM, 149-150

installing Windows Vista from, 181

installing Windows XP from, 198

CD-RW, 150

data storage, 149-150, 153

cellular connectivity, 448

Cellular WAN, 337

CF (CompactFlash) cards, 161

changes to computers, identifying (problem identification process), 11

changing passwords, 466

cheat sheets (exam preparation), 515-516

chipsets, 29

ICH (I/O Controller Hubs), 26

bus connections, 28

IDE buses, 28-29

SATA buses, 29

IOH (Input/Output Hubs), 26

MCH (Memory Controller Hubs), 26, 80

video card chipsets, 356

chkdsk command, 307-308

Class A networks, 418

Class B networks, 418

Class C networks, 418

Class D networks, 418

Class E networks, 418

Classic mode, reverting to, 238

clean power, 107

cleanup programs, HDD (hard disk drives) maintenance, 140, 270-271

clear speaking, 508

clearing data, 461

clock rates, 56-57

external clock speeds, 57

internal clock speeds, 57

motherboards, 57

CMOS (complimentary metal-oxide semiconductors), 39

password resets, 42

CNR (Communications and Networking Riser) buses, 32

coaxial cable, 435

color depth, 364-365

Command Prompt, 219, 307

starting/stopping services, 234

working with directories in, 251-252

Command Prompt option (Recovery Options), 284

command-line interface, opening, 437

commands

attrib, 486

bootrec, 311

chkdsk, 307-308

convert, 308

copy, 311

defrag, 309

diskpart, 309

drwtsn32, 296

dxdiag, 227

edit, 310-311

expand, 311

FDISK/MBR, 480

FIXBOOT, 312

FIXMBR, 312, 480

format, 309

ipconfig, 437-438

net, 441-442

netstat, 440-441

nslookup, 441

ping, 438-439

regedit, 239

regedit32, 239

SFC (System File Checker), 308

SYS, 480

taskmgr, 229

tracert, 439-440

xcopy, 309

communication skills, developing, 508-510

communications, laptop, 336-337

compatibility

DRAM (dyanmic random-access memory), 98

power supplies, 116-117

printer installation, 399

compliance, security, 463

Component Video, 354

compression, 485

CompTIA A+, post certification development, 519

CompTIA A+ 220-701 practice exam

exam answers, 540-552

exam questions, 521-539

CompTIA A+ 220-702 practice exams

exam answers, 573-586, 598-608

exam questions, 553-572, 587-597

Computer Management, starting/stopping services, 233

Computer window, 215-216

comsetup.log, 205

configuring

BIOS (Basic Input Output System), 40-41, 472

IPv4, 414-417

network adapters, 422-424

password policy, 466-467

printers, 400

managing print jobs, 401

managing printer permissions, 405

pooling printers, 404

print spooling options, 402-403

separator pages, 406

setting printer priority, 401-402

sharing printers, 405

XPS (XML Paper Specification) feature (Windows Vista), 404

video settings

color depth, 364-365

drivers, 363-364

Multiple Monitor (DualView), 370-371

OSD (on-screen display), 369-370

refresh rate, 368-369

resolution, 365-368

connectors, video card, 354-355

consumables, 394

continuity testers, 433

Control Panel, 218

convert command, 308

cooling
  CPU (central processing units)
    fans, 65-66
    heat sinks, 64
    liquid cooling systems, 66
    thermal compound (TIM), 65
  power supplies, 127
copy command, 311
copying folders, 492
CPU (central processing units), 55, 66-68
  32-bit CPU, 58
  64-bit CPU, 58
  AMD CPU, 63-64
  caches, 60-61
  clock rates, 56-57
  cooling systems
    fans, 65-66
    heat sinks, 64
    liquid cooling systems, 66
    thermal compound (TIM), 65
  function of, 56
  HT (Hyper-Threading), 61
  installing, 69
    ESD prevention, 69
    LGA sockets, 70
    motherboard preparation, 69
    PGA sockets, 72
    testing installations, 72-73
  Intel CPU, 63-64
  laptop CPUs, 345-347
  memory controller integration, 80
  multi-core CPU, 61
  power consumption, 62
  RAM access, 80
  sockets, 58
    compatibility, 59-60
    LGA sockets, 59, 70
    PGA sockets, 59, 72
  TDP (thermal design points), 62
  troubleshooting, 74-76

CPU-Z, 73
CRT (cathode ray tube), 362
Ctrl+Alt+Del login functionality, 468
customers, listening to (professionalism), 508
customizing user environment, 238-239

D

data backups, 461
data removal, 461
data security
  data sensitivity, 462-463
  security compliance, 463
  technologies, 460-462
  threats, 460-461
data sensitivity, 462-463
data storage
  Blu-Ray, 154
  CD (Compact Discs), 149, 153
    CD-R, 150
    CD-ROM, 149-150
    CD-RW, 150
  CF (CompactFlash) cards, 161
  DVD (Digital Versatile Discs, 151-153
  floppy disk drives, 143
    boot disks, 145
    installing, 144
    troubleshooting, 144
  HDD (hard disk drives), 132
    antimalware, 141
    backups, 272-273
    caches, 138
    cleanup programs, 140, 270-271
    components of, 132
    data transfer rates, 137
    defragging, 141, 271
    determining drive specifications, 137-138
    installing, 139
    latency, 138

manually deleting Internet files, 270

manually deleting temporary files, 270

NAS (Network Attached Storage), 143

PATA (Parallel ATA), 133-135

preventive maintenance, 140-141, 270-271, 275-276

restore points, 274

rotational speeds, 138

SATA (Serial ATA), 135-136, 140

SCSI (Small Computer System Interface), 138-139

troubleshooting, 141-143

Ultra ATA hard drives, 139

magnetic storage media, 132-147

optical storage media, 149-155

SD (Secure Digital) cards, 159

SDIO (Secure Digital Input Output) cards, 160

solid-state storage media, 156-162

tape drives, 145

USB flash drives, 156-157

formatting, 158

memory, 158

troubleshooting, 158

data transfer rates, HDD (hard disk drives), 137

date/time (BIOS configuration), 41

DC (direct current), 104

DDR (Double Data Rate), 84-85

DDR2 (Double Data Rate 2), 86

DDR3 (Double Data Rate 3), 87

DDR4 (Double Data Rate 4), 88

Debugging Mode option (Advanced Boot Options menu), 281

defrag command, 309

defragging HDD (hard disk drives), 141, 271

degaussing, 370

deleting. See removing

desktop, 210

destroying data, 462

device drivers, video drivers, 363-364

Device Manager, 225-226, 290-293

dial-up connectivity, 446

dialog boxes, Windows Security, 467

digital cameras, 387

digital optical ports, 376

digital signatures, 227

digital subscriber line (DSL), 447

Digital Visual Interface (DVI), 354

direct-sequence spread spectrum (DSSS), 449

Directory Services Restore Mode option (Advanced Boot Options menu), 281

directory structure for Windows Vista, 248

dirty power, 107

Disable driver signature enforcement option (Advanced Boot Options menu), 281

disabling

fast user switching, 467

visual effects, 238

Welcome screen, 467

Disk Cleanup, 140, 270-271

Disk Defragmenter, 271

disk images, installing from

Windows 7, 169

Windows Vista, 182

Windows XP, 199

Disk Management, 253-256

diskpart command, 309

disks. See also HDD (hard disk drives)

formatting, 253-256

mounting, 257-258

partitioning, 253-256

RAID, 259-260

display controls, 324-325

displays

CRT, 362

LCD, 361-362

projectors, 362-363

troubleshooting, 19

example of, 15-16

disposal of hardware/equipment, safety, 505-506

distractions, avoiding (professionalism), 509

docking stations, 335

documentation

findings/solutions (six-step troubleshooting process), 13

display issue example, 17

power issue example, 18

motherboards

installing, 25-26

Technical Product Specification PDF, 27

MSDS (material safety data sheets), 505

reviewing (problem identification process), 11

double-sided memory modules, 90

Downlevel phase (Vista installation), 190

downloading

BIOS (Basic Input Output System), 43

updates, 478

Dr. Watson, 296

DRAM (dynamic random-access memory), 82

compatibility, 98

installing, 94-95

ESD prevention, 95

motherboards, 95

testing installations, 96

RDRAM (Rambus DRAM), 88

SDRAM (synchronous DRAM), 82-83

troubleshooting, 98-101

Driver Signing, 227

drivers, video, 363-364

drives. *See* **disks**

drwtsn32 command, 296

DSL (digital subscriber line), 447

DSSS (direct-sequence spread spectrum), 449

dual channel RAM (random access memory), 89

DualView, 326-327, 370-371

duplex settings, 423

DVD (Digital Versatile Discs), data storage, 151-153

DVD-ROM, installing from

Windows 7, 169

Windows Vista, 181

DVI (Digital Visual Interface), 354

DxDiag, 227-228

dynamic IP addresses, 415

E

Easy Transfer, 237

ECC (Error Correction Code), RAM, 91

edit command, 310-311

EEPROM (Electrically Erasable Programmable ROM) chips, 39

EFS (Encrypting File System), 257, 493-495

electrical safety, 500

AC outlets, 500

ESD (electrostatic discharge), 502-504

monitors

CRT monitors, 500-501

LCD monitors, 501

power supplies, 500

printers, 501

surge protectors, 502

UPS (uninterruptible power supplies), 502

EMI (electromagnetic interference), 506

Enable Boot Logging option (Advanced Boot Options menu), 281

Enable low-resolution video (640x480) option (Advanced Boot Options menu), 281

Encrypting File System (EFS), 257, 493-495

encryption, 461
  asymmetric key encryption, 493
  definition of, 492
  symmetric key encryption, 493
  in Windows, 493-495
  wireless encryption, 453

ergonomics, 505

error reporting, 300-301

errors
  boot errors
    Windows 7 Boot Errors, 287
    Windows Vista Boot Errors, 285-287
  error reporting, 300-301
  stop errors, 298-300

ESD (electrostatic discharge), 18-19, 502-504
  CPU installation, 69
  DRAM installations, 95
  troubleshooting motherboard-related issues, 50

Ethernet, 336, 424

Event Viewer, 294-296

exams. See also practice exams
  post certification development, 519-520
  preparing for
    cheat sheets, 515-516
    exam day tips/tricks, 516-518
    exam preparation checklist, 513-515
    scheduling exams, 513, 516

exFAT (Extended File Allocation Table), 257

expand command, 311

expansion buses, 352-353
  AGP (Accelerated Graphics Port), 31, 33
  AMR (audio/modem riser), 32
  CNR (Communications and Networking Riser), 32
  PCI (Peripheral Component Interconnect), 29, 32
  PCIe (Peripheral Component Interconnect Express), 31, 33

expansion devices, 334-336

expectations, setting/meeting (professionalism), 508

Extended File Allocation Table (exFAT), 257

external clock speeds, 57

F

fans, 65-66
  troubleshooting, 124

FAST (Files and Settings Transfer) Wizard, 237

fast user switching, disabling, 467

FAT16, 257

FAT32, 257

FAT64, 257

FDISK/MBR command, 480

file security
  definition of, 485
  file attributes, 485
  folder sharing
    copying folders, 492
    moving folders, 492
    overview, 486-487
    permission inheritance and propagation, 491
    in Windows Vista, 490-491
    in Windows XP, 488-489
  hidden files, 486

file systems, 257

File Transfer Protocol (FTP), 429

files
  boot files, 249
  comsetup.log, 205

file security
definition of, 485
file attributes, 485
folder sharing, 486-492
hidden files, 486
file systems, 257
hidden files, 486
indexing, 250-251
miglog.xml, 191
NetSetup.log, 205
PostGatherPnPList.log, 191
PreGatherPnPList.log, 191
setup.log, 204
setupact.log, 191, 204
setupapi.app.log, 191
setupapi.dev.log, 191
setupapi.log, 204
setuperr.log, 191, 204
setuplog.txt, 204
Windows 7 setup log files, 174
Windows Vista installation log files, 191
Windows XP installation log files, 204
Winsat.log, 191
Files and Settings Transfer (FAST) Wizard, 237
findings, documenting (six-step troubleshooting process), 13
display issue example, 17
power issue example, 18
firewalls
updates, 275
Windows Firewall, 443, 479
FireWire, 385
FireWire (IEEE 1394a) ports, 33
FIXBOOT command, 312
/fixboot option (bootrec command), 311
FIXMBR command, 312, 480
/fixmbr option (bootrec command), 312

flash drives, 156-157
formatting, 158
memory, 158
troubleshooting, 158
flashing BIOS, 43-44, 472
flicker, 368
floppy disk drives, 143
boot disks, 145
installing, 144
troubleshooting, 144
folders
copying, 492
moving, 492
sharing
overview, 486-487
permission inheritance and propagation, 491
in Windows Vista, 490-491
in Windows XP, 488-489
format command, 309
formatting
disks, 253-256
USB flash drives, 158
front panel ports, 34
FRU (field replaceable units), power supplies as, 500
FSB (Front Side Buses), 28
external clock speeds, 57
FTP (File Transfer Protocol), 429
full-duplex, 423
function keys, 318-319
functionality, verifying (six-step troubleshooting process), 12-13
display issue example, 16
power issue example, 18
fuses, troubleshooting power supply fuses, 124

G

garbage printouts, troubleshooting, 408
gateway addresses, 416

Ghost, 304

ghosted images (printers), troubleshooting, 408

GPF (general protection faults), troubleshooting, 100

GPU (graphics processor unit), 324

video card GPU, 356

H

half-duplex, 423

hard drives. *See* HDD (hard disk drives)

hard faults (page faults), troubleshooting, 100

hardware

compatibility

for Windows Vista, 180

for Windows XP, 198

disposal of, 505-506

recycling, 505-506

requirements

for Windows 7, 167-168

for Windows Vista, 179-180

for Windows XP, 197

hash algorithms, 493

hashing, 493

HD (high definition), 324

HDD (hard disk drives), 132

antimalware, 141

backups

Windows 7, 272-273

Windows Vista, 273

Windows XP, 273

caches, 138

cleanup programs, 140, 270-271

components of, 132

data transfer rates, 137

defragging, 141, 271

installing, 139

testing installations, 140

Internet files, deleting manually, 270

laptops, 342-343

latency, 138

NAS (Network Attached Storage), 143

PATA (Parallel ATA), 133, 135

cable select drive configurations, 135

master drive configurations, 134

single drive configurations, 134

slave drive configurations, 135

preventive maintenance, 140-141, 270-271, 275-276

restore points, 274

rotational speeds, 138

SATA (Serial ATA), 135-136

installing, 140

SCSI (Small Computer System Interface), 138-139

specifications, determining, 137-138

temporary files, deleting manually, 270

troubleshooting, 141-143

Ultra ATA hard drives, installing, 139

HDMI (High-Definition Multimedia Interface), 354

Health Insurance Portability and Accountability Act (HIPAA), 463

heat, physical safety, 504

heat sinks, 64

heavy items, physical safety, 504

hibernation, 235

Hidden file attribute, 485

hidden files, 486

high definition (HD), 324

High-Definition Multimedia Interface (HDMI), 354

HIPAA (Health Insurance Portability and Accountability Act), 463

hives (Registry), 240

HKEY_CLASSES_ROOT Registry hive, 240

HKEY_CURRENT_CONFIG Registry hive, 240

HKEY_CURRENT_USER Registry hive, 240

HKEY_LOCAL_MACHINE Registry hive, 240

HKEY_USERS Registry hive, 240

hot components, physical safety, 504

hot docking, 336

hot swappable devices, removing, 229

HT (Hyper-Threading), 61

HTTP (Hypertext Transfer Protocol), 429

hubs, 424

I

i.Link (IEEE 1394a) ports, 33

I/O ports. *See* **ports**

ICH (I/O Controller Hubs), 26

bus connections, 28

IDE buses, 28-29

SATA buses, 29

icons, 211

IDE (Integrated Drive Electronics) buses, 28-29

BIOS configuration, 42

identifying

changes to computers (problem identification process), 11

problems (six-step troubleshooting process), 10-11

display issue example, 15

power issue example, 17

IEEE 1394, 385

IEEE 1394a (FireWire/i.Link) ports, 33

impact printers, 396

impedence, 104

Indexing service, 250-251

Infrared, 337

inheritance, permissions, 491

ink/toner cartridges, disposal of, 506

inkjet printers, 395

peizoelectric inkjets, 395

printing process, 395

thermal inkjets, 395

input devices, 386-387

laptop input devices

function keys, 318-319

keyboards, 318-322

pointing devices, 323

stylus, 323

installing

CPU (central processing units), 69

ESD prevention, 69

LGA sockets, 70

motherboard preparation, 69

PGA sockets, 72

testing installations, 72-73

DRAM (dyanmic random-access memory), 94-95

testing installations, 96

floppy disk drives, 144

HDD (hard disk drives), 139

testing installations, 140

laptop memory, 344-345

motherboards, 46-47

documentation, 25-26

power supplies, 122-123

printers

calibrating printers, 400

compatibility, 399

device connections, 399-400

printer driver installation, 399

testing installations, 400

snap-ins, 221

sockets

LGA sockets, 70

PGA sockets, 72

sound cards, 377-378

speakers, 377

video cards, 357-360

Windows 7
  installation methods, 169-170
  step-by-step installation process, 170-173
Windows Vista
  installation methods, 181-182
  partitions, creating, 186-187
  step-by-step installation process, 183-185
Windows XP
  installation methods, 198-200
  step-by-step installation process, 200-203
Institute of Electrical and Electronics Engineers (IEEE) 1394, 385
Integrated Services Digital Network (ISDN), 448
Intel CPU (central processing units), 63-64
interference
  EMI (electromagnetic interference), 506
  RFI (radio frequency interference), 506
internal clock speeds, 57
Internet files, manually deleting, 270
Invalid boot.ini (error message), 287
inverter boards
  replacing, 328-329
  troubleshooting, 328
IOH (Input/Output Hubs), 26
IP addresses, configuring, 415
ipconfig command, 437-438
IPv4
  Classes, 417-419
  configuring, 414-417
  IPv6 versus, 420
IPv6, 420-421
IrDA wireless ports, 337
ISDN (Integrated Services Digital Network), 448

J

jams (paper), troubleshooting, 406-407
jump drives. See flash drives

K

keyboards, 387
  function keys, 318-319
  laptop keyboards
    overview, 318-319
    replacing, 320-322
    troubleshooting, 320
KVM Switches, 387

L

LANs (local area networks), 426
laptops
  audio subsystem, 329-330
  communications, 336-337
  components, 318
  CPUs, 345-347
  expansion devices, 334-336
  function keys, 318-319
  hard drives, 342-343
  keyboards
    overview, 318-319
    replacing, 320-322
    troubleshooting, 320
  memory, 343-345
  optical discs, 330
  overview, 315-316
  pointing devices, 323
  ports, 317
  power, 330-333
  stylus, 323
  system board, 345-347
  video subsystem, 324
    display controls, 324-325
    DualView, 326-327
    GPU, 324

LCD, 324

resolutions, 324

troubleshooting, 328-329

laser printers, 392

advantages of, 394

electrical safety, 501

printing process, 393-394

toner cartridges, 394

Last Known Good Configuration option (Advanced Boot Options menu), 281

latency, 423

HDD (hard disk drives), 138

RAM, 90

LCD (liquid crystal display), 324, 361-362

troubleshooting, 328

LGA (Land Grid Array) sockets, 59

installing, 70

Libraries, 217

lines/smearing (printers), troubleshooting, 407

liquid cooling systems, 66

liquid crystal display (LCD), 324, 361-362

listening to customers (professionalism), 508

lithium batteries, 332-333

BIOS password resets, 42

CMOS, 39

local area networks (LANs), 426

Local Group Policy Editor, 467

local printers, 397

log files

Windows 7 setup log files, 174

Windows Vista installation log files, 191

Windows XP installation log files, 204

logic, using while troubleshooting, 19

logon process, security, 467-469

loose connections, troubleshooting, 320

Love Bug virus, 475

low on virtual memory errors, troubleshooting, 100

lumens, 362

M

macro viruses, 476

magnetic storage media, 132, 146-147

floppy disk drives, 143

boot disks, 145

installing, 144

troubleshooting, 144

HDD (hard disk drives), 132

antimalware, 141

backups, 272-273

caches, 138

cleanup programs, 140, 270-271

components of, 132

data transfer rates, 137

defragging, 141, 271

determining drive specifications, 137-138

installing, 139

latency, 138

manually deleting Internet files, 270

manually deleting temporary files, 270

NAS (Network Attached Storage), 143

PATA (Parallel ATA), 133-135

preventive maintenance, 140-141, 270-271, 275-276

restore points, 274

rotational speeds, 138

SATA (Serial ATA), 135-136, 140

SCSI (Small Computer System Interface), 138-139

troubleshooting, 141-143

Ultra ATA hard drives, 139

tape drives, 145

maintenance, HDD (hard disk drives), 140-141, 270-271, 275-276

malware, 460

  definition of, 475

  spyware

    definition of, 477

    preventing and troubleshooting, 481-483

  trojan horses, definition of, 477

  viruses

    definition of, 475

    preventing and troubleshooting, 478-481

    types of viruses, 475-476

  worms, definition of, 476

managing

  devices

    Device Manager, 225-226

    Driver Signing, 227

    DxDiag, 227-228

    System Information Tool, 227

  power, 235-236

  printers

    print jobs, 401

    printer permissions, 405

master drive configurations (PATA), 134

mATX (microATX) motherboards, 36-37

MCH (Memory Controller Hubs), 26

memory

  laptop memory, 343-345

  low on virtual memory errors, troubleshooting, 100

  memory controllers

    CPU integration, 80

    MCH (Memory Controller Hubs), 80

  out of memory errors, troubleshooting, 100, 407

  RAM (random-access memory), 79, 91-93

    CPU access to, 80

    DDR, 84-85

    DDR2, 86

    DDR3, 87

    DDR4, 88

    double-sided memory modules, 90

    DRAM (dynamic random-access memory), 82, 94-96, 98-101

    dual channel RAM, 89

    ECC (Error Correction Code), 91

    memory latency, 90

    nonparity, 90-91

    parity, 90

    RDRAM, 88

    SDRAM, 82-83

    single channel RAM, 88-89

    single-sided memory modules, 90

    SRAM (static random-access memory), 81-82

    volatile RAM, 81

  ROM (read-only memory), 82

  USB flash drives, 158

  video card memory, 356

  virtual memory, 232-233

memory buses, 28

metadata, 217

metafolders, 217

microATX (Advanced Technology Extended)

  motherboards, 36-37

  power supplies, 118

microphones, 387

microprocessors. *See* CPU (central processing units

Microsoft Challenge-Handshake Authentication Protocol (MS-CHAP), 495

Microsoft Management Console (MMC), 221

Microsoft System Configuration Utility. *See* Msconfig

MIDI (Musical Instrument Digital Interface), 387

miglog.xml, 191

migrating user data, 236-238

minimum requirements. *See* **hardware, requirements**

MMC (Microsoft Management Console), 221

modems, 337

monitors

CRT monitors, electrical safety, 500-501

LCD monitors, electrical safety, 501

troubleshooting, 19

example of, 15-16

motherboards, 23, 37-38

ATX (Advanced Technology Extended) motherboards, 24, 35-37

BTX (Balanced Technology Extended) motherboards, 36-37

buses. *See also* expansion buses

AGP (Accelerated Graphics Port), 31, 33

AMR (audio/modem riser), 32

CNR (Communications and Networking Riser), 32

DSB (Front Side Buses), 28

expansion buses, 29, 31-33

IDE (Integrated Drive Electronics), 28-29, 42

memory buses, 28

parallel buses, 28-29

PCI (Peripheral Component Interconnect), 29, 32

PCI Express x16 Interface, 28

PCIe (Peripheral Component Interconnect Express), 31, 33

SATA (Serial ATA), 29

speed ratings, 28

chipsets, 29

ICH (I/O Controller Hubs), 26, 28

IOH (Input/Output Hubs), 26

MCH (Memory Controller Hubs), 26, 80

clock speeds, 57

CPU installation, 69

CPU sockets, compatibility, 59-60

documentation

installations, 25-26

Technical Product Specification PDF, 27

DRAM installations, 95

front panel ports, 34

I/O (input/output) ports, 33

installing, 46-47

documentation, 25-26

main components of, 24

microATX (mATX) motherboards, 36-37

NLX (New Low Profile Extended) motherboards, 36-37

troubleshooting, 47-49, 51-52

BIOS-related issues, 50

component failures, 51

ESD-related issues, 50

manufacturing defects, 51

mounting drives, 257-258

mouse devices, 387

moving folders, 492

MS-CHAP (Microsoft Challenge-Handshake Authentication Protocol), 495

Msconfig, 231-232, 298

MSDS (material safety data sheets), 505

multi-core CPU (central processing units), 61

multicast addresses, 421

multimeters

AC outlet tests, 106, 108

testing power supplies, 126

multipartite viruses, 476

Multiple Monitor (DualView), 370-371

Multiple Monitor technology, 327

Musical Instrument Digital Interface (MIDI), 387

My Computer, 215-216

N

NAS (Network Attached Storage), 143
native resolution, 361
net command, 441-442
NetSetup.log, 205
netstat command, 440-441
network adapters, 422-424
wireless network adapters, 450-453, 455
network installation
of Windows 7, 169
of Windows Vista, 181
of Windows XP, 199
network interface card (NIC), 414
network printers, 397
Network window, 218
networking
cables, 432-435
EMI (electromagnetic interference), 506
hubs, 424
IPv4
Classes, 417-419
configuring, 414-417
IPv6 versus, 420
IPv6, 420-421
LANs (local area networks), 426
latency, 423
network adapters, 422-424
network interface card (NIC), 414
overview, 413-414
ports, 427-430
protocols. *See* protocols
proxy servers, 425
repeaters, 424
routers, 425
SOHO (small office home office) networks
802.11 wireless, 449
Bluetooth, 449-450

cable Internet, 447
cellular, 448
dial-up, 446
DSL (digital subscriber line, 447
ISDN, 448
overview, 446
port forwarding, 454
port triggering, 454
routers, 450-453, 455
satellite connectivity, 447
wireless network adapters, 450-453, 455
switches, 425
troubleshooting network connectivity
applications, 442-443
ipconfig, 437-438
net, 441-442
netstat, 440-441
nslookup, 441
ping, 438-439
tracert, 439-440
VPNs (virtual private networks), 426
WANs (wide area networks), 426
WAPs (wireless access points), 425
NIC (network interface card), 414
NLX (New Low Profile Extended)
motherboards, 36-37
power supplies, 118
nodes, 419
nonparity, RAM, 90-91
northbridge. *See* MCH (Memory Controller Hubs), 80
nslookup command, 441
NTBackup (Windows XP), 273
NTDETECT failed (error message), 287
NTFS (NT File System), 257
NTFS permissions, 488
NTLDR is missing (error message), 287

O

OFDM (orthogonal frequency-division multiplexing), 449

ohms, 104

on-screen display (OSD), 369-370

Online configuration phase (Vista installation), 191

opening command-line interface, 437

operating system optimization

with Msconfig, 231-232

with power management, 235-236

with Task Manager, 229-231

with virtual memory, 232-233

optical discs, 330

optical storage media, 149, 154-155

Blu-Ray, 154

CD (Compact Discs), 149, 153

CD-R, 150

CD-ROM, 149-150

CD-RW, 150

DVD (Digital Versatile Discs), 151-153

optimizing operating system

with Msconfig, 231-232

with power management, 235-236

with Task Manager, 229-231

with virtual memory, 232-233

orthogonal frequency-division multiplexing (OFDM), 449

OSD (on-screen display), 369-370

out of memory errors, troubleshooting, 100, 407

outcomes, documenting (six-step troubleshooting process, 13

display issue example, 17

power issue example, 18

outlets. *See also* **power**

electrical safety, 500

regulating output, 107

testing

via multimeters, 106, 108

via receptacle testers, 105

Outlook, 442

overheating power supplies, 127

P

page faults (hard faults), troubleshooting, 100

page printers, 392

paper, troubleshooting blank paper, 407

paper jams, troubleshooting, 406-407

parallel buses

IDE (Integrated Drive Electronics), 28-29

BIOS configuration, 42

SATA (Serial ATA), 29

parallel ports, 386

parity, RAM, 90

partitioning disks, 253-256, 259-260

partitions, creating during Windows Vista installation, 186-187

passwords

BIOS

configuring in, 42

resetting in, 42

changing, 466

password policy, 466-467

strong passwords, 465

PATA (Parallel ATA) hard drives, 133, 135

cable select drive configurations, 135

master drive configurations, 134

single drive configurations, 134

slave drive configurations, 135

patch testers, 433

PC Check, 168, 180

PC Diagnostic tools, 168, 180

PCI (Peripheral Component Interconnect) buses, 29, 32, 352

PCI Express x16 Interface, 28

PCIe (Peripheral Component Interconnect Express) buses, 31, 33, 352

PCMCIA (Personal Computer Memory Card International Association), PC Cards, 32

percentage signs (%)$217

Performance tool, 297-298

Peripheral Component Interconnect (PCI), 352

peripherals, 386-387
   monitors
      CRT monitors, 500-501
      electrical safety, 500-501
      LCD monitors, 501
      troubleshooting, 15-16, 19
   printers
      disposal of ink/toner cartridges, 506
      electrical safety, 501
      laser printers, 501

permissions
   inheritance and propagation, 491
   NTFS permissions, 488

PGA (Pin Grid Array) sockets, 59
   installing, 72

physical safety
   cable, 504
   ergonomics, 505
   heavy items, 504
   hot components, 504

piezoelectric inkjet printers, 395

ping command, 438-439

pixel dimensions, 365

plans of action, establishing (six-step troubleshooting process), 12
   display issue example, 16
   power issue example, 18

pointing devices, 323

pointing sticks, 323

polymorphic viruses, 476

pooling printers, 404

POP3 (Post Office Protocol Version 3), 429

port forwarding, 454

port replicators, 336

port triggering, 454

ports, 427-430
   audio clusters, 34
   definition of, 382
   digital optical ports, 376
   front panel ports, 34
   I/O (input/output) ports, 33
   IEEE 1394, 385
   IEEE 1394a (FireWire/i.Link) ports, 33
   laptop ports, 317
   PS/2, 386
   RJ45 LAN ports, 34
   serial versus parallel, 386
   Sony/Phillips Digital Interconnect Format (S/PDIF), 376
   USB (Universal Serial Bus) ports, 33, 382-385

positive outlook, maintaining (professionalism), 508

POST (power-on self-tests), 40

Post Office Protocol Version 3 (POP3), 429

PostGatherPnPList.log, 191

power, 103, 115
   AC (alternating current) outlets, 104
      electrical safety, 500
      regulating output, 107
      testing via multimeters, 106, 108
      testing via receptacle testers, 105
   amperage (A), 104
   blackouts, 110
   brownouts, 110
   clean power, 107
   DC (direct current), 104
   dirty power, 107
   impedence, 104
   ohms, 104
   power connectors, 119-120
   power strips, 110-111

power supplies, 128-129

    ATX form factor, 116-117

    BTX form factor, 118

    capacity requirements, 118-119

    compatibility, 116-117

    cooling, 127

    electrical safety, 500

    installing, 122-123

    microATX form factor, 118

    NLX form factor, 118

    overheating, 127

    power connectors, 119-120

    testing, 126

    troubleshooting, 123-127

    wattage (W, 118-119

sags, 110

spikes, 110

surge protectors, 111-112

surges, 110

UPS (uninterruptible power supplies), 112-113

voltage (V), 104

    sags, 110

wattage (W), 104

    power supplies, 118-119

power consumption

    CPU (central processing units, 62

power issues, troubleshooting, 19

    example of, 17-18

power management, 235-236

    BIOS configuration, 42

power supply

    FRU (field replaceable units), 500

    for laptops, 330-333

PowerShell, 219

practice exam 1

    exam answers, 540-552

    exam questions, 521-539

practice exam 2

    exam answers, 573-586

    exam questions, 553-572

practice exam 3

    exam answers, 598-608

    exam questions, 587-597

PreGatherPnPList.log, 191

preparing for exams

    cheat sheets, 515-516

    exam day tips/tricks, 516-518

    exam preparation checklist, 513-515

    scheduling exams, 513, 516

preventing

    spyware, 481-483

    viruses, 478-481

preventive maintenance, HDD (hard disk drives), 140-141, 270-271, 275-276

printers, 391, 397-398

    configuring, 400

        managing print jobs, 401

        managing printer permissions, 405

        pooling printers, 404

        print spooling options, 402-403

        separator pages, 406

        setting printer priority, 401-402

        sharing printers, 405

        XPS (XML Paper Specification) feature (Windows Vista), 404

    consummables, 394

    impact printers, 396

    ink/toner cartridges, disposal of, 506

    inkjet printers, 395

        piezoelectric inkjets, 395

        printing process, 395

        thermal inkjets, 395

    installing

        calibrating printers, 400

        compatibility, 399

        device connections, 399-400

        printer driver installation, 399

        testing installations, 400

laser printers, 392
  advantages of, 394
  electrical safety, 501
  printing process, 393-394
  toner cartridges, 394
local printers, 397
network printers, 397
page printers, 392
thermal printers, 396
troubleshooting, 406-411
prioritizing printers, 401-402
private addresses, 419
probable cause (six-step troubleshooting process)
  establishing theory of, 11
    display issue example, 15-16
    power issue example, 17
  testing theory of, 12
    display issue example, 16
    power issue example, 17
Problem Reports and Solutions, 296
problems, identifying (six-step troubleshooting process), 10-11
  display issue example, 15
  power issue example, 17
professionalism, 508-510
Program Compatibility Wizard, 244
program viruses, 476
projectors, 362-363
PROM (Programmable ROM) chips, 39
protocols
  APIPA (automatic private IP addressing), 416
  FTP (File Transfer Protocol), 429
  HTTP (Hypertext Transfer Protocol), 429
  IPv4
    Classes, 417-419
    configuring, 414-417
    IPv6 versus, 420
  IPv6, 420-421

  POP3 (Post Office Protocol Version 3), 429
  ports, 427-430
  SMTP (Simple Mail Transfer Protocol), 429
  TCP/IP (Transmission Control Protocol/Internet Protocol), 414
  TELNET, 429
proxy servers, 425
PS/2 ports, 386
public addresses, 419
punctuality (professionalism), 508
purging data, 461

Q

quality of audio, 378-379
questioning users (problem identification process), 10
Quick Launch, 212

R

RAID (Redundant Array of Inexpensive Disks), 259-260
RAM (random-access memory), 79, 87, 91-93. *See also* **memory**
  CPU access to, 80
  DDR (Double Data Rate), 84-85
  DDR2 (Double Data Rate 2), 86
  DDR3 (Double Data Rate 3), 87
  DDR4 (Double Data Rate 4), 88
  double-sided memory modules, 90
  DRAM (dynamic random-access memory), 82
    compatibility, 98
    installing, 94-96
    RDRAM, 88
    SDRAM, 82-83
    troubleshooting, 98-101
  dual channel RAM, 89
  ECC (Error Correction Code), 91
  memory latency, 90

nonparity, 90-91

parity, 90

single channel RAM, 88-89

single-sided memory modules, 90

SRAM (static random-access memory), 81-82

volatile RAM, 81

RDRAM (Rambus DRAM), 88

Read-only file attribute, 485

/rebuildbcd option (bootrec command), 312

receptacle testers, AC outlet tests, 105

Recovery Command Prompts, 310

copy, 311

edit, 310-311

expand, 311

recovery environment commands, 311-312

Recovery Console, 284-285

recovery discs, installing from

Windows 7, 170

Windows Vista, 182

Windows XP, 200

recovery environment commands, 311-312

recycling hardware/equipment, safety, 505-506

Redundant Array of Inexpensive Disks (RAID), 259-260

refresh rate, 368-369

regedit command, 239

regedt32 command, 239

Regional and Language Options, 239

Registry, 239, 241

Reliability and Performance Monitor, 297-298

Remote Assistance, 242

Remote Desktop, 242-243

removing

hot swappable devices, 229

Internet files from HDD (hard disk drives), 270

snap-ins, 221

temporary files from HDD (hard disk drives), 270

repair tools, 279

Advanced Boot Options menu, 280-281

Recovery Console, 284-285

WinRE (Windows Recovery Environment), 282-284

repeaters, 424

replacing

inverter boards, 328-329

laptop keyboards, 320-322

reporting errors, 300-301

resolution, 365, 367-368

changing, 367

of laptops, 324

native resolution, 361

table of, 366

resolving problems (six-step troubleshooting process), establishing plans of action, 12

display issue example, 16

power issue example, 18

restore points, 274. *See also* backups

restoring Windows, 301

to an earlier condition, 303

with System Restore, 303-304

from Windows Vista complete PC backup, 302

from Windows XP's ASR backup, 302

results, documenting (six-step troubleshooting process), 13

display issue example, 17

power issue example, 18

reviewing documentation (problem identification process, 11

RFI (radio frequency interference), 506

RJ45 LAN ports, 34

ROM (Read-Only Memory) chips, 39, 82

rotational speeds, 138

routers, 425, 450-453, 455
    SOHO routers
        port forwarding, 454
        port triggering, 454
        security, 453

S

S-Video (Separate Video, 354
S/PDIF (Sony/Phillips Digital Interconnect Format) port, 376
Safe Mode, 482
Safe Mode option (Advanced Boot Options menu), 280
Safe Mode with Command Prompt option (Advanced Boot Options menu), 280
Safe Mode with Networking option (Advanced Boot Options menu), 280
Safely Remove option, 229
safety, 507
    disposal of hardware/equipment, 505-506
    electrical safety, 500
        AC outlets, 500
        CRT monitors, 500-501
        ESD (electrostatic discharge), 502-504
        LCD monitors, 501
        power supplies, 500
        printers, 501
        surge protectors, 502
        UPS (uninterruptible power supplies), 502
    MSDS (material safety data sheets), 505
    physical safety
        cable, 504
        ergonomics, 505
        heavy items, 504
        hot components, 504
    recycling hardware/equipment, 505-506
sags (power), 110

sanitizing data, 461
Sarbanes-Oxley (SOX), 463
SATA (Serial ATA)
    buses, 29
    hard drives, 135-136
        installing, 140
satellite connectivity, 447
Scan Line Interleave (SLI), 360
/ScanOS option (bootrec command), 312
scheduling exams, 513, 516
screen switching, 325
SCSI (Small Computer System Interface) hard drives, 138-139
SD (Secure Digital) cards, 159
SDIO (Secure Digital Input Output) cards, 160
SDRAM (synchronous DRAM), 82-83
SDSL (Symmetrical Digital Subscriber Line), 447
security
    administrative privileges, 221
    authentication
        biometrics, 473
        BIOS security, 471-472
        logon process, 467-469
        passwords, 465-467
        smart cards, 472
        UAC (User Account Control, 470-471
        usernames, 465
    data security
        data security technologies, 460-462
        data sensitivity, 462-463
        security compliance, 463
        threats, 460-461
    encryption
        asymmetric key encryption, 493
        definition of, 492
        symmetric key encryption, 493
        in Windows, 493-495
        wireless encryption, 453

file security
  definition of, 485
  file attributes, 485
  folder sharing, 486-492
  hidden files, 486
malware
  definition of, 475
  preventing and troubleshooting, 478-483
  spyware, 477, 481-483
  trojan horses, 477
  viruses, 475-476, 478-481
  worms, 476
overview, 459
smart cards, 473
security compliance, 463
Separate Video (S-Video), 354
separator pages (printers), 406
serial ports, 386
servers, proxy servers, 425
service packs. See SP (service packs)
services, 233
  Indexing, 250-251
  starting/stopping
    in Command Prompt, 234
    in Computer Management, 233
setup.log, 204
setupact.log, 191, 204
setupapi.app.log, 191
setupapi.dev.log, 191
setupapi.log, 204
setuperr.log, 191, 204
setuplog.txt, 204
SFC (System File Checker), 308
sharing
  folders
    overview, 486-487
    permission inheritance and propagation, 491
    in Windows Vista, 490-491
    in Windows XP, 488-489
  printers, 405

shielded twisted pair (STP), 434
Sidebar, 212
SIM (Subscriber Identity Module) cards, 160
SIM (System Image Manager), 169, 181
Simple Mail Transfer Protocol (SMTP), 429
single channel RAM (random access memory), 88-89
single drive configurations (PATA), 134
single-sided memory modules, 90
six-step troubleshooting process, 10, 14, 304-305
  display issue example, 15-16
  documenting solutions, 13
    display issue example, 17
    power issue example, 18
  establishing plans of action, 12
    display issue example, 16
    power issue example, 18
  establishing theory of probable cause, 11
    display issue example, 15-16
    power issue example, 17
  identifying the problem, 10-11
    display issue example, 15
    power issue example, 17
  power issue example, 17-18
  testing theory of probable cause, 12
    display issue example, 16
    power issue example, 17
  verifying system functionality, 12-13
    display issue example, 16
    power issue example, 18
slave drive configurations (PATA), 135
Sleep, 236
SLI (Scan Line Interleave), 360
small office home office networks. See SOHO networks
smart cards, 472-473
smearing/lines (printers), troubleshooting, 407

SMTP (Simple Mail Transfer Protocol), 429

snap-ins, adding/removing, 221

SO-DIMMs, installing into laptops, 344-345

social engineering, 460

sockets

CPU sockets, 58

compatibility, 59-60

LGA (Land Grid Array) sockets, 59

installing, 70

PGA (Pin Grid Array) sockets, 59

installing, 72

software, malware

definition of, 475

spyware, 477, 481-483

trojan horses, 477

viruses, 475-476, 478-481

worms, 476

SOHO (small office home office) networks

802.11 wireless, 449

Bluetooth, 449-450

cable Internet, 447

cellular, 448

dial-up, 446

DSL (digital subscriber line), 447

ISDN, 448

overview, 446

port forwarding, 454

port triggering, 454

routers, 450-453, 455

satellite connectivity, 447

wireless network adapters, 450-453, 455

solid-state storage media, 156, 162

CF (CompactFlash) cards, 161

SD (Secure Digital) cards, 159

SDIO (Secure Digital Input Output) cards, 160

USB flash drives, 156-157

formatting, 158

memory, 158

troubleshooting, 158

solutions documenting (six-step troubleshooting process), 13

display issue example, 17

power issue example, 18

solutions, implementing (six-step troubleshooting process), 12

display issue example, 16

power issue example, 18

Sony/Phillips Digital Interconnect Format (S/PDIF) port, 376

sound cards

installing, 377-378

overview, 375-376

SOX (Sarbanes-Oxley), 463

SP (service packs), Windows updates, 264-265

speakers, installing, 377

speaking clearly, 508

spikes (power), 110

spooling (printers, 402-403

spyware

definition of, 477

preventing and troubleshooting, 481-483

SRAM (static random-access memory), 81-82

standby, 235

Start menu, 212

configuring, 214-215

Start Windows Normally option (Advanced Boot Options menu), 281

starting services

in Command Prompt, 234

in Computer Management, 233

startup issues, troubleshooting, 19

example of, 17-18

Startup Repair option (Recovery Options), 284

Startup Restore option (Recovery Options), 284

static IP addresses, 415

status indicators, 422

stealth viruses, 476

stop errors, 298-300

troubleshooting, 99

stopping services

in Command Prompt, 234

in Computer Management, 233

storing data

Blu-Ray, 154

CD (Compact Discs), 149, 153

CD-R, 150

CD-ROM, 149-150

CD-RW, 150

CF (CompactFlash) cards, 161

DVD (Digital Versatile Discs), 151-153

floppy disk drives, 143

boot disks, 145

installing, 144

troubleshooting, 144

HDD (hard disk drives), 132

antimalware, 141

backups, 272-273

caches, 138

cleanup programs, 140, 270-271

components of, 132

data transfer rates, 137

defragging, 141, 271

determining drive specifications, 137-138

installing, 139

latency, 138

manually deleting Internet files, 270

manually deleting temporary files, 270

NAS (Network Attached Storage), 143

PATA (Parallel ATA), 133-135

preventive maintenance, 140-141, 270-271, 275-276

restore points, 274

rotational speeds, 138

SATA (Serial ATA), 135-136, 140

SCSI (Small Computer System Interface), 138-139

troubleshooting, 141-143

Ultra ATA hard drives, 139

magnetic storage media, 132-147

optical storage media, 149-155

SD (Secure Digital) cards, 159

SDIO (Secure Digital Input Output) cards, 160

solid-state storage media, 156-162

tape drives, 145

USB flash drives, 156-157

formatting, 158

memory, 158

troubleshooting, 158

STP (shielded twisted pair), 434

strong passwords, 465

stuck keys, troubleshooting, 320

stylus, 323

surge protectors, 111-112

electrical safety, 502

HDD (hard disk drive) maintenance, 275

surges (power), 110

switches, 425

symmetric key encryption, 493

Symmetrical Digital Subscriber Line (SDSL), 447

SYS command, 480

system boards, laptop, 345-347

system failure, 460

System file attribute, 485

System File Checker (SFC), 308

system functionality, verifying (six-step troubleshooting process), 12-13

display issue example, 16

power issue example, 18

System Image Manager (SIM), 169, 181

System Information Tool, 227

System Recovery Options window, 283-284

System Restore, 274, 303-304

system tools

Device Manager, 225-226

Driver Signing, 227

DxDiag, 227-228

Msconfig, 231-232

Program Compatibility Wizard, 244

Registry, 239, 241

Remote Assistance, 242

Remote Desktop, 242-243

Safely Remove option, 229

System Information Tool, 227

Task Manager, 229-231

virtual memory, 232-233

Windows XP Mode, 244

System Tray, 212

systray, 212

T

tape drives, 145

Task Manager, 229-231

DRAM installations, testing, 97

opening, 97

Task Scheduler, 239

taskbar, 212

configuring, 214-215

TCP/IP (Transmission Control Protocol/Internet Protocol), 414

TDP (thermal design points), 62

TDR (time-domain reflectometers), 434

Technical Product Specification PDF, 27

TELNET, 429

temporary files, manually deleting, 270

testing

AC outlets

multimeters, 106, 108

receptacle testers, 105

CPU installations, 72-73

CPU-Z, 73

Windows, 72

DRAM installations, 96

HDD (hard disk drive) installations, 140

power supplies, 126

printer installations, 400

theory of probable cause (six-step troubleshooting process), 12

display issue example, 16

power issue example, 17

twisted pair cable, 433-434

tests. *See* exams

theory of probable cause (six-step troubleshooting process)

establishing, 11

display issue example, 15-16

power issue example, 17

testing, 12

display issue example, 16

power issue example, 17

thermal compound (TIM), 65

thermal inkjet printers, 395

thermal printers, 396

thinking logically while troubleshooting, 19

threats, 460-461

throughput (data). *See* data transfer rates

TIM (thermal interface material), 65

time-domain reflectometers (TDR), 434

time/date, BIOS configuration, 41

toner cartridges

disposal of, 506

laser printers, 394

tools, 279. *See also* commands
  Advanced Boot Options menu,
    280-281
  Recovery Console, 284-285
  WinRE (Windows Recovery
    Environment, 282-284
touch pads, 323
touch screens, 387
tracert command, 439-440
TrackPoint, 323
Transmission Control
  Protocol/Internet Protocol (TCP/IP),
  414
trojan horses, definition of, 477
troubleshooting, 20-21
  BIOS (Basic Input Output Systems)
    memory errors, 99
    motherboard-related issues, 50
  boot errors
    Windows Vista Boot Errors,
      285-287
    Windows XP/2000 Boot Errors,
      287
  BSOD (Blue Screen of Death), 99
  command-line tools, 307
    chkdsk, 307-308
    Command Prompt, 307
    convert, 308
    defrag, 309
    diskpart, 309
    format, 309
    SFC (System File Checker), 308
    xcopy, 309
  CPU (central processing units),
    74-76
  DRAM (dyanmic random-access
    memory), 98-101
  error reporting, 300-301
  ESD (electrostatic discharge), 18-19,
    502-504
  fans, 124
  floppy disk drives, 144
  fuses, power supply fuses, 124

  GPF (general protection faults), 100
  hard faults (page faults), 100
  HDD (hard disk drives), 141-143
  laptops
    audio subsystem, 329-330
    communications, 336-337
    CPUs, 345-347
    expansion devices, 334-336
    hard drives, 342-343
    keyboards, 320-322
    memory, 343-345
    optical discs, 330
    power, 330-333
    system board, 345-347
    video issues, 328-329
  low on virtual memory errors, 100
  monitors, 15-16, 19
  motherboards, 47-49, 51-52
    BIOS-related issues, 50
    component failures, 51
    ESD-related issues, 50
    manufacturing defects, 51
  network connectivity
    applications, 442-443
    ipconfig, 437-438
    net, 441-442
    netstat, 440-441
    nslookup, 441
    ping, 438-439
    tracert, 439-440
  out of memory errors, 100
  page faults (hard faults), 100
  paper jams, 406-407
  power issues, 17-19
  power supplies, 123-127
  printers, 406-411
  recovery Command Prompts
    copy, 311
    edit, 310-311
    expand, 311
    recovery environment commands,
      311-312

repair tools, 279

Advanced Boot Options menu, 280-281

Recovery Console, 284-285

WinRE (Windows Recovery Environment), 282-284

restoring Windows, 301

to an earlier condition, 303

with System Restore, 303-304

from Windows Vista complete PC backup, 302

from Windows XP's ASR backup, 302

six-step process, 10, 14, 304-305

display issue example, 15-16

documenting solutions, 13, 17-18

establishing plans of action, 12, 16, 18

establishing theory of probable cause, 11, 15-17

identifying the problem, 10-11, 15, 17

power issue example, 17-18

testing theory of probable cause, 12, 16-17

verifying system functionality, 12-13, 16, 18

spyware, 481-483

startup issues, 17-19

stop errors, 99, 298-300

thinking logically, 19

USB flash drives, 158

user error, 19

video cards, 357-360

viruses, 478-481

Windows 7 installation, 174-176

Windows tools

Device Manager, 290-293

Dr. Watson, 296

Event Viewer, 294-296

Msconfig, 298

Problem Reports and Solutions, 296

Reliability and Performance Monitor, 297-298

Windows Vista installation, 190-193

Windows XP installation, 204-205

TV tuner cards, 360

twisted pair cables, 432

U

UAC (User Account Control), 470-471

Ultra ATA hard drives, installing, 139

unauthorized access, 460

unicast addresses, 421

Universal Serial Bus (USB), 382-385

unshielded twisted pair (UTP) cables, 432

updates

antimalware, 275

BIOS, 43, 275

downloading, 478

firewalls, 275

Windows updates, 268-269, 275

SP (service packs), 264-265

Windows Update, 266-267

Upgrade Advisor, 203

upgrading

to Windows 7, 173-174

to Windows Vista, 188, 190

to Windows XP, 203

UPS (uninterruptible power supplies), 112-113

electrical safety, 502

HDD (hard disk drive) maintenance, 275

USB (Universal Serial Bus) ports, 33, 382-385

USB flash drives, 156-157

formatting, 158

memory, 158

troubleshooting, 158

User Account Control (UAC), 470-471

user error, troubleshooting, 19

user state, 237

User State Migration Tool (USMT), 237

usernames, 465

users

  customizing user environment, 238-239

  ergonomics, 505

  logon process, security, 467-469

  migrating user data, 236-238

  passwords

    changing, 466

    password policy, 466-467

    strong passwords, 465

  questioning (problem identification process), 10

  state, 237

  UAC (User Account Control), 470-471

  user awareness, 462

  usernames, 465

USMT (User State Migration Tool), 237

UTP (unshielded twisted pair) cables, 432

V

verifying

  system functionality (six-step troubleshooting process, 12-13

    display issue example, 16

    power issue example, 18

  Windows 7 installation, 174-176

  Windows Vista installation, 190-193

  Windows XP installation, 204-205

versions

  of Windows 7, 166-167

  of Windows Vista, 178-179

  of Windows XP, 196-197

vertical refresh rate, 368-369

VGA (Video Graphics Array), 354

video subsytem

  laptop video subsystem, 324

    display controls, 324-325

    DualView, 326-327

    GPU, 324

    LCD, 324

    resolutions, 324

    troubleshooting, 328-329

  overview, 351

  video cards, 352

    chipsets, 356

    connector types, 354-355

    expansion busses, 352-353

    GPU, 356

    installing, 357-360

    memory, 356

    SLI and TV tuner/capture cards, 360-361

    troubleshooting, 357-360

  video displays

    CRT, 362

    LCD, 361-362

    projectors, 362-363

  video settings

    color depth, 364-365

    drivers, 363-364

    Multiple Monitor (DualView), 370-371

    OSD (on-screen display), 369-370

    refresh rate, 368-369

    resolution, 365-368

virtual memory, 232-233

  low on virtual memory errors, troubleshooting, 100

virtual private networks (VPNs), 426

viruses

  definition of, 475

  preventing and troubleshooting, 478-481

  types of viruses, 475-476

Vista

  Backup Status and Configuration, 273

  boot errors, 285-287

  boot files, 249

  directory structure, 248

  folder sharing, 490-491

hardware compatibility, 180
Indexing service, 250-251
installing
    installation methods, 181-182
    partitions, creating, 186-187
    step-by-step installation process,
        183-185
minimum requirements, 179-180
restoring
    to an earlier condition, 303
    from Windows Vista complete PC
        backup, 302
troubleshooting installation, 190-193
upgrading to, 188, 190
verifying installation of, 190-193
versions, 178-179
XPS (XML Paper Specification)
    feature, 404
visual effects, disabling, 238
**volatile RAM (random access
    memory), 81**
voltage (V), 104
    sags, 110
VPNs (virtual private networks), 426

W

WANs (wide area networks), 426
WAPs (wireless access points), 425
wattage (W), 104
    power supplies, 118-119
webcams, 387
Welcome Center, configuring, 215
Welcome screen, disabling, 467
wide area networks (WANs), 426
**Widescreen Extended Graphics Array
    (WXGA), 324**
**Widescreen Super Extended Graphics
    Array Plus (WSXGA+), 324**
**Windows. See also Windows 7;
    Windows Vista; Windows XP**
    applications
        Command Prompt, 219

Computer, 215-216
Control Panel, 218
Network, 218
PowerShell, 219
Windows Explorer, 216-218
components
    application windows, 212
    desktop, 210
    icons, 211
    Quick Launch, 212
    Sidebar, 212
    Start menu, 212, 214-215
    System Tray, 212
    taskbar, 212, 214-215
    Welcome Center, configuring, 215
    Windows Aero, configuring, 215
CPU, testing installations, 72
encryption, 493-495
firewalls
    HDD (hard disk drive) maintenance,
        275
    updates, 275
tools
    Device Manager, 290-293
    Dr. Watson, 296
    Event Viewer, 294-296
    Msconfig, 298
    Problem Reports and Solutions, 296
    Reliability and Performance
        Monitor, 297-298
updates, 268-269
    HDD (hard disk drive) mainte-
        nance, 275
    SP (service packs), 264-265
    Windows Update, 266-267
Windows 7
    Backup and Restore, 272-273
    boot files, 249
    installing
        installation methods, 169-170
        step-by-step installation process,
            170-173

minimum requirements, 167-168

troubleshooting installation, 174-176

upgrading to, 173-174

verifying installation of, 174-176

versions, 166-167

Windows 7 Logo'd Products List, 173

Windows Aero, configuring, 215

The Windows Boot Configuration Data file is missing required information (error message), 286

Windows Compatibility Center, 168, 173

Windows Complete PC Restore option (Recovery Options, 284

Windows configuration

administrative tools, 220-221

boot files, 249

directory structure, 248

disks

formatting, 253-256

mounting, 257-258

partitioning, 253-256

RAID, 259-260

file systems, 257

Indexing service, 250-251

MMC (Microsoft Management Console), 221

power management, 235-236

services, starting/stopping, 233

in Command Prompt, 234

in Computer Management, 233

system tools

Device Manager, 225-226

Driver Signing, 227

DxDiag, 227-228

Msconfig, 231-232

Program Compatibility Wizard, 244

Registry, 239, 241

Remote Assistance, 242

Remote Desktop, 242-243

Safely Remove option, 229

System Information Tool, 227

Task Manager, 229-231

virtual memory, 232-233

Windows XP Mode, 244

user customizations, 238-239

user migration, 236-238

Windows Easy Transfer, 237

Windows Explorer, 216-218

Windows Firewall, 443, 479

Windows Logo'd Products, 168

Windows Memory Diagnostic Tool (Recovery Options), 284

Windows Preinstallation Environment phase (Vista installation), 191

Windows Recovery Environment (WinRE), 282-284

Windows Security dialog box, 467

Windows System Image Manager (SIM), 169, 181

Windows System Information tool, 168, 180, 198

Windows Update, 266-267

Windows Upgrade Advisor, 173

Windows Vista

Backup Status and Configuration, 273

boot errors, 285-287

boot files, 249

directory structure, 248

folder sharing, 490-491

hardware compatibility, 180

Indexing service, 250-251

installing

installation methods, 181-182

partitions, creating, 186-187

step-by-step installation process, 183-185

minimum requirements, 179-180

restore points, creating, 274

restoring

to an earlier condition, 303

from Windows Vista complete PC backup, 302

troubleshooting installation, 190-193

upgrading to, 188, 190

verifying installation of, 190-193

versions, 178-179

XPS (XML Paper Specification) feature, 404

Windows Vista Logo'd Products List, 180, 188

Windows Vista Upgrade Advisor, 188

Windows Welcome phase (Vista installation, 191

Windows XP

boot errors, 287

boot files, 249

folder sharing, 488-489

hardware compatibility, 198

Indexing service, 250-251

installing

installation methods, 198-200

step-by-step installation process, 200-203

minimum requirements, 197

NTBackup, 273

restore points, creating, 274

restoring

to an earlier condition, 303

from ASR backup, 302

with System Restore, 303-304

troubleshooting installation, 204-205

upgrading to, 203

verifying installation of, 204-205

versions, 196-197

Windows XP Logo'd Products List, 198, 203

Windows XP Mode, 244

WinRE (Windows Recovery Environment), 282-284

Winsat.log, 191

wireless access points (WAPs), 425

wireless network adapters, 450-453, 455

wizards

FAST (Files and Settings Transfer) Wizard, 237

Program Compatibility Wizard, 244

worms, definition of, 476

WSXGA+ (Widescreen Super Extended Graphics Array Plus), 324

WXGA (Widescreen Extended Graphics Array), 324

X-Z

xcopy command, 309

XP

boot errors, 287

boot files, 249

folder sharing, 488-489

hardware compatibility, 198

Indexing service, 250-251

installing

installation methods, 198-200

step-by-step installation process, 200-203

minimum requirements, 197

restoring

to an earlier condition, 303

from ASR backup, 302

with System Restore, 303-304

troubleshooting installation, 204-205

upgrading to, 203

verifying installation of, 204-205

versions, 196-197

XPS (XML Paper Specification) feature (Windows Vista), 404

zombies, 477

Get prepared for the CompTIA® A+ Exams

Pearson Certification has the learning tools that you need to get ready for the CompTIA® A+ exams. From foundational learning to late-stage review, practice, and preparation, the varied print, software, and video products from Pearson Certification can help you succeed!

Book/CD Learning Products

CompTIA A+ Certification Guide, Second Edition

ISBN-13: 9780789747907
ISBN-10: 0789747901

Comprehensive A+ learning from best-selling author Scott Mueller

CompTIA A+ Exam Cram, Fifth Edition

ISBN-13: 9780789747921
ISBN-10: 0789747928

The best-selling late-stage A+ study book of all time

CompTIA A+ Practice Questions, Fourth Edition

ISBN-13: 9780789747914
ISBN-10: 078974791X

Prepare with 1,000+ practice questions in print and electronic test engine formats

Online Learning Services and Late-Stage Electronic Kits

myITcertificationlabs: A+ Second Edition

ISBN-13: 9780132566087
ISBN-10: 0132566087

Online service assesses knowledge, creates customized learning plans, and delivers study materials

CompTIA A+ Cert Flash Cards Online, Third Edition

ISBN-13: 9780132674553
ISBN-10: 0132674556

Online flash cards provide review, practice, and enhance memory retention

CompTIA A+ Cert Kit

ISBN-13: 9780789742438
ISBN-10: 0789742438

Expert video training and other electronic learning tools like online flash cards and exam quick references prepare you for the A+ exams!

PEARSON · **EXAM/CRAM**

For more information on this and other Pearson Certification products, visit pearsonITcertification.com

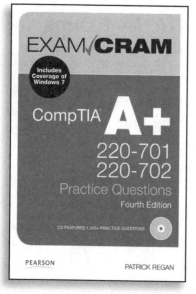

FREE Online Edition

Your purchase of **CompTIA A+ 220-701 and 220-702 Exam Cram** includes access to a free online edition for 45 days through the Safari Books Online subscription service. Nearly every Exam Cram book is available online through Safari Books Online, along with more than 5,000 other technical books and videos from publishers such as Addison-Wesley Professional, Cisco Press, Que, IBM Press, O'Reilly, Prentice Hall, and Sams.

SAFARI BOOKS ONLINE allows you to search for a specific answer, cut and paste code, download chapters, and stay current with emerging technologies.

Activate your FREE Online Edition at www.informit.com/safarifree

> **STEP 1:** Enter the coupon code: YBSTOXA.

> **STEP 2:** New Safari users, complete the brief registration form.
> Safari subscribers, just log in.

If you have difficulty registering on Safari or accessing the online edition, please e-mail customer-service@safaribooksonline.com